Third Edition

NATIVE AMERICAN HERITAGE

Merwyn S. Garbarino

Robert F. Sasso

University of Wisconsin—Parkside

Prospect Heights, Illinois

For information about this book, write or call:
Waveland Press, Inc.
P.O. Box 400
Prospect Heights, Illinois 60070
(708) 634-0081

Cover design by John Stanicek; cover photo courtesy of Milwaukee Public Museum.

ISBN 0-88133-773-0

Printed in the United States of America

7 6 5 4 3 2

INTRODUCTION

This new edition of *Native American Heritage* is accompanied with my great gratitude to Dr. Robert F. Sasso who has so ably done the revision of Part I: Prehistory. It seemed to me important to have the help of a professional in prehistory and archaeology because of the many new discoveries and revisions in dating that have occurred recently.

Dr. Sasso received his Ph.D. from Northwestern University, and he has participated in and directed a number of archaeological research projects and excavations in the Upper Mississippi Valley and Western Great Lakes regions. He has also participated in Paleolithic excavations in southwestern France. He is currently serving on the faculty at the University of Wisconsin-Parkside. He brings his experience and expertise to this book, and I know that it will benefit immensely from his participation.

When Waveland Press decided to publish a new edition, they asked instructors who had used the book for their comments. Those critiques have proven invaluable in my revision. Their suggestions and requests fall into three categories: those wishing more tribal ethnography; those asking for more contemporary information (especially on Canadian Indians); and the preponderance, those asking for a new format and more illustrations. Waveland Press has responded to the last, and I have addressed the first two.

In Part II I have maintained the construct of culture areas because I believe, based on my own years of teaching, that the culture area formula is the clearest and simplest means for understanding the relationship between culture and adaptation as well as an excellent mnemonic device for sorting out the diversity of American Indian cultures. The section on culture traits, Part III, on the other hand, remains an efficient device for summarizing similarities as opposed to diversities across the continent.

I have enlarged some of the tribal descriptions, but I decided not to add new ethnographic sketches. One could add ever more examples within each culture area, but this book was never intended to do more than give a broad but accurate sampling of the lifeways and different levels of socio-cultural development. It is always to be hoped that students will read at least one complete ethnography. Some possible selections have been given at the end of each chapter. I had to put finite bounds on this volume and, after all, nothing can take the place of professional ethnographic monographs, many of which should be available in college libraries.

Addressing the request for more current information, I was faced again with the problem of length. Some respondents said that they found Part IV very valuable, while others replied that contemporary Indian life was a separate course at their institutions with different readings so that they did not find Part IV useful. Calling upon my own classroom experience, I decided that even if current conditions were not part of the course, students always asked many questions abut Indians today. Therefore, I have brought Part IV up to date and have added more information about Canada in response to those who remarked that it was difficult to find data on Indians of that country.

I am grateful to the editors at Waveland Press for their interest and support. They have been ever pleasant and helpful, and I know the new graphics and illustrations they have introduced will make the people and their lives more vivid.

Merwyn S. Garbarino, 1994

TABLE OF CONTENTS

Maps xi
Charts xiii

Part I Prehistory: Before Europeans Came **1**

1 First Settlers in the New World **5**
The First Americans 6
The Peopling of the New World 8 / How the Earliest Americans Lived 13 / A Society of Bands 15
The Paleo Indians: Big Game Hunters 16
People on the Great Plains 17 / How They Hunted 20 / A New Diet 22
The Archaic Period 23
Desert Archaic People 24 / People of the Coastal Archaic 27 / Living in the Arctic and Subarctic Archaic 29 / Forest People of the Eastern Archaic 30
The Woodland Tradition 33
Adena People 35 / Hopewell People 38
The Question of Transoceanic Contacts 42
Botanical Evidence 42 / Cultural Evidence 43
Summary 45

2 Cultivation and American Cultures **49**
Corn, Beans, and Squash 50
Changing Culture 51
The Southwest 54
The Beginnings of Agriculture 55 / Three Cultures 57 / Mogollon: The Earliest Farmers 58 / Hohokam: The Irrigators 61 / Anasazi: The Pueblo Farmers 65 / Nonagricultural Areas of the West 73
The Eastern Area 73
Late Woodland Cultural Developments 73 / The Mississippian Tradition 76
The Great Plains 86
The Plains Village Tradition 87
Summary: The Results of Cultivation 89

Part II Culture Areas of North America 93

3 The Arctic and the Subarctic 101

The Arctic 102
The Environment 103
The Eskimo 104
Adapting to the Arctic 106 / Regional Variations 107
Alaska: The Seasonal Pattern of Life 108
Spring Whaling 109 / Summer Activities 110 / Winter Life 112
Eskimo Life in General 115
Technology 116 / Social Organization 118 / Eskimo Religion 121
The Subarctic 125
The Environment 126
Aboriginal Population 127
Life in the Subarctic 127
Food 128 / Technology 128 / Religion 130 / The Chipewyan 133 / The Ojibwa 134

4 The Plateau and Northwest Coast 139

The Environment 141
Prehistory 141
Life on the Plateau 143
Resources 144 / Communities 144 / Religion 146 / The Nez Perce 147 / The Klamath of Southern Oregon 150
The Northwest Coast 154
The Environment 155
Prehistory 156
Native Life 157
Technology 158 / Social and Political Organization 160 / The Potlatch 162 / Northwest Coast Art 165
Tribes of the Northwest Coast 166
The Tligit 166 / The Nootka of Vancouver Island 170 / The Chinook, Traders at the Dalles 173 / The Kwakiutl Warriors 175

5 California 181

The Environment 183
Northern California 173 / Central California 185 / Southern California 185
California Peoples 186
The Promised Land 186
Food Resources 186 / Technology 188 / Political Organization 189 / Religion 190

The Yurok 190

Subsistence 192 / Social and Political Organization 192 / Wealth and Property 193 / Religion 195

The Pomo 198

Abundant Food 198 / The People 199 / Organization 199 / Technology 200 / The Sexes 202 / The Kuksu Cult 202 / Ghosts and Spirits 204

Southern California Indians 204

The Mission Indians 205 / The Luiseño 206

6 The Great Basin and the Southwest 215

The Great Basin 216

The Environment 217

Basin People 219

Exploiting the Environment 219 / Social Organization 221 / The Paiute 222 / The Ute and Shoshoni 225

The Southwest 225

Early Peoples of the Southwest 227

The Upland Yumans 228 / The River Yumans 229 / The Pimans 231

The Pueblo 233

The Environment 234 / Religion 235 / Social Organization 235 / Technology 236 / The Hopi 238 / Cochiti 242 / Pueblo Organization 244

The Southern Athabaskans 245

The Migration South 245 / The Apache 246 / The Navajo 248

7 The Plains 259

Plains Prehistory 263

The Horse Comes to the Plains 264

The Plains at the Time of Contact 265 / The Horse Culture 265

Changing Patterns of Life 266

Changing Technology 266 / Communication 271 / Economic Change 272 / Social Organization 273 / Values and Beliefs 275

How Plains Culture Developed 277

The Blackfoot 278 / The Cheyenne 283 / The Comanche 286 / The Crow 289 / The Mandan 291

8 The East 297

Early Life in the East 299

Prehistory 299 / The East at Contact 301 / Resources and Technology 303 / The People 305

The Northeast 307

New England Algonkians 307 / The Iroquois League 313

The Western Great Lakes 318
Early Life Around the Great Lakes 318 / Migrations and Changes 319 / The Prairie People 321 / The Menominee 322
The Southeast 325
Early Southeastern Culture 326 / The Central Atlantic Algonkians 328 / The Natchez 331 / The Seminole 334

Part III Native American Culture **341**

9 Technology, Art, and Religion **345**
The Food Quest 346
Gathering 346 / Hunting 347 / Fishing 351 / Cultivation 351
Preparing Food 352
Grinding and Pounding 352 / Food Preservation and Storage 353 / Cooking 354 / Fire-making 354
Housing 355
General Forms of Housing 355 / Specialized Forms of Housing 357
Transportation 358
Water Transportation 359 / Land Transportation 360
Clothing 360
Kinds of Apparel 360 / Body Decoration 362
Arts and Crafts 363
Woodworking 364 / Bone and Horn 364 / Pottery 364 / Stone Working 365 / Leather Work 366 / Metal Work 367 / Basketry 368 / Painting, Dyes, and Pigments 368 / Textiles 369 / Toys 370
Dramatic Arts 371
Dance and Music 371 / Folklore 371
Religious Beliefs 374
Supernatural Power 374 / Souls 376
Religious Behavior 376
Visions and Personal Power 376 / Religious Specialists 377
Religious Ceremonies 380
Regional Rituals 381 / Sacrifice 383 / Religious Paraphernalia 384

10 Social and Political Systems **387**
Marriage 388
Arranging a Marriage 388 / Polygamy 390
The Family 391
Adoption 391 / Childhood 392
Rites of Passage 393

Birth 393 / Naming 395 / Puberty 396 / Death 397
Clans and Other Large Groupings 398
Clan Rights and Duties 400 / Other Kin Groups 400 / Pseudo-kinship 401 / Associations 401
Games and Recreation 403
Women's Status 404
Slavery 405
Political Organization 406
Bands 407 / Tribes 407 / Chiefdoms 408 / Other Political Classifications 409 / Councils 409
Social Control 410
Supernatural Control 410 / Control of Adults 411
Economic Systems 412
Property Rights and Land Tenure 412 / Inheritance 413 / Trade and Commerce 413
Warfare 415
Going to War 416 / Scalping 417

Part IV Conflict Between Cultures 423

11 Indian-White Relations 423
Early European Exploration 424
Areas of Investigation 425 / European Goals 427
Consequences of Contact 430
Religious Reaction 430 / The Spread of Diseases 431 / The Spread of New World Cultigens 431
Government Policies toward Indians 432
The Colonial Period 432
Local Culture Contact and Change 436
The Northeast 436 / The Atlantic Seaboard 437 / The Southeast 438 / The Midwest 439 / The Plains 441 / The Southwest 445 / California 449 / The Plateau and the Basin 450 / The Northwest Coast 453 / The Arctic 454
Canadian Government Policy 455
Brief History of Canadian Nationhood 455 / Relations With the Native Peoples 455

12 Contemporary Indians 459
Reservations 462
Indian Rights on Reservations 462 / Reservation Facilities 465 / The Bureau of Indian Affairs 466 / Reservation Land 470 / Reservation Housing 470 / Reservation Life 471 / Reservation Culture 473
Changes after World War II 473
The Development of Indian Policies 473 / Termination 474 /

Relocation 475
Education 477
Sequoyah 478 / Early Indian Schools 479 / Education Today 479
Health 481
Religious Change 482
Indians in Today's World 483
Economic Success 484 / Economic Hope 485
Political Movements 488
National Indian Youth Council 488 / American Indian Movement 489 / Occupation of the BIA Building 489
Preservation of Human Remains and Repatriation of Indian Property 490
Current Conditions in Canada 492
Land Claims 492 / Economic Development 493 / Hunting and Fishing Rights 494 / Education 495
Conclusion 495

Glossary 497
Bibliography 507
Films and Videos 517
Photo and Illustration Credits 525
Index 527

MAPS

Pleistocene glaciers and Bering land bridge **10**
Early sites in North and South America **12**
North American Archaic and Woodland cultures **34**
Early Mesoamerican sites important in the development of agriculture **52**
Late Mesoamerican sites **63**
Late Woodland effigy mounds **75**
Culture areas of North America **95**
Geographic distribution of language families **98**
Arctic and Subarctic culture areas and their tribes **105**
Plateau and Northwest Coast culture areas and their tribes **142**
The California Culture area and its tribes **184**
Great Basin and Southwest culture areas and their tribes **218**
The Plains culture area and its tribes **262**
Huff site **291**
The Eastern culture area and its tribes, showing the subcultural divisions **300**

CHARTS

New World cultures, traditions, and events covered in Part I **46–47**
Characteristics of the Arctic tribes **123**
Characteristics of the Subarctic tribes **135**
Major groups and languages of the Arctic and the Subarctic **138**
Characteristics of the Plateau tribes **153**
Characteristics of the Northwest Coast tribes **176**
Major groups and languages of the Plateau and Northwest Coast **179–180**
Characteristics of California tribes **210**
Major groups and languages of California **213–214**
Characteristics of the Great Basin tribes **223**
Characteristics of the Southwest tribes **254**
Major groups and languages of the Great Basin and the Southwest **257–258**
Characteristics of the Plains tribes **293**
Major groups and languages of the Plains **296**
Characteristics of the Eastern tribes **336**
Major groups and languages of the East **339–340**
Indians and Alaskan Natives in the United States: 1980 and 1990 populations compared **461–462**
Organization of the BIA **467**

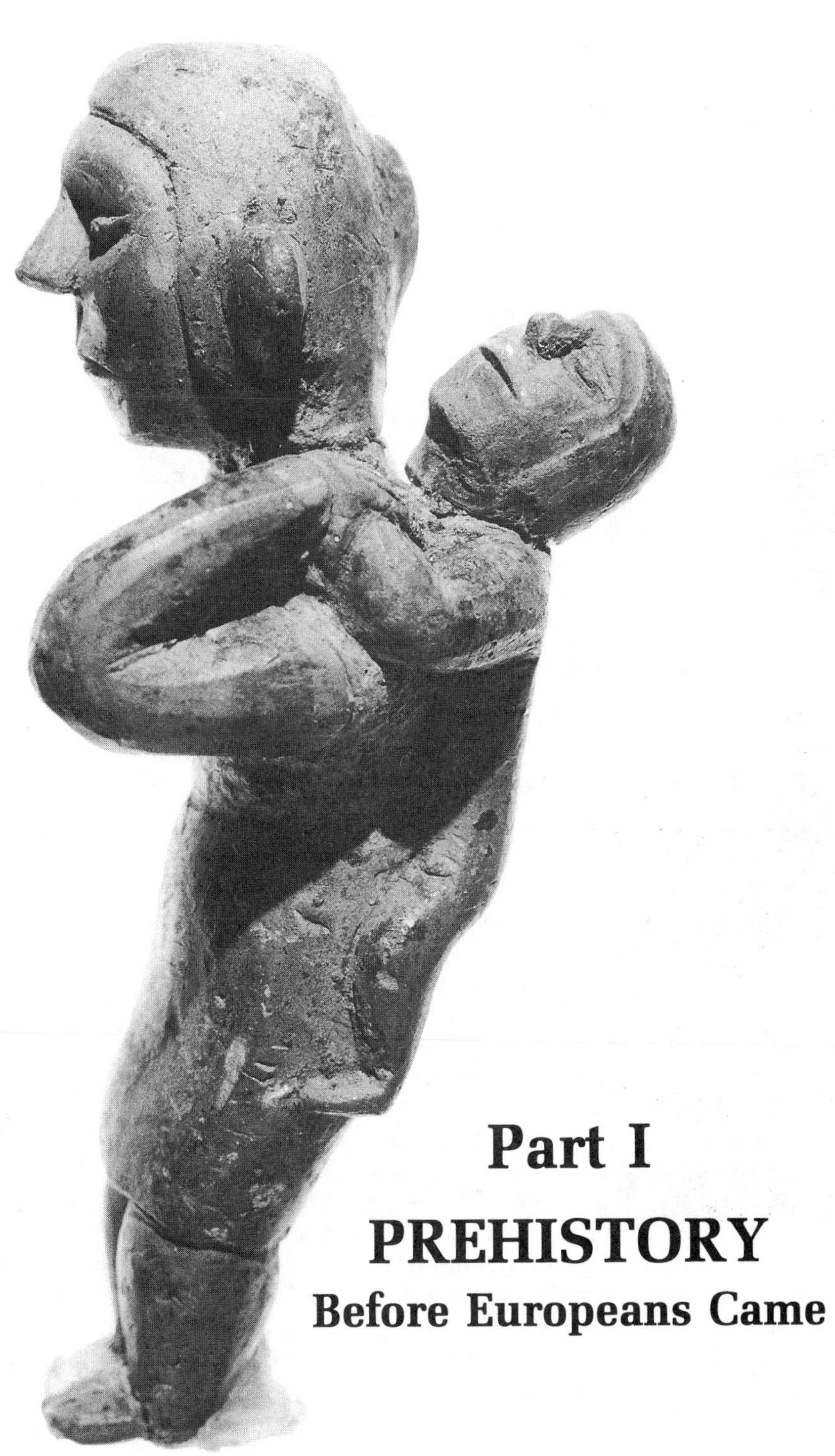

Part I
PREHISTORY
Before Europeans Came

In 1492, Christopher Columbus sailed westward across the Atlantic Ocean from Spain in search of a passage to the Orient. He never found it. Instead, he landed on islands off the coast of a continent unknown to Europeans of that time, though Norsemen had landed on the northeast coast almost five hundred years earlier, sometime during the eleventh century. Thinking he was in the Indies off the coast of southeast Asia, Columbus called the native inhabitants "Indians."

The so-called Indians had been living in the New World for many thousands of years before any Europeans knew of their existence. By the time Columbus "discovered" them, they occupied all the land from the far northern reaches of Arctic North America to Tierra del Fuego at the southern tip of South America. They spoke many different languages, and had no single word to describe themselves as a racial or cultural group that would be the equivalent of our word "Indian." Each group had its own term for itself, usually meaning something like "we, the people" or "the real people," and each had other words for those who did not belong to the group. Navajo, for example, called themselves *Dine*, meaning "the people" or "people of the surface of the earth."

We continue to use the name Columbus gave the native people, although some scholars have suggested that "Amerind" is more accurate. Many people today prefer "Native American," although others have pointed out that this name literally refers to anyone born within the Americas, regardless of ancestry or cultural background. In Europe, especially in Britain, the American Indians are often called Red Indians to distinguish them from the natives of India, and the slang terms "redskin" and "red man" were once popular in stories and films. Since Indian skin is not red, but shades of brown, these terms may have arisen from the Indians' use of red body paint for their religious and battle dress.

No single way of life characterized all of the Indians. Just as Indian groups each had their own languages, so too did they possess their own distinct cultures. Indian societies varied, ranging from simple hunting and gathering bands to populous urban centers supported by highly elaborate agricultural systems. Some groups spent their lives in one place, cultivating the soil; others lived part of the time in villages, leaving them only for seasonal activities; still others led a nomadic life-style involving a fairly constant pattern of group movement throughout the year hunting game and gathering wild plants. It was many years before Europeans realized the variety of Indian cultures and how different each was from all the others. The Indians Columbus met in the West Indies, those the Pilgrims lived among on the northeast Atlantic seaboard, and those the Spanish found in Mexico and Peru were as unlike each other as the Pilgrims and the Spanish themselves. They had countless languages—linguists believe that more than three hundred different languages were spoken north of the Rio Grande. Though only some Mexican Indians had written languages, other groups had various less elaborate visual means of recording events, censuses, and other important information, and all groups seem to have possessed highly developed oral traditions. Physical characteristics varied among different groups as well. Some Indian populations were characterized by tall individuals, as among the Mojave and Yuma, while others were typically short and stocky. Some looked like the Indian on the old buffalo nickel, with hawklike noses and high cheekbones. Others had flat noses, round and generally oriental faces. There never was a typical Indian, culturally or physically.

The Europeans who were curious about where these unknown people had come from suggested many theories of which a few have survived and are still heard from time to time. One of the earliest and most persistent traced the Indians to the ten lost tribes of Israel, who had somehow made their way to the New World. Others linked Indians with a variety of peoples, both real and mythical. One tale tells how the soldiers of Alexander the Great sailed east from India after their leader's death and eventually populated the Americas. The Indians' origin has also been attributed to the Trojans, Phoenicians, Romans, Egyptians, Welsh, and the people of the mythical lost continents of Atlantis and Mu.

A few of the imaginative histories came very close to the one the scientific community now accepts. Early explorers and scientists speculated that Indians had come to the continent from the northwest and that animals from the Old World had come in at the same place. They pointed out physical likenesses between Indians and people of northeastern Asia. How this migration must have happened is the story that opens chapter 1.

Suggestions for Further Study

Bibliography

Fagan, Brian M. 1987. *The Great Journey: The Peopling of Ancient America.* New York: Thames and Hudson, Inc.

______. 1991. *Ancient North America: The Archaeology of a Continent.* New York: Thames and Hudson, Inc.

Both of these offerings from Brian Fagan are well researched, interesting, and well worth reading. *The Great Journey* provides a detailed discussion of recent theories and data pertaining to the earliest occupation of the Americas. *Ancient North America* presents an updated view of the prehistory of the North American continent as revealed through more than a century of archaeological research.

Jennings, Jesse D., ed. 1983. *Ancient North Americans*. New York: W. H. Freeman and Company.

This is a very useful edited volume that combines writings on prehistoric cultural developments in the various culture areas of the North American continent, including a section on pre-Columbian transoceanic contacts.

Jennings, Jesse D. 1989. *Prehistory of North America*. 3rd ed. Mountain View, CA: Mayfield Publishing Company.

An introductory college text in North American archaeology. This is a highly regarded and well illustrated book which deals with methodology and definitions as well as prehistoric cultural developments. It contains an excellent bibliography for beginning students, as well as a glossary.

Other Pertinent Works

Fiedel, Stuart J. 1992. *Prehistory of the Americas*. 2d ed. New York: Cambridge University Press.

Griffin, James B. 1967. Eastern North American Archaeology: A Summary. *Science* 156(3772): 175–191.

Hoffecker, John F., W. Roger Powers, and Ted Goebel. 1993. The Colonization of Beringia and the Peopling of the New World. *Science* 259: 46–53.

Mason, Ronald. 1981. *Great Lakes Archaeology*. New York: Academic Press.

Snow, Dean R. 1989. *The Archaeology of North America*. New York: Chelsea House Publishers.

Williams, Stephen. 1991. *Fantastic Archaeology: The Wild Side of North American Prehistory*. Philadelphia: University of Pennsylvania Press.

1

FIRST SETTLERS IN THE NEW WORLD

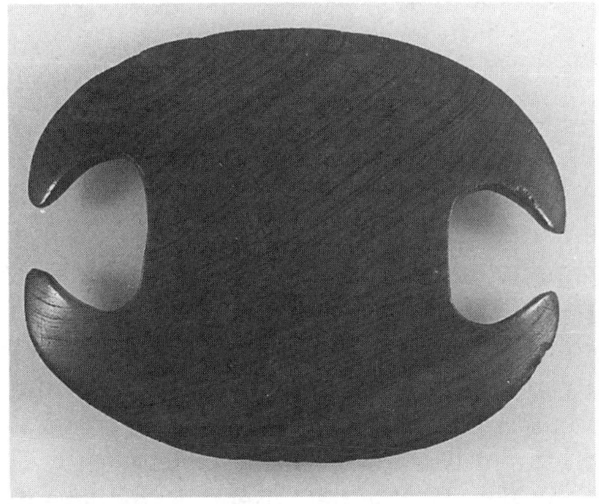

Archaic bannerstone from a prehistoric site in western Wisconsin. This specimen was a weight from an atlatl.

As a starting point for discussing prehistoric Native American cultures, we must address a number of important questions regarding the origins and antiquity of humans in the New World. How long have people lived in North America? How and when did they arrive here, and from what other area (or areas) of the world did they come? Is there significant evidence for earlier forms of humans than our own species? Where did the earliest inhabitants enter the New World? Do modern Native American peoples represent a single episode of migration to the New World from elsewhere, or perhaps multiple episodes?

While our understanding of human antiquity in the Americas is hardly complete, we can go far in answering many of these questions based upon the currently available biological, archaeological, and cultural data. The present evidence points to Asia as the Old World source area for ancestral Native American peoples. As research continues, our understanding of the origins of Native American populations will become even clearer.

The First Americans

What were the earliest Americans like, and how did they live? Physically, all that we know of them comes from relatively few skeletal remains, most of which date to uncertain times in the past. Even these fragmentary traces, though, show clearly that they were of our own species, *Homo sapiens*. To date, no substantiated fossil finds of any biologically archaic (or primitive) forms of humans have been made anywhere in the New World, such as *Homo erectus* or earlier forms of *Homo sapiens*. Likewise, we have found no fossil remains of any apes or human-like forms in the New World. Thus, humans did not evolve in the New World, but entered in modern physical form. In other words, the New World was first settled by biologically modern humans. This in turn indicates that, relative to Old World regions such as Africa, Asia, and Europe, the human occupation of the New World occurred in comparatively recent times.

Reconstructing a human being's physical appearance from bone material is moderately chancy. Judging from skeletal remains and descriptions of Indians by early European arrivals as well as the appearance of contemporary Indian people, physical anthropologists believe that early Americans were of a Mongoloid type, less oriental in appearance than today's East Asians, but with dark hair and eyes, light to medium brown skin, and relatively little facial and body hair. Generation after generation of adapting to new environments would have left them with the variations in height and body build that the European visitors found in North America at the time of contact. Nothing in the New World, though, compared with the physical differences to be found in Africa, where stature ranges from the tallest to the shortest people on earth, living just a short distance apart.

Physical anthropologists have noted that all Native Americans and North Asian peoples share strong dental similarities that are not common among other populations of the Old World, such as East Asians or Europeans. These similarities include distinctive molar and premolar root configurations, as well as strongly "*shovel-shaped*" *incisors*. This is a kind of hollowing out of the inner side of the upper central incisor teeth, giving them a scoop or shovel shape. The fact that this trait is common in both Native American and North Asian populations is very strong evidence that they had a common ancestry.

The Eskimo (or *Inuit*) population is not considered Indian but a distinctly separate group physically and culturally, which in turn suggests that they arrived later than the ancestors of the Indians in a separate population movement. Physically, they are a more specialized Mongoloid type than the Indians, with *epicanthic eye folds*—the so-called slanted eyes—as well as yellower skin and flattened noses. The Eskimo are the only society on earth whose geographical range coincides with a climate zone, the Arctic, and who have a common language and culture with only minor variations.

Genetic studies of blood serum proteins also indicate north or northeastern Asia as a likely place of origin for Native Americans. The genetic evidence also suggests that the ancestors of modern Native American populations arrived in the New World as the result of three separate migrations. The most recent migration apparently gave rise to Athabaskan (or *Na Dene*) populations. At an earlier time, the ancestors of Eskimo (*Inuit*) and Aleut peoples came into North America. Earliest

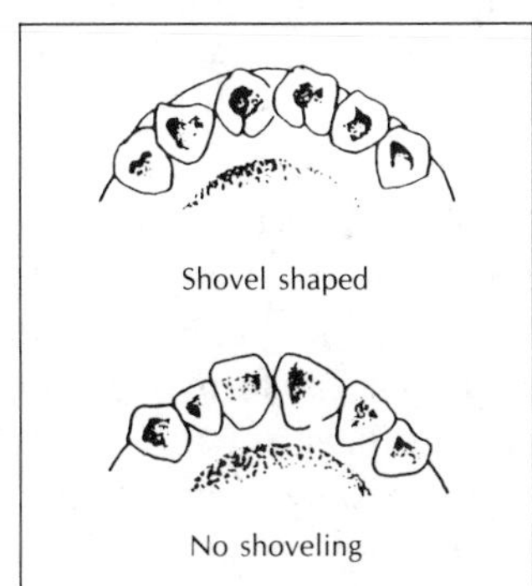

Shovel-shaped incisors (top), characteristic of American Indians, Eskimo, and East Asians, are compared with incisors with no shoveling.

of all was the original migration of the people ancestral to all other native populations of both North and South America. The chronological order of the two most recent migrations is presently a matter of some debate, and some prehistorians would view the Athabaskan migration as preceding the Eskimo-Aleut.

While the biological evidence for the north Asian source of Native American peoples is fairly strong, we know far less about their cultural roots. Upper Paleolithic sites from northeast Asia and early sites in the New World show some weak cultural similarities between material remains such as stone tools. Yet there are curious distinctions between the artifact assemblages of both areas that remain unexplained. For example, one of the most common tools associated with well-dated early New World sites is a type of projectile point, or spear point, with a distinctive shape and flake feature. No similar artifacts have ever been found in the Old World, and such tools are similarly absent from the assemblages from early sites in Alaska.

The Peopling of the New World

Just how recently people came into North and South America has long been the subject of considerable debate. However, most archaeologists agree that the peopling of the New World took place toward the final stages of the Pleistocene Epoch, a period in the earth's geologic history that began roughly two million years ago and ended about 10,000 years ago. Human entry into the New World probably took place sometime just prior to the latter date.

The Pleistocene Epoch was characterized by the repeated development of huge glaciers that periodically expanded to cover large parts of several continents, including much of North America, Europe, and Asia in the northern hemisphere. Not all of North America was covered by the glaciers, however. Surprisingly, even some areas located in the northern part of the continent remained mostly or completely free of glaciation for much or all of the Pleistocene. One such area includes much of western and central Alaska.

Glaciers are masses of ice that include rock and soil material scoured from the earth's surface as they spread from a central area outward. The largest of the North American glaciers are thought to have been one to three miles deep over most of their extent. Such a glacier would incorporate an enormous amount of water locked up in the form of glacial ice. The ultimate sources of that water were the oceans, and as the glaciers grew in size, sea level worldwide dropped. Lowering sea level exposed large areas of the continental shelves that would ordinarily have been submerged under shallow seas along the edges of the continents.

One expansive area exposed as more or less "dry land" was situated between northeast Asia and western Alaska, in the location presently occupied by the Bering Strait. The Bering Strait today measures a minimum of fifty-six miles across, and represents the narrowest water separation between the Old and New Worlds.

The land connecting the two continents during times of lower sea levels has come to be called the Bering land bridge. The area including the land bridge and adjacent portions of northeast Asia and western Alaska is commonly referred to as *Beringia*. At its maximum, the land connection may have measured a thousand miles in width, from the Arctic Ocean on the north to the Aleutian Islands on the south. It has been estimated that the land bridge was exposed for thousands of years at a time, and that this occurred at several distinct times over the past 100,000 years. The most recent exposure of the land bridge occurred during the last glacial maximum and may have continued until as recently as 10,000 to 11,000 years ago.

It is clear that migrating herds of large grazing mammals wandered back and forth across this land connection whenever it was exposed by lowered sea levels. Mammoths, mastodons, wild horses, ancient bison, reindeer or caribou, and camels all moved between the two continents. By approximately 28,000 years ago, Paleolithic people were living in the northeastern part of Siberia, with a way of life that focused on hunting these types of large game for their subsistence. It is believed that sometime between this date and 12,000 years ago, people began following these herds of animals across Beringia into Alaska, no doubt unaware that they were entering a different continent. This migration began the original settlement of the Americas.

It has been suggested that when the Cordilleran Glacier covering the Rocky Mountains was undergoing expansion, it spread northeastward toward the concurrently expanding Laurentide Glacier, which covered the north central portion of North America. Whenever the masses were joined together, glacial ice would have spanned virtually the entire continent from west to east. At such times of glacial expansion, the movement of people and animals southward into the interior of the continent would likely have been prevented. However, as the glaciers periodically receded, ice-free corridors opened along the east side of the Rocky Mountains, allowing people to move south and eastward into southern Canada, the United States, and beyond. Perhaps they followed one of the temporary corridors north of the Brooks Range or up the Yukon River Valley into the MacKenzie River Valley and then southward along the east slope of the Rockies and into the Dakotas. The corridors themselves may not have been very favorable for human occupation in terms of climate and presumably the availability of plants and animals. Some have suggested that populations may have been able to move southward

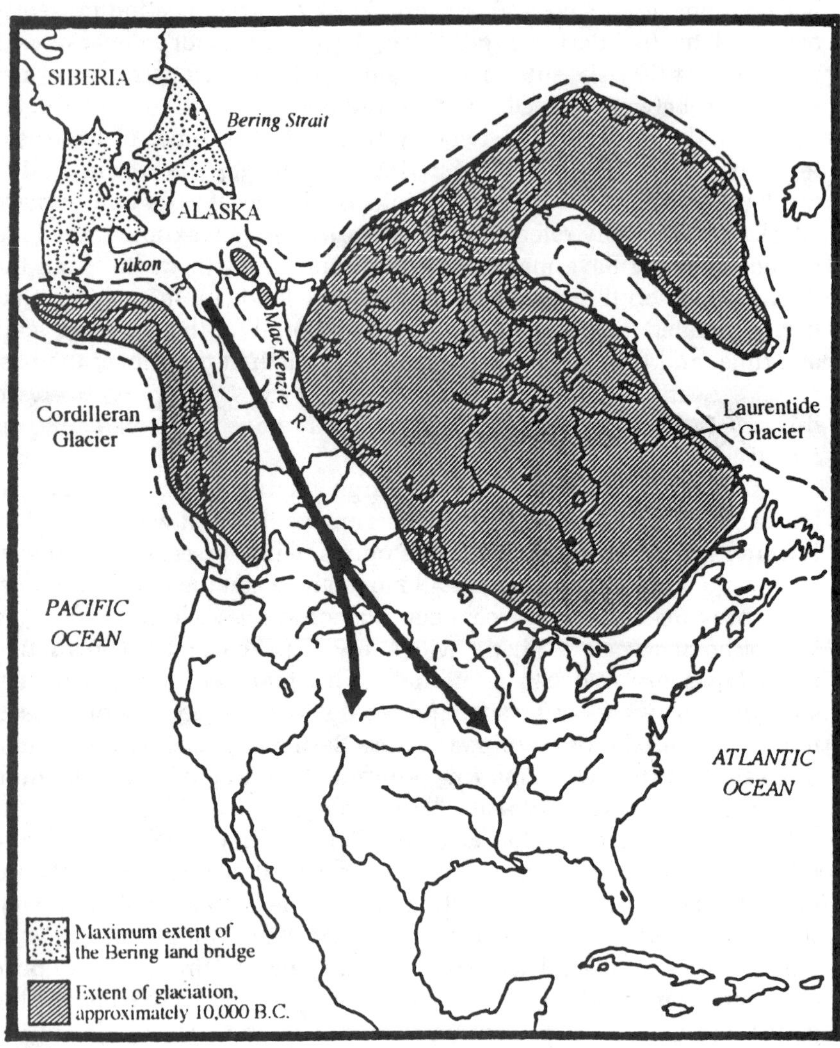

Location of the Pleistocene glaciers, the Bering land bridge, the ice-free corridor, and the probable route of human entry into the interior of North America (arrows). The dashed line indicates the approximate extent of glacial coverage around 17,000 B.C., when glaciers spanned the continent from east to west and no corridor of ready passage existed.

along the islands and bays of the Pacific Northwest coast, although no archaeological evidence has yet been obtained to show that they did in fact traverse or occupy these areas during late glacial times.

The exact date of the first entry of people into North America may never be known. The evidence for the earliest entry may be lost beneath cold ocean waters, destroyed under advancing and retreating glaciers, or lying undiscovered in Siberia or Alaska. It is clear that they came, and almost certain that they did so by the route just described. But when the first people arrived continues to be the subject of controversy among North American prehistorians.

The earliest well-dated evidence of human occupation in the Americas dates to approximately 11,500 years ago. However, a small number of excavated sites have revealed archaeological deposits that may date from before 15,000 years ago. The most important of these sites are the Meadowcroft Rockshelter in southwestern Pennsylvania, Pedra Furada in northeastern Brazil, and Monte Verde in northern Chile. None of these three sites has been completely accepted by archaeologists, for one or more reasons. Until recently, many archaeologists believed that people had begun settling the New World as much as 20,000 or more years ago. In general, the current view holds that while earlier settlement may have taken place, the first significant or widespread human settlement of the New World occurred *at the very latest* by approximately 11,000 to 12,000 years ago.

It appears that humans spread relatively quickly from northwestern North America through the interior of the continent, into Central America and subsequently into South America. Once south of the glaciers in open environments of interior North America, it may have taken only a few thousand years for populations to expand into open areas as far south as southern South America. Beyond any doubt, people had reached Tierra del Fuego, the southern tip of South America, before 6000 B.C. This spread may have involved a rapid population increase among mobile hunting and gathering peoples in a land with plentiful game resources. How long would a hunting and gathering group, following the migratory herd animals that comprised its primary source of food, take to travel from Alaska to the end of the South American continent? Many, many generations must have lived and died as the people drifted southward. Some may have stopped, settling and adapting to local conditions—one possible reason that Indian societies are so numerous and so different. In one hundred centuries or more, even people with the same ancestry can develop marked cultural and physical differences. The Indians may be descended from many successive waves of immigrants, but they could just as well have sprung from two or three groups arriving from Asia a few millennia apart.

The locations of certain early sites in North and South America.

How the Earliest Americans Lived

To reconstruct a picture of these early American settlers, we can draw much indirect evidence from geology, archaeology, anthropology, and other disciplines. Another useful tool is *ethnographic analogy*, comparing the facts we have about prehistoric peoples with what we know about tribal people who live today or who lived in the recent past. Such comparisons can be very helpful if they are used with careful control. The people compared must have some historical connection with one another, living in about the same environment and being similar in terms of technology. To reconstruct ancient Indian groups, we have used knowledge about more recent American Indian societies with low population density and simple tools, making their living in difficult environments. From this information, we can arrive at informed guesses about how the Indians' very early ancestors lived.

The early people had simple tools. They needed protection from the cold, so we can assume that they knew techniques for working hides into clothing and probably into simple shelters—though their shelters may well have been no more than windbreaks. Remains of ashes are good evidence that those people certainly knew how to make and control fire, which would have also been important, considering the climate. What we probably know most about is their stone tool technology. The scarce stone remains tell us that their tools were relatively simple. They possessed projectile points, representing spear points or knives for killing and butchering game. While these people did not possess bow and arrow technology, they did have weapons such as lances or spears that could be hurled at game animals. Finds of scrapers bear out the idea that these people knew how to work hides. They also had engraving tools for working such materials as wood, bone, antler, and ivory. In addition to these tools, the people also used simple flakes of stone for a variety of jobs, including cutting, punching, and chopping.

Without question, these people lived primarily by hunting large game animals. In the Arctic and Subarctic they would have little choice but to hunt for most of the year, even today. The short northern summers would have presumably brought a greater variety of foods to their diet: vegetable foods, edible roots, seeds, and berries. Regrettably, we have little archaeological evidence of the sorts of plant foods these people consumed as part of their diet. Eggs would have been available from the migrating birds that nest at that time of the year by the millions, and perhaps even clams and mussels were gathered along the beaches and tidal flats. Fish and sea mammals would likely have been available as well, although we know very little about their use by the earliest inhabitants of North America. But for most of the year, then as now, that northern land was frozen, snow-covered tundra. The plants were

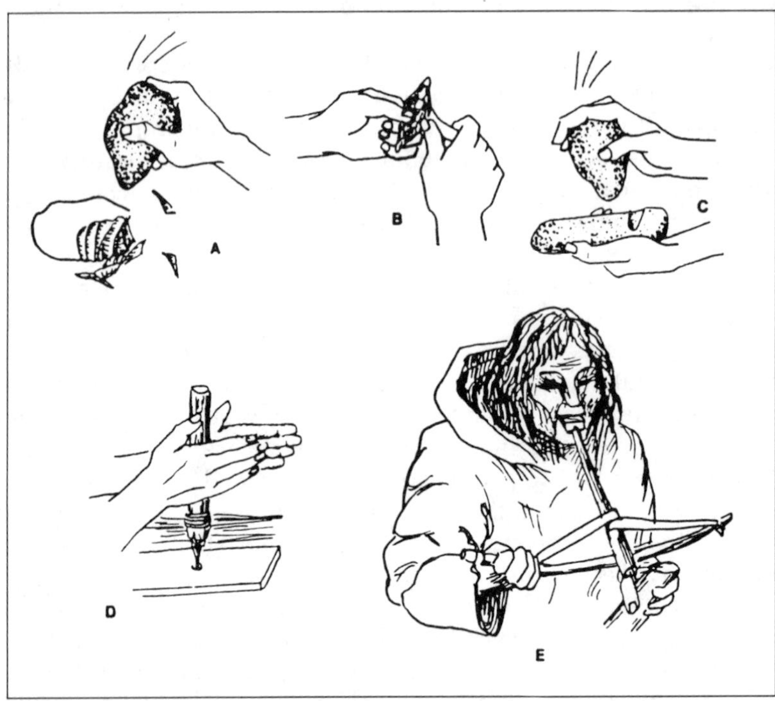

Tool technology. Stone tools were manufactured by various steps. First, a suitably hard stone was selected and flakes were chipped off it by means of a hammer stone (A). Next, the edges of a flake were chipped by applying pressure with a bone tool, thus making a sharp-edged tool (B). Finally, by pecking (C), grinding, and polishing, such tools as axes and chisels were manufactured; a hammer stone was used to peck tiny bits from the tool's surface to make it smoother.

Drilling. Holes in stone and bone tools could be drilled by different methods. The simplest tool was a hand drill (D), made of a wooden shaft with a point of stone, bone, or copper; the shaft was rotated in opposite directions by rolling it back and forth between the hands. The Eskimo and some other northern tribes used variations of the bow drill (E). The Eskimo steadied the drill by holding the bone mouthpiece in his teeth and revolved the drill by moving the bow back and forth; a bow drill can also be worked by holding the top of the drill with one hand and working the bow with the other. A simpler version of this drill has a mouthpiece but no bow—only a cord that is pulled to turn the drill.

buried or dormant, and the birds had migrated to the south. Shellfish beds were locked under ice, and streams were frozen over. It was hunt or starve, and the remains of stone tools tell us that the hunt was vital.

Hunting must have often been difficult and tiring, and the hunters would have sometimes returned to camp empty-handed. At such times, they may have lived off any stored meat or dried plant foods, or fresh plants gathered during the growing season. We lack fossil evidence of the plant foods because they decay quickly, but we know that primitive hunting tribes today commonly depend on wild plants as a stable food supply. It is likely, then, that the men hunted, and the women and children gathered wild plants. When the hunt was successful, everyone feasted on meat; but when the hunt failed, people may have been forced to consume any other foods that were available at the time. Plant foods may have been a more reliable daily food in some regions, at least on a seasonal basis.

A Society of Bands

One of the most difficult aspects to reconstruct for a prehistoric society is its social organization. In general, there are few preserved archaeological traces that can tell us much about this fundamental aspect of an ancient lifeway. Once again we use ethnographic analogy and assume that as groups became more populous—and they must have done so sometimes in spite of the rigorous climate—some families probably moved off to fresh hunting and gathering grounds. The amount of food the environment could produce would have strictly limited population size; even later people with more complex technology such as more effective hunting tools could not escape that limitation. Also the population limits set by the technology and the food supply would have kept political structures simple. We describe their social organization as *band level*, groups of fifty to one hundred people in families or other kin groups that lived and found food together. Bands probably were composed of brothers with their wives and younger children, the oldest brother or the best hunter usually acting as leader, making suggestions and offering guidance. No one would have held the leadership except by community agreement, and no one would have had coercive power to enforce his decisions. Group decisions would have been made after thorough discussion and by unanimous agreement. Cooperation and intimate knowledge of animals, surroundings, and weather conditions were essential for efficient hunting. Brothers would have been a good core for a band of hunters because, having grown up together, they would know how to most effectively hunt together and would have detailed knowledge of their environment. Strangers brought together as husbands of a group of sisters would exploit the environment for hunting far less effectively, but women who started as strangers would not suffer as much disadvantage in gathering wild plant foods for their families.

Although the land was vast and the populations were small, bands must have met from time to time, perhaps by arrangement to organize marriages or engage in communal hunts. Such hunts would have required more hunters than any one band usually could muster. Some of the animals they hunted—as we know from bone remains—were large; the best way to hunt them would be to stampede them over cliffs or into bogs where they would be mired down, killed, or disabled. The bands probably planned such activities together, and, if the hunt was successful, followed it with communal celebrations and feasting. When the supply of meat dwindled, the bands would break up, perhaps planning to meet during a good hunting season when they could find enough food for the larger population. We can also guess that bands sometimes met each other unexpectedly; the results of such contact may not always have been peaceful.

As the earliest Americans wandered, following the game they hunted, they moved southward and eventually entered new environmental zones within the interior of the continent. The southward movement was gradual enough that it generally brought no abrupt changes in climate, vegetation, or animal life. The people had plenty of time to adapt their traditional ways to new environmental requirements. The food quest would have changed as the need arose, modified by past customs. People would have responded to new circumstances, but their responses must have varied widely, depending not only on new geographic conditions and old accustomed ways, but also on the frequency of contact between bands. Various groups would doubtless have exchanged information and techniques, a process called *diffusion* or *cultural borrowing*. Those who lived where people often passed through would show more variety than those who became isolated from contact with others. The people who moved into environments rich in natural resources would begin to show a richer material life. As the years passed and groups adapted to different environments, cultures would have diversified.

The Paleo Indians: Big Game Hunters

The country stretching from the Rocky Mountains to the Mississippi and south to Mexico had a chilly and moist climate in late Pleistocene times. Winds blowing off the continental glaciers to the north cooled the Plains and brought enough rainfall to sustain lush vegetation even in regions that later turned arid or semiarid.

On the northern Plains, the lower and wetter areas were forested with pine, spruce, and tamarack; the higher land, except for wooded lake margins and river valleys, was open and carpeted with grass. Farther south along the Missouri River the Plains extended hundreds of miles in a broad belt of prairie grasslands scattered with lakes and ponds, and with woodlands of birch, alder, and other deciduous trees as well as many conifers. Toward the Rockies the long-grass area was mostly treeless. West of the Rockies, parts of today's Nevada and Utah were covered by Lake Bonneville, and even Death Valley was well vegetated.

The Plains area was an enormous open zoo, filled with some of the largest and most remarkable mammals the continent has known: giant moose, beavers as large as modern bears, ground sloths twenty feet long, long-horned bison, caribou, musk-oxen, camels, gigantic mammoths, and in the wooded areas, mastodons. Peccaries, rabbits, and smaller animals were everywhere. In season, waterfowl formed a living blanket on the prairie ponds. A fearsome array of carnivores—meat eaters—preyed on the plant eaters. The dire wolf, nearly half again as large as the later timber wolf, was armed with powerful, bone-crushing jaws. There were also bobtailed saber-toothed cats, and a panther larger than the biggest modern lion. The giant short-faced bear was much larger than today's grizzly and had a body well-designed for running with very long legs; this was probably the most dangerous carnivore of its time.

People on the Great Plains

Human beings, lured by game, wandered southward, and were drawn toward the Great Plains by the promise of even better hunting. Why did they go south? They could not have known what awaited them there, but consider the sights that met their eyes yearly. As daylight decreased in the northern latitudes, watchers saw swans, geese, ducks, curlews, plovers, and other birds fly southward from arctic breeding grounds. The birds were followed by the great browsers and grazers. The snow drifted deeper and deeper, and less and less game appeared. People would have needed no great imagination to deduce that by following the vanishing sun as the birds and the beasts did, they might find more game. And so the early hunting people, referred to by archaeologists as Paleo Indians, came to the Great Plains.

Few traces of these first pioneers of the American West have been found, but enough to tell us that as they entered the Plains their hunting and living practices began to change from the ways of their northern forefathers. The food resources of the Plains were radically different from those in the northland; plants in particular were far more plentiful. The new resources could not help affecting people's ways of life. As the glaciers began to retreat, people moved into the grassland areas. These included not only the places that are the Plains today, but also the prairies and woodlands that extended to the east beyond the Mississippi, as well as the grassland territory that later became the desert of the Southwest.

In this vast area, people specialized in the hunting of large herd mammals. The period of the Paleo Indian Big Game Hunters began by approximately 9500 B.C. and generally lasted until about 7500 B.C., although it lasted longer in the true Plains than elsewhere—long after the desert area had grown so arid that it could no longer support the herd animals.

Folsom People. Archaeological research in the Plains area has helped us understand the Big Game Hunters, and has also established the antiquity of humans in the New World. Scholars long believed that the first migrations from Asia had come as recently as 2000 B.C. During the first quarter of this century, in fact, no one even bothered to search for evidence of an earlier arrival, so convinced were scientists that human entry was recent.

Then one day, in 1925, riding in search of lost cattle near the town of Folsom, New Mexico, a man named George McJunkin noticed a layer of bleached bones twenty feet down in a deep gully. He was familiar with cattle bones and recognized immediately that the bones, though resembling modern cattle bones, were not quite like any he had ever seen. Among them McJunkin found several bits of worked flint, somewhat like arrowheads he had seen, but of a different shape—parallel instead of tapered edges, with the base chipped into a concave curve. Both sides of the points had been grooved or fluted.

News of McJunkin's discovery spread eventually to archaeologists and *paleontologists* (scientists specializing in fossils), who identified the bones as those of a bison that had become extinct about 8000 B.C. The bison's antiquity was not startling, but its clear association with human-made flint points was most exciting. The official theory at that time was that humans had not yet arrived in the New World until long after that species of bison had become extinct. Either the bones and flints had become mixed long after the bison died or else the date of human arrival in the New World had to be changed.

Unanimously the scientific world agreed that the association of bones and artifacts was no mere accident: the points had actually been used in hunting the bison. That bison pursued by ancient Folsom hunters was *Bison antiquus*, a long-horned beast that stood six feet high at the shoulder and weighed a ton. At the original Folsom site, the arrangement of the bones shows that twenty-three animals had been trapped and killed as a group in a blind gully. Here, and at some other Folsom kills, the hunters' main object seems to have been hides rather than meat; the bones are not scattered as they would have been if the bison had been butchered, and the tail bones, which would have come away with the hide when it was removed, are nearly all missing.

Clovis People. In 1932, another New Mexico site, near Clovis, yielded the bones of extinct animals accompanied by stone points different from those found at Folsom. But these Clovis points were discovered beneath layers of earth containing flints of the Folsom type, indicating that Clovis was older, and pushing the time of human arrival in North America still further back. Clovis-like spear points have turned up from coast to coast, as far north as Alaska and as far south as Mexico. Folsom points, on the other hand, are far less common beyond the high Plains. The Clovis point is larger than the Folsom, and the fluting on the Clovis does not extend as far along the blade. We have some evidence suggesting that the Clovis point may be more commonly associated with mammoth hunting and the later Folsom point with bison hunting.

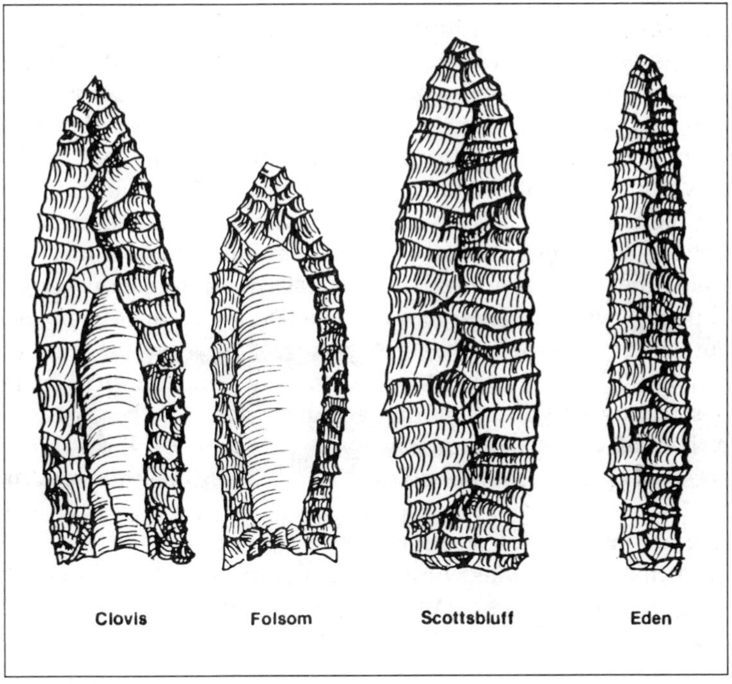

Points used by the Plains Big Game Hunters, with the names of the sites where the points were found.

How They Hunted

The hunters of the Paleo Indian tradition were probably not physically different from the earliest immigrants to the New World. But the difference in their skill at manufacturing stone tools is noticeable. The Clovis and Folsom points are extremely well-fashioned tools, and while the fluted points look delicate, they were lethal to giant animals.

The fluted points were probably set into wooden spear or lance shafts and hurled from an implement called an *atlatl* (an Aztec word) or spear thrower. The atlatl may have been brought over from Asia or it may have been independently invented in the New World. It could be used to propel a spear with triple the force of the unaided arm, a force great enough that the spear would penetrate the tough hides of the large game animals; the force came from the length the atlatl added to a hunter's arm and the extra joint that created more leverage. The atlatl was a truly revolutionary tool which allowed the hunter to attack a dangerous animal from a relatively safe distance. The bow and arrow did not appear in the New World until much later.

Even with spear throwers, it was hard to kill the large animals, and as in earlier times, the hunters often used drive strategies to provide themselves with an advantage. One approach involved driving the animals into natural cul-de-sacs such as box canyons where they were disabled and could not escape. Other methods included setting grass fires in predetermined locations; the spreading flames sent game in a panic over cliffs or into swamps. At one site the bones uncovered are all from young animals, suggesting that the hunters had managed to separate the less dangerous and more tender individuals from the herd. They had other ways of minimizing the risks of hunting large game. The Clovis people who hunted mammoths seem to have made a practice of lying in wait at water holes where the animals drank, and attacking them there. In one Clovis kill site, the leg bones of a mammoth were found intact, standing upright just as they had been when the beast was mired down. The rest of the skeleton was scattered about as if the hunters had butchered their kill from the top down, ignoring the hard-to-reach rear legs.

The great number of scrapers recovered from Paleo Indian sites indicates that they worked hides from the animals they hunted. The hunters used stone knives to cut the hides and butcher the animals. They possessed other tools as well: drawshaves, chisels, and gravers for woodworking and for engraving or splitting bone, antler, horn or ivory. Because these people wandered, like the earlier people, we would not expect to find remains of permanent shelters, and their housing appears to have been nothing more than rude windbreaks or simple tents of brush and grass or perhaps hides. In fact, with the exception of a small number

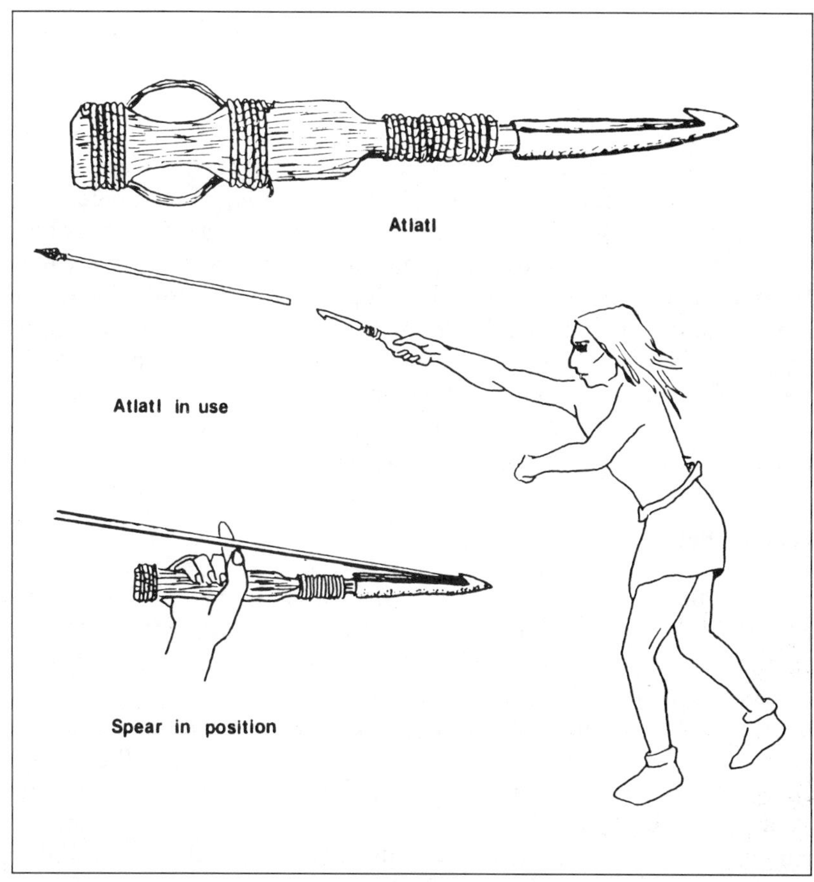

The atlatl, or spear thrower, has a wooden handle and a hooked tip into which the haft of the spear was fitted (length, about 2 feet). The use of the atlatl enabled the hunter to add range to this spear—he could stay at a distance from his prey—and to increase the speed of his weapon by the flipping action with which it was thrown. The round weights around the atlatl were probably adjusted to the individual hunter.

of sites, such as Lindenmeier in northeastern Colorado, camp sites from the time of the Paleo Indians are all but unknown; most of our knowledge comes from kill and butchering sites.

The fact that so few habitation sites have been excavated means that we may have a somewhat skewed picture of Paleo Indian life. We know more about their hunting practices than we do about other aspects of life, including what vegetal foods they relied upon. Although most of the remains that would tell us how these people used plants either have long since decayed or have yet to be discovered, we can guess from the amount and variety of vegetation that grew around them that plants were important in their food supply. Their bands came together during good hunting season to hunt game communally, interact with one another socially, perhaps exchange marriage partners and otherwise reaffirm social ties. Mass bison drives suggest that at least several dozen individuals cooperated in these. One archaeologist estimated that something like 60,000 pounds of meat must have been butchered at one site; at least 150 people would have been required to carry away even a third of it. While most of the archaeological evidence for Paleo Indian hunting comes from the Great Plains, archaeologists strongly suspect that contemporary Paleo Indian peoples in other regions of North America had similar means of subsistence and similar life-styles. Unfortunately, we have only limited evidence telling us about Paleo Indian lifeways in other regions of the continent.

A New Diet

Around 8000 B.C., though the people continued to depend upon game, they seem to have turned more and more to plant foods. Sites of the late Paleo Indian period show more equipment, such as grinding stones, for processing plants. Why the shift in eating habits? The answer is tied up with a hotly debated puzzle: why did many of the big game animals disappear? The phenomenon is often referred to as the Pleistocene extinctions. Between about 10,000 and 5000 B.C., more than a hundred species of mammals became extinct in North America, among them the mammoth, the mastodon, the horse, the camel, and all but the modern variety of bison, often called buffalo. We know that the climate of North America underwent dramatic change at the end of the Pleistocene. Geographic regions experienced significant changes in vegetation, such as the Southwest which went from grassland to desert in a matter of several hundred years, perhaps less. Was climatic change responsible for the die-offs? On the other hand, many of the species that became extinct at the end of the Pleistocene were large herd mammals that were primary food sources for Paleo Indian hunting peoples. The number of kill sites with tens or hundreds of individual game animals represented certainly suggests the possibility that human hunting may have played a significant role in these extinctions. Were the animals wiped out by human overhunting, by climate change, by both, or by causes yet to be determined?

While the answer to this question is far from settled, in the future, we may be better able to address this issue with environmental and archaeological data. In any case, the extinctions made people change their subsistence patterns and caused important changes in their ways of life. In some places hunters began to seek small game; in others fish became a major food; in still others the food was mostly wild plants. In many regions, people changed their diets to include several such food sources. People in the majority of regions tended to shift their diets to include a wider array of plant and animal food resources than they had previously used. Those new subsistence patterns led to other new patterns. Instead of wandering over broad areas searching for large game, hunters began to use more of the food resources they could find in limited areas. In one way this restricted the food search: people no longer ranged over great distances; in another way, it expanded their diet: they began to use more kinds of foods. The new local conditions varied from place to place, and as a result the individual groups of people began to differentiate according to the specific regions they inhabited.

Although the Paleo Indian tradition had seen regional modification, it was recognizable as one more or less coherent tradition from the tools the people used. The shift from Big Game Hunting to an economy varied by plants and animals introduced the cultural stage or period we call the Archaic, to which we add a word describing the region: Desert Archaic, Eastern Archaic, and others. With different regional patterns of life emerging, there was no longer just one major way of life in North America.

The Archaic Period

The stage called Archaic spans generally the years from 7500 to 1000 B.C., though its length varied from region to region. From the kinds of tools that were most common in that period, we can see the changes the people went through in finding subsistence. People made new kinds of tools, and developed new techniques for making and using already existing tools. Instead of fluting their projectile points, they began to make points with notches along the sides for hafting to spear shafts. Special devices for spearing, hooking, netting, and trapping fish showed how sophisticated technology was becoming. Stone itself came into broad use in a new form—many tools were ground into shape instead of being chipped or flaked. This change in manufacturing was much more than a refinement. It enormously expanded the supplies of raw materials from which tools could be made. Almost any tough stone, such as basalt, could now be ground into a serviceable ax, and an easily split material like slate, which cannot be chipped as well as flint because it splits too easily, could be ground into a very good spearhead, and soft stone could be hollowed out to make containers.

In this period we see the first evidence of many significant cultural developments among prehistoric North American peoples, including regional domestication of various plant food species and the first widespread evidence for domesticated dogs. Far-flung regional trade networks developed, allowing for the exchange of raw materials, food items, and perhaps many other goods. Important inventions also occurred: boats, baskets, and cloth woven of plant fibers, and in the late Archaic in the Lake Superior region, even some tools and adornments made of copper. The size and complexity of the tool kit and the changes it made in people's ways of life varied according to environment. In the western deserts, resources were sparse, and the possibilities were somewhat limited. In the eastern woodlands, countless new possibilities opened up to the inhabitants, who worked out a highly efficient technology for exploiting them.

About 8000 B.C., the North American climate began to change. Conditions became drier and as a result the grasslands and forests began to shrink. The continental ice sheets had withdrawn and the land that had been under ice was exposed. The melt-water from the ice sheets ran into river beds, filling the Great Lakes and others, and the ocean began to submerge the Bering Strait. The shorelines of the continents began to change as the oceans grew deeper. The Southwest and parts of Mexico became so hot and dry that they turned into deserts. All these new climatic and geographic conditions altered the animal life and also forced the people into different ways of life. Big Game Hunting gave way to more intensive plant collecting and small game hunting.

Desert Archaic People

The first evidence that Big Game Hunting was declining comes from the Southwest and Basin areas, which were turning into arid zones by 8000 B.C. This vast region lies between the Rockies and the Sierra Nevada and Cascade ranges, covering all of Nevada, Utah, Arizona, and parts of Oregon, Idaho, California, New Mexico, and northern Mexico. As the Pleistocene closed, it was becoming desert land, one of the most rigorous habitats in North America, imposing severe limitations on human existence. Fortunately for us, the typically dry conditions, particularly in western caves, have helped preserve ordinarily fragile items (made, for example, from wood, leather, or plant fibers) that in most other regions would quickly decompose. This has afforded us an unprecedented knowledge of the material culture of Desert Archaic lifeways.

Life in the Desert. People in this area had to shift from hunting to foraging—some would even call it scavenging. They diversified their dietary habits to include rats, snakes, lizards, gophers, birds, and other small desert species, though unquestionably most of their diet was desert seeds, tubers, and other vegetable foods. Small game and birds were sometimes caught with loop snares. Deer and elk must have been rare delicacies in the desert, though the hunting of big game continued in the grasslands to the east. Some desert peoples had at least occasional access to other large game, including pronghorn antelope, wild sheep, and bison. For the new, largely vegetarian diet the Indians developed grinding stones, which they used to reduce the vegetable foods, indigestible when raw, to a condition suitable for cooking. Baskets for harvesting and storing wild plants became common household utensils. The women gathered all kinds of seeds including those of pickleweed, sunflower, and yucca, from good-sized acorns to tiny Indian millet seeds. Placed on a surface of a grinding stone and ground with a small stone held in the hand, the seeds were reduced to a coarse meal. This milling equipment was the prototype of the stone slab (*metate*) and hand-held stone (*mano*), still widely used in rural Mexico to grind corn. The cooks then either formed the meal into cakes to be baked or boiled it into a mush in watertight baskets by dropping hot stones into them—a method known as stone boiling.

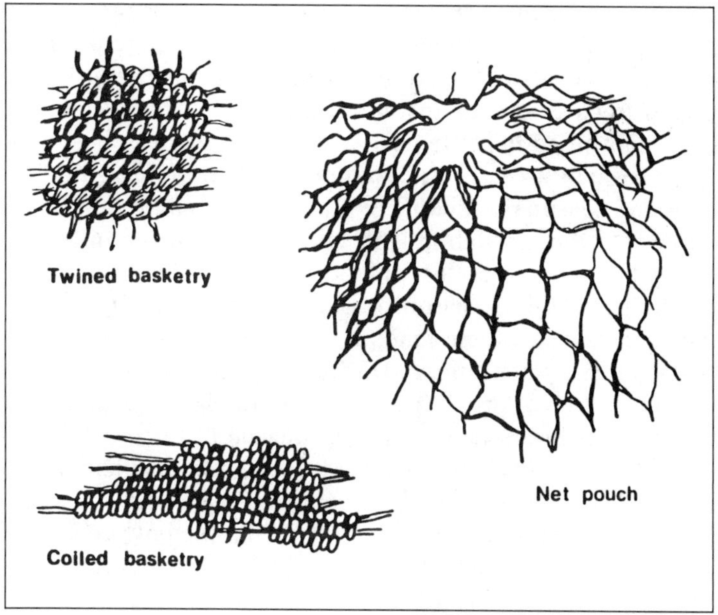

Examples of basketry fragments from the Desert Archaic. The net pouch was probably used like a shopping bag.

These people had a domesticated animal, the dog, certainly by mid-Archaic times, around 4000 B.C., and perhaps as early as 8000 B.C., as indicated by finds such as that of Jaguar Cave in Idaho. Dogs helped in hunting, as scavengers about the camp, as a warning if animal predators or human enemies came near—and occasionally as a source of food.

The once large lakes of the region were drying up and turning brackish by Archaic times, but migrating fowl stopped by, attracted by realistic decoys made of reeds sewn together with fiber threads and covered with duck feathers. The people trapped waterfowl in nets, searched the reedy shallows for eggs in the nests of grebes or mud hens, and caught fish in fiber nets weighted on the bottom edge with stones: six or seven boys or men waded out waist-deep to bring the net around in a loop to scoop up the fish. They also apparently caught fish on bone hooks attached to fiber lines. In and along the marshes they collected the seeds of bulrush, cattail, and panic grass (*Panicum sp.*).

By the early summer, the heat was intense, and the waterways and lakes began to dry up. No longer did people have to wear fur blankets and robes; breechcloths for the men and short hide aprons for the women were all the summer clothes they needed. Brush shelters that had given protection against winter cold gave shade during summer midday heat. Women harvested the seeds and plants as they ripened, carrying the foodstuffs in tall, conical collecting baskets and roasting them by shaking them with live coals on wickerwork trays. The heat split the inedible husks and freed the seeds inside for grinding.

People continued to settle near whatever lakes, marshes, or streams remained in their area. They developed a highly mobile life-style that incorporated seasonal scheduling practices to ensure that they would have access to the most abundant wild food resources in their region. Thus they foraged and collected foods in various environmental zones during their individual seasons of availability. Sometimes they stored quantities of less desirable foods in caves and natural rockshelters as a hedge against winter famine. During later Archaic times, piñon nuts became a resource of prime importance to the Desert Archaic peoples. Throughout the prehistoric period in these areas, we detect a pattern of flexibility in life-style that allowed the people to adjust to changing local conditions that periodically fluctuated between dry and more moist. Toward the later stages of the Desert Archaic, the bow and arrow were introduced, as was the practice of making and using pottery.

This life-style spread to nearly all the arid and semiarid regions of the West. In some places it persisted until historic times (documented after European contact), as in the cultures of the Shoshoni, Ute, and Paiute tribes, from whom we get our descriptions of the rabbit hunt.

The Rabbit Hunt. An important cooperative activity, hunting for rabbits, added meat to the mostly vegetable diet. Rabbits were caught in nets more than two hundred feet long but only about two feet wide, woven of milkweed fiber. Only the very old and mothers with babies did not take part in the hunt. Some of the people tied nets together and set them up, and others served as beaters, thrashing the underbrush with sticks. Rabbits ran from their hiding places into the nets, where they were met with throwing sticks and clubs. As the animals approached, the hunters killed as many as they could short of the net, because if too many rabbits hit it they could tear the delicate net fibers. A second line of hunters disposed of animals engaged in the mesh and caught many of those that managed to get through the net.

The hunt was followed by a rabbit feast, and then the women dressed the skins. Beginning at the outer edge of a pelt and cutting around and around in a spiral, they converted the skins into long strips and stretched them between trees until they dried. Thirty or so six-foot lengths of fur rope woven side by side with bits of skin made a winter robe or blanket.

People of the Coastal Archaic

Along the borders of the western desert and in the lands stretching to the Pacific coast, life was much less harsh, but the people's adaptations were much the same. The main difference was the amount and variety of food available: the supply of animals and plants was more bountiful beyond the desert, and fish and seafoods abounded along waterways and coasts. In central California, where oak trees were plentiful, the main crop was acorns, which women gathered and ground into meal for cakes or mush. In southern California, people gathered tubers, bunchgrass seeds, and abundant buckeye seeds that required leaching before they could be eaten. The foraging groups along the seacoast exploited the rich food resources there: abalones, clams, mussels, many kinds of fish, and even marine mammals like seals and sea otters. In the California area, communities were larger than in the desert, and life went on around more or less permanent base camps.

The northwest coast, then as now, was mountain terrain with deep valleys whose rivers rushed to the sea. The archaeological record, still very incomplete, shows Archaic adaptations to the plentiful fish and shell foods of the rivers and coast. Bone remains tell us that people also took sea mammals such as otters and seals as well as land mammals like elk and deer. The hunting and fishing adaptations of the northwest coastal people appear to have begun 5,500 or more years ago. The picture emerging from the archaeological record for the northwest coast is one of gradual change and long-term continuity, eventually culminating in

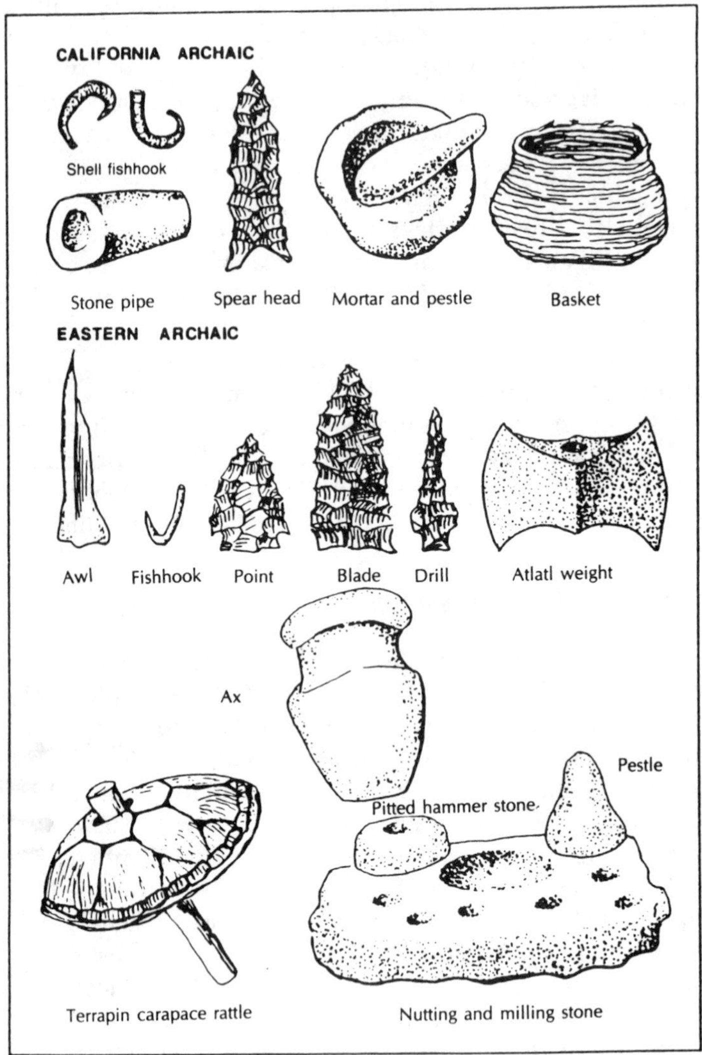

Archaic artifacts. Artifacts of the California Archaic made of shell, fiber, and stone (top; variable scale). Eastern Archaic artifacts (bottom; all one-fourth actual size except the weight, the ax, and the milling stone). All these items are of stone except for the awl and the fishhook, which are made of bone, and the carapace, or turtle shell, which is a restored rattle.

the characteristic lifeways documented by European visitors in the contact period. The relatively stable and abundant resources of the northwest coast, most notably a surplus of fish, contributed to the establishment of large, permanent or semipermanent settlements in favored coastal locations near the mouths of rivers. The coastal areas experienced greater population growth over the centuries than did drier areas to the east.

Living in the Arctic and Subarctic Archaic

Scholars agree that North America's native populations entered the continent from the extreme northwest, but the archaeological material they have from the far north is much scantier than from almost any other region. The reason is obvious: the excavators face formidable obstacles in a land of permanently frozen soil. Some ancient sites are accessible—one is conveniently on the campus of the University of Alaska—but others lie in remote and almost unmapped regions, reachable only recently by helicopter. Digging still can be done only during the very brief summer, and even then it poses unique difficulties. After removing one shallow level, the excavator must wait for the sun to thaw a few more inches of soil before digging deeper. This natural deep-freeze has the advantage, of course, of preserving otherwise perishable materials. Ancient refuse does smell as it begins to thaw, but it is full of information about prehistoric diet.

Tiny tools known as *microblades*, dating from about 8000 to 800 B.C., have turned up in the Arctic. This stone tool technology represents initially the Paleo-Arctic tradition (8000 to 5000 B.C. and later in certain areas), as well as more recent cultural developments eventually culminating in the Arctic Small Tool tradition (2000 to 800 B.C.). The blades were probably set in antler and bone to make composite tools, one of which was a kind of toothed saw, useful for working hides. Other types may well have been serrated points used for spears and harpoons. People of the Paleo-Arctic tradition probably were not Eskimo, but many of their tool designs were similar to those of subsequent people in the Arctic Small Tool tradition who undoubtedly were Eskimo, and who appear to have migrated to the Alaskan Arctic from Asia approximately 2000 B.C. The Small Tool makers spread rapidly across the northern part of the continent in the Arctic and Subarctic from Alaska to Hudson's Bay and eventually to Greenland. Archaeologists think that their tools resemble certain Asiatic types. Some of those people seem to have hunted sea mammals in summer and passed the winters farther inland hunting caribou, elk, musk oxen, and small game. They also fished, for net sinkers have been found among the stone equipment, especially in sites in the subarctic forests.

The people of the Arctic Small Tool tradition possessed a distinctive tool kit with microblade tools, including the earliest bows and arrows in North America. It is believed that the bow and arrow was introduced into the Arctic region from northeastern Asia approximately 4000 years ago. From the Arctic, the bow and arrow eventually spread to cultures throughout North America. While the bow and arrow were originally used so long ago in the Arctic, they were not introduced into the interior of North America until much more recently. Peoples on the far northern plains probably began using this new technology during the first few centuries A.D., while it was apparently not introduced into the Great Lakes, Mississippi Valley, and eastern woodlands until approximately 500 or 600 A.D.

We know from a relatively small number of excavated archaeological sites that other people also lived in the frigid zones across Alaska and northern Canada. In some regions, for example along the northern Atlantic coast, Archaic cultures began to develop in distinctly different directions, largely in relation to the available natural resources and environmental conditions. While we are learning more about these cultures as time goes on, the picture is still so incomplete that relatively little can be said about them.

Forest People of the Eastern Archaic

From the Plains eastward to the Atlantic, forests were prominent in the environment after about 8000 B.C. Those eastern forests were not scattered patches of woodland as they are today, but endless tracts of trees covering mountains, rolling hills, and valleys. The forests sheltered countless woodland animals; deer were most common, but squirrel, opossum, bear, raccoon, and wildcat also inhabited the forests. The region was well watered by rainfall and by rivers and streams. Those watercourses and the many lakes and large and small ponds held many species of fish and turtles and attracted a number of waterfowl and wetlands mammals, including otter, beaver, and muskrat. The Indians of the East lived in the forests, where trees that provided the materials for their houses and equipment could be found, in addition to plentiful game.

The women gathered many forms of wild plants, seeds, nuts, fruits, tubers, and roots. It is possible that the people living around Lake Superior may have begun to exploit a grass seed that we now call wild rice. Archaeological evidence indicates that, in addition to harvesting such wild foods, later Eastern Archaic peoples had begun to harvest intensively and even cultivate certain plants by approximately 3500 to 5000 years ago. *Cucurbits* (gourds and possibly squashes) and bottle gourd represent domesticated plants with apparent Mexican origins. These were likely cultivated in dump areas or other disturbed ground near Archaic camps along with several native Eastern plants, including sunflower, marsh elder, goosefoot, and maygrass. Taken as a group, these indigenous seed plants have been referred to as the *Eastern Agricultural Complex*. All evidence indicates that these comprise the first agricultural activities north of Mexico.

The forests residents constructed rather elaborate dwellings, as we can tell from the patterns of postholes found at some Eastern Archaic sites. They must have been more settled than the desert or arctic people of the same period. While they were far from fully sedentary, it appears that they relocated less frequently, occupying certain base camps for most of the year and making fewer moves over the course of any season. The enormous heaps of fresh-water shells along inland rivers and seashells on the coast imply a population that was not only more settled, but also more numerous. In addition to supplying food, shellfish also provided raw material for utensils and shell ornaments.

The tools the easterners used reflect increasing technological elaboration, and included many implements for exploiting the wood that was so plentiful: axes, drills, gouges, and other woodworking tools of ground and chipped stone. They made specialized items, too: many styles of fishhooks, harpoons, and nets for game and fowl as well as for fish, and mortars and pestles for crushing and grinding plant foods. Out of bone and shell they carved beads, pendants, and awls. Archaic peoples living around the Great Lakes approximately 2300 to 1200 B.C. hammered tools as well as ornaments out of the copper nuggets they found—the first instance of metalwork in the New World. The copper was hammered as if it were another form of stone; the people had no knowledge of smelting, and the copper workers never learned to cast metal. Consequently, metal craft was primarily restricted to the region around Lake Superior where lumps of pure copper could be found ready for use. Archaeologists have given the name "Old Copper Culture" to the Archaic development of copper technology in the Great Lakes region.

It is not unlikely that the birchbark canoe was invented during the late Archaic in the densely forested north woods that stretched from Wisconsin and Minnesota into Canada and to the eastern seaboard. Such a boat would have been particularly useful in this environment, where thousands of lakes are connected by a network of streams and rivers, but with gaps in the connections. Only a lightweight vessel could negotiate shallows and be carried across land between waterways. Once available, the bark canoe opened up the formerly impenetrable north

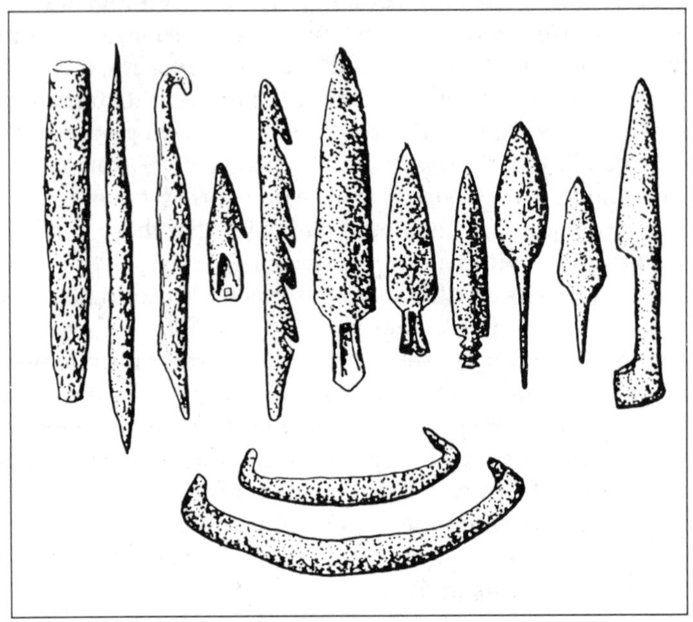

Copper tools of the Archaic period (about one-half actual size).

woods and converted the region's web of lakes and streams into routes for trade and communication.

In the East, Archaic people not only hooked and netted fish, they also trapped them. One huge fish trap, or weir as it is called, was built about 2500 B.C. in what is now Boston. It was an enclosure extending over two acres of a shallow lagoon, allowing water to pass through but keeping fish back. Building the weir would have required an estimated 65,000 stakes, sharpened with stone axes and set in double rows interlaced with brush. The labor it took shows that it was not intended for short-term use, but to bring in a sure food supply for many years—enough for the fairly large population that would have been needed to build such an extensive installation. The large number of workers required meant that there must also have been some central authority to mobilize people and materials for such a large public work.

Like the Desert Archaic, the Eastern Archaic tradition left a record telling of a remarkably stable way of life over a long period. Unlike the Desert, though, the Eastern shows a big difference in population growth, because resources there could support many more people. Although the wooded eastern region as a whole may be characterized as we have done here, this one general tradition included an infinite variety of local environments and thus considerable diversification. Over time, Eastern Archaic adaptations became more regionally specialized, resulting in noteworthy differences in the cultures between, for example, coastal and interior areas. We also witness the development of long-distance trade of raw materials (including copper and marine shell), foods, or finished goods among groups living in various areas of the East and perhaps beyond.

The Woodland Tradition

In the East, two major new developments set off the period from about 1000 B.C. to A.D. 800 from the Archaic: the construction of large earthen mounds and the use of pottery. Building upon the practices begun during the Archaic, Eastern peoples also continued to cultivate and harvest certain favored plants that had by this time become at least semidomesticated. While many Archaic cultural traits continued over much of the East until European contact, a number of significant changes took place in a number of geographic areas. Some areas showed such intensified development and so much new sophistication that most prehistorians feel it is reasonable to separate this period or cultural stage from the Archaic. It has become known as the Woodland tradition.

Within the Woodland tradition, different groups constructed spectacular earthworks as burial and effigy mounds, and apparently traded luxury items like freshwater pearls, marine shells, copper, mica, and obsidian (or volcanic glass). What has been called a revolution in container technology occurred in eastern North America, resulting in the development of waterproof pottery vessels for storing and cooking foods. Thus the period is not only of great interest but also of great importance. Those local changes showed how bountiful natural resources, complex and sophisticated technology, social organization, and opportunity for new ideas to enter (probably by the connecting river routes) all came together to create a new social and economic pattern. This led, though indirectly, to even more complex societies. Important stimulus may have come from as far as Mexico, although archaeologists by no means agree about Mexican influence in this early period, or even during later prehistoric periods.

Two of the most fascinating and elaborate Woodland cultures are known as Adena and Hopewell. As you read these descriptions, keep in mind that Adena and Hopewell are a biased sample of Woodland culture. Many contemporary eastern groups were not so technologically or socially sophisticated, but merely added pottery and occasional rather insignificant mounds to their mostly Archaic adaptations. Indeed, for some societies, Woodland has been described as "Archaic with pottery."

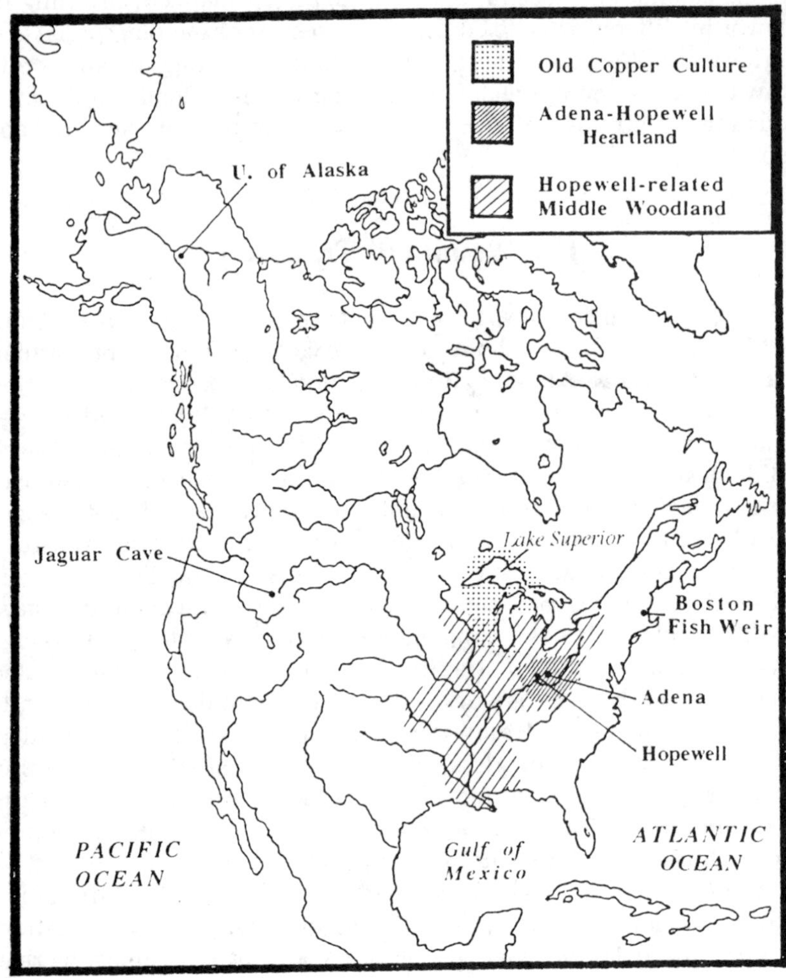

North American Archaic and Woodland cultures and prehistoric sites discussed in text.

Other more highly developed Woodland groups, while not truly Adena or Hopewell, interacted directly or indirectly with these cultures, and to varying extents appear to have adopted or imitated aspects of Adena or especially Hopewell cultural elaboration.

Adena People

For reasons not yet known, around 1000 B.C. some eastern people began a new type of construction. From the eastern plains to the Atlantic Ocean, people constructed earthen mounds of various sizes and shapes, most of which covered burials. While a rich lore has developed about the so-called "Moundbuilders," implying that a single culture was responsible for creating these features on the landscape, in fact the mounds were not all built at the same time, nor by the same people. Many Woodland and later cultures constructed mounds for various reasons, frequently as a part of their burial ceremonialism. Even a few late Eastern Archaic groups had apparently built mounds to bury their dead.

Serpent Mound, longest of all mounds ever constructed in the shape of animals (a quarter mile), contained no burials as far as can be determined; it is located in southwestern Ohio. The construction of this mound probably had religious or other symbolic significance, but no one really knows.

The first of the major mound-building peoples were the Adena, an Early Woodland culture named after an estate near Chillicothe, Ohio, where earthworks were excavated in 1901. The Adena mode of subsistence largely followed the Archaic pattern. The people lived by harvesting wild foods in a systematic way, taking advantage of a great variety of available plants, and hunting woodland animals, especially white-tailed deer. The Adena people and their contemporaries in other areas relied very heavily upon wild or semidomesticated plant foods, and obtained most of their subsistence from a relatively small number of species. In particular, they harvested and even cultivated several annual grasses that produced an abundance of small, either oily or starchy seeds: sunflower, marsh elder, goosefoot, maygrass, pigweed, and possibly little barley. Several of these plants had apparently been utilized since at least the late Archaic period, as noted earlier. What began with intensive harvesting of wild plant seeds likely led to intentional sowing of seeds. Agriculture, or true cultivation, seems to have developed over a long period of time in the East, probably in response to growing population and more restricted territories and food resources. Squashes and gourds were also cultivated by Adena and other Woodland peoples, as were pumpkins, which appear to have been domesticated somewhere in eastern North America by this time.

We do not have much excavated evidence of Adena habitations, but the remains that have been found show that their houses were round, built of posts leaning outward with mats hung from them to form walls. The roofs were thatched. The finest remains of the Adena people are their burial mounds and the structures that went with them. People began erecting these mounds sometime around 600 B.C., surrounding many of them with ridges of piled-up earth through which long avenues, similarly bordered, approached the mounds. The mound structures are clearly associated with important aspects of Adena ceremonial life.

Because so much excavating has been done in the Adena people's ceremonial complexes and so little in their villages, we know much more about their ornamental objects than about their ordinary tools and equipment. For the most part, these tools differed little from those of the Archaic people except that they had been developed further and show differences in temporal and regional style to some degree. The Adena people made pottery, pendants of ground stone, and pipes. The latter indicates the smoking of plant materials, possibly including tobacco, although the direct archaeological evidence for tobacco in the East postdates the Adena by some three hundred years. During the historic period, other plant materials were also smoked by eastern peoples, including hemp, grasses, and the leaves or bark of certain shrubs; such practices may extend well into the prehistoric also. Adena people wove

A reconstructed Adena house (diameter, 26 feet) based on a circular floor plan.

cloth from plant fibers and made items of copper: body ornaments like bracelets, pendants, and rings, as well as some tools.

The burial mounds were large, up to 65 feet tall, and much care was lavished on them. The people built them through cooperative efforts by piling up small basketloads of earth, one after another, atop a prepared ground surface. The dead interred in these mounds were probably high-ranking people in Adena society, because not all bodies got this treatment. Some were laid on the ground and merely covered with earth; others were placed in pits lined with logs and roofed with more logs, over which a mound was built. Some bodies were cremated and some were merely buried.

Grave goods placed with the dead included designs cut from sheets of mica, and ground and polished stone tablets elaborately carved with an image of a bird associated with the Adena people. This was probably meant to represent a *raptor* or bird of prey like a hawk or eagle, along with an eye motif, and is found in this culture and later eastern and southern cultures. Some burials show evidence of having been painted or sprinkled with natural pigments. Grave goods reflect exotic materials obtained through widespread trade with peoples living in regions far from the Ohio Valley, including North Carolina, New England, Ontario, and the Lake Superior region. Although Adena certainly influenced other cultures in the East, it appears to have been confined mainly to parts of Kentucky, West Virginia, southeastern Indiana, and southern Ohio.

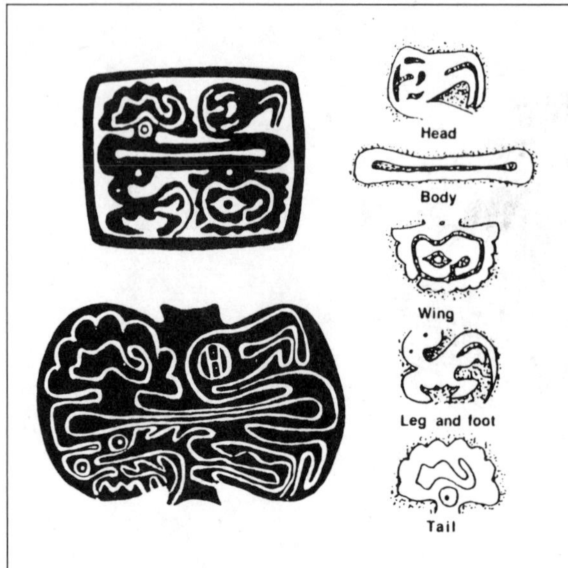

Elements of the Adena bird design and two engraved tablets which show the elements.

Hopewell People

Early Hopewell existed around the same time as Adena and was directly influenced by that culture. Adena was earlier and Hopewell probably lasted longer, though they had generations of overlap. Hopewell and contemporary cultures are commonly referred to as Middle Woodland. While Hopewell may have started in west-central Illinois or more likely Ohio, it clearly reached its peak in Ohio, where it got its name from a mound-studded farm in Ross County that was owned by a man named Hopewell. The Hopewell people, like the Adena folk, were mound builders, but their mounds were even more sophisticated and complex, and their burials were much more richly furnished with personal adornments.

Hopewell Trading. The Hopewell peoples also are distinguished by their far-flung trading system. Trade had been going on throughout the Midwest and East since at least the Archaic, especially trade in copper nuggets, but it was informal, not systematic. Hopewell trade appears to have involved at least semiprofessional traders. The Ohio Hopewell sites were well suited to such commerce. To the north, rivers gave access to the Great Lakes and the copper and silver resources of Lake Superior. To the east, through Lake Ontario, were routes to the St. Lawrence, Mohawk, and Hudson valleys. The Ohio River led south into the

Appalachians, where mica and other useful minerals were found. From the Gulf of Mexico and the southern Atlantic coast, trade in shells moved north via the Mississippi and other river systems. Up the Missouri River, to the west, traders could get grizzly bear teeth and obsidian. The upper Mississippi Valley apparently participated in the trade as well, providing cubes of galena and passing along exotic stone material from the Dakotas. Other high quality stone materials (flints and cherts) also were traded from southern Illinois and southern Indiana.

What did the Hopewell people trade for these items? The complexity of their society implies much specialization of labor, at least part-time, so they probably had craftsworkers turning imported raw materials into finished goods for trade. Pipes, beautifully fashioned stone tools, and finely crafted pottery appear to have been distributed widely from the center of Ohio Hopewell activity. In addition, the Ohio Hopewell peoples had a valuable raw material of their own, a flint of distinctive and fine quality dug from a deposit known today as Flint Ridge. Another local product was a fine-grained stone used for making pipes, much desired throughout the East and Midwest.

Traders did not have to travel as far as Lake Superior, the Gulf, or the Rockies. Articles from those areas were almost unquestionably passed from tribe to tribe along a network of commercial routes. But Hopewell traders probably sought business as far as several hundred miles away.

Burial Complexes and Crafts from the Tomb. The Hopewell peoples of Ohio and adjoining areas buried their dead in large artificial earthen mounds. Frequently these mounds were of quite impressive size and were arranged in systematic fashion. Many, particularly in Ohio, were constructed in groups within encircling enclosures of geometric design. The approaches to these ritual enclosures were in many cases lined by other earthworks, effectively creating avenues that connected individual mortuary areas to one another.

The majority of the Hopewell populace were apparently cremated prior to burial; however, the elite of their society were buried intact in log-lined tombs with a rich variety of grave goods. Proof of the wealth that trade funneled into Hopewell communities is plentiful in these tombs. Accompanying the burials are not only spear points and tools, but also embossed breastplates and ornaments of hammered copper, delicately chipped obsidian knives, fragile silhouettes cut out of sheet mica, and conch shells engraved with designs representing men and beasts. Some skeletons have been found covered with thousands of fresh-water pearls, which had apparently decorated a cloak or blanket.

These rich goods do not always reflect the results of trade, however. Some show how culturally sophisticated the Hopewell were themselves. Pipes of local stone were beautifully carved into naturalistic animal or

Mica silhouette. The brittle, transparent mineral from which silhouettes were cut was traded by the Indians of the Hopewell culture. Found in Ohio several hundred miles from the nearest source of mica, this silhouette had been buried with an Indian who lived about 1,500 to 2,000 years ago.

human forms by artisans. Pottery shows imagination and remarkable skill in its shapes and decorations. Instead of painting their pottery, the potters produced their designs by engraving and by varying its texture. One design element many Hopewell peoples used is a bird of prey, resembling the Adena design.

In addition to carved pipes and almost sculptural pots, the Hopewell peoples produced true sculptures: little pottery figurines that show how the people sat, stood, and dressed. A woman, seated with her feet to one side, wearing a mid-length skirt, suckles her baby; another stands beneath an elaborate headdress, long hair hanging down her back in a sort of tassel, a crescent-shaped necklace around her neck and wide bands of either beads or tattooing around her wrists, upper arms, and ankles. And a little kneeling man, clad in a breechcloth, holds a war club or a hoe.

Cultivating Crops. The Hopewell folk definitely cultivated their crops. In addition to several of the weedy or grassy plants described earlier, such as sunflower, marsh elder, maygrass, goosefoot (also called lamb's-quarters), and little barley, we find some indication of *maize*, the grain known as corn in the United States. Squashes and gourds were also cultivated by Hopewell and other Middle Woodland peoples. While maize only became an economically important crop some hundreds of years later, the several native small-seed species were apparently being cultivated by what has been described as intensive horticulture.

The large, stable settlements, the broad geographic range of the culture, the wealth, and the elaboration of burials all indicate that the Hopewell had some sort of central authority and a large, organized work force, and also an assured food supply they could have gotten only by combining some domestication with the wild plant and animal foods.

Around A.D. 400, the prosperity that had marked the Hopewell culture diminished. The great earthworks were no longer built, and the funeral offerings became crude and sparse. The elaborate trade between widely separated regions of eastern North America collapsed. What caused the decline is unknown, though some scattered evidence of invaders and warfare has been found. Booming population growth may have caused competition for resources. The introduction of the bow and arrow into eastern North America around the middle of the first millennium A.D. may have resulted in significant changes in both hunting practices and warfare. On the other hand, it has been suggested that cultivated foods took on increasing importance as the Woodland tradition progressed, and that this may have brought about new subsistence strategies or changes in leadership. The cause behind the downfall of Hopewell culture is not precisely known, but the people generally abandoned the ceremonial centers, and simple local forms developed in place of the once grand and widespread Hopewell tradition.

The Question of Transoceanic Contacts

It would not do to conclude our discussion of the early history of the New World without a brief look at the question of pre-Columbian transoceanic contacts other than those which may have come across the Bering Strait. There is no serious doubt that the New World was populated from Asia over land that emerged during the Pleistocene. The early immigrants had a very simple technology: they could control and make fire, work stone by chipping, work hides, and apparently make very little else. In much later periods, however—from 3000 B.C. to perhaps A.D. 1000—some traits show up in the New World that are strikingly like traits in the Pacific Islands, Southeast Asia, or Africa. To explain this similarity, some archaeologists have suggested contacts between people across the Pacific or Atlantic Oceans.

The items that may be signs of contact with the Old World are cultural and botanical, and most are not more than similarities between remains from South America and trans-Pacific cultures. Some botanists and archaeologists believe the similarities are too striking to have been independently invented, and that they must have been carried by voyagers across the ocean: examples of what anthropologists refer to as *cultural diffusion*. Certainly some resemblances came about as adaptations to similar conditions. Or the forms may look alike where function and meaning are quite different—in other words, they are sheer coincidence. Some similarities, though, cannot be so casually dismissed, and at least one is cultural. Whatever the case, it is essential that archaeologists and prehistorians consider the available evidence critically in assessing the potential influence or impact of Old World cultures on the pre-Columbian cultures of the Americas.

Botanical Evidence

Before any Europeans had arrived in North America, certain domesticated plants appear to have been known both in the New World and in the Old World and some of the Pacific Islands. The most important of these—those for which we have what has been considered the best evidence—are cotton and the bottle gourd. Some people have taken the existence of these two cultivated plants in both hemispheres as evidence that people brought them from the Old to the New World. Since domesticated plants must be carefully tended to survive, whenever they appear outside the area where they were originally domesticated it usually means that they were moved by people.

The arrival of the domesticated bottle gourd in the New World has been variously attributed to either West African or Southeast Asian travelers. Those who oppose the theory of transoceanic contact have long pointed out that the seeds of the gourd can still grow even after long soaking in ocean water, and therefore could have come to the New World simply by floating across the ocean. More importantly, to date, there is no indisputable evidence of any direct prehistoric contact between New World peoples and the proposed Old World carriers of the bottle gourd. It is currently believed that bottle gourds originally arrived in Brazil long before they were domesticated. They have been recovered in Mexican sites dating to around 7000 B.C., and in at least two Archaic sites in Illinois dating to circa 5000 B.C. However, it is unknown whether or not they had been domesticated by the time they reached eastern North America around 4000 years ago.

Cotton is a botanically complicated puzzle, but recently scientific opinion seems to have swung to the point of view that modern forms could have arisen independently by natural crosses between two wild New World species. Cotton, then, is no longer considered very good evidence for the transoceanic theory. The presence of other cultivated plants in both Old and New Worlds, such as the sweet potato and the yam, might have explanations other than transmission by prehistoric cultivators, and all in all, domesticated plants do not seem very convincing evidence for contact. It is particularly weak when we consider that voyagers would have had to cross either the Pacific or the Atlantic *before 2000* B.C. to bring these domesticates to the New World, because archaeological remains show that they were already here by that date.

Cultural Evidence

A number of investigators have been interested in stylistic similarities between the Old and New Worlds, such as decorative designs using crosses, serpent deities, and intertwined ribbons or laces. The question is: are those designs so complex that they would not have been thought up more than once in the vast history of humankind? Another objection to proving contact by anything so tenuous as art styles is that the spread of style would have required more interaction than just a few people landing from a boat. On the other hand, if a flood of people came across the ocean, so many that they would make an impression on the native population, how can it be that they left anything so nebulous as an art style, but not one object of material culture, not one tool or pot from their homes? We may also ask if those sailors or fishermen would have been so artistic that they could reproduce the art styles of their homelands. It seems more likely that some design components turn up almost everywhere in art, like spirals and scrolls; finding such items in two widely separated areas does little to prove human contact between the two places.

The appearance of more complex items in both the Old and New Worlds has been considered by some to represent sounder evidence of contact: items such as panpipes and blow guns, and a way of casting metal that was known in South America. These are elaborate enough that it seems unlikely they would have been invented independently. Nevertheless, no one has determined how complex or complicated an item must be before it definitely could not have been independently invented in several areas. Proponents of contact between cultures of the Old and New World often fail to explain precisely why a particular element or an art style would be adopted from an outside society. Brief cultural contact by itself does not necessarily create significant change; on the other hand, longer-term interaction between distinctly different cultures usually leaves a quantity of indisputable evidence of the contact. While many cases have been proposed, overall, the archaeological evidence for pre-Columbian contact between cultures of the Old World and the New World is very limited indeed.

One of the most often discussed examples of potential contact concerns the Valdivia complex on the coast of Ecuador. Valdivia complex pottery was thought to be the earliest known pottery in the New World, dating to around 3000–2500 B.C. When first investigated, this very sophisticated pottery posed a mystery for archaeologists, since no earlier, simpler forms had been found to indicate how it developed. It was suggested that, because it was so well made and of such advanced design, it must have come in full-blown from somewhere else. Researchers noted that the dates of the Valdivia ceramics were consistent with dates of pottery made in Jomon, Japan, and the shapes and surface designs were also consistent with the Jomon forms and decoration. This was viewed as making a strong case for contact across the Pacific between the Jomon culture and the Valdivia culture, perhaps accomplished by fishermen driven far off course from their Japanese homeland waters.

Other scholars argued that the nature of the Jomon canoes and the great distance and time involved in making such a journey made such contact four to five thousand years ago extremely unlikely, and suggested instead that the similarities in pottery were more likely coincidental. More recently, less sophisticated ceramics have been recovered at Valdivia that predate the Valdivia complex pottery and appear to bear little resemblance to Jomon. While it is still not understood where the stimulus for this earlier, yet still well-made, pottery originated, it now seems that

Colombia rather than Japan represents a far more likely source.

The best documented case of pre-Columbian transoceanic contact between the Old and New World cultures are the Norse voyages to northeastern North America, approximately one thousand years ago. Viking traditions indicate attempts to explore and settle the northwestern Atlantic region around A.D. 1000, including the establishment of settlements in southern Greenland, lasting several hundred years, and in a land they called Vinland (probably Newfoundland) for a mere two years duration. In this case, we have encountered indisputable archaeological evidence of the Norse presence and of contact between the Norse and Native American cultures in these areas, notably the Inuit (Eskimo) and probably also the Algonkian-speaking Beothuk. Norse artifacts have been recovered in several areas, and a Norse habitation has been excavated on Newfoundland. Interestingly, this single well-documented example of transoceanic contact between vastly different cultures appears to have left no detectable impact on the native cultures of these regions.

Even if other cases of contact are proven eventually, it is still clear that most aspects of high civilization in America were truly indigenous. The important *cultigens* (that is, cultivated plants), especially corn, are native to the New World, and we know that early Americans manipulated them over many years to bring them from their wild state to domestication. The same is true for urbanization and complex political, social, and economic structures, as well as native art styles.

Summary

At some time before 10,000 B.C., small groups of people moved into the New World over the open land that at that time connected northeastern Asia and northwestern North America. They were not deliberately migrating to a new land, but simply following the herds of animals they hunted. Those early people had relatively unsophisticated technology: simple stone tools to butcher the game they killed and to work the hides. They hafted their carefully made stone points to spear shafts for use as hunting weapons, and made other stone tools for chopping, scraping, hammering, and other tasks. Over the millennia, moving through the ice-free corridor between the eastern and western ice sheets, succeeding generations came to the Great Plains area to the east of the Rocky Mountains.

The Great Plains were home for a number of species of large herd animals, and as time passed, the hunters began to concentrate on these large browsers and grazers. Thus the period from around 9500 to 7500 B.C. is known as the Paleo Indian, or Big Game Hunting, era. Because

NEW WORLD CULTURES, TRADITIONS, AND EVENTS COVERED IN PART 1.

DATE	Arctic	Subarctic	Northwest Coast and Plateau	California
Modern times				
A.D. 1600				
A.D. 1500	THULE TRADITION			
A.D. 1000			PLATEAU AND NORTHWEST COAST TRADITION	CALIFORNIA TRADITION
A.D. 1		NORTHERN ARCHAIC TRADITIONS		
1000 B.C.	ARCTIC SMALL TOOL TRADITION			
2000 B.C.	?			COASTAL ARCHAIC TRADITION
3000 B.C.				
4000 B.C.	?		COASTAL ARCHAIC TRADITION	
5000 B.C.				?
6000 B.C.			?	
7000 B.C.	PALEO-ARCTIC TRADITION			
8000 B.C.				
9000 B.C.				
10,000 B.C.				
	Entry of Asiatic population into New World			

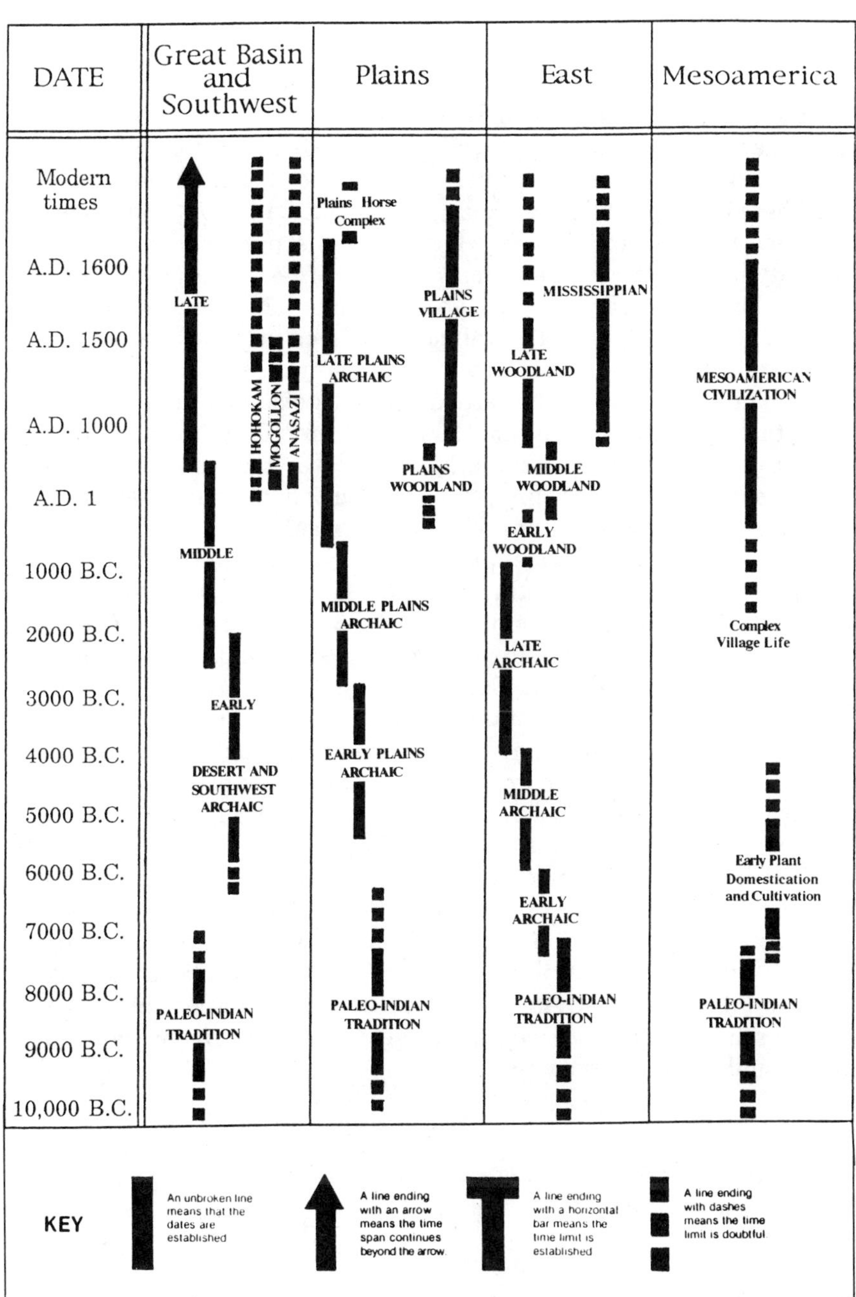
DATE
Great Basin and Southwest
Plains
East
Mesoamerica
Modern times
A.D. 1600
A.D. 1500
A.D. 1000
A.D. 1
1000 B.C.
2000 B.C.
3000 B.C.
4000 B.C.
5000 B.C.
6000 B.C.
7000 B.C.
8000 B.C.
9000 B.C.
10,000 B.C.
LATE
HOHOKAM
MOGOLLON
ANASAZI
MIDDLE
EARLY
DESERT AND SOUTHWEST ARCHAIC
PALEO-INDIAN TRADITION
Plains Horse Complex
PLAINS VILLAGE
LATE PLAINS ARCHAIC
PLAINS WOODLAND
MIDDLE PLAINS ARCHAIC
EARLY PLAINS ARCHAIC
PALEO-INDIAN TRADITION
MISSISSIPPIAN
LATE WOODLAND
MIDDLE WOODLAND
EARLY WOODLAND
LATE ARCHAIC
MIDDLE ARCHAIC
EARLY ARCHAIC
PALEO-INDIAN TRADITION
MESOAMERICAN CIVILIZATION
Complex Village Life
Early Plant Domestication and Cultivation
PALEO-INDIAN TRADITION
KEY
An unbroken line means that the dates are established
A line ending with an arrow means the time span continues beyond the arrow
A line ending with a horizontal bar means the time limit is established
A line ending with dashes means the time limit is doubtful

of climate change, human overkill, or causes yet undetermined, the animals began to die out, and slowly the Paleo Indian tradition gave way to less specialized ways of life that varied regionally. That period of diversification and adaptation to many local environments we call the Archaic.

In the Southwest, the climate became hotter and drier. The desert dwellers began to use more plant food, for the desert animals were small and scarce. Many archaeological remains of implements for collecting and grinding seeds have turned up in desert regions. The desert people also gathered berries, bulbs, and roots, and ate nuts in season. Sometimes they added meat to their diet in the form of rabbits, prairie dogs, snakes, rats, and larger game such as deer.

In the North and East, where ice and snow once covered much of the land, great forests grew up. The animals that lived in those forests were smaller and swifter than the mastodon and many other earlier species. The Archaic Indians of the Eastern Woodlands changed their tools to exploit the new environment and its animal life. They invented axes and adzes for woodworking, and around the lakes and along the rivers the people increased their fishing and trapping of ducks and other water birds. Along the new coastlines they began to gather and eat shellfish. Indians of the Archaic left great piles of shells along some of the coasts and inland waterways, indicating that quite large populations lived on those foods. In some areas, people began to experiment with intensive harvesting and eventually cultivation of squashes, gourds, and small seed foods such as sunflower, marsh elder, and maygrass. Eventually, this resulted in the domestication of several native species.

In some areas of North America, notably in areas such as California, the Great Basin, and the Subarctic, the basic Archaic adaptation lasted until historic times. In other regions, the introduction of pottery, an increase in cultural complexity, and population growth produced more advanced lifeways that warrant a new classification; thus the eastern adaptations are referred to as the Woodland tradition. One new practice that arose during this period was the building of burial mounds. The deliberate selection and cultivation of plant foods that had begun during the Archaic led eventually to corn horticulture, an introduction that made possible social and technological complexity unattainable in hunting and gathering societies.

2

CULTIVATION AND AMERICAN CULTURES

A Mimbres design from a pottery bowl.

In the highlands of Central Mexico, the Archaic cultural stage followed much the same course as the Desert Archaic north of the Rio Grande. The climates were not very different after the continental ice melted, and in each region the people adapted to differences in altitude, water, and supplies of plants and animals. The changing climate, in Mexico as in the north, brought an end to the hunting tradition specializing in big game such as bison and mammoth. Archaeological evidence indicates that people shifted from big game hunting to dependence on plant foods in both areas. While the Rio Grande would have provided something of a natural barrier prehistorically, it seems unlikely that it would have prevented peoples from crossing back and forth between the areas to its north and south. Although we somewhat arbitrarily designate Mexico and the rest of Mesoamerica a separate cultural region from the other areas of the North American continent, cultural traits and practices may have been exchanged across this region innumerable times in the past. After all, the border between Mexico and the United States is the result of political history, and did not keep prehistoric southwestern peoples from carrying their way of life into what is now northern Mexico.

Corn, Beans, and Squash

The archaeological record of the mid-Archaic in some Mexican sites clearly tells us that people were subsisting more and more on plants. One new food, maize or corn, was not native to the more northern regions. It became the heart of the diet for Indians in Mexico as well as the outlying regions where cultivation spread. Corn, beans, and squash are the major cultigens of the Americas, the trinity of Native American agriculture. Most important of these crops was corn, and by the time Europeans came, it was being grown in most areas of North America where conditions would allow it to be successfully cultivated. Varieties ranged from the bushy form suited to desert conditions to the tall corn of the eastern area, and came in more than six colors.

Corn has been studied for many years by the archaeologists and botanists trying to trace its origins, spread, and varieties. Botanical information pointed to a wild ancestor that was probably a popcorn with its kernels in pods. In its undomesticated state, this plant would have probably lacked any true cob and provided only a small number of kernels per plant. It has been suggested that the wild ancestor of corn was a wild grass still common in Mexico known as *teosinte*. Drilling for a subway in old lake beds under Mexico City unearthed pollen grains of ancestral wild corn dating back to 80,000 B.C., long before the arrival of humans in Mexico let alone any efforts at domesticating plants. The area around the Valley of Mexico was therefore certainly one logical place for archaeologists and botanists to hunt for the earliest domesticated corn. After years of research, the earliest domesticated corn yet recovered was found in the Tehuacán Valley, somewhat south of Mexico City. The archaeological record there shows a sequence of change from early Archaic wild plants and animals to domesticated corn. Domesticates show up alongside increasingly abundant equipment for grinding and processing plant food, indicating that people were depending more on vegetable foods. We can see in the record that the human population was slowly growing over several thousand years. The increase may have been related to a favorable change in climate; however, it may have stemmed from a change in the culture—the presence of cultigens—which allowed a more secure food supply. People of that time ate plants we recognize as edibles and also other plants we now think of as mere weeds. Some of today's weeds were truly domesticated, and though these are no longer cultivated, we cannot ignore their significance in early times.

Corn was probably undergoing the process of domestication by sometime between 7000 and 5000 B.C. Squash was apparently domesticated at approximately the same time as corn, and possibly even earlier. Squash remains from Tamaulipas to the north have been dated as early as 7000 B.C., while squash seeds from the Valley of Oaxaca slightly further to the south may date from between 7400–6700 B.C. The people of the Tehuacán Valley were using domesticated squash by 5000 B.C. The earliest variety of corn found in Tehuacán was not much more productive than its wild ancestor, having a very short cob with relatively few kernels. Until a hybrid appeared, corn was apparently not a big part of the diet. It has been estimated that between 5000 and 4000 B.C., domesticated foods may have contributed as little as 10 to 15 percent of the overall diet of these otherwise foraging and hunting peoples; however, more recent studies suggest they may have actually been far more important. Whatever the timing of the onset of heavy usage of these foods, there can be no question that, as time progressed, the role of domesticated plants increased tremendously.

Changing Culture

In the early period, domestication was just one of the many adaptations we have described as typical of the Archaic. Around 2300 B.C., however, when the Mexican Indians were growing several corn hybrids, cultural change speeded up among the cultivators. By 1500 B.C. the people had

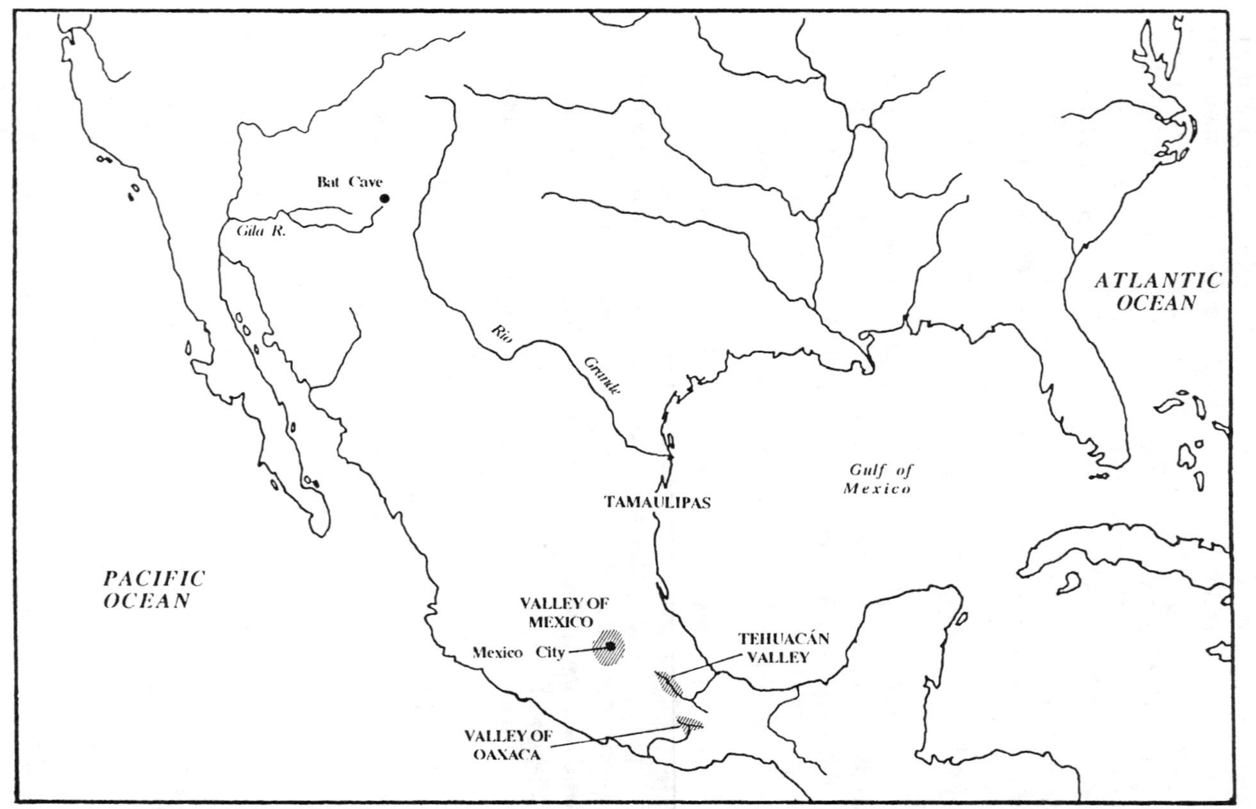

Early Mesoamerican sites and geographic areas important in plant domestication and the development of maize agriculture.

a complex, settled village life, were making pottery, and were depending on cultivated crops for their staples. Pottery, first used on the coasts, was an important invention for agriculturalists because it provided a rodent- and insect-proof storage container and a superior vessel for boiling foods. It is probably no coincidence that the spurt in cultural development that led to complex village life began when superior strains of maize had been hybridized and the use of pottery began to spread.

The shift from the wild food gathering of the Archaic to settled village life relying on domesticated plants was gradual. As the shift went on, the flow of culture change reversed and went from Mexico to the north. No longer did peoples and ideas drift primarily from north to south as they had from the time the Asians came into the New World until about 4000 B.C. Even pottery appeared earliest to the south and apparently diffused from there to the more northerly cultures.

The only domesticated mammal north of the Rio Grande was the dog. We do not know much about how domesticated dogs originated on this continent: were they tamed here or brought over after domestication in Asia? The archaeological evidence is as yet inconclusive on this matter. Whatever their source, as we noted in the first chapter, domesticated dogs existed in North America as far back as 10,000 years ago. The dog was sometimes eaten but was never an important food animal; it was helpful in hunting, as a scavenger, for protection, in carrying small packs, and pulling sleds, sledges, or travois. Besides dogs, the only other New World mammal put to service was in South America, where the peoples of the Andes domesticated the llama, using it as a pack animal and a source of wool. Because the Indians outside the Andes had no suitable domestic animal, they did not have dairy foods or large animals to ride or to haul substantial loads. Without farm animals, the New World never developed the mixed farming complexes that arose in the Old World. Until the Europeans brought sheep, cattle, and swine, wild animals remained the main source of meat protein.

Many plants that began in America have become very important to the rest of the world. Today corn and potatoes (a South American cultigen) are second only to wheat and rice as commercial food crops everywhere. Other plants domesticated by Indians of North and South America and now used by many peoples include beans, manioc (the source of tapioca), squash, pumpkin, peanuts, cashews, pineapple, tomato, chili peppers, sunflower, cacao (chocolate), vanilla, and tobacco. Among the medicinal herbs used by pre-Columbian Indians are quinine, curare, and cocaine.

The paths by which corn, beans, and squash diffused to the north are not precisely known. That Archaic peoples in the East and possibly elsewhere were experimenting with tending and perhaps even planting native small-seed plants suggests that basic concepts and practices of cultivation may have existed in some regions north of Mexico long before maize and the other Mesoamerican domesticates arrived. Seeds and more elaborate cultivation practices may have later passed from group to group, or migrating groups may have transmitted them, but we have no clear archaeological evidence.

The earliest domesticated corn recovered north of the Rio Grande comes from the Southwest and dates to around 1000 B.C. Squash was apparently introduced into the Southwest at the same time, although some squash was clearly being cultivated much earlier in the East. Corn cultivation spread from the Southwest to the East somewhat later. The exact date has not been determined, but it appears that corn was first grown in the East sometime between 500 and 300 B.C. However, at that early period it was not an important foodstuff. Keep in mind that maize was a tropical domesticate. Evidence indicates that after its initial arrival in North America, native peoples gradually developed hybrids that were far better adapted to the environmental conditions of the temperate regions of North America (including shorter growing season and shorter nights as it moved northward). Only after such adaptations had taken place did corn become a significant food in virtually all regions where it could be successfully cultivated. The bean was the last of the three Mexican domesticates to arrive in both the Southwest and the East. Evidence suggests that beans were first cultivated in the Southwest around 500–300 B.C., and spread from there into eastern North America much more recently, sometime between A.D. 800 and 1200. Together, corn and beans provided cultivating peoples an excellent nutritional base in the form of highly complementary vegetable proteins.

The Southwest

The environment of the Southwest after 2000 B.C. was much as it is today. While the environment is characterized by diversity, there were no lush green fields or fertile bottom lands as in the East. Stony, dry desert was common, hot in summer, cold in winter, swept by winds, dotted with straggly mesquite and spiny cactus. It may very well have been this poverty of the land that eventually influenced its inhabitants to try farming where water supplies allowed it. Vegetation was too slight to attract large animals that were very common in most other areas of the continent. The numbers of small animals that could be found were only enough to support a relatively small human population. So the idea of helping food plants to grow had great appeal for the southwestern Indians when at last it reached them.

The Beginnings of Agriculture

These people were well acquainted with the life cycles of plants, having followed for many generations the ripening vegetation of the area on foot. Like all Archaic folk, they had learned to use all of the food resources of their environment because they had to, and in the desert that meant focusing on plant foods. In the process of gathering wild plant foods, they may have unwittingly tended useful plants or intentionally encouraged them to propagate through a variety of practices. The tools they had developed for wild plant gathering and preparation were usable on domesticated plants without modification. Thus, if not ready and waiting to turn to cultivation, they were at least well disposed toward it. They were also geographically located close to Mexico, so it is not surprising that the idea of farming, as well as the most important cultigens, showed up first in the desert Southwest.

It was a long time, just as in regions farther south, before agriculture could provide even half the food supply of the southwestern peoples. For centuries they continued to get much of their subsistence by foraging. The challenging climate probably held back agricultural advances, and so did the plants themselves. The earliest maize grown in the Southwest

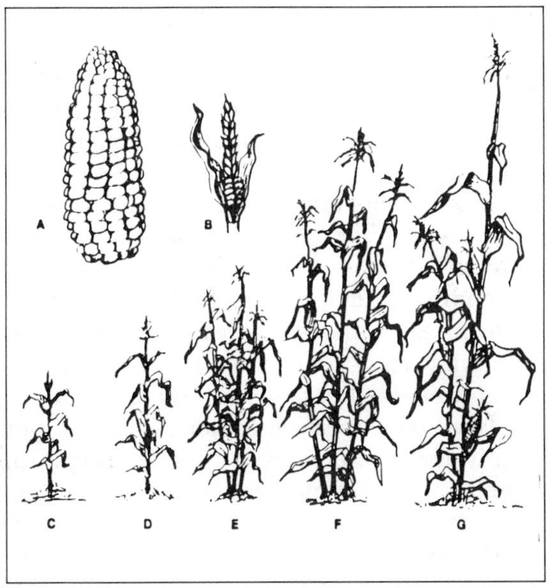

The development of corn (not to scale): (A) an ear of today's corn; (B) the probable look of the ancestor of wild corn; (C–G) domesticated corn's evolution.

was only a step or two removed from its wild ancestor. Its cobs were much shorter than those of modern varieties, holding far fewer kernels. These miniature ears, unlike those of modern corn, were not enclosed and protected in a tight husk, so the grains were exposed to competitive foraging by birds and rodents, and they shattered easily when ripe, not waiting for people to harvest them. The types of corn that followed were only a little more productive, but gradually over the centuries the people acquired and developed improved plant strains. Some unquestionably were imported from Mexico, but some came from natural crossing, probably helped along by human selection.

The environment of the desert Southwest also held a number of problems for potential cultivators. Besides the need for improved, more adaptable hybrids, the people also had to face and overcome the shortage of water. High evaporation rates and especially the limited rainfall to this day makes simple dry-land farming, without irrigation, painfully uncertain in much of the region. In addition, while the southwestern soils are typically rich in minerals they lack organic matter compared to those of other regions.

Precipitation in most parts of the Southwest comes mainly in summer, usually as brief thundershowers. With little vegetation to slow the movement of water across the land surface, such rainfall events are so intense that the precious rainwater runs off downhill before much seeps into the ground, often eroding soils in the process. To make the most of the limited moisture, the early farmers learned to build artificial features including dams of loose stones across the small gullies that channeled the runoff. These dams slowed the rushing water to help the ground absorb more of it, and also trapped sediment, forming terraces of better than average fertility. Where a spring seeped out along the base of a cliff, a group of farmers might wall off a small area, filling it with dirt and trash to make a garden. On lower ground, along the larger streams and rivers, a community would arrange its fields to take advantage of flooding from showers or from melting snow in the mountains upstream. Some people probably employed "pot irrigation," like that still used in parts of Mexico and the Southwest, carrying water to the fields in clay-caulked baskets, skin bags, or pottery containers. And in a few places southwestern Indians ultimately built irrigation systems, storing water in reservoirs and distributing it through canals.

Farming techniques also improved, though tools seem not to have developed much beyond the simple digging stick of pointed hardwood, useful for unearthing wild roots, punching holes in the soil to plant seeds, gouging out a new irrigation canal, or cleaning the sediment out of an old one. Crops were sown in early spring when the lower levels of soil were still moist with winter seepage. The people planted corn in deep holes, in clumps widely scattered over the plot, to make the

"Waffle Garden," Zuñi Pueblo, New Mexico, 1911. Gardens such as these were one way the Indians of the Southwest conserved precious moisture needed for growing domesticated plants.

best use of the limited water. Each clump contained enough seeds to produce ten or twelve stalks. As the stalks grew—seldom more than three or four feet high—the outer plants shielded the inner ones from the hot, dry winds of summer, so that they could live long enough to yield a few ears at harvest. In some areas people adapted to variable rainfall by maintaining several cultivated plots located in different nearby environmental settings. In such cases they might plant some of their crops in the river bottoms, along terraces, and even on slopes and hilltops as a hedge against the potential for either too little or too much moisture in a given season.

Three Cultures

Between 300 B.C. and A.D. 400, three local cultures began to develop in the southwestern area, the Mogollon, the Hohokam, and the Anasazi. All were farming societies, but they devised different agricultural techniques that were well suited to their individual environments. They did have traits in common—pottery, cultivated plants, and permanent settlements—and probably had some interaction in the form of trade. In all three, wild plant collecting was still of some importance, and wild game was their major source of meat. At some time during the generations that these three regional cultures took to develop, the people began to raise turkeys, the only domesticated creature native to North America except for the dog. Exactly when and where turkeys were first domesticated is not yet known. At the very least it seems certain that domestication occurred either in the Southwest or in Mexico.

The Anasazi of prehistory became the Pueblo Indians of historic times. The sequence for the Mogollon and Hohokam is less clear. Archaeological evidence indicates that both cultures fade after about A.D. 1400. The Hohokam may have given rise to the Pima and Papago Indians, or perhaps some other groups. The Mogollon area apparently underwent a rapid population decline in the fourteenth century A.D., with complete abandonment following very shortly thereafter. What became of the Mogollon remains a significant question in southwestern prehistory. It has been suggested that the Mogollon may have merged with the Anasazi, or perhaps joined with some Hohokam groups. It is possible, but not proven, that the Zuni Indians are in part descended from the Mogollon.

Mogollon: The Earliest Farmers

By about A.D. 200 some cultivators had begun to settle in villages in the valleys of the Mogollon mountain range in New Mexico. Because they found little land suitable even for modest farming in the steep mountains and narrow valleys of their Mogollon heartland, they still counted heavily on hunting and gathering to supplement their limited crops. In this early period, their villages rarely amounted to more than about a dozen pithouses.

These dwellings were built over roughly circular or rectangular excavations no more than two or three feet deep, above which rose a framework of stout posts supporting a roof of saplings laid across poles. The entire structure was probably covered with woven reeds and a mud plaster that would keep out all but the worst of the infrequent rainstorms, and the earth into which the house was dug was effective insulation against the desert heat. In the Southwest, temperatures often go over 100 degrees Fahrenheit in the summer, but a few inches below ground level they are far less extreme. The kangaroo rat and half a dozen other species of desert animals long ago learned to take advantage of this difference by spending the hottest hours of the day in their holes or burrows.

Just as important was the fact that the pithouses would have insulated

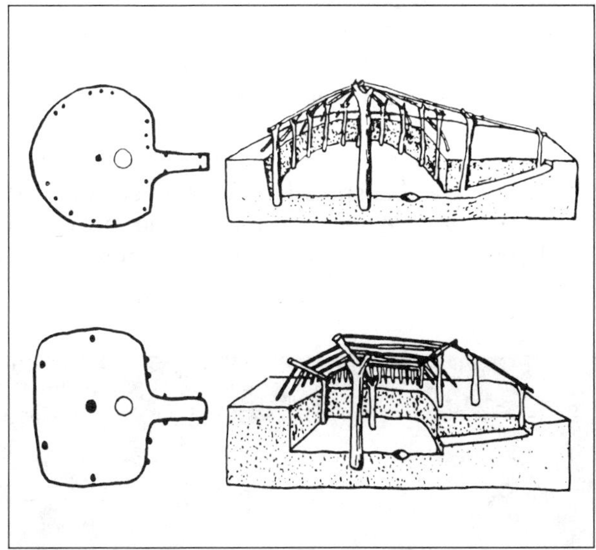

Two Mogollon house styles, showing floor plans and reconstructions of cross-sections, from the Harris village site.

equally well against the cold, which is not as rare in the desert as one might think. The clear, dry air that characterizes the Southwest cools far quicker than more humid air. As a result, 100 degree temperatures in the early afternoon can drop close to freezing by dawn the next morning. Winter cold snaps, particularly at high altitudes, can be even more biting. The well insulated pithouses required less effort and fuel to heat during the winter, a very important benefit in a region where wood and other fuel sources were limited.

While early Mogollon settlements were ordinarily small, as time went on villages commonly grew in size. Some later settlements contained far greater numbers of pithouses. Later still, around A.D. 900, the Mogollones had become influenced more heavily by their Anasazi neighbors to the north and began to put together dwellings in the pueblo style, clusters of rooms with walls in common, making one large structure containing many families.

Mogollon equipment shows how much of the diet was obtained from plants: digging sticks, several types of metates and manos, and baskets for gathering and storage. Their hunting implements were snares, bows and arrows, nets, and many styles of flint points for spears. The Mogollones were some of the earliest potters in the Southwest, and over time pottery became increasingly important and well made. One region of Mogollon settlement known as Mimbres became known for its fine ceramics with whimsical painted designs of insects, animals, and people. Many consider the Mimbres pottery the artistic climax of the prehistoric Southwest.

Mogollon seems to have been the earliest farming culture in the Southwest, a style of life that spread to the other subareas. While it may have been the first, the Mogollon lifeway did not prove to be the most enduring. Perhaps because it developed in a region so difficult to live

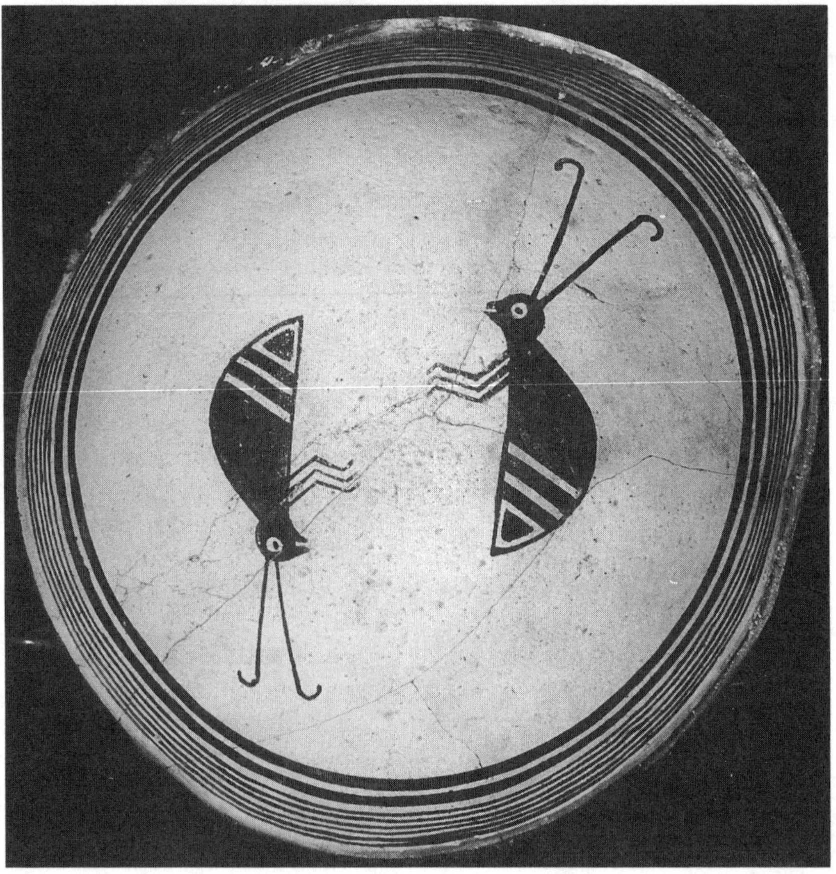

A Mimbres pottery bowl (diameter, 9 inches). The Mimbres potters excelled in their craft and decorated their typically black-on-white pottery with whimsical animals, insects, and people. Bowls with damaged bottoms ("killed" on purpose) have been found in graves with their owners' bodies.

in, it appears to have quickly reached its cultural climax, to have undergone major change, and later to have disappeared. Anasazi influences resulted in the adoption of a pueblo life-style around A.D. 1000; within four hundred years' time the Mogollon subarea had been completely abandoned.

Hohokam: The Irrigators

To the west of the mountainous Mogollon territory, much more elaborate farming communities arose in the valleys of the Salt and Gila rivers in southern Arizona. Here conditions might seem even less promising for agriculture, since the two watercourses flow through some of the bleakest desert in North America. Rainfall usually amounts to less than twelve inches per year. Though the region appears forbidding, its soil is made surprisingly rich by deposits of silt laid down each spring as the rivers, swollen with rain and melted snow from the mountains to the east, overflow their banks. A people whom archaeologists call the Hohokam developed a system to take advantage of this rich soil and the limited water resources. The name for this prehistoric culture comes from a Pima word whose meaning has been reported as "all used up" or "those who have gone."

Flood Irrigation. Perhaps as early as 2000 years ago, the Hohokam began practicing a crude form of flood irrigation, building dikes and little dams and diverting water from the Salt and Gila to cultivated plots near the riverbank terraces. As time progressed, irrigation methods became more elaborate and the people constructed systems of canals and ditches to carry the life-giving water farther from the rivers. The Hohokam's first simple efforts are hard to trace today, most having been obliterated by modern irrigation, agriculture, and urban development (the remnants of several Hohokam settlements and irrigated field systems lie beneath the Phoenix metropolitan area). However, it has been estimated that the early irrigation ditches were as much as fifteen feet wide, although no more than one or two feet deep. Later, presumably to cut down evaporation of precious water by reducing the surface area exposed to air, canals were built only eight feet or so wide, but six or more feet deep. Many were lined with clay to reduce loss by seepage.

In a few places the Hohokam built large earth dams to divert the water from the riverbeds into their canal system. Some of their major canals carried water thirty miles, with branch canals leading into fields along the way. The flow of water was controlled, as in many modern irrigation systems, by a series of *head gates*—movable devices for blocking and unblocking a branch channel. The Hohokam are thought to have made the head gates of tightly woven grass mats, backed by stakes, which could be raised or lowered as needed.

The Hohokam works are the most complex of any New World irrigation systems north of Mexico. Such elaborate systems clearly required imaginative engineering, enormous amounts of labor, and organized management. The ditches apparently were gouged out entirely with digging sticks, the marks of which have been found on the walls of canals uncovered by archaeologists, and the loosened earth was carried off in baskets. Once built, moreover, the canals had to be maintained. Silt deposited by the muddy spring floodwaters had to be removed periodically in order to keep the canals functioning properly. A flash flood from a summer thunderstorm could break through the sides of a canal and cut gullies across fields at a lower level. In exchange for their exertions, the Hohokam canal system could carry water to the rich valley soil far from the rivers, making possible a denser population and larger communities than those of the Mogollon. Some Hohokam communities are estimated to have included up to a thousand individuals.

Hohokam Subsistence and Settlements. Archaeological evidence indicates that the Hohokam subsistence practices were very similar to those of the Pima and Papago tribes described by early Spanish visitors to the region. Agriculture was clearly the Hohokam mainstay, and they may have even grown two successive crops of maize, squash, and drought-resistant tepary beans in a given year. In addition, they grew cotton and amaranth, and may have cultivated tobacco. The Hohokam gathered wild plant foods of the desert, particularly cactus fruits and mesquite pods. While plant foods apparently made up most of the diet, they also hunted deer, rabbits, and birds. Early Hohokam dwellings were similar in many ways to the simple Mogollon pithouse. At first these houses were scattered about settlements of various sizes, but some later settlements possessed a more formal arrangement of structures within a walled compound.

Mexican Contacts. The Hohokam appear to have much stronger connections than any other prehistoric North American societies to cultures further south in Mexico. Certain architectural features and a variety of artifacts reflect a significant degree of contact with Mesoamerica. Perhaps the most intriguing evidence noted by many researchers are the pyramid-like mounds and so-called ball courts that have been found at a number of Hohokam sites.

The Hohokam ball courts had oval playing floors made of clay, some as small as a modern basketball court, others as large as a football field. At both ends of the court were stone markers or basins that have often been interpreted as goals. A few rubbery balls, probably made from the coagulated juice of a desert plant called *guayule*, have been found on

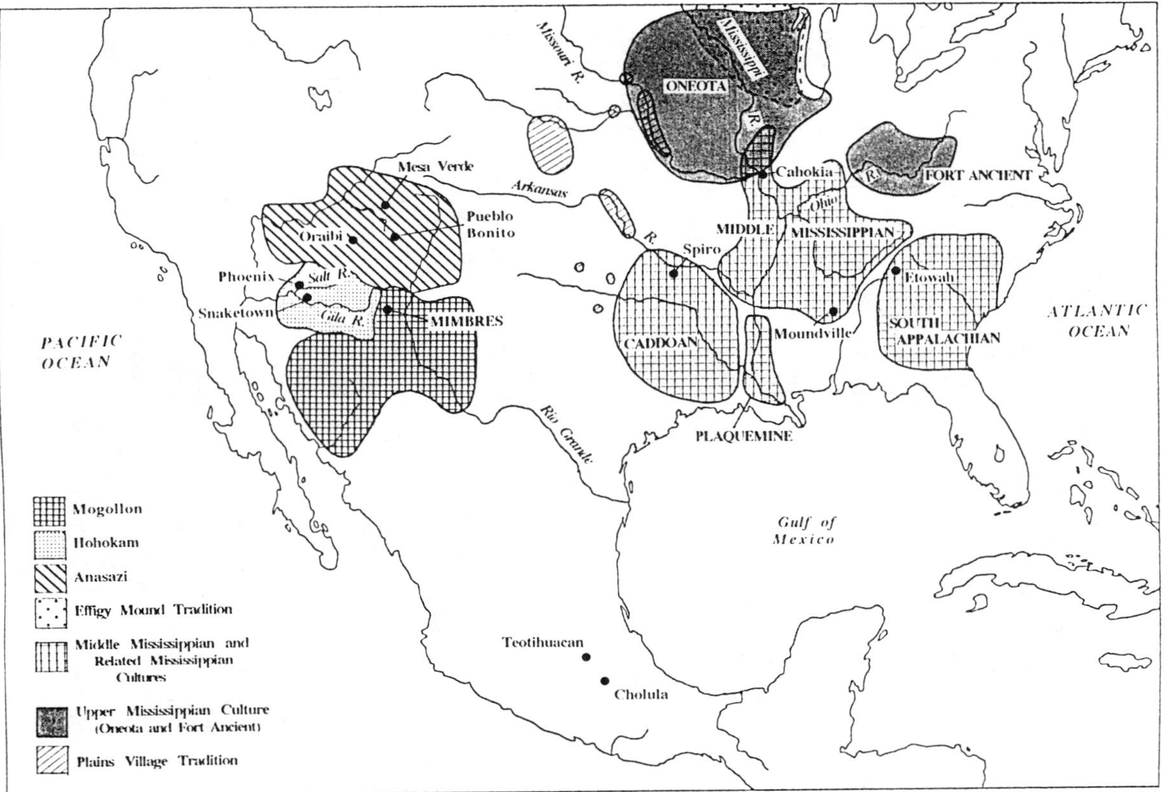

Late prehistoric sites in Mesoamerica and agriculturally based cultures and sites in the Southwest and the East.

Hohokam sites, although unfortunately they weren't directly associated with any of the ball courts. Still, some researchers have suggested that these balls were utilized in games on the courts, presumably being passed or struck into the goals. When one looks at a Hohokam ball court it seems strikingly likely that its builders were strongly influenced by more advanced societies in Mexico. Yet southwestern prehistorians are not in complete agreement that these interesting features are even what their name would indicate; some archaeologists have suggested that they may have actually been used by the Hohokam as communal dance floors.

The possibility of Mexican influence is even more apparent in the pyramidal platform mounds that the Hohokam built in some of their larger settlements of later periods. Made of earth and hard-packed clay, they are clearly smaller, simplified versions of the enormous stone-faced platforms of Mexico. The Hohokam platform mounds, like their Mexican counterparts, may have been topped by temples or other special-purpose structures.

More evidence of contacts with Mexico appears in the Hohokam artifacts and art motifs. One motif painted on some Hohokam pottery shows a serpent being attacked by a bird. This resembles an ancient Mexican design, the serpent and the bird motif, which is displayed today on the Mexican flag. Polished slate mirrors, iron pyrite mirrors, little copper bells, and the remains of Mexican macaws have been unearthed at several Hohokam sites and are clearly Mexican imports.

Curiously, the precise nature of the Hohokam connections with Mexican cultures remains uncertain, even after many years of study. Some researchers have hypothesized that the Hohokam represent an immigrant Mexican group that settled in the southern Arizona region, bringing with them knowledge of irrigation agriculture and an elaborate material culture. Others have pointed to several lines of evidence that suggest that the Hohokam culture represents an indigenous development from a local Archaic cultural base, heavily influenced by contacts with Mexico. One problem hindering a resolution to the question of Mesoamerican influence concerns dating the Hohokam culture sequence. Some early Hohokam sites have been estimated as dating to as early as 300 B.C., while other interpretations suggest that these same sites are actually much more recent, perhaps dating to around A.D. 400–500. Many researchers feel that the dating question must be resolved before the overall nature of Mexican influence can be properly understood. At the very least, it now seems clear that Hohokam peoples had trade contacts with peoples further south. Beyond this, only further research can enlighten us regarding questions of Mesoamerican immigration or cultural diffusion.

What Became of the Hohokam? The other question of interest with regard to the Hohokam concerns what eventually happened to them. The Hohokam settlements show remarkable long-term continuity and stability until shortly after A.D. 1400. About that time, for reasons unknown to prehistorians, the cultural stability that had characterized the Hohokam region for a thousand years or more was interrupted. Overall population declined, and in particular the larger settlements decreased in size. At the same time, some elaborate cultural practices ceased, including the construction and use of large irrigation canal systems and public architecture in the form of ball courts and platform mounds. While it appears that the modern descendants of the Hohokam include the Pima, Papago, and other historic groups, there is still some debate on the matter. Just why the Hohokam culture changed so dramatically, more than one hundred years prior to contact with the Spanish, remains an important unanswered question for those trying to understand the course of cultural development in the Southwest.

Anasazi: The Pueblo Farmers

Hohokam agricultural practices were sophisticated, but their way of life was confined to river valleys that were broad enough and had water enough to make large-scale irrigation possible. The Anasazi flourished to the north of the Hohokam and Mogollon, spreading at their climax over more territory than any other prehistoric southwestern farmers. Their name was given to them by archaeologists using an old Navajo term. The meaning of *Anasazi* has commonly been given as "the old ones," though it may more properly be translated as "the ancient enemies" or "the ancient alien ones," a reference to the ancestors of the several groups of Pueblo Indians who were the traditional enemies of the Navajo during the historic period.

The Anasazi were not only successful farmers, they were just as clever at building. They were the first to raise the remarkable structures that come to mind when we hear southwestern Indians mentioned—that is, the apartment-like dwellings of clay, mud, and stone that the Spanish explorers called *pueblos*, meaning "towns." The most unusual pueblos are built into natural clefts or rockshelters high in the walls of steep canyons. The best known of these, in Mesa Verde National Park in southwestern Colorado, is still almost livable 650 years or more after its last inhabitants left. Other pueblos were constructed atop the *mesas*, or tablelands. One of the most important of these is Oraibi on the southern end of Black Mesa in northeastern Arizona, which has been occupied for several hundred years.

The Anasazi originally occupied a fairly limited area known today as the Four Corners, where Arizona, New Mexico, Utah, and Colorado meet. At their peak, around A.D. 1200, their villages were scattered across much of those four states. Wide, barren tracts there make any sort of agriculture difficult if not impossible, but much of the region over which the Anasazi eventually spread is better suited to farming than the rugged Mogollon country and needs less irrigation than the river valleys cultivated by the Hohokam. Its high mesas and plateaus guarantee relatively copious rainfall; some of this water could be stored in reservoirs, so that in most years the people could farm without building extensive irrigation systems. In this region too are some of the Southwest's highest mountains, the Rockies in Colorado, the Sangre de Cristo in New Mexico, and the Wasatch range in Utah, with many vigorous rain-nourished streams that the Anasazi used for flood irrigation in the foothills and valleys.

The earliest Anasazi settlements, dating from around the beginning of the Christian era, give little hint of accomplishments to come. The more westerly Anasazi groups constructed deep pithouses that more closely resembled the Mogollon and Hohokam pithouses. However, in most areas of Anasazi settlement, communities were small, comprised of dome-shaped structures that were built over shallow saucerlike depressions cut into the gentle slopes along the bases of the cliffs. Built up of concentric layers of logs laid in a sort of rail fence arrangement and cemented with mud mortar, they seem to have lacked one feature that most prehistoric people considered essential, an interior fireplace. Probably the homes were heated by stones warmed in outside fires and then laid in a pit in the house floor. Such heating pits have been found during excavation. A possible reason for this arrangement is that the log houses were covered with flammable brush or grass, making an interior fire dangerous. A few centuries later, though, the Anasazi were building more conventional pithouses with more usual heating, a central fireplace, the smoke from which escaped through a hole in the roof. Perhaps to prevent sudden flareups caused by gusts of wind through the doorway, the fireplaces were protected by deflectors, low screens made of stone slabs. These must have also helped block off uncomfortable drafts in winter.

The Pueblos. It was not until sometime between A.D. 800 and 900 that the Anasazi began to build pueblos. These singular structures are unlike anything elsewhere in North America. The early Spaniards correctly named them towns, for an entire village could be housed in a compound structure that was, in effect, a single building. Many small pueblos were no more than a helter-skelter collection of roughly cubical units added at different times. Other pueblos were considerably larger, and while they too were frequently built up over time by the addition of room units, some of the larger pueblos show remarkable planning in their arrangement and construction. Pueblo Bonito, whose ruins lie in the valley of the Chaco River, was four or five stories high and had approximately eight hundred rooms arranged in an immense ''D'' around twin plazas. The pueblos were elaborately constructed of stone masonry covered over with a plaster of mud or adobe. They possessed roofs made typically from beams of pine, fir, or spruce obtained from the surrounding highlands. In many cases the wooden beams would have had to be transported fifty miles or more in order to be used in the construction of a given pueblo in Chaco Canyon.

Curiously, the pithouse, or something very like it, survived amid the new style of architecture, though its traditional earthen walls were now lined with stone. These circular, semiunderground chambers, entered by ladder through an opening in the mud-covered, wooden beam roof, were prototypes of the *kivas* that some southwestern tribes still use for ceremonial purposes. Probably they served the same function among the Anasazi peoples. Smaller settlements might only possess one or two kivas, but the larger pueblos often had a far greater number of such structures with different sizes. Pueblo Bonito had five larger or ''great'' kivas as well as thirty-three smaller ones.

We can only guess what inspired the Anasazi to devise their pueblos in the first place. One possibility is a growing shortage of timber as their increasing population, nourished by successful agriculture, was compelled to build more and more dwellings. Substituting locally abundant stone and clay for timber would almost necessarily have given the pueblos their vertical walls, limiting the shape a building could take, but at the same time would have made it easy to add a room by simply attaching three more walls to one in the original structure.

A possibly more pressing influence than lack of timber may have been a need for physical security. The expanding population of the pueblo dwellers could have caused friction between the groups, leading to conflicts. While the archaeological evidence for hostilities is limited, many pueblos occupy defensible positions on the landscape and certainly have the look of walled fortresses. On the first story, at least, doors and windows open only to the enclosed interior courtyard. The only way of getting in from the outside is by ladder, and ladders can, of course, be drawn up to leave only the blank exterior walls to confront hostile strangers.

Security seems to be the best explanation for the development of the cliff dwellings. They are among the most inaccessible homes ever inhabited. Built among the high mesas deeply scarred with narrow canyons, they occupy lofty ledges in faces of sheer cliffs. Most were too high to be reached from the canyon floors, and from the mesas above could be gotten to only by steep paths down the cliffs, some pathways

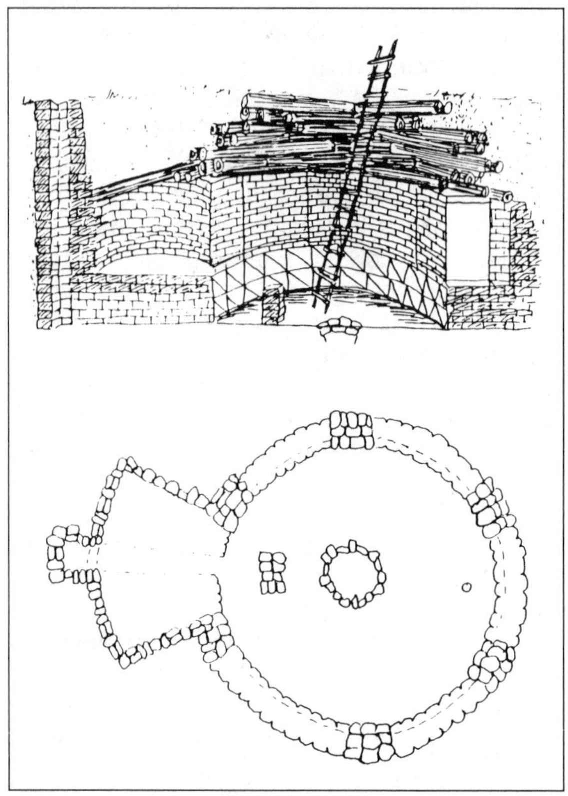

A kiva of the Mesa Verde type, showing the cross-section (above) and the floor plan (diameter, 14 feet).

no more than a series of shallow toeholds hacked out of the rocks. A few of the dwellings can be reached today only by experienced mountain climbers, who must lower themselves down the cliff face on a rope. Yet the Anasazi, men and women carrying babies and bundles of food and jars of water, climbed several times a day between the pueblos and the croplands on the mesas above. Many of the cliff dwellings possess walls, towers, and what were apparently protected entryways that likewise suggest a concern for defense. Yet their position and inaccessibility are clearly their most striking defensive features. One of the largest and most impressive pueblos, Mesa Verde's famous Cliff Palace, is sheltered in an enormous cave 325 feet long and 90 feet deep, with a rocky ceiling that arches to a height of 60 feet. It contains more than two hundred rooms and must have housed several hundred people. From the cave

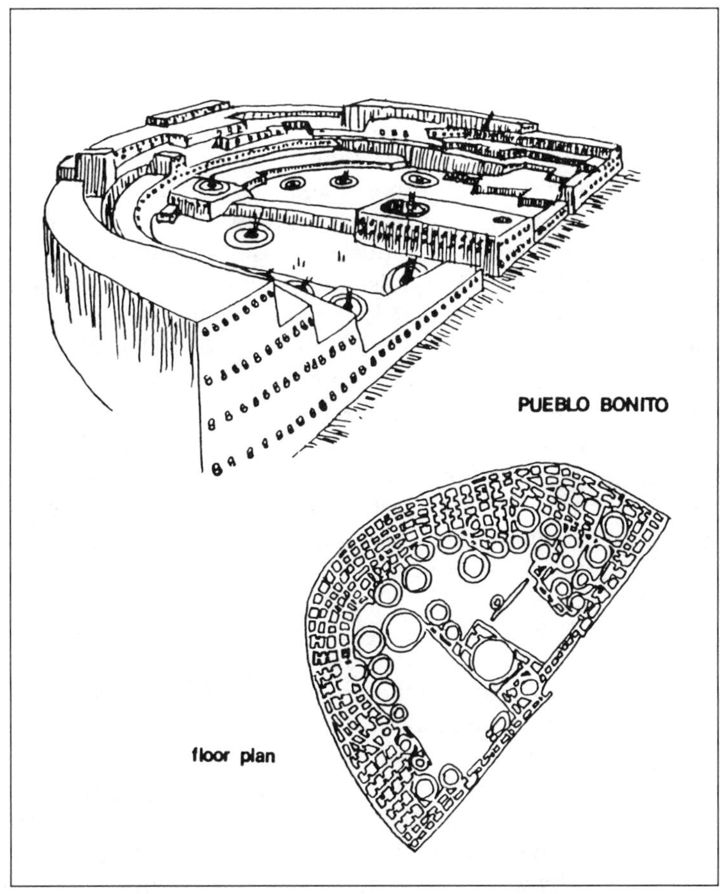

Pueblo Bonito, New Mexico. This Anasazi community, built during A.D. 900–1100, was four to five stories high and contained about 800 rooms and 30 kivas.

to the mesa above stretch 100 feet of vertical cliff; the canyon floor lies a dizzying 700 feet below.

The Anasazi diet was diverse. Among their domesticated plants were corn, squash, and beans. To these they added wild plants such as piñon nuts, mint, onions, amaranth and chenopod seeds, and berries. They kept domesticated turkeys and hunted rabbit and deer to provide themselves with animal protein. Women made pottery for cooking and storing, and also for ritual containers. Men wove nets or baskets, made simple bows, and chipped arrowheads; they were cultivators as well as hunters, unlike the males in most Woodland cultures, who characteristically left cultivation to the women. Fishing equipment and fish bones do not appear in the remains; archaeologists believe that although there were fish in the nearby streams, they were not used for food.

In some areas of Anasazi settlement, specifically in the Chacoan region, clear evidence exists for an extensive and complex trade system. Pueblo Bonito and several other major neighboring towns were apparently connected by an elaborate network of roads to outlying communities of various size and possibly also to sources of important trade materials, including turquoise. More than 250 miles of straight roads, up to almost thirty feet wide, have been discovered emanating from Chaco Canyon. Where the roads encountered obstacles such as canyon walls, the Anasazi cut stairs into the stone to allow the road to continue in a straight fashion, rather than going around such an impediment. The roads presumably facilitated the exchange of food and important trade goods between the Chacoan centers, outlying towns, and, very likely, areas well beyond. It has also been suggested that the roads may have functioned as "pilgrim roads," allowing inhabitants of various communities to travel to sacred Chacoan centers for ceremonies, festivals, and rituals.

The Pueblos Abandoned. For reasons not completely understood at present, Pueblo Bonito and the other towns in the Chaco area apparently underwent a collapse around A.D. 1130. Population declined in the area, and many pueblos were abandoned in the following century. It has been suggested that most of the people of Chaco Canyon may have moved to pueblos in other areas, and that some may have even reverted to a hunting and gathering way of life. The dramatic change in the Chaco area was followed by what appear to be similar developments in other areas of Anasazi settlement. Between A.D. 1200 and 1300, dozens of Anasazi pueblos began to undergo abandonment, most notably within the northern areas of settlement on the Colorado Plateau, including the cliff dwellings of Mesa Verde.

The apparent discontinuity has led researchers and laypeople alike to raise many issues regarding the later prehistoric situation among the Anasazi. What could have caused an apparently successful culture to undergo such profound change? What cultural changes actually occurred? Do the abandonments represent the effects of people dying at the hands of invaders, or due to conflicts with other pueblo dwellers, or from starvation or the ravages of disease? Did the people die off or simply move elsewhere? Researchers have discussed a variety of scenarios and have identified a series of factors that may have contributed to the sequence of change.

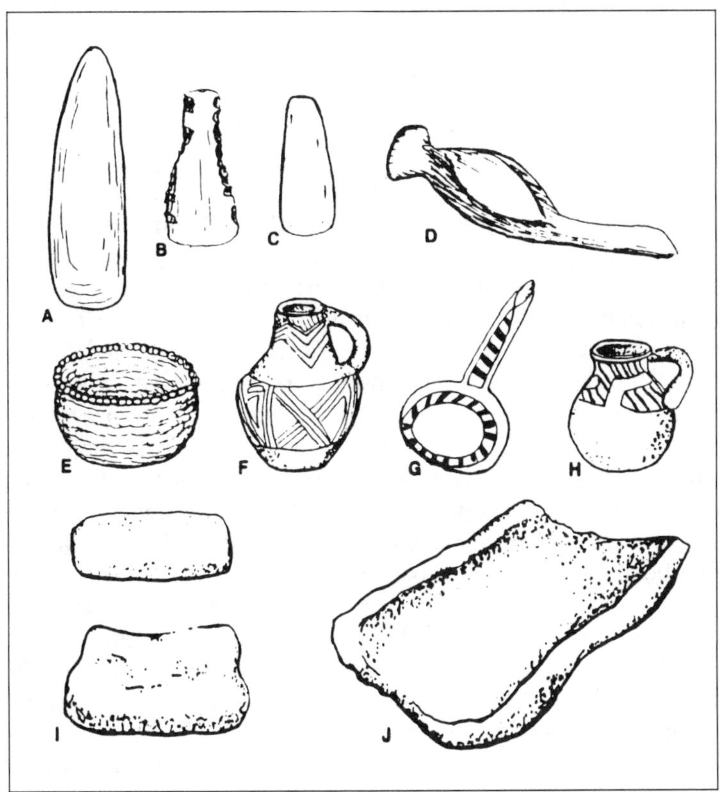

Pueblo III period artifacts (A.D. 1100–1300): (A-C) polished stone hoes or celts; (D) carved wooden bird; (E) basket; (F) black-on-red pottery jar; (G) black-on-white pottery ladle (Mesa Verde); (H) black-on-white pottery jar; (I) manos; (J) metate.

Since the dwellings seem to have been designed for security, their desertion might suggest a retreat after a period of attack, but nowhere do we find evidence of widespread warfare. Many people accept as explanation a long, generally droughty period that gripped much of the Southwest, generally coinciding with the period of abandonment. For some areas, the drought may not have begun until the second half of the thirteenth century, but on the Colorado Plateau at least, the onset of a period of cooler and drier climate occurred around A.D. 1150. The evidence for that dry spell is unmistakable, recorded in the shrinking annual growth rings of trunks of ancient trees. This climatic change appears to have forced a migration to places with more water, principally the Rio Grande valley, where sixteenth-century Spanish explorers found many flourishing pueblos. But drought may not be the entire answer—the settlements were never reoccupied after the drought passed. Perhaps the pueblo people did try to return to their former villages, but found the land occupied by other Indian settlers too formidable to be driven out.

If that happened, who were the new people? Perhaps they were typical Archaic desert foragers like the Utes, who had long lived in the Great Basin on the outskirts of the pueblo country. Some evidence in the form of pottery remains suggests they were hunters from the north—as far as Canada—Athabaskan Indians, the ancestors of the Navajo and Apache. These tribes are unrelated to their southwestern neighbors. Comparison of the languages suggests that their nearest tribal connections are to be found in the interior of Alaska and northwestern Canada today. For reasons still unknown, these northern hunting people began to drift into the Southwest, and there is limited evidence that their arrival may date as early as the thirteenth century. However, the vast majority of the evidence suggests that the Athabaskan movement into the Southwest occurred later, likely around A.D. 1500. As a result, most archaeologists believe that the period of pueblo abandonment took place far too early to have been forced by Athabaskan attacks.

A more recent theory about how the pueblos came to be abandoned is now more widely accepted. Many Southwest archaeologists and ethnologists believe the cause was an ecological crisis. The drought, combined with severe deforestation, rapid runoff of rainwater, and resulting soil erosion reduced the areas that could effectively be cultivated, and forced the people into a more restricted territory. These environmental conditions brought about a sort of energy or resource crisis: there was no longer enough timber for building and fuel, and the land could no longer support enough agriculture to feed the population. What had essentially been a successful adaptation under more favorable climatic conditions may have led to population growth and resource exploitation that could not be sustained in many areas, particularly as wood resources became exhausted and the climate worsened.

While warfare and environmental crisis are favored by many as the likely causes of late prehistoric change among the Anasazi, these are not the only explanations that have been offered. Some researchers have pointed at the potential for factionalism within pueblo communities to divide the population and result in movements of people to new settlements. Others have argued that the relatively crowded living conditions of the pueblos may have created sanitation and health problems, resulting in an outbreak of infectious disease that could have severely reduced the population. While many ideas have been offered on the subject, the archaeological record does not entirely support any particular hypothesis over all others. This has led some researchers to consider the possibility that a host of factors, perhaps including some not yet identified, may have brought about the changes observed for the pueblo dwellers in the four hundred years before the arrival of the Spanish.

Nonagricultural Areas of the West

In early America west of the Rockies, agriculture never spread beyond the Southwest. Why was agriculture never adopted by native peoples in other areas of the West? Certainly in some areas, it may simply not have been possible, whether due to unfavorable climate or unproductive soils. In most of the Great Basin, dry farming was impossible and irrigation was difficult at best, though we know of a few desert tribes who used crude irrigation techniques to encourage the growth of some wild plants whose seeds they gathered. In most of California, dry farming was no easier; summers were almost as dry as in the desert, and that region's most important food staple, the acorn, did not lend itself to cultivation. Foraging was so easy in California, though, that agriculture was not a pressing need. Natural food resources were plentiful and easily reaped. Incentives for agriculture were even less along the coast and in the Pacific Northwest, where wild foods, particularly fish and marine resources, were even more abundant and reliable. However, east of the Rockies, particularly in the Mississippi Valley and the eastern woodlands, agriculture spread widely, producing societies that were true urban centers by the time Europeans arrived.

The Eastern Area

Late Woodland Cultural Developments

After the decline of Hopewell and related Middle Woodland cultures in the eastern area around A.D. 400, a series of significant cultural developments transformed the lifeways of prehistoric native peoples and ultimately created the cultures known to the earliest European visitors to the region. While the causes are still debated, several changes are apparent. The bow and arrow were probably introduced to the East around A.D. 500, undoubtedly leading to more efficient hunting of large and small game animals. Maize became an increasingly important cultigen in the East, particularly after A.D. 800. By that time, Late Woodland peoples in most areas of eastern North America south of the Great Lakes and St. Lawrence River had begun to rely upon corn for a significant (though not likely the primary) portion of their diet. Corn cultivation was essentially added to an existing diet that was based upon some combination of hunting, wild food gathering, fishing, and the cultivation of one or more eastern cultigens described earlier.

The Late Woodland period witnessed continued population growth that was accompanied by changes in settlement practices and intergroup relations. Over time, groups became larger and more sedentary, making fewer moves over the course of a given year and occupying individual settlements for longer periods of time. Once maize cultivation became an integral part of the eastern lifeways, greater sedentism was a natural result, since planted crops more effectively tie groups of people to their gardens or fields. There appears to have been an increase in the overall number of settlements occupied in different regions within the East, again suggesting that populations were growing. A growing body of evidence indicates that warfare and raiding activities increased during the Late Woodland period. Skeletal remains show higher rates of traumatic injuries and violent death, and for the first time in eastern North America, many settlements began to be encircled by protective palisades or stockades. In addition to improving hunting practices, the bow and arrow may have changed the dynamics of warfare and contributed to an increase in hostilities at a time when population growth was already beginning to test the relations between neighboring groups in many areas of the East.

Late Woodland Mortuary Practices. In general, Late Woodland peoples continued the practice of burying their dead in earthen mounds. Compared to the very large Hopewell and Adena mounds discussed in the first chapter, though, the majority of Late Woodland burial mounds were much smaller. In most areas these mounds were invariably constructed in a circular or conical shape. In one region of the Upper Midwest, however, so-called "effigy mounds" were built in a variety of shapes including both geometric and animal forms. Effigy mounds are known primarily from Wisconsin, and have also been found in adjacent areas of eastern Minnesota, northeastern Iowa, and northern Illinois. The geometric shapes include crosses, ovals, bar-bells, linear, and simple conical-shaped mounds. Animal shapes include birds of several types, turtles, panthers, deer, bears, and a host of other mammals. There are even a few mounds that were apparently built with a human shape.

Why the Late Woodland peoples of the Upper Midwest constructed their burial mounds in such shapes continues to be a question for modern researchers. They are found in groups that vary both in the number of mounds—from one or two to as many as three hundred or more—and in the shapes represented. Many of the effigy mound groups included several different shapes, both geometric and animal. It has been suggested that effigy mounds were built to convey clear meaning in their

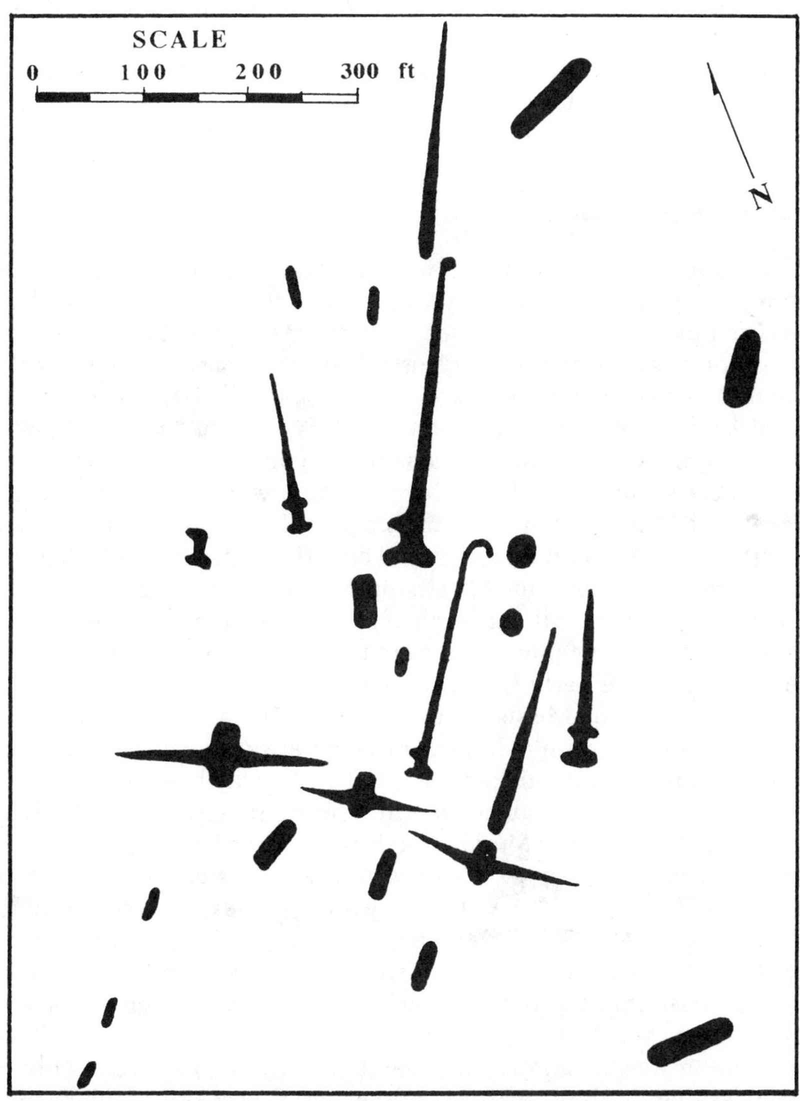

A plat of the Late Woodland effigy mounds at a site along the Fox River near Mukwonago in southeastern Wisconsin. This group included examples of shapes commonly termed birds, panthers, turtles, a small tailless mammal, linear, tapering, oblong, and conical. After Lapham 1855: Plate XVI.

day, possibly even reflecting the clan or other social group whose members were buried there. As has been suggested for eastern burial mounds in general, they may have functioned as territorial markers as well as repositories for the dead. Of course, it is entirely possible that their shapes had a significance that we today cannot even imagine.

The Mississippian Tradition

While groups lived in small villages throughout the East, communities grew in population and complexity along the lower reaches of the Mississippi River and in Florida. The Mississippi Valley became the primary focus of settlement for a new prehistoric cultural tradition that we first recognize around A.D. 700 to 800. This tradition, called Mississippian, eventually spread over many of the tributaries draining into the great river, from Louisiana to Wisconsin and from Oklahoma to Tennessee and beyond, and by about 1200 had developed into one of ancient America's most remarkable cultural traditions. By any criterion—wealth, population, social complexity, or technological and artistic sophistication—the Mississippians included the most advanced of any Indian societies living north of Mexico, and their vigorous culture lasted in one form or another long enough to be witnessed by Hernando de Soto and other early European explorers.

Those we call the Mississippians were neither a single society nor a single linguistic group. Although it is not always possible to connect historic tribes with prehistoric sites or cultures, archaeologists believe that at least three language families were represented within the Mississippian tradition: *Muskogean*, including the languages spoken by the Creek and the Choctaw among others in historic times; *Siouan* tongues as spoken by Yuchi and many other groups; and in areas of the Midwest and South, some *Algonkian* languages. Overall, there was a great deal of diversity among the various cultures that together made up the Mississippian tradition; some societies were highly elaborate while others were by comparison somewhat simpler. What they all had in common was the adoption, to varying degrees, of a host of cultural practices that set them apart from other eastern societies of their time. Typically these included a major reliance upon maize cultivation, the construction of pottery vessels made from clay mixed (or "tempered") with crushed shell, the use of bows and arrows tipped with small triangular-shaped points, the occupation of larger and more permanent settlements, and various other practices that reflect the development of greater social complexity.

Mound Building and Ceremonial Objects. While not all Mississippian societies built earthen mounds, truncated pyramid mounds are the hallmark of the most elaborate Mississippian cultures, often collectively referred to as *Middle Mississippian*. Also called platform mounds, they are not primarily burial mounds, although some burials are found in them. Rather, they are flat-topped pyramids that had structures on the top that were apparently temples and the houses of the elite members of their societies. The mounds were commonly much larger than those of Hopewell and Adena construction. The great size of the larger Middle Mississippian mounds was the end result of additions over many years, in some instances perhaps eight or ten layers altogether. Many had log stairs laid up a ramp on one side for access to the temple on top.

Comparing these mounds with the huge pyramids raised by the ancient Egyptians and the people of Mexico and Central America, we see that the Mississippian structures were monumental by any standards. The largest Mississippian mound is located at Cahokia in what is now southern Illinois. Referred to by archaeologists as "Monks Mound," it is a hundred feet high and has a base several times larger than that of the Great Pyramid of Egypt, covering approximately eighteen acres. In the Americas, it is smaller only than the Pyramid of the Sun at Teotihuacán and the great pyramid at Cholula, both in Mexico. And this monster mound is just one of eighty or so still standing in this area; probably another forty have been leveled by farmers in the recent past.

From the number of these platform mounds and their size, as well as information left us by early European explorers who visited some of the surviving Mississippian centers in the sixteenth and seventeenth centuries, it appears that Mississippian society was strongly ceremonial. In fact, ceremonial items such as figurines, plaques, and headdresses have been found at major sites virtually throughout the Mississippian area; these are so striking that archaeologists have long talked about them as representing a major prehistoric cult referred to as the Southern Cult, or sometimes as the Buzzard Cult or Southern Death Cult. It now appears that, rather than representing a single religious faith uniting groups across the entire Mississippian area, the many Mississippian societies probably had somewhat distinct religious beliefs that incorporated many of the same symbols we see on ritual items wrought from materials like shell, copper, stone, and clay. The weeping-eye motif, circles, crosses, sun symbols, elaborate arrows, serpents, hawks, thunderbirds, human-bird figures, and engraved representations of human sacrifice have been discovered. The artifacts include earrings, pendants, tablets, and elaborately crafted pottery.

The Question of Influence from Mexico. Many of the ceremonial objects have to do with death, and this prompted many scholars to speculate that they showed some contact with or influence from Mexican cult practices, with their human sacrifices. Many of the Mississippian

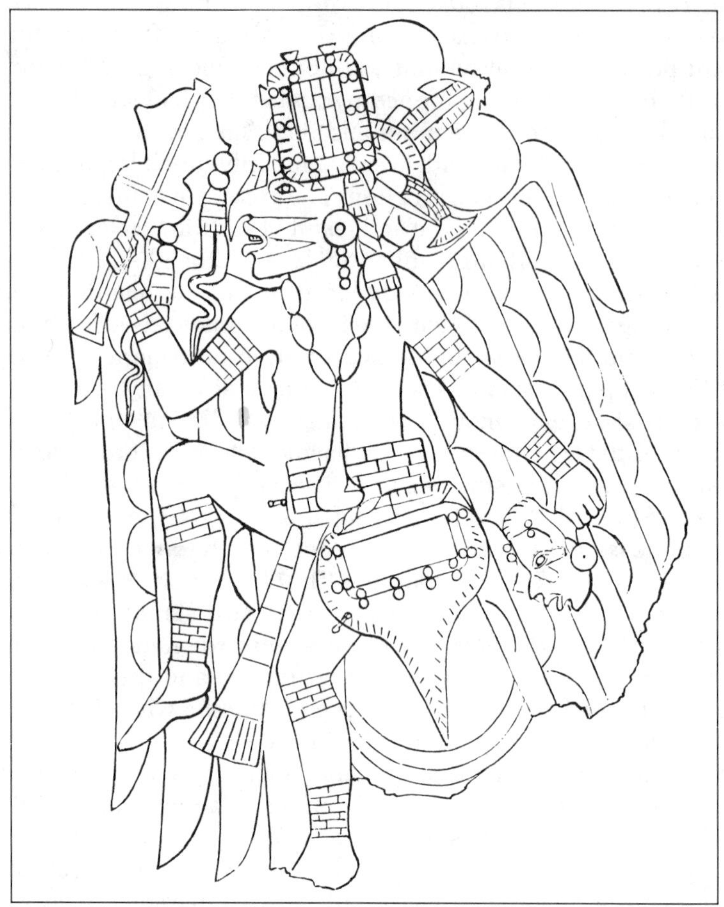

Winged human figure engraved on a copper plate found in Etowah Mound, Georgia.

designs appeared earlier, though, in Adena and Hopewell sites, most particularly the raptorial bird and the eye motifs. In fact, overall, the Mississippian motifs more closely resemble the symbolism of earlier Eastern Woodland cultures than any Mesoamerican designs. Others argue that another indicator of Mesoamerican influence is obvious in the Mississippian ceremonial centers, whose layout and style of mound building in many ways resemble the Mexican centers with their pyramids. Since the Mississippians were dependent upon Mesoamerican cultigens, first maize and later beans, it is suggested that their advanced, intensive agricultural way of life may have been imported. The presence of these cultigens is perhaps the best evidence for some sort of contact with Mexico, yet it hardly need have been direct contact. If Mississippians were interacting directly with any Mesoamerican societies, we would expect to encounter artifacts of Mesoamerican origin in Mississippian sites. Yet to date, no such finds have ever been recovered. Since more evidence now supports the indigenous development of elaborate Mississippian societies, archaeologists largely or entirely dismiss the possibility of Mesoamerican influence or contact in eastern North America.

Mississippian Cities. It is unfortunate that far fewer people have ever heard of the ancient Mississippians of eastern North America than are aware of the elaborate civilizations of Mesoamerica. While the heights of the great Mexican civilizations were never attained by the Mississippians, in many ways they came very close. It is true that they never developed a system of writing, but it is likely that they had some other effective means for record keeping. We know that they attained at least some degree of practical proficiency in engineering and apparently astronomy, as reflected in some of their constructions.

Their largest center was Cahokia, a city covering an area of approximately five square miles. Cahokia's population has been estimated by many to have approached 30,000 people, putting it in a class with other ancient centers such as Ur in Mesopotamia, Mohenjo Daro in India, and Tikal in Mesoamerica. Other large Mississippian centers included Etowah in northern Georgia, Moundville in Alabama, and Spiro in eastern Oklahoma. None of these other sites ever approached Cahokia in size or population, but all reflect a high level of cultural complexity. Some of the late Mississippian sites are considered to have been occupied by the ancestors of historically known groups including Creek, Choctaw, Chickasaw, Cherokee, and others. However, it is difficult to match archaeological remains in the Southeast and Midwest with known groups, first because of late prehistoric cultural changes that took place during the century preceding the arrival of the earliest Europeans, and second because of the way the population was dislocated after European exploration and settlement.

Populous communities and monumental mounds show how much the Mississippians achieved, but their specialized crafts and industries are equally good evidence. Their elaborate pottery, stone carvings, and metalwork—the latter still hammered from copper found in nuggets, not from smelted ores—suggest that some of this work was done by full-time craftsworkers. Nor was manufacturing limited to luxury goods. One community near Cahokia mined chert, a flintlike rock, and converted it into knives and hoe blades. Another may have specialized in evaporating salt from the waters of nearby salt springs; the demand for this commodity grew among people who ate more and more bland plant food and less meat.

Most of the larger Mississippian centers show evidence of social distinctions often interpreted as reflecting the existence of different classes within these societies. Typically there was also a hierarchy of settlements within any area: while the largest center in an area of Mississippian settlement was probably the focus of most of the social, political, commercial, and religious activity, it is unlikely that most of the people actually lived there. Other members of the society inhabited smaller centers, while many people lived in farming hamlets comprised of perhaps three to five households each in the surrounding area. The large Mississippian towns were commonly encircled by palisades supporting stockade walls or were located in settings that provided natural barriers—such as streams or lakes that may have effectively served as moats—to those trying to enter. While it is likely that the Mississippians used these as a means of defense against enemies, it has also been suggested that they may have served to restrict the access of their own people to the religious and political centers.

Cahokia. The central part of the city of Cahokia was well fortified by a stockade of stout posts, foot-thick logs set close together and plastered over with clay. Every hundred feet or so a square bastion of similar construction projected from the palisade. Each had a raised floor from which the defending archers could shoot down on their enemies. The gateways of the city were screened with curtain walls, L-shaped projections of the stockades that forced attackers to approach an entrance from the side instead of head on, slowing the attackers down and exposing them to heavy fire from the main wall. In addition to the palisade surrounding the center of Cahokia, there was another defensive wall of larger circumference protecting the northern half of the city.

Within the stockade, everyday life of Cahokia had its center in the large open area that probably served as a marketplace. Here came stone hoe blades, furs, hides, dried meat, copper nuggets from 400 miles away in Wisconsin, and a variety of other materials from near and far. Many of the wares offered in the market were made in workshops scattered about the city, where Cahokian craftsworkers turned out goods for both local consumption and export. Not only toolmakers, hide dressers, potters, and weavers gathered here, but also craftsworkers who hammered ornaments from imported copper, engraved designs on shells brought from the Gulf, and manufactured beads by drilling shells with hardwood bits and fine sand. On special occasions the focus shifted from the market to the city's several broad plazas. Here the people gathered for festivals, religious services, or games of *chunkey*, a sport in which, at least during the historic period, the players tossed or rolled a heavy

A reconstruction of Cahokia (circa A.D. 1150), a Mississippian city near East St. Louis, Illinois. Monk's Mound stands at the center. On the opposite side of the central plaza stand Twin Mounds. A stockade wall fortification encloses the central precincts where the elite lived. To the left is Woodhenge, a solar calendar. Agricultural fields surrounded Cahokia.

disk-shaped stone ahead of them and then, throwing their spears, tried to pinpoint the place where the chunkey stone would finally come to rest.

Cahokia's most striking feature was not its protecting palisades or its market and spacious plazas, but the many mounds, large and small, that rose above the city. Some had conical shapes and others resembled ridges, triangular in cross-section. Both of these types of mounds were apparently used for burial of the important citizens of Cahokian society. The larger flat-topped mounds served as platforms for temples or the houses of the more important Cahokians. However, the biggest, most impressive mounds had even more important public uses. One of them, a truncated pyramid not far from the city's southwestern entrance, was a place for ceremonies and religious rituals.

Dwarfing all was Monk's Mound, the great steep-sided mound that was Cahokia's religious and political center. More than a thousand feet long and nearly eight hundred feet wide, it rose in several enormous steps. On its topmost level, one hundred feet above the city, was a temple built of post and wattle (poles interwoven with branches), with a sharply

Aerial view of Cahokia today. Twin Mounds in foreground and Monk's Mound at top center.

peaked roof of thatch. On the lower terraces were homes that appear to have been residences of high-ranking personages. These, like the larger building above them, faced the principal plaza and the avenue leading toward the pyramid and a large conical burial mound.

From the top of the great mound another structure beyond the city wall could be observed, an immense circle of posts, more than a hundred yards across, which may have been used as a solar observatory and a kind of calendar. A person seated on a post near the circle's center could keep track of the shifting seasons. The position of the sun in relation to the surrounding posts as it rose over the bluffs half a mile east of the city would tell when to plant crops.

The structure of Mississippian society can be pieced together from many kinds of evidence. Many facts can be deduced from the remains of the houses used by these people. Houses were constructed by setting posts upright in excavated wall trenches, interlacing the posts with branches, and covering this wood and wattle frame with mud or clay. House sizes presumably depended upon their owner's rank—they ranged from huts to buildings thirty feet square. Burial goods found in tombs also tell us much about the status of those interred. And we have eyewitness accounts of the life of the later Mississippians from Europeans

A Middle Mississippian house. The diagram shows the wattle-and-post construction—mud plastered over poles laced with branches.

who observed the culture in its final stages among tribes of the lower Mississippi Valley. Combining these sources, we have a fairly detailed picture of a complex, socially stratified society.

The Decline of the Cities. Why Cahokia and nearby communities were abandoned is uncertain. It was once thought that infectious diseases introduced by early European visitors to the New World spread among the Mississippian societies and decimated their populations, causing widespread cultural collapse and the abandonment of Mississippian centers such as Cahokia. However, excavations and scientific dating show that the city reached its peak between approximately A.D. 1050 and 1250, by 1400 all significant construction had ceased, and by 1450 the city had been virtually abandoned, long before any European arrivals. Cahokia was empty when the first French explorers passed that way in the 1670s. There have been many theories offered to explain the abandonment of Cahokia and other large Mississippian settlements in the Midwest and Southeast. Some try to account for the decline on the basis of environmental deterioration or climate change, while others emphasize cultural factors including warfare, population growth, and changing subsistence practices.

One theory traces the decline to social disintegration and warfare brought about by increased populations. Unquestionably the intensive agriculture on which all Middle Mississippian life was based would have sharply increased their numbers, which in turn would have forced them to expand the cultivated area. And that may have presented a problem. Once the richest river valley lands had been thickly populated, the northerly Mississippian communities could have expanded only in two directions. One way was into the numerous islands of long-grass prairie around them, but there the compacted soil with its thickly rooted tough grasses created a sod that was impossible to cultivate without iron plows drawn by horses or oxen. The other route for expansion was into the forests, where trees could be cut down and burned to create fields for crops. Forest soils, however, unlike those of the annually flooded lands along the rivers, are thin. Even with a top dressing of wood ash they can be farmed for only a few years and then must be abandoned for as much as a generation or more. Thus the Mississippian communities would have had to push their cultivation even farther into the forest—and away from the rivers on which most of their trade depended. This change could have also produced problems in political control. Collecting taxes (as the Mississippian rulers must surely have done to keep up their elaborate standard of living) may have been simple enough when their subjects were situated along a riverbank, but not so easy if the tribute-paying villages were scattered in several directions forty or fifty miles into the woodlands.

Other theories suggest that a major climatic change leading to a cold period known as the Little Ice Age may have shortened the growing season for Mississippian farmers and reduced the reliability of Mississippian yields. While the onset of cooler conditions does generally coincide with the end of the Middle Mississippian cultural climax, we really have no idea just what impact the climate may have had on maize farmers in the central or lower Mississippi Valley. We do know that various farming cultures on the fringes of Mississippian settlement were apparently able to cope quite well with the new climatic situation, suggesting that the impact on Middle Mississippian culture may not have been terribly significant. Others have suggested that the introduction of the bean to the Mississippian diet may have reduced their dependence upon floodplain animal protein resources, resulting in a movement away from the rich valleys and a decentralization of political power.

While the answer to what caused the late prehistoric decline in Mississippian cultural development remains uncertain, there is no mystery about what destroyed the more southerly Mississippian communities that lasted into the early historic period. When the French trader De la Vente visited the Natchez Indians of the lower Mississippi Valley in 1704, he found them, according to their own accounts, much reduced in numbers by the diseases introduced by Europeans. The Indians, because of their long isolation from the Old World, had little or no immunity to European germs, so that outbreaks of smallpox, influenza, measles, or even the common cold could devastate or completely wipe out an entire community. De la Vente himself wrote that thanks to smallpox, the Natchez population had dropped by as much as a third in a mere six years, and similar catastrophes must have overtaken many other tribes; germs as well as goods can travel along trade routes. A generation after De la Vente, the French finished the job that the microbes had started. In a war against the Natchez they killed most of the population and dispersed the remnant.

Upper Mississippian Cultures. A number of somewhat less complex late prehistoric societies referred to as Upper Mississippian cultures existed over much of the Midwest beginning a few hundred years after the development of the earliest Middle Mississippian cultures. We find these cultures scattered across the region from the eastern fringes of the plains, across the northern part of the Mississippi Valley, and into the western Great Lakes and central Ohio Valley. At best, few of these cultures are recognizable in the archaeological record before A.D. 1000. However, a number of them survived into the period of contact with European people. Certain Upper Mississippian cultures and sites have been connected archaeologically with individual groups described in early historic accounts of the Midwest.

These cultures shared many practices with the Middle Mississippians already described. They had at their core a heavy reliance on maize agriculture combined with large mammal hunting; the exploitation of smaller marshland animals, waterfowl, and fish; and the gathering of various wild plant foods. Many Upper Mississippian groups manufactured pottery from clay tempered with crushed shell, and utilized a number of similar artifact types and styles. Defensive earthworks and stockades were not uncommon in many areas of Upper Mississippian settlement. However their major villages, while essentially permanent, were typically neither as large nor occupied as long as the larger Middle Mississippian centers. The Upper Mississippians apparently built relatively few mounds, and virtually no platform mounds. They apparently shared in some of the religious ideology of the Middle Mississippians. However, it is not likely that they ever attained similar levels of socio-political or economic complexity.

On the eastern prairies of Minnesota, Iowa, Wisconsin, Missouri, Illinois, and in portions of northwestern Indiana and southwestern Michigan, the Upper Mississippian lifeway is represented by the *Oneota* culture. The area of the Midwest having Oneota sites actually extends as far west as eastern Kansas and Nebraska. Archaeological evidence clearly indicates connections between specific Oneota sites and the Siouan-speaking Ioway, Oto, Missouri, Kansa, and Omaha. In other cases, there are strong suggestions of cultural links that remain to be firmly established between other Oneota sites and other related Siouan-speaking peoples, most notably the Winnebago. Some archaeologists have suggested that a few Algonkian-speaking peoples may be represented by the Oneota, although the evidence for such connections seems less conclusive.

In the Ohio Valley region, a similar group of Upper Mississippian cultures are collectively referred to as the *Fort Ancient* culture. While clearly not identical to Oneota, they shared many similarities in general culture and overall way of life. At present, the archaeological evidence seems to indicate a likely archaeological connection between the Fort Ancient inhabitants of the Midwest and several Algonkian groups, including the Shawnee, Illinois, and Miami.

The Great Plains

The Great Plains of North America extend from the edge of the floodplains of the Mississippi River on the east to the Rocky Mountains on the west, and from the southern third of Alberta, Saskatchewan, and Manitoba to mid-Texas. They blend in gradually with the desert Southwest; nowhere is the change sharp. Moving from east to west, the general plains division has three zones: the low plains on the east, marked by tall prairie grasses, the sods of which are too tough to cultivate with stone or bone equipment; the high plains, with shorter grasses and less annual precipitation; and the mountain foothills, driest of all and having the shortest varieties of grasses. The gradual rise in elevation from east to west means that the rivers flow swiftly to the east, and each spring, as the mountain snows begin to melt, they flood, refertilizing the lands around them with productive silts. The great rivers of the region are the Missouri, the Arkansas, and the Red, along with their many tributaries. The area from north to south may be subdivided into northern plains, central plains, and southern plains, the difference here being one of temperature rather than altitude or precipitation.

We have examined one cultural tradition of the Plains: the Paleo-Indian big game hunters. By 5000 B.C., hotter and drier climate began to change the vegetation on the plains, and many of the large game species had died out, including mammoths and giant bison. While other bison still survived, overall the tradition of big game hunting diminished. A generalized Archaic tradition followed that in many areas of the plains apparently involved a largely nomadic life-style with varying degrees of dependence on bison and smaller animals as well as the gathering of seeds and other plant foods. Unfortunately, we know relatively little about the Plains Archaic cultures since very few sites of this period have been studied.

Over much of the region, the Plains Archaic tradition was followed by a Woodland tradition that was most likely brought into the region by Woodland peoples from the East a little more than 2000 years ago. This period is usually called Plains Woodland, and was eventually succeeded around A.D. 900 by a Village tradition based on river valley agriculture and heavily influenced by the developing Mississippian cultures to the east. However, the most westerly plains area never took on any sort of cultivation but remained stable in an Archaic way of life that was essentially most similar to that of the Desert Archaic tradition, with sparse population and little social or technological complexity.

Although we may see a connection with the Desert Archaic in the ways of life that followed the Paleo-Indian tradition of big game hunting, the most important events that resulted in widespread corn cultivation appear to have come in from the East rather than the Southwest. While it appears that maize was originally introduced from the Southwest across the plains and into the East, probably by 200 B.C., for a long time it was little more than a minor plant in Plains Woodland gardens. Eventually the development of strains of corn that were very well adapted to the region occurred several hundred years later, not in the Southwest but within the Midwest. Just as importantly, the eastward flowing river system provided an easier and more inviting route for interaction between the Plains peoples and burgeoning Mississippian agricultural societies than a trek across the arid desert to those of the Southwest.

The river regions on the eastern plains show strong Woodland connections, beginning during the time of the Hopewell cultural development. Starting around 250 B.C., small groups of Woodland cultivators moved into the river valleys of the plains from the East. Those Indians had a mixed economy, relying on hunting of various animals of all sizes, gathering of wild plant foods, and also gardening. They made pottery and lived in small, fairly permanent villages or camps along the rivers and streams. The pottery styles alone show eastern Woodland characteristics, and mound burials of the Woodland type appear as well in some areas.

The Plains Village Tradition

Between about A.D. 900 and 1700, or until the period of European contact, the Plains settlements along rivers and streams reached a climax. The inhabitants planted and harvested crops on the fertile river floodplains where they had some shelter from the bitter winds that whipped over the flat land in winter. Extensive settlements with numerous storage pits much larger than any known from Plains Woodland sites also hint at more productive cultivation and larger population; crop yield must have been great.

The Plains Village settlements consisted of sizable earth lodges, built partly underground, on stream terraces close to the cultivated fields that lay in the river-bottom lands. Away from the river valleys, the plains were vacant of human population for most of the year, but during the late spring or early summer, as tender grasses watered by early rains attracted the mating buffalo, the villagers moved out from their settlements to hunt. The men must have hunted bison as in past centuries: stampeding the animals over cliffs; driving them into traps or swampy areas where they were disabled or mired down; and using grass fires to supplement feeble human muscle, spears, and bows and arrows. Long before horses were reintroduced to the plains, Plains Village peoples had developed highly successful means for hunting on foot the large and formidable bison that along with maize represented essential components of their diet, and in a much broader sense, of their overall lifeway.

Influence from the East. We find even more evidence of eastern connections in this later period than in the time just before it, including items of trade and commerce from the Mississippian peoples. In addition, many villages were surrounded by protective stockades and ditches, features also commonly encountered in large Mississippian settlements in many parts of the East. Here, in contrast with the Southwest, the principal cultivating tool was a hoe having a blade made from a bison scapula (shoulder blade). Grinding stones were not common, suggesting that the villagers probably used wooden grinding equipment like the mortars and pestles of the East.

Some Mississippian cultures probably spread to the west by migrations. Though the direct evidence for such movements is still limited, the easy route the rivers offered makes the idea seem logical. Beyond the practices mentioned already, such as increased agricultural efforts and larger, protected villages, no sharp break separated the new way of life from that of the earlier Plains cultivators. The people continued many of their practices without noticeable change. Hunting, still very important, was done mostly with the bow and arrow. Many people added the fish in the rivers to their food supply, much as in the general Eastern Archaic.

Burials. The Plains Villagers had many ways of burying their dead, starting with simple interments. They used secondary burials as well, placing the corpse on a scaffold or platform until the flesh had decayed, and burying the bones in communal pits called *ossuaries*, in natural hills, or beneath small artificial mounds. Some bodies were even buried under the lodges. These varied means of disposing of the dead might indicate that people from a number of eastern groups moved westward, or perhaps local tradition or adapting to local environmental conditions was responsible for the differences. By the time of European contact, certainly, the Plains people had several linguistic divisions, though their styles of living were similar throughout.

Few sites where the Plains Villagers lived have been matched archaeologically to groups in existence when written history began in this part of the continent. On the upper reaches of the Missouri River were the ancestors of the Hidatsa, Mandan, and Arikara. Those around the Lower Loup River in east-central Nebraska were ancestral to the Pawnee. The early Wichita settled in the western Arkansas River Valley in central Kansas and were visited by Coronado in 1541 at the place the Spanish named Quivira.

Summary: The Results of Cultivation

By 5000 B.C. in Mexico the warmer, drier climate led to a way of life like that in other desert areas, with a vital difference. The people, depending more and more on plant foods, began to cultivate grasses native to the central Mexican region that were forerunners of maize. Between about 5000 and 2000 B.C., the Mexican Indians improved corn until it was very productive, with plants providing large ears filled with grains. Cultivation of early maize and other useful plants encouraged greater sedentism, and reduced the necessity for constant movement in the quest for food. This eventually allowed the development of settlements that were occupied for longer periods of time than previously had been possible. However, until Europeans came to North America, no animals like horses, cattle, sheep, or swine had been domesticated. Only two animals were apparently domesticated in North America. The dog, probably domesticated at an early date in the New World, served many purposes. At a much later date, the turkey was domesticated. However, neither of these animals proved to be a major food source for prehistoric North American societies, and hunting remained the predominant source of meat.

The idea of cultivation could have developed independently in a number of separate areas of North America, as Archaic peoples began to depend upon wild plants for an increasing percentage of their food. However, it seems that the idea of cultivation spread from Mexico to the north, as tropical cultigens were passed along into new areas. In the desert regions of the southwestern United States, along rivers and in the few spots where they could find water, people began to settle down and cultivate crops. Some of these earliest farmers were the ancestors of later Pueblo people. Elsewhere in the desert, people had to continue their life of wandering, for without a water supply they could not farm. The two ways of life went on side by side: farming where there were adequate sources of moisture, and nomadic hunting and plant collecting in waterless places. The wandering hunting-gathering people probably raided the farmers, who may have developed their special type of house, the pueblo, to protect themselves from marauders.

In the East during the Woodland period, groups of Indians had already begun to follow a more settled way of life in river valleys, where they found they could encourage the growth of wild plants in a way that approached cultivation. They were thus ready to accept the new cultigens that filtered in from the south. Squash had been introduced into the East several thousand years ago, and maize was introduced approximately 2000 years ago. Initially, corn was not an important food source, but by A.D. 800 or so, strains of maize had been developed in the East that were better adapted to the more northerly environment. Soon the eastern diet included a considerable amount of corn and squash as well as the local cultigens they grew and the wild plants they continued to gather. The Woodland populations increased and villages grew. Farming in the river valley lands was easy and productive because the soil was deep, rock-free, easy to work with primitive tools, and replenished each year when the river floods brought new silts. River-bottom farming along the Ohio and Mississippi rivers and tributaries was rich enough to support large populations. Within a few hundred years, beans were introduced and added another important element to the subsistence base. Between about A.D. 900 and 1500, cities such as Cahokia in Illinois grew to great size, and the larger populations organized into new kinds of social groups. Farmers produced enough so that some people could devote their time to crafts, government, religion, or trade, and not spend all their time seeking food. When farmers were not busy in the fields, they probably provided the labor to build the mounds, temples, and other public works, under the direction of some sort of centralized leadership.

Variations of this general Mississippian way of life penetrated into the river valleys of the East, the Midwest, and the Plains. In these areas we find a variety of cultures that adopted many central features of the Mississippian lifeway, including a major reliance on maize, settlement in large villages, and concern for protecting themselves against warring or raiding enemies. Within the plains and eastern prairies, the river valleys were the only part of the vast grasslands that could be tilled—elsewhere lay the densely rooted prairie grasses that defied cultivation with digging sticks and bone, shell, or stone hoes.

By the time Columbus bore news of the American continent back to Europe, Indian people already had true urban centers along the river systems of the Southeast and Midwest, and people led less complex village lives in the rest of the eastern Woodlands and along the rivers and streams of the Plains. In the southwestern deserts, the Desert Archaic way of life continued alongside settled agricultural communities where water and human modification of the landscape made farming possible. In the Great Basin, in the far West, and in the foothill area of the western Plains, the Archaic ways also lingered. In the Subarctic and Arctic regions, Archaic ways of life likewise persisted, except by then the people in the Arctic were the Eskimo, not the Indians.

Part II

CULTURE AREAS OF NORTH AMERICA

Spreading gradually down and across the continent, the American Indians built new societies wherever they stopped to settle. People slowly adapted themselves to each new environment, developing new ways of life. These collective ways of life are called *cultures*. The many kinds of environments and resources the Indians encountered inspired many kinds of *adaptations*, and thus the Indian societies were surprisingly varied. Differences among societies also came about through change over time, or *cultural evolution*. It would be astonishing if any of us in this country, Indians or non-Indians, lived today as our ancestors did centuries ago. Even if Columbus had never seen this side of the Atlantic, none of us would live now as people did in his time. Indian societies also grew unlike each other because of *cultural isolation*: tribes that lived by themselves, separated from others by great distances or bitter climate, changed little.

Other tribes settled close together, in more or less the same environment, with much the same resources, and developed similar adaptations. Often they borrowed useful traits from each other. Those who lived closest to the innovators would, of course, pick up a new invention earliest. This sharing is called *cultural diffusion*. People living close to each other, with much happening around them, exposed to novel ways of life, changed or evolved quickly.

All these ways in which cultures change—adaptation, evolution, isolation, diffusion—make it clear that no such person as a typical Indian ever lived. The people who adapted to coastal living were very different from those who learned to live in the desert, plains, or mountains. Because we cannot take the time to study each of the hundreds of Indian cultures, we will focus on groups of tribes within geographically distinct regions where similar ways of life developed. These regions are called *culture areas*.

The Culture Area Scheme

The boundaries of the culture areas as indicated on the map on p. 95 appear more distinct and definite than they were in reality. The boundaries were not fixed limits as much as transitional zones, where one culture area more or less graded into the adjacent one in terms of environmental and cultural characteristics. That is because life in boundary areas was a cultural mixture, and tribes there could reasonably be classified in more than one area. After all, they too borrowed ideas from each other and lived in similar surroundings. Thus different anthropologists have come up with somewhat different dividing lines.

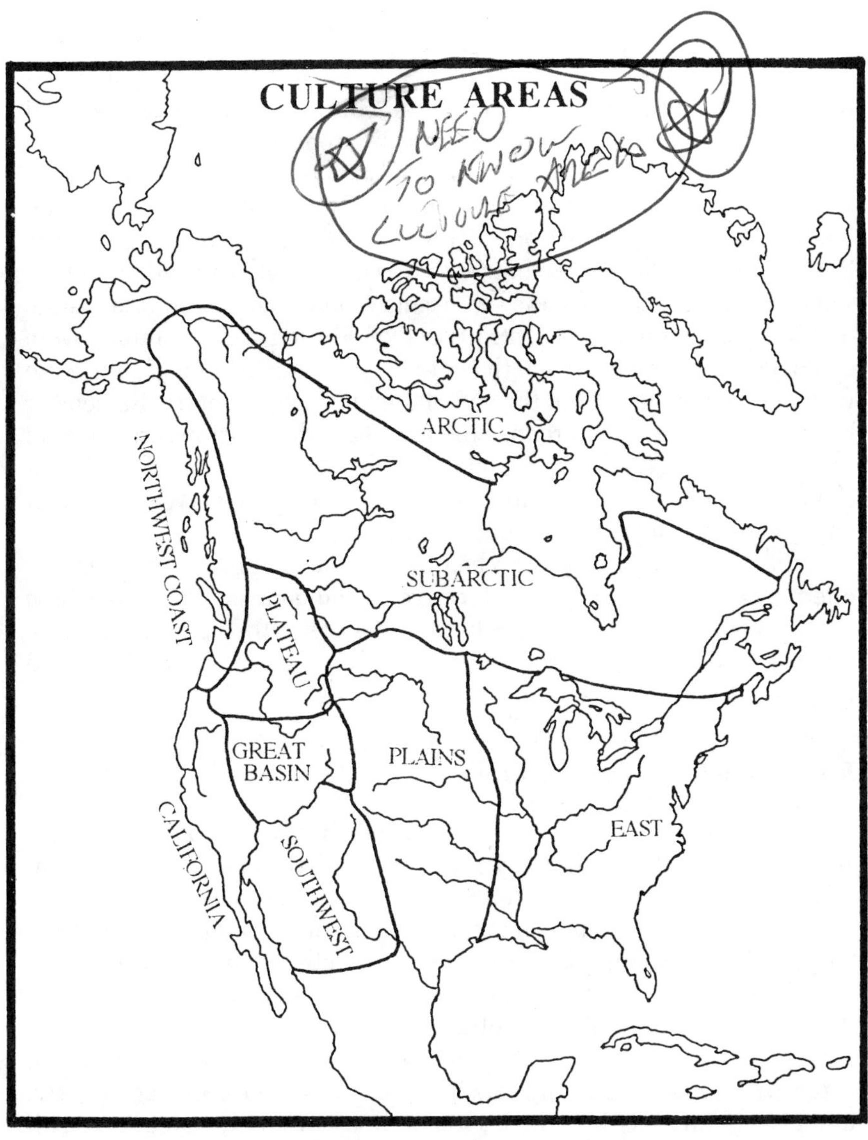
CULTURE AREAS
ARCTIC
SUBARCTIC
NORTHWEST COAST
PLATEAU
GREAT BASIN
PLAINS
CALIFORNIA
SOUTHWEST
EAST

Still, the culture area is a very useful device. Considering that there were at least four hundred distinct Indian groups at one time, most of which are unfamiliar to many of us today, the culture area scheme is a good way to study general similarities and differences.

The culture areas we will examine here are not historically equivalent. We will see most of them at their climax, just before European disturbance. The Plains horse culture is an exception, since it was Europeans who introduced horses to this continent. Thus you will find some cultures described as they were generations or even centuries before others. People on the Atlantic coast of Florida, for example, were contacted in the early sixteenth century, yet some Eskimo groups were unknown to outsiders until the end of the nineteenth century. Remember this time difference, and realize too that these descriptions are no more true of American Indians today than a description of colonial Philadelphia tells us anything about that city today. We will treat contemporary Indians in a later section.

In discussing Indian cultures before the time of European contact, we often speak of them as aboriginal, native, or indigenous. Words like these carry no suggestion of inferiority or superiority: they simply indicate that the adaptations in question occurred before colonists, explorers, and traders came along.

Reconstructing Ways of Life

You may wonder how we can study societies that left no documentary records and boldly say that this or that was the way of life at the moment of outside contact or of climax. The answer is that we build our reconstructions on archaeological information and ethnographic analogy. We depend not only on present-day ethnographic descriptions, including legends that are still told, but also on earlier written data, like diaries of settlers; economic, political, and military reports of explorers; personal accounts, letters, and traders' records. We use such information carefully, always balancing it with what we know about geography, climate, plants, and animals. Sometimes we can come up with remarkably good reconstructions; sometimes we are not so fortunate.

Although it is reasonable to talk about cultures in terms of the areas where they occurred, that is not at all the same thing as saying that environment *causes* culture. It simply means that environment cannot be ignored: every society has to respond to it in one way or another. The same human ingenuity has invented many ways of responding to each environment. Responses that take the form of material culture naturally are easier to see than such things as social organization and religion.

The Culture Areas

In Part II we will consider nine culture areas, starting with the hunters and gatherers and going in the direction of increasing complexity to the agriculturalists: Arctic, Subarctic, Plateau, Northwest Coast, California, Great Basin, Southwest, Plains, and East. Each chapter begins with a legend typical of the area; this is one way we learn how people saw their world and nature's wonders. For those who had no written history, legends were an important means of understanding the world.

Population

All our figures on population at the time of European contact and earlier are estimates, and they vary enormously. We do not even have accurate, documented population records for later periods. Today, figures on American Indians are probably the least reliable of all census data. Estimates on the number of people north of Mexico before European contact range from 1 million to 10 million, and in California alone, from 100,000 to 1 million. There is no way of proving any of these numbers. However, we do know something about relative density. Aboriginal population was highest in California, the Northwest Coast, and the Southeast, and sparsest in the Arctic, Subarctic, and Great Basin areas.

Language

Many people have the idea that all Indians shared one language. Actually, at least three hundred languages were spoken north of Mexico at the time of European contact, though many of those are extinct today.

Phyla and Families

Linguists group all languages, including the hundreds of Indian languages, into major categories called *phyla* (*phylum* in the singular), and within each phylum into divisions called *families*. To give a familiar example, English is in the Indo-European phylum. It belongs to the Teutonic family, like Dutch and German. French is an Indo-European language too, but it belongs to another family, Romance languages. Just as speakers of English and French cannot understand each other without special training, Hopi and Paiute could not understand each other even though their languages were both of the Aztec-Tanoan phylum. Thus when we refer to Algonkian speakers, for instance, we do not mean they could talk together, but that they spoke related languages.

Geographic distribution of the language families of native North America. After Voegelin and Voegelin 1966.

Linguist Carl Voegelin established the language divisions which we use in this book. He has proposed seven phyla for the languages north of the Rio Grande: Paleo-Siberian, Na-Dene, Macro-Algonkian, Macro-Siouan, Hokan, Penutian, and Aztec-Tanoan. There remain some language families for which the phylum affiliation is uncertain. After each culture area chapter a list of the cultural units and their major linguistic affiliations appears.

It will become obvious in Part II that people speaking widely different languages adapted as neighbors to the same environment with almost identical responses. The many languages found among Plains Indian societies are demonstration of this point. On the other hand, the great geographical separation of some groups speaking closely related languages illustrates migrations of people across the continent over many years. Through a technique known as *glottochronology*, linguists can estimate the time of separation of such groups. Thus we can say that some Athabaskan speakers of the Subarctic moved into the Southwest 500 to 700 years ago. Furthermore, it is interesting to note that the languages spoken by the dwellers of the Great Basin, whose cultural elaboration was minimal, are closely related to that spoken by the Aztec of Mexico, who created one of the most complex urban societies of the New World. Thus people of a single phylum or linguistic family adapting to disparate and diverse environments could become radically different. It is a serious error to assume that culture areas and linguistic areas show significant correspondence.

Relationships among language groups, therefore, give insight into the migrations of people and may aid in reconstructing ancient social connections. However, reconstruction and analysis of this sort are highly specialized and are the domain of trained linguists.

Tribal Names

Our names for Indian societies are not often the names they took for themselves. Most societies called themselves something like "we, the people," or "the men." For other societies they used descriptive words. Our word for Chippewa comes from another tribe's description of them, meaning "those whose moccasins have puckered seams." Creek was the name given that tribe by British settlers, referring to the location of their towns. Fox got their name from a misunderstanding: A French party asked a group of Indians who they were and they replied with their clan name, which in English is Fox. The name they called themselves was mesquaki, meaning "red-earth people." The Pima got their name from another misunderstanding with Europeans: *pima* means "no." Ottawa is an Algonkian word meaning "to trade or sell," and was applied to the tribe because of their trading activities.

Bibliography

Kroeber, Alfred. 1939. *Cultural and Natural Areas of Native North America.*

Relates culture areas and environment, vegetation, and physiographic zones. The book includes many helpful maps and Kroeber's population estimates.

Murdock, George Peter. 1970. *Ethnographic Bibliography of North America.*

Bibliography by culture area and tribe. Every student should be familiar with this important reference book.

Sturtevant, William C., gen. ed. 1978 *et seq. Handbook of North American Indians.*

This series will eventually contain 20 volumes, of which about half are currently available. It is an important reference work.

3

THE ARCTIC AND THE SUBARCTIC

Mask representing an Eskimo in a winter hood, with labrets and tattoo marks.

The Arctic

Eskimo Creation Myth

Once upon a time a widower lived alone with his daughter, Sedna, who had grown to be a handsome woman sought in marriage by many young men. None of them pleased her, for she had lost her heart to a seagull who flew over the ice and wooed her with an enticing song. "Come with me to the land of the birds where there is never hunger, where my tent is made of the most beautiful skins. You shall rest on soft bearskins. Other gulls will bring you all your heart may desire; their feathers will clothe you; your lamp will always be filled with oil, your pot with meat." Sedna could not resist, and they went together over the vast sea.

When at last they reached the country of the gull after a long, hard journey, Sedna discovered that her new husband had shamefully deceived her. Her new home was not built of beautiful pelts but was covered with wretched fishskins, full of holes, that gave free entrance to wind and snow. Her bed was harsh, and she had to live on miserable fish which the birds brought her. In her wretchedness she called to her father to rescue her. "Oh, father, come to me in your boat and carry me home across the waters. Oh, come and take me back home."

When a year had passed and the sea was again stirred by warmer winds, the father went to Sedna, and, hearing of her woes, determined upon revenge. He killed her husband, the seagull, took Sedna into his boat, and they quickly left the country of the birds. But when the other gulls returned home and found their companion dead and his wife gone, they flew away in search of the fugitives. They were very sad over the death of their comrade and continue to mourn and cry until this day.

After a short flight, the gulls discovered the boat and caused a terrible storm to break out. The sea rose in immense waves that threatened the pair with destruction. In this mortal peril the father determined to offer Sedna to the birds and flung her overboard. She clung to the edge of the boat. The father then took a knife and cut off the first joints of her fingers. Falling into the sea, they were transformed into whales, the nails turning into whalebone. Sedna held more tightly to the boat, but her second joints fell under the sharp knife and swam away as walrus. Then the father cut off the stumps of the fingers, and they became seals.

Meantime the storm subsided, for the gulls thought Sedna had drowned. Sedna took up abode in the depths of the ocean whence she controlled the sources of nourishment. She sent out all the animals that served for food or sometimes withheld the supply, causing want and famine. When the people of the earth displeased her by their behavior or neglect of the taboos, she punished them with starvation.

In a nearly treeless land of cold, snow, and ice, with continuous darkness for three or four months each year, life offers few comforts and few products of the soil. Most of the native people of the northern land made their living from the ocean, and the ocean mammals also provided the raw materials for their clothing, housing, and tools. Small wonder, then, that the Sedna myth—in many versions—was told and retold by almost all Eskimo across 6,000 miles of Arctic coast.

The Environment

The landscape of the Arctic is rolling plains called tundra, with little vegetation other than mosses and occasional scrub bushes. It has no trees, for the Arctic lies beyond the northern tree limit. The Arctic Ocean freezes solid in winter, but in summer the ice cracks into pieces along the shores and drifts south with the ocean currents. Hunters can get trapped if the ice breaks up unexpectedly in the spring.

Cold is the outstanding feature of the Arctic environment. The Arctic winter is severe not only because of extreme cold, but also because daylight is so short. Surprisingly, snowfall is comparatively light; the winds build high drifts because no wooded areas are there to act as windbreaks. Summer winds are less violent than the winter gales that sweep with intense force across the barren land. The summer wind may even be welcome, because it blows away the insect pests—flies and mosquitoes—that appear with the warmer weather and mercilessly attack human and animal populations.

During the brief summer, temperatures do rise above freezing, and it can become quite warm, though never long enough for the sun's heat to penetrate far into the earth. This is the land of permanently frozen subsoil, called *permafrost*. When the topsoil thaws, it turns into muddy mire over the frozen lower layer, through which water cannot drain away.

Some Arctic areas, especially northeastern Canada, have hardly any soil where the land was scraped down to bedrock by the Ice Age glaciers. Because of this, the short growing season, the low summer temperatures, and the intense wind, the plants are small, tough varieties—dwarf willows, lichens, mosses, sedges, and low grasses. Limited though the vegetation is, it nourishes large herds of caribou and musk-oxen and tiny animals like the vole and lemming, which in turn support foxes, wolves, and weasels.

After spring thaw, the small lakes, the uncountable ponds, and the pools are full of fish and attract hordes of waterfowl. The sea ice melts, and ice floes break off. Fogs are frequent during the spring melting, and sunlight diffused through the fog can create a white-out, which may cause snow blindness.

At the North Pole the winter nights are the longest—six months—but even during that night the visibility is not as poor as one might expect. There is a good deal of twilight, and the snow reflects moon and starlight. Winter temperatures average below zero, dropping at times to 50 degrees below. Storms alternate with spells of quiet weather in which the little heat that remains in the earth radiates away into the clear, dark skies. Most herds and birds move south, and the remaining animals hibernate.

The Eskimo

The Arctic is one of the most unpromising and demanding environments inhabited by human beings. Probably the aboriginal population never reached 120,000 in the entire area. The people who settled this forbidding land, the Eskimo, spread from Alaska, where they had entered North America, across Canada and on to Greenland. Archaeology is difficult at best in the Arctic, but excavations indicate that the Eskimo, a subdivision of the Mongoloid group, began entering North America between 3000 and 2000 B.C. By that time the land connection between Siberia and Alaska had been submerged under water for several thousand years, so they must have crossed the strait over ice floes or, what seems far more likely, in boats. The life they had led in northeastern Siberia appears to have been well suited to the new territory across the strait and all the way east along the Arctic coast, for many Asian tools continued in use in the New World.

Over most of the great area inhabited by the Eskimo, a single language was spoken, though local dialects occurred. With the exception of the areas south of the Yukon River, where at least five distinct Eskimo languages are recognized, the remainder of the Eskimo areas show remarkable similarity in sharing a single language between regions as geographically separate as western Alaska and Greenland. The Eskimo language group has been classified with languages spoken in northeastern Siberia—Chukchi, Kamchadal, and other tongues—as belonging to the Paleo-Siberian linguistic phylum. It bears no resemblance to American Indian languages, and is the only North

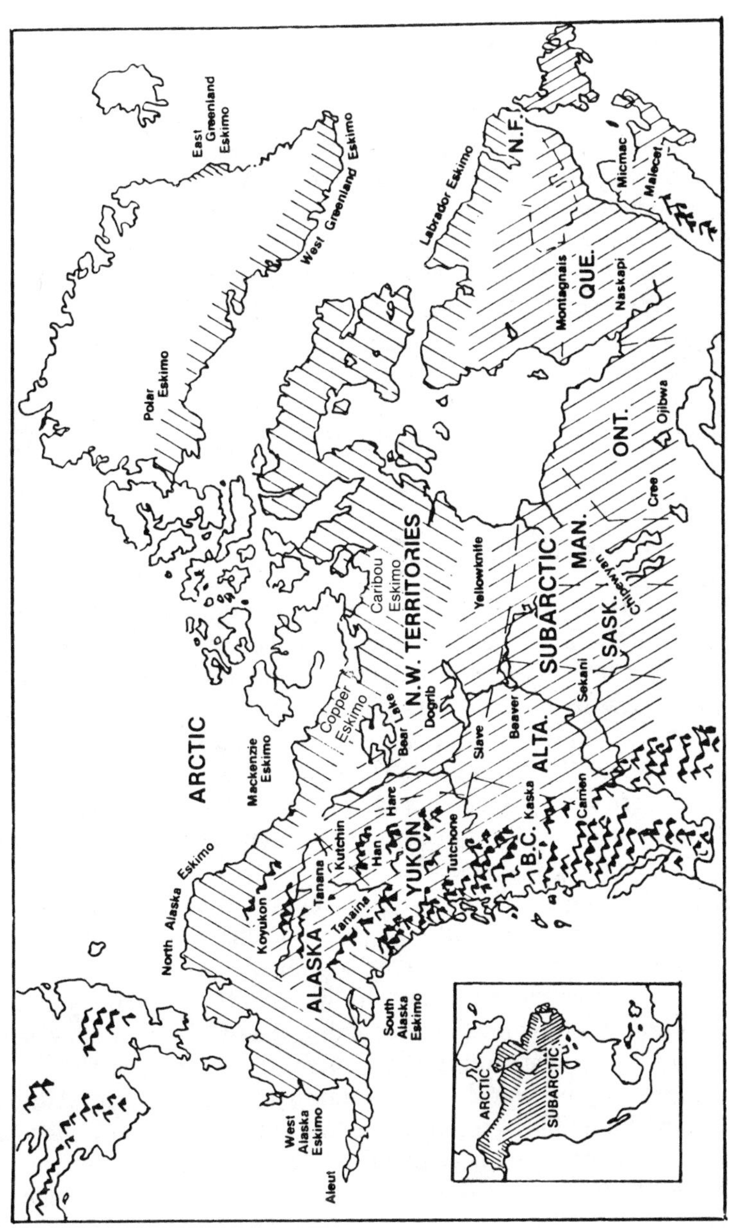

Arctic and Subarctic culture areas and their tribes.

American language group that shows clear linguistic ties to any Old World tongue. Also within this phylum is Aleut, spoken by the natives of the Aleutian Islands, who were closely related to the Eskimo. The linguistic homogeneity suggests the relatively recent spread of the Eskimo across the continent.

Several other kinds of evidence also support the idea that the Eskimo reached America fairly recently, and spread eastward along the Arctic coast relatively quickly. For one thing, the oldest artifacts recovered in the New World that can be reasonably linked to ancient Eskimo culture are only about 4,000 years old. Archaeological evidence across the entire Arctic region to Greenland indicates that it was first inhabited by Eskimo people at approximately that same date. Moreover, the Eskimo resemble the peoples of northeastern Asia much more than they do other American aborigines. Their skin is relatively light, their profiles are almost invariably flattened, their cheek bones are wide, and their eyes are narrowed by the fleshy lids and epicanthic fold found in eastern Asiatic peoples.

Adapting to the Arctic

The bleak land occupied by all these peoples and their descendants was a tremendous challenge to their ingenuity. The way of life that existed among the earliest Eskimo arrivals and ultimately spread from Alaska to Greenland was regulated everywhere by the environment. People wore layers of fur and hide clothing, carefully tailored and airtight, because they would freeze if they did not. The women made undershirts of bird skins to be worn with the feathers against the body for added insulation. Babies rode naked in fur pouches on their mothers' backs; mothers packed the hoods with moss or used fur or bark diapers.

The climate forced the Eskimo to live, at least during the long winter, in well-insulated shelters—pithouses of wood and whalebone in Alaska, and igloos built of snow blocks in the central and eastern Arctic. As they entered their homes, the people carefully beat off ice crystals and snow so that their clothing would not become wet and heavy in the warmth. They had to dry all wet clothing carefully or it would freeze when they went outside. Drying was done on a frame over an oil lamp. Although some Eskimo hunted land animals the year around, most lived primarily off the sea by hunting seals, whales, and other marine mammals. The endurance of an Eskimo hunter is amazing to anyone raised in the temperate world. Almost never did they turn back once they got on the trail of an animal, and they learned to wait hours, motionless, for a seal at its breathing hole in the ice.

Eskimo wasted nothing, eating every edible part of animals and making bones, teeth, and antler into implements. They made sleds of antler and whalebone, wood of course being rare. Women rendered (melted down) fat into oil, and made hides into shelter, clothing, boat coverings, or other equipment. Sinew became the thread that held skins together.

Arctic survival required heat as well as food and shelter, and where timber was not available and driftwood was too precious to burn, the Eskimo burned oil from sea mammals. The best heating oil was rendered seal blubber, which burned with a clean, smokeless, hot flame. The Eskimo poured the oil into a soapstone lamp, a shallow stone carved with a depression, and added a wick of moss. The women could regulate the flame, which burned continually, and kept it low at night. For daytime, they fixed the wick to create more light and heat. The women cooked on the oil lamp and melted snow and ice over it for drinking water. (Water was rarely used for washing because it was too scarce.) It may be hard to believe, but Eskimo dwellings, both igloos and the semiunderground structures of Alaska, were comfortable, not drafty or too cold. Inside, the people went almost naked.

Regional Variations

The differences among the various Eskimo groups were slight. In Alaska where there were some trees and the environment was slightly less harsh, Eskimo built wooden dwellings and communal houses. For transportation they had two types of boat, the one-person *kayak* and the *umiak*, a large open boat made of hide stretched over a framework of lashed wood. They made some pottery and had complex trading relationships and ritual activities. *Labrets*—ornamental lip plugs—appear to have been confined to Alaska, as were a few other traits such as masks and basketry. These traits were also common to tribes of neighboring Indians and may have been derived from them and added to an older Eskimo culture.

Farther east, in the area called the Barren Grounds, the Caribou Eskimo severed all connection with coastal life. Geological data reveal that about six hundred years ago, in the central part of Canada, the earth's crust was uplifted, leaving the sea there too shallow for whales and other large sea mammals. To replace that main source of food, Eskimo there turned to the caribou and also fished in inland waters. Life there was so hard that they abandoned many cultural elaborations of the Alaska Eskimo in their struggle for sheer subsistence.

Another division of Eskimo, living around Coronation Gulf, followed the common Eskimo pattern of hunting sea mammals, but there nuggets of copper could be picked up and made into implements; thus these people became known as the Copper Eskimo. The Eskimo of eastern

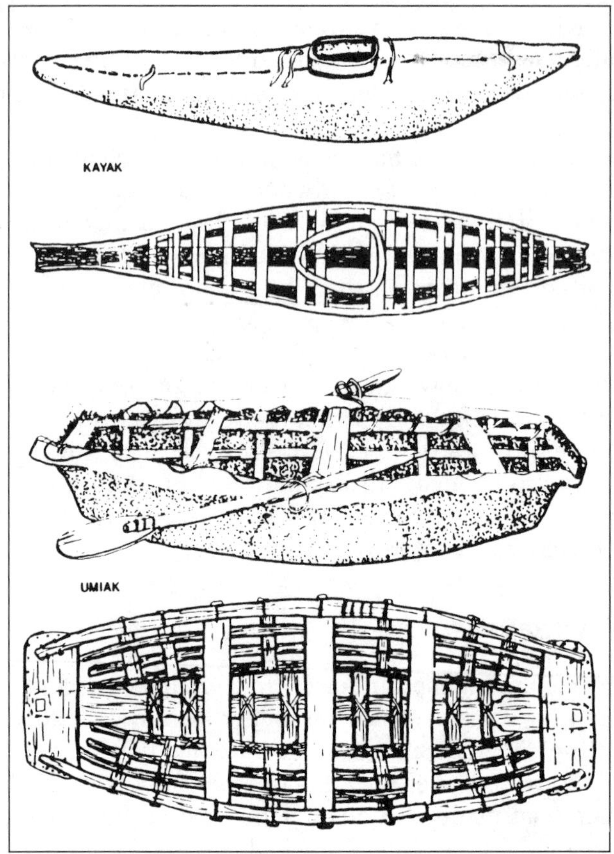

A kayak and a umiak, showing exterior views and framework.

Canada in Baffin Land and Labrador also depended on sea mammals, occasionally including whales, as did the Greenland Eskimo. All these people used the kayak and umiak except the Polar Eskimo of North Greenland, who did all their transporting on their own backs, not even using sleds.

Alaska: The Seasonal Pattern of Life

From our brief review of Eskimo life we can see that most traits typical of the Alaska Eskimo, except those taken from Indian peoples nearby, were carried east by the early people who spread in that direction. They seem to have abandoned a few traits as environmental conditions dictated; but on the whole, the people who moved eastward from Alaska, hunting both inland animals and sea mammals, were already adapted to life under all the conditions they met. The eastern migrants merely dropped some of their traditional ways, modifying others. Thus, if one way of life can be called typical and "purest Eskimo," it is the coastal, from which all the others developed.

Spring Whaling

The earliest Eskimo were the so-called Old Whaling People. Relics of their pursuit of whales, found on Cape Krusenstern in northwest Alaska, date from around 2000 B.C. These people left large flint blades which presumably tipped heavy-duty harpoons, and though no preserved bits of boats have turned up, Old Whaling sites have yielded plentiful deposits of whalebone, sure signs of the whalers' skill as hunters on the open sea.

By the end of April, when daylight stretches over nineteen hours each day, ice in the Arctic Sea begins to break up, leaving open lanes of water. The bowhead whales, huge animals sixty feet or more in length, move north through wide cracks in the ice in Bering Strait. As soon as the whales began their northward migration, Eskimo hunters rushed to load their umiaks onto sleds and moved out to the edge of the shore ice. Thanks to the long, sunlit days and vigorous tides, by that time of year the ice had broken up to within a mile or so of the village. Chanting songs urging the whales to come and be caught, hunters pulled on waterproof suits made of sheets of walrus gut.

When they sighted spouting whales offshore, they quickly launched the boats, each manned by the owner-steersman and six paddlers plus a harpooner in the bow. As the whales dived, the paddlers in the lead umiak paddled furiously while the captain steered toward the area where he expected the animals to surface. When a whale broke water, the paddlers, following the harpooner's gestured directions, edged the bow of the boat to within a few feet of the whale. Then the harpooner hurled his weapon at the animal. As the head of the harpoon sank in, the shaft fell away to be retrieved later. For the moment the crew was totally occupied keeping clear of the whale's thrashing. The line whizzed overboard, carrying drags of inflated sealskins to slow the whale's progress. The whale dived, the boat followed its underwater course, and the harpooner aimed a second harpoon and perhaps a third as the animal emerged. At last, tired by its wounds and the tug of the sealskin drags, the whale could no longer dive, but rested quietly on the surface.

Then came the most dangerous part of the whale hunt. Cautiously the whalers paddled up to the side of the great beast. The harpooner thrust his spear into the whale's side, searching for a vital spot. As the animal thrashed convulsively, he thrust again and again till the whale spouted not white but crimson. The paddlers had to backwater quickly to keep the boat clear of the animal's death throes.

In ten minutes or so, the whale floated dead, and the crew raised a shout of triumph. Hearing it, the other boats closed in to help with the slow job of towing the immense catch to shore. Long, steady paddling brought them at last to the shore ice, where the whole village joined in dragging the carcass, inch by inch, onto the ice for butchering. First the head was severed, and the wife of the victorious boat captain ceremonially offered it a drink of fresh water. "We thank you for coming," she intoned. "You must be thirsty." She then urged the whale's spirit, released when the head was cut off, to return to the land of the whales and tell its fellows how well it had been treated. Without this ceremony, the people feared, the whales would not return next year. After butchering, the heaped tons of whale meat were buried in storage pits for the coming period of cold. Also, blubber—whale fat—was made into oil or exchanged for furs and caribou skins with people of inland settlements.

Summer Activities

In early summer, whaling dwindled, and both groups and individuals began a variety of summer pursuits and outlets. Usually the winter village communities broke into smaller family groups, with some individuals splintering off as solitary hunters or traders. Some stayed on the coast, some moved to interior hunting grounds or fishing sites, and others trapped or traded. Interior Eskimo groups who had to depend on caribou rather than whales were always eager to trade with the whalers, and trading trips to the interior took long enough that hunting, trapping, and fishing could be done on the way. Meat, fish, and furs obtained during the summer travels were stored in pits cut in the subsoil, used as a huge freezer. If whole families moved together, they might stop midway at a convenient spot where the women and children stayed in a temporary camp in skin tents until the husbands and fathers returned. At these summer camps the women made clothing for winter, processing the furs and hides for the tailored garments no one could live without in the Arctic. The camp might also be a fishing station where a net was stretched across a stream to be emptied of the catch when the traders returned.

Dogs. The dog team accompanied the family and hauled the foods, supplies, and clothing obtained or made during the summer. If the

An Eskimo squaw strings tomcod to prepare it for smoking. Nome Beach, Alaska, 1904.

journey was by stream, the dog team, walking along the bank, pulled the umiak. If snow was on the ground, they pulled a sled which, during warmer weather, was itself transported on the umiak.

Families rarely owned more than three or four dogs because food, even for people, was scarce, and a dog team could eat many pounds of meat each week. However, dogs were important for hunting and transport. The tough, strong huskies—just one breed throughout the Arctic—could pull heavily laden sleds over great distances. Each dog was hitched separately to the sled, and the team spread out like a fan with the lead dog in the center, a short distance ahead of the others.

Solitary hunters often took along one dog, especially on seal hunts, for a good dog could smell out and locate a seal's breathing hole much more quickly than even the most skilled and experienced hunter. The Eskimo of interior Alaska and those of the eastern areas used their dogs during large hunts for caribou and musk-oxen. The dogs kept the herd at bay while the hunters shot arrows at a selected animal. Although dogs were work animals, not pets, the Eskimo often became emotionally attached to them and mourned the loss of a favorite animal.

Trading. Toward the end of the short summer, as signs of cold weather became noticeable, the family packed up the products of their summer activities and returned to the winter village. They usually traded with any groups they met on the way, exchanging seal and whale oils, hides, ropes of hide, birds packed whole in seal oil, driftwood, furs, and artwork such as carved ivory labrets. Exchanges were handled by recognized trading partners who had established formal, enduring trade relationships. Trading partners were usually not relatives because one already has a formal relationship with a relative; the wise thing was to spread out loyalties and dependence by forming non-kin relationships. In a world where cooperation was essential to survival, it made sense to create interdependence with as many others as possible, especially with those in another ecological zone, to obtain items not available in one's own area. It was usual to cement such partnerships with a sexual bond also. Partners had access to each other's wives, and these sexual relations made a quasi-kinship bond stronger than all other bonds except those of family.

Winter Life

Back at the winter home where the families once more congregated to form a small village community, there was a period of sociability as people told of their summer pursuits and prepared for the severe weather ahead. Boats were repaired, houses were caulked and readied for cold, traps were set, and perhaps men carved a piece of bone or walrus ivory into labrets or a hunting charm.

The Eskimo carved animal and human figurines as charms and toys and engraved geometric and naturalistic designs on many of their implements and utensils. Bone, stone, ivory, and horn took the place of wood. The Alaskan masks (almost no other Eskimo made them) were of hide, whalebone, fur, and, when it was available, wood, sometimes trimmed with shells and feathers. The masks were produced in great variety, representing the many Eskimo supernaturals.

The Seal Hunt. Sometimes in the spring, when the seals and their pups were sunning on the coasts, several men would join to hunt them, but winter sealing was a different matter; it was solitary. In Alaska, seal hunters usually speared the animal as it rose to breathe. Seals swim under the ice, but they must have several widely spaced breathing holes through the floes, and keep these holes ice-free during the winter. The hunter and perhaps a dog searched for the holes, and might wait beside one of them many hours until the seal returned. The hunter often tried to attract one by scratching gently on the ice with a pointed strip of whalebone, imitating the sound of a seal's claws on the ice.

When the hunter found a seal's breathing hole, he would enlarge it with a flint blade mounted in an antler handle so that he could set a trap. He bored four small holes around the breathing hole and then lowered into the hole a tough net of thin whalebone strips, topped with ivory rattlers to warn, by their noise, when the seal had come. He attached the four corners of the net through the small holes he bored in the ice so that an approaching seal could swim over the net to reach the hole. Once the animal gulped a new supply of air, it dived, only to become entangled in the net that lay directly beneath. The rattlers shook and warned the hunter, who hauled up the net and killed the animal with a blow. Then he might take a drink of blood, perhaps his first fresh food for months. Wounds in the animal were plugged with a whittled stopper because blood was far too precious to waste. The hunter might set his net again or go home. To haul his catch home, he might form a coating of ice on the runners of his sled by urinating on them, making the vehicle slide more easily when loaded. He lashed the seals and his tent on the sled, and over his boots he slipped creepers—strips of corrugated carved ivory to give traction on the smooth ice.

Home Life. In Alaska, home was a stone dome covering a pit about ten feet square and three feet deep; the stone was braced with whalebone or driftwood and topped with an insulating layer of earth. An Eskimo entered the house by stepping down into a passageway dug lower than the floor to trap cold away from the living quarters. There was no door, but a skin lashed across the entry could close it tight. On one side of the passageway was a small storeroom for harpoons and other bulky equipment. Inside, the walls were festooned with extra clothing, hide nets containing snares for trapping small game, and tools for working flint and hide. A sleeping platform situated at the back of the house, large enough for the whole family to stretch out comfortably on fox and polar bear skins, was only about three feet below the roof, where the warm air collected.

In the evening, the hunter might go over to the men's house. This building—common in Alaska, but rare farther east—was considerably larger than any family dwelling, but of the same construction. There the adult males of the village spent time eating, sleeping, repairing hunting equipment, and making new gear. At intervals, their wives brought in food, and from time to time work stopped for a wrestling contest or an insult match in which the men competed to see who could compose the most scurrilous songs about one another, to the uproarious delight of the listeners. These contests were only partly serious: the men were hunting partners and friends. Such competitions usually were a harmless way of working off grudges, relieving the tensions built up during the long, dark winter, or letting others know when they had behaved badly. Other amusements were quieter: telling tales of great hunters now dead or the clever exploits of Raven, the trickster spirit,

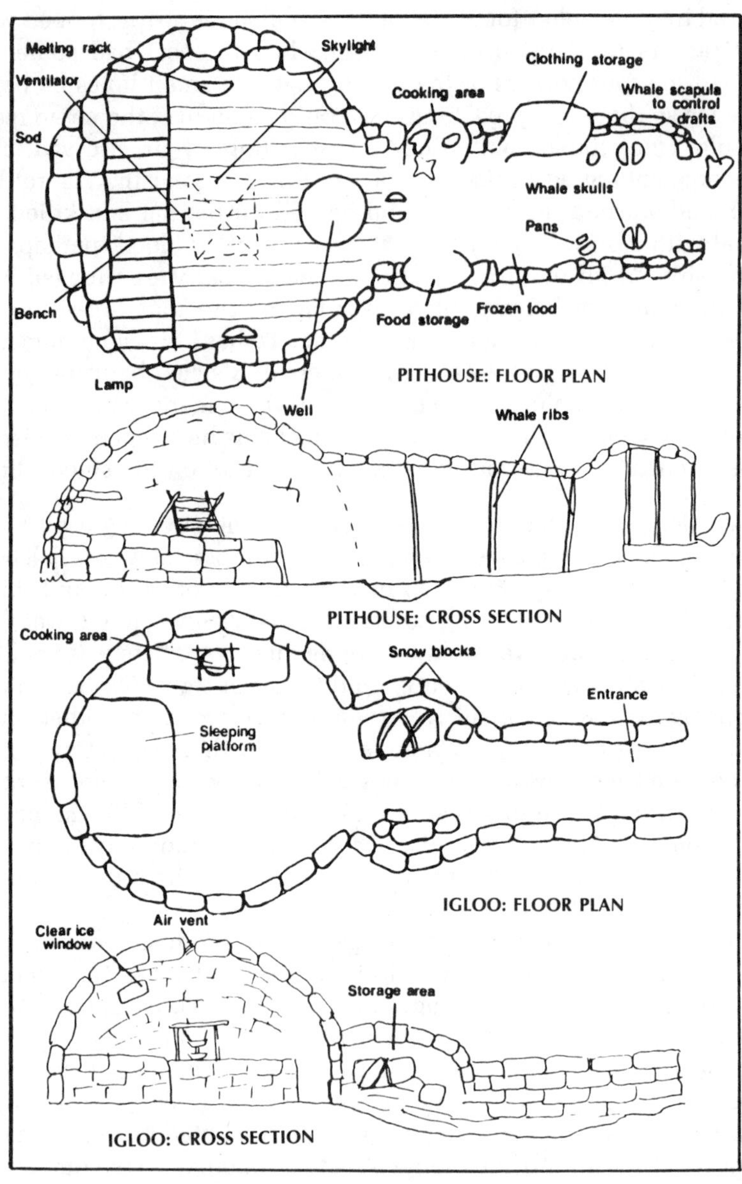

Diagram of an Alaskan pithouse, showing the floor plan (top) and cross-section. Supported by whalebone or driftwood, the house framework was covered with stone and earth. Diagram of an igloo (bottom), showing similarities in its layout to the pithouse.

or watching the shaman (a religious specialist) perform his feats, such as pulling a fur mitten from an empty tambourine.

As long as the hunting remained good, the men spent much of their leisure time in the clubhouse, leaving it from time to time for another expedition after seals, a trapping trip for foxes or hares, or, after the spring's migrant birds had arrived, a hunt for eggs. And then again in April, the whale hunts recommenced.

Eskimo Life in General

Like the Alaskans, the central and eastern Eskimo made the seasonal change from winter communities to summer dispersement by family or individual. Whaling, although known on the Atlantic coast, was more typical of the northern and western Alaskan groups; interior peoples depended more on the great caribou herds. Indeed, the Caribou Eskimo, exploiters of the Barren Grounds, abandoned coastal adaptations entirely and lived off the caribou alone.

The main difference between the Caribou Eskimo and all other Eskimo groups was their restricted subsistence. Caribou herds migrated through the Barren Grounds twice a year, and human life there depended on those migrations. The scarcity of food produced among the Caribou Eskimo the simplest material culture of all Eskimo groups, and they had no mythology involving Sedna, the sea goddess, being far from the ocean and its supply of food. The only large mammals they hunted besides caribou were musk-oxen, which did not appear regularly. These Eskimo believed that caribou were the only good food, but fish could relieve the monotony and were important when caribou were scarce. Hunters did prefer, though, to spend time on an unsuccessful caribou hunt rather than go fishing. Eskimo usually hunted caribou communally by driving them into ambush or into water where men in kayaks killed the animals with stone-tipped spears.

The Caribou Eskimo did have some dwarf trees in their environment, so they made fire from wood, not oils. None of the Eskimo subdivisions used much of the plant life available to them, though, which is surprising considering how intensively they exploited the rest of their environment. Plant life in the Arctic has a short, but very flourishing, season. The long hours of sunlight in the Arctic summer produce a brief burst of bloom, which the Eskimo thought important only as it affected the browsing and grazing animals that migrated northward for food. Caribou, moose, musk-oxen, and deer were hunted intensively by some groups and occasionally by others, but the plants on which the animals fed were not sought as nourishment by the people themselves.

Eskimo ate some fish and meat raw—the word Eskimo is Algonkian for "those who eat raw flesh"—but they cooked most foods as stews of meat chunks, blubber, water, and sometimes blood. Their cooking pots were usually ground stone vessels, but in Alaska might be poor-grade clay pottery. The cook suspended the "kettle" from a horizontal pole supported on a four-legged frame or from a tripod above the lamp.

Technology

Boats. Eskimo used two types of boats, the umiak and the kayak. The umiak, large enough to transport a dozen or more people, was used in whaling and hauling. It was often called the women's boat because it was the only kind they used. Kayaks were one-person boats, their framework covered with sealskin, except among the Caribou Eskimo, who used caribou skin. The opening fit snugly around the paddler so that with his waterproof jacket he was protected against the waves and could even right himself with his paddle if he capsized.

To the basic necessity, seaworthy boats, the Eskimo added a great array of special tools and devices specially invented or adapted for every requirement of Arctic living. Their harpoons were often assembled from half a dozen parts. One widely used type had a detachable walrus ivory head fitted with a tip of flint or ground slate, in which a hole was drilled for attaching a line. The head was lashed not to the main harpoon shaft but to a flexible bone foreshaft. For still more flexibility, the foreshaft was seated in an ivory socket fitted onto the main shaft, and foreshaft, socket, and shaft were lashed together with hide or sinew. The shaft itself was further equipped with a bone or ivory thumb support for leverage in throwing.

The Igloo. Eskimo ingenuity also produced the *igloo*, one of the most unusual shelters ever devised. This house, built entirely of snow and ice, kept living quarters above freezing while outside temperatures dropped to 40 degrees below zero. We know that it was used in the central Canadian area, but we cannot trace its origin because when igloos melted they left no sign that they had ever existed. In prehistoric times they probably differed hardly at all from those made until recently by people of the central Arctic.

An Eskimo and his wife could build a family-sized igloo, nine to fifteen feet in diameter, in an hour or so. First the man drew a circle on firm snow to outline the structure. Then, with a spatulalike bone or antler knife, he cut the hard-packed snow inside the circle to make rectangular blocks about four inches thick. Standing in the circle, he trimmed the blocks and arranged them in an ascending spiral that gradually closed in to form a dome. Architects point out that this is the only type of dome that can be constructed without scaffolding, which was out of the

Eskimos build an igloo in Arctic Canada.

question in the treeless northern Arctic. For a draftproof entry, he built a tunnel like the one used on a pithouse, but made of blocks of firm snow. The entrance was usually to the south, away from the north wind. Meanwhile, his wife, working outside the igloo, shoveled a plastering of loose snow over the walls to fill any cracks or holes. Children often helped close up the slits.

Once the shell was completed, the man built a sleeping platform of packed snow around the inside, covering it with furs and hides. The family used this area for dining and sitting as well as sleeping. A window of clear ice or seal gut in the wall near the entrance let in some light, and outside the window a large block of snow might be set to reflect light inside. Heat from the oil lamp transformed the inner surface of the roof into a smooth ceiling of ice that rarely dripped. Instead, a film of meltwater flowed toward the floor, where it froze. Often hides were suspended a few inches from the dome, creating a dead air space with great insulating efficiency. Three or more igloos might be built together, connected like rooms, one as a storeroom for equipment, another for clothing; the dogs often slept in the entrance tunnel.

More tools. Excavations at a north Alaskan site near Point Barrow, dating from around A.D. 500 and containing the remains of only about a half dozen pithouses, have turned up a large number of tools that helped the people adapt to their rigorous environment. The hunting gear included spear throwers and spears, nine kinds of bone missiles for bringing down birds, and half a dozen types of harpoon heads. Along with bows were implements to tighten bow strings, arrow shafts, and six varieties of bone arrowheads—some with multiple barbs for killing large prey. There were also mouthpieces for blowing air under the skin of a harpooned seal so that the body would not sink. Along with this hunting and fishing equipment, the Point Barrow site disgorged enough gear to fill an ancient hardware store: antler snow-shovel blades, probes for testing treacherous-looking stretches of snow or ice, whetstones, engraving tools, bow drills, whalebone digging tools, stone knives and adzes for working driftwood, needles and needle cases of bone, and dozens of other specialized tools.

Other ancient Point Barrow Eskimo had wrenches for straightening arrow shafts, hooks for hauling blubber off a whale carcass, and *gorges*. These last were double-pointed pieces of bone with lines attached to the middle—when a fish gulped one down, it jammed in the throat. For traveling over snow and ice, there were sleds as well as toboggans made of whalebone strips lashed together. The dog sled may very well have spurred the spread of Eskimo culture across Canada. Dog sleds not only would have given hunters greater mobility, but also would have made winter hunting much more efficient: seal catches, particularly, could be handled far more easily. And an abundance of boat remains showed that by 1,500 years ago, the skin-covered kayak and the umiak used in whale hunting had developed into forms closely resembling their nineteenth-century counterparts.

One anthropologist has called the Eskimo "gadget-burdened." They were well equipped to deal with the frigid zone in which they lived, but their equipment was not so much extensive as intensive. Although the Eskimo developed an almost unbelievably fine assortment of tools and mechanisms for adapting to the environment, their tool kit was not nearly so extensive as that of many Indians to the south.

Social Organization

Eskimo society was not complex. The family and the household were the basic social units; occasionally the two were the same. Most often, though, the household—those residing together at least in their winter homes—was some sort of extended family grouping. This meant that the *nuclear family*—man, woman, and their children—shared a home with grandparents, or grown brothers or sisters and their families, or another wife, or even combinations of all three. The closest ties were within the nuclear family, but the household was the most important economic unit for both production and consumption.

The division of labor was sharp and essential. Male and female tasks were complementary, and both were necessary. There were no unattached individuals, for no one could last long alone in the tough Arctic conditions. If a woman's husband died, she expected to become the wife of his brother. If a man's wife died, he expected her family to send him another woman, usually a sister of his dead wife.

A very successful hunter might take a second wife to help with the domestic work, but few had more than two wives. Together a man and a woman were an efficient unit: the man was the provider with his hunting, fishing, and trapping, and the woman prepared the clothing from hides, cooked the food, and cared for the young and the home. The arduous life in the frigid zone gave little extra time for doing another's work; each took care of his or her own.

Beyond the nuclear family, any others in the household—grandparents, brothers and sisters, and more distant relatives such as cousins, aunts, and uncles—were expected to pitch in to accomplish any other domestic tasks. Within the household everyone lived with complete economic reciprocity: they produced together and consumed together; occasionally they starved together.

Partnerships. Some men's tasks, such as hunting, trading, or whaling, made it necessary to widen their circle beyond that of kinfolk, and to build up other loyalties and dependencies. A special relationship existed among the men in a whaling crew or the members of a caribou hunt. Those groups were semipermanent and formed and dispersed according to the seasons year after year. Only if feuds broke out, or if the leader of the crew or hunt seemed to have lost his powers, did those groups disband.

A man became and remained a leader only because he was competent, never because his father had been a leader before him. The owner of a whaling umiak persuaded his crew to remain with him because he was an effective whaler, not because he was anyone's relative, though he probably enticed the men to join him in the first place by giving them gifts. The relationship between the owner and his crew was like that between the leader of a caribou hunt and his hunting party. Each held his position by merit: the leader had demonstrated quite clearly that he was competent and wise, and men were willing to follow him because they expected success under his direction.

The trading partnership was another relationship that extended beyond kin ties. Those partnerships endured everything but a feud, and they were exclusive; one did not trade with just anyone, only with those who had entered into a special trading pact. Trading partners became a sort of pseudo-kin, and such associations usually carried with them a kind of bantering camaraderie; the partners were good buddies.

The Eskimo world, then, was divided into kinfolk—"us"—and non-kin—"them." Kin included blood relatives, traced through both maternal and paternal lines, and the sort of "secondary kin" of trading or hunting partnerships—those whom one could trust and count on. All others were looked on as at least potential enemies. For aid in daily activities, one called first upon close kin, next upon more distant relatives. For special assistance, as in trading or hunting, there were those in the specialized relationships. All these networks of association were practical; no government or system of laws decided who traded together or who would be in charge of a hunt. One man might dominate a household, just as the hunt leader or crew captain dominated his men—because of wisdom and competence. But outside of this tentative sort of leader position, social control was in the hands of society at large. Someone who misbehaved might be ridiculed gently or harshly in song, or scorned by his fellows. In extreme cases he might even be abandoned, his household packing up and leaving the undesirable behind. He then had to mend his ways, for otherwise he became truly a person without a country or even a house. Many people thought that supernatural forces would punish the wayward with sanctions too dreadful even to contemplate. These ways of promoting socially acceptable behavior usually proved effective, for it was through their social relationships that the Eskimo survived.

Marriage. Marriage was not formalized by any ceremony. It was an agreement between man and woman not only to live together but to take on their respective roles in the domestic economy, which in the Arctic was far more important than sexual union. Divorce was as simple as marriage; the couple separated. Sexual relations between men and women not married to each other were often used to cement relationships between men who were not related by kinship. That is, trading partners, members of a hunting or whaling party, or whatever, might exchange wives in recognition of their mutual bond. This special relationship between men who exchanged wives also extended to their children, making them, in effect, cousins.

A man who eloped with another's wife could expect to keep her only if he mustered more support from his kin and quasi-kin than the husband could from his. In many ways, might was right, but the result was endless feuding between the two kin groups, for most men were outraged to be cuckolded and sought vengeance. The two kin groups were then caught up in a very undesirable situation involving murder and further murder in retaliation, for they had no courts or policing agencies to settle such disputes. Consequently, families always tried to keep their own members in hand to avoid destructive feuding. Knowing that he lacked kin support, an Eskimo would think twice about any kind of wrongdoing.

Song Duels. When Eskimos felt they had been injured by others, they composed a satirical song, which was sung at a public challenge performance. The target of the song responded, and the audience acted as judge and jury. When the decision on who was winner was announced, the contestants had to be friends again and not continue the quarrel. These song duels were both comic entertainment for the spectators and revenge for one of the participants. The duel stopped most physical aggression within the group and calmed hostile feelings and personal grudges; all parties had their say in public and released aggression and resentments vocally. No matter who was adjudged winner, all could then go about their daily business having had their day in court—the court of public opinion.

Abandoned Infants and Elders. The extreme conditions of life in the Arctic resulted in both infanticide and geronticide. Infants who could not be fed for any reason—their mother's death, food shortage, illness—and old people who could no longer make an economic contribution to the group might under some dire circumstances be abandoned. Such an act was never done lightly; infant mortality was already high, and children were greatly desired; old people were loved. If circumstances became severe, however, it was considered wisest to select those most apt to live and reproduce the community, and concentrate resources on them. The aged recognized the hardship and also the sorrow of such a decision, and they usually left quietly, unnoticed, to die rather than be a drain on supplies. All Eskimo grew up recognizing the possibility of such a fate.

Eskimo Religion

Eskimo religion, like other aspects of Eskimo culture, varied little from east to west. Eskimo everywhere believed in the existence of spirit powers in charge of the universe. In Alaska, male spirits predominated; elsewhere, the principal powers were usually female. Sedna, the sea goddess, for example, was less important in Alaska than in most other areas. The Caribou Eskimo, having turned to pursuing land animals, had for their principal deity Mother of the Caribou, a guardian of both human and animal life. In Alaska, a major divinity in charge of the universe was the Moon Man, who ruled the sky and the souls of game animals and human beings.

Eskimo relied on religion mainly for controlling subsistence and the forces of nature, preventing disease, and foretelling future events and conditions. Eskimo believed that nature was basically harmonious and that the supernaturals—all elements and beings that were "non-natural"—were either neutral or benign. They could be angered, though, by human negligence or disobedience. People thus were essentially responsible for their own problems and distress; their failure to behave properly and observe taboos and rules was thought to cause discomfort, disease, famine, and the other ills that beset humankind. Means of atonement were confessing sin and promising improved behavior.

Beliefs. Eskimo believed that humans and animals were in a special mystical relationship, the animals allowing themselves to be hunted and caught because they were sorry for the humans, though charms and other types of magical practices might force their capture too. Among the Eskimo, as well as most of the hunting peoples of North America, belief was strong that animals had souls or spirits that left the body at death to be reincarnated in another body. Hunters helped game animal spirits to reincarnation by offering them a drink of fresh water. Under no circumstance should a hunter offend the hunted animal, which might then withhold itself and all others of its class from humans. Consequently, slain animals were addressed with words of esteem and requests that their spirits tell other animals that humans had treated them well.

Proper etiquette toward the animal world required separation of land and sea mammals. Many taboos prohibited mixing flesh from the two types in meals or using the same weapons on them, and it was thought that whales were insulted if dogs gnawed on their bones or licked their blood. Among the Caribou Eskimo, it was taboo for dogs to chew the antlers or bones of caribou. If taboos were broken, the game animals, essential to the people's very existence, would be outraged and no longer allow hunters to capture them.

Human beings also possessed souls, according to Eskimo belief. A human soul might get lost or stolen, a situation that was a major cause of disease and very frightening to the owner, who then called upon a shaman (a religious figure and a curer) to locate the missing soul and return it to its proper place. Human souls were fragile things, especially when compared to animal souls, and that fragility symbolized the Eskimo feeling of helplessness in the face of capricious and inexplicable nature.

In addition to the body and the soul, Eskimo believed each person had a third aspect, a name. A name was a very important thing, and when someone died, his or her name was not spoken until it was given to some newborn infant, who made the name come alive again. The Eskimo thought that the newborn cried at birth because it wanted a name. Eskimo names had no gender; they were used for males and females alike.

Eskimo belief included other categories of supernaturals: demons that were potentially dangerous because they could work evil, and a sort of psychic projection called the *inua*, which could come from animals, objects, and even places. In Alaska, inua were sought as personal

CHARACTERISTICS OF THE ARCTIC TRIBES

Clothing	Food production	Equipment	Shelter	Social and political organization	Religion	Warfare
Tailored skins (fur and hide)	Fishing	Harpoons	Igloo (central and eastern Arctic)	Nuclear families	Myths	Feuds between kin groups
Parkas	Hunting (sea mammals and land mammals)	Spears and spear throwers	Skin tents	Extended families	Spirits (control universe)	Song duel
Mittens	Some wild-plant gathering	Fishhooks	Semi-subterranean housing	Bands	Shamans	Warfare rare or unknown
Boots		Gorges	Pit houses of wood and whalebone (Alaska)	Social control in hands of society at large	Guardian spirits	
Undershirts of birdskin with feathers		Flint tools			Songs and other rituals	
Fur pouches for babies		Bone needles			Mother of the Caribou (Caribou Eskimo)	
		Nets and weirs			Souls present in both humans and animals	
		Bone and antler knives				
		Oil lamps				
		Sleds				
		Toboggans				
		Kayaks				
		Umiaks				
		Ground stone vessels				
		Pottery				
		Basketry (Alaska)				

guardian spirits that might be called upon for aid, good weather, good hunting, and good health.

Besides observing their many taboos, Eskimo performed magical rites to ensure welfare or success in their pursuits. Such rites included singing songs, reciting formulas, and carrying charms. Owners of umiaks, successful harpooners, and caribou hunt chiefs were semireligious figures, who all had special songs and charms to bring success to their expeditions. Eskimo songs, charms, formulas, and other magical activities can be compared to good luck charms like rabbits' feet, talking to dice, and lucky numbers. All people of the world have practices like these.

The Shaman. The important religious figure was the shaman. He was only a part-time specialist in religious activities, also participating in the subsistence pursuits of his community and being a father and husband. All the people had ties with the supernatural world, but a shaman's were closer, and he could use those ties to cause good or harm. He was both respected and feared. He might be employed for the good of the community as a diviner to learn the cause of some misfortune or to predict weather conditions or hunting success. If game was scarce he might travel to Sedna to compel her to release the animals. On the other hand, he could unleash the fury of the supernatural world against others.

The shaman was also very important as a curer. The Eskimo were very anxious about disease, not only in the practical sense of broken bones, but in terms of disturbances we would classify as psychosomatic—responses to the tensions in Arctic life. Such disturbances were blamed on failure to carry out rituals, attacks by hostile shamans, soul loss, soul theft, and intrusion of a mysterious object into the body. Illness due to neglect of rituals was cured by confession and some prescribed atonement; a disease inflicted by a shaman was cured by going to a more powerful shaman. For the others, cures were done by the shaman, who located the soul and restored it or sucked out the object causing the illness. If a patient died, the shaman explained that he had been opposed by a shaman with greater power or by malevolent spirits. Though shamans could treat general injuries like broken bones and cuts, almost any adult knew how to care for those practical disabilities, and the shaman's real value was in psychological curing.

Most of a shaman's activities took place before an audience and included an element of entertainment. He used a variety of what we might call tricks to produce the required results: ventriloquism, sleight of hand, and human helpers or apprentices who gave the desired atmosphere by manipulating objects with strings invisible in the dim light. Some of the performances were spectacular, and it is no wonder that the shaman often worked cures on the psychological problems he encountered. The shaman was, of course, aware that he was using trickery, but he believed in his supernatural power, and his patient and audience believed in it too.

A person with potential for or interest in becoming a shaman either sought out spirit help on his own or apprenticed himself to an older shaman. Both men and women were eligible, but few women of childbearing age ever entered the profession; most women shamans were past menopause. Age seemed to be a factor in success, for it was generally thought that the most powerful shamans were old people, whether male or female.

It is hard for us to keep separate all the classes of supernatural and religious practices, and probably they were often confused in Eskimo thought. All of them symbolize the unreasonable and unpredictable aspects of nature that could be ignored only at one's peril. Life, nature, and the supernatural were uncontrollable and had to be appeased, pleased, and calmed with the many taboos of diet and behavior. The result would be an easier and more secure life, they hoped. The Eskimo took no chances; it was not a matter for debate.

The Subarctic

Northern Athabaskan Legend

Long ago when the world was new, an Indian man was traveling in the wintertime. He had a long way to go, and the snow was deep and cold. It was so hard to walk that he could hardly go on. He asked aloud, "Why does the North Man do this? Why does he send such winter weather?"

Suddenly he saw a man all in white standing before him. At first he could not imagine who would be out in the winter cold, but as he drew near, he realized that it was a man made of snow. When the Snow Man saw the Indian and how cross and tired he looked, he asked, "What is the matter?" "Such terrible snow. It is so hard to travel. The North Man is no good." The Snow Man said, "I will try to help you: just keep on your way." And the Snow Man disappeared. The hunter went on with his journey.

Finally spring came and warmer weather. The lakes melted, and the hunter wondered, "What did the Snow Man mean when he said he was going to help me?" He began to hunt, and he saved all the fat from the animals he caught and stored it in bladders. He also cut lots of wood, which he arranged in deep piles. And he went on all summer and into the fall storing grease and piling up wood. He did not know why he did these things; something seemed to impel him.

As fall turned into winter, the snow began again. It snowed and it snowed, and there were great drifts around the hunter's camp and over his wigwam. The hunter built a fire, and one day the Snow Man came to the hunter's camp. "How do you like the weather this winter?" the Snow Man asked. "All right," replied the hunter. And the cold increased and the snow drifted higher. The hunter kept putting wood on the fire. and then he began to pour grease over the wood. The fire burned stronger. By and by the Snow Man asked again, "How do you like the weather now?" "All right," answered the hunter as before. He really had had enough cold weather, but he would not give in. He stood the cold better than ever before because he had plenty of grease and wood. He made the wigwam hotter and hotter.

At last the heat was too much for the Snow Man and he began to melt. Soon, he went away entirely. As he left, he said to the hunter, "You are a stronger man than I am. You have conquered me, and now I must leave." Soon the cold began to moderate, and the winter continued just the way winters should be, not too cold, not too warm. It was a good winter, and the winters have been good since then.

Perhaps for the Subarctic peoples who told and retold this tale, it was an explanation of summer and winter, why winter was not eternal and how people learned to survive it. Certainly the intense cold and deep snows of the Subarctic must have been a constant concern for the people who lived there.

The Environment

As the name suggests, the Subarctic is the zone just south of the Arctic. It includes most of Canada and Alaska, except for the coastal regions. The boundary between Arctic and Subarctic shows up most clearly in the vegetation change from treeless tundra to forest, evergreens in the west and evergreens mixed with deciduous species (birch, elm, maple, oak) in the southeast. Subarctic animals include the small woodland types such as squirrel, rabbit, fox, beaver, and porcupine, as well as the larger fauna: caribou, musk-oxen, moose, deer, and bear. The region has many lakes and bogs, rivers and streams, filled with whitefish, salmon, pickerel, trout, perch, and sturgeon, and waterfowl make stops there in their yearly migrations. Along the Atlantic seacoast are shellfish. Plant foods throughout the area are limited, and the climate prohibits agriculture.

In the West, the Canadian Rockies are a powerful influence on weather, blocking the moderating force of the Pacific Ocean and letting polar air masses flow southward and spread out, circulating toward the East. Conditions reverse in the summer, when subtropical air masses move into the Subarctic across the prairies and lowlands of the Great Lakes by way of the Mississippi River system. The seasonal extremes are pronounced: winters are long and cold, and summers are relatively short but hot, with plagues of biting insects. Most of the precipitation falls in storms, snow in winter and violent rainfall in summer. In winter, the interior is even colder than the Arctic, which has the ocean to moderate its temperatures. In spite of the many game species, the harsh environment meant that food was seasonally scarce and famines were frequent for the native hunting peoples. Often winter cold and snow lying deep and forbidding were together almost unbearable. To leave home was to face agony; to stay home was to starve.

Aboriginal Population

We divide the Subarctic into eastern and western divisions by the languages spoken there. Algonkian was the language of the East and Athabaskan of the West. Although the two language families belong to different phyla and have no more in common than English and Chinese, the cultural adaptations—the general ways of living—of the native peoples were very similar across the continent. There were regional variations in style and detail, but throughout, food was obtained by hunting, fishing, and some gathering.

Population was never great in the Subarctic—one estimate puts it at less than 60,000 for the whole area at the time of European contact. Perhaps that is on the low side; twice that is probably more accurate. When European intruders began to transmit their diseases to the natives, nearly half of those people died. One whole tribe, the Beothuk of Newfoundland, became extinct.

We know less about the Subarctic Algonkians than about almost any other aboriginal group in North America because of their small numbers and also because they were badly disrupted by early contact with European fur traders. The early European explorers had little or no interest in recording information about the northern Algonkians and have left us few descriptions. We know more about the Athabaskans because many bands still survive; in fact, their numbers seem to be growing.

Life in the Subarctic

The Subarctic hunters and fishers wandered in small bands. In the East there was a slight patrilineal trend, with brothers remaining together or close by, and wives moving into their husbands' territory. The Athabaskan area seemed to have a matrilineal preference. However, European contact and its disturbing influence altered the culture, gathering people into the composite *band*—a group formed by kinship, either maternal or paternal, primarily for economic expediency. The bands went where they thought they would have access to good hunting territory and fishing sites. Food was never abundant enough to allow a large population, and there was no political structure outside of kin organization or achieved leadership. A competent, wise man acted as group leader, deciding when to move on to new hunting grounds and generally seeing that the traditional customs and taboos were followed by the group. Only when the hunting was extraordinarily good (and that was very rare) did a large number of people gather and feast.

Food

The lives of most Subarctic people revolved around caribou, their most important food. As among the Caribou Eskimo, caribou hunts were often communal: hunters surrounded a herd and drove it into a trap or enclosure, or perhaps a lake, where others waited in canoes to kill the floundering animals. In deep snow, a hunter on snowshoes could run down a caribou, and the Subarctic people also used snares for both large and small game. Game was supplemented with fish, especially salmon from the western rivers that flowed into the Pacific. Plant foods were sparse and contributed far less to the diet than among any native Americans except the Eskimo.

Subarctic dwellers stored food for lean months in caches (hiding places), sometimes pits in the ground, sometimes bags suspended from poles. In winter it was easy to preserve food by freezing, but summer heat was too high to keep foods frozen. To store meat, then, the women dried it, pulverized it, and mixed it with suet or other fat, making a classic Indian dish—*pemmican*—which remained edible for more than a year. In spite of their efforts at storage, however, most Subarctic bands were perpetually close to starvation in winter. Like the Eskimo, they sometimes had to abandon those who could no longer care for themselves.

Technology

Subarctic technology included many items to help people adapt to snow, although in general the tools were not so complex or ingenious as those of the Eskimo. The Subarctic people may have been the first to invent the toboggan and snowshoes, which they needed for swift movement over deep snow. The pattern or style of snowshoe varied from place to place. Some were round, some had a pointed heel, some had turned-up toes, but all were formed of a wooden framework, usually made pliable enough to bend easily by steaming, with a webbing or mesh of rawhide strips, called *babiche*. A thong of rawhide was woven into the netting and tied over the instep. These shoes kept the wearer from sinking into snow. They were not for speed, unlike skis. Different styles were adapted to different kinds of snow, and a tribe could usually be identified by its snowshoe style.

Another important item in the Subarctic snow was the toboggan made of bark, wood, or hide, pulled by human muscle—often by women. The word *toboggan* is Algonkian. The Subarctic people also used the bark canoe, a very important technological advance where waterways were plentiful. Birch bark made a lightweight canoe that could be carried over portages—the trails between waterways.

A characteristic that set Athabaskans and Algonkians apart was the emphasis each placed on stone as a raw material. The Athabaskans used far more wood, horn, antler, and bone than the easterners, even preferring beaver teeth to stone for knives. The easterners made few utensils from animal products, preferring stone.

Although much of their territory was in the great northern conifer forest, the Subarctic people had no tools for hewing or working full-grown trees. They fashioned their wooden equipment from saplings, brush, and bark. In the West, the Athabaskans made containers of spruce roots and fibers as well as bark, and bags, ropes, binding, and nets of babiche. The Algonkians made most of their containers, even those for cooking, from birch bark. The women sewed the bark with vines and made it watertight with pitch, and used bark containers not only for stone boiling, but also for direct boiling—bark vessels actually can be hung close enough to a fire to boil water inside without burning the bark. Women used both the white outer layers and the light brown inner layers of birch and heated them over fire or in steam to make them pliable, bending them to the desired shape. Once the container cooled, the shape became permanent. Often the women decorated the bark by scraping designs through the white layer, letting the brown layer show through, or they added moosehair embroidery, paint, porcupine quills, and, after European goods became available, beadery. The constant quest for food left little time for activities like art, but the women of many tribes decorated not only the containers but also the clothing with porcupine quill or moosehair embroidery, and the Algonkian Naskapi painted geometric designs on their garments. The embroidery they produced was some of the finest of its kind in North America.

Housing. All Subarctic peoples were on the move much of the year, following the caribou and other migratory game, going north in summer and returning to river valleys and deep forest in winter. They could not live in permanent villages and built shelters that were easy to put up and take down. The Naskapi of northern Quebec lived in conical *tipis*, some covered with caribou hides, some with birch bark. The Athabaskans also favored the tipi of skins or bark, and in both areas people built more temporary shelters of brush or spruce boughs. The Indians of interior Alaska and some of those in British Columbia built the most durable structures of the Subarctic—houses of logs or planks. Many tribes, among them the Naskapi, built domed sweathouses, primarily for ritual purification. The common form was a circular framework of saplings bent over to meet at the top. Bark or hide covered the framework.

Clothing. Women made semi-tailored clothing to protect against the bitter winter cold. Their sewing was not as fine as that of the Eskimo, and they probably borrowed some clothing ideas from the Eskimo, such as mittens, and leggings attached to moccasins. Men's leggings extended from foot to thigh and were held up by a thong attached to a belt. Along with leggings, men wore breechcloths, long shirts or hide coats, and fur hats. Generally women's leggings covered only the legs below the knees and were held by garters that were sometimes decorated with porcupine quills, or later, after European trade goods were available, with beadery. Women wore longer overgarments than men, and their loose, belted shirt-dresses kept their thighs warm. In cold weather both men and women wore fur robes as well as mittens and caps, and moccasins lined with furs for added warmth. Even in summer most Subarctic people covered their bodies as protection against insect bites.

Women did the work of preparing hides. The furs used for hats, mittens, and other clothing came from hare, fox, muskrat, beaver, and mink. These furs were the object of the European fur trade in later times.

Religion

Subarctic beliefs were simple and ceremonies few. Across the continent people believed in a multitude of spirits and other supernatural beings such as monsters, giants, and demons. Both Athabaskans and Algonkians attributed misfortune and lack of success to witchcraft or to the supernaturals, and hunters normally sought supernatural aid in the form of a spirit helper.

Like the Eskimo, the Subarctic peoples believed that animals had souls. Indeed, they believed that animals were more powerful than humans, that they had been the original inhabitants of the earth and could take human form if they wished. These powerful beings had to be treated with respect. They were appealed to and thanked for the good they bestowed on human beings in the form of food and raw materials. Although hunters were forced to kill animals, the souls or spirits of those slain returned to their spirit home, and the mortal remains, the bones, had to be treated properly or else the animal spirits would withhold others of their kind from other hunters. Among most caribou hunters, special rituals and beliefs were connected with the caribou. A "chief caribou spirit" lived in the mountains; unless proper respect was shown the slain caribou, the "overlord" would stop sending animals, and the people would starve. Often hunters would hang up the skull of a slain animal and offer it prayers and ceremonial smoke. Caribou bones were carefully kept away from dogs and also from menstruating women.

Every hunter hoped for a vision as a sign that he was under the protection of a spirit. Such a mark of favor helped him to face the perils of life, if not with complete confidence, at least with belief that he had support from the spirit world.

The fact of menstruation was overlain with fear that this female occurrence was dangerous to men and animals. During menstrual periods, childbirth, and for a while after, women were segregated from the male community. At such times, women were thought of as having almost an excess of spirit power—power dangerous to hunters and distasteful to the animals they hunted. At their first menstruation, girls were isolated and taught how to care for themselves and how to avoid men and animals taboo to them. The supernatural aura surrounding menstruating women was common to most Indians, but in some areas, including the Subarctic, segregation and taboos were very rigid.

As among the Eskimo, the sole religious practitioner was the shaman. Most of the Subarctic had no priesthood, although the Midewiwin society of the Ojibwa (to be discussed later) was an exception. The shaman's techniques included drumming, purifying people and objects with the smoke of tobacco (obtained by trade, since it could not be grown that far north), and in some areas, tent shaking. The shaman arranged the latter by techniques that we would call trickery, pulling slender cords to get the tent flapping as a sign to the followers that the spirits were present and listening. The drum was of great ritual importance to the shamans for divining the future and ensuring success in the hunt. Rattles were also used to catch the attention of the spirits who presumably advised the shamans and guided their actions.

The Windigo. Beliefs among the peoples of the Subarctic were inspired by their particularly harsh environment. One prominent and sometimes gruesome belief involved the Windigo, or cannibal monster. People's belief in the Windigo, and their resulting behavior, has been called

Windigo psychosis. It occurred mostly among the Algonkian speakers, most particularly the Montagnais-Naskapi, the Ojibwa, and the Cree. Since the food quest in the Subarctic was a constant struggle, the ever-present threat of famine gave a common character to all the cultures of the area. That pressure and the tensions it caused are central to Windigo psychosis.

The Windigo monster was a superhuman giant about thirty feet tall, who lived in the forest and preyed on human beings. The Algonkians believed many spirits inhabited the forest, but only this one was a cannibal. He was described as having a heart of ice, no lips, huge jagged teeth, and protuberant eyes rolling in blood. His feet were a yard long with pointed heels and only one toe. His hands were like claws. He hissed and made long-drawn-out thundering sounds, accompanied by gruesome howls. His speed and strength were enormous. The Windigo ate rotten wood, swamp moss, and mushrooms, but above all he loved human flesh. It was believed that he sought his victims hauntingly and relentlessly, but waited for darkness before he seized and ate them. Whenever a hunter failed to return from the forest, the Indians knew that he had probably fallen victim to the Windigo.

It was thought to be almost impossible to kill a Windigo. Some people believed that only a silver bullet could kill him—obviously a European addition to Windigo beliefs. A powerful shaman who could enlist the help of other supernaturals might be able to conquer a Windigo, but few ordinary mortals could.

The Indians had a number of ways of explaining this monster's origin. One explanation was that he had been a human being and was transformed by the spirits. Others held that he had been created out of a sorcerer's dream and sent out into the world to do malevolent deeds. Another belief was that the Windigo embodied all the people who had died of starvation. After contact with missionaries, some Indians came to believe that God had made the Windigo, presumably to punish evildoers.

Windigos and Cannibalism. The Windigo's compulsive desire to eat human flesh was his most fearsome habit. While such desire appalled the Subarctic people, cannibalism was a fact in their lives during times of famine. Because most people spent the winter in small family hunting groups, desperate hunger often meant eating a close relative, even a spouse or a child. A person who resorted to cannibalism became a Windigo. Consequently, anyone with a craving for human flesh—real or fancied—was considered a Windigo, possessed by the spirit of the Windigo monster. Once someone had tasted human flesh, he was thought to develop a burning appetite for more. Anyone who became a Windigo could not control his actions, and because he could not be cured, he had to be killed. It is reported that victims even asked to be destroyed.

The connection between cannibalism and becoming a Windigo could work either way. Among the Subarctic hunters, the search for a spirit helper was common, and some people acquired a Windigo spirit helper. A Windigo could select a person as his protégé, and if the individual did not reject the Windigo, he came to resemble his guardian in all respects, even to his heart of ice and his cannibal cravings. Or a shaman might send the Windigo spirit to an enemy to possess him or to become his spirit helper. A clever sorcerer could create Windigos by using his supernatural power to cause starvation, which forced the object of the sorcery to turn to cannibalism. Both males and females could become Windigos, which is surprising considering that it was the men who were the hunters, responsible for securing food and acquiring spirit helpers. Of the recorded cases, 40 were male, 29 were female, and the sex of one was not recorded. The records show that 44 of those cases involved an actual act of cannibalism; a family member was eaten in 36. Once a person had been designated a Windigo by others of his community, he probably turned to cannibalism even if he had not practiced it before because he believed it was futile for him to resist. Other symptoms of the Windigo psychosis were deep depression and delusions in which other people were perceived as animals. The Windigo-bewitched individual withdrew from human society and did not eat, sleep, move, or talk—he sat preoccupied with cannibalistic thoughts. It was believed that in this state of apathy he might still be helped, but once he had progressed to violence, his case became hopeless and he ought to be killed for the good of society.

Seventy cases of Windigo psychosis are recorded in the literature, most of them back in the nineteenth century. The peak of the recorded incidents came during the greatest time of stress in Indian-white relations, which hints that extreme Windigo psychosis may have been a contact phenomenon, at least in its full-blown form, though cases recorded by Jesuits in the seventeenth century indicate that it was an aboriginal development.

The Chipewyan

Among the Athabaskan groups, the Chipewyan (not to be confused with the Algonkian Chippewa) were the most populous and spread over the greatest area. They were caribou hunters primarily, but they also pursued buffalo, musk-oxen, and smaller game, as well as waterfowl and fish. Their life was not easy, and did not vary much from the typical Subarctic ways of exploiting the environment. The one big difference was the very low status of Chipewyan women and their hard life compared to women of most other groups. They were so little valued that they were last to be fed and first to perish in times of famine. Female infanticide was practiced, and adult women are reported to have expressed the wish that they had perished in childhood, so hard was their lot in adulthood. Women took the place of pack animals, hauling the household goods on their backs during seasonal migrations. They were at the mercy of their husbands, whom they married in early adolescence and who were often middle-aged men. Women were considered inferior to men in all ways. They prepared food for men, but they did not eat until the men were full, when little food might be left.

The women did have one way of escaping the burdens their men imposed upon them. Like all Subarctic men, the Chipewyan men feared and isolated menstruating women. But they seemed not to understand the timing. Consequently, when a woman wished to escape her husband, she moved to the menstrual hut, as often as several times a month, where she could be sure no man would pursue or bother her.

That kind of abuse might seem to lead inevitably to broken marriages, but in fact divorce was not more frequent among the Chipewyan than elsewhere. The harsh life meant, as in the Arctic, that the male-female division of labor was complementary and essential. Neither men nor women could easily manage alone. Sexual exchange of wives, here as in the Arctic, bonded two men together in a quasi-kin relationship, and if one of the men died, the other would be responsible for the wife and children of the deceased.

The difficult life affected the elderly, the sick, and the disabled, who might be neglected or abandoned when food was scarce. The Chipewyan may stand out as inhumane, but their environment was harsher than anything most of us can imagine. Hardships in the Subarctic were so great that society had to give its few meager benefits to those most likely to survive. The central Subarctic zone took a terrible toll among those hardy enough to live there.

The Ojibwa

Probably the largest tribal unit in the Subarctic were the Ojibwa, Algonkian speakers who lived along the northern shores of the western Great Lakes. They spread southward from the Subarctic into the agricultural district to the south. The name Ojibwa is applied to the group that remained in the Subarctic, while those who moved into territory that became the United States are usually referred to as Chippewa. Both names come from the Algonkian word meaning "those whose moccasins have puckered seams"; they were simply transcribed differently. If you

CHARACTERISTICS OF THE SUBARCTIC TRIBES

Clothing	Food production	Equipment	Shelter	Social and political organization	Religion	Warfare
Tailored skins Hide coats Leggings Skin dresses Long shirts Fur robes Hats Mittens Breechcloths Moccasins Snowshoes	Fishing Hunting Gathering wild plants	Bows and arrows Harpoons Traps Weirs Nets Toboggans Canoes Birchbark containers	Skin or bark tipis Log or plank houses Domed sweathouses	Nuclear families Bands Patrilineal trend in the east Matrilineal trend in Athabaskan area The Three Fires (alliance between Ojibwa, Ottawa, and Potawatomi)	Myths Spirits (monsters, giants, and demons) Shamans Witchcraft Spirit helpers Midewiwin Society of the Ojibwa Windigo Spirit Souls present in both humans and animals	War more frequent among Ojibwa than more northerly peoples

say each one several times, you will notice that they begin to sound very similar.

The Subarctic Ojibwa got many benefits by living on the border between regions. Life was never so rigorous as farther north, giving many more options for survival. Winters were neither so long nor so fierce; people enjoyed a delicacy in the form of maple sugar; and trade with fully agricultural groups to the south brought foods and equipment unavailable to the more northerly Algonkians. Some of the Ojibwa even did some rudimentary cultivation, and others availed themselves of the grain now called wild rice that grew in abundance around Lake Superior.

At one time, the Ojibwa joined with their kinfolk, the Ottawa and the Potawatomi, in a loose alliance known as the Three Fires. Before that, all three had been bands or separate units within a larger tribal organization. Although the individual groups or bands were mostly independent, with their own hunting territories, they were connected by language, common customs, kinship, and intermarriage. Separation into the divisions Ojibwa, Ottawa, and Potawatomi probably was due more to European classification and treatment than any self-perceived division, but as the Europeans treated the groups separately, in time they came to think of themselves as separate.

The Ojibwa fought more wars than the more northerly peoples did, perhaps because their life was easier. They used bows and arrows, clubs, knives, and hide shields in war, and carried home scalps of vanquished enemies. After a victory celebration, conquering warriors who had slain an enemy wore an eagle feather indicating their success. Their war practices probably were adopted from their enemies, tribes of the Great Lakes and the eastern Woodlands, some of whom spoke Algonkian and some Iroquoian.

The biggest difference between the Ojibwa and most other Subarctic people was not their much greater use of plant foods and their warfare, but their religious organization. Ojibwa religion had a more social and organized form, an association known as the Midewiwin, the Grand Medicine Society.

The Midewiwin was a religious and curing organization to which both men and women might belong if they were willing to spend the time and pay the heavy fees. There were four grades of membership, and each required long instruction and high payment. The initiate was expected to have a vision and personal contact with the supernatural. At an annual ceremony new members were inducted into the lowest grade. Very few ever attained the highest grade.

The Ojibwa had shamans, who followed the individualistic practices we have seen, but in this tribe, shamanism was less important and had less prestige than membership in the Midewiwin. The members' primary function was curing, mainly of psychological disabilities. Yet unlike curing elsewhere, it is said that members had much knowledge of natural drugs and many herbal remedies for nonpsychological problems. Their power came from the group, not from the individual, and membership brought very high prestige. Ritual was extensive. As a memory device, birchbark scrolls were inscribed with symbolic figures; these could not be called writing, but were closer to it than anything other groups north of the Rio Grande produced.

Suggestions for Further Study

Bibliography

Birket-Smith, Kai. 1958. *The Eskimos*. 2nd ed.

A general survey of Eskimo people by a distinguished European anthropologist.

Boas, Franz. 1888. *The Central Eskimo*.

An older classic about the Eskimo of Baffinland with many excellent line drawings of artifacts.

Jenness, Diamond. 1928. *The People of the Twilight*.

Describes the annual round of the Copper Eskimo.

______. 1955. *The Indians of Canada*.

A comprehensive survey of the Subarctic tribes with much information hard to locate in any other source.

Mowat, Farley. 1954. *People of the Deer*.

A gripping narrative about the hard life of the Caribou Eskimo.

Spencer, Robert. 1959. *The North Alaskan Eskimo*.

Ecology and social adaptation in North Alaska.

Other Pertinent Works

Lantis, Margaret. 1947. *Alaskan Eskimo Ceremonialism*.

Leacock, Eleanor. 1954. *The Mantagnais Hunting Territory and the Fur Trade*.

Osgood, Cornelius. 1936. *Contributions to the Ethnography of the Kutchin*.

Osgood, Cornelius. 1937. *The Ethnography of the Tanaina*.

Price, John. 1979. *Indians of Canada*. Scarborough, Ontario: Prentice-Hall of Canada, Ltd.

Speck, F. G. 1935. *Naskapi*.

Teicher, Morton I. 1960. *Windigo Psychosis*.

MAJOR GROUPS AND LANGUAGES OF THE ARCTIC AND SUBARCTIC

Language phylum	Language family	Cultural division
ARCTIC		
Paleo-Siberian	Eskimo-Aleut	Aleut Eskimo
SUBARCTIC		
Macro-Algonkian	Algonkian	Cree Malecite Micmac Montagnais Naskapi Ojibwa
	Undetermined	Beothuk
Na-Dene	Athabaskan	Bear Lake Beaver Carrier Chipewyan Dogrib Han Hare Kaska Koyukon Kutchin Sekani Slave Tanaina Tanana Tutchone Yellowknife

4

THE PLATEAU AND NORTHWEST COAST

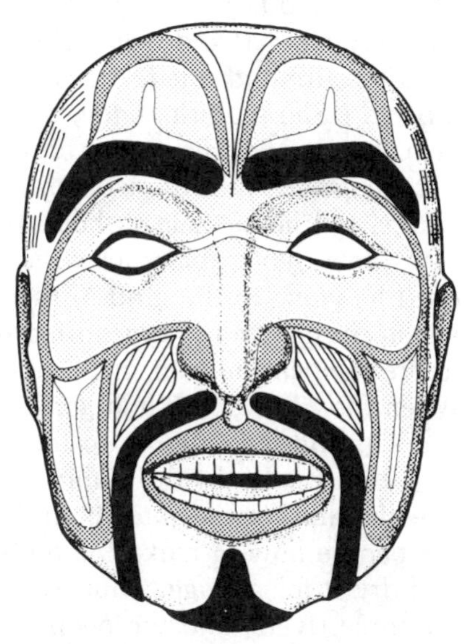

Painted wooden mask.

Salishan Trickster Tale

Long ago Coyote tried to cross a flooded stream leading to the Thompson River. He started across a log, but lost his balance and fell into the water. He was in danger of drowning so he turned himself into a piece of wood and was swept downstream to where the Thompson flowed into the Fraser River, and on from there into unknown waters. He sailed along until he was stopped by a fish weir owned by two old women. One of the women picked up the piece and said, "This is good wood. It will make a nice bowl. I will take it and carve it."

When the old woman had made the bowl, the other brought a fresh salmon to put in it. But the salmon disappeared before the women could eat it. They put more salmon in the bowl, but each piece disappeared quickly, and at last the women in anger threw the bowl into the fire. Suddenly from the fire came the sound of a baby crying. The old woman who had carved the bowl pulled it from the fire and cried, "It is a baby, and I have always longed for a baby!" She took the baby, a little boy, and raised him as her own. But he was a difficult child, disobedient, stubborn, and hard to manage. At first the women took him along fishing and gathering plants, but he became so headstrong they finally left him home.

Now Coyote, for he was the little boy, had never eaten salmon until he came to the land of the old women. There were no salmon in his country, and he acquired a taste for the fish. He determined to break open the weir and lead the fish to his people up the rivers. When the old women had gone, Coyote ran down to the weir, broke it open, and led salmon up the Thompson and Fraser rivers; then he went over to the Columbia River and led salmon up it and the streams that flowed into it. And all along the rivers Coyote taught the people how to make the tools to catch the fish, and how to cook and dry it for storage. That was how salmon came to the land of the three rivers, and the people called Coyote their ancestor, the ancestor of all tribes living between the Cascade and Rocky Mountains. The people since that day have been known as Coyote people.

The Thompson, Fraser, and Columbia rivers, and others such as the Snake, the Okanagon, the Umatilla, and smaller ones, were the lifeblood of the Plateau. The rivers made possible a relatively large native population—maybe 200,000—for they teemed with salmon. It is not surprising that salmon and the rivers were often the focus of myths.

The Environment

The Plateau is an interior highland area bounded by the Cascade mountain range in the west and the Continental Divide or the eastern slope of the Rocky Mountains in the east. On the south it bends into the Desert Basin, and to the north its boundary is less well-defined running roughly along the tributaries of the Fraser and Mackensie rivers. It is an elevated basin with deep river canyons and mountain and hill zones. Much of the area is desert, so low is the annual precipitation, yet it is watered well enough by the river systems that the low rainfall is less important than in regions without rivers. Winters are cold, but not nearly so cold as in the Subarctic, and summers can be hot. The southern vegetation is dry land forms: cactus, sagebrush, scrub trees. The northern mountain slopes are covered with forests of conifers mixed with some deciduous forms.

Culturally, the Plateau is a transition zone. The cultures of most of its inhabitants resembled those of groups in neighboring areas: the Plains on the east, the Northwest Coastal peoples to the west, or the desert dwellers to the south. The differences are not strong, but the Plateau adaptations are distinctive enough to identify the region as a separate culture area. It includes the western quarter of Montana, southeast British Columbia, eastern Washington, most of Idaho, and northeast and central Oregon.

Prehistory

Remains of the earliest human occupations in this area show that salmon fishing was common among the earliest Plateau dwellers. Some of these people later moved on to the North Pacific Coast; the rivers offered natural passages through the Cascade and coastal ranges to the lowlands of the seaboard. Rugged badlands and lava flows cover much of the Plateau, making the river valleys not only the major avenues for travel but also the primary locations for settlement and subsistence activities. Flint blades and fishbone debris at the Dalles, a series of major rapids on the Columbia River, have been dated to between 8000 and 6000 B.C. Other ancient remains, of pithouses and earth ovens dating from early periods, indicate their long history on the Plateau. Long ago, as in historical times, the ovens were used to bake the vegetable staple of the Plateau, the camas bulb, a starchy root somewhat similar to the potato.

Another ancient form that lasted into historic times was a ground-level pole and mat dwelling. It appears that such dwellings may have been first used several thousand years ago on the Plateau. Other dwellings used in the region included semi-subterranean pithouses and earth

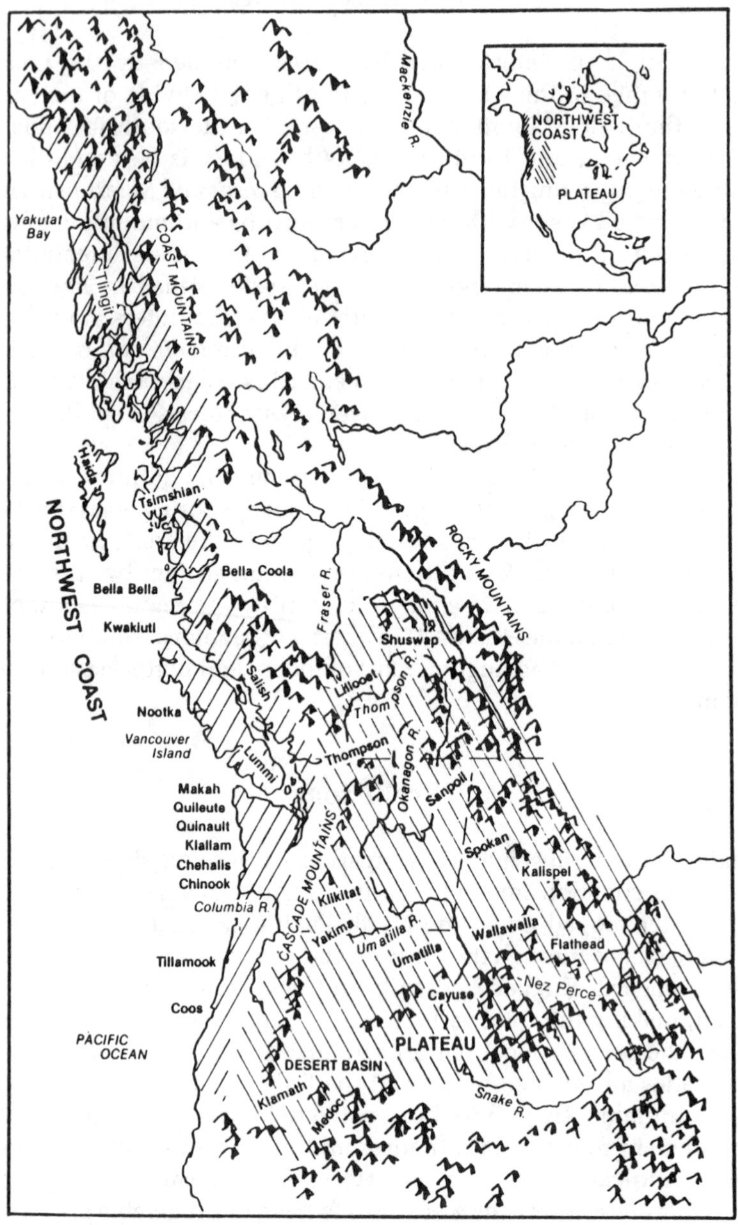

The Plateau and the Northwest Coast culture areas and their tribes.

lodges. As was the case for much of the West, the Plateau peoples developed and continued a life-style that took advantage of naturally occuring plants and animals in their wild forms. It seems that the earliest people to move into the Plateau region made for themselves a way of life not really very different from that of their descendants who were visited by Lewis and Clark on their famous expedition from 1804 to 1806.

The Plateau is significant as a transitional area through which people passed in ancient times as they populated the continent. Here descendants of the original settlers coming from the Subarctic developed a new way of life, which would adjust and prepare their own descendants for the areas beyond—the Coast and California. It appears that people passed through the Plateau in small groups, not year by year but generation by generation. As they moved, they learned and invented new ways of adapting to new environments. Those who stayed within the Plateau region adapted to its own environmental challenges and benefitted greatly from the relatively few significant offerings that existed there. The Dalles, mentioned above, was not only a prime fishing area but also developed into a primary center for trade of many important products and resources among the peoples of the Plateau, Northwest Coast, California, Great Basin, and the Plains.

Life on the Plateau

As you read this quick description of the Plateau people, remember that the area they lived in was transitional. It had few clear-cut, unique characteristics and did not become a center of technological elaboration.

From ancient times, Plateau tribes moved seasonally to take advantage of many foods. Their winter villages usually were on the banks of one of the area's many rivers, where they served as fishing stations in all seasons, including the major fishing season from May to November. Groups left the winter homes to fish in new streams or to hunt in the hills in spring, summer, and early fall. Each community recognized a large territory as its own for gathering berries, roots, and other plant stuffs, and for hunting game.

Houses in the winter villages were permanent, large, and well-insulated. Many were pithouses built of logs and covered with sod. Light came from a hole in the roof, which also let out the smoke from the fire. With the addition of a notched log ladder, this hole served as an entrance as well. In the summer, the people moved to lighter, less durable shelters. These usually were built of poles and covered with mats of rushes or cattails. Some of them were community dwellings, up to sixty feet long, constructed over shallow pits; others were made of the same materials but housed only one family. Openings in the roofs let smoke out and light in.

Resources

None of the Plateau tribes practiced agriculture, for the region was too cold and too dry for cultivating the early corn species. The food important above all others was salmon, though other fish such as trout and sturgeon were eaten. Salmon was not only the favorite but the basic food, eaten fresh in season and dried for the rest of the year. Plant and animal foods filled out the diet of fish: camas bulbs, nuts, and seeds; and deer, elk, and mountain sheep, as well as smaller animals such as rabbit. Food was neither so scarce as it was in the north in the Subarctic, nor so bountiful as along the Northwest Coast or in most of California. The Plateau population was therefore denser than in the north, though sparser than in culture areas to the west.

The most important resources other than food were the plant fibers of grasses, rushes, reeds, and vines, which could be used in basketry. Basketry was important throughout the area from ancient times not only for containers and cooking, but for bedding, house covering, sandals, cradles, and shrouds for the dead. Justifiably famous for their fine work, the Plateau women made many forms: large cylindrical baskets of Indian hemp and beargrass for gathering and storing roots; flat winnowing baskets of willow; mortar baskets of the same shape, but bottomless and fastened to a stone upon which the women pounded seeds or roots; cooking vessels of willow splints; flat bags or pouches for holding small personal possessions, and larger ones for holding clothing and family equipment. Matting was the principal house covering and also served as mattresses or tables.

Communities

With dependable subsistence from salmon and wild plants, the Plateau people could settle in stable, independent village communities. Villagers recognized ties between themselves and those in other villages in their common customs and dialects, not in any political unification. Varieties of four language families were spoken in the Plateau: Salishan (of uncertain derivation), Sahaptin (a branch of Penutian), Algonkian, and Athabaskan.

The village rather than the tribe was the main political unit in the Plateau. Among villages using the same language, people shared ceremonies, intermarried, and traded regularly. Each village set aside territories exclusively for those who belonged to the village, letting others use those resources only as guests; some groups would let others use their land only by invitation.

Some large and productive fishing sites were communally owned, and the catch was distributed among all members of the village. Fishing on

Salmon, a food staple of the Plateau tribes, was caught in a weir made of slender poles. Once the fish was entrapped, it would be speared through an opening in the top of the weir and withdrawn. A fish spear with two detachable bone points lashed to form a V (above) was commonly used.

such a large scale was done with the large traps or dams called fish weirs. Individual fishing spots were owned or controlled by small kin groups or by individuals. The large weirs were built and repaired by all the men in the community, while the small weirs and fishing platforms were built by their owners. Fishing rights were important and zealously maintained.

In most cases, the village was governed by a *headman*, sometimes referred to as a chief. He was chosen in some groups by the village adults and in others got his position by inheritance. Even the hereditary leaders, however, held power only by competence, and none was more than adviser to the community. If disagreement arose within the community, the headman negotiated a settlement agreeable to all. The position was his for life unless he displeased the village people, but his authority rested on their consent, and a council both assisted him and limited his power. In some groups women belonged to the council, and in a few cases they were chiefs.

The Plateau people were generally peaceful. Some had a reputation for making great efforts to avoid a fight. If raids or retaliation were felt to be necessary, the people chose a war chief or leader, but they rarely looked for prestige in warlike feats until after European contact. Then the Plateau peoples felt the influence of the Plains tribes, who believed a man's best way to success and prestige was in war. When Plateau people did any raiding, it was almost always against another linguistic group, and the raiding party was no more than a few volunteers. They occasionally took prisoners in the western Plateau, where influence from the Northwest Coast was strong. Those captives became slaves, but in time, they were assimilated into the community.

Religion

Spirit Helpers. The Plateau Indians believed that success in life depended on the good will and aid of the spirit world, and that it was essential for every man to have a spirit helper. For a woman the helper was less important, but many women sought a guardian spirit anyhow. Having more than one spirit helper gave anyone a greater chance of success. Since so many of the people were in touch with the supernatural world, the line between shamans and others was not clear-cut in the Plateau country.

Indians believed that spirits took the form of animals, plant life, or even places, and that they often taught a song or a chant as a kind of talisman or charm to their devotees. Because spirits appeared only when someone sought them, a person who wished to make contact with the spirit that was to become his or her guardian retired to an isolated spot to undergo what is called the *vision quest*. The spirit might take several nights before it appeared in a vision. After that the spirit would appear in time of trouble, or in dreams, or sometimes at a ceremonial dance given by those who had received it as a vision. Shamans found their guardians in the same way, but they had more helpers, and their helpers were more powerful.

Throughout life, people called on their spirits for help, but if the personal spirits could not or would not help, one could go to a shaman. As in the Arctic and Subarctic, shamans were curers of bad luck and unnatural disturbances brought on by broken taboos, unfriendly spirit contact, or intrusion by foreign objects. They might also be village headmen or leaders of fishing or hunting parties, because their ritual abilities were bound to give a better success than an ordinary man could expect. However, men whose guardian spirits were salmon or deer would lead the fishing and hunting, being especially favored by the spirit in control of the activity. Thus the position of hunt leader had definite ritual and supernatural overtones.

Ceremonies. Men who shared the same spirit helpers often joined during the winter to hold public ceremonies and dances. These gatherings renewed contact with the guardian spirits, and also with people from neighboring villages. They were also a welcome emotional release, breaking the monotony and working off anxiety and tensions during the cold and dreary months of the year.

Other public activities with ritual significance included the first-fruit ceremonies, celebrating the first catch or plants of the season. As the salmon began their journey to spawn in the inland waters of their birth, a salmon chief, who usually had a salmon spirit helper, thanked the salmon for coming and then caught and ate one, carefully disposing of its bones so that its spirit would not be offended. Such services were designed to placate the spirits of the animals and plants, thank them, praise them, and keep them plentiful in years to come.

Women's Taboos. Another main focus of the Plateau people's supernatural interests was girls' puberty. Many Indian societies considered the menarche—the onset of menstruation—a time of supernatural importance, and the Plateau people regarded this period with particular awe. As in the Subarctic, it was an event heavy with spiritual meaning; the pubescent girl was supposed to be supercharged with power dangerous to males and their pursuits. Girls were taught never to touch their heads during the menstrual period because for the supernaturals the head was the most important part of the body. If her head itched, a girl learned to scratch with a special scratching stick. In some tribes, girls were taught to drink through straws or tubes, never allowing water to touch their lips. They were separated from the male community, living in a special hut while they were taught by older women to learn and observe menstrual taboos and to keep busy all day long. Such training prepared a girl for an industrious life as wife, mother, and plant collector.

Women did not usually think of menstrual taboos as a burden, but as a way to get out of daily chores and thus a welcome rest. Life for most Indian women was no less hard than that of the men, but they were given little prestige and honor. They were glad to be left alone.

The Nez Perce

Nez percé is French for "pierced nose," but the people of the tribe known by that name never did pierce their noses, as far as we know. Perhaps French explorers attached the name to a variety of tribes, some of which did have that custom. The name is no longer given a French pronunciation, but now is usually pronounced *nez purs*.

The first encounter between the Nez Perce and non-Indian outsiders occurred when the Lewis and Clark expedition passed through their territory in 1805. At that time the Nez Perce population was probably around 5000.

Seasonal Life. The Nez Perce lived in settled villages in the southeastern part of the Plateau area, the land that is now Idaho. Individual bands were autonomous though each group recognized others of the same linguistic and cultural stock. It was the coming of the Europeans that brought about the unification into a distinct tribal entity. The villages were their winter dwelling place and also their permanent homes, but individual bands were widely dispersed during the summer to exploit the wide range of ripening plant food, summer fishing sites, and animal life. The summer hunting territory was vast, hundreds of square miles.

Spring saw the dispersal from the winter villages in the search for plant grounds where starchy tubers and bulbs abounded. The Nez Perce harvested a favorite food, the camas bulb, in June and July, and at that time, food being plentiful, various bands met in the harvest areas. They had time for games, gambling, and general festivities, and they enjoyed being out in the open after the hard winter of boredom, isolation, and frequent hunger. In summer clothing was minimal: breechclouts (or breechcloths), skirts and possibly capes of shredded bark.

At mid-summer, the bands moved on to reap other ripening plants, and by late summer, they were at favorite fishing sites where they remained until October. The whole summer season was lived in the open in general freedom and plenty.

When it was no longer pleasant to be outdoors, they returned to their permanent encampments, their winter homes, in small communities along streams. Those winter homes were semi-subterranean, some for nuclear families—parents and children—some for the larger extended family. In both cases, the structures were insulated with earth, and roofs had smoke holes along the ridge poles. The larger habitation was merely a lengthened version of the smaller to allow space for several families of the kinship group with individual fires down the center.

The winter dress included fur robes and leg wrappings. Around 1800, under the influence of the Plains tribes, the Nez Perce began to use tailored hide clothing with shell and elk teeth decoration and European beads acquired by trade.

Though the Nez Perce practiced some food storage, there was rarely enough for the long winters, and hunger was common by early spring. The meat supply was most uncertain but became more plentiful after the Nez Perce acquired horses. Until that time, the food quest—gathering, fishing, and hunting—required constant work. One advantage the Nez Perce hunter had was a special bow made from mountain sheep horn backed with deer sinew. It was very powerful.

Chiefs. The Nez Perce group was made up of loosely bound villages or bands, each with its own headman or chief. This position of chief, though officially inherited, was really elective, for public opinion made the final decision in seating a new chief. The chief was assisted by an advisory council of important men such as warriors and shamans, who held their positions by prominence and recognized ability. Anyone who proved unworthy was soon replaced, and each village or band was independent of the others in choosing its representatives. The Nez Perce had no overall chief.

Guardian Spirits. Young Nez Perce sought guardian spirits to help them win success in life. Both boys and girls hoped for a vision, and usually before age ten a child left home to go into mountain wilds and commune with the spirits. Parents decided when children were ready to set out on the vision quest, and told them about the land they would travel through. But outside of that advice, the child was alone. He or she had been told how one might expect to hear from the spirits, and that one should fast so that the spirits might come quickly. Expecting them to come in the form of an animal, the child, hardly more than an infant, hungry and perhaps frightened, would see an animal or a bird and be more than ready to believe that the supernatural had manifested itself. The child would usually find a symbol or fetish of this vision—a strangely shaped or colored stone, a feather, or perhaps a bone, something that seemed to show the spirit had just been there. That was the proof, to be carried whenever spirit help was needed. The spirit also might teach the initiate a song which, like the object, came to be a symbol of spirit power.

The child returned home secure in his or her vision. The initiate usually sought other spirit helpers, too, making the vision quest a number of times. By adulthood, most Nez Perce thought they had made contact with many supernatural beings. It is easy to imagine what that must have meant. Indians with many guardian spirits could hear them calling in the forest as trees whispered in the breeze, as clouds drifted across the sky, and as birds flew overhead. What a sense of confidence these signs from their guardians must have given them! The supernatural revealed itself in many ways every day.

Marriage. Parents arranged the marriages, the father of the young man visiting the girl's father, discussing plans, and offering gifts. The bride went to the groom's home when arrangements were complete. After a few weeks, the couple and the man's kinfolk took the gifts to her father's home, where they all partook of a grand feast. The groom's family then received gifts from the girl's family.

Only a few men had more than one wife. No ceremonies honored the later marriages, and no gifts were exchanged, for usually the other wives were sisters of the first. Divorce was simple, occurring at the wish of either husband or wife.

Plains Influence. By the time the Lewis and Clark expedition (the main source of our information) had reached their territory, the Nez Perce had taken on many aspects of Plains culture. They had horses, and were known by other Plateau tribes as rather aggressive. The date the Nez Perce first obtained horses is uncertain, but it was sometime in the early eighteenth century. Horses were a blessing for hunting and traveling, and by the mid-eighteenth century the Nez Perce were true equestrians. The rich grassland of the Plateau area provided excellent fodder and an opportunity to increase the herds, and when winter snows came, the same river valleys that sheltered the villages protected the horses from the worst of the cold. The Nez Perce took to horses with gusto, and so successful were they that they learned selective breeding, a practice shared by the Cayuse and Comanche, but by almost no other tribes. They were in a favored economic position, being close to the buffalo-filled plains, and they took buffalo hides on regular trade excursions to the rapids on the Columbia River, the Dalles, to exchange for goods from the coast, especially shells.

The Klamath of Southern Oregon

Environment. The Klamath are difficult to place in a culture area. They were geographically and culturally transitional and showed traits of the Plateau, the Northwest Coast, California, and the Desert Basin. The isolation and separatism of the local groups were typical of California, as was the importance of seeds in the diet. Characteristic of the Basin were seasonal deficits in food supply and the absence of hereditary chiefs. The importance of fish in the Klamath diet, their simple first-fruit rituals, and their practice of head deformation show influence from both the Plateau and the Northwest Coast. Other Plateau characteristics were their house types and their linguistic affiliation. The Klamath probably took their armor of rods or tough hides from the Northwest Coast. The crude snowshoes that helped them move through the deep snows were ultimately derived from the Subarctic. The Klamath language belongs to the Penutian phylum, having its closest affiliations in the Plateau.

Klamath territory was mostly stream-watered marshland, and their greatest food resources were fish, mussels, and water birds. Compared to the Desert Basin, subsistence was bounteous for the Klamath; compared to the Northwest Coast, it was meager. Winters were long and cold with heavy snowfalls. Food was scarce at that time of year, and had to be stored in summer for the lean months.

Home Life. The winter settlement was a village of earth lodges and communal storage pits and a few domed, mat-walled huts. The earth lodges were excavated two or three feet down for better insulation and the entrance was a hole in the roof, which also let smoke out. Lodges were taken down each spring, because they became soggy from melting snows and vermin-ridden and odorous from the people and fires inside. Each fall when the families returned from their summer rounds they rebuilt the lodges.

The Klamath also built small semiunderground sweathouses, in which they created steam by pouring water over hot stones. Both men and women used the sweathouses, though not at the same time. The men would sweat before a hunt to purify themselves ritually, but sweating was often just a relaxation as well. It was followed by a plunge in a stream, even in the cold of winter.

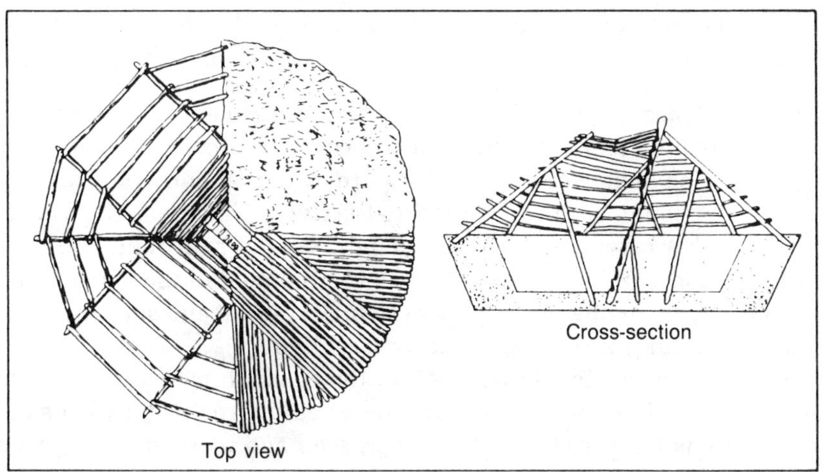

A reconstructed pithouse. The roof, as seen from above, showing hatchway, rafter construction, sheathing of poles, and covering of earth (left); cross-section displaying pit, center posts, roof framework, and notched log ladder (right).

The Klamath's main social unit was the nuclear family, but the extended family was almost as important. They traced their kinship through both males and females, with slight emphasis on the male line. Most earth lodges were occupied by extended families, though the shaman might have one to himself, and the hamlet was governed by a loose council of respected men limited by group consensus. No leader had power without support of the community. In contrast with the social pattern of the Northwest Coast, wealth did not confer decision-making powers.

Clusters of hamlets or villages made up the group called a *tribelet*, of which the Klamath had six. They sometimes fought each other; the Klamath never had strong tribal identity, though they recognized themselves as related and a cultural unit speaking the same language.

Shamans. Shamans were the only specialists, serving as part-time curers and entertainers. With the guests supplying the food, their performances were given in midwinter and lasted five days and nights. For part of the time children were not permitted because the spirit power might be too dangerous for them. The shamans had assistants who helped summon the spirits and generally aided in the performance, which involved dancing and singing, calling the spirits, and tricks such as swallowing fire. It helped while away the long winter hours, and it was also an important ritual that demonstrated the shaman's spiritual competence and connections with the supernatural world.

The Food Quest. By late winter, food supplies ran low, and some years brought real hunger before fresh food became available. In March, the suckers, fish that were to the Klamath what salmon were to more northerly people, began their runs up the rivers. The Klamath observed a first sucker ceremony, and also caught salmon and trout. They had dugout canoes, which they submerged in the mud of the marshes and streams during winter to keep them from drying out and splitting. They also fished on the lakes at night by torchlight.

After spring fishing slowed down, the Klamath moved to flats and meadows to find camas bulbs and other edible roots and plants and cattail reeds for basketry. All summer, seed and berry gathering went on. Huckleberries, chokecherries, wild plums, and others were eaten fresh or dried and stored for winter. However, it was the use of water-lily seeds as a food resource that set the Klamath and the Modoc, their closely related neighbors to the south, apart from other tribes. In the thousands of acres of marshland and lake, pond lilies grew, and in August their seeds ripened. So important was this crop that the seeds were not harvested until a shaman had performed a simple first-fruits

CHARACTERISTICS OF THE PLATEAU TRIBES

Clothing	Food production	Equipment	Shelter	Social and political organization	Religion	Warfare
Fur and fiber robes Leggings Tunics Skirts Sandals Snowshoes (Klamath)	Fishing Hunting Gathering	Spears Nets Hooks Weirs Traps Basketry Armor of rods and hides (Klamath) Dugout canoe (Klamath)	Ground-level, pole-and-mat dwellings Pit houses of logs and sod Earth lodges Sweathouses	Families Bands Villages — the main political unit, governed by headmen Chiefs and councils (Nez Perce)	Myths Spirit helpers First fruit ceremonies Shamans Vision Quest	Generally peaceful Small raids

ritual. Women, children, and old men collected the wild pond-lily seeds from dugout canoes while the younger men hunted deer, elk, and mountain sheep. The summer encampments at the lily beds were a time of recreation and relaxation, but as summer came to an end, the Klamath returned to the winter sites to rebuild their earth lodges and prepare for the cold weather.

Work and Success. The Klamath philosophy of life was that hard work would be rewarded with tangible goods and respect from others. Poverty was the result of laziness. Headmen were those who demonstrated by their many possessions and their ability to support several wives that they had labored long and hard. The Klamath never amassed as much wealth as the Northwest people, but the idea of getting ahead was dominant, and even those born poor had a chance to work hard and make a success in life. The successful shared with their kinfolk and neighbors, of course, but it was considered demeaning to be dependent on others. It was a very individualistic philosophy, and everyone was expected to strive constantly to better his lot in life. Klamath believed it was good to work, and judged people by their industriousness and material achievement.

The Northwest Coast

Tlingit-Haida Creation Myth

Before the world came into being, a spirit ruled from the clouds. Beneath his realm was nothing but water. Raven was servant to the spirit. One day Raven was far from his home in the sky and became very weary. He flew on and on over the vast body of water, but could find no place to rest. Finally, he began to beat the water with his wings. He beat so hard that waves on each side of him rose up high, almost to the clouds. The waves suddenly became rocks that increased and spread into islands. Sandy beaches formed, and eventually plants grew from the sand.

Raven decided the land would be his, but after a while he grew lonely all by himself. He took two large piles of shells and from them he created two human beings, both women. Soon the women complained that Raven should not have made two women; one should have been a man. So Raven transformed one into a man, and that made everyone happy. That first pair was the ancestor of the Indians who lived on the islands.

Unfortunately, it was not long before the people began to quarrel, and they quarreled and quarreled. At last the spirit came down from his cloud kingdom and warned them that they would be destroyed if they could not learn to live in peace. And for a while, the quarreling ceased. It started once again, however, and the spirit decided to punish the people. He took the most obstinate and changed them into cedar trees. He then told the others, "If you can learn to live in peace, you will have these lovely trees for many things: planks for houses, trunks for canoes, bark and roots for mats and baskets. From inner bark you will make clothing." The people had learned their lesson well, and from that time they have used cedar trees for all those things.

The Environment

The Northwest Coast culture area reaches more than 2,000 miles from the panhandle of Alaska on the north to the northern tip of California on the south. It is called coastal because it covers very little territory east to west; it is hardly a hundred miles at the widest, confined between the Pacific Ocean on one side and the Coast Mountains of Canada and the Cascade Mountains of the United States on the other. It includes a partly submerged offshore mountain chain forming many large and small islands, of which the most important are the Queen Charlotte Islands and Vancouver Island.

The ocean, warmed by the Japanese Current, moistens and tempers the prevailing westerly winds, and even in winter the mountains block off most cold air coming from the interior. These geographic conditions cause intense fogs and precipitation, for as the moisture-laden ocean winds rise against the mountain slopes, the air is cooled to the precipitation point. The native people needed little clothing, and used it for protection against rain more than cold.

The western mountain slopes are covered with temperate-zone rain forest of spruce, hemlock, cedar, and giant Douglas fir, some rising 250 feet above the ground and fog to reach the sunlight. Firewood and building materials came from these forests, and materials for basketry, cord, rope, mats, clothing, and bedding, as well as canoes, boxes, implements, and utensils. The fringes of these great forests are home to game animals, including deer, moose, elk, and several varieties of bear. There are mountain goats and sheep, and fur-bearing species like mink, beaver, and fox. However, the sea is a far richer resource, providing whale, porpoise, seal, sea lion, sea otter, and many kinds of fish. Halibut may weigh up to a quarter ton each; sturgeon are twice as large. And there are shoals of herring and smelt, cod, and the *oulachon*—the candlefish—so called because, with a wick run through the body, it burns like a candle. Salmon were once so plentiful that it has been said the people could have lived on them alone. The tidal flats yield shellfish, one of which, the geoduck clam, is so large that six of them might provide a meal for a large family. In spring and fall, clouds of waterfowl fly by on their migrations, challenging hunters. This wealth of food supported an estimated native population of 250,000.

Prehistory

Until recently, relatively little archaeology has been conducted along the Northwest Coast, leaving us with a fairly incomplete understanding of prehistory of the area. It now appears that the region was first occupied long ago by peoples entering from two or more different areas adjacent to the Northwest Coast. Coastal-dwelling groups came southward from Alaska, and interior Plateau groups descended along the major rivers that flowed westward into the Pacific. Still other groups from coastal areas further south also may have migrated northward into the region. There is evidence that Paleo Indian peoples occupied some areas of the interior as early as 9000 B.C. By 5000 B.C. we can see many of the basic features of the traditional Northwest Coast marine-oriented lifeway well established on some of the major islands and along the shore of British Columbia. In this early period, Northwest Coast peoples combined large terrestrial and sea mammal hunting with fishing and shellfish collection. Eventually, prehistoric Northwest Coast peoples came to rely more and more upon the marine resources, particularly fish such as salmon, that were so plentiful and reliable in their region.

Contact and exchange between the Northwest Coast and the Alaskan coast are evident in the presence of tools and other artifacts, and reflect a major cultural influence. While evidence for Eskimoid or Asiatic influences is indirect and rather tenuous, certain whaling practices and myths suggest contact between Eskimo and Northwest Coast Indians in late prehistoric times. Archaeologists have suggested that a thin veneer of Asiatic or Eskimo traits diffused into the area, probably by way of the coast. The latter traits show up archaeologically in tools such as semicircular knives of ground slate and harpoons, and also in the physical anthropology of the region. The skin tone of the northern people was much lighter than that of other Indian peoples before contact. Alexander Mackenzie, the first European to reach one of the tribes, the Bella Coola, wrote in 1793 that he saw Indians with brown rather than dark brown or black hair, and with light-colored eyes. The Northwest Coast people also have much heavier facial and body hair than other Indians, and the epicanthic eye fold is more common among these people. All this suggests an infusion of Eskimo or Aleut genes.

Many of the details of prehistoric cultural change and development within this region remain for archaeologists to discover. Wherever the people came from, by 1000 B.C. they had established a genuine Northwest Coast tradition, and by A.D. 1000 that tradition reached the form and covered the territory in which Europeans found it. Large permanent villages, ranked societies, warfare, extensive trade, elaborate woodworking, and the characteristic art of the region had developed as central features of Northwest Coast culture by late prehistoric times. Hundreds of years before the arrival of Europeans, the societies of the Northwest Coast had developed ways of life that rank among the most complex and sedentary for nonagricultural peoples anywhere.

Native Life

In aboriginal times, the richest providers of food were the rivers. As often as seven times a year, spawning salmon filled the waters so thickly, observers said, that one could walk across the water on their backs. Northwest people speared, netted, or trapped them by the ton, and dried or smoked them for future use.

In terms of the food supply, the usual standard for wealth among nonindustrial people, the native peoples of the Northwest Coast were wealthy indeed. Food stocks of course must have varied from tribe to tribe, and were not always bountiful, yet the people of this area were so blessed with natural resources that they reached the limits of complexity attainable in a hunting and gathering economy. They built huge, durable houses; they made large dugout canoes that could carry sixty people or more; they were excellent craftsworkers and artists, decorating nearly everything they made; they staged elaborate musical dramas and ceremonies; they engaged in intricate economic activities; and they developed a complicated system of social stratification.

We separate the ethnographic area of the Northwest Coast into northern, central, and southern divisions. Their basic adaptations were strikingly similar, but regional differences make the division useful. The best known northern groups were Tlingit, Haida, and Tsimshian; central groups were Bella Coola, Kwakiutl, and Nootka; and in the south were Coast Salish, Quileute, and Chinook. Near the present California-Oregon boundary, the culture areas blended, and we have to assign tribes to one area or the other arbitrarily. We place the Yurok, Karok, and Hupa in the California area, though others have put them in the Northwest Coast area.

The nature of the region's resources made it inevitable that all the inhabitants would settle on the coast or river banks and spend their lives near the water instead of the mountains inland. The topography meant that travel was easier and faster in coastal waters than overland. From

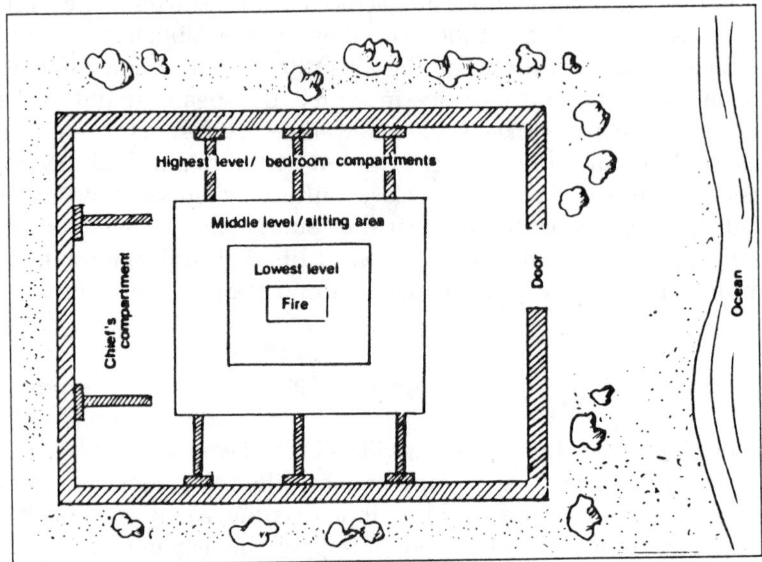

A generalized floor plan of a Northwest Coast house. On the lowest level this rectangular dwelling had a fire in the center, with a smoke hole above it. The middle level contained the sitting area, while the highest level provided spaces for bedroom compartments and the chief's compartment. The house contained no windows and usually only one door.

Puget Sound northward, mountains rise steeply from the sea, and the coast is cut by deep fjords. With boats men could move among protected channels and exploit the marine life.

Technology

In this densely forested country, the main building material was wood, above all yellow and red cedar. It was durable, yet soft enough to work with stone or bone adzes and chisels. And because this kind of wood has long, straight, parallel fibers, great planks could be split off the logs with hardwood or antler wedges to make siding for houses. The planks were grooved or notched so that they could be joined without pegs. The result was rectangular dwellings sixty feet long and perhaps fifty feet wide, their gabled roofs supported on enormous cedar beams held up by massive cedar posts. The frameworks of most houses were designed to be permanent structures, but their siding was not part of the weight-bearing structure and could be dismantled whenever their owners had reason to do so, as when they set up housekeeping at seasonal fishing sites. At each site, the family maintained a house frame to which they attached the siding and roof planks. When moving time came again, the planks were stripped off and carried to a new site on the canoes that also moved the family. Sometimes the planks were lashed across two canoes, forming a useful deck.

Boats and Totem Poles. The people stretched cedar logs, hollowed with fires and adzes, into canoe shape by partially filling them with heated water to soften the wood. They built canoes in many sizes, small ones for travel on streams, larger ones for ocean fishing and whaling, and great sixty-foot canoes for trade, warfare, and ceremonial visits. Cedar logs also were the medium for an important art form, now known as the *totem pole*. Elaborately carved with figures of animals and supernatural beings, the poles honored dead chiefs, marked the graves

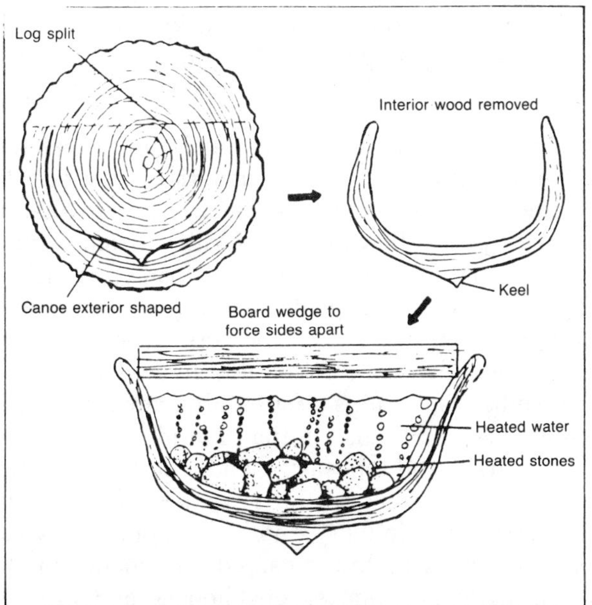

Dugout canoes were constructed by various steps. First a log was split, and the exterior of the canoe was shaped. The interior wood was then removed with adzes and fire. Next, the interior was filled with water heated by hot stones. The sides of the canoe were forced apart while heated and moist, and a crossbeam was wedged in to stabilize the shape of the sides. The water and stones were subsequently removed, the dugout dried, paddlers' seats installed, and a prow and stern might be added and decorated.

of important people, served as portals to houses, and generally were a sort of coat-of-arms indicating the owner's rank and title.

Boxes and Masks. Cedar planks also provided the boxes that served as home furnishings, for storage, and for coffins. These wooden boxes were ingeniously made. Woodworkers cut a board to the shape of a cross, then scored it so that the side pieces could be folded up into place and pegged or sewn together. Fitted with covers, smoothed with abrasive sandstone or sharkskin, and usually intricately painted or carved, these containers stored almost everything from whale, seal, or candlefish oil to sinew cords and spare points for arrows.

Wood carvers turned blocks of cedar into ceremonial masks, conventionalized yet vivid representations of men, beasts, and supernaturals, sometimes equipped with leather hinges and strings by which the faces could be opened to reveal another mask inside. Even cedar bark had multiple uses. Its tough fibers were woven into blankets, mats for covering walls and floors, openwork baskets for carrying fish, or baskets so tightly made that they held water. Woven cedar fibers also made hats and raincoats.

Other Materials. Though wood was the main natural resource, the craftsworkers also used other raw materials. Various fibers were inventively used, such as strands of kelp, twisted into fishlines. Coastal people fashioned projectile points and knives from horn, bone, and stone, but in general they used far less stone than other Indians. Perhaps the most important stone implements were the axes and adzes for hewing wood. But craftsworkers also used woodworking equipment with blades of bones and especially shell, honed to a fine edge.

Men made tambourine drums by stretching rawhide over a hoop, but hide was otherwise of little use in that humid climate: when soggy it stretched out of shape and tore easily, and when dried, it became stiff. Matting was far more useful, and the women wove poncho-like rain garments and basketry rain hats. Another important raw material was mountain-sheep horn, which was carved into spoons or steamed and spread to make bowls. Deer hooves, goat hooves, and puffin beaks made rattles or jingles when attached to dance aprons, bracelets, or anklets.

Social and Political Organization

Tribes. It will be convenient to use the term *tribe* to refer to the linguistic groups of the Northwest Coast, but it is a term that must be used with caution, since it does not really correspond to the native unit. In fact, this English word has caused quite a bit of legal trouble in attempts to determine economic and political rights and claims. The anthropologist's use of the name Tlingit, Kwakiutl, or any other name really indicates a linguistic group that had no political unity in the people's minds. They saw themselves instead as villages or kin groups such as lineages, clans, or extended families.

The tribe—that is, the linguistic group—had no political figure with power or authority over the whole group. For instance, the Tlingit had no chief or leader who could speak for them as a whole. Those who spoke Tlingit recognized a relationship in their common language, and they had marital and kin ties in many communities, but their real loyalties were to the local group and not the linguistic group. While this is true of Indian societies generally, it applies especially to the peoples of the Northwest Coast, where villages speaking the same language might raid each other, a situation far from common elsewhere. The local groups were independent, and though they might form alliances with each other, the entire linguistic group never acted as one nation.

The northern tribes of the Northwest Coast were *matrilineal*; that is, they traced descent through the women. All the others reckoned descent through both mother and father, with some emphasis on the paternal side in matters of group membership and inheritance. In the north the local leadership was hereditary; in the south, wealth generally determined social rank and political position.

Social Rank. The northern and central emblems of rank were crests or coats of arms that showed the owner's ancestry; totem poles were one kind of crest. The system of social ranking among the Northwest Coast people was unique in native America. One anthropologist has called it rank without social class, because individuals were graded rather than classes of individuals. However, loose general groupings were discernible as chiefs, nobles, commoners, and slaves. Within each of these general categories, except for the slaves, there was a ranking of statuses from high to low.

The individual's social position was not totally rigid. One could raise his own rank or that of his children or heirs, sometimes by using wealth, sometimes by inheriting a higher position from another branch of the family that was in danger of dying out through lack of suitable heirs. Some promotion in social rank was in the chief's power—he could reward one of his group with a higher title.

Social position was certainly tied in with kinship much as the rank and position of king is inherited in European societies. Yet inheritance was subject to limitations. The right to assume a higher position had to be validated formally at a potlatch (to be discussed in the next section), and the rest of the group had to approve the new heir. Consequently, social rank did not depend solely on heredity or wealth, but was a combination of the two, plus the individual's achievements. Even people

A Northwest Coast village, probably Kwakiutl, showing house construction, canoes, and totem poles.

with very low rank, however, still had basic rights within their local group. Only slaves were truly without rights, and even they could be ransomed (for most slaves were war captives) or could sometimes buy their own freedom. Slavery was often a temporary condition, but it was a shameful one. Occasionally an owner would kill slaves to show his wealth and power. Male slaves were killed more often than women and children, probably because they were harder to control.

The Potlatch

Events of social importance were proclaimed at the feast called a *potlatch* from a Chinook word. Potlatching took many forms within a group, and varied considerably from group to group. At the potlatch, social position was formally validated. For instance, when an old chief died, the new chief gave a potlatch to announce his new rank, and all the guests showed by their presence that they accepted his claim and supported him. A potlatch given for a position as important as that of chief always lasted several days, with singing, dancing, drama, and games as well as feasting. The hosts invited entire nearby villages and spent months on preparations for feeding the guests— sometimes more than a year. Large numbers of people were fed, and important guests were given valuable gifts. Among the Northwest Coast people, it was a virtue to distribute wealth, not accumulate it. One accumulated only to have something to redistribute.

The chief depended on his entire kin or local group to support him in preparing and building up supplies. Though much food was eaten and many presents were given, a potlatch was a kind of investment, for the givers were guaranteed a return potlatch in the future. The potlatch, then, was a type of social security regardless of its immediate purpose, because future return was assured. It was also a way of redistributing the community's wealth not only with food but with gifts, for everyone in the community came. The poor (even this area had some orphans, widows, and people of very low rank) all got food, blankets, and equipment, and had an enjoyable time they could not have afforded on their own. The giver's kin group expressed its solidarity by helping with preparations and acting as co-hosts, and shared in the glory and esteem of giving a great potlatch. They too would be included in future potlatching when the guests repaid their obligations.

Other events worth celebrating had their potlatches too, but their style was far less lavish. The *rites of passage* when a boy came of age or a girl reached marriageable age, a new career, unusual success, even birthdays, all called for formal recognition. One could give only two or three really grand potlatches in a lifetime, but having lesser ones was a regular thing.

Potlatches also were given for services rendered, like help in a house-raising, and as a face-saving device. The guests would help to build the house, carve and raise the posts, and perform ceremonial offices—that is, guests of low rank helped with the hard labor while their chiefs visited with the host. But the host paid the guest chiefs in bounteous gifts, which they then distributed to their followers who had done the work. A high-ranking individual upon whom some misfortune fell or who suffered an embarrassment or an indignity might give a potlatch to wipe out his embarrassment, and at the same time demonstrate his right to high rank. The publicity following such a potlatch reestablished his self-esteem. He had acted the part of an important man and was recognized as one by the community.

In later times, when European disease had reduced the population, many titles fell vacant as whole family lines died out. A wild, sometimes quite destructive form of potlatching, the rival potlatch, developed.

The interior of the home of a Tlingit chief features some of the goods involved in a potlatch.

Potlatching had always been competitive, but in the last decades of the nineteenth century it seems to have gone beyond any past extremes. People who had no inherited rights to titles but who had become wealthy in trade goods beggared themselves giving away presents, to gain the community's recognition for their assumed titles and crests. Anyone who had the wealth could compete for these titles, and such rivalry produced some potlatches at which goods were destroyed, foods thrown away, and occasionally houses set on fire (whether by design or accident is uncertain). These flamboyant potlatches have had a lot of attention, and were important in showing how the culture was changing, but they were not typical. They were merely the way the newly rich tried to win the prestige of "old money."

With their potlatches the Coastal people confirmed their social positions, distributed wealth to the community, and used food (much of which was not storable). Potlatches helped integrate social groups by making kinfolk more dependent on each other, and were investments that would be returned, often with interest, in the future. They probably also channeled aggression into a harmless kind of rivalry that helped avoid more physical and socially destructive conflict.

Northwest Coast Art

The Northwest Coast people produced what many consider the finest aboriginal art north of Mexico. To see the Northwest style is to recognize it forever. Regional variations are visible, but the whole central and northern area did have one recognizable style. It is highly conventionalized art, its stylistic traditions rigidly adhered to by the makers; it should appeal to those who enjoy cubism and geometric designs. The style was applied in clothing, basketry, and the many forms of wood carving: totem poles, boxes, masks, grave markers, and house posts. It was a style unique in native America, resembling nothing in the art forms of the Southwest, Plains, East, or other areas. Authorities who suggest that the style shows influences from Asia or Polynesia have offered no evidence beyond stylistic inferences of the sort that are suggested as proof for trans-Pacific contacts.

Decorative art in the northern area was mostly two-dimensional, applied to flat surfaces. Lateral symmetry was the hallmark of this art: the figures were treated as though they had been split down the spine and spread out to either side of it. Northern artists disliked bare space, filling all areas with their designs. Central area artists had a style more like sculpture in treatment and use, and stressed mass and movement. Southern art forms were less dramatic, confined to simple tool embellishment, not large-scale design. Anyone who speaks of Northwest Coast art normally has the central and northern areas in mind.

Many scholars believe that the Haida of the Queen Charlotte Islands and the Tsimshian on the coast across from the Haida represent the center of art development. Their art shows a purity of style and organization, and the designs may well have spread out from this area. As the style is found both north and south of the Haida, it tends to weaken and gradually to pick up elements from neighboring peoples, the Eskimo to the north, the Salish and others to the south. The basic elements are found among what may be called the "core group": the Haida and Tsimshian and to a lesser extent, the Tlingit and Kwakiutl, but each tribe and indeed each artist throughout the area developed their own characteristics within the conventional patterns.

Northwest Coast designs depicted the supernatural or animal ancestors of lineage or kin groups, displayed as symbols of noble descent. Bear, Beaver, Eagle, Raven, Whale, and Wolf were the clan ancestors that appeared most often as crests or symbols. Artists followed the traditional ways of representing the animals by emphasizing one or two features: the whale was indicated by its large dorsal fin, the beaver by its large front teeth and broad, crosshatched tail, and the bear by its sharp claws. This was a thoroughly social kind of art, demonstrating, for all to see, the crests which were so highly esteemed.

The Chilkat division of the Tlingit tribe was famous for the fabrics they wove from cedar fiber and mountain-goat hair, used as ceremonial blankets, dance shirts, and skirts. The true loom was unknown on the Northwest Coast. The Chilkat blanket weaver twined horizontal threads with her fingers through vertical threads, suspended from a bar, and worked from top to bottom of the design. Like art applied to containers, houses, and crests, the Chilkat woven goods were designed as proof of prestige and wealth.

Copper brought from deposits at the Copper River in Alaska was beaten into one- to four-foot shield-shaped plaques called coppers, which were important in potlatch exchanges. Later artists engraved or embossed designs on sheet copper obtained from traders. Coppers were valuable and thus made gifts of great prestige and significance. Each time a copper was given away, its value grew; on extraordinary occasions, such as the succession of a major chief, one might be broken and thrown into the sea or the fire. In later times when potlatching became fiercely competitive, destroying a copper would challenge guests to give an even grander potlatch or sacrifice a copper of equal or greater value.

Tribes of the Northwest Coast

The Tlingit

The Tlingit language is related to Athabaskan. The most northerly of the Northwest Coast peoples, the Tlingit occupied the coast from Yakutat Bay in Alaska south to Cape Fox in British Columbia. They were divided into fourteen subtribes, the best known being the Chilkat, who made the blankets we have described. Being far to the north, the Tlingit showed traits also found among Eskimo groups. The two cultures probably were in contact, and borrowing moved both ways. The Tlingit also carried on trade with the interior Athabaskans of the Subarctic, getting from them copper, furs, and tools.

Like the Northwest Coast in general, Tlingit territory had high rainfall and mild temperatures. All the raw materials and vegetable foodstuffs of the lush, temperate-zone rain forest were available to the Tlingit. However, their northerly location meant greater snowfall than in the south. Consequently many artifacts of the Subarctic, like snowshoes, appeared in Tlingit territory.

Seasonal Life. The Tlingit had winter homes in villages on the coast or at the edge of a river. A stockade ran around the winter village for protection from raiders. The dwellings were large plank houses of the sort described, each housing several matrilineally related families. Each family had its own apartment within the house, divided by partitions along the walls. The center of the house was on a lower level than the sides and contained the hearth. Fish were hung from the beams to dry. Outside, racks were set up for drying fish during sunny weather. Lean-tos against the outer walls of the dwellings housed menstruating women or those giving birth. At one side of the village was the community cemetery.

Summer encampments were more casual. Families built temporary houses (Tlingit did not bring sideboard planking from the winter homes), but they lived in the open too, moving throughout the territory that belonged to their kin group. Kin groups also owned the fishing sites and controlled the hunting and collecting areas. The people followed their summer pursuits only in the areas where their kin connections gave them rights.

In winter, the Tlingit caught halibut and trout for their main diet and collected mussels along the coastline back at their "home" settlements. They also hunted fur-bearing animals at that time because the pelts were in prime condition. In spring the Tlingit women began their task of plant collecting, which lasted until late fall. Men caught candlefish with dip nets and traps. Those fish were boiled with hot stones in a wooden container, sometimes in a canoe, and the oil was skimmed off and stored. Throughout the year animals were hunted and fish caught and processed, some to be eaten immediately, some to be stored for winter when food was less easily obtained. Drying was the common means of preservation, although some food was stored in oil. As everywhere in this culture area, salmon was an important food; the Tlingit caught many varieties, among them coho, chum, and sockeye, from July through December. They took most with weirs that directed the fish into a trap. The Tlingit also hunted sea mammals like seals, sea otters, dolphins, and sea lions.

Social Organizations. Tlingit society was divided into two groups, each called a *moiety*, from the French word for "half." The moieties were Raven and Wolf, and every Tlingit belonged to one or the other. A man had to choose a wife from the other moiety, and children belonged to the moiety of their mother because descent was matrilineal. That is, Wolf men had Raven wives, and all their children, boys as well as girls, were Ravens. Each moiety was further divided into smaller groups called lineages, or matrilineages, because membership in them too was inherited from the mothers. One had to marry not only outside his own moiety, but outside his lineage. The lineages had names, owned crests and ceremonies, and were headed by chiefs.

Moiety division, common among American Indian societies, often was a way of giving mutual help. Among the Tlingit, a midwife assisted at births in the opposite moiety, never at births within her own, and the opposite moiety members performed all tasks connected with death, such as care of the body and preparations for cremation, which was standard with the Tlingit. The opposite moiety members mourned ritually and carved mortuary poles and mortuary boxes to contain the remains. The moiety of the deceased gave a potlatch and presented gifts to those of the opposite moiety who had taken part in the mortuary services.

Adult Tlingit of the higher ranks were expected to conduct themselves with restraint and dignity, and they encouraged their children to copy adult behavior. Parents rarely punished children physically; instead they shamed them when they behaved badly and praised them for good behavior. A regular part of childhood training was in behavior suitable to their rank. At the tender age of six or seven, boys moved to the home of one of their mother's brothers, where they learned how to fill their positions in life and became familiar with the traditions of the matrilineage.

The maternal uncle had authority over his sister's children. Because children belonged to their mother's matrilineage, the adult males of their lineage group were the uncles on the mother's side—never the fathers, who belonged to a different lineage. Usually one uncle took on the responsibility for a boy; the choice was expected to be mutual in that the boy took an interest in his uncle's calling (carver, hunter, shaman, or whatever), wished to be trained in that career, and expected to inherit his uncle's position. The important titles and their crests, however, usually passed to the oldest nephew if the child was generally competent.

Marriage. Daughters of high-ranking families were carefully guarded, not only to secure their virginity but also to keep them out of the sunlight, for light skin was prized. At her first menstruation a girl of high rank was secluded for a whole year (a commoner, two or three months), during which the women of her matrilineage taught her about lineage traditions and also the behavior expected of her high estate. A female slave attended her during this seclusion. Soon after its end it was expected that she would marry. Her parents' wealth and position were known, and her own rank depended mostly on the *bridewealth* that had been paid for her mother. This bridewealth consisted of gifts the family of the groom gave to the bride's family, not as payment for her, but to compensate the family for her loss and because giving gifts was common at any social event in the Northwest Coast area. Just as individuals were graded, bridewealth followed rank, important parents receiving more for their daughters than low-ranking families. Parents hoped of course for a favorable marriage with a high bridewealth.

The bride had to marry outside both her lineage and her moiety. A mother's brother's son or a father's sister's son was the most frequent choice; that union kept wealth within a close kin group and between people of relatively equal rank. The bride's parents sponsored the wedding and feasting, but the groom gave a potlatch for his new in-laws, and the couple usually moved in with one or the other set of parents. High-ranking, rich men often had more than one wife, but the first wife held the highest position.

Aggression. In spite of the mutual obligations binding members of opposite moieties, hostilities sometimes erupted between them, and even between matrilineages within the same moiety. To settle disagreements, feuds, or other conflicts, the hostile parties exchanged goods. There was a well-developed sense of "blood money," that is, payment for transgressions.

The Tlingit often conducted raids to take slaves or get revenge. Warriors wore armored jerkins or jackets made of rods or tough hide coverings, masks, and wooden helmets; they carried spears, clubs, and copper-bladed daggers. Warring groups took scalps, and sometimes impaled whole heads on poles and carried them home on exhibit. Warfare was glorified, and to be defeated was shameful. To restore peace, the combatants gave a series of potlatches at which hostages were exchanged and captives might be ransomed. Those not ransomed remained as slaves.

Tlingit Religion. Shamanism was the heart of the Tlingit religious practices. The shamans were thought by other Tlingit and by members of other Northwest Coast societies to be very powerful. They controlled supernatural spirits which they inherited matrilineally; that is, shamans passed their spirits to their sisters' sons. The spirits were thought to leave the body at death and enter the body of the new shaman, who revealed that he had been chosen by going into a deep trance. The new shaman then had to demonstrate his power, after which he inherited his uncle's ritual paraphernalia. Shamans were distinguished from the rest of the community by their hair, which was never cut or combed. They identified the spirits they could contact with representative masks, and they also possessed charms, amulets, and rattles that they used in ceremonies. As in many other tribes, shamans were curers of unnatural afflictions, which they relieved by sucking or blowing out the cause. Women could be shamans, but very few were.

Like the Plateau peoples, Tlingit observed simple first-salmon rites as well as rituals to honor other species that supplied their sustenance, but none of these public ceremonials was as important to them as to tribes in the south. Tlingit men were expected to have spirit helpers, but might inherit them as the shamans did their powers. The vision that a man sought came from among the spirits associated with his matrilineage.

An unimportant man of low rank could develop into a shaman by finding more spirits, and more potent ones, than ordinary persons had. Being able to contact the spirit world was a means of raising one's status and increasing prestige and wealth, for clients paid for shamans' services. No one, though, could accumulate enough wealth by shamanistic practices to rival a high-ranking wealthy man.

The Nootka of Vancouver Island

The Nootka occupied the western coast of Vancouver Island, a region buffeted by strong winds and heavy ocean waves caused by the violent southeasterly storms crashing into narrow bays. Fishing and whaling encampments were built on the seacoast, but the villages were sheltered on inlets some distance from the coast.

In most ways, Nootka life varied little from that of other tribes in this culture area. The winter village was the permanent community site, with houses of removable plank walls. As elsewhere, these planks were taken down and carried to the summer camps.

Social Organization. The Nootka had no moieties, clans, or lineages. They were organized *bilaterally*: their placement in social groups and inheritance ran through both men and women, with perhaps a slight preference for the paternal line. Extended families were the real units of society. They held land, including fishing grounds, berry and plant tracts, and shellfish beds, and also intangible property such as the rights to crests, titles, and ceremonies. Each extended family had a family head. Heads of the important families were the village chiefs. At a wedding, the father of the bride could bestow some of his family crests on his daughter, to be held in custody by his new son-in-law for his future grandchildren.

Among the northern Nootka groups, extended families joined into larger units, sometimes referred to as confederacies, but among the southerners the extended families and the village in which they lived remained the only social and political units. In the north, the highest-ranking chief (chiefs too had recognized grades) acted as representative of the confederacy under pressures from the outside, like war. Where the people did not organize in confederacies, each settlement was governed by the highest-ranking head of the extended families composing the community. A few noble families were the core of each local group, and they were responsible for its well-being, because they performed the rituals and saw that the taboos were obeyed. These were the privileged, but the commoners were related to them, usually being younger lines of the family. They owed the chiefs allegiance in return for participating in the rights to fishing and hunting grounds. Here again, social classes were not clear-cut; individuals, not classes, were ranked, and the chiefs depended on their non-noble followers and relatives for help in many pursuits, especially potlatching, which no one could manage alone.

Whaling. The Nootka differed most from other tribes of the Northwest Coast in their way of pursuing whales, which suggested contact with Eskimo whalers. A whaling party set out in a dugout canoe large enough to hold a crew of eight and to stow lines and floats. The whalers and oarsmen wore nothing but oils and clay smeared on their skin and hats for protection from the sun. Sometimes their faces were painted in designs with ritual meaning.

The perils of whaling were recognized by the Nootka community and by the crew, who observed rituals and taboos before going out to sea. The canoe owners and harpooners, men of high rank, had contact with important spirits. Their positions were handed down in family lines, as were charms helpful in whaling. One charm might be the skull of an ancestor who had been outstandingly successful as a whaler. The charms and spirit tokens were kept in a box that was taken along on the canoe. The captain also spoke to the whale spirits, though without using the word "whale," which was taboo during a hunt. Whales were referred to as "noble ladies," and the captain spoke magic words to entice them to come and be caught.

While the crew was on a hunt, the captain's wife lay without moving at home. She symbolized the whale and by lying quietly she kept the whale quiet. Her husband had not slept with her for some time before the hunt, nor had any of the crew had sexual relations with their wives. Besides these sexual taboos, the crew observed dietary restrictions, and if any of the crew or the captain broke the taboos, there would be no kill or it would be a very difficult hunt.

When the captain's wife was informed of the strike, she began a chant asking the whale to come to the village, where it would be most welcome. After the exhausting battle, swimmers from the boat would tie the dead whale's mouth shut and attach tow lines to pull the animal laboriously to shore. The villagers greeted the crew joyously on the beach, and the captain's wife came to continue her ritual observances on the shore. She greeted the dead whale, welcomed it to the village, and brought it a drink of fresh water.

With blubber knives, the whale was cut up, a piece being carefully conserved for the captain for a special ritual. Women turned the blubber to oil by stone-boiling it in cooking boxes after cutting off pieces for guests, chiefs, and commoners in order of rank. The captain's own kinfolk received their shares in private, then everyone joined in a feast.

Dead whales sometimes drifted ashore, and the Nootka treated these chance events as another form of whale hunting. They performed rituals to make them happen more often, just as they did to ensure successful hunts by harpooning. Human corpses or skulls were used in the whaling ritual, not because the Nootka lacked respect for the dead—indeed, they feared and respected them greatly—but because remains were considered extremely potent magic. Whalers built a shrine away from the houses, where they placed the bodies, or sometimes carved images, around the figure of a whale. The chief, the harpooner, or the captain from families owning these rites (no one else could use them) was always a ritual specialist along with his other activities. He bathed, abstained from food and sex, and spoke his incantations and sang his songs nightly in front of his shrine.

Canoes. The Nootka also had a smaller sailing canoe that might hold three people. It was almost as long as a whaling canoe, but it was not nearly so wide. Captain Cook, the eighteenth-century explorer, fresh from his voyages to Polynesia, saw it and marveled that it did not roll over without a stabilizing outrigger. Large canoes were a specialty of the Nootka, who were admired for their craftsmanship by neighboring tribes. Nootka canoes had high prows and low sterns, both pieces separate from the main body and lashed on with fiber cords threaded through holes bored in both sections. The owner's crests were carved and painted on the stern and bow.

Only a wealthy man could afford a large canoe because of the amount of labor required to make one. The job took many days, and all workers had to be fed. A large cedar tree had to be felled and split in half. One half was selected and charred with fire and then chiseled out. Craftsmen who specialized in canoe building used adzes for the finer work of trimming the walls and finishing the outside. When the hull was thin enough, it was filled with water into which hot stones were dropped, so the craftsmen could spread the hull, inserting cross-beams to hold the width.

Because cedar was easy to work, canoes could be made in about a month. The largest canoes, reaching sixty feet and carrying ninety to a hundred people, were used for war, transport to summer camps, and visiting. They were too large and clumsy to be safe whaling vessels. None of the canoes had rudders; the paddles were used for steering. Both men and women paddled; according to a European visitor of the late eighteenth century, women's paddles were blunt at the tip but men's were sharp for use as weapons in sea battles.

Dentalia. The Nootka controlled a resource greatly prized on the Northwest Coast—beds of shellfish called *dentalia*, named after their toothlike appearance. It was the shells, not the animal, that were valuable, and they were not easy to reap. A tool like a stiff broom was rammed down on them with just enough force to clamp a few of the long, thin shells in its points and hold them while the fisher pulled the catch back up. Dentalia beds were far enough offshore that shellfishing had to be done from a boat. Like fishing stations and berry tracts, dentalia beds belonged to families who kept their exact position a carefully guarded secret. The shells, divided into three sizes by length, were important in trade with the north, the interior, and down into California.

The Wolf Dance. The Nootka had an important winter ceremony, performed by a group called the Dancing Society. Because it involved a myth about wolf spirits, it is referred to as the Wolf Dance, and it was a kind of initiation rite. The elaborate performance lasted for days. Children and adolescents practiced their parts, and there were many feasts and dances, along with a lot of comedy and mirth, though the ceremony itself was serious.

The myth was about a Nootka ancestor, who intruded into the home of the Wolf Spirits. They taught him their songs and dances and ritual behavior, which he in turn taught to his people when he got back home. Each year the Wolf Dance taught these things to the initiates. Every child of the community participated at least once. Children were given their family crests to carry, and high-ranking children went through the ceremony several times to receive all the crests of their distinguished line. This ceremonial taught and reinforced each child's place in society and entertained the community as well. The whole ritual ended with a potlatch.

The Nootka attitude toward the supernatural followed the usual pattern. They believed that spirit helpers were necessary to success and sought them in spirit quests, and shamans who had many spirit helpers were needed to relieve unnatural illness or bad luck.

The Chinook, Traders at the Dalles

At the Dalles, a series of rapids on the Columbia River, a rather small tribe called the Chinook built up a reputation as traders and intermediaries controlling the flow of products up and down the river. All people coming along the river had to stop and carry their canoes around the rapids, and this portage took them through Chinook territory. Less is known about the Chinook than the other tribes we have sketched, but the information that has been recorded is a fine example of precontact trade.

Many items of their material culture as well as their language suggest that the Chinook were closely related to Plateau peoples. Yet in grasping the economic opportunity laid before them by their strategic location at the Dalles, they developed a unique adaptation. They were certainly in contact with the Plateau people, as well as with coastal societies and groups from the Great Basin. The rapids and waterfalls of the Dalles were swift, slowing both people and salmon as they traveled. The Chinook found the fish easy prey, and used their fortunate position to set up a sort of trade depot where people of varied tribal backgrounds met.

To the Chinook trading station at the Dalles, then, came peoples from areas of poor fishing to trade pelts of animals from the interior for dried salmon. Warring tribes brought captives, the Nootka brought valuable dentalia, and Basin peoples brought basketry and woven rabbit-skin robes. Candlefish oil was an important trade item, as was oil from seals and whales. Commercial interaction extended from Alaska into California and the Desert Basin and across the Rocky Mountains into the Plains. The Dalles was the hub of a wheel with spokes radiating in all directions, and the Chinook controlled the hub.

The first Europeans who saw these people left us little ethnographic description. The Lewis and Clark expedition passed through with Sacajawea, a Shoshoni woman interpreter; and an artist, George Catlin, visited the Chinook later. But they stayed just long enough to record the most obvious data. Consequently, reconstruction is difficult, and our picture of the Chinook is tenuous.

The Chinook language, belonging to the Penutian phylum, became the core of a trade language in historic times. The words *potlatch* and *hootch* (liquor) are derived from Chinook, which also gave its name to the desiccating wind that blows down the eastern slope of the Rockies. Chinook trade jargon was a combination of Chinook, words from other Indian languages, and some European words. With this tongue peoples who met at the Dalles carried on their business.

Although the Chinook subsistence basis—salmon—was typical of the Northwest Coast area, the rest of their culture was a modification of the Northwest culture. The Chinook had no totem poles, masks, or dramatic art; they lived in pithouses with only the gabled roofs above ground level, suggesting the Plateau much more than the Coast. Chinook obtained most of their canoes by trade as well as the box containers and the bowls (fashioned from mountain-sheep horn) they used.

Like some other people of both the Northwest Coast and the Plateau, the Chinook practiced head flattening, using a cradle that pressed down on the infant's forehead to produce a slanting or flat-fronted skull. The result was considered attractive. The Flathead Indians of the eastern Plateau got their English name from this practice, but strangely, it was not the Flathead people themselves, but visiting Chinook, or Chinook slaves, whom the Europeans saw; the Flathead did not practice head deformation.

The Chinook apparently had a social ranking system, but it was less rigid than those farther north. Their sociopolitical unit was the village, and kin lines were traced through both maternal and paternal sides, although paternal lines appear to have been emphasized. The eldest of the kin group became the headman if he was competent.

Chinook religion emphasized the vision quest and first-salmon rites; villages conducted their own ceremonies. Both males and females sought spirit helpers in visions, although guardian spirits were vital only for males because success in hunting and fishing depended upon supernatural contacts.

The Kwakiutl Warriors

The Kwakiutl, who lived on Vancouver Island and the nearby mainland, were much like the Nootka in their general way of life. The Kwakiutl had no tribal identity outside of their common language; they lived in villages that were essentially independent of each other. We consider them here because they were prominent in an area we have not previously discussed: warfare.

The Kwakiutl fought not for political power or economic gain, but for social prestige or to avenge the death of a relative or fellow villager. Kwakiutl wars were usually between villages of the same tribe; sometimes a few local groups joined together for an attack, but the resulting war could not be considered national. Most Kwakiutl wars were ceremonial in nature and did not involve massive killing or destruction: killing one individual usually satisfied the attacking party.

The most common reason for war was revenge for a death from warfare or murder, or even death from disease or accident. Death was considered a blow against the group, shameful and insulting as well as grievous, and it could be obliterated only by the death of someone else of equal social rank. The object of revenge might not have been responsible for the first death, and might not even have been a relative or a member of the same group as whoever committed the initial act of violence. Even if death had resulted from sickness, revenge through another death was necessary. The attitude of those who had suffered a death, from whatever cause, was to make someone else mourn for a loss. A high-ranking man might get up a war party saying, "Why should I mourn? Let someone else wail."

Another reason Kwakiutl went to war was for social prestige. A man could acquire the social rank, privileges, and symbolic crests of another by killing him and taking over his position, usually keeping his women and children as slaves. Except for slaves, plunder was of little importance, and Kwakiutl never waged war to gain land.

Although a war party might include as many as two hundred men,

CHARACTERISTICS OF THE NORTHWEST COAST TRIBES

Clothing	Food production	Equipment	Shelter	Social and political organization	Religion	Warfare
Very little clothing Woven ponchos for rain Fiber shirts and skirts Furs Basketry rain hats Tunics Sun hats (Nootka)	Fishing Hunting (sea mammals and land mammals) Gathering (plants and shellfish)	Spears Bows and arrows Clubs Copper daggers (Tlingit) Slate knives Harpoons Canoes Mats Weirs Traps Woodworking tools Cedar boxes Horn, bone, and stone projectile points Sheephorn spoons and bowls Armor of rods and hides	Large, gabled plank houses	Families Lineages Clans Moieties (Tlingit) Villages Northern tribes matrilineally organized; others bilateral Social stratification: chiefs, nobles, commoners, and slaves Extended families joined in confederacy (Nootka)	Myths Spirits Spirit helpers Shamans Wolf Dance (Nootka) Vision Quest First Salmon rites	Exchange of goods to settle disagreements Raids Warfare prominent among Kwakiutl

only a few were specialists. Boys of the proper social position and disposition—younger brothers of chiefs, usually—were trained early for roles as warriors. They were taught to be cruel; they learned to use weapons, to run and swim to keep themselves physically fit, and to perform feats of endurance. These warriors were humorless and always ready to fight. Few married and raised families.

Kwakiutl weapons were bows and arrows, clubs, spears, and slings. The men wore body armor made of wooden slats, and war canoes capable of carrying fifty people bore them to the enemy village.

War parties attacked by surprise. Although no village knew exactly when attack might come, there was a conventional fighting season from about the middle of August to the first of October, when the water was not rough and frequent fogs helped conceal the approach of attackers. At that time of year, villagers moved to stockades, fortified hills, or other spots that could be defended easily. Kwakiutl also used trickery in attack, such as dressing as women and posing as harmless travelers or visitors. Although the frequency of Kwakiutl warfare should not be exaggerated, combat could be fierce. Kwakiutl always attacked at night, and might kill or behead sleeping enemies. After such an assault, they displayed any head taken as a trophy on a pole in front of their villages. The Kwakiutl had a reputation as ferocious fighters, and apparently they enjoyed that reputation.

Suggestions for Further Study

Bibliography

Codere, Helen. 1966. *Fighting with Property.*

An analysis of the Kwakiutl economic system of the potlatch and its implications for social structure, as well as a study of the relationship between the potlatch and warfare during the period of acculturation.

Drucker, Philip. 1955. *Indians of the Northwest Coast.*

A general survey of cultures and aspects of culture.

Krause, Aurel. 1956. *The Tlingit Indians.*

A translation of a study made by a German in the last quarter of the nineteenth century.

Price, John. 1979. *Indians of Canada.* Scarborough, Ontario: Prentice Hall of Canada, Ltd.

Ray, Verne F. 1963. *Primitive Pragmatists.*

An ethnography of the Modoc Indians based on the memories of native informants, discussing problems of change and the Modoc War.

Spier, Leslie. 1930. *Klamath Ethnography.*
The classic study of the Klamath tribe of the Plateau area.

Spinden, Herbert J. 1908. *The Nez Perce Indians.*
A general study of the aboriginal society and change resulting from contact with Europeans.

Other Pertinent Works

Boas, Franz. 1966. *Kwakiutl Ethnography.*

de Laguna, Frederica. 1960. *The Story of a Tlingit Community.*

Drucker, Philip. 1951. *The Northern and Central Nootkan Tribes.*

Ford, C. S. 1941. *Smoke from Their Fires.*

Josephy, Alvin. 1965. *The Nez Perce Indians and the Opening of the Northwest.*

Rohner, Ronald, and E. C. Rohner. 1970. *The Kwakiutl Indian of British Columbia.*

Steward, Julian H. 1938. *Basin Plateau Aboriginal Sociopolitical Groups.*

MAJOR GROUPS AND LANGUAGES OF THE PLATEAU AND THE NORTHWEST COAST

Language phylum	Language family	Cultural division
PLATEAU		
Penutian	Klamath-Modoc	Klamath Modoc
	Cayuse	Cayuse
	Sahaptin-Nez Perce	Klikitat Nez Perce Umatilla Wallawalla Yakima
Undetermined	Salishan	Flathead Kalispel Lillooet Sanpoil Shuswap Spokan Thompson
NORTHWEST COAST		
Na-Dene	Haida	Haida
	Tlingit	Tlingit

MAJOR GROUPS AND LANGUAGES (continued)

Language phylum	Language family	Cultural division

NORTHWEST COAST (continued)

Language phylum	Language family	Cultural division
Penutian	Chinookan	Chinook
	Coos	Coos
	Tsimshian	Tsimshian
Undetermined	Salishan	Bella Coola Chehalis Klallam Lummi Quinault Salish Tillamook
	Wakashan	Bella Bella Kwakiutl Makah Nootka
	Chimakuan	Quileute

5

CALIFORNIA

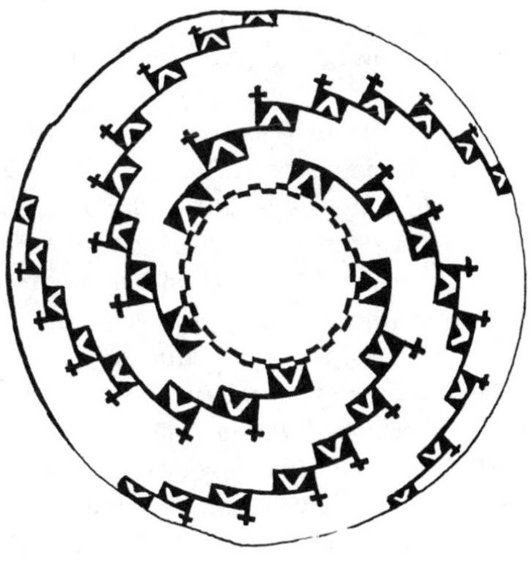

Mission Indian basketry design.

Maidu Creation Myth

Long ago there were no stars, no moon, no sun. There was only darkness and water. A raft floated on the water, and on the raft sat a turtle. Then from the sky, a spirit came down and sat on the raft. "Who are you?" asked Turtle. "Where do you come from?" "I came from above," answered the spirit. "Can you create some land for us?" asked Turtle. "We need dry land and some people to live on it."

Creator said, "To create land I must have some earth to make it from." So Turtle offered to dive to the bottom of the water and bring up some earth. He was gone a very long time, and when he came back to the surface, he had only a small amount of earth under his nails because the rest had washed away in his long swim to the surface.

Creator scraped the earth from under Turtle's nails and rolled it around in his hand. At first nothing happened. Then the earth began to grow. It enlarged until it became as big as the world. The raft was grounded, and mountains stretched toward the sky. But it was still dark, so Turtle asked, "Can you make it light?" The spirit said, "I will tell my sister to come up," and to the east the sun began to rise. For a while it was bright and warm, and Turtle sat in the light, but then the sun went down, and Turtle asked the spirit to make more light. Creator said, "I will make my brother come," and the moon rose.

Then turtle said, "What else are you going to do?" The Creator said, "I will show you," and he made a great tree grow. It had many different kinds of acorns on it. Turtle and the Creator sat for several days in the shade of the tree. They were pleased with the things the spirit had made. In a few days Coyote and Rattlesnake came up out of the ground. Then the spirit called birds from the sky and made more trees and animals to live in the woodland.

Then the spirit said that something else was needed, and he made people. He took earth and mixed it with water and made two figures, a man and a woman. The first man was called Kuksu, and the first woman was called Morning Star. And by and by there were many people on the earth.

For a long time everyone spoke the same language, but suddenly people began to speak in different tongues. Kuksu, however, could speak all the languages, so he called his people together and told them the names of the animals in their own languages, taught them to get food, and gave them their laws and rituals. Then he sent each tribe to a different place to live. Then he too left. He went to the spirit house that was up above.

The Environment

The culture area called California has somewhat different boundaries from the state of California, though it includes much of the same territory. The eastern edge of the state is part of the Great Basin culture area, while the southeast section fits best in the Southwestern culture area. In the north the transition from Northwest Coast into California is so gradual that border groups like the Yurok could reasonably be considered with either culture area. We have placed them in this chapter although, as you will see, they showed characteristics of Northwest Coast culture as well.

Within the culture area of California, three different geographic regions exist: northern, central, and southern. Set off by climate, altitude, and land forms, each region has different kinds of animals and plants; thus the people too adapted differently to each area. The native languages followed this geographic pattern as well, with one or two language groups dominant in each area.

All over California, the numerous streams, rivers, valleys, and mountains created secluded pockets where people could settle and flourish cut off from the other societies around them, and a denser population developed in California than in most other regions. This area, geographically only about 1 percent of America north of Mexico, sheltered about 10 percent of the native population.

Because the California area shows so much diversity in such a small space, you may wonder why we think of it as a separate culture area instead of dividing it among the other culture areas around it. There are three things that unify California and set it off as a single area: people everywhere used wild foods, especially seeds; populations were dense and moved around very little; and elaborate death ceremonies and puberty rites were common. Of the three regions of California, the one most typical in these respects was the central area.

Northern California

In the northern region, the coast is rocky, battered by weather and waves into palisades and cliffs. Swift rivers rush down into valleys from the high mountains, and rainfall is plentiful. The mountains are well watered, and heavily wooded with tall sequoia, ponderosa pine, and Douglas fir. Some peaks are high enough to be snow-covered all year round; and both Mount Lassen and Mount Shasta were still active volcanoes in the early days of Indian occupation. In the mountains and forests, deer, bear, wildcat, coyote, and wolverine were abundant, and before the Europeans came the bighorn mountain sheep and wapiti were

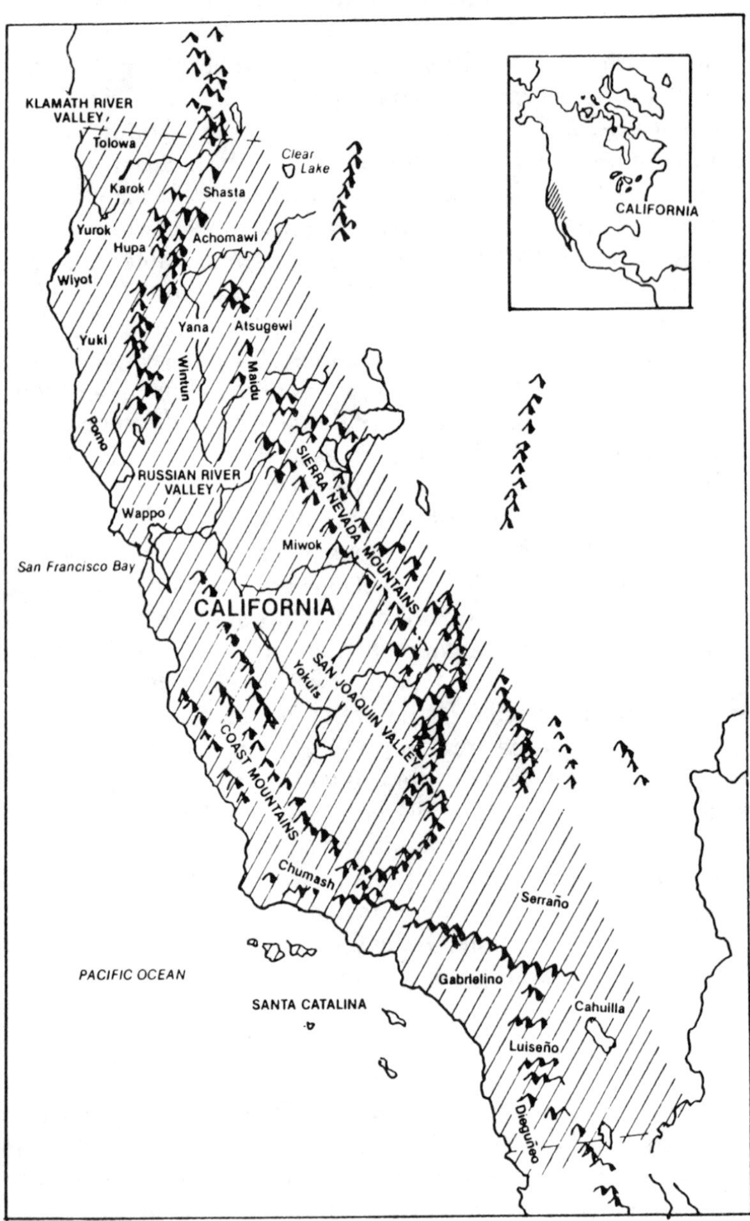

The California culture area and its tribes.

common. Many of these animals provided food, but even more important to northern Californians were the fish and shellfish along the coast, and the bass, trout, salmon, and sturgeon in the many rivers. Hokan languages were predominant in the north.

Central California

This is a land of contrast and great diversity: inland lakes and ponds nestled among foothills, spectacular mountains with cascading rivers and streams, broad lush valleys, and coasts rich in shellfish. The variety of plants provided the California basketmakers with a wide selection of fibers, and the especially abundant oaks supplied acorns and hardwood. Fish and game were plentiful in the days before cities and industrial and commercial development. The climate is mild, except occasionally in the central valley, where the temperature may go above 90 degrees in summer and sometimes drops to freezing in winter. Heavy fogs often blanket the coast, though rainfall is less than in the north. This region is larger than the other two and can be considered "classic" Californian. It was home for many groups of Penutian speakers, each having enough food and building supplies in its own rather small territory. They could gather plenty of one food or another in nearly every month of the year, and the acorns and seeds that were the staple part of their diet could be stored in anticipation of any shortage.

Southern California

Today, through extensive irrigation, southern California has become a major garden and agricultural area, but the land is naturally dry, and the mountains are less timbered than in the north. There are fewer rivers, and they flow through steep, barren canyons where fishing is difficult. The climate goes from warm to hot in winter as well as summer, though the mountains are cooler. The sandy beaches slope gradually to the water, without the high, abrupt cliffs of the north. Rainfall is scant, and lakes are rare. The tropical plants that grow in the area today survive only with artificial watering. Native forms are desert vegetation— such as chaparral, mesquite, and sagebrush—and oak, which is not as abundant as farther north. Indians of the area ate acorns and also seeds from plants like mesquite, which also provided wood for building, fibers for baskets, and a black dye. Animals of the region include kangaroo rat, horned toad, pronghorn antelope, squirrel, and rabbit, all hunted by the Indians. Great mounds of seashells from ancient times tell us that people lived on the coast even then and ate shellfish. Shoshonean was the dominant language.

California Peoples

Two mountain systems, the Coast Ranges and the Sierra Nevadas, run through California from north to south, roughly parallel to the coast. We have assigned the territory east of the Sierras to either the Great Basin or the Southwest. Between the two mountain systems lie fertile valleys where many small groups lived. Most of their names sound unfamiliar today: Maidu, Miwok, Yokuts, Wintun. California tribes were small, rarely larger than a few hundred people, and most stayed close to home. They had no need to travel, for wild foods were plentiful almost everywhere, and no one needed materials that could not be found in home territory. Their society was simple, but they had economic security.

In the remarkably diverse California culture area, the people spoke more than one hundred languages, from every major North American Indian phylum except Aleut-Eskimo and Macro-Siouan. While some other culture areas had as many languages, none is so small. Why was California so rich in variety? Many believe the "fishtrap" theory explains it. The narrow coastal plain is blocked off from the rest of the continent by its north-south mountain ranges. The only way people could enter was by crossing the mountains, which have few passes, or by making their way over the southeastern California deserts. Thus, migrants were mostly small groups from diverse linguistic and cultural backgrounds who found their way into California from less desirable places. Once there, they found living conditions so favorable that they settled down and adjusted their ways to the pleasant conditions, like fish swimming into a trap.

The Promised Land

Our reconstructed picture begins, then, with people migrating from Asia, moving slowly southward over thousands of years. Most groups turned east, or continued south, or settled in intermediate territory. But splinter groups from almost all linguistic and social divisions must have made the trek over the mountains into a place that may well have seemed like the promised land.

Food Resources

What was the promise in this land? Anthropologists generally measure the wealth of a nonindustrial society by the amount of food available to the people. The early Californians had so much wild food within easy reach that agriculture held no appeal—even simple farming would have required more labor for less food than gathering wild plants. The climate too was agreeable, with almost no freezing weather except in high

Hupa Indian woman leaching tannic acid out of acorn meal.

mountains, and temperatures rarely above 90 degrees outside the desert. Only the Northwest Coast was richer in easy-to-find food. California's aboriginal population may have reached one million.

So important were acorns in California cultures that they are worth describing. The many species of oaks there produce acorns big enough to amaze people from the East, who are accustomed to an inch-long nut. The western acorn is about three inches long and very plump and nutritious. It has one serious disadvantage: it contains tannic acid, which causes severe gastrointestinal disturbance and can kill infants. At some remote time, lost to both archaeology and ethnography, the California people learned to grind acorns to flour, which they then leached with water by spreading it in a shallow pit in clean sand and pouring water over it. The water rinsed the acorn meal, washing away the tannin. The acorn harvest was reliable year after year, with little or no fluctuation, and the nuts and flour were easily stored for winter, which, indeed, was not severe.

Acorns were not the only means of subsistence. Pine nuts too were plentiful, along with mesquite beans, sage, and grass seeds. Also important were game—deer and many other species—and fish, particularly in the central and northern regions. With these resources, California developed the densest population north of Mexico in aboriginal times.

Technology

California people made almost no pottery, but they were among the best basketmakers in the world. It was the women who wove baskets, and they developed the craft into an art. Their raw material ranged from yucca fibers—used for sandals, straps, mats, and nets as well as baskets—to grasses, stems, and roots of ferns, bushes, and trees such as Douglas fir and the many species of oak.

The Californians made many kinds of canoes, from dugouts and planked boats in some areas to the common raft made of tule reeds (bulrushes). All were made for fishing, for the Californians traveled very little. Only the Chumash seem to have gone beyond their home grounds, exploring the ocean coastal regions north and south of what is now Santa Barbara. The Chumash built stronger vessels of planks to weather the rough coastal waters and the turbulent currents. Indians at the edge of the Northwest Coast made smaller versions of the dugout canoes typical in the northerly areas, while the inland tribes made tule canoes.

In the mild California climate people could get along with very little clothing, wearing nothing elaborate except perhaps on ceremonial occasions. Children went naked, older girls and women wore fiber or hide skirts, and men wrapped skins around their hips. When they needed footwear it was of hide or fiber, but many people went barefoot most of the time. A skin cape slung over the shoulder provided protection from rain and wind. Fancy apparel being unnecessary, the Indians often decorated their bodies with paints and tattoos, and wore shell, bone, wood, and stone necklaces and feathered hair ornaments.

The mild climate also made durable housing unnecessary. It was almost always simple, and often temporary, made of grass, tules, brush, or bark, occasionally covered with soil. The people lived outdoors much of the time. In the hot southern areas, shelter from heat and sun was far more important than protection from cold or rain. Some dwellings housed several families; some housed only a couple and their children. The Yurok and their neighbors in the north needed sturdier homes than those in the south, so they built plank houses that were similar to those of the Northwest Coast, though smaller.

Sweathouses were important in this culture area. They were

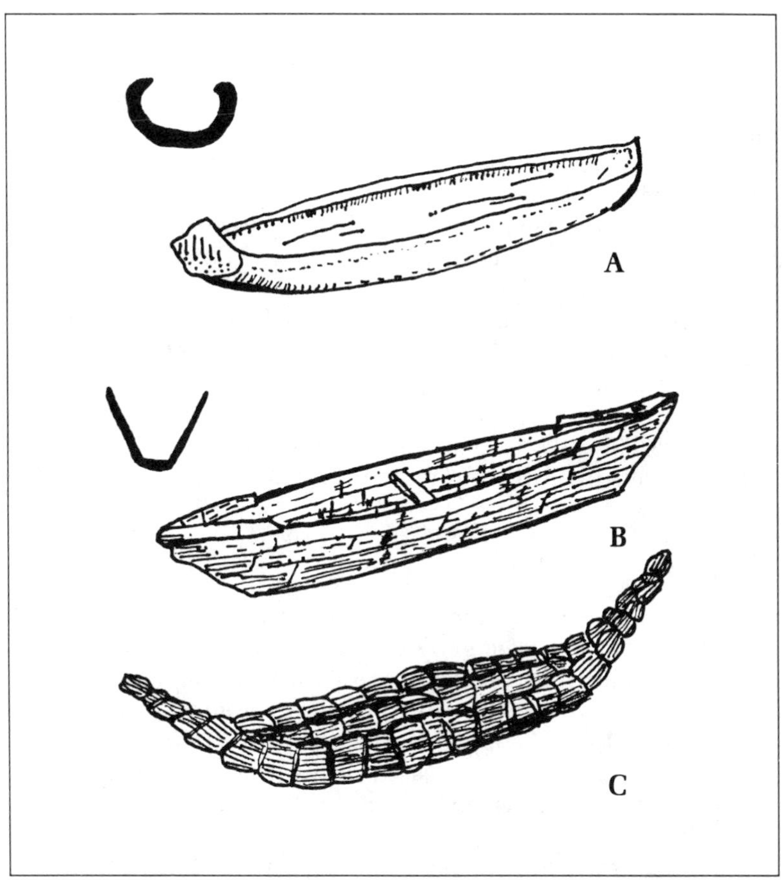

Yurok river canoe (A), Chumash plank canoe (B), and tule-reed canoe (C). Not to scale.

substantial structures often partially underground, covered with earth or sod over a framework of branches, bark slabs, or planks in the northwest. A hole in the roof let smoke escape. Here men induced sweating by direct heat from a fire, not from steam generated by pouring water over hot stones. Women almost never entered sweathouses, which were men's sites of ritual purification, medical treatment, and relaxation. They have been likened to men's clubs. They existed throughout the culture area with the exception of the southern desert.

Political Organization

Clan organization was largely lacking in California, the basic unit being the small village. Some villages were just a few families living together, but others had up to two or three hundred people. In the San Joaquin Valley, all the Yokuts villages together may have totaled 20,000 people, an unusual size for California.

The local groups, the villages, were really autonomous, though people from associated villages recognized their common customs and language. Such groups of independent villages made up the unit anthropologists usually call a tribelet. Villages almost never waged war against others in the same tribelet, and even between tribelets war was very rare. These were peaceful people, if for no other reason than that aggression brought no benefits.

The village leader, usually called the headman, governed the local group. Although he generally inherited his position, others obeyed him only as long as they respected his wisdom and experience. He had no police support nor any other means of coercing his fellow villagers. Throughout California, no one, not even the headman, was considered above the others by birth, and there was little social inequality of any kind.

Religion

The shaman was often the most powerful and respected person in the community. He or she frequently played an important part in selecting the village headman by revealing the will of the supernatural. Some shamans obtained power from dreams, others from visions induced by hallucinogenic drugs. People believed shamans could control weather and cure disease, and often feared as well as respected them: the shamans' contact with the supernatural made them dangerous as well as powerful.

Ceremonies were most elaborate in central California, where long series of rituals took place every year. The people celebrated girls' puberty as well as boys' initiation into men's societies. Costumes for the dances that accompanied these rituals were often very elaborate. In the north people honored the first salmon fishing each year and often had lavish death and mourning rites. The dead were usually buried in the north; in the south, cremation was the custom.

Indians in California had many kinds of cultures, yet within the three natural divisions the ways of adjusting to the environment and the styles of life had much in common. We will describe one society from each region, north, central, and south, to give some of the flavor of life in California in those early times.

The Yurok

Outsiders first contacted the Yurok in the middle of the nineteenth century when aboriginal culture was still intact. In addition, tribal elders

Yurok house made of planks.

remembered and described the old ways for ethnologists who visited the Yurok at the beginning of the twentieth century. Consequently, we have a much clearer picture of the unacculturated Yurok than we have of tribes where the Spanish brought vast change much earlier.

The Yurok lived in the lower Klamath River Valley, about two hundred miles north of San Francisco Bay. Situated in this transition zone between the potlatch-givers to the north and the "classic" Californians to the south, they blended a northwestern California culture with that of the Northwest Coast.

The Yurok built their villages near water—on the riverbank, at the river's mouth, or on the seacoast. From all the fifty or more permanent, year-round villages, people hunted deer and gathered seeds, acorns, and firewood in the hilly, heavily wooded land extending away from the rivers and the coast. At the time of first contact, the Yurok population totaled about 2,500, clustered into seven population centers. A typical village consisted of six or seven redwood plank houses—smaller and less elaborate than the Northwest Coast houses—and one wooden sweathouse for the men, which also served as their clubhouse and alternate sleeping quarters.

The Yurok shared their valley and their way of life with their neighbors upstream, the Karok and the Hupa. In fact, most of the three groups' material and nonmaterial culture was identical: legends, costumes, ceremonies, houses, and behavior. But there was one difference—the tribes spoke totally unrelated, mutually unintelligible languages. The

Yurok language belonged to the Macro-Algonkian phylum, the Karok language to the Hokan, and the Hupa to the Na-Dene. The cultural similarities and the linguistic differences have led anthropologists to believe that the Yurok were there first, and that when the others arrived, they adopted Yurok culture.

Subsistence

The Yurok lived on salmon and acorns supplemented with deer, seeds, bulbs, and mussels. Very rarely they killed a sea lion or found a whale stranded on the beach. Food was abundant, at least enough to support permanent settlements, but it was never wasted. The Yurok felt two sparse meals a day were enough, and they ridiculed gluttony.

Men fished individually with nets, usually at privately owned fishing spots chosen for their productivity. When the salmon were running, one man could catch enough fish in a day to feed his family for a whole season. The salmon ran mostly in the spring and autumn, but since there were several species, there were fish in the river almost every month of the year. Men who did not own or share in a special fishing spot had to fish in the open river, where the catch was less bountiful.

The heart of Yurok life was the river. All nourishment and human contact, all transportation and communication, followed the watercourse. The Yurok reckoned direction not by north or south, but by words for "upstream" and "downstream," even along the seacoast. As one follows the river, upstream is at various times north, south, east, and west.

Prime deer-hunting lands were also privately owned. Wealthy men controlled large areas of good deer land where they could hunt with little effort, while poor men had to journey far from the village to the unclaimed lands. The Yurok concepts of wealth and prestige clearly came from the Northwest Coast, but without the accompanying crests and symbols.

Gathering acorns and seeds was women's work. After the women pounded the acorns and leached them to remove the tannic acid, they usually boiled the meal with hot stones in a basket to make porridge. The Yurok made no pottery, using instead wooden containers and baskets so finely made that they held water.

These Indians cultivated just one plant, a strong native variety of tobacco, which men smoked to make themselves drowsy before retiring.

Social and Political Organization

The Yurok, Karok, and Hupa all were so loosely organized that it is more accurate to call each an ethnic group than a tribe. All the Yurok shared a culture and a language, interacted and communicated, intermarried and traced relatives, but still they did not think of themselves as a unit. People saw themselves as village residents, not as tribal members. Yurok folk tales are full of references to homesickness and love of one's birthplace. This kind of local attachment and loyalty to kin and lifelong friends are typical of all the California Indians.

Yurok leaders were the wealthy individuals; they drew power and status from relatives, followers, and semidependents and gave them back assistance, food, and protection. A village acted as a unit only if its entire population was one wealthy man's entourage. This was a transition zone, as we have noted, blending the rigid ranking of the Northwest Coast and the more democratic society of central California.

Besides having no chiefs, the Yurok had no priests. Each village ceremony was directed by an elder male who knew most about it from his years of participation.

War and murder were the same thing for the Yurok, who undertook both for revenge, never for plunder or prestige. The revenge they wanted was retaliation for a death thought to have been caused by witchcraft. Deaths caused feuds that could have totally disrupted society if there had not been a means of settling them: blood money. When murder had been committed, wealthy men from both sides met to calculate the value of all property lost, injuries sustained, and people killed. They then set retribution to be paid in dentalia shells and other material. Representatives from each side met, examined the items offered for retribution, and danced over them. Once the payments were accepted, the conflict was settled; anyone who held a grudge after that was not behaving properly. Each side paid the other for losses and injuries instead of subtracting the lesser from the greater and paying the difference.

Compensation for the degrees of injury from insult to murder was finely scaled. How much was a man's life worth? The Yurok said it was worth as much as had been exchanged for his mother when she married his father, the bridewealth. A man whose mother had brought much bridewealth—dentalia, deerskins, other furs, and perhaps a canoe—was worth a great deal in blood money.

All Yurok rights were individual rights, and all crimes were committed against individuals. There was no state or township to administer punishment; compensation in a dispute had to be agreed on by the parties involved. The kin on both sides shared that responsibility, not as a group but as a succession of individuals; the closer the relationship to plaintiff or defendant, the greater the degree of responsibility.

Wealth and Property

The Yurok and their neighbors were obsessed with wealth, which they counted primarily in dentalia. These shells were used as a standard of value and a medium of exchange, the closest thing to all-purpose money found anywhere in aboriginal times. The dentalia were graded into standard sizes and strung on a measured string. A string containing ten shells was more valuable than one with eleven smaller shells, even though the strings were the same length; larger shells, especially without blemish, were more valuable. The Yurok graded the dentalia far more precisely than did the Nootka from whom they obtained the shells.

Being wealthy meant having a well-built house on a desirable site, with chests of treasure in its rooms. The finest houses had names, like English manors. Wealth meant owning good fishing and hunting lands that could be leased out, and paying high bridewealth for wives from other wealthy and prestigious families, thus increasing one's own wealth and status. It meant too that one's daughters would be sought after and would marry into wealthy families who pay handsomely.

Only a few men were so wealthy. Most owned a simple house and some small share in a fishing place. They might take years to pay for their brides, partly with their labor. Any friendship, kinship, or other attachment with a wealthy man was a great security to the common man. A few were so poor or so deeply in debt that they had to give themselves up into debt slavery to a rich man. A slave or servant to a rich household often had a more comfortable life than a poor but free man.

Everyone wanted to be rich. They thought about wealth constantly, prayed for it, and behaved according to standards of moderation and good manners that were believed to bring it. But in fact they could do very little to become wealthy. A very few men were traders or built dugout redwood canoes that they sold to the neighboring tribes, but wealth generally stayed among the wealthy. The Yurok did not hold potlatches like the tribes of the Northwest Coast, and when a man died, his sons received most of his possessions, the rest going to his daughters, kinfolk, and hangers-on.

Being wealthy did have its obligations. A wealthy man paid for most of the World Renewal Ceremony (to be discussed shortly), often including payments to the mourners of the year's dead. Any transgressions he might commit cost him more than they would a poorer man, and his ownership of land was so absolute that trespassers who injured themselves while on his land could claim compensation—usually a share in the land involved.

The Yurok systems of laws and values depended on mutual agreement. Because of this flexibility and their concept of private property, they accepted contact with whites more easily than did most other tribes. They translated their shell money into American money (at one time a string of twelve shells was worth ten dollars). A few of their descendants still live today in their river valley, a wilderness not yet destroyed.

Religion

Guardian spirit quests were not very important among the Yurok. Their shamans were women curers who received powers in dreams with help from an ancestor. The shamans obtained their supernatural power in the form of "pains," which could enter a person and cause illness. Yurok believed that possessing one or more pains made the shaman able to cure or extract similar pains—sicknesses—from others. Those who became successful healers were respected and commanded high fees for curing, but they never gave up their duties as wives and mothers. Shamans received pay for their cures according both to the severity of the illness and the importance of the sick person. The charges were frequently so high that considerable wealth exchanged hands. If, however, the cure was not successful, the wealth was returned.

World Renewal. The Yurok placed more emphasis on ceremony than belief. Ethnographers give the name "World Renewal" to the cycle of about a dozen ceremonies the Yurok, Karok, and Hupa held every year. Each ceremony always was held in the same place, and each was different from any of the others. All, however, included the public performance of one or both of two distinctive dances, the Jumping and the Deerskin. This dance cycle was typical of the northern California area, as the Kuksu Cult performances were of the central and the Chungichnish of the southern areas. All these ceremonial cycles were meant to keep the world in order and running properly for another season and to ensure abundant food and prevent disaster.

Each ceremony in the World Renewal cycle had two parts, the esoteric or secret rites and the public performances. In the secret part, a long formula was narrated about the first performance of the ceremony by a member of an ancient, prehuman, half-spirit race, and its immediate beneficial effect. The recitation demonstrated the efficacy of the first and therefore of the current performance. It was spoken in sections by an old man, generally accompanied by a young assistant, before rocks and other places believed to be the abodes of the spirits. All the prescribed symbolic acts were performed by these two alone. They fasted and otherwise refrained from their ordinary activities, stayed in a house sanctified by tradition for this purpose, and spent a number of nights in a sweathouse.

Dances and Regalia. The public part of the ceremony was the dancing, which began after the secret rites had been completed. The dancing went on every day for five, ten, or more days. The dance outfits, songs, and steps were standardized by custom, and were neither symbolic nor sacred. The dancers, all men, were not impersonating spirits but displaying wealth in front of the audience. A large part of every rich man's wealth was dance adornment, and men came from miles up and down the river, bringing their treasures to show. Dance regalia was almost as highly valued as strings of dentalia. A wealthy man's dance outfits consisted of enough albino deerskins, red woodpecker scalp headdresses, and giant obsidian blades to outfit many dancers and thus display his worth to all.

On the first day the dance was brief and performed by a few young men and older boys, but as days passed, it built up in duration, intensity, splendor, and number of dancers, accentuated by competition among the rich men of the several villages involved. As days went by, they handed out more and more of their own and their friends' valuables for their dancers to wear in the next dance. The finest regalia, the most dancers, the longest dances, and the largest audience all formed the climax on the last day.

The Jumping Dance and the White Deerskin Dance were different from each other in costumes, steps, and songs. If both dances were performed, the Deerskin always came first, with costumes of deerhide or civet cat kilts, masses of dentalia necklaces, and wolf-fur bands around the forehead. The dancers carried poles with stuffed deer heads mounted at the end and white or light deerskins draped below. Bright woodpecker scalps decorated the heads. A row of dancers, each carrying skins thus displayed, was headed and followed by dancers holding large ritual obsidian blades of fine handiwork. The dance step was very simple, merely a stamp of the feet, but the rhythmic swing of the mounted deerskins was impressive.

The Jumping Dance was slightly more active, though it had only two movements, a high leap and a stamp. The costumes for this dance were elaborate: a headdress, for instance, consisted of fifty large woodpecker scalps attached to a forehead band, topped with long white feathers. The dancers wore strings of dentalia around their necks, and deerskin robes around their hips.

Before the ceremonial dances began each year, some payment was made to grieving families of Yurok who had died since the last ceremonial cycle. The payment was to compensate for intruding upon the mourners' privacy and sorrow. Contributions might come from the villagers, or a wealthy man might donate the entire sum. Death brought mourning before and during burial. Among the Yurok, as everywhere in California, the names of the dead were never mentioned.

Kepel Fish Dam. The Yurok held one other large annual gathering that was both a ceremony and a cooperative food producing venture. Every autumn hundreds of people from several miles up and down the Klamath River gathered at the village of Kepel. There they spanned the river with a structure of logs, poles, and small stakes. The dam was really a fish

The White Deerskin Dance being performed.

weir: it did not halt the water flowing downstream, but its mesh was fine enough to keep salmon from passing upstream to spawn. It had ten sections, each with a gate and a pen behind the gate. Fish passed through a gate and were trapped in a pen, from which they were pulled out with nets and divided among the men who had built that section of the dam. For ten days the men pulled the fish out of the pens while the women split and dried them for storage. Each pen provided enough fish to last several families an entire year.

The Yurok never cooperated in nonreligious ventures, so it is understandable that they could build the dam only by associating it with religious ceremonies. Before work on the dam began each year, an elder male, well-versed in the formulas, led a ritual for success, a young apprentice assisting him. After the fishing period was over, the people followed the dam's dismantling with a Deerskin Dance and then a Jumping Dance. Another rite, the first-fish ceremony, similar to the first-salmon rites of the Northwest Coast, was held many miles away at the mouth of the river. No fish were pulled from the dam until word arrived that the ritual specialist in charge had completed the first-fish ceremony.

The Pomo

The Indian peoples we refer to as the Pomo once occupied many villages over a large area of California north of San Francisco Bay. The population extended from Clear Lake on the east to the seacoast on the west; its center was in the Russian River Valley, which runs roughly north and south. The Pomo generally did not occupy the dense redwood forest of this region, but settled mainly along waterways and in the open valleys. The deep forest supplied only deer and acorns, while the valleys with their rivers and meadows provided an almost unbelievable variety of foodstuffs.

Abundant Food

Hunger was unknown to the Pomo. They had a liberal food surplus, not because of agriculture (for they had none) or methods of storing food, or an abundance of any one food (compare the Indians of the Northwest Coast, with their never-ending supply of salmon), but because of the sheer diversity of their wild foods. No one item was so necessary to their diet that its sudden disappearance could not be made up by other items. Exploiting so many food sources was time-consuming, however, and left the Pomo little leisure time.

Women gathered acorns in the fall and stored them in large baskets until needed. Then they ground the nuts with pestles in sturdy basket mortars, leached the flour, and stone-boiled the mush in watertight baskets or baked acorn meal bread in warm ashes. The acorn was not as important to the Pomo, however, as it was to some other California Indians. The Pomo relied as well on tubers and roots (arrowroot was popular), berries and bulbs (used for soap and fish poison as well as food), ferns, flowers, and leaves (some raw in salads, some boiled as we do spinach), and seaweed cooked into cakes. They made sugar from sugar pine sap, took salt from seaweed and natural salt licks, and used many plants for medicines. For meat and skins the men hunted and trapped deer, elk, bear, mountain lions, seals, sea lions, sea otters, rabbits, squirrels, and wood rats. They also caught birds such as quail, woodpeckers, pigeon, grouse, ducks, and geese, other animals such as turtles and lizards, and occasionally insects such as grasshoppers. Grasshoppers were caught and cooked in one neat operation: several Indians set a ring of grass on fire, and as the ring closed on the grasshoppers, they were confined to a smaller and smaller space, and finally toasted.

Fish, another main source of food, were caught from shore and from boats with hooks, traps, snares, nets, weirs, spears, and harpoons, and also by means of poisons that paralyzed the fish's breathing mechanism but were harmless to humans. Salmon, panfish, and many other kinds of fish were taken in the fresh water of the rivers and Clear Lake; abalone, many other shellfish, and octopus came from the ocean. Some residents of the Clear Lake area became professional fishers, selling their catch for other necessities. These people used boats of a type called the "balsa canoe" by anthropologists, which were neither canoes nor made of balsa wood. They were really rafts, made of loosely bound tule reeds gathered into a canoe shape, depending on the buoyancy of the individual reeds to keep afloat rather than a watertight hull.

The People

The meaning of the word *Pomo* is not clear. It is a native word, but not a name they used for themselves. It is reported to mean "red clay," used as a name because most of those people added a red clay to their acorn bread to give it color. All the Pomo spoke dialects of a language of the Hokan phylum. The dialects were so closely related that speakers of each could understand the others, but distinctive enough for linguists to group the tribelets into seven major divisions. None of these groups had political identity or unity, however.

The Pomo appear to have been in California a very long time, longer than most of their neighbors. White contact affected them rather quickly, so even though they were not all driven from their lands, we know little of what their culture was like in precontact days. The Russians encountered them in 1808, trading with them until 1847. The Spanish tried to convert them to Christianity beginning in 1823 with the mission at Sonoma. From 1834 to 1847, Mexicans moved into Pomo territory. In 1848, gold was discovered in central California, and the whole area was invaded first by gold seekers and later by settlers who ruthlessly took Pomo lands for their own. Those contacts and disturbances, added to the usual mortality from European diseases, make it hard to guess at precontact population. A figure often cited is 8,000 for all Pomo. At the time much of the ethnographic data were gathered, in 1910, there were 1,200 left. Of those that remain, the southwest Pomo, called the Kashia, have kept more of the old ways than the others.

Organization

During winter and spring, the Pomo lived in permanent villages along streams. Each community claimed its own territory, within which all its members were free to hunt, gather, or fish, though tracts on the shores of Clear Lake were family owned. During the summers, which were always dry, the population spread out, some building temporary shelters like lean-tos away from the village, some sleeping out while on food quests, and some remaining at the village. The permanent winter quarters varied from small, single-family tipilike structures of redwood bark to circular or elongated multifamily houses of brush, up to fifty feet in diameter. Besides living quarters, each village had a men's sweathouse and a dance house. Both of these were round and half-buried in the ground, the sweathouse being small and the dance house the largest structure in the village. The men congregated in either of these—the home was for women and children and storing property, cooking, eating, and other domestic activities.

The largest unit of social organization was the tribelet, of which there were about seventy-five throughout the Pomo territory. Each consisted of one large village where the head chief lived and most of the ceremonies were held, and the surrounding small villages, each with its own lesser chief. The lesser chiefs inherited their positions, but social pressure could force their replacement if they were not competent. It is not clear whether the head chief was from a kin group in the main village or whether he was somehow selected from among the lesser chiefs. Those chiefs had little direct power but great influence as peacemakers, advisers, organizers, and, strangely perhaps, preachers on ethics and proper behavior to the assembled townspeople. They were not war chiefs; in fact no one could be described as a war leader. The society had no regular organization for war. A "battle" would sometimes start over a supposed wrong done to an individual or small group, but it ended as soon as an important man on either side was wounded or killed. When that first blood was drawn, the headmen or chiefs arranged a settlement and determined payments for losses.

Technology

Most of the material culture of the Pomo and other central California peoples conformed to the general description given early in this chapter. Their everyday clothing was typical of the whole West Coast, women wearing only a skirt, men wearing a simple, short wrap-around skirt or, more often, just going naked. In cold weather both sexes wore rabbit-fur blankets.

Large carrying baskets with headstraps were also common to the whole area, and the Pomo shared most basket forms, sizes, and manufacturing techniques with other California tribelets. They were unique, however, in the elaborate feathered decorations that the women wove into their fine baskets, often acclaimed as the most beautiful in the world. The baskets were an item of some status and wealth; the finest were never

Pomo woman weaving a large, beautifully decorated basket.

sold but were given as gifts or kept in the family. The Pomo combined the coiling of basketmakers to the south and the twining technique of those to the north, added a greater variety of materials (at least twelve), and with great skill and care wove finely and tightly meshed baskets, beautifully decorated with bright feathers, shells, and beads. Their almost endless variety was rare among American Indians, a truly individual art, and the sizes ranged from those so small the weave cannot be seen to those large enough to hold a grown person.

Unlike the Indians in northwestern California, the Pomo had a rich musical life. They knew many songs and accompanied their songs and dances with flutes, whistles, drums, rattles, a musical bow, the bull-roarer (a sort of slat, whirled on the end of a rope), and a huge wooden drum that the dancers stomped on.

The Pomo made strings of shell beads and strung disks made of a mineral called magnesite, using these much like money. They did not hoard these things, however, or attach to them the value and status that the northwestern California tribes did. They were spenders rather than savers; a family might spend all its bead money on a visit to Clear Lake to feast and relax in the company of relatives and friends. Pomo were wealthy, but not obsessed with wealth. They did much traveling, using both the waterways and overland trails, and traded such items as bows, salt, woodpecker scalps, seaweed, beaver skins, shells, magnesite, baskets, and obsidian.

The Pomo developed an arithmetic and knew some astronomy. Special men learned such things and maintained the calendar, which not only kept track of the passing seasons, but also counted the passing years.

The Sexes

One gets the impression that the Pomo had an unusual degree of equality between the sexes. Marriage was accompanied by an exchange of gifts between both families rather than a one-way exchange of goods for a bride. Women could own and inherit personal property, and they won prestige as master basketmakers. Whether Pomo traced kinship *unilineally* (solely through males or solely through females) is not certain, but they do seem to have settled wherever they wished after marriage. A newly married couple could live with his family, her family, or in a new location.

Only men could become shamans, however. There were both good and evil shamans. The evil ones were the "bear doctors," who went about in bearskins and were greatly feared, though they probably existed as much in legend as in reality, and "poisoners," who could convince people that they were being poisoned. The good shamans were healers, some healing by sucking out the cause of illness, some by administering herbs and performing magic. The Kuksu dancers appear to have been healers also. They knew the medical properties of plants and herbs and used them for doctoring. A man became a shaman in one of two ways: either he inherited the paraphernalia from his father or some other shaman whose assistant and student he had been, or he received power directly from a spirit, often during an illness.

The Kuksu Cult

Our information about the Kuksu Cult is scanty. We know that its ceremonial performances were of great importance to many peoples of central California, and we have some descriptions of the dances. However, we know little about the beliefs behind the practices. Kuksu ceremonies were shared by the Pomo with several other central California tribes, most notably the Wintun and the Maidu. This cult probably took form about a thousand years ago among these people, but no one knows where. Perhaps it was brought in by outsiders, like the modern Ghost Dance, and spread from tribe to tribe. Kuksu may be the name of the man who began the cult.

Among the Pomo, Kuksu was believed to be a spirit, but some of the other central California tribes, the Maidu, for instance, believed that he was the first man. (The myth at the beginning of this chapter is from the Maidu.) The Maidu performed the Kuksu ceremonials to dramatize the creation myth, but the Pomo performances carried other meaning, and they involved impersonating the spirit.

Kuksu Ritual. The Pomo form had a secret society to which all men belonged and into which all boys were initiated by older members, who symbolically killed the boys and then brought them back to life as members of the society. Cult activities, such as initiations, almost always took place in a ceremonial chamber, a large, earth-covered, semiunderground structure a little like a Pueblo kiva. Members of the cult may have used this building for leisure-time lounging or sweating in addition to the ritual observances.

The Kuksu dancers beat rhythm on a foot drum, a six- to ten-foot log slab on which they danced. The disguised and costumed dancers impersonated spirits: they did not dance to show off their costumes as the Yurok did. The Kuksu ritual was part of a cycle of dances and ceremonies that went on throughout the winter—the Pomo were dispersed in summer. A major ceremony was held in any one place only once in several years, which was just as well because it usually involved the expense and labor of building a new dance house. Between times, people visited and took part in their neighbors' ceremonies.

The whole cycle of dances was presumed to bring rain and nourish the earth, to bring a bountiful natural crop, and to ward off epidemics, floods, and earthquakes. The Kuksu dancers themselves brought renewed spiritual life to the community and took away sins and illnesses; the Kuksu was thus a world renewal ceremony.

Ceremonies began with social dances by men and women, though later in the presentations only men participated. Then came the "fire-devils," painted naked men who frightened the women and children, especially those about to be initiated. Finally came the true Kuksu, with painted bodies and huge, elaborate headdresses with radiating feathered sticks and a cover for the face such as a big red feather nose that hid the wearer's identity. The word Kuksu refers to both the dancer and the headdress. Each dancer danced separately about the dance house, moving in circles and turning his body in symbolic harmony with the universe. All the men of the village participated as dancers, drummers, fire tenders, or master of ceremonies. As the dancers left the village, the people believed they took with them all the community's sickness and sin.

During the ceremonial performances, the Kuksu danced in the assembly house at least once each day. The people spent the intervals eating, gambling, playing games, and watching other dances.

Ghosts and Spirits

There were other rituals in the cycle besides the Kuksu, such as the Coyote Dance and the Ghost Ceremony. The Coyote was the son of the creator who brought life to man, and the dance was a retelling of the origin myth. The ancient Ghost Ceremony—not to be confused with the Ghost Dance of the 1870s—was like the Kuksu in many ways. The "ghosts" were fearsome for the women and children, who were not allowed in the dance house to see the dance itself. The two kinds of ghost dancers were "ash ghosts" and "ghosts" proper, both having painted bodies and fancy head coverings. The ash ghosts had white ash on them and, it was believed, ate live coals. They probably were connected with the Pomo practice of cremating the dead.

The Pomo were unusual in that they believed in a creator god. However, their main religious concern was an ever-present fear of the spirits of field and woods. This dread kept them on good behavior, causing them to wash themselves, to take care of their children, to respect nature, to be honest and truthful, and to sing prayers day and night. Doing these things, they believed, kept the spirit world friendly. Boys and girls underwent a painful and frightening initiation to adulthood, which both scared and controlled the children and reminded all that fear and pain were a part of life.

Southern California Indians

On the coast, transitional between central California and the south, were groups we refer to as Costanoan, from the Spanish word meaning "coastal people." They lived to the south of San Francisco Bay in an area famous for many large seashell mounds, the result of mussel dinners on the same spot for thousands of years. From the little we know of the Costanoan culture, we believe that their food quest, material culture, death practices, and religious beliefs must have been similar to others of the central and south coastal areas.

The Chumash were another group who lived along the coast and on the islands just north of the present city of Los Angeles. Spaniards first arrived among them in 1542, but so little was recorded about their aboriginal settlements and subsistence that almost all we know about them comes from archaeology. We do know that they fished from and traveled in oceangoing boats made of planks sealed with asphalt from natural deposits in their territory.

The Mission Indians

The Indians who lived along the seacoast from San Francisco Bay south to the Mexican border were first disrupted by white contact—Spanish missionaries—more than two centuries ago. The missionaries took them over, reorganizing them into groups around the closest mission with little regard for tribal origins, cultural unity, or native languages. All had been hunters and gatherers; the missionaries forced them to become cultivators and cattle herders. So complete was mission control, backed up by Spanish soldiery, that old life-styles were lost within a generation or two. These tribes, known to us mostly by Spanish names (usually names of missions), are often called "Mission Indians." Early descriptions of those Indians by missionaries and travelers relate their lives at missions, not their ways of living in native villages, especially not their "pagan" beliefs and ceremonies, which the Spanish were most eager to change. We are not likely ever to know all the original tribes and their distributions, populations, or cultures.

"Mission Indians" usually means the coastal tribes from Los Angeles to the Mexican boundary, though all the Indians from the Costanoans south have been given that name at various times. The cultures of these Indians were similar, and all but the Diegueño spoke Shoshonean languages. Their ways of life showed relationships with the Shoshonean speakers of the Great Basin to the east. They probably moved into California from the Basin relatively late, displacing other groups already in California, possibly the Diegueño and the Chumash, who moved south and north respectively. The easier food quest in California produced greater social and religious complexity and elaboration than the Great Basin tribes had. The southern Californians' own names for themselves and for each other were lost in years of mission living; today we know them only by the names of the missions where they settled in historic times.

Among the better known of these mission groups were the Fernandeño, named after the mission San Fernando, and the Gabrielino, after San Gabriel. They appear to have been closely related and in pre-mission times probably were part of the same large ethnic group. The two tribes occupied most of the present area of Los Angeles and Orange counties, the islands of Santa Catalina and San Clemente, and most of the fertile lowland of southern California.

The Juaneño were named for the famous mission San Juan Capistrano, south of Los Angeles. Next in order south were the Luiseño, after the mission San Luis Rey de Francia, and the Diegueño, who occupied the last strip of coastline before the present Mexican border. They were named after the mission San Diego, as was the present city. They spoke a language of the Yuman family, and probably resembled the Yuma and other tribes to the east more than the other Mission Indians did.

The Luiseño

The Luiseño lived mostly in the hills, not on the coastal lowlands like most of the other southern mission tribes. Perhaps that is why more of their old villages and ways of life lasted long enough for the early ethnographers to record. They spoke one language, with differences in dialect from the extreme north to the far south. They had no tribal name for themselves, but they did have names for local groups. Their pre-European population has been estimated at three to four thousand.

Life-style. The main part of the Luiseño diet was acorns and seeds; they also ate shoots, fruit, berries, and roots, and used at least twenty plants as household medicines. They ate some venison and lots of rabbits. Other supplementary meats were wood rats, mice, ground squirrels, quail, ducks, grasshoppers, mollusks, and fish. They hunted with the bow, but probably trapped and snared as much game as they shot.

If the early reports are accurate, the Luiseño used all three types of canoes found in California: the balsa or tule canoe like the Pomo, the dugout canoe like the Yurok, and the tarred plank boat like the Chumash. They built their houses in pits about two feet deep and eight across and often covered them with earth. Women cooked outside under a thatch roof shade, open on all sides. The men's sweathouse was small, used only for daily sweating, not as a clubhouse or sleeping quarters. The dance and ceremony house was not a building at all, but a circular area ringed with posts and without a roof. Spectators could watch by looking in the entrances or peering over the posts. The Luiseño made big baskets, mostly for storage, but not the fine watertight ones, for, unlike most California Indians, the Luiseño (and the Diegueño) made pottery, probably having learned how from the Southwest. They also made pottery pipes in the form of tubes, which the men smoked lying down just before retiring.

Organization. Little is known about the structure of Luiseño society before the Spanish, Mexicans, and Americans displaced them and reduced their numbers. They had patrilineal family groups, perhaps clans, which joined together to form ceremonial groups. Many of the southern Mission Indians had a moiety organization, but we do not know that the Luiseño observed this dual pattern. Most kin groups were small, almost the equivalent of large extended families. Several smaller groups clustered about a large group and its chief or headman for the ceremonial grouping. The chief ordered the ceremonies, so a group without a chief depended on joining with other groups for religious activities. Chieftainship was hereditary; it was not wealth that brought honor, status, and leadership as in the Northwest, but the office that brought wealth. The followers supplied the wealth needed to carry out the ceremonies the chief directed, which were a cultural focal point for the participants.

Because we know so little about these precontact Mission Indians, we tend to assume that they shared most traits, but it might be simply mission influence that made them seem alike. Some things about the Luiseño ceremonies do apply to the other mission and inland southern California tribes, some we assume were shared, and some are unique, or at least are recorded only for the Luiseño.

Religious Rituals. Luiseño religious life focused on initiation rites and mourning rites. Both these basic tribal ceremonies involved the Toloache Cult, which the Luiseño shared with the neighboring tribes. Members of this cult used the narcotic, vision-producing jimsonweed or datura plant, and believed in a deity, Chungichnish, who gave the ritual to the Indians. The cult was centered on the boys' initiation into the secret society of the Toloache. In addition to weeks of fasting and physical and mental ordeal, the youths were expected to attain a new perspective on life in a "new vision," a violent mystical experience induced by the drug. The dreams a boy had at initiation he remembered all his life, and they determined much of his behavior and beliefs.

Songs, an important part of all Luiseño ceremonies, were unvarying myths and descriptions of rituals, though some were secular. Interestingly, some of their songs were in the Gabrielino language, which may mean that the Toloache Cult spread from the Gabrielino to the Luiseño.

The Luiseño had only two or three standard dances, which were used in most of the rituals. The most spectacular was the Fire Dance climaxing the Toloache initiation. It began with a huge bonfire and a ring of barefoot men dancing around it. By rhythmically closing in on and retreating from the edge of the fire, stamping on the hot embers, they snuffed it out.

Like the Pueblo and Navajo, the mission tribes made sand paintings by dribbling colored sands into designs three to twelve feet in diameter. They used these paintings in the Toloache initiation for boys, in the girls' adolescence ceremony, and in the death rites for members of the Toloache society. The circular sand painting was not quite representational, but had elements that stood for serpents, stars, and mountains—

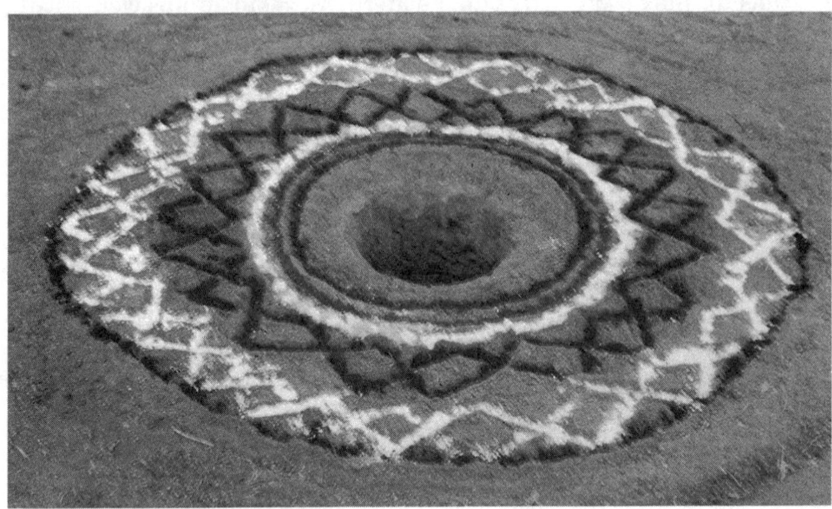

A circular Luiseño sand painting created for the "Burial of Feathers" ceremony.

making a sort of picture of the world. At the center was a small pit or depression called the "Hole of the Dead" or the "Navel of the Universe," symbolizing death and burial of cremated remains.

The usual dance costume was a net skirt decorated with eagle feathers that swung out as the dancer spun around. Its simplicity compared to the dance regalia of northern and central California may be a result of the jimsonweed psychic effect; the dancers supposedly had their attention turned inward, recalling their own visions when they had been initiated.

Toloache Ceremony. A Toloache initiation ceremony was held only once every few years, whenever there were enough boys of the right age. All the boys, plus any older boys, men not initiated in childhood, or men who had married into the tribe, were brought together and given the drug to drink. The potion was very carefully administered, for too large a dose could have been, and sometimes was, fatal. Only the initiates took the drug; no one ever drank the Toloache more than once in his lifetime. The boys passed out and dreamt while the adults danced all night around the fire. A boy usually dreamt about an animal, and never again killed that animal.

The ceremony ran for about six days, the boys dancing at night and sleeping during the day, fasting all the while. Even after six days of dancing, other rituals went on, the initiation tapering off slowly. For months the boys ate no meat and took part in occasional night dances.

Older men taught them special knowledge during this time, such as the secret of the Fire Dance and other magic. The sand painting was made right after the fast. After a long lecture on proper moral behavior, a lump of meal was placed in each boy's mouth, which they all spat into the center pit of the painting. The painting was swept into the pit so that noninitiates would never see it.

As part of the ordeal of passing into manhood, the boys underwent a trial in which they were covered with biting red ants. They had to endure the pain solemnly, without complaint. On another occasion they had to walk carefully through a trench on stepping stones laid out in the shape of a corpse; a stumble foretold an early death.

The other major ceremony of the Toloache Cult came at a society member's mourning anniversary. The members made a sand painting about Chungichnish, then swept the dead one's dance feathers and other ceremonial possessions into the pit and destroyed the painting.

The Girls' Ceremony. A female adolescence ceremony, though supposed to take place whenever a girl reached puberty, usually was not performed until several girls could undergo the rite at the same time. Probably a rich man's daughter celebrated her first menses and other girls participated, avoiding the costs or sharing them. The sponsoring parents were expected to feed the guests who attended the ceremony.

The girls' ceremony did not involve the Toloache drug. First the girls swallowed balls of tobacco. Anyone who vomited was thought to be unchaste. Then the girls were "roasted," laid out in a pit lined with warm stones and covered with more stones. They had to lie perfectly still for three days in the pit. During the night the men, and during the day the women, danced around them. They were let out once a day for bodily functions and given a light meal while the stones were being reheated. When they emerged, their faces were painted by the village chief's wife, and their bodies were decorated, sometimes tattooed. Exactly a month later, the girls gathered for a sand painting, after which their bodies were touched with balls of meal, which were then placed in their mouths. They spat them into the pit and the painting was destroyed.

Death Rites. Most of the southern California Indians held elaborate death ceremonies. Luiseño ceremonies had two distinct parts: immediately after death the body was cremated and possessions were burned, then about a year later, images were made of the deceased and then burned.

When death was imminent, or immediately upon death, kinfolk dug a pit about two feet deep running north and south. They filled it with brush, erected a log pyre over it, and placed the body on top, face

CHARACTERISTICS OF THE CALIFORNIA TRIBES

Clothing	Food production	Equipment	Shelter	Social and political organization	Religion	Warfare
Hide or fiber skirts Skin capes (in bad weather) Aprons Breechcloths Rabbit-fur blankets Hide or fiber footwear, sandals	Gathering (seeds, acorns, wild plants, shellfish) Hunting Fishing Grasshoppers (Pomo)	Bows and arrows Hooks Mats Nets Canoes Traps Snares Weirs Harpoons Rafts (Pomo)	Simple dwellings of grass, brush, or bark Gabled plank houses (in north) Wooden sweathouses Subterranean shelters Temporary lean-tos (Pomo, in summer) Redwood bark tipi-like structure (Pomo, in winter)	Families Small villages Clans (occasionally) Headmen	Elaborate death ceremonies and puberty rites Shamans Witchcraft Women curers (Yurok) Myths World Renewal Ceremonies First Fish Ceremony Kuksu Cult Ghost Ceremony (Pomo) Toloache Cult (Luiseño) Drug use in some areas Creator god Long series of rituals (central California)	Generally peaceful Feuds settled by payment

upward, head to the north. One relative supervised the cremation while others sat nearby, weeping and wailing. It often took twelve hours for the flames to consume the body; if the heart were slow to burn, it was punched full of holes to speed destruction. When the body was consumed, the bones and ashes were gathered and placed in a basket. Saving garments for a later ceremony, kinfolk burned all other possessions, while singing, dancing, and mourning went on all night.

The next morning, or as soon as enough food had been gathered, the dead one's clothes were washed, then they too were burned. This released the deceased from all earthly ties.

Usually only relatives were present at the cremation and the burning of possessions; that was a private ceremony and a time for grief. The effigy burning was a public ceremony which honored all the year's dead. All the neighboring people were invited, sometimes as many as five hundred, and food had to be provided for all for a week. Thus it was sensible to combine mourning for several people into one great public observance.

Mourners made the effigies of sticks and brush, with buckskin heads, and dressed them in men's or women's clothing. These images represented all the dead of the community since the last effigy burning. The ceremony lasted a week; on the last night all images and offerings to the dead were piled up and ignited as the assemblage mourned.

On the anniversary of a chief's death, his kinfolk held a night-long dance during which they killed, skinned, and cremated an eagle. Its feathers became part of a dance outfit.

The Spanish missions—San Diego de Alcala, established in 1769, was the first—brought great hardship and cultural loss to the Indians of southern California while the Indians outside that area were not severely disturbed until after the discovery of gold in 1848 and the ensuing gold rush. The great damage and cultural trauma suffered by the California Indians resulting from contact with outsiders is recounted in Part IV.

Suggestions for Further Study

Bibliography

Kroeber, Alfred L. 1925. *Handbook of the Indians of California.*

An encyclopedic work on the cultures of the California area by an outstanding specialist. This book should be the starting point for all studies on California Indians.

Kroeber, Theodora. 1961. *Ishi in Two Worlds.*

An account of the last surviving Yana Indian, who surrendered himself to the white world on August 19, 1911. A sensitive and fascinating book that conveys the heartbreak that comes from having one's way of life destroyed. Unforgettable.

Other Pertinent Works

Heizer, Robert F., and Alan Almquist. 1971. *The Other Californians.* (Indian-White relations)

Heizer, Robert F., and M. A. Whipple. 1951. *The California Indians.*

Strong, William D. 1929. *Aboriginal Society in Southern California.*

MAJOR GROUPS AND LANGUAGES OF CALIFORNIA

Language phylum	Language family	Cultural division
Aztec-Tanoan	Uto-Aztecan	Cahuilla Gabrielino Luiseño Serraño
Hokan	Chumashan	Chumash
	Karok	Karok
	Palaihnihan	Achomawi Atsugewi
	Pomo	Pomo
	Shastan	Shasta
	Yanan	Yana
	Yuman	Diegueño

MAJOR GROUPS AND LANGUAGES (continued)

CALIFORNIA (continued)

Language phylum	Language family	Cultural division
Macro-Algonkian	Wiyot	Wiyot
	Yurok	Yurok
Na-Dene	Athabaskan	Hupa Tolowa
Penutian	Maidu	Maidu
	Miwok-Costanoan	Costanoan Miwok
	Wintun	Wintun
	Yokuts	Yokuts
Undetermined	Yuki	Wappo Yuki

6

THE GREAT BASIN AND THE SOUTHWEST

Hopi pottery jug.

The Great Basin

Shoshonean Legend

There was a time when only animals and birds lived on the land, and they had no fire. Coyote knew that there was fire someplace, for he could see smoke in the distance. He did not know where it was coming from, so he sent the birds into the sky. Woodpecker went up and out of sight, but he returned without learning the source of fire. "Let me try," said Hawk, but he too returned without seeing it. Finally Eagle set out, and when he returned, he said, "There are flames on the other side of the mountain." They all decided to go to the fire, Coyote leading, followed by Woodpecker, Hawk, Bluejay, Rabbit, Roadrunner, and others. Coyote was very clever. He thought, "We must not let the fire-owners know why we are coming. We will carry firedrills to make them think we already have fire."

When they crossed over the mountain, they said to the fire-owners, "We have come to have fun, to gamble and play with you." The hosts gave them all food—to each bird a different kind of seed, to Coyote, berries. After they had eaten they began to gamble. This is what they did. They made three piles of dirt and hid a stone in one pile. Others had to bet on which pile held the stone. Whoever guessed right won the game. The hosts said, "You have not come to gamble; you have come to steal our fire." The Coyote showed them the firedrills and said, "No, we have fire ourselves." Toward morning, they began to dance. Coyote wore a headdress over his hair and danced close to the fire. He danced closer and closer. Suddenly he bent over the fire and a spark caught in his headdress. The animals all ran toward home followed by the fire-owners. Before long, Bluejay was caught and killed by the pursuers. The animals were getting tired. One after the other they carried the fire. Finally Roadrunner said, "Let me carry it," and he ran making his feet point in many directions so the pursuers could not tell where he had gone. He escaped and built a big fire back on the other side of the mountain.

That evening it began to rain. Coyote and his people carried plenty of wood to the fire, but the rain put it all out save one coal. Rabbit covered that with his tail until the rain stopped. But all the wood was wet then, and they could not find any tinder. Rat said, "I have a dry nest. We will use that." Soon they had fire again. Then Coyote dried his bow and arrow and killed Rat and roasted him in the fire. After that he killed Rabbit, skinned him, and made a blanket of the skin. He said, "From now on people will do this."

The upland area known as the Great Basin covers Nevada, Utah, and parts of California, Idaho, and Wyoming. On the east, north, and west it is surrounded by mountain ranges, but its southern boundary is not sharp—one of many reasons to consider the Southwest and Basin as extensions of each other. Another is the desert conditions in both areas.

The foragers in the Basin and the cultivators in the Southwest, and the ways of survival both learned, reach back to a common base in the Desert Archaic period. Abundant milling equipment dating back to 8000 B.C. indicates that by then people were shifting away from big game hunting, depending more and more on wild plants for food. People of that period left behind other evidence of their way of life: wooden digging sticks, netting, and basketry. As thousands of years went by, these tools, plus leather, fur, and fiber clothing, remained vital for human adaptation to an environment that to modern people seems nearly barren of life-sustaining materials.

The Environment

The few streams in the Basin flow down from the surrounding mountains into the central depression rather than to the oceans. The area receives little precipitation and evaporation is high, so the water bodies in the Basin are quite salty. The Great Salt Lake of Utah is all that remains of ancient Lake Bonneville, which once covered an area about 350 miles long and 150 miles wide. Alkaline flats, the dry traces of old water beds, are common in the Basin. Those rivers that still carry water have cut canyons so deep that there are no flood plains to make cultivation easier.

Summers in the Basin and Southwest are hot, often over 100 degrees, and winters are cold, with temperatures sometimes falling to 20 degrees below zero. Precipitation there is never more than ten inches a year, and in many areas it is far less because the western mountains receive all the moisture brought by winds coming in from the Pacific. The streams depend on the mountain snows rather than rainfall. Patches of grass and clumps of desert vegetation like sagebrush are as much as the land can manage with so little rain. When Europeans first tried to cross the Basin, many died of starvation and thirst.

Though smaller areas within the bleak Basin varied in altitude and amount of available water, nowhere could people depend on a plentiful year-round food supply. Plant resources fluctuated yearly, each one being in short supply at least every two or three years. They also grew and matured at different times, forcing the Indian harvesters to move regularly from zone to zone. However, while no one plant was abundant enough to support people, many species could be eaten, and the people gathered every bit of the sparse vegetation: seeds, berries, nuts, leaves,

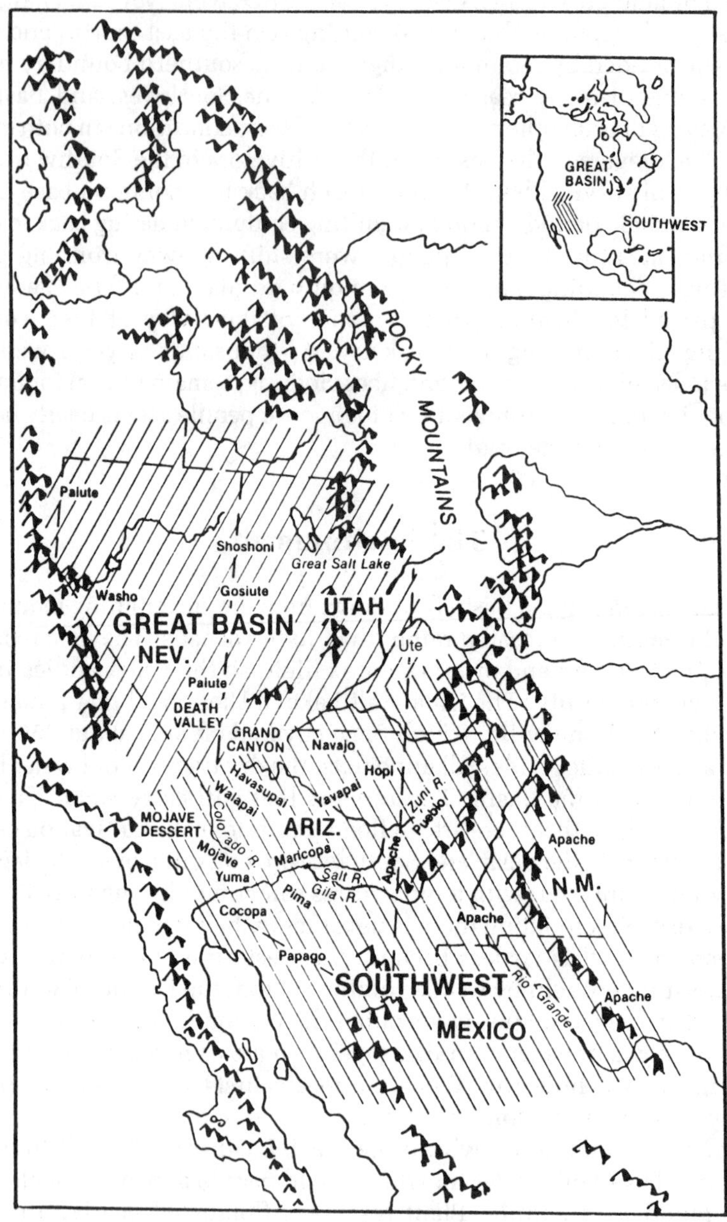

The Great Basin and the Southwest culture areas and their tribes.

stalks, tubers, roots, and bulbs. So thoroughly did they exploit underground plant parts with digging sticks that they were called "Diggers" by Europeans, a term that later came to imply contempt for their poverty.

The animal food supply also fluctuated. Occasional antelope, and rarely a mountain sheep, were the only animals of any size to tolerate Basin conditions, so the people ate many species that others considered inedible—rats, snakes, and insects. Most of their meat, however, came from rabbits, whose populations exploded every few seasons and at other times became quite scarce. Where streams cut through the Basin, the people added fish to their diet—trout, salmon, and suckers—and also waterfowl and their eggs. When salmon were running, people could catch them in quantity.

In the thousands of years between the Desert Archaic and European contact, Basin Indians did little to change their way of life, though survival became still harder as the climate grew drier. Indeed, studying the ways of life of modern Shoshoni and Ute has given us a reasonably good picture of the Desert Archaic.

Basin People

The harsh environment held the human population down and spread it thin; probably it never grew beyond 65,000 or 75,000 for the whole Basin area. All the groups in the Great Basin spoke Shoshonean languages of the Uto-Aztecan family, except for the Washo near the California boundary who spoke a Hokan language. As in so many other areas, people of the same linguistic group did not think of themselves as anything like a tribe. They lived in bands of perhaps fifty to a hundred people, and though they recognized common customs and dialects, they had only the vaguest notion of unity.

Exploiting the Environment

Bands occasionally came together to hunt rabbit or antelope or share a good crop of pine nuts and enjoy a bit of relaxation and sociability while there was enough for all to eat. Then they broke once more into smaller units—often individual families—to continue the never-ending hunt for subsistence. During winters people usually congregated in small settlements, separating into foraging bands and family groups again when the weather grew warmer.

Within the territory that belonged to the general unit we call a tribe, the bands moved in a fairly regular pattern over perhaps fifty to one hundred square miles. They took plant foods as they ripened, harvesting everything available in one small area and then moving on to another. Even with this diverse food supply, people suffered many lean years, and populations stayed small. The least productive territory was the southwest, the Mojave Desert and Death Valley. Life was not as hard in the mountain areas of California, Idaho, and Wyoming, where more water, game, and plants were available. But nowhere could people stop their search for food to settle down long, and with their simple technology, agriculture was impossible.

Housing. In winter, a structure called a *wickiup* sheltered families in the central and northern areas of the Basin. This was a conical or domed hut of poles covered with brush, matting, or bark strips, with a center fire pit and a smoke hole in the roof. Summer housing consisted of temporary huts or windscreens of brush, mostly for shade. Most housing in the very arid regions of the south was brush.

Some Basin people built sweathouses of brush or hides, making the interior steamy by pouring water over heated stones in a center pit. Sweathouses were built near a stream if possible so people could plunge into the water after sweating. As in other areas, sweating served as a kind of ritual purification, and it was also thought to have medicinal value. In some parts of the Basin, the heat for sweating came directly from an interior fire; this kind of sweathouse usually was a larger structure also used as a meeting house.

Food. As their ancestors had done for thousands of years, the Basin people held communal rabbit hunts when the rabbit population increased. Piñon nuts, grasshoppers, and antelope also showed a periodic spurt in numbers. Piñon nuts ripened in late fall, but like everything in the Basin, the crop was highly unpredictable from year to year. Women did most of the gathering, beating the cones that held the nuts from the piñon pines. In a good year, they might collect enough to store for a year or more, because the nuts kept well. When the grasshoppers swarmed, it was a joyous affair. People beat the grass, driving the insects into a pit, then boiled them, roasted them, or pounded them into a paste which was dried for storage.

Whenever antelope were available, the bands came together to hunt them communally, driving them into an enclosure of sagebrush and stone. Directed by an antelope shaman, who was believed to have supernatural power over antelope, the men, dressed in antelope headdresses, sang songs to lure the animals into the trap. Other hunters waited in ambush to kill them.

Women learned many ways of preserving plant food to help tide their families over the winter. They ground seeds, made them into cakes, and dried them to be consumed later. They dried berries whole or pounded them into a powder, and stored nuts in hide bags. All these provisions were kept in grass-lined storage pits at the site of the winter encampment.

Winter brought the best hunting, but even then animals were not plentiful. In the drier southern areas, game was so scarce that there was very little hunting at any season, However, Basin people used all food resources with such thoroughness that though they rarely feasted, they were rarely faced with starvation.

Technology. The Basin people's clothing and equipment stayed essentially the same for thousands of years: buckskin breechcloths and leggings in winter for men; aprons of shredded bark, fibers, or hide for women; and in cold weather, woven rabbit-skin cloaks and blankets and hide moccasins for both. Snowshoes made it easier to walk over deep snow. The most developed part of Basin technology was willow basketry, as it was among most seed gatherers of western North America. Basin women made carrying baskets, seed beaters, trays, and bottles tightly woven and coated with pitch to hold water. They used natural vegetable stains to dye strands that could be woven in with the uncolored fibers to make designs.

Social Organization

In some parts of the Basin food was so scarce that people could gather into band-sized groups only once every few years. Between times they lived as isolated extended families, joining others only in years of rabbit hunts, good piñon harvests, or the like. Kinfolk on both the mother's and the father's sides were equally important. Anyone could marry anyone as long as no blood relationship could be traced between them. Marriages were made within the band and between bands, and the couple joined the family of one spouse or the other, often alternating as economic conditions changed. Among some groups, a man might have two wives (usually sisters), but monogamy was the rule, and divorce was simple: the couple merely separated.

These people had no tribal leadership at all. During band gatherings the temporary position of rabbit boss or antelope shaman provided an authority who could direct the hunt successfully. Those leaders acted while the group congregated and saw that people behaved during any recreation and dancing. When the group disbanded, their leadership ended, for it was no longer necessary. Individual families then followed the suggestions of the family elders.

Along with the help they gave in hunting antelope, shamans healed the sick and could appeal to the spirit world on behalf of the people. No one was a full-time specialist; shamans lived like everyone else, hunting, fishing, and so on. Each individual's relationship with the supernatural was his or her private business. There were no community rites, though the people enjoyed watching the shaman's curing activities as a moment of entertainment in a difficult way of life. People did seek spirit guidance, but the vision quest was much simpler here than in the Plateau and Northwest Coast.

The Paiute

All Basin peoples lived much the same kind of life, and the Paiute furnish a good example of it. Their territory spread from north to south over the western part of the Basin, interrupted only by the Washo. The Owens Valley Paiute, who lived just east of what is now Yosemite National Park, had the streams flowing from the Sierras to make their lives a little easier; but most Paiute lived in very small groups, often just extended families, and never stopped moving in their search for food. They had no tribal organization, but several bands would get together for dances and feasts on the rare occasions when they had enough food.

Food, Clothing, and Technology. The Paiute followed a regular seasonal pattern of food-getting within the band's traditional territory, knowing which roots and bulbs to dig in spring, where seeds and berries ripened in summer, and so on through fall, when the piñon crop came in. As they pursued plant foods, the Paiute also collected almost anything that walked, flew, or crawled—larvae and adult insects, grasshoppers, locusts, and ants. Men hunted for meat too, but in a land where plants were scarce, animals were scarce. With long sticks the men prodded rats, lizards, and ground squirrels out of their burrows, and they set traps for rabbits. If rabbits were plentiful, the community held a rabbit hunt. A real windfall was an antelope or two.

Women treated nuts and especially seeds by grinding them into flour which they then boiled or baked into porridge or cakes. It was this preparation that rendered the otherwise inedible seeds into digestible and nourishing food. First the seeds were toasted with hot coals on flat baskets, the women tossing the containers constantly to prevent burning. Then, if making mush, the women stone-boiled the ground seed flour in a basket container. For baking, women added water to the flour to make a dough which they then baked in hot ashes. Prepared flour could also be stored for some months in anticipation of later need.

Men's hunting tools were bows and arrows, spears, clubs, and throwing sticks. Paiute bows were not very efficient and consequently the Paiute were inefficient in hunting large animals. However, antelopes were exceptions. Communal hunts occurred every six or seven years under an antelope shaman who directed the effort to drive antelope into

CHARACTERISTICS OF THE GREAT BASIN TRIBES

Clothing	Food production	Equipment	Shelter	Social and political organization	Religion	Warfare
Leather, fur, and fiber clothing Buckskin breechcloths and leggings Skirts Bark, fiber, or hide aprons Rabbit-skin cloaks and blankets Hide moccasins Snowshoes Woven hats	Foraging Hunting Fishing Grasshopper drives	Digging sticks Bows and arrows Nets Clubs Hide bags Basketry Seed beaters	Wickiups (winter) Temporary huts or windscreens (summer) Sweathouses	Nuclear families Extended families Bands	Shamans Simple form of Vision Quest Spirits (animals, plants, and natural phemonena) Ghosts Witchcraft	Warfare rare Short-lived feuds

a surround where hunters killed them. The shaman was very important and highly respected because it was believed he or she had power to charm antelope into the trap to be killed.

For hunting rabbits when the rabbit population was high, the women made nets two or three feet high and as long as a hundred yards. Under the guidance of a rabbit boss, the net was stretched out and secured, then hunters drove rabbits into the net where they were dispatched by waiting Paiute. Like the antelope drive this was a communal project, but an individual hunter might kill rabbits anytime with a bow and arrow or a throwing stick. Rabbits were prized for their fur almost more than for their meat.

The men could not catch enough animals to make much buckskin, and the people wore little hide clothing—only a loincloth for men and sometimes a skirt for women. Most of the time women wore fiber aprons, and sandals, if worn at all, were made of fiber too. Both sexes wore skin moccasins in winter, and woven rabbit-skin robes. To make these, the men cut each rabbit skin spiral-fashion into one long strip, which they twisted so that fur stuck out on all sides. The strips were twined with a fiber thread into a blanket or robe. Sometimes bird skins with the feathers still on were treated in the same way. Both kinds of robes were light and warm.

Paiute women were basketmakers of great skill. Working with reeds, grasses, bark fibers, or twigs, they made almost every implement except the men's hunting equipment: cradles, mats, seed beaters, hats, and above all, baskets. Baskets served as water jars, dishes, and containers. Large carrying baskets had vertical poles sticking through the bottom to hold them upright on the ground. The women carried those on their backs suspended by a strap called a tumpline across the forehead. To keep the tumplines from cutting into their skin, the women wore basket hats.

Dreams and Curing. Men and women found spirit power in dreams, in which the spirit appeared as an animal or plant, mountains, clouds, or other natural phenomena. This power brought strength, skill, endurance, and good fortune, and to shamans it also gave the ability to cure. Dreams also could cause illness, not necessarily to the dreamer: a member of an individual's family or a friend might become ill if a person dreamed it.

Ghosts too caused illness, for they attempted to steal souls. Witches sickened a victim by magically making some object like a small stone, worm, or lizard enter the person's body. Shamans cured the illness by sucking out the foreign object or going into a trance to retrieve the lost soul. Singing and dancing usually went on along with curing performances, providing entertainment for onlookers. Both men and women could become curers by getting spirit help, either involuntarily from dreams or by a quest in special mountain areas where it was thought the spirits would come to the seeker.

The Paiute never had enough of anything to make them targets for attacks by other Indians. Disagreements in the form of feuds sometimes erupted within the band, but they never lasted long, simply because the job of getting food left little energy for fighting. However, it is instructive to compare the Paiute, who were thoroughly familiar with their territory and how to adapt to and exploit it, to some white pioneers in 1847 who were snow-bound in Paiute territory. Not knowing or ignoring Paiute adaptations, many starved; others survived only by engaging in cannibalism. The Paiute could live in a land where whites perished.

The Ute and Shoshoni

If the Paiute may be considered a continuation of the Desert Archaic people in their struggle for life, some bands of Ute and Shoshoni may stand as examples of people with the same meager tradition but who seized the opportunity to acquire a powerful new technology. That acquisition was the horse, which was of little advantage to most Basin dwellers for their arid land provided no pasturage; in fact, the desert dwellers ate the first horses they obtained.

Although originally as hard pressed as the Paiute for an assured, stable food supply, some Ute and Shoshoni—they too were called diggers—became mounted nomads. By about 1825, horses allowed the consolidation of their previously dispersed bands. They began to raid other Indians as well as white settlers and pioneers who by that time were either pursuing irrigation farming in the Basin or were traversing the land on their way to the West Coast. The horse also allowed some eastern and northern Ute and Shoshoni bands to participate in the Plains bison culture (see chapter 7). Mounted raiding bands quickly became the object of action by the United States Army, but for about 40 years, raiding on horseback resulted in political union under a chief or war leader, a previously unknown figure in the Basin. One anthropologist has called this new political form "predatory bands." It should not, however, be thought that these raiding bands were representative of most of the Basin people.

The Southwest

Keresan Origin Myth

In the beginning, the earth was square and flat, and below its surface were four layers. All people, birds, and beasts lived in the bottom layer or world. Everything was in darkness. There was no sun, no moon. It was dark and it was crowded, but the people did not know how to get out. At last two boys pierced the roof of the lowest layer, making an opening. The people tried all the plants that grew one after the other, hoping that one would be tall enough to allow them to climb out. Finally after many trials, they found a reed so tall that it grew through the opening. The people climbed it to the second layer.

At first there was room for all, but that layer too became crowded, and like the first world, it was dark. Again the people placed the plant under the roof opening and climbed out. The third world too was dark. The two boys found fire and set torches ablaze. In that light the men built kivas. Things were not well, however. The women became crazed and neglected their children. They danced all the time, ceasing only to sleep, and fathers took care of the children. The men soon had enough of that and ascended into the fourth world, this world. But it too was dark, and people worked by the light of torches and fires.

Other beings of the world had come out with the people: one was Spider. Spider tried to make it light. She spun a pure white cloth that gave some light, but it was not enough. It was sent to the west and became the moon. The people prepared a very white deerskin that made a brilliant light. From the skin they formed a shield and sent it to the east, where it became the sun. Now there was light.

Now that people were living in the upper world, some of them began to explore, and quarrel, and marry and beget children. Animals lived in the world of light too, and some of them helped the people while others played tricks on them.

In many ways the Southwest is a continuation of the Great Basin, but the river valleys are wider to the south, and some of the area has extensive plateaus. The plateau region is divided into flat-topped eminences called mesas, and steep-walled canyons; the Grand Canyon of the Colorado is the most dramatic. The mouth of the Colorado River, where it empties into the Gulf of California, is much lower than the plateau region to the northeast; winters are warmer there, and it is even drier than in the Great Basin. The Rocky Mountains, with peaks rising over 10,000 feet, have forests of firs at high altitudes, with juniper and dwarf pine on lower slopes. In the valleys cottonwood trees, willow, and alder grow among bushes, vines, and other small growths. This non-mountainous territory has scanty vegetation, poor grassland, low shrubs, many kinds of cactus, and other plants adapted to dry conditions, such as yucca and agave.

Early Peoples of the Southwest

The cultures of the Southwest, like those of the Great Basin, grew out of the Desert Archaic. Their diet similarly emphasized plant food, which predisposed them toward using more and wider varieties of plant species. When farming techniques and corn spread north from Mexico, probably around 1500 B.C., some people in the Southwest added this new food to their diet.

Slowly the idea of cultivation spread around the Southwest, wherever there was enough water for it. Three typical early farming cultures were the Mogollon, Hohokam, and Anasazi. Descendants of the Anasazi and probably some Mogollon became the Pueblo Indians of historic times, and the Hohokam seem likely to have been the ancestors of the historic Pima and Papago. During the thirteenth century, many Anasazi settlements were abandoned. It seems likely that the reason was an ecological crisis resulting from drought, worn-out soil, and erosion. Regions that under more favorable conditions had supported Anasazi population growth were no longer capable of providing adequate food for these settlements.

By the time the Europeans came, three distinct ways of life had developed in the Southwest. One of these was farming near the area's rivers. Settled along the Colorado River were groups speaking Yuman languages, and along the Salt and Gila rivers were Piman speakers, the Pima and Papago. The Yumans on the Upper Colorado were marginal cultivators, getting only a little of their food by farming. Downriver, cultivation was much more productive. The Piman speakers too mixed cultivation with hunting and gathering. The Pima emphasized domesticated crops, while the Papago obtained more of their food from wild plants and animals.

Living in what the Spanish called *pueblos* were fully agricultural, settled peoples referred to collectively as the Pueblo. (*Pueblo* with a capital *P* refers to the Indians themselves; with a lowercase *p* it means their dwelling.) The Pueblo, including such groups as the Hopi and Zuni, were true farmers, drawing at least 80 percent of their food from their gardens.

A third way of life was followed by the Navajo and Apache, latecomers to the Southwest. They were hunters and gatherers and knew nothing about cultivation when they arrived in the region approximately 500 years ago. The Navajo raided the settled Pueblo, taking from them some knowledge of farming, as did a few Apache groups. Other Apache remained hunters and gatherers, raiding cultivated fields. In fact both names, *Navajo* and *Apache*, come from a Zuni phrase meaning "raiders of the fields."

There was great linguistic variety in the Southwest. In addition to the

Piman and Hopi languages of the Aztec-Tanoan phylum and Yuman, of the Hokan phylum, there were those Athabaskan languages spoken by the Navajo and Apache, the Penutian tongues, and a few more languages of uncertain affiliation. Population in the Southwest was much greater than in the Basin, perhaps 300,000, but unevenly distributed. More people lived in farming areas than in the open land where hunting and gathering people moved.

The Upland Yumans

Beside the Colorado River, from the Grand Canyon to where the river empties into the Gulf of California, lived a prehistoric people whom archaeologists have labeled *Patayan*. This name comes from a Yuman word with the same meaning as Anasazi: "the old people" or "the ancient ones." Archaeologists know less about the Patayan culture than about the Hohokam or Anasazi, but they believe these people were ancestors of the Yuman speakers who lived there later.

The Yumans who lived farther up the Colorado—the Havasupai, the Yavapai, and the Walapai—are often called the Upland Yumans. These three groups probably were closer to the old Desert Archaic tradition than others in the Southwest; we include them in this area because they did practice some agriculture. Their simple social organization, religious practices, and material culture were typical of the Basin tribes. They had no unilineal descent groups (clans or lineages), and the family was the basic unit for producing food and making decisions. The Upland Yuman's territory was too dry for cultivation much of the time, and their settlement patterns and population density varied according to where and when they could find water.

The Havasupai. We cannot leave the Upland Yumans without a look at the extraordinary environment of the Havasupai. Their home was the floor of Cataract Canyon, an arm of the Grand Canyon. The gorge of Cataract Creek, a small tributary of the Colorado, widens for a little way, making room for banks deep in rich earth laid down by floods over the ages. Here the canyon walls tower several hundred feet straight up, with only two frighteningly steep trails to the top. The cultivable floor is less than half a mile wide, split by the clear blue-green stream that gave the Havasupai their name, which means "the people of the turquoise water."

The Havasupai combined a Basin way of life with some cultivation. They dammed Cataract Creek to force the water into irrigation ditches that ran to fields on the narrow canyon floor. During the summer both men and women cultivated the fields, then in the winter they shifted to hunting and gathering up on the canyon rim. The quantity and kinds of their basketry equipment, like their winter way of life, showed Basin connections.

After fall harvest, when the cultivated food was processed and stored, the families scattered. Women left the canyon seeking seeds and piñon; men hunted or went on trading journeys to the Pueblo or to the Mojave lower down the Colorado, where they exchanged skins for pottery, beads, and woven blankets.

In summer, the Havasupai built four-post, brush-roofed shelters without walls as a defense against the searing heat. These structures, often called *shades*, blocked the sun and let air circulate freely. In winter the people made dwellings of framework covered with brush or reeds, sometimes with an outer covering of earth. During the hunt in the upper canyon the men built wickiups of branches and bark to live in while they sought deer, mountain sheep, and an occasional bear.

The River Yumans

Leaving its steep-sided canyon, the Colorado flows south into a much flatter valley. Annual floods fed by melting winter snows and spring rains in the mountains spread over the lower Colorado plain and delta, dropping new, rich soils every year. This yearly inundation transforms the hot desert in the south into a green oasis along the river plain. Here along the lower Colorado lived the Mojave, the Yuma, and below them the Cocopa, close to the river's mouth. Together with the Maricopa, who lived along the Gila River near its junction with the Colorado, these tribes are called the River Yumans.

Exploiting the Environment. Native cultivation depended wholly on the yearly flooding of the Colorado. Besides leaving deep silts for farm plots, the flood waters also nourished a dense growth of wild food plants and cane, willows, and rushes for basketry and housing. The wild foods and the cultivated corn, beans, and squash could feed a population much larger than that of the Basin or even the Upland Yumans to the north. The Indians helped the wild plants along by scattering their seeds on the less fertile or less well watered patches.

Hunting provided very little food for the River Yumans. Game, even rabbit, was hard to find, so most of their nonvegetable protein came from the fish they caught in the river.

The river people's villages consisted of houses scattered along the river and its delta, high in the valleys or on steep slopes to escape flooding. In this hot desert land, protection from the sun was far more important than protection from cold or rain. Consequently, most housing consisted of open-sided shades with flat, slightly slanting woven roofs. There were also some more substantial structures, large earth-covered dwellings which, since there was so little rain, stood for years.

The River Yumans did not need much clothing. Their garments were simple: breechcloths for men, and for women a short skirt of the fibrous inner layer of willow bark, softened in water and woven into coarse cloth. Both men and women wore rabbit-skin robes in cooler weather. Moccasins were unknown, but occasionally the people wore hide sandals. Both sexes painted and tattooed their bodies. Material culture, including basketry, was also simple and rather poor in quality and durability. Trade with other tribes brought in better goods than home manufacture could produce.

Social Organization. The River Yumans had loose patrilineal clans, which did little beyond regulating marriage. People married outside their clan. The family was the basic economic and social unit, and families moved freely from settlement to settlement. Perhaps because of this movement among villages the Yumans had a strong sense of tribal identity. They had a tribal chief, whose leadership was hereditary: a dead chief's nearest male relative was the next leader so long as he was satisfactory to the rest of the people. His main functions were to give advice and to be dignified and wise. Within each settlement, local leaders acted as advisers, but their authority was no more than general esteem. The tribal chief himself had no means of enforcing his rulings.

Unlike the Pueblo or the Indians of California and the Basin, warfare was frequent among the River Yumans. Usually they fought with one another, though the Mojave and Yuma were generally allied with each other. Battle among these people had an almost ritual quality; it was thought of as a spiritual necessity and was strongly mystical. Encounters were stylized: the opposing forces drew up in battle array, advancing close enough for hand-to-hand fighting with clubs. Warriors might also carry bows and arrows or spears, usually specializing in one type of weapon. Often leading warriors fought duels in front of the assembled fighters before the battle, and sometimes the "war" was won by the side whose champion won the duel. Renown as a warrior increased a man's social status. War also involved raiding settlements for captives, usually female, who were made slaves. During both raids and battles fighting could be fierce, and scalps were taken from fallen enemies.

Religion. Among the River Yumans, religion was very individualistic. Dreams rather than vision quests were the source of power and success. Dreaming about spirits gave men aid in curing the sick or success in war or other endeavors. Respected men and chiefs were thought to receive their inspiration and wisdom from revelations in dreams. Dreams were supposed to be destined for each person before birth, part of the Yumans' strong sense of predestination. They believed each life was already "set up"; one had merely to learn one's lot from dreams. People made their dreams public so that their powers would be known to all.

Because dreams came naturally, the Yumans felt no need for the fasting, isolation, body punishment, or drugs common in many other societies. Dreams were not always of power, but all were felt to have supernatural content or symbolic meaning which could be used to predict the future. Except for the supernatural nature of dreams, the River Yumans had no developed religious theory or practices. The only religious specialist, the shaman, got his power like the rest of the people, from dreams. Women dreamed, but rarely had real power dreams and did not become either shamans or political figures. So strong was the belief in dream power that to wish a person good luck, one said "good dreams."

Like the people of southern California, the Yumans cremated their dead. The body was laid, face downward, in a trench filled with dry brush, and dry wood was piled high over the whole. To this were added personal belongings of the deceased and any offerings the mourners wished to make. After the fire had burned down, the ashes were covered with earth. No one ever again spoke the name of the dead person.

The Pimans

Both Piman tribes, the Pima and the Papago, occupied the southwestern section of what today is Arizona. The Pima lived along the Salt and Gila rivers, and the Papago lived in the desert along the Mexican border. Probably they were once a single group, almost surely descended from the prehistoric Hohokam. The two groups spoke the same language, differing only in dialects. Their only other cultural difference was that cultivation in Pima territory was easier than in the Papago, which had no permanent flowing water. Thus the Pima were sedentary, while the Papago followed the ancient life of seasonal movement, seeking new water sources as old ones dried up and exploiting the wild plant and animal life of their desert.

Subsistence. Primarily farmers, the Pima depended on water brought from the rivers by irrigation ditches to their fields of corn, beans, and squash. They supplemented their diet with wild plants and animals, which they badly needed in years of drought and crop failures, and with fish from the rivers. With such a relatively stable food supply, the Pima lived in permanent villages led by a headman who had considerable authority in directing labor in the irrigation works. And the Pima had a tribal chief, elected by the combined village chiefs.

The Papago depended mainly on hunting and gathering and supplemented that food with a small amount of farming. Violent July and August rains soaked the Papago fields and ensured water in the flat plains and in the water holes and ditches they constructed to control runoff. Their farming was possible only because of this summer rainfall. Men did most of the cultivating of the maize, tepary beans, and squashes, while women gathered wild plant foods. When summer rains ended, the fields dried and even drinking water disappeared from the plains. Then families wandered to the mountains to hunt or went to trade with neighboring groups.

Fish, important to the Pima, were unavailable to the Papago, whose territory had no waterways. The Papago had no choice but a semi-nomadic life, and their villages were autonomous units with no tribal structure. One of the ceremonial practices, rare north of the Mexican area, was to gather the fruit of the giant cactus and ferment it, making a wine which they drank with solemn ritual until they were drunk. This was a symbolic drunkenness; the people were saturated with alcohol as the fields were drenched by the summer rains. Long ago, the Pima too followed this practice, but they appear to have abandoned it shortly after European contact.

In that desert climate, neither of the Piman tribes needed much clothing: men wore breechcloths, women wore wraparound skirts. Both went barefoot most of the time, putting on leather or yucca fiber sandals to cross rocky terrain. Desert trees such as ironwood and mesquite provided the Pimans with wood for implements, and the women gathered grasses and reeds to make the fine basketry for which they were known. They also made some pottery in the ancient Hohokam style. For houses they had slightly domed structures, perhaps fifteen feet in diameter, with earth or sand piled against the sides, and roofs of brush thatching. They also enjoyed open-sided shades like the other Southwest groups during the intense summer heat.

Social Organization. The Pimans were peaceful and went to war reluctantly when faced with the need. Their principal enemy was the Apache who raided their fields. A warrior who killed an enemy had to go through rigorous purification. The enemy's ghost was greatly dreaded, and a man who had killed might endanger the entire village. Consequently, far from being honored and praised, any warrior who killed was put with his polluted weapons into isolation, far from the village. After a quarantine, observing strict dietary taboos and ritual behavior, he was allowed to come back into the community. Warriors never bragged of their exploits, and even the scalps they took were purified and ever after were given offerings of tobacco smoke.

Villages of both tribes were large groups of patrilineally related families. Men were expected to choose wives from villages other than their own and bring them back home to live. Girls were secluded at puberty and all later menstrual periods, and women gave birth in a hut away from the dwellings, remaining there for a month. Boys sought visions of spirits to help them in hunting. Like the River Yumans, shamans' power came from dreaming. They cured diseases (which were sent by animals or caused by failures in ritual), either by sucking out a foreign intruded object or by repeating the poorly performed ritual properly.

The Pueblo

The Southwest origin myth at the beginning of this section was recorded in many versions in the legends of the Keresan-speaking Pueblo. Some Pueblo myths strikingly resembled Judeo-Christian or Greek mythology in content and plot. In one of them, all the people of the world but two were destroyed for their wickedness, as in the Noah myth. In a kind of "Tower of Babel" story, two people quarreled so much that Earth Mother (one of the divinities) changed their language, causing each to speak a tongue the other could not understand.

Myths and legends carried a common theme: all the people should work together, behave properly, and respect ancestors and the supernatural, so that everything would go well and rain would come to water the crops and feed the people. From their many legends, the Pueblo developed their own cardinal points of the compass—six instead of four because they included up and down. Each direction had a color, a god, an animal, a woman, a tree, a snake, and a warrior associated with it. In such a well-ordered world, there was always strong public pressure to do everything just right. Ingenuity and originality were not highly regarded; the "right" was the traditional way.

The people's critical problem was getting enough to eat. Game was rarely plentiful, and everyone had to work hard and pray for rain. With good hearts, powerful songs, prayers, paraphernalia, and proper ritual, the Pueblo believed they could accomplish anything.

The agricultural Pueblo were descended mainly from the prehistoric Anasazi and Mogollon, who had populated the mesas and canyons of the Southwest. They lived in the highlands of northern Arizona, in a valley in west-central New Mexico, and along the upper Rio Grande and tributaries on the eastern slope of the Continental Divide in New Mexico. The Pueblo usually are divided into two groups: the Western including the Hopi who live on the tablelands and promontories of northern Arizona, the Zuni in New Mexico close to the Arizona border in the valley of the Zuni River, the Acoma, and the Laguna, and the Eastern or Rio Grande Pueblo. We speak of both the people and their village or pueblo with the same name: "The Zuni live at Zuni."

Three distinct language groups are represented among the Pueblo: Aztec-Tanoan (Hopi, and many Rio Grande people), Keresan (Cochiti, Acoma, and others), and Penutian (Zuni).

The Environment

Although Pueblo settlements spread over a fairly broad territory, their physical surroundings did not vary much. Pueblos were built in high, semiarid country where temperatures went from intense heat on a summer day to cool summer nights, and cold winter days were moderated by weeks of unbroken sunshine. Summer storms were sudden and often violent, but some rain fell throughout the year. Rainfall was somewhat greater in the higher altitudes of the east, and the river systems there helped in dry periods, whereas the western area depended upon rainfall and seepage entirely. Wild plants and animals were sparse, although not so rare as in some areas to the south and west inhabited by other Southwestern Indians, or in the Great Basin to the north.

Pueblo farmers grew corn, beans, squash, tobacco, and cotton. Water for these crops had to come from several sources because rainfall alone was never adequate and was always uncertain, varying widely from one year to the next. In the west, the Hopi counted on small, intermittent streams running from the highlands to the valleys, and underground water that seeped through the sandstone of the plateau top southward, reappearing in small springs and pools close enough to the pueblos to be used for the crops. In July and August, a crucial time for corn, the land received enough water from rain and these other sources to ensure the harvest for most seasons. The threat of too little water always hung over them, however, and much of Hopi life was devoted to using the water as efficiently as possible and to performing ceremonies to produce greater rainfall.

Zuni also lived in arid country, but they had the advantage of a permanent though meager water supply, the Zuni River, as well as more springs and somewhat greater rainfall. The pueblo of Acoma, sometimes referred to as Sky City, sat high on a mesa which had only small springs at the foot; the people built large reservoirs on the top to trap rainfall and supply the town with water. Their fields were some distance from the town and were watered by both the springs and rainfall.

Eastern Pueblo could get water from the Rio Grande close by, and they dug irrigation canals to bring the water to their fields. Farming was far more risky in the west than among the Rio Grande Pueblo: besides the ever-present threat of inadequate moisture, there was always the chance that violent summer storms would wash out the crop. To hedge their bets, the Western Pueblo planted in many different spots, each receiving water from different sources, so that if one planting failed, they would have others to fall back on. They ensured against crop failure with magical precautionary measures, rites to compel the supernatural to help them obtain a successful harvest. The Rio Grande peoples also had elaborate ceremonial practices.

Men were the cultivators, and labor was clearly divided. Women were responsible for raising the children, general domestic duties, gathering wild plants, and making pottery. Men farmed, made their own equipment, built the houses—though women added finishing touches like plastering—and did the weaving. They also hunted, though hunting was less important than elsewhere in North America. Men from the Rio Grande pueblos ventured into the plains occasionally to pursue buffalo, and all hunted antelope, deer, and especially rabbit.

Religion

All Pueblo cultures had a complex ceremonial life. Ceremonial activities were communal, with curing societies, priesthoods, and ritual associations taking part. Especially in the west, personal crises passed quietly, often unnoticed. Vision quests were not important, and even shamans were considered suspect because of their individuality. The Pueblo ideal was to avoid individualism.

Religious societies performed their ceremonies exactly as their ancestors had done. And like their forefathers the people made *prayer-sticks*, lengths of wood with feathers and perhaps shells attached. Prayer-sticks were messages to the spirits to send rain and other needed things. People prayed to the gods and spirits for rain. Good spirits, called *katcinas* by the Hopi of Arizona, brought rain when they visited. They had come from the underworld with the people, and men were permitted to impersonate them. Dressing as katcinas, men danced to get the rain to fall. Cloud, rain, and lightning symbols were everywhere, even on the headdresses of the katcina dancers.

Ceremonial activities took place in the open for the benefit of all the community and also, in most pueblos, in kivas, chambers often partially underground, to which only members of the religious order or society were admitted. Religion was a part of almost all aspects of life, and government was a civil and religious combination of the type we call theocratic, although there was usually a war chief; his responsibility was confined to warfare, raiding, defense, and communal hunting.

When a Pueblo died, the body was buried, but the soul went back to the place of emergence to return to the womb of the earth. That was the way it had been, and that was the way the people thought it should be.

Social Organization

The Western Pueblo were organized very differently from those of the Rio Grande. Westerners were matrilineal, belonging to their mother's clan, and newlyweds moved in with or close to the bride's mother's household. Women owned and inherited houses and land, and clans controlled ceremonial activities devoted to manipulating the weather. The Rio Grande peoples had greater variety. The Keresan-speaking people had matrilineal clans, but those were not responsible for performing ceremonies, as they were among the Westerners; associations rather than kin groups usually had that responsibility. Relatives on the mother's side were generally less important than in the west. The father and his family had more authority over the young in the east, and the nuclear family was more important.

The other Rio Grande Pueblo did not have clans, but traced kinship through mother and father equally, and the extended family was the basic social and economic unit. An extended family might include a man and wife and adult sons or daughters and their spouses and children. Rights in lands passed through both sons and daughters, whereas under the matrilineal system those rights passed through women only. All Pueblo people were monogamous, but divorce was easy and common.

The Pueblo peoples have frequently been described as peaceful, and compared to many other societies, they doubtless were. Childhood training as well as religious exhortation focused on development of tranquil adults dedicated to the difficult food quest rather than to feuding or the glory of warfare. However, the fact that the Pueblo lived surrounded by nomadic raiders intent on ravaging the Pueblo's scattered fields, so carefully and arduously maintained, meant that even the Pueblo had to fight. And so they did. Trained warriors protected Hopi buildings, lands, and crops. A war chief headed the Warrior's Society by virtue of his recognized superiority in warfare. He also helped the village chief maintain order within the community, and with a war party, went into battle when necessary and if successful returned with scalps of slain enemies.

Technology

With timber scarce in the desert, the Pueblo turned to the raw material most abundant—stone. As their ancestors had done, they built flat-topped rectangular rooms side by side and often several stories high. Some of those structures they covered with a thin plaster of *adobe*, a kind of clay. Adobe formed into sun-dried bricks became a major building material after Spanish contact. Some pueblos were built around a square or plaza; others were built in a row. Often the first-floor rooms were entered from the roof, as in ancient times. Most rooms were dark; windows, if any, were small; and the people carried on most of their activities outside—pottery making, preparing hides, preserving foods.

Women ground corn on a slab of stone called a *metate* (an Aztec word),

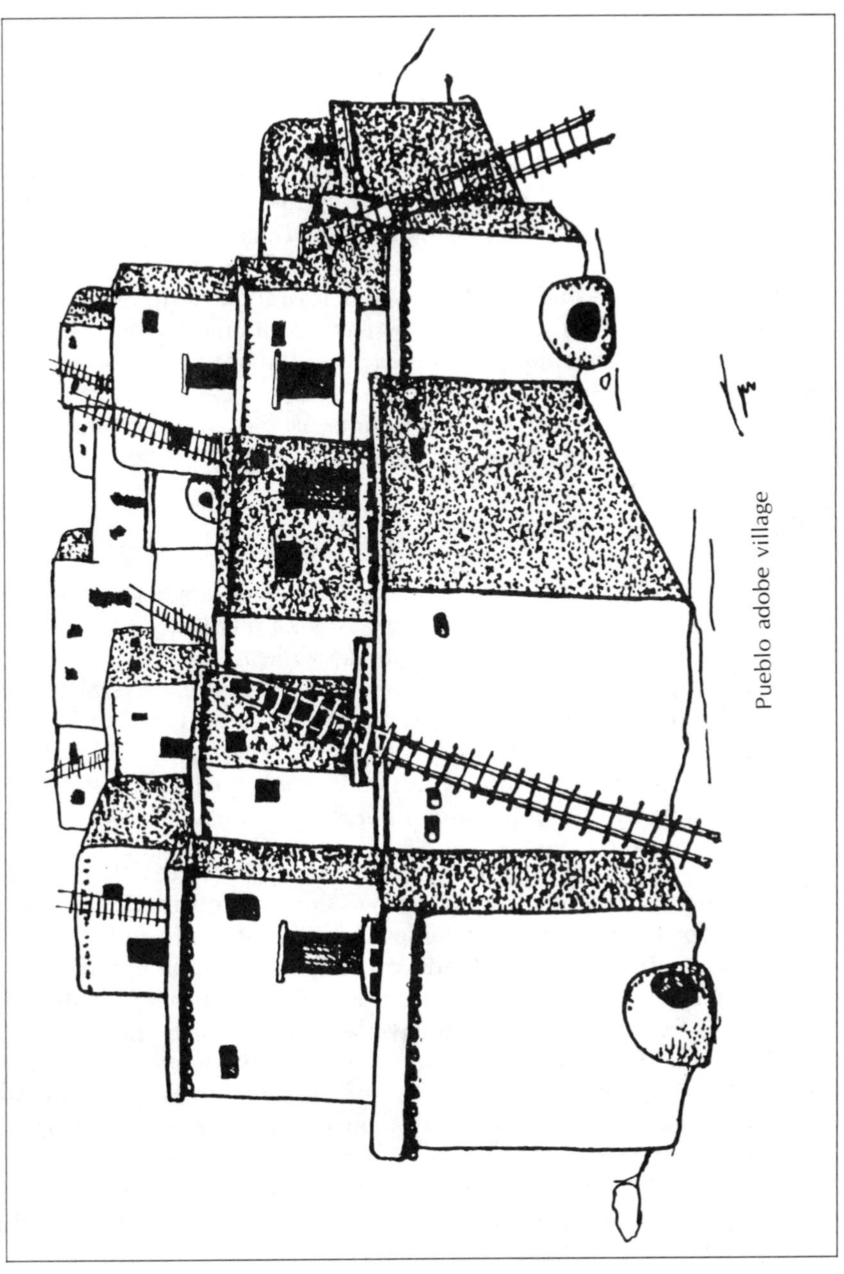

Pueblo adobe village

using a smaller stone, a *mano* (Spanish for "hand") to pulverize the grain into meal. Women also made many pottery utensils: ladles, bowls, dishes, cups, pitchers. They decorated some of the pottery with painted designs, but containers used directly on the smoky fires were left plain. Shapes and designs varied from pueblo to pueblo, and a Pueblo could tell from looking at an item where it had been made.

The Pueblo made much of their clothing from cotton cloth: breechcloths, belts, skirts, and dresses that fastened over the right shoulder, leaving the left shoulder bare. They made sandals from plant fibers such as yucca, and moccasins from hide. Women wrapped strips of buckskin around their lower legs. Men and women wore rabbit-skin or turkey-feather robes in the winter, and they decked themselves out gaily with beads and pendants of stone, shell and minerals—turquoise was a favorite. Traders carried the handicrafts as far away as Mexico to exchange for shell and other raw materials.

The Hopi

Westernmost of the Pueblo people, the Hopi spoke a language belonging to the Uto-Aztecan family in the Aztec-Tanoan phylum. They lived in villages on mesas with their fields in the valleys.

Hopi housing was the usual pueblo structure of stone, several stories high, often terraced with the upper stories set back. Two hundred or so people lived in each pueblo or village, grouped by clans. Sometimes the pueblo was built to enclose a courtyard. People got into the dwellings through a hole in the roof, using a notched pole as a ladder.

Cultivation. Because they never got enough rain for their crops, the Hopi scattered their planting in many fields where runoff water and ground seepage supplemented the scant precipitation. In addition they had to face sudden summer cloudbursts that might wash out the crops or bury them under a load of mud. Consequently the farmers dug ditches around the fields and built protective barriers of brush and logs.

Most important of the crops was corn, followed by squash, beans, and cotton. Corn was planted earliest, in April and May. The young plants had to survive not only spring drought but also severe sandstorms. Squash was planted soon after the first corn, and then more corn and squash were planted with beans, spreading the planting so that fields were under cultivation at varying times, there were always plants in many stages of growth, and crops reached maturity and harvest at different times. Plants were widely spaced, sown in spots that had not been used the year before. Ten to twenty corn seeds were planted in the same hole, a foot or more deep to give the roots room to develop and protect them from drying out or being washed out. Sowing many seeds helped make sure that some plants would survive to maturity.

Cultivable land was allotted to each of the matrilineal clans, who marked off their plots with boundary stones. A clan's fields were never all in one place, nor was all the clan land under cultivation at any one time. Such dispersal improved the chance of a successful harvest—though some fields might fail, others would not. The men tended their wives' crops; women sometimes helped at harvest. Women were considered the owners of the land as well as of the houses.

Each stage of cultivation and plant growth had its ceremonial activity following the ritual calendar. The calendar was based on the sun's position at sunrise, which moves gradually from the southernmost point on the horizon at the winter solstice to its northernmost point at midsummer. The Sun Watcher, a religious functionary, took daily observations and announced the important dates. When the sun rose from behind a certain hill, he declared that planting time had arrived and all danger of frost had passed.

Hopi women and sometimes men supplemented the diet of domesticated crops by collecting a variety of wild plants, for example, mesquite beans, piñon nuts, and juniper berries, and the men hunted antelope, deer, coyote, rabbits, and prairie dogs among others. They hunted the larger animals with bows and arrows, and the smaller with curved throwing sticks. The Hopi kept domesticated turkeys for their feathers and for occasional food. In addition they often caged eagles and hawks for their plumage though they did not eat them.

People obtained salt after a long and fairly difficult journey to mineral springs. Salt was relished especially where the diet was composed largely of plant foods, so it is no wonder that the quest for salt was sacred, made with much ritual and ceremonialism.

Katcinas. At the winter solstice, all the adult Hopi men held the Soyal Ceremony. It was the responsibility of one clan, and was meant to force the sun, now at its southernmost position on the horizon, to return north so that the crops would grow. It was at the Soyal that katcinas appeared, staying until the summer solstice, when they presumably returned to their mountain homes.

The katcinas were supernaturals, cloud beings and bringers of rain, beloved by the Hopi. Their appearance each year was portrayed by the katcina dancers, men in katcina masks who performed at ceremonials during the first six months of the year, when the katcinas were thought to live among men. Children were given small images of them, usually called *katcina dolls*, mostly to teach them about the many katcinas. All adult Hopi belonged to the Katcina Cult, though normally only men portrayed katcinas. For six months every year, the Katcina Cult members had to see that performances of ceremonies and rituals designed to

Katcina dancers performed at Hopi ceremonies to ensure good crops. They were also a means of social control, visiting children to learn if they had been good.

summon the clouds and bring rain were done correctly.

In addition to their ritual performances, the katcina impersonators were a means of social control. They visited the houses, asking whether the children had been good for the past year. Children who had misbehaved were threatened with being hauled away in baskets the katcinas carried. Parents pretended to defend the children, who must have been terrified by the huge masked beings trying to snatch them from their homes. When children entered adulthood and were accepted as full members of the tribe, they were told that the katcinas were just their male neighbors and relatives. All this might seem to have been cruel to little children, yet katcinas were thought of as good and kind spirits.

Other Ceremonies. Another important ceremony, Powamu or bean planting festival, took place in February at the new moon and lasted until beans sprouted in the kiva that belonged to the Powamu Society. Early in the ceremony, seed beans had been planted in basins of sand in the kiva. In the warmth from fires kept burning and with kiva members watering them well the seeds germinated quickly. These beans were considered omens of the year's crops—if they grew well, the yield would be good. Members of the Powamu and Katcina Societies had ritual duties, and their traditions, rituals, and lore were secret.

Every year in late summer, societies put on another ceremonial. The Antelope and Snake Societies performed together, alternating every other year with the Flute Society, conducting prayers and making offerings to bring rain to the crops and fertility to the women. But the best known Hopi ceremony is the Snake Dance, a nine-day ceremony. For the first four days, members of the society went out to the north, south, east, and west to collect snakes. The next few days were for secret rites carried on in their kiva. The ninth day brought a public dance in the square. Members of Snake Society danced with snakes—both poisonous and harmless—held in their mouths or around their necks. After the dance, all snakes were released to return to the gods with messages asking for rain.

Tribal initiation in November was the year's last major ceremony. Men were initiated into the Katcina Cult, boys into one of the four men's societies, and girls into women's societies. By this initiation they became full, functioning adult members of the tribe.

These and the other ceremonials during the year, each one a series of dances and rituals, might last a few days and nights or a month or more. There was little time during the year when one ceremony or another was not under way. Hopi life was always and intimately tied to ceremony and religion. Most Hopi thought and endeavor were directed toward obtaining blessing and help from the supernatural. The main contact with the supernatural was the societies, who devoted their efforts to rain, fertility, crops, and good behavior.

Hopi Deities. The Hopi populated their cosmos with many supernaturals—including the spirits of their ancestors, called the Six-Point-Cloud-People. They believed that success in the food quest and life in general depended upon appeasing and pleasing those incorporeal beings. Chief among deities was the Sun, and many other sky and weather gods were associated with the Sun, for instance Eagle, Rain, and Thunder, while among lesser gods or spirits were the Wind and Rainbow deities. Serpent spirits had power over the water supply and dwelt in springs. The Six-Point-Cloud-People also aided in bringing water to the Hopi, causing rain to fall from the clouds that carried them to their descendants. The Hopi decorated their ritual paraphernalia such as Katcina masks with symbols of rain, lightning, and fertility.

There was a god of fire and death, Masau'a, a fearsome being. Muyingwa supervised the germination of crops. The Spider Woman, also known as the Salt Woman, dwelt near the Hopi villages with her grandsons, the Twin War Gods. In addition, the Corn Mother and her Corn Maidens cared for the corn plants, and the Mother of Wild Animals watched over the game supply. The preceding were only the major figures. The Hopi conceived of all nature inhabited by spirits that must be propitiated, and a body of mythology developed to teach children the appropriate behavior and to explain the universe.

Witchcraft. The Hopi explained crop failure, bad behavior, and all other undesirable happenings as having been caused by witchcraft. Witches might be either men or women; they could be recognized by their un-Hopi behavior—they behaved differently. A proper Hopi (*hopi* means "good") was cooperative, unassertive, generally undistinguished, and calm. Anyone who stood out as aggressive, ambitious, flamboyant, or offensive was suspected of being *kahope*, the opposite of Hopi, and probably was a witch. To call someone a witch was the worst possible accusation. Witches were referred to as "Two Hearts" because they were believed to have one heart of their own and another of the animal spirit that gave them their witch power. Witches were greatly feared as killers of people, animals, and crops. Although most Hopi religious activity was social, not individualistic, they did have some shamans, and it was to the shamans that the Hopi turned to cure illness caused by witches. However, shamans themselves were highly suspect, for they were too individualistic and might well be witches.

Cochiti

The pueblo of Cochiti, on the Rio Grande about thirty miles southwest of what is now Santa Fe, was inhabited by Keresan speakers. In climate and weather Cochiti was not much different from Hopi, but the presence of the river contributed to important differences in social organization. The work of irrigation required more political centralization than kin groups could provide, so Cochiti depended more on non-kin units.

Social Organization. The Cochiti did have matrilineal clans, but they were less important in religion and government than at Hopi. The matrilineal extended family brought up the children, but Cochiti fathers, not mothers' brothers, were the disciplinarians; the nuclear family was more significant here. The religious and economic functions taken care of by clans in Hopi were assumed by associations or cults at Cochiti, though the clan stayed in charge of marriage arrangements. Associations watched over village activities, disease, warfare, crop fertility, and communal well-being and harmony. Specific associations handled specific problems, seeing that the proper rites were performed. The Cochiti were much less absorbed by weather control such as rainmaking, and emphasized the importance of the sun.

Cochiti society was divided into moieties. Everyone belonged to either the Pumpkin (sometimes called Squash) or the Turquoise division, each with its own kiva. Children became members of their father's kiva, but a woman might transfer to her husband's at marriage. In fact, anyone could leave his father's moiety if he chose, though clan affiliation could never be changed.

The moieties had social, religious, and political influence. Some political officials were chosen from one kiva, some from the other, and those offices alternated between the two kivas. Each kiva was also responsible for putting on some of the ceremonials and dances, functions of the clan at Hopi. Cochiti also had a katcina cult, called Shiwana. Most of its ceremonies were secret, unlike the very public Hopi katcinas, but some of its dances were public, and the dancers' masks were as elaborate as the Hopi's. The Shiwana Cult was controlled by medicine societies.

Medicine Societies. Cochiti medicine societies were very influential—the real basis of government, in fact. The head of the town, called by the Spanish a *cacique*, was always the head of a medicine society. He served as both government chief and head priest, and was constantly concerned with the general welfare, living a frugal life and fasting often to set a good example for everyone else. He was aided in the practical matters of government by a council composed of officers of the societies.

The village had four medicine societies, two in each moiety, which took charge of solstice ceremonies, performed cures, and destroyed witches. These societies were so highly organized that they have been called priesthoods. Joining a medicine society took up to four years of preparation. The head of the society saw to it that candidates spent that time observing the proper dietary and sexual restrictions, ending with a rigorous four-day purge. Then the candidate joined the other members in seclusion to be prepared for initiation. After songs, prayers, ceremonial whipping, and dancing, the initiate was given a new name. His was the lowest position in the society; and he moved up only as members ahead of him died. Medicine societies were never large.

Clowns. Another form of association, besides the medicine societies and Shiwana Cult, was the clowns, called Koshare. They hid their identities not by masks and clothing, but with paint and hair: they were painted with horizontal black and white stripes from head to toe, black circles outlining their mouths and eyes in white faces, and their hair was arranged into two upright "horns" on each side of a central part. Koshare helped the cacique in communal activities. Both men and women could become members of the association of clowns, but women worked mostly on preparing food.

Social control may have been the clowns' most important job. Anyone behaving improperly could be sure of being publicly ridiculed or even humiliated by the clowns, and that was usually enough to make people conform. The clowns' antics also supplied comic relief, some of it bordering on the obscene. They behaved as other citizens could not, offering a vicarious experience in forbidden activity that greatly amused the spectators.

Cochiti had other associations, like the Warriors and the Hunters, that were less important than the medicine societies because they dealt with less significant parts of Pueblo life. These organizations duplicated some functions of medicine societies, but did not have their prestige or power.

Witchcraft. Fear of witchcraft was strong at Cochiti, and people were as afraid of being charged with witchcraft as they were of the practice itself. It was terrifying to think you might be a witch and not even know it. Witches took many forms—human, animal, reptile, or even red fireballs with black centers. Members of the medicine societies could exorcise or cast out the witches, but sometimes it was hard to rid the community of sorcery. The tension would build up as each citizen wondered who might be a witch. Like the Hopi, the Cochiti blamed witchcraft for things that went wrong even when all rituals had been faithfully performed.

Pueblo Organization

We might call Cochiti, like Hopi, a small theocracy, combining government and religious functions in associations and individuals. The basic organizational difference between the two was their ways of recruiting people into the major public groups. The Hopi used kinship; in Cochiti it was membership in associations which cut across kin ties. Some anthropologists suggest that the non-kin organizations made it easier to mobilize the community for the necessary public work in irrigation. Except for that, all the Pueblo people were much alike, especially in religion, which was the key to Pueblo life, and in their continuous ceremonial activity.

All Pueblo believed that their chiefs or caciques should set an example of the perfect Pueblo, keeping calm and remote from petty, personal squabbles. Chiefs should be above ordinary emotions such as anger, hate, or vindictiveness. Anthropologist Ruth Benedict described the desirable leadership quality as the golden mean—all things in moderation. Although such a personality served as a model for the average citizen, all knew that most people would fall short of it, and of course they did. Still, the societal standard the chief was expected to exemplify was very different from that of the Indians of the Northwest Coast, the Plains, or the East. The chiefs felt this pressure for perfection, and that is probably one reason why few men were interested in the position.

The Southern Athabaskans

Arriving in the Southwest later than other Indian groups were the Athabaskans, whose nearest linguistic relatives were the Athabaskan-speaking peoples of western Canada. Some anthropologists and archaeologists believe that advance groups of Athabaskans may have come to the Southwest as early as the thirteenth century, but most feel they probably were not there before the fifteenth. They were hunters and gatherers, more aggressive and less settled than the Pueblo; their raids on the farmers' fields and homes were perhaps the first contributions toward a long lived tradition of emnity between the southern Athabaskans and the Pueblo. Eventually they came to live in the area, and today their descendants are known as Apache and Navajo.

The Migration South

Probably the advance of these nomads from the north caused the settled farmers only limited problems at first—a few fields plundered, a few women stolen. The pueblos themselves, entered from the roof, were easy enough to defend. However, as more of the intruders entered the Pueblo territory and preyed on the inhabitants and their crops, relations worsened, and it is easy to see how the invaders became more than a nuisance. One of their advantages was their superior weapon, the sinew-backed bow, which could shoot farther, straighter, and with more deadly effect than the Pueblo people's simple bow. The Athabaskans appear to have been enthusiastic and skillful warriors, and even today Zuni mothers frighten naughty children by telling them to behave or a Navajo will get them.

We do not know why the Athabaskans moved south into Pueblo country. Hunters and gatherers, they lived off wild foods as they moved, carrying their weapons and very little else. Probably their immigration continued over many decades. Some may have come through the Great Basin; others appear to have taken an eastern route along the foothills of the Rockies. By the time Europeans came, Athabaskans were living in the southern plains as well as in central Arizona.

As the Athabaskans moved, they not only raided the settled cultivators but began to take on some of the local skills and customs, modifying them to fit with their own traditions. Some groups of newcomers borrowed more of the Pueblo customs than others. Those who came to be known as Navajo learned to cultivate crops, as some western Apache groups did later, while eastern Apache remained hunters and gatherers, some of them later taking part in the thoroughly typical Plains way of life, which will be discussed in the next chapter. In spite of this mixing with a new culture, most of their dialects remained mutually intelligible at first, and the groups held onto a deep layer of common custom that stayed different from the Pueblo ways. As time passed, however, the Athabaskan groups became more and more differentiated.

The Apache

The southern Athabaskans probably did not become two groups, Navajo and Apache, until long after they wandered in from their northern homeland. They must have come in bands, which over the generations sometimes came together for a time, sometimes broke up. We have no facts about the Athabaskans before about 1600. By then Apache were clearly separate from Navajo. Though the Navajo mixed with the Pueblo and the Spanish, the Apache long remained aloof from both. To learn something about older Athabaskan practices and customs, then, our best source is the Apache. The Apache had no tribal identity; their allegiance was to their local bands. Those bands have come to be known as the Chiricahua (the band of the famous leaders Geronimo and Cochise), the Mescalero, the Jicarilla, and an offshoot of the Jicarilla, the Lipan, who moved into Mexico under pressure from the Comanche. All these bands ranged from southern Colorado to the Texas border, and the Chiricahua also extended into Arizona. Other bands, collectively known as the Western Apache, lived in east-central Arizona, where they grew far more like the Navajo than the eastern Apache did. One eastern group joined Kiowa of the southern plains and was later called the Kiowa Apache. After the horse appeared in the area, the Apache became raiders feared by all agricultural neighbors; even the Western Apache raided, though they also did some cultivating.

Apache Life. Among the Western Apache, the women tended the crops, and collected the same wild plants favored by their neighbors to the west, the Pimans. The Apache made a kind of beer from the fruit of the mescal cactus or from maize, a practice they probably learned from Mexican Indians or perhaps the Pimans. In the west, where it was too mountainous for horse transportation, horses were more often eaten than ridden at first.

The nomadic eastern Apache had very little agriculture; they were hunters, gatherers, and raiders. Before they had horses, they hunted buffalo on foot, using dogs and *travois* to carry meat and equipment; the travois consisted of two poles trailing from the animal's back and acting as shafts between which a net or platform was constructed to bear the load. They were among the first Indians to take a mounted life when horses became available. It was from the eastern Apache that the great Apache warriors came. Men had little trouble raising enthusiasm for a raiding party—that was a way of life and the means to success and social recognition. Raiding and warfare were considered proper male occupations, and boys were trained to be aggressive and brave. Warriors collected scalps of fallen enemies, but since all Apache greatly feared the dead, the scalps had to be purified to make them safe. Then warriors often wore them on their shirts as a sort of battle insignia.

Apache women were excellent basketmakers, but not very adept at making pottery, which is of little value to people on the move. Clothing was of buckskin, and most Apache lived in wickiups of brush-covered saplings; some Apache of the plains built hide tipis.

Social Organization. Apache bands were independent of one another and had no overall leader. Each band had an informal chief who held his position by his ability and the willingness of band members to follow him. Raiding parties were volunteers who joined a war or raid leader they respected. The bands themselves consisted of groups of extended families that had a strong sense of band unity, especially when faced with external threats such as enemy raids.

The Western Apache's matrilineal clans probably grew out of their contact with Navajo, who reckoned descent matrilineally; the other Apache bands traced their kinship equally through males and females. Almost all Apache practiced what has been termed *mother-in-law avoidance*. When he could, a man was supposed to avoid his mother-in-law; if he found that impossible occasionally, he should avoid looking at her. Men could have more than one wife, but the wives were always sisters.

Religion. Every Apache had a horror of death, burying the dead one swiftly and burning his house and possessions. Then the mourning family purified itself ritually and moved to a new place to escape the ghost of the deceased, The ghost, not the body, was fearsome because ghosts might harm the living or take them away to their ghostly dwelling place.

A girl's first menstruation brought a four-day ceremony: a shaman sang songs, a woman instructed the girl in proper behavior, and masked dancers performed at night to bring the girl a blessing from the supernatural. This girls' puberty rite was one of the most important Apache ceremonies and may have been derived from the northern Athabaskan traditions in which the puberty ceremony was of great importance. Several Apache girls went through ritual together, and the whole community participated at some time during the four days, if only as chanting spectators.

Masked dancers also appeared at ceremonies, for curing and to ensure success in hunting or warfare. Shamans got their powers from individual visions, but the dancers' rites and dance steps were learned.

The Navajo

Navajo land was and is desert with such typical desert vegetation as sage, piñon, and juniper. It is hot in summer and cold in winter, and drought is an ever-present threat; even in the mountains, rainfall never exceeds twenty inches per year. When it does come, the rain forms raging, land-eroding torrents. Over the centuries, rain and wind have carved the earth into spectacular mesas and canyons, fantastic buttes and skyscraping basalt columns.

Today the Navajo are the largest Indian tribe in the United States. They live in north-central Arizona, southern Utah, and western New Mexico. Little is known of them before 1600, when Spaniards entered their country. The Navajo are more like the Pueblo than the Apache are, perhaps because the Navajo were neighbors of the Pueblo Hopi for 500 years, and because many Rio Grande Pueblo refugees went to live with the Navajo after an unsuccessful war against the Spanish from 1690 to 1692. Though the Navajo took up the Pueblo dress, loom and weaving practices, and many ceremonies, they kept their distinctive house. This was the *hogan*, a log-framed, earth-covered, circular structure with the doorway always on the east. Later forms were often six- or eight-sided. Although many Navajo have moved into contemporary housing in recent years, the hogan still is important for ceremonials.

Under Pueblo influence, the Navajo turned from their hunting and gathering economy to farming, and after contact with the Spanish, to herding sheep and raising livestock. Sheep gave wool for weaving, and all livestock was used for food, because most of the wild game was gone and the sheep and other grazers ate whatever vegetation there was in the desert.

Special Patterns. The seventeenth-century Navajo way of life mingled Pueblo, Spanish, and ancient Athabaskan customs, adding cultivation from the Pueblo and herding from the Spanish to old traditions to produce a unique culture. Like the Pueblo, the Navajo developed matrilineal clans, but they kept their local group or band autonomy—often to the despair of the federal government agents, who tried to bind the Navajo with treaties, only to learn that no band felt obliged to observe agreements made by any other band.

The band was a scattered group, not a village, because to herd sheep

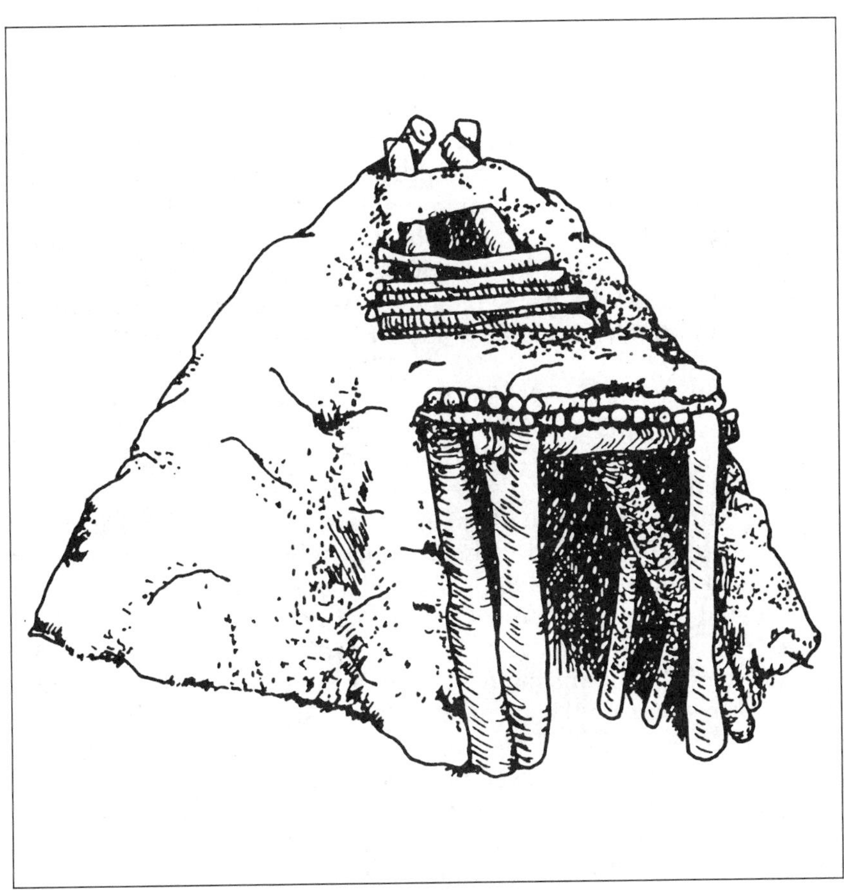

Traditional hogan. Logs set in the ground form a point with a covered entrance. Earth covers the structure which always opens to the east. Later hogans were made with horizontal logs, six or eight sided, also covered with earth.

in that environment people had to cover a wide area. They were bound by their common language, rituals, and kinship, which extended from band to band by marriage.

An outstanding contrast between the northern Athabaskan and the Navajo lay in the status they accorded women. As you may recall, the position of northern Athabaskan women was not high; among some groups, it was distinctly inferior. The Navajo woman held a strong and respected place in society. She was important economically because she controlled lineage property, which passed through women. As weaving paid more and more, the woman who did the weaving got the income from her work. She also owned the sheep, so that the proceeds from selling wool or sheep went to her. Socially, the woman was the center of the nuclear family. Newlywed couples generally moved into hogans near the wife's mother; if they divorced, the man returned to his mother's house. Children were closer to their mother's relatives because they usually lived nearby, and also because the matrilineal relatives formed the groups that did the daily chores and had most of the responsibility for rearing children. Like the Apache, the Navajo observed the mother-in-law taboo: a man was never to look at his wife's mother or even be in the same room with her, which must have kept in-law quarreling to a minimum but also inspired many Athabaskan mother-in-law jokes.

Kinship and Sociopolitical Groups. Another group the Navajo formed was the *outfit*, composed of matrilineally related extended families living fairly close together. Each outfit farmed within a defined territory, clearing and planting new fields as old ones became infertile, and also herded within their own domain. The outfit was an organization cemented by kin ties and common land rights. It had a headman or spokesman who was an older, respected member of the outfit and who represented the group in disputes or dealings with outsiders.

Larger than the outfit was the clan, which was matrilineal (each member belonged to his mother's clan) and exogamous (each member had to marry outside the clan and also outside his father's clan). Clan elders were responsible for clan members' behavior and for training their children. Clan members felt responsible for one another and supported each other in time of need or danger. The mother's brother was in charge of his nephews and nieces, disciplining as well as instructing them: his opinion had great weight in matters of marriage.

Social and political control thus was handled by the family, the clan, and the outfit, not by political or legal structure. Sometimes the outfits in a territory did gather into bands, under the leadership of a headman; these groups were territorial rather than based on kinship. As elsewhere, the headman's leadership depended on his wisdom and ability; he had no coercive power. Communities or bands made their decisions after discussion and unanimous agreement among the adults of the group, both male and female.

Navajo Sings. As among the Apache, a girl's puberty was a time for ceremony, one among many in an elaborate cycle of rituals in which all adult Navajo took part. The girl's ceremony lasted four days and was intended to mold her into a virtuous young woman. While she was in seclusion, family and friends gathered to sing and ensure the girl's future.

Some of the ceremonials, called sings, were meant to cure ailments of any kind, from disease to laziness, from drunkenness to marital problems. A specialist often prescribed chants, songs, or rituals. Sometimes referred to as a *hand trembler*, he did part of his diagnosis by holding his hands over the sick one's body until they trembled where the disorder lay, then he recommended the ceremony that would work a cure. Then the sick person or a relative hired a singer who knew that ritual and was willing to conduct the sing, which would last from one to five days. To start the ceremony, the singer usually made a design on the ground by dribbling colored earths, pollens, powdered minerals, or ground charcoal between his thumb and fingers. Often referred to as *sand paintings*, these designs might better be called dry painting, because many substances besides sand were used. The singer then directed a continuous chant toward the patient; if it was not letter perfect, the ceremony would be ineffective.

The Navajo singer or chanter, sometimes called a medicine man, learned the sacred songs by being apprenticed to an older singer. Everyone sang sacred songs, but only the chanter could cure. Curing and chanting were part-time occupations, supplemented by tending flocks, farming, and hunting.

Community Ceremonies. Larger, public ceremonies, including whole communities, were like the family curing sings but more complex, and they often were meant for more than one patient. Social activities evolved around two of those ceremonies, making them something more than curing sings. The most famous and most often performed was the Enemy Way. *Way* is used as an English alternative for "sing." This ritual was designed to remove the evil influences from warriors returning from a raid. It was recently revived for soldiers returning from world wars and other military actions such as the Viet Nam conflict. Held in the summer months, the ceremony lasted four days. Anyone who felt the need for a ritual cure might decide to have the ceremony, though this decision was usually confirmed with a diagnostician. Enemy Way was performed to render the ghost of an outsider, an enemy ghost, ineffective. "Way" applies to the whole ceremonial, consisting of chants, rituals, and a dance. The dance part itself was social, having nothing to do with the ritual, and was a kind of courtship dance at which young unmarried women, dressed for the occasion, appeared each night to select male partners for the dance and as possible mates. That is why Enemy Way has in recent years been called the Squaw Dance.

Other dances, the Yeibeichai, took place in winter: nine days and nights of chants and rituals. This ceremonial was more spectacular than the dances of Enemy Way because the dancers were masked and costumed and, in the part called the Fire Dance, performed with firebrands. It was also a more powerful ceremonial, as evidenced by its

Navajo sand painting performed for the benefit of a sick child.

greater complexity. Learning the necessary songs and paraphernalia took years of apprenticeship to an older singer. An apprentice paid for instruction in service, money, or livestock, which gave the younger singer the right to the performance. Stolen knowledge lost its power.

Ghosts and Witchcraft. Like other southern Athabaskans, the Navajo deeply feared the dead. They believed in ghosts, and believed that all ghosts were evil. Ghosts came back to cause trouble among the living, even to enter the bodies of the living, which was good reason for avoiding the dead. Anyone exposed to a corpse had to undergo long and expensive ritual treatment, and when someone died inside a hogan, it was abandoned. Often a seriously ill person was moved out of the hogan so that he or she would not die inside and force the family to seek a new home. As one would imagine, burial was quick, without much ceremony, and funerals and people near death were avoided whenever possible. So great was their dread that many Navajo would not go out at night when they believed ghosts were abroad. The Navajo were delighted when white undertakers took over the care and disposal of the dead.

The Navajo believed that just as some medicine men were good, laboring and paying to learn blessing chants, others did the same to learn evil chants. Those witches, both male and female, could bring illness and disaster, and the Navajo greatly feared them. Every Navajo believed that some people actually were initiated as witches and possessed evil power. They told many stories of "black Sabbaths," incest, nakedness, and murder.

Of all witches, the Navajo feared the Wolf-man and Wolf-woman most. Those beings could transform themselves into wolves or coyotes, and bewitch their enemies by sprinkling ground parts of human infants through the smoke hole, into the hogan. Bullets could kill a Wolf-man or Wolf-woman, but the witch's kin would seek vengeance against the executioner, and any kinfolk of witches were probably witches themselves.

Other Beliefs and Practices. Navajo accompanied every one of their daily activities, no matter how mundane, with ritual. At sunrise the eldest male of the household began the day by singing a sacred song and dropping corn pollen, which was sacred, to the four directions, north, east, south, and west. Sacred songs were sung all day—in the fields, while driving the herds, as household tasks were performed—calling for blessings or protection for the family and herds. Men took sweat baths together in semi-underground rooms, combining cleanliness with worship. During the sweating, they sang songs that were mostly prayers, asking for good health, good crops, good herds, rain, and wealth.

Navajo religion was not so much a theological system as a means of keeping humans in harmony with the universe and maintaining order and balance. The world was a dangerous place, and only ceremonials could bring security and serenity. Religion therefore was largely a guide to behavior from situation to situation and a way of atoning for neglect, ignorance, and errors in judgment, as well as countering the malevolence of others. Unlike the Pueblo, the many Navajo religious specialists did not form a body of priests, but were alternative sources of power or means of manipulating the supernatural. If one practitioner failed a Navajo sought help from another.

The Navajo word for themselves, Diné, meant "people of the surface of the earth." Their creation myth is a key to the Navajo relationship with the Pueblo. Having borrowed from the Pueblo many ideas in myth and ceremony, the Navajo added their own special emphases and elaborations. The origin myth described their ancestors coming to the earth's surface and the happenings that ultimately produced the Navajo way of life. The Navajo believed that below the surface of the earth were twelve worlds, inhabited by powerful Holy People or Powerful Ones

CHARACTERISTICS OF THE SOUTHWEST TRIBES

Clothing	Food production	Equipment	Shelter	Social and political organization	Religion	Warfare
Leather, fur, and fiber clothing	Cultivation (corn, beans, and squash)	Digging sticks	Pueblos	Bands	Shamans	Warfare frequent among River Yumans (raids, duels, and battles)
Woven cotton (Pueblo)	Hunting	Throwing sticks	Kivas	Nuclear families	Ghosts	Warfare rare among Pimans
Breechcloths	Gathering	Basketry	Wickiups	Patrilineal clans (River Yumans)	Spirits	Raids common among Apache
Fiber skirts	Fishing	Nets	Hogans (Navajo)	Matrilineal clans (Western Pueblo and Navajo)	Witchcraft	
Rabbit-skin robes	Livestock-raising (post-contact Navajo and Apache)	Bows and arrows	Tipis (some Apache)	Patrilineal families (Pima and Papago)	Dreams as a source of power	
Dresses		Spears	Shades (Havasupai)	Bilateral extended families (Rio Grande Pueblos)	Rituals for farming success	
Moccasins		Pottery	Domed structures with thatched roofs	Tribal chiefs (River Yumans and Papago)	Curing societies	
Sandals		Clubs	Semi-subterranean houses		Priesthoods	
		Manos and metates			Ritual associations	
		Stone bowls and cups			Katcina dancers	

(Yei). Two of the Holy People, created from two ears of corn, were First Man and First Woman, who, some accounts say, created the universe. They were the parents of Changing Woman, the most important person in Navajo mythology. She personified the earth, like Mother Nature; her "changing" was seasonal change. Changing Woman mated with the Sun and with Water and produced twin sons. They grew up and received from the Sun weapons and knowledge with which they killed the monsters that were on earth. The Navajo saw evidence of all this in natural land formations (mountains, lava flows, basalt columns) which they took to be the remains of the monsters. The Twin Monster Slayers' lives were a model for proper, traditional Navajo male behavior, just as witches were the model for improper, undesirable behavior.

There were many other Holy People—each associated with natural land features, other Yei, the weather, vegetation, mineral deposits, or animals. The Yei were not gods; their behavior was not perfect, and they could be controlled and persuaded by ritual acts, which were the guides for Navajo life. The whole Navajo mythology explained the otherwise inexplicable, creating traditions of knowledge, ceremonial practices, and proper behavior.

Suggestions for Further Study

Bibliography

Downs, James F. 1972. *The Navajo.*

A study of Navajo sheepherding, describing the general reservation culture as well as the historical background.

Dozier, Edward P. 1970. *The Pueblo Indians of North America.*

A general ethnographic and historical survey of Pueblo cultures by an eminent American Indian scholar and professor of anthropology.

Lange, Charles H. 1959. *Cochiti, a New Mexico Pueblo.*

A historical and ethnographic study of one of the Rio Grande pueblos.

Ortiz, Alfonso. 1969. *The World of the Tewa Indians.*

Written by an American Indian anthropologist, this is a study of the Pueblo peoples of the Tewa linguistic group.

Simmons, Leo W. 1963. *Sun Chief: The Autobiography of a Hopi Indian.*

A memorable study of the life of a Hopi man. This book puts the reader into the Pueblo culture as few others have done.

Other Pertinent Works

Basso, Keith. 1970. *The Cibecue Apache.*

Beaglehole, E. 1935. *Hopi of the Second Mesa.*

Downs, James 1966. *Two Worlds of the Washo.*

Joseph, Alice, R. B. Spicer, and J. Chesky. 1949. *The Desert People: A Study of the Papago Indians.*

Opler, Morris E. 1941. *An Apache Life-way.*

Steward, Julian H. 1933. *Ethnography of the Owens Valley Paiute.*

Stewart, Omer C. 1941. *Northern Paiute.*

Underhill, Ruth. 1956. *The Navahos.*

MAJOR GROUPS AND LANGUAGES OF THE GREAT BASIN AND THE SOUTHWEST

Language phylum	Language family	Cultural division
GREAT BASIN		
Aztec-Tanoan	Uto-Aztecan	Bannock Gosiute Paiute Shoshoni Ute
Hokan	Washo	Washo
SOUTHWEST		
Aztec-Tanoan	Kiowa-Tanoan TEWA DIVISION	Hano Nambe San Ildefonso San Juan Santa Clara Tesuque
	TIWA DIVISION	Isleta Picuris Sandia Taos
	TOWA DIVISION	Jemez
	Uto-Aztecan	Hopi Papago Pima

MAJOR GROUPS AND LANGUAGES (continued)

SOUTHWEST (continued)

Language phylum	Language family	Cultural division
Hokan	Yuman	Cocopa Havasupai Maricopa Mojave Walapai Yavapai Yuma
Na-Dene	Athabaskan	Apache Navajo
Penutian	Zuni	Zuni
Undetermined	Keresan	Acoma Cochiti Laguna San Felipe Santa Ana Santo Domingo Zia

7

THE PLAINS

Painted shield cover, Sioux Indians, North and South Dakota.

Assiniboine Creation Myth

At one time there was nothing but a vast expanse of water. No earth existed then. Inktomi looked around and said, "If I had some soil, I would make some land." "Muskrat said, "I can find soil for you," and he dived into the water. Many times he dived, and many times he came back to the surface without soil. Finally he took a very deep breath and plunged deep into the water. Inktomi waited for a long time before he saw Muskrat, but finally Muskrat came to the surface with a ball of mud in his paws. Inktomi took the mud and made the earth with grasslands stretching as far as the eye could see, and some streams flowing over the grasslands.

Muskrat and Inktomi enjoyed the earth. Besides the two of them, there were Rabbit, Fox, Coyote, Bear, Eagle, and Frog. Always the grass grew, and the weather was pleasant. Inktomi and his friends just sat around doing nothing or playing tricks on each other. Frog said, "It is always too nice. It is tiresome always to have weather like this." Inktomi thought Frog was criticizing, so he made it snow. And it snowed and snowed. Snow stayed on the ground for a long time. It was never warm anymore. Frog begged Inktomi to change the weather, and after a while Inktomi said, "When it was always nice, you complained, and I grew tired of your complaints. Now you are sorry; but I will make part of the year warm, and part cold. We will have ten months of cold, and two months of warm weather." But the animals begged Inktomi to make more warm weather than that, and he said, "Very well, we will have seven months of cold and five months of warm." And that is the way it has been ever since.

Then the animals said, "We are alone in the world. There ought to be some other beings." They talked to Inktomi. Inktomi thought, "I would like some other beings too." So he took some dirt and from it made a man and a woman. The new people asked Inktomi what they should eat. Inktomi did not want people to eat his friends, so he created buffalo. He told the people that they should eat buffalo. He said, "Everybody get ready. I will teach you how to hunt." He taught the men to kill the buffalo, and how to skin the animals. He showed them how to make knives to remove the skin, and he taught the women to make scrapers and how to scrape the skin so that it was soft and pliable. He showed the people how to butcher the buffalo and what parts could be eaten. He broke open a leg bone and showed the people the marrow. Then he said, "From now on, this is what you will eat, all the parts of the buffalo. And you will make tools from his bones and horns.''

After a while there were many people in the world. Inktomi's people hunted the buffalo as he had taught them, with bows and lances and on foot. But one day his people saw that other men did not hunt on foot. They rode on the backs of large animals. The animals could go much faster than people on foot. On the horses, for that is what the others rode, the other people could keep pace with the buffalo, and they could kill more buffalo and they could carry more buffalo meat. Inktomi's people begged him to get horses for them too. But Inktomi said, ''I have given you all that I intend. You will have to learn to steal horses from the other tribes.'' And that is what Inktomi's people learned to do, and that is how they got their horses.

The Plains of North America stretch from southern Canada into Texas, from the Mississippi River to the Rocky Mountains. Treeless grassland except for wooded river valleys, the gently rolling territory was home to millions of bison, popularly called buffalo. In the valleys and hills other animals lived: deer, elk, antelope, bear, beaver, and, in the mountains at the western edge of the Plains, mountain sheep. In the rivers were fish, and waterfowl nested in trees, shrubs, and reeds along the banks.

This description of how Indians adapted to the Plains will be different from that of the other culture areas. For most areas we have tried as nearly as possible to recreate the aboriginal cultures, untouched by European contact. Plains Indian life, however, did not reach its climax (with a population of about a quarter of a million) until after Europeans introduced the horse to this continent. The Plains culture was not an aboriginal development but a contact phenomenon. We will see how life was lived on the Plains from about 1670 to 1870. After that the mounted nomads' flamboyant way of life slowly disappeared along with the buffalo they lived on. White settlers moving west from the Mississippi fenced in the land. No longer could Indians make their living on the open prairie; it belonged to ranchers and homesteaders.

To many people, the Plains life-style represents *the* American Indian, the Indian of the eagle-feathered warbonnet, galloping across a movie screen after buffalo or enemies. This Hollywood stereotype is not entirely imaginary: for about two hundred years, the Plains Indians did lead an exciting life focused on masculinity and youth. The Plains way, however, though easy to romanticize, was just one of many Indian adaptations in North America.

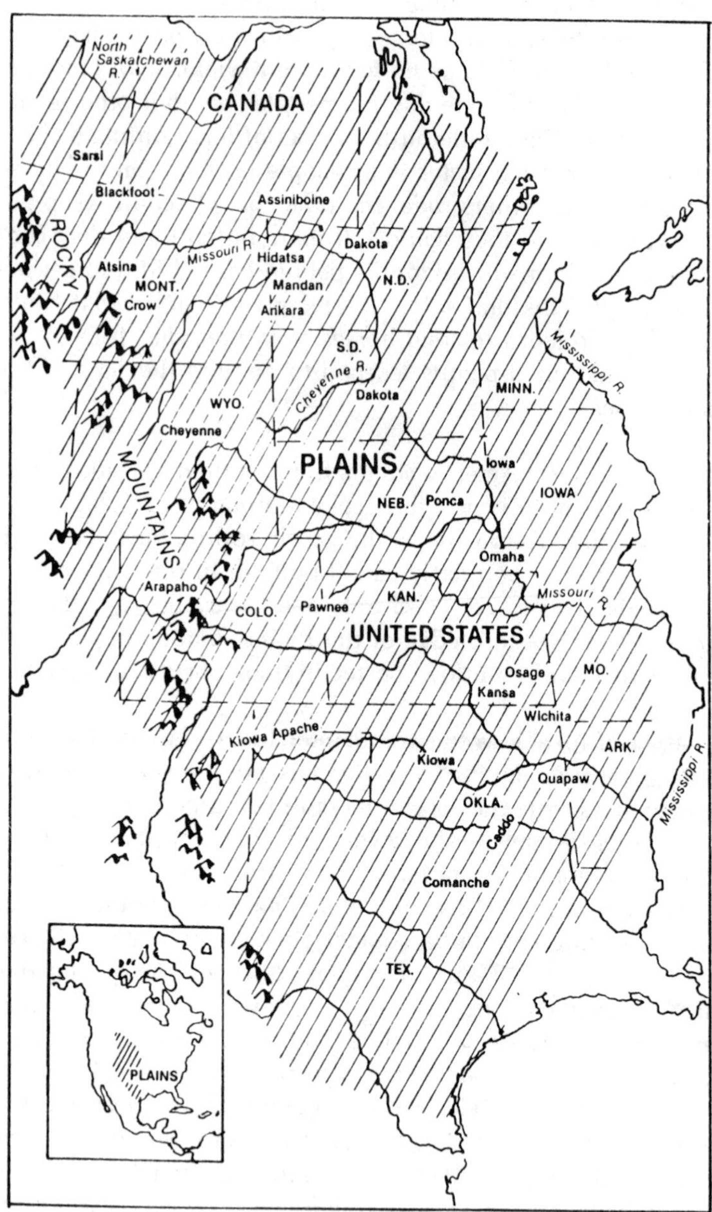

The Plains culture area and its tribes.

Plains Prehistory

As you may recall from Part I, after about 8000 B.C., the climate of the Plains region slowly became much drier, and many of the large game sought by the Paleo-Indian hunters became extinct. By 5000 B.C., a shift in subsistence practices had occurred, with the large game hunting tradition almost disappearing. Over time Plains people increasingly turned to gathering wild plants in combination with hunting smaller forms of game as well as some bison. Archaeological evidence suggests that human population in the region shrank greatly as the climate change created a different sort of Plains environment.

Much later, about 2000 years ago, Woodland people moved in from the east and settled in small villages along the Plains rivers. The lifestyle of the so-called Plains Woodland people eventually came to include a fairly significant reliance upon cultivated foods, including maize and squash. We know from archaeological evidence that they hunted buffalo and other game as well. By A.D. 900 or 1000, the Plains Village tradition had developed more fully into an agricultural way of life. While the Plains Villagers continued to hunt buffalo, they cultivated large gardens or fields of corn, beans, and squash. By the time Europeans came into contact with New World peoples, Plains villages were good-sized. The people of this tradition lived in villages spread out along the major river systems, and left their valleys only seasonally to hunt the bison. Few people dwelt in the grasslands of the Plains, for the tough, thick root masses of the vegetation there were almost impossible to penetrate with stone and bone digging tools, with the result that cultivation was impossible. Moreover, unlike the valleys, during the cold season the wide-open grasslands offered no natural protection against the elements for any would-be human inhabitants.

When hunters ventured out on the Plains to chase buffalo, they typically did not go far from their settlements, for they were on foot and had only their dogs, equipped with packs or travois, to help carry the proceeds of the hunt back to their villages or winter camps. In most cases, they probably skinned and butchered the bison where they fell, cutting the meat into strips to be dried before departing. Several days might be spent in gathering and processing the meat, hides, and other useful parts of the carcasses for the journey home. Like their mounted descendants, the villagers turned the buffalo they caught into much more than food. They made robes, shields, tents, and containers from hides; bones became implements like scrapers, knives, axes, awls, and hoes. Women used the sinews for sewing; men used them for bowstrings and for tying points to arrow or spear shafts. Horns could make cups, spoons, or ladles, and the shaggy buffalo hair was spun into cordage, woven into netting, or used for stuffing and padding. Buffalo heads were sometimes made into headdresses. Even the dung, often called buffalo chips, was useful as fuel in a region where firewood was scarce or nonexistent, as European settlers also found when they arrived.

For thousands of years before horses became available to the peoples of the Plains, buffalo hunters used techniques that included the time-proven methods first used by the Paleo Indian inhabitants of the region. Beating the brush and making noise or using fire to drive the game, they stampeded the animals over cliffs or into pens; drove them into marshes, gullies, or deep snow to immobilize and disable them; and separated the weaker, younger animals from the herd. Disguised with animal skins, the hunters crept close to the herd to drive in a lance or discharge an arrow. Buffalo were the biggest game these villagers preyed on, but they also hunted pronghorn antelope, deer, elk, bear, and prairie wolves.

Buffalo hunting practices, with or without horses, changed with the Plains seasons. Men did some hunting in winter snow, but spring and summer brought great communal drives. Winter forage was scanty, keeping the buffalo in small groups. When the tender grasses sprouted and the mating season approached, the herds grew; mating went on from July to October. Calves were born in the late winter and early spring, and the herds were slowed down by the less swift, more easily fatigued young animals. Hunting was good then. During the warmer months of the year, villagers on communal hunts might encamp on the grasslands themselves, living in temporary settlements of skin tents.

In summer, women planted corn, beans, squash, and sunflowers, and men cultivated tobacco in fields along the rivers where the soils were deep, fertile, and free of the thick-rooted prairie grasses. Some of the villagers also engaged in fishing during summer, using traps or weirs to provide themselves with fish from the nearby rivers.

The Horse Comes to the Plains

A few times in history, technology has changed so sweepingly and dramatically as to alter a whole way of life. The invention of the automobile is one example. In the Plains during the seventeenth century it was the horse that changed Indian life.

Horses came to the Southwest with the Spanish, first appearing on the southern Plains around 1650, but the tribes in the northern Plains had none until nearly 100 years later. Having no word for horse, Indians called it the "mystery dog" or "big dog." One tribe, the Sarci, gave it the practical name "seven dogs," implying that one horse could turn out that much work. (When the machine came along we did the same, measuring its strength in horsepower.)

At first Indians used horses as food. The Spanish had tried to keep the animals from them, knowing that Indians on horseback would be hard to control. But the Spaniards could not hide their riding skills from the Southwestern Indians, who learned by watching how the Spaniards broke and rode horses. Working for the Spanish, the Indians learned to care for horses and make bridles and saddles. From the Southwestern Indians the Plains Indians learned that horses were more useful for riding than for food. On horseback hunters could go farther and faster. A whole new way of life began, one that attracted people from surrounding areas and brought a wave of Indian immigrants to the Plains.

The Plains at the Time of Contact

As the horse began to spread northward in the seventeenth century, this is how tribes were distributed in the Plains: Along the upper Missouri River were agricultural village people, Siouan speakers—the Mandan and Hidatsa. Other farmers, also Siouan, were farther south—the Omaha, Osage, and Kansa. Caddoan speakers—Pawnee and Wichita—were in Nebraska and Kansas and the Caddo in Texas. The Arikara split off from the Pawnee and joined the Mandan and Hidatsa in the north sometime in the seventeenth century.

Few nonagricultural tribes lived on the Plains before horses came along. The Blackfoot, who were Algonkian hunters, lived in the northern Plains, and the Comanche, Shoshonean speakers, were then moving away from the Basin and into the southern Plains. The Kiowa originally lived near the headwaters of the Missouri; they moved south into the Plains on foot before the horse was introduced. The Blackfoot, Kiowa, and Comanche appear to have been the only noncultivators who lived there before the horse arrived. The other Plains hunters were latecomers, among them those familiar in cinema and legend: the Cheyenne, Crow, and Dakota. Some newcomers saw advantages in Plains life and moved there of their own accord. Others, from the east primarily, were pushed into the Plains by the struggles between the Iroquois and the white settlers.

People who came from the west, like the Shoshoni and Nez Perce, had never practiced cultivation as far as we know, but some newcomers had been farming people before entering the Plains. Cultivators like the Cheyenne, Crow, and Arapaho adjusted their ways and subsistence patterns, eventually abandoning settled life for hunting nomadism.

The Horse Culture

By 1700, the Plains Indians, old and new, had taken seriously to horseback riding. Though at first they got horses by trading with the

Spanish to the south, later they commonly stole them. They never captured many of the horses that ran wild, nor did they breed horses much—except for the Comanche, who often did both.

The old Plains villagers changed their traditional ways after acquiring the horse, though not as drastically as others. They did not abandon their villages or their cultivated fields, but combined hunting with farming. The villages remained permanent homes; the village hunters left for long trips in summer, returning for the rest of the year. Old folks, women, and children mostly remained in the villages, where the women tended the crops, cured hides, and prepared food for winter.

Even the nomads were not constantly on the move. They camped for varying periods of time—longest in the winter—but they had no home base, and they carried their skin tent housing with them. The whole band moved—no one stayed behind. The nomads never thought of farming, for their hunters could supply more food in a day than the women could in months of cultivation.

The Plains, which were nearly vacant before the Indians acquired horses, quickly became a region of riders, fighting over territory, on the move most of the time (except for the villagers), creating the new way of life we have come to call the Plains culture. Though it was born and flourished quickly, it was so appealing and the changeover was so complete that the memory of past ways faded swiftly. The new Plains dwellers came to believe that they had always been nomads of the Plains.

Changing Patterns of Life

The horse made a vast difference in the Plains people's ways of settlement, subsistence, and technology. It also caused changes in the social organization of many tribes, and produced a new value system. Tradition already placed great value on the life of the warrior; the Plains horsemen expanded that tradition and elaborated it into a kind of military hierarchy with symbols of military distinction. They glorified bravery, individualism, and stoicism, and their whole way of life came to focus on manhood and youth.

Changing Technology

Housing. The villagers still lived in their traditional dwellings along the rivers. The Missouri River people (Mandan, Hidatsa, and Arikara) had large earth lodges of log framework over shallow pits, covered with poles, brush, and sod. Smoke from the fireplace found its way out through a smokehole in the roof. Entryways were large enough to let

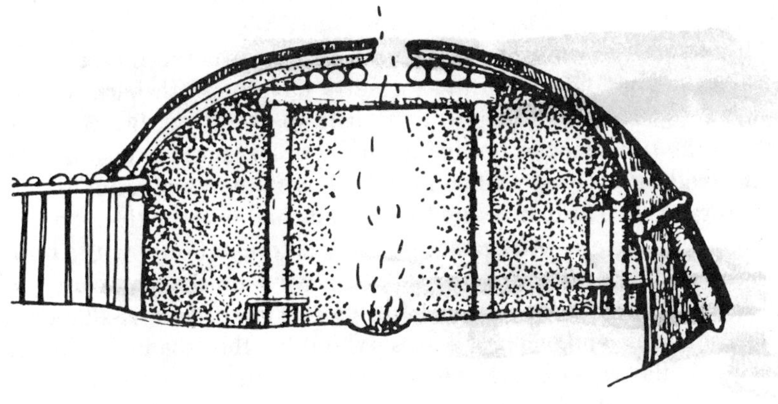

Earth lodge, section.

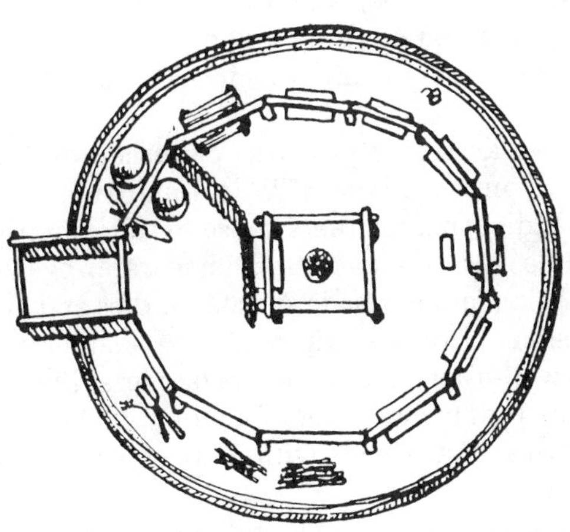

Earth lodge, plan.

a horse through, and during severe winter weather, the people often kept their favorite and most valuable horses in their homes. The Pawnee and neighboring villagers built similar large, durable structures. The Wichita and Caddo, however, built thatched beehive-shaped houses with the hearth in the center of the floor, but with no smokeholes—smoke filtered through the thatching. These two tribes lived where winters were less severe.

The main change in housing on the Plains was the increase in size of the tipi, a conical building formerly covered with bark, brush, or deerhide, five or six feet high, with little space inside. But with horses to haul the tipi, packed on its own lodgepoles, Indians began to build their dwellings twelve to fifteen feet high with plenty of room for people and storage. The only housing the nomads had was the tipi, made with buffalo-hide covers. Villagers used the tipi too, but only while hunting away from home. The Plains nomads, always on the go, carried other belongings as well as their housing on the travois, an A-shaped drag with the narrow end over the horses's shoulder, the broader end dragging behind. This was a bigger version of the older, dog travois. Babies, children, household equipment, and aged relatives might also ride on the travois.

Equipment. Pottery was far too easily broken to be useful to those traveling by horseback. Instead, possessions and even food went along in containers of leather. The fully nomadic people who had previously made pottery turned entirely to leather containers, but the villagers still used some pottery at home. The commonest container, known by the French name *parfleche*, was made by women from rawhide. Unpacked, it looked like a giant envelope; packed, it expanded to the size and shape of a small chest. It stored clothing and other belongings conveniently and often carried food, especially the dried meat and berry concoction called *pemmican*.

Much of the Indian riding gear was patterned on Spanish designs, modified for use on the Plains. While some riders, including most women, used saddles, many others chose to ride bareback. In style and decoration, saddles, bridles, and other horse trappings varied from tribe to tribe. Many Plains Indians made special saddles and horse decorations for dress occasions. Horse equipment was leather until trade with Europeans was well-established; then metal parts, like bridle bits, came to the Plains. The Indians were very fond of good horses and took great pleasure in decking their steeds with gaily colored designs of bead or quill work.

Long after guns became available, Indians continued to use bows and arrows and lances for hunting and warfare. The early rifles, like the old one-shot muzzle loaders, were much too slow and hard to reload on

A travois used by Plains Indians to transport their possessions as well as their housing.

horseback, and were less accurate than bows. In fact, guns were not used much on the Plains until the late nineteenth century. The horse did not make the traditional weapons obsolete, though the people did begin using shorter bows that were easier to handle on horseback. Eventually, as traders made metal available, Indians replaced their stone, bone, and horn arrowheads with steel points. In addition to bows and spears, warriors carried clubs of various styles and a protective shield of bison rawhide painted with magical symbols to make it more effective. *Pectorals*, large chestplates of bone, were more for adornment than protection.

Clothing. Clothing changed little, still being made of deerskin except for the great buffalo-hide robe people wore in winter and used for bedding. Men wore leggings and shirts or coats over breechclouts, and women wore skirts, jackets, or sometimes one-piece dresses. Moccasins, too, were made of hides, and were so distinctive in style that a good tracker could tell the wearer's tribe from a moccasin print. The main change in basic clothing was the addition of more decoration. Fringe trimming on the buckskin increased, and as Europeans brought beads in trade, women decorated garments with elaborate beaded designs as well as quill embroidery. Porcupine quills had been used for designs on the Plains in earlier days, but not so much as farther east.

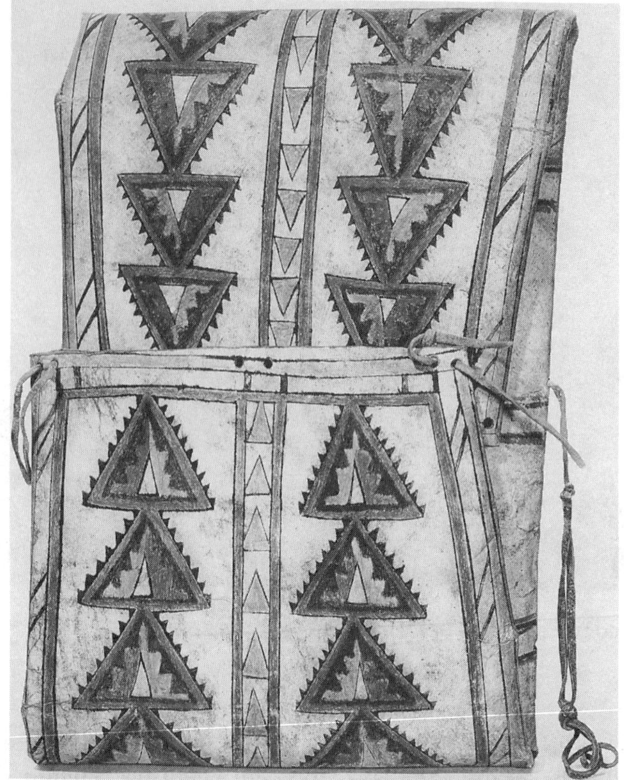

A parfleche, made of rawhide, was strapped to a horse's side and usually was filled with dried food, clothing, and other belongings.

The one really new piece of clothing was the tailed warbonnet, more a symbol of prestige than a garment. This feathered headdress with its long, flowing streamers could hardly be worn except on horseback, it was so heavy and cumbersome. Plains warriors prized their bonnets. Only men who had done some brave deed were entitled to wear eagle feathers, and even those warriors wore them only on ceremonial occasions. Today not many people realize that only the mounted Indians of the Plains wore the feathered bonnet; now, tribes all over North America have taken the warbonnet as their trademark.

Most decoration done by Plains people consisted of geometric forms, except on shields and shield covers, men's robes, and tipis. Only men painted these, using representational designs that showed their feats, honors, or visions, or the year's main events. Women did the other decorating, the geometric art on the parfleches, and the quill and beaded work.

Blackfoot painted tipis. The symbols could be painted only by men and represented important events, honors, or visions. Smoke escaped through the smoke-flap at top, which could be controlled by the flap poles. The cover was pegged down on all sides during the winter, but during warmer weather might be raised on one side for greater ventilation.

Communication

In spite of hostility among the Plains tribes as they jockeyed for good positions in hunting and war, there were many times when people of one linguistic group had to communicate with another. Even if they spoke varieties of the same language they might need an interpreter, and many of the groups who came into the Plains after the advent of the horse spoke languages totally unintelligible to each other. To get along in this babble of languages, the Indians developed a standardized way of communicating, the so-called sign language. It belonged strictly to the Plains; Indians of California or Virginia, for instance, did not use it nor could they understand it without instruction. It could not express many abstract ideas, but it was enough for trade, parleys, and treaty making. White explorers, traders, trappers, and soldiers also came to use it.

Economic Change

The New Materialism. As men accumulated horses and buffalo hides, a new feeling about material wealth spread, and a kind of capitalism grew up on the Plains. Horses and sometimes hides were put to use as money, a medium of exchange. The value of other goods was counted in horses or hides, and even a man's bridewealth payments to his wife's family were determined in horses. Horses came to be traded for just about everything; they represented a man's accumulated wealth. Trade in stolen horses grew brisk, and horse stealing came to be much admired, a proof of manhood.

Until the coming of the horse, Plains Indians lived in egalitarian bands. No one had more than the other tribe members, and sharing was part of life. Material possessions did not bring recognition or a commanding position; prestige came only from achievement. The horse changed all that. Men were ranked by wealth. With a large supply of horses, a man could be sure of having food, clothing, and other things for himself and his family. He could afford to add a wife or two—extra wives meant more hands to cure the hides that added to his wealth. An average family required a dozen horses just to move their belongings.

Sharing did not vanish, however. A wealthy man made himself bigger in the eyes of his neighbors and kinfolk by holding a give-away. This was a big affair, with feasting for the community and many gifts, even for enemies (to make them friends). Buffalo robes, decorated clothing, weapons, and foods were given away as well as horses, though horses were the real measure of stature. While the Plains give-aways were never so formalized as the Northwest Coast potlatches, both were investments in the future, for the recipients (except for the really poor) always repaid the generosity.

As a result of the economic abundance created by the horse, three loosely structured classes developed: a privileged class that was expected to be generous and responsible for the band's welfare, a middle class sharing most benefits of the upper class but with fewer possessions, and a lower, underprivileged class of people poor in horses and other possessions and dependent on the powerful upper class. Though these classes tended to perpetuate themselves by inheritance, a man could gain wealth as a warrior and hunter and change his class standing.

Trade. For many centuries, Plains people had traded with each other and with those of other regions. After the spread of the horse, trading accelerated. At Taos, in what is now New Mexico, the Pueblo Indians had long held trade fairs. The Indians of the southern Plains began to go to Taos to trade dried meat, animal skins, and other products for agricultural produce and European goods. Villages of the Mandan, Hidatsa, and Arikara became trade centers in the north. White traders also set up trade posts to deal in furs, hides, and other native commodities. Enormous quantities of buffalo hides changed hands for metal implements, and eventually for guns.

One wholly unfortunate item of exchange was liquor, which many Indians sought above all else. European traders later used it to cheat Indians, getting one warrior after another intoxicated and unable to manage his affairs. Eventually the government forbade the sale of liquor to Indians, but the liquor merchants evaded that law.

Social Organization

Kinship patterns were one aspect of Plains life that did not change much after the horse's arrival. Some Plains people, such as the Mandan, Hidatsa, and Crow, traced descent matrilineally. Some, like the Omaha, Oto, and Kansa, had patrilineal clans. But on the Plains, clans had little function except in the regulation of marriage: people had to marry outside their own clan. The family was most important everywhere. Often close ties among people of the same age also were essential for mutual help in hunting and warfare.

The major political unit was the tribe. The nomads broke their tribe into bands for much of the year but came together for communal hunts and ceremonies in the summer. Tribe members shared a common language and common territory, intermarried, and put up a united front to all outsiders. Some tribes were governed by a tribal counsel, like the Crow and Cheyenne. Others had no permanent tribal leader but would find leaders for specific events—to lead raids or direct hunts. Wealthy men commanded much respect, many of them gathering followers who obeyed them. Decisions that bound the whole community were made throughout the Plains by groups of tribal elders, that is, respected older men.

Associations. Most Plains tribes had societies or associations for men, gathering members from many kin groups and bands within the tribe. Thus the associations were a cross-section of the tribe, not one kin or local group. Members were faithful to the tribe as a whole, making these organizations a strong unifying force. Members always felt great loyalty to the association and always stood united. Some of these associations were *age-graded*, with all members of one grade moving together to the next, much like our school system.

These brotherhoods are often called warriors' societies because of their policing and military functions. Members went on raids together; in fact, most warfare was carried on by associations, though raiding parties smaller than the brotherhoods were also common. Rarely did the whole tribe engage in military action. The chiefs and elders, no matter how violent and aggressive they had been in their youth, were expected to be beyond the age of rashness and strive for peace. Full-scale fighting, approaching total warfare, became more frequent when United States soldiers came to fight the Plains Indians.

Some of the warriors' societies were so renowned for bravery that it was a great honor to be asked to join. The most prestigious were the Dog Soldiers, a military society in several tribes. The Dog Soldiers of the Kiowa were especially famed for their bravery. In addition to their military side, these associations had religious aspects, as we might expect among people to whom the supernatural was of vital importance in hunting and warfare. Many brotherhoods had their own ceremonials and sacred objects as well as the members' personal spirit power. In some tribes, all men belonged to an association; others left it to individual choice.

Some tribes also had women's societies, usually with strong magical or ritual aspects. They used their magic to summon the herd or make the crops more fruitful. Other women's societies were like craft associations—groups of hide workers or bead workers, for instance.

Status of Women. Horses did not relieve women of much work, though they did carry the belongings women or dogs had formerly borne on their backs so the men would be free to fight or hunt. Horses even increased women's labors by helping the hunters bring in more hides for the women to prepare. Thus, as the hunters were more and more successful, *polygyny*—multiple wives—also increased. A good hunter needed several wives because they were the only source of labor. As hides and work piled up, the first wife might even suggest that her husband bring in another wife. Jealousy was never reported as being much of a problem among Indian women, probably partly because a man's second wife was likely to be a sister of his first wife.

Women were far less important in the Plains than they were among the Pueblo, Navajo, and Eastern agriculturists. They were most valued for their services to males. Successful hunters needed women to cure hides, prepare meat for storage, and put up and take down tipis. The successful man was known not only by his emblems of accomplishment, but by the number of his wives, though few men, no matter how successful, had more than three wives. Because women did help determine a man's wealth by their labor on his buffalo hides, they sometimes became influential, though not on a public or tribal level. A few women were able to become independently wealthy by accumulating horses in payment for their services.

Values and Beliefs

Though Plains Indians earned respect for their competence in hunting, glory came to them from feats of courage in warfare. Everyone in a war party helped each other, but honor gained in battle was individual. From the time they were boys, male Indians prepared for combat; at about fourteen they were initiated into one of the military societies. From then on their standing in the tribe depended mainly on their conduct in war. The sort of achievement that led to greatest prestige was an act of daring; we might call it foolhardiness. Helping a wounded tribesman to escape from the enemy was praiseworthy. Killing an enemy or stealing his horses also brought praise, but glory was reserved for the man who touched a live enemy without killing him and came back to brag about it. It was the custom to carry a small stick, a *coup stick* (*coup* is French for a "blow"), into battle or on raids, to touch the enemy. The warrior told about his acts of bravery on his return home by striking a pole with his coup stick each time he recounted an act of courage. That was called "counting coup."

The Vision Quest. The vision quest was of great importance to a warrior, who devoutly believed that he could win supernatural aid by fasting, prayer, and body mutilation. To communicate with the spirits was not a task for priesthood or communal religious effort—each man was on his own in appealing for the supernatural's pity and beneficence. Shamanism was played down in many tribes, and in some was even absent, for each person shared in sacred power. Other tribes, mostly those practicing some cultivation, did have shamans.

If no spirit granted him a vision after long fasting and isolation, a warrior would resort to self-torture, hoping the powers would take pity on him in his human helplessness. Torture could take many forms: chopping off a finger (certainly not one he needed for wielding weapons, however), cutting away strips of flesh, or driving bone pins several inches long through his back muscles, attaching a weight that he would pull until muscles and flesh tore, or until he collapsed. Trials like these, added to hunger, would call up a vision almost without fail.

Warriors kept strangely shaped stones, bones, or feathers—symbols of their visions or animals that sent them power—in sacred containers called *medicine bundles*. The items were *medicine*; they had power. We could liken them to good-luck pieces, sacred talismans, or religious relics. Often a sacred song came with a warrior's vision, and it too became part of his medicine. Some tribes owned sacred tribal bundles, and the people believed that the tribe's well-being depended on the proper care and protection of those bundles.

The warrior had to make repeated contact with his source of power. Facing any important event, he could appeal for guidance and protection from the supernatural through another vision. If prayer and fasting did not bring contact, he would again try self-torture or perhaps stare at the sun for hours until he went into delirium or hallucination.

The Sun Dance. Warriors often sought visions during the big summer ceremonials, the best known of which is the Sun Dance. This was a ceremony put on for the good of the tribe, to keep the buffalo running and ensure a plentiful food supply.

Indians never took nature's bounty for granted. If people did not perform proper rites, the animals would withhold themselves from hunters, plants would wither, and the people would slowly starve. To prevent this ultimate disaster, twenty or more Plains tribes resorted to the Sun Dance. Its name came from the Sioux "gazing-at-the-sun dance," but the Cheyenne name for the structure in which the ceremony was held—translated "new life lodge"—reveals its purpose, which was to do no less than make the whole world over.

The Sun Dance took various forms. The most elaborate types were held by the Arapaho, Cheyenne, and Sioux, but its variations overlapped enough everywhere to make it one ceremony. It lasted about seven days and always took place in summer or early autumn when all the bands of the tribe had come together for the buffalo hunt. A pledger or sponsor gave the dance to fulfill a vow he had made at a time of danger or when the spirits had given him some special attention. It was his way of thanking the supernatural.

Sun Dance Ceremony. Although one person sponsored it, the Sun Dance was performed for the whole tribe, and almost everyone participated in some phase of it. The people put up their tipis in a circle with the dancing area in the middle. A large lodge, facing east, was specially built within the dance area for the ceremony. A group of renowned warriors cut down a straight tall tree, carried it to the dance site with solemn ritual, and erected it as a center post. The participants danced around and around the center pole for long periods, staring at sacred objects hung from it, perhaps sending themselves into hypnosis. Spectators sang and drummed, and both they and the dancers blew whistles.

Dramatic self-torture highlighted the Sun Dance. The warrior participants went without water and food, danced to exhaustion, and sometimes slashed their flesh to appeal to the spirits. In some tribes, a young man who had vowed self-mortification in the ceremony had a medicine man cut two small holes through the skin and flesh on each side of his upper chest. Sticking wooden skewers through the holes, the medicine man secured them to two ropes, the ends of which were fastened to the top of the central pole. The young warrior then danced, straining against the ropes until he broke free or the medicine man cut his flesh to release him. The pain and sacrifice of flesh was the ultimate proof of sincerity: he was giving up the only thing that really belonged to him.

When the ceremony was over, the Indians could again count on enjoying health, fertility, and food. The world was renewed, its complex harmonies restored, its many supernatural powers revived and ready once again to work for the tribe's welfare.

While the Sun Dance was underway, the tribal council or the elders usually met to make plans and decisions for the coming season. It was also a time for festivity and feasting, when marriages were made and friendships renewed. It caused some social strain, however, and the great size of the gathering could bring trouble. Social control was difficult when hot-blooded young men were whooping it up and trying to go on raids, and overly eager hunters could endanger the tribal food supply by stampeding the herds before the men were ready to hunt. During the summer a special police force was created to keep order just for the dance season. Usually one of the men's associations did the policing.

The Misfits. What of the man who had no taste for the life of a warrior, which, after all, was very dangerous? There was a socially acceptable way out: a man could choose to become a *berdache* and lead the life of a woman. A berdache was not necessarily a homosexual; he merely chose a way of life other than the ideal masculine pattern. He was denied honors, but he did not suffer public scorn or ridicule. In some tribes, notably the Blackfoot, women who found the average female role dull and uninteresting had a similar choice: they could become "manly-hearted" women and hunt and raid with the men. They were far fewer, however, than the berdaches.

How Plains Culture Developed

Although it was the nomadic horsemen who created the Plains culture, the villagers too found their lives reorganized by the horse and buffalo. Plains culture from north to south, both the cultivating and the hunting tribes, was remarkably homogeneous. The Plains became a melting pot of American Indian cultures, since without natural geographic barriers there was no way to maintain physical or cultural isolation among such mobile societies. The Plains area shows how people of widely different backgrounds living in the same environment (the Plains and the buffalo) came up with very similar adaptations when they encountered new technology (the horse).

In the Plains culture too we can see how quickly major cultural change can come about when people are willing to accept transformed subsistence patterns, value systems, and social organization. Contrast with that the change forced on the Indians in the late nineteenth century. By then, overkill and the encroaching frontier had wiped out the buffalo herds; proud warriors were debased into government wards. That cultural change is still being fought.

Although the Plains culture was strikingly similar everywhere, there were enough differences to support tribal individuality—a few examples of which we shall now examine.

The Blackfoot

The Blackfoot of historic times included three independent divisions with a common origin: the Siksika, the Blood, and the Piegan. Their territory was almost all north of today's Canadian-United States border in the province of Alberta. That makes them, along with the Sarci and the Plains Cree, the most northerly of the horse nomads.

The Blackfoot spoke a distinct variety of Algonkian. Just how long they had been residents of the northern Plains is uncertain, but several lines of evidence suggest that they may have lived in the grasslands of southern Alberta for several hundred years or more before European contact in the 1750s. On the other hand, there is also some indication that they may have arrived in their historic Plains homeland far more recently, having moved there during the early 1700s from an area further east or northeast along the Plains-Northwoods boundary. Whatever their prehistory and however long they had lived on the Plains, the Blackfoot had acquired European guns as well as horses from neighboring groups twenty years or more before Europeans first visited them. At the time of first direct contact with Europeans, the Blackfoot were in the process of developing an equestrian way of life.

The Pedestrian Blackfoot. The pre-horse Blackfoot were hunters and gatherers. They hunted buffalo by using the *surround*, men encircling the herd and killing as many of the outer animals with lances and arrows as they could before the beasts broke out, or by luring the bison into a corral or pound. Women followed the hunters and skinned and dressed the carcasses on the spot. Meat and hides were carried back to camp on dog travois. Buffalo hunting on foot was so difficult and dangerous that the Blackfoot hunters settled for occasional buffalo kills, supplementing this source of meat by trapping wolves, foxes, and badgers, and hunting deer and antelope. The Blackfoot especially valued deer and antelope hides for clothing. They would drive antelope into a pit at the end of a high brush fence, where concealed men clubbed the animals to death as they fell or tried to escape. Blackfoot also hunted mountain sheep, which were prized for their meat and horns. Meat from one animal or another theoretically could be had all year round, but in the northern Plains the intense winter cold and deep snow made hunting difficult and very uncomfortable. Consequently, in those pre-horse days, women dried all the meat they could during the short summer for use in winter.

Meat was the favorite Blackfoot food, but they also used the many nourishing plants available to them. In preparation for winter scarcity, they dried plant foods and stored them like meat. The Blackfoot never ate fish, though fish were in the rivers. The only cultivated plant was tobacco, which the men planted each spring and harvested in the autumn. They smoked tobacco ritually and for pleasure.

The Blackfoot religion of pre-horse times probably grew from common Algonkian beliefs. One belief was that animals had supernatural power, which they would share with those who sought it by praying and fasting. Another was the Shaking Tent Ritual. A bound shaman was placed inside a tent, which soon began to shake; this meant the powers were communicating with the shaman, giving him the ability to predict where game could be found or to foretell the band's future. Religious beliefs and practices were simple in pre-horse times and there were no large community ceremonials.

Even before the horse appeared, people won prestige from personal courage and achievement and from the supernatural power they might attain. A woman's status was the same as her husband's unless she had supernatural power of her own.

The Equestrian Blackfoot. Horses spread slowly to the northern Plains, both because it was so far from the source of supply in the Southwest and because of the difficulties of bringing a string of horses across the great rivers, such as the Missouri. In the early days, Blackfoot people apparently got their horses from the Shoshone or other Plateau peoples to the southwest, rather than more directly from the south.

The Blackfoot alone among Plains Indians received the horse and the gun at the same time. They were among the last of the Plains people to get horses, in about 1730 or 1740, and by that time the Cree, whose territory was just to the east, were trading guns to them. For the most part, whites stayed outside Blackfoot territory until about 1780, leaving the Cree as intermediaries for the gun trade.

The Seasonal Pattern. With spring coming late in Blackfoot territory, and a semidrought settled in by midsummer, the grass was in prime condition for only about two months. Horses, buffalo, and other grazers feasted on fresh grass in spring, but after a summer of scanty forage, they rarely entered winter at their strongest. Blackfoot horses had a hard time, especially through the winters when fodder was short. Bison stayed in the area only as long as grazing was good, scattering to better pastures for the rest of the year. The people too broke into bands in winter to seek the protection of valleys and woods.

During the spring and early summer, when bison formed great herds on the northern Plains, the Blackfoot bands united into larger groups for a communal hunt. The rest of the year, people traveled in smaller units within their own territory. Each band was usually based on the *patrilocal* family—brothers, their wives, and children—but unrelated individuals or families might also form bands. Though wealthy men (that is, successful hunters) had more than one wife, most men were monogamous. Only economic expedience determined who combined into groups of kin or held territory in common.

The summer encampment that followed the concentrated hunting season was a scene of feasts and dances. Medicine bundles were sold (a Blackfoot practice; not all tribes sold them), as were robes and horses. Brotherhoods performed their ceremonials, initiating boys into the first stage and transferring some members to the next rank. After they acquired horses, the Blackfoot also began to take part in the Sun Dance, the culmination of summer activity. The tribe dispersed soon after and moved to winter camps.

Organization. Band leaders were chosen for their competence. There were no inherited political positions. The outstanding men from all bands formed a tribal leadership, but they had no coercive powers and they depended on the rest of the population for support.

Most Blackfoot men belonged to associations that took turns controlling the larger gatherings formed for the summer hunts. The association in charge was responsible for keeping the peace and regulating individual hunting; its members also had ritual duties. Blackfoot societies were age-graded: about every four years one grade moved or graduated to another level, taking that level's rights and rituals and transferring its own practices to the next junior rank. Junior members paid with horses or goods for the position they took in the next grade. Because payment was required, it was possible to skip a grade or to remain longer than normal in one grade. The oldest or highest grade formed a sort of council of wise men, a senior rank called the Bull Society.

Religion. The Blackfoot Sun Dance was a display of wealth and self-torture. It probably came to them from the Arapaho, and it became their major tribal religious ceremony. The Blackfoot Sun Dance was unique in that women had a big part in it. A medicine woman pledged the dance and was responsible for its success. Women as well as men mutilated themselves for blessings from the supernatural, though the women's torture was milder—at most they would cut off bits of flesh or chop off a finger joint.

Along with the Sun Dance, the equestrian Blackfoot adopted the vision quest and the medicine bundle. The search for power from animal spirits of pre-horse days became more intense and more complex once they had horses. The warrior expected the spirits to reveal sacred items to him which he would then keep in his sacred bundle. Selling a medicine bundle was an important commercial transaction, for the bundle was always worth at least what was paid for it, and if it brought the buyer success, it became worth more.

Shamans or medicine men often became wealthy by charging high fees for successful cures. Many of the curers were women, who found this a way to buy horses of their own. Blackfoot women were valuable and influential not only as curers but as laborers. Good hunters depended on their wives for curing buffalo hides and other skins. Women were respected too as childbearers.

Warfare: Ambush and Battle. Once the Blackfoot had horses, they became distinctly expansionist, taking over territory from neighboring tribes and profiting by a geographical position which allowed them to control the spread of both horses and guns. By 1850, Blackfoot territory stretched from the North Saskatchewan River to what is now Yellowstone Park. They also changed their war tactics, from infantry to cavalry. Before the horse, the Blackfoot pattern of warfare had been either ambush or battle. In an ambush, a few armed men fell upon a small group of unsuspecting enemies, capturing the women and children and killing the men. The women and children were married or adopted to replace killed Blackfoot, or taken as slaves. The battle was more complex. Opposing warriors chose the battleground by mutual consent. Then the two forces formed long lines facing each other, just within arrow range, and warriors fired arrows from behind large shields. Dancing and singing went on both before and during the conflict. Most of these contests were indecisive.

Mounted warfare swept away the large-scale battle, replacing it with the raid. Warriors of one band or age-grade formed the war parties, and stealth and maneuverability were crucial to their success. Casualties went up immensely. War became commercial, and aimed at accumulating horses, and prestige came to be counted in numbers of horses, not courageous deeds.

Raiding for Horses. Only one path led to wealth and social standing for the male Blackfoot—raiding. Many in the raiding parties were poor but ambitious young men, willing to risk their lives to get horses. There were also a few who loved the excitement. The raid leader, an older, proven warrior, chose his volunteer party of eager, competent men, and refused anyone he thought unreliable. Raiding parties rarely were larger than twelve men, for larger groups were hard to conceal and control. Sometimes young childless wives went along with their husbands.

Raids were less common in winter than in spring and summer because of the severe cold and deep snow, but some winter raids did occur. The blown snow covered tracks quickly, making it hard for the enemy to follow. Often the raiders covered themselves with white Hudson's Bay blankets, not only to ward off cold but also to help them blend in with the snow. In warmer weather they wore only the bare essentials: breechclout, leggings, and sometimes a shirt.

Though he trained to be skillful, resourceful, and swift, the Blackfoot warrior credited his success in raiding not to his physical prowess but to the power of his war medicine. No people relied more on war charms than the Blackfoot, who wore their personal medicine in buckskin bags hung around their necks or as hair decoration. In the bags might be herbs and a bear claw representing strength, a weasel skin for speed, or a bone disk symbolic of the sun. Feathers were commonly the hair ornaments. Men learned the formula for their medicine and battle songs from dreams, in which a dream spirit would take human or animal form. They might also buy war medicine from old men who had been successful warriors.

The Raid. The raiding party might travel several hundred miles, the first part on horseback, the last on foot. Along with their war medicine, the men carried pemmican, ropes to control the horses they expected to steal, and knives, often butcher knives made in Sheffield, England. The Blackfoot got these knives from Canadian traders and used them to butcher animals for food, cut firewood, or lift an enemy scalp if an opportunity presented itself. Raiders also carried a bow and quiver of arrows or a gun.

When they came close to enemy territory, they hid by day and traveled by night. Near the target they built a shelter, a bark- or brush-covered tipi or lodge where they would prepare for the assault, using it as a base camp for scouting and concealing supplies. From the camp, scouts located the enemy encampment and studied the layout and how horses were pastured.

The raiders scheduled the attack for daybreak. Creeping stealthily into the enemy camp, they tried to cut horses from their picket lines or to steal range horses without waking the enemies. If dogs barked, they could be pacified with chunks of meat. With their stolen horses, the men took off for home so that the enemy could not catch up. If they were caught, they had to fight for their lives. For the first day or day-and-a-half the raiders rode without stopping, except to change horses as the animals tired. Bringing back fifty or so horses was considered very good, and each man was entitled to the animals he had run off. If any arguments broke out, the leader settled them, and might even give up horses he had captured to those who had taken none. Such generosity increased his stature as a leader. After three or four days of travel, the party slowed down to a more leisurely pace. Near home they painted their faces as a sign of victory before they entered camp, where people greeted them with shouts and drumming.

The Cheyenne

The Cheyenne were once typical Algonkian agriculturalists living in the woodland region to the west of Lake Superior. Late in the seventeenth century they began slowly moving into the Plains, probably driven by pressure from dislocated Indian peoples to the east and white traders and settlers closing in. They came to the Plains still practicing cultivation, but probably also hunting buffalo like the traditional Plains villagers. By 1700 they were living along the Cheyenne River in North Dakota, and by 1830 they had enough horses to become fully nomadic, abandoning all agriculture.

As equestrians, the Cheyenne controlled a region of dry grassland on the high plains where trees grew only along watercourses in the mountain foothills. Most precipitation came in early summer, often in severe thunderstorms. In late spring and early summer, the grass grew luxuriantly, and great herds of buffalo gathered in Cheyenne territory. As the weather grew hotter and drier, the herds broke up into widely scattered foraging groups.

This pattern of animal life in turn controlled the Cheyenne seasonal rhythm of gathering into a tribe and dispersing in bands. In winter the mounted hunters left the unwatered upland because too little grass grew there to feed the horses, and they set up smaller camps in sheltered spots near watering places. In small groups the Cheyenne could find enough forage for the horses, and the hunters could cover a wider area in the foothills to search for deer, elk, antelope, and other game.

Most bands included a number of related families, led by men of proven ability who might also be tribal chieftains or leaders of one of the brotherhoods. Labor was strictly divided. Women gathered wild plants, tanned hides, cooked the food, and brought up the children. Men were hunters and warriors, making the weapons and performing all the rituals. Subsistence techniques generally were well adapted to the environment and provided a balanced diet in good times. Famine was always a threat in winter and early spring, though, so appeals to the supernatural were part of every aspect of procuring food.

The Council of Forty-four. During the spring and summer, when Cheyenne bands joined forces for communal hunting and ceremonials, the tribe was governed by the Council of Forty-four. Four headmen from each of the ten bands and four general chiefs formed the council, each having tenure for ten years. Their decisions and tribal rules were backed up by the Cheyenne military societies.

The council was concerned with internal affairs, the general public good, and external relationships like treaties. (War was in the hands of war chiefs.) Although it was the only body with authority to make decisions affecting the whole tribe, the council recognized that without public support those decisions would be meaningless, and held debates and discussed issues thoroughly. Decisions had to be unanimous, thus ensuring support from the whole society since the council was composed of representatives from all the bands.

Ceremonials. The tribal gathering in summer, when food was abundant and easy to find, was a time of spiritual renewal. It was then that rituals were performed to regenerate the tribe's vitality and bring success in hunting and warfare. Very important for tribal well-being was the Arrow Renewal Ceremony, a dance pledged by an individual to thank or praise the spirits, or perhaps because one Cheyenne had murdered another. (Murder within the tribe was considered very bad luck for everyone and required expiation.) There were four Medicine Arrows: two held power over buffalo, two over people. They were very sacred and were kept under the protection of an official appointed for that purpose. The Medicine Arrows stood for the tribe's collective existence; as long as they were cared for, the tribe would flourish. This supernatural power covered all Cheyenne, controlling both people and buffalo. The arrows, then, were the Cheyenne's greatest resource against severe anxiety, failure of the food supply, and extermination by enemies. The Arrow Renewal Ceremony brought the whole tribe together in sacred observances, after which all the hunters joined in a communal buffalo hunt. Anxieties relieved, the hunters went off confident that they would be successful, and certain that the whole earth and all therein had been revitalized in their favor.

Another ceremonial was the Cheyenne version of the Sun Dance, which they called the Medicine Lodge, or New Life Lodge, for its world renewal function. Usually the Cheyenne Sun Dance and Arrow Renewal Ceremony did not occur in the same year, but if they did, the Arrow Renewal Ceremony was more important and was given first. In the eight-day Sun Dance, warriors went through self-torture, suspending themselves from the central lodgepole by skewers through their chest muscles.

Religious Beliefs. Apparently the Cheyenne had no theory about how the world came to be; creation did not matter to them. They saw the world as composed of related parts, each governed by a kind of generous spirit. While the spirits had not created the world, they did know how to keep it operating properly, and they would give that knowledge to those who sought and listened respectfully. Human beings could not control nature, but they could learn to control themselves and know their place in nature. Careful self-control and the performance of exact symbolic rites would keep a man in tune with the environment, rejuvenate the earth, and maintain good health, good hunts, and victory in warfare. Self-discipline thus played a large part in Cheyenne conduct, from extreme sexual repression to bravery in the face of impossible odds.

The Cheyenne sought supernatural power through a vision quest, and shared the belief in guardian spirits common to many tribes, calling them "spirits who told me in sleep." To seek personal healing power or safety in a coming raid, a man would find a lonely place to fast and pray to the spirits. If a spirit was inclined to grant his requests, it appeared as a vision and told him how to prepare special charms, paint himself, and sing to summon his guardian. He was also given taboos to protect his new power. Under stress such visions came unsolicited, but they could also be called forth by the same sorts of gifts, offerings, or sacrifice used elsewhere in the Plains.

Prestige and Self-control. Like all the nomadic tribes of the Plains, the Cheyenne were relative newcomers. Because they were constantly having to defend their hunting territory against other groups that might deplete the buffalo supply or stampede the herds, they placed much emphasis on military prowess. Prestige in war was socially important; counting coup against the enemy established the warrior's place in his people's eyes and gave him great psychological satisfaction. Dozens of ritual occasions allowed an outstanding warrior to count coup, receiving public acclaim each time.

The Cheyenne have often been described as sexually repressed because cf their attitude toward sex and self-control. They believed that long-term continence gave a man great endurance and ability in warfare and hunting; it was not unheard of for a man to vow to abstain from sexual relations for years. Women were just as sexually constrained, and their virginity was very highly valued. Adultery was rare, and sexual continence was highly praised even for married couples. Ten years was the ideal spacing between children, bringing praise to men for abstinence and self-restraint.

Boys had no puberty ceremonies, but a girl's first menstruation was an important event. The girl's father would give away horses if he were rich, while her mother gave her a chastity belt to wear until she married and then whenever her husband was away.

The Comanche

The Comanche differed in many ways from the other Plains groups we have discussed. Their warfare was very individualistic, they never developed the military societies other Plains people had, and they did not perform the Sun Dance. What made them true Plains people was their total focus on horses: their superb riding skills surpassed all others. The Comanche spoke a Shoshonean language and apparently split off from the Shoshone after their arrival on the western Plains, sometime after A.D. 1500. They had been Basin foragers who moved onto the Plains a century or more before horses came.

How They Got Horses. By the time the Comanche came into history they were already riders. They were among the first Indians to acquire horses, though no one knows exactly how it happened. We know where they were in the mid-seventeenth century, though, and that gives us a clue. The eastern groups of Apache had come by some horses while the Comanche were settled nearby, around what is now Amarillo, Texas. The Comanche must also have come into contact with Spaniards, who, of course, had horses. In any event, by 1700 they were raiding the Spanish not only for horses but for mules and making a reputation for themselves as extremely skillful equestrians and clever traders. Once horses became common on the southern Plains, they spread quickly northward, and the Comanche benefited from being strategically located intermediaries between the supply in the Southwest and the demand to the north. Most other tribes had to trade through them, at least in the early days, so it is not surprising that the Comanche had more horses than any other tribe.

As time went on, the Comanche got their horses from many sources: trade with the Spanish and with other tribes, theft, raiding, breeding, and capturing wild mustangs. Even the poorest Comanche had at least one horse; the wealthy might have hundreds. It is said that some Comanche had more horses than did whole tribes in the northern Plains.

Eventually the Comanche ceased trading for horses; they traded horses for other things.

Horse stealing was prestigious, fun, and easier than breaking wild horses. The Comanche built quite a reputation for clever horse theft, inspiring many stories about thievery taking place despite "impossible" conditions: under the noses of guards or soldiers, or in stables where men were sleeping. The Comanche also stole mules, using them for backpacking and carrying war captives, since mules were slow.

The Comanche also bred their horses, unlike most other Indians. They castrated all stallions but those chosen for their fine qualities to breed the mares; riding horses were almost always gelded. The most desirable horse was wiry, swift, and easy to turn and train. Comanche did not shoe their horses, but toughened the hooves by walking the animals near a fire. Sometimes they made a sort of rawhide boot for a horse with a sore hoof. To break a wild horse, a Comanche usually rode it into water for the first few attempts so that when he was tossed by the bucking animal, he would land safely.

Skilled Equestrians. The Comanche were described as such fine riders that they looked like part of the horse. They rode both with saddles—modified from Spanish originals—and bareback, controlling their mounts with their knees and a simple rein. Babies on their mothers' backs became accustomed to riding before they learned to walk, and at four or five a boy had a horse of his own. Girls were as accustomed to riding as boys, though girls did not ride in hunts or raids. Boys were so competent that they were really trick riders, practicing daily like an athlete or dancer. They learned to pick up things from the ground while riding at full speed, and by adulthood they could swing a man up from the ground onto a horse. They often used this trick to rescue fallen comrades in battle; leaving a wounded Comanche to his enemies was about the worst thing another rider could do. Usually a pair of riders made the rescue, one on either side, leaning down to grasp the prone man at the same instant and raising him onto one of the horses. Men and horses practiced that feat until their timing and coordination were perfect.

Training Horses. A superior animal would be trained by its owner as a war or buffalo horse or both. A war horse had to be able to stand the whooping and screaming of the fight, and to respond alertly to commands the rider gave by pressing with his knees or shifting his weight while his hands were busy with weapons. An attacker galloped in a straight line, hanging over one side of the horse with only one heel showing over his mount's back. In that position he could loose arrows from under the horse's neck, shielded by its body. The rider was

Charles M. Russel's painting captures the drama of the buffalo hunt.

supported by a loop of horse or buffalo hair woven into the animal's mane and slung around one of the man's shoulders. He locked one leg over the horse's back and the other under its belly.

For buffalo hunting, a horse had to have many of the characteristics needed in battle—speed and fearlessness to enter the fringes of a nervous, thundering herd without guidance from his rider's reins, quickness to avoid the charge of a wounded bull, and deep wind to stay with the herd for miles. Comanche ponies were perfect machines of the hunt. They were trained to ride up to a fleeing buffalo, then veer aside as soon as they heard the twang of the bow. The hunter approached a buffalo from the rear, coming up swiftly and shooting an arrow into the soft, vulnerable area between the rib cage and the pelvis. At such close range, the arrow did tremendous damage. The hunters also killed with lances, but success in either case depended as much on the steed as the rider. It is not surprising that races and other contests on horseback were favorite Comanche sports.

A Comanche had great esteem for his favorite horse. He combed it and petted it, and for safety's sake usually picketed it at night near his tipi. To kill a man's favorite horse was about the same as committing murder.

The Crow

Old age is evil; it is far better for a man to die young in battle than to live to comfortable old age. So believed most of the Plains Indians, among them the Crow of southern Montana. Consequently boys trained young to become warriors, learning from games that imitated adult war conditions. Boys counted coup on animals as their elders did on enemies, and girls danced with the hair of a wolf or coyote as though it were an enemy scalp. On his first war party, a youngster might find himself the butt of practical jokes, and he was expected to carry the meat, do menial tasks, and locate water for the older men. But all such incidents prepared a young man for the time when he would be on his own, facing an enemy with only his meager weapons and his wits.

Warfare and military feats were the way to gain social standing and a chieftaincy among the Crow. War was a focal point for all Crow, not just those of one class or sex. Women's social status came from their husbands' military feats: they danced wearing scalps their husbands had accumulated, and proudly displayed their weapons. Nothing was more effective in whipping up emotion for a raiding party than a woman's grief over a fallen son or husband. There were even a few women warriors, one of whom was reported to have struck a coup and scalped a fallen enemy Blackfoot.

Crow warriors carried home scalps as evidence of a killing, but scalping in itself had no special merit. Cleaned, dried scalps were displayed as trophies at the end of a long stick.

Raids. The most frequent type of aggression was a raid organized by one man, consisting of a small party under his personal care. Men followed him because they expected success—the winning of horses and glory. As among the Cheyenne, the tribal leaders were expected to keep the peace and might veto the raid if it looked ill-advised, so they were not usually informed of plans for raids. The leader found all the approval he needed in a dream or vision giving him full details on where to go, whom to raid, and what loot to expect. A man who could not get the right kind of vision could go to someone known to have war medicine for direction from his dreams. Skeptics did not follow a raid leader if they doubted the power of his vision. Members of the party observed taboos during the raid to make sure it would be a success, and carried along the leader's sacred bundle for its medicine.

Raiding parties usually set out on foot, after dark. Bivouacking in simple shelters, they would send out scouts to find the enemy. Once the enemy was sighted, rituals were begun: men sang around a pile of buffalo chips, and one of the scouts announced the sighting by kicking over the chips. On the raid each man wore sacred objects on his body and designs painted on his face. The sponsor would pray to the sun for a safe and successful raid. Their goal was to steal or free enemy horses, and if they were able to do so the party returned home satisfied.

Enemy camps often caught the intruders at their work, and would try to fight them off or pursue them on horseback. If a member of the raiding party was killed, someone would go ahead to tell the camp by firing a gunshot and signalling to the people with a blanket. Those in camp went into mourning while the unlucky raiding party stayed in isolation for ten days. Then they would try again. If they were able to steal horses on the second attempt, the grieving ended, though the dead warrior's family would continue mourning until an enemy had been killed.

Although death in battle was considered glorious, the war party always tried to avoid losing people. Any man who got a reputation for leading raids on which men were often killed began to have a very hard time finding followers.

Winning Glory. A man could do four things in battle to win glory; when he had accomplished all four, he won the title of chief. The deeds were: (1) striking coup by touching a live enemy (the first coup of battle was ranked higher than any later blow), (2) snatching away an enemy's weapon in a hand-to-hand encounter, (3) stealing or freeing a horse in the enemy camp, (4) leading a successful raid.

Warriors wore symbols telling about their brave deeds. A coup striker might wear wolf tails on the heels of his moccasins; a gun-snatcher might decorate his shirt with ermine skins. Any warrior also had the right to picture his deeds on his robe and to recite his own praises on public occasions.

Other Reasons for Raids. Aside from the honor and social status warriors could win in battle, the desire for loot, horses above all, was motive for raiding. Although gaining horses from any source was profitable, the Crow felt it showed more valor to cut loose a picketed or hobbled horse than to make away with many that were wandering free; and of course a picketed horse was more apt to be valuable. Whatever loot the raiders got the leader theoretically could claim for himself. In practice he always shared it, not only with others of the raiding party, but often with those who had remained at home.

Another reason for raids was revenge: avenging a slain tribesman, or replacing Crow horses that had been stolen by taking as many or more from the enemy. If they killed an enemy, the warriors returned with blackened faces. They might take prisoners, often marrying captured women into the tribe. Male captives might also be spared, but not so commonly as women and children. If the Crow had suffered losses during the raid, or the enemy had put up great resistance, prisoners might be tortured and killed. It was a custom everywhere to adopt captured children.

The Mandan

A Siouan-speaking people, the Mandan had settled on the upper Missouri River long before Europeans reached the New World. By the time European explorers met them, two other sedentary tribes lived close by, the Hidatsa, also Siouan, and the Arikara, a spin-off of the Caddoan-speaking Pawnee. All lived in settled villages on terraces or cliffs along rivers. Archaeological ruins indicate that before A.D. 1400, relatively few of these villages were fortified. However, some villages such as the Huff site, a prehistoric Mandan village with more than one hundred lodges, had defensive earthworks and log palisades with bastions set up at regular intervals. Nineteenth century Mandan built stockade fences on the sides of the villages not naturally protected by cliffs.

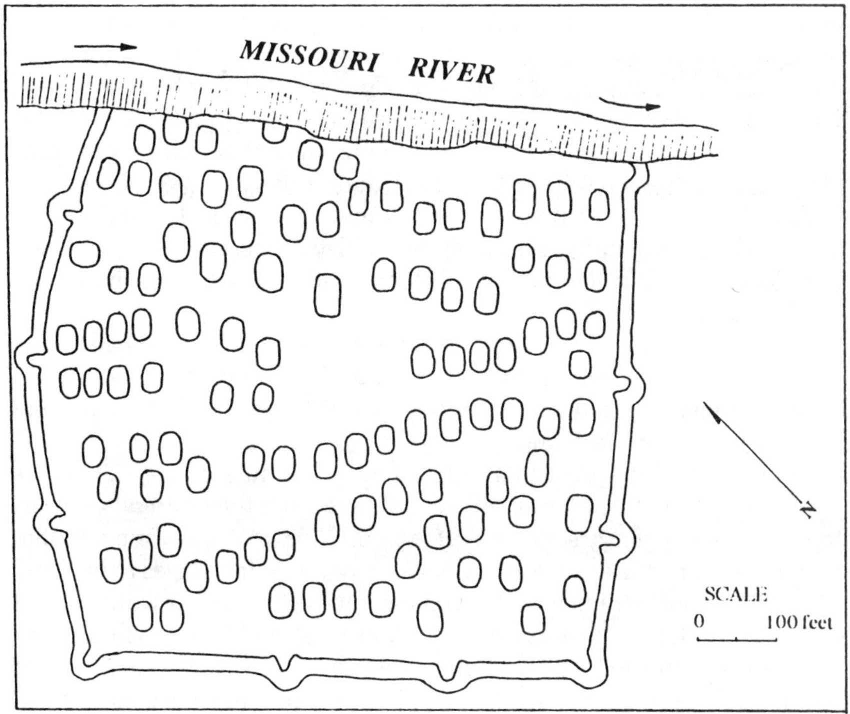

A plan of the Huff Site, a fortified prehistoric Mandan village on the west side of the Missouri River in Morton County, North Dakota. Note the bastions spaced at regular intervals along the palisade line. After Wood 1967.

Mandan villages had sturdily constructed earth houses fifty to eighty feet or more in diameter, large enough to house an extended family and a few horses during cold weather. Ground was excavated about two feet deep, above which a superstructure of heavy center posts and cross-beam logs was raised, walled with poles and roofed with rafters, over which branches were entwined. The entire building was covered with earth and sod, leaving only a center hole for smoke to escape. A short tunnel with a wind baffle of planks just inside the lodge was the entrance. People often sat on the roofs, where many foods were spread to dry before the women moved them to storage pits sunk into the lodge floors. These houses were warm in winter and cool in summer. They were built around a central area used for ceremonies and sports, a sort of village plaza or square. On the summer communal hunt, the Mandan lived in hide tipis.

Cultivation and Hunting. The Mandan participated in the mounted life of the Plains, but they also cultivated gardens. Cultivation was mostly women's work, but men helped clear the fields, and old men and children did some of the cultivating. They planted their gardens in fields along the river, after clearing off the trees by cutting them down and burning them or saving them to use for building houses. The women planted corn, beans, squash, and sunflowers in the rich river-bottom land, which they turned up and cultivated with hoes, digging sticks, and rakes. Tobacco, much used for ritual, was cultivated by old men. Unlike the fully nomadic tribes, the Mandan lived on their crops and had well-developed ceremonials for agriculture. They also traded corn to nomadic people for horses and hides. Village tribes ate nearly as much buffalo as corn, but the mounted Indians had only whatever corn they got by trade.

Fishing too was more important for Mandan subsistence than it was to most other Plains tribes—not surprising, since they lived on the river. Large numbers of bones in the village garbage heaps prove they were especially fond of catfish.

After the major spring planting came a lull in farming. Then the Mandan hunters turned from elk and deer, which they hunted all year, to the bison and the great summer communal hunt. They rode out onto the plains, sometimes for long periods, leaving their villages to be cared for by old people, some women, and the youngsters. Other women went with the hunters to process their buffalo meat and hides. Though the Mandan had hunted buffalo before they had horses, it was far more important later because, like the other Plains tribes, the horse made them more productive hunters.

Religion: The Okipa. The Mandan had no Sun Dance, but they had a midsummer ceremony for tribal well-being called the Okipa that was much like it. The Okipa was sponsored by an individual to fulfill a pledge; if several people wanted to sponsor one, several might come in one season, both before and after the buffalo hunt. Much self-torture went on during the Okipa, more than in many versions of the Sun Dance. An Okipa society directed the ceremony and guarded the sacred Okipa bundle that ensured the tribe's safety. The ceremony was for the good of the whole tribe. During its performance, the Mandan creation myth was acted out; it was much like the myth at the beginning of this chapter. The first part of the ceremonial celebrated the subsiding of the flood, then dancers, costumed or painted as mythical personages such as First Man, acted out the coming of the buffalo. The final parts of the ceremonial—the torture—were initiation rites to induct young men into manhood and ordeals to harden warriors for extreme trials of endurance.

Social Organization. The Mandan tribe was divided into two moieties, each with a part in the political organization. In each village, the peace leader came from one moiety and the war chief from the other. Within the two divisions were matrilineal clans, which controlled the fields, allotting them for cultivation to individual families in the clan. Women were important in land use and inheritance of rights in this matrilineal system, belonging to age-graded associations like the men. Membership in the grades was purchased. One rank of young men, the Black Mouth Society, was responsible for social control during tribal hunts. The Mandan also had a tribal council of leaders from the villages, which had no coercive powers but led by example and persuasion.

Raising Corn and Hunting Buffalo. The Mandan are typical of Plains villager life, though villages varied, of course, in customs, environment, and particularly climate. But the village tribes kept the pre-horse cultivation practices at the same time that the new, swift transportation enriched and elaborated their hunting activities. The two ways of getting subsistence meshed without strain. Before the buffalo hunt, the fields were prepared and sown. Women with children old enough for the occasion and all able-bodied men moved onto the plains to hunt bison, the women curing meat and tanning hides as the men killed the animals. Though matrilineal at home, hunting parties generally shifted to patrilocal or patrilineal arrangements, because brothers preferred to work together. When they had killed as much game as they could haul, the people returned to their permanent sites to harvest crops and process food for winter storage. Belief and ceremony among the village tribes included both rituals for good hunting and success in warfare (including the Buffalo Dance and the Okipa Ceremony) and a Rain Dance for good crop-growing weather.

CHARACTERISTICS OF THE PLAINS TRIBES

Clothing	Food production	Equipment	Shelter	Social and political organization	Religion	Warfare
Buffalo robes Leggings Shirts Coats Dresses Breechcloths Skirts Jackets Moccasins War bonnets	Nomads: hunting, gathering, fishing, some cultivation of tobacco, and trading with villagers Villagers: cultivation (corn, beans, and squash), hunting, and gathering	Bows and arrows Spears Scrapers Awls Hoes Clubs Shields Pectorals Axes Pottery (villagers) Parfleches Basketry Buffalo horn spoons and cups	Skin tents Large tipis Earth lodges of log framework over shallow pits Thatched beehive-shaped houses Sweathouses	Local bands Matrilineal and patrilineal clans Tribes Tribal associations Age grades Moieties (Mandan) Council of Forty-Four (Cheyenne)	Shamans Spirits Guardian spirits Vision Quest Sun Dance Arrow Renewal Ceremony (Cheyenne) Okipa Ceremony (Mandan)	Warfare — the most important source of glory for men Frequent raids "Coup" counting Scalping

Suggestions for Further Study

Bibliography

Lowie, Robert. 1954. *Indians of the Plains.*

An excellent survey of the Plains Indians after they acquired the horse.

Nabokov, Peter. 1967. *Two Leggings: The Making of a Crow Warrior.*

Good biographical and ethnographic information about the Crow during 1840–1920, and one man's quest for leadership.

Neihardt, John G. 1961. *Black Elk Speaks.*

A description of a Sioux medicine man's dreams and the influence they had on his life.

______. 1951. *When the Tree Flowered.*

A compilation of the life stories of many real Sioux into one fictional man. This excellent ethnographic work should be more valuable to students than the more esoteric *Black Elk Speaks.*

Price, John. 1979. *Indians of Canada.* Scarborough, Ontario: Prentice Hall of Canada, Ltd.

Other Pertinent Works

Ewers, John. 1955. *The Horse in Black foot Indian Culture.*

______. 1958. *The Blackfeet.*

Fletcher, Alice, and Francis LaFlesche. 1906. *The Omaha Tribe.*

Grinnel, George B. 1923. *The Cheyenne Indians.* 2 vols.

Lowie, Robert. 1922. *Plains Indian Age Societies.*

______. 1935. *The Crow Indians.*

Mishkin, Bernard. 1940. *Rank and Warfare among Plains Indians.*

Secoy, Frank R. 1953. *Changing Military Patterns of the Great Plains.*

Wallace, Ernest, and E. A. Hoebel. 1952. *The Comanches, Lords of the South Plains.*

Wilson, Gilbert L. 1924. *The Horse and the Dog in Hidatsa Culture.*

MAJOR GROUPS AND LANGUAGES OF THE PLAINS

Language phylum	Language family	Cultural division
Aztec-Tanoan	Kiowa-Tanoan	Kiowa
	Uto-Aztecan	Comanche
Macro-Algonkian	Algonkian	Arapaho Atsina Blackfoot Cheyenne
Macro-Siouan	Caddoan	Arikara Caddo Pawnee Wichita
	Siouan	Assiniboine Crow Dakota Hidatsa Iowa Kansa Mandan Omaha Osage Ponca Quapaw
Na-Dene	Athabaskan	Kiowa Apache Sarsi

8

THE EAST

Iroquois wooden mask of the False Face Society.

New England Algonkian Legend

Many years ago a young Indian man built a small lodge away from the home of his family. He had arrived at the proper age to undertake a fast and learn what kind of spirit would be his guide and guardian through life. He entered his little lodge where he would not be disturbed, and prepared himself to receive a spirit.

He sought to clear his heart of every evil thought, and to think only good, beautiful, and kindly things. He ate nothing and he meditated for two days. Nothing happened, and the young man felt despair. On the third day, weak and faint, he wondered whether any spirit would come to him. He lay on his bed, and suddenly saw a bright light at the lodge door. At first, the man was frightened, but then he saw that a beautiful woman had entered his lodge. She was richly and gaily dressed in many flowing garments of green and yellow colors. She had a plume of waving feathers on her head, and she had long, light hair, very different from Indian hair.

She spoke in a soft, musical voice. "I have come in response to your fasting." The man tried to approach her, but she seemed to move away. He told her he was lonely and he wanted her to stay with him. She told him that if he did just exactly as she said, she would be with him always. She would return to him the next day and tell him what to do.

When the woman returned, the man was very faint in body, but strong at heart. He said, "I have continued my fast to show you my good heart. Now you have promised that you will never leave me." "You have won your desire," she said, "and your fast will soon be over. This is what you must do." And she took the man by his hand and led him from the lodge.

Outside, some distance from the lodge, was a meadow of dry grass. The woman told the man to rub two dry sticks together quickly, holding them in the grass. Soon sparks flew, and the grass caught fire. Then the woman said, "when the sun goes down, you must take me by my hair and drag me across the field. After that you may eat." The man did not want to drag her, but she told him he must, and if he did, he would never again be hungry. When evening came, he did as he had been told. The woman disappeared, but wherever he had dragged her, a tall and graceful plant arose. On it were golden clusters of grain, and on each cluster the man could see the light, silky hair of the woman. It was corn, the friend of all mankind, and every spring it grows again as the Indians plant the kernels in the ground.

The Eastern culture area stretches from the Mississippi River to the Atlantic Ocean, and from the Gulf of Mexico to the Great Lakes and slightly north of the Canadian border (as far north as maize can be cultivated). In this very large area with its many regional variations, most Indian groups adapted themselves to woodland living. All practiced agriculture, but though corn was very important in the diet (as in the myth introducing this chapter), rarely did cultivation make up much more than half the diet. Game, fish, and wild plants were abundant and could be taken with little effort. In two parts of the East, farming was not done at all: the Calusa area of south Florida, where the people lived entirely on wild foods, and the extreme northeast, where the growing season was so short that crops very often failed. Yet even there people had corn, getting it in trade with more southerly neighbors.

Early Life in the East

The East had three distinguishable subareas, which we can call the Northeast, Southeast, and the Western Great Lakes regions. Though cultures in all three areas shared woodland living and corn cultivation, a number of differences in environment and cultural adaptations make the three regions distinct.

Languages, however, followed a different pattern. Algonkian speakers lived from the Western Great Lakes to the New England coast and down the coast into North Carolina. Piercing this expanse of Algonkians was a wedge of Iroquoian speakers, concentrated around the Eastern Great Lakes and spreading into the Appalachians. Separated from this northerly Iroquoian group by Algonkians was another set of Iroquoian speakers around Virginia, eastern Tennessee, and North Carolina. Some Siouan-speaking tribes lived south of those Iroquois, and a few isolated Siouans had established themselves along the Gulf coast. By far the most common tongues of the Southeast were languages of the Muskogean family, and Muskogean is limited to the Southeast.

Estimating aboriginal population in the Eastern Woodlands is difficult, but the area was large and life there was fairly easy, so as many as three-quarters of a million to one million people may have lived there.

Prehistory

The earliest Easterners hunted large game animals like mammoth, bison, mastodon, and caribou. Around 8000 B.C. they started to shift from big game to smaller animals and wild plant foods, exploiting many local environments such as lakes, rivers, coastlines, and especially forests. By about 2000 B.C. the people in many parts of the East had begun to

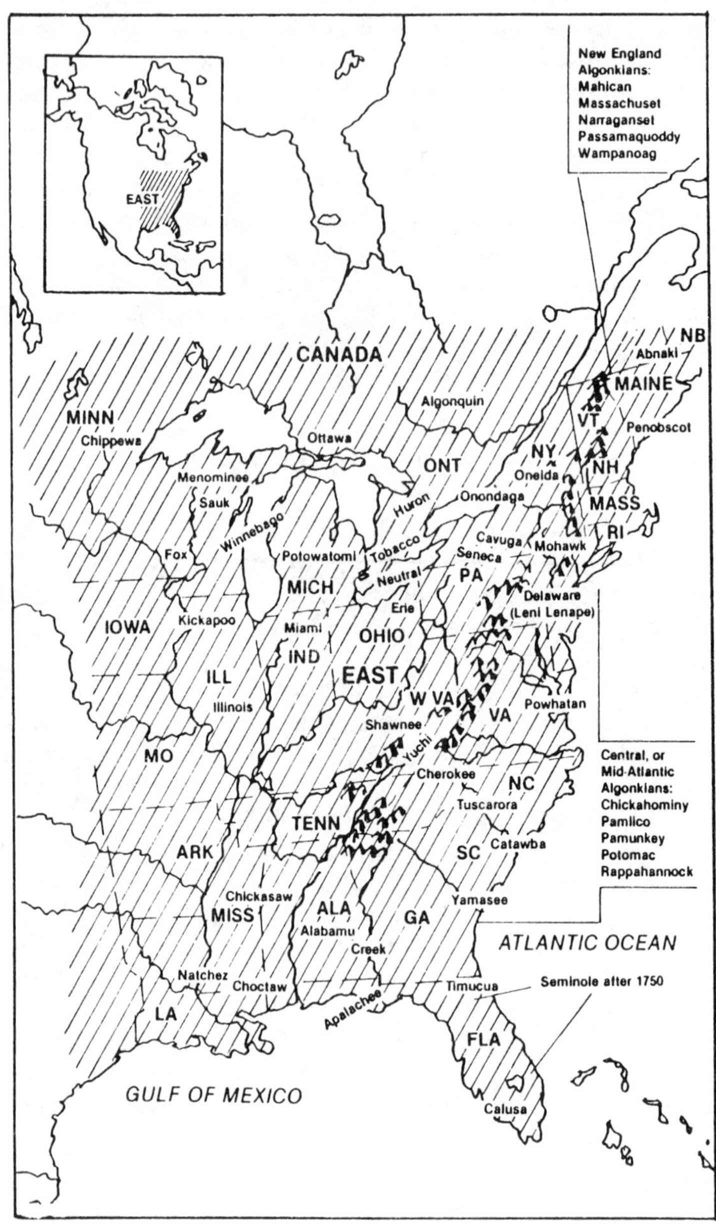

The Eastern culture area and its tribes, showing the subcultural divisions.

cultivate both native and introduced plants that they found to be useful food sources. We call this time of growing local diversity the Eastern Archaic.

About 1000 B.C. groups in the northern part of the area began to build mounds of earth, usually over burials. They also started to use some plants more intensively and to make pottery. These new adaptations marked the beginning of the Woodland Tradition, which underwent further cultural development as time progressed. The earliest presence of the tropical cultigen corn in the East dates from a little over two thousand years ago, though at first it is only indicated by a very small quantity of kernels at a few Woodland sites. By A.D. 1000 corn had become a dietary staple among many cultures in the East. The Woodland Tradition held on nearly unchanged in some places until the Europeans came.

Other groups of mound-building people began their own tradition after about A.D. 800, mostly in the upper and lower parts of the Mississippi Valley and the Southeast. Upon their flat-topped mounds they constructed temples and the houses of important individuals, and some were part of real urban centers like Cahokia in Illinois. The people of the Mississippian Tradition farmed intensively along fertile river floodplains, raising large crops of corn, beans, and squash. The greatly improved corn they grew had ultimately originated in Mexico, though how it came into the East and how it became adapted to the more northerly environmental conditions are not yet fully understood.

The East at Contact

The Atlantic seaboard was the scene of the first European colonies, and consequently of the first and most complete damage and destruction to Indian societies. Native American life was so disrupted that little was left to be recorded by the time scholars realized what had happened. By the nineteenth century, the coastal tribes were gone; unlike the Plains, Southwest, or other areas, no one was left to preserve any of the old traditions. Most of our information about the seaboard tribes at the time of first contact comes from a few early observers who wrote down their impressions. Even these records are not as complete or as competent as we might wish. After all, these English, French, and Spanish observers were not ethnologists. They did not always understand what they saw and often they misinterpreted what the Indians were doing: one described an initiation ceremony as a sacrifice of young boys. Sometimes references are made that excite our curiosity, but no descriptions come with them. Much of the time we have to reconstruct the aboriginal life by leaning heavily upon ethnographic analogy, archaeology, and general anthropological theories of kinship and political structure.

Tribes in the Southeast and around the Great Lakes lasted longer than those of the coast, and we know more about them. However, our picture of European-Indian contact is one-sided; almost everything we have is from European sources. Indians recorded very little, and nobody seems to have cared much about what Indians thought of it all.

Ancestors and Descendants. Often we cannot connect historic tribes with prehistoric sites; all we can do is make reconstructions from language comparisons, and even those often defy explanation in detail. For example, the northern speakers of Iroquois were culturally similar in many ways to the Southeastern peoples. In fact, northern Iroquois were much more like the Southeasterners than their own northern neighbors. Northern Iroquois were matrilineal, lived in large dwellings with extended families, practiced intensive agriculture, and tortured war captives, all Southern traits. Their nearest linguistic relatives were southern Iroquoian speakers, the Cherokee and Tuscarora, from whom they were separated (at the time of contact) by a solid block of Algonkians.

Comparing language and other cultural relationships, we might guess that some Iroquois speakers moved north and settled around the Eastern Great Lakes not too long before Columbus. Yet archaeological findings indicate that the Iroquois of the north had been there much longer than that. The connection over time, then, between southern and northern Iroquoian speakers is not at all clear; we have too little information.

The same is true of the relationship between Southeastern Siouans and Algonkians. The Siouans built their villages and sowed their fields in the broadleaf forest of the Piedmont, while the Algonkians lived on the sandy soil and marshlands of the tidewater zone. We have no doubt that the Algonkians pushed down from the north where most Algonkian speakers apparently lived long before Europeans came to North America. Did the Algonkians come before the Siouans? Or did they invade the Siouan people and drive them from the coastal plain? Or did the Siouans come from the west and drive the Algonkian onto the coast? No one knows for sure.

Ohio and the Southeast. Where Adena, Hopewell, and Fort Ancient people had lived, in and around Ohio, an abrupt decline in population appears to have struck just before the Europeans arrived. In fact, the population fell so sharply that some maps of tribal locations in the early historic period show that region as uninhabited. Soon, however, people driven from their homes farther east by the many European-Indian struggles filled that void. Cultural hybrids, groups composed of Indian-white mixtures as well as remnants from many fragmented tribes, made their temporary home around Ohio.

A similar situation can be seen in the Southeast, where the relation between history and prehistory has been obscured by changes around the time of European contact. Connections have been proposed between a number of the historic Southern tribes and the prehistoric Mississippians and other cultures of the Southeast. Sites of the prehistoric Pisgah culture, for example, can be connected to the historic Cherokee. Several Mississippian sites in the Lower Mississippi Valley are clearly connected to the historic Natchez. Late prehistoric occupants of the major Mississippian center of Etowah in northern Georgia were likely ancestors of some of the Muskogean speakers who later became members of the Creek Confederacy in historic times, along with other fragmented groups from the area of northern Alabama and Georgia. Moundville, a major prehistoric Mississippian center along the Black Warrior River in western Alabama, may be related to the historic Choctaw. The Little Egypt site in northern Georgia was likely the main village of the Coosa, occupied well into the sixteenth century and visited by Hernando de Soto and other Spanish explorers. Another significant Mississippian center in eastern Oklahoma, the Spiro site, was probably occupied by prehistoric Caddoan-speaking people, although any connection to a specific tribe is not presently possible.

It should be kept in mind, however, that many such identifications are tentative or speculative for most areas of the East. One complicating factor in attempts to connect archaeological cultures to historic tribes is that closely related tribes speaking almost identical languages can possess very different lifeways and artifacts; it is equally possible that linguistically and genetically remote groups can share in nearly identical life-styles and possess very similar material culture. Many factors can affect our understanding of past tribal locations and make direct tie-ups between archaeological cultures and historic tribes difficult, including population reduction due to the impact of infectious disease and warfare, population movement, group fragmentation and amalgamation, the shifting balance of power between opposing groups, and the lack of adequate historic accounts for particular tribes or areas.

Resources and Technology

Indians of the East had natural resources in abundance: the great forests, which provided wood, game, and wild plant foods; the rivers, coasts, and lakes, which had fish and shellfish; and the rainfall which came at the right season and provided enough water for farming. Men hunted, fished, fought, and made equipment for those pursuits. Women gardened, gathered wild plant foods, cared for the home and the young, and made utensils for those tasks.

Food. We still eat many of the dishes Indian women made from corn. They made succotash by boiling beans and corn with a chunk of fat. Hominy was made by boiling corn with wood ashes: lye from the ashes loosened the hulls, then the plump corn kernels were washed free of ash and hulls and boiled some more. From corn meal, made by pounding corn kernels to a fine flour, women produced corn cakes, bread, and a corn porridge. Sometimes they added nuts or berries to their corn bread. Corn soup was a favorite all over the East. Parched corn could be brewed into a drink something like coffee.

Other foods, of course, were also important to Eastern Indians. Eastern Indians ate berries, both raw and cooked, and dried them for storage; they also steeped them in water to make fruit drinks. Other beverages came from sunflower seeds and roots of the sassafras tree. The Woodland Indians had several seasonings, though most of them did not use salt. Indeed, among the Onondaga, a tribe of Iroquois speakers, salt was taboo. Instead, the women added wild onion, ginger, and maple sugar to their dishes.

Shells and Pottery. The Indians who lived along the seacoasts and rivers used shells for many kinds of utensils, like spoons, cups, cutters, and scrapers. The men even used bivalve shells as pincers or tweezers to remove whiskers. (Fortunately for Indian men, they had very scant facial hair.) Eastern Indians had raw materials for just about anything they needed from food to construction to adornment.

Almost all Eastern Indians made pottery. Before shaping and firing it, women mixed clay with fine bits of stone, shell, or fiber (called *temper*), which kept the clay paste from splitting and cracking as it heated. Shell-tempered pottery was a hallmark of the Southeast and was also common among the long-resident cultures of the Midwest prairie. Indians could tell the tribe of the potter from the shape and temper of the pottery.

Clothing. Garments varied with the climate and season. Indians in the colder parts of the Northeast wore fitted skin garments most of the year. Women's dresses were made from two skins, one hanging down the front, one down the back, from the shoulders. In the winter sleeves were added for extra warmth. Men wore breechclouts, and put shirts, coats, and leggings over them when it was cold. Leggings were made in pairs, but not sewn together; each leg was separate. They were held by a cord fastened to a waistband, usually the waistband holding the breechclout. Farther south, people wore little more than breechclouts and skirts. Women there made their skirts of plant fibers. Most moccasins throughout the East came up to the ankles, where they were tied. Women often decorated the clothing with flattened porcupine quill embroidery.

An Eastern Indian whose scalp lock has been styled into a roach to which deer's tail hairs have been fastened.

Hair Styles. Women usually wore their hair in braids, and men often did too. Another common male style was the *roach*, a stiff ridge of hair two or three inches high, running from the forehead to the back of the neck and sometimes padded out with red-dyed deer hair. The rest of their hair they plucked, shaved, or burned off with hot stones. A popular arrangement for men left only a *scalp lock*, a lock of hair grown long as a challenge to enemies to "come and get it." Both sexes sported many hair ornaments of shell, feathers, stone, and copper. Bear fat was a common hair dressing for both men and women, sometimes mixed with soot to make the hair blacker.

The People

Warfare. It may be impossible to explain why some people seem more belligerent than others. Whatever the reason, warfare in the Northeast and Southeast seems to have been almost continuous at the time Europeans arrived, and the Europeans provoked the hostilities still more. Even before contact, many of the tribes quarreled and feuded constantly—Iroquois speakers against Algonkian, Algonkian against Algonkian, Muskogean against Muskogean—seeking revenge for injury, theft, or trespass. The renown and glory that war honors brought throughout the East were no help in keeping things peaceful.

Fighting was by ambush and hit-and-run raiding. Warring groups were seldom large; one or two dozen men made the usual war party. Bows and arrows, stone and bone knives, and stone- or wooden-headed clubs (called *tomahawks* by the Algonkians) were their weapons. After Europeans introduced iron implements, tomahawks had iron heads and some knives and arrows were made with iron blades or tips.

Scalping and similar cultural practices existed among native Eastern cultures hundreds of years before the arrival of Europeans, as prehistoric skeletal evidence shows. Scalping, however, apparently became more common among the native inhabitants after Europeans began offering rewards or bounties for them. In most areas of the East, the prevalance of raiding and warfare induced native groups to locate their settlements in naturally defensibile settings and encircle them with protective stockades.

Warriors had rituals to perform before going to war, and they observed taboos while fighting. If they returned victorious, the community celebrated with a victory feast or dance. If the war party lost a man, the warriors and villagers observed mourning rites and vowed revenge.

Religion. Eastern warriors, like those in western culture areas, sought guardian spirits and supernatural help. Most found their spirit help in dreams or visions after fasting and isolation. Like Indians elsewhere, the Easterners looked not to one god but to spirits and natural power. They felt themselves to be a part of nature, certainly not superior to it, and religion was a powerful factor in their lives. They held elaborate ceremonies and carried out detailed rituals to thank, placate, or appeal to the supernatural.

Shamans were curers who had much spirit help to cure disease. In the East, curing was often combined with an ability to bring good weather, foretell the future, and ensure success in warfare and hunting. But Easterners also had medicine societies, and in the Northeast and Western Great Lakes regions shamanism was secondary to medicine societies.

The Indian character is often painted as silent, unsmiling if not sullen, and generally aloof or unfriendly. This portrait probably came from a time of oppression or was painted by people who made no effort to be friendly. Early reports showed Indians to be eager to meet newcomers and generally interested in and delighted by European goods. Bitterness and hostility grew as their lands were taken away.

The Northeast

The Northeast subarea includes what is now New England, the Atlantic states as far south as Virginia, the Ohio valley, the Eastern or Lower Great Lakes (Erie and Ontario), and Canadian territory about one hundred miles north of the Lower Great Lakes. It is a region cold in winter, with deep snows, and often hot in summer. The Appalachian mountain ranges extend southward from the northeast into Alabama, and include the Catskills, Alleghenies, Blue Ridge, Cumberland, and other ranges. The Appalachian is an old, worn-down mountain system with no very high peaks. Two ridges run north and south parallel to the coast, and the valley between them is very fertile. On the east the primary rivers draining the Appalachians are the St. Lawrence, Hudson, Potomac, and Delaware; and on the west, the Ohio and its tributaries. Many lesser rivers also drain the area, which gets enough rainfall for agriculture everywhere.

The forests are a combination of deciduous trees—elm, oak, ash, birch, and maple—and various needled evergreens, such as the hemlock. They provide a home for many woodland animals like squirrel, deer, fox, and bear. Nuts and berries of many species are everywhere, and many varieties of fish fill the lakes and rivers. The climate is suitable for farming, and the ground is fertile. Thus subsistence for the Northeastern tribes was varied, combining corn cultivation, hunting, fishing, and wild-plant gathering.

Women were the cultivators, but men helped in cutting and burning the trees to prepare the fields. The fields were farmed until they were no longer fertile, then new fields were cleared while the old lay fallow—a practice known as *slash-and-burn agriculture*. After a generation, the fertile fields were often some distance from the village, and whole communities moved to be closer to the garden plots. Some groups, especially the Iroquois, got more food from cultivation than others; the Algonkians of New England found winter severe and the land rocky and hard to cultivate.

New England Algonkians

The earliest European colonists landed on territory belonging to the coastal Algonkians. What thoughts passed through the minds of those Indian New Englanders when they saw such strange ships and strange people land on their shores? We can only guess. But during the early years of European settlement, relations between European and Indian were most often friendly. The New England Algonkians of the vicinity kept the Pilgrims alive, in fact, for European wheat and other grains could not be sown in the rocky soils. An Algonkian of the Wampanoag tribe, Squanto, taught the newcomers to plant maize in little hills and fertilize each mound with an alewife, a species of fish. Much American literature on the early settlers is about the Atlantic Algonkians, including *The Last of the Mohicans* and other works by James Fenimore Cooper. Few descriptions, though, give accurate ethnographic information. Since the way of life of those Eastern tribes has long since disappeared, we must flesh out our attempts at reconstruction with analogy, theory, and some guesswork.

Algonkian Village Life. The Northeastern Algonkians fought off heavy snowfall and winter cold with many of the same techniques the Subarctic Algonkian folk used. The great difference between the two was their way of handling the food quest: the New England Algonkians could grow maize. And this led to another difference: they were also more settled. They lived in villages among their fields in *wigwams*, domed structures of bent poles or saplings tied together and covered with sheets of bark, hide, or woven matting. Wigwams usually housed small families, just the parents and their children, instead of extended families, though some New England Algonkians made wigwams large enough for two or three families.

Like their Subarctic cousins, the New England Algonkians treated animal bones respectfully. Also, they segregated women at their first menstruation, during menstrual periods thereafter, and at childbirth. They traveled the streams in bark canoes, gathered wild plant foods, hunted and fished, and cultivated corn, beans, and squash. New Englanders exploited coastal resources such as clams and lobsters, and like their northern Algonkian relatives, tapped sugar maple trees for the sweet sap. From them we have taken into English the words *succotash*, *hominy*, *moccasin*, *squaw*, *papoose*, and *wigwam*, and many place names such as Massachusetts, Narraganset, and Alleghany. The words *podunk*, referring to a small, provincial town, and *mugwump*, a renegade in politics, both came from Algonkian.

Political Order. Algonkian tribes of the Northeast were divided into villages that had their own names, and the tribes also formed alliances that have often been called confederacies. But these relationships probably were too temporary and limited in power to be true confederacies. Our information is so scant that it is hard to tell just what aboriginal politics were like. Probably the confederacies were alliances among independent groups speaking the same language with differences only in dialect. Such alliances probably formed and broke up quickly in a generation or less, depending mainly on the personal magnetism of a leader from one of the member tribes. When he died or lost power,

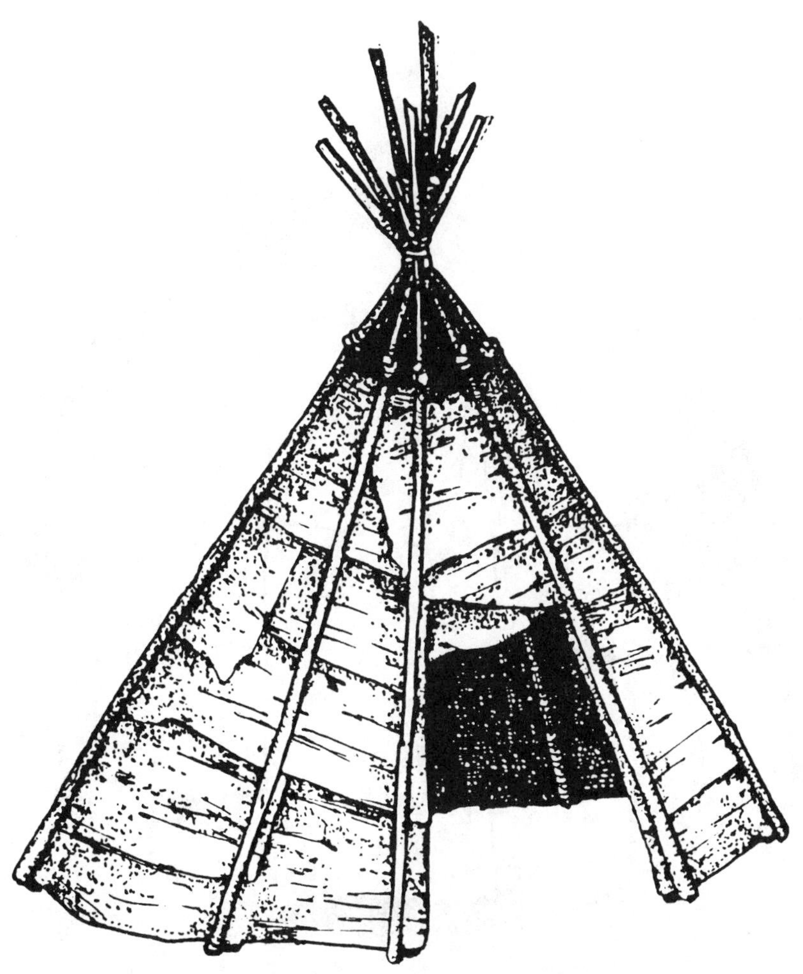

Bark Tipi (the Northeast)

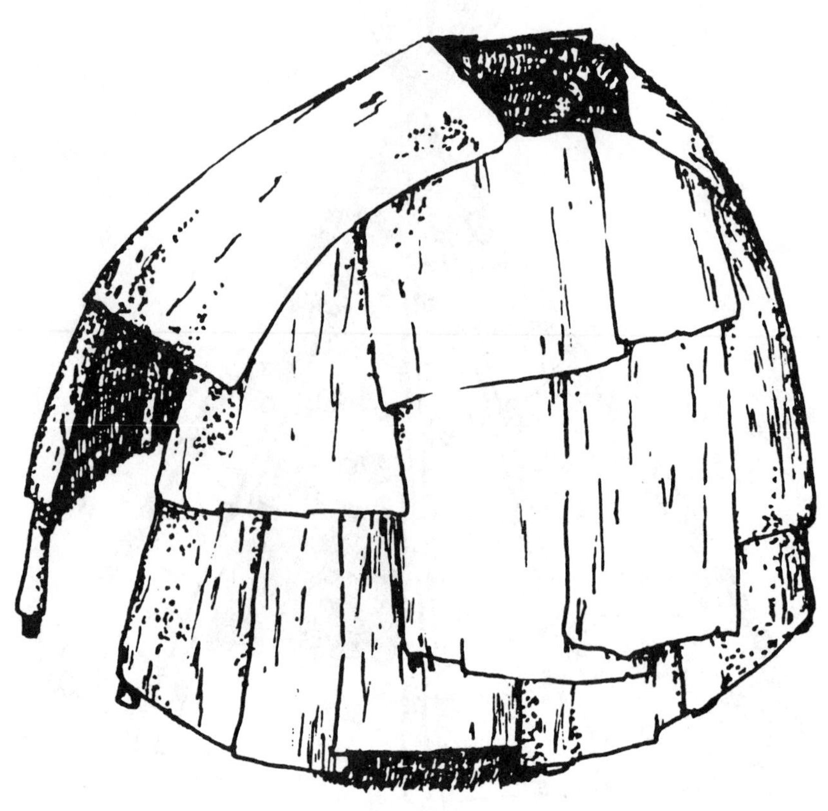

Wigwam (Northeast or Western Great Lakes)

the alliance would fall apart. However, some authorities do think the connections among the New England and Atlantic seaboard Algonkians were real confederacies, somewhat lasting, with some kind of supreme leadership, usually a council made up of leaders of the member tribes. It is a futile debate, for the Atlantic Algonkians were so disrupted by European settlement that we have no records to decide the issue. Early in the colonization by European powers, though, leagues of some sort existed among many Indian societies in the Eastern area. In fact, most of the names by which we know the seaboard Algonkians are not their tribal names but names of the alliances.

After Europeans interfered with aboriginal life, such alliances grew more structured in defiance of the common enemy. They never quite developed into a potent adversary force, though, for the member tribes always ended up fighting each other as much as their foe, the Europeans.

Some of the Algonkian groups known as confederations during the historic period were the Abnaki of Maine, including the Penobscot and the Passamaquoddy; the Massachuset, around the present city of Boston; the Narraganset in Rhode Island; the Mahican of the upper Hudson Valley and in Connecticut (where they were known as the Mohegan); and the Leni Lenape or Delaware in New Jersey, Pennsylvania, and Delaware.

The Abnaki. Tribes in the Abnaki alliance were at the northern limits of cultivation and resembled people of the Subarctic in many ways. Though they had a reputation for being peaceful and gentle, they went in for the raiding typical of the Easterners. They often tortured male prisoners, but women captives were absorbed into the tribe and treated kindly. The Abnaki lived in multiple-family bark- or mat-covered wigwams in stockaded villages. Each village was governed by a council of elders that met in a council house much larger than the dwellings. Each tribe had both a peace chief and a war chief, and corresponding tribal councils, one in charge of civil matters, the other of warfare.

The Abnaki favored the French over the English in the colonial struggle in the Northeast, but after the French lost power, they made peace with the English. Most of the Abnaki moved to Canada, although two subdivisions, the Penobscot and Passamaquoddy, remained in Maine.

The Leni Lenape. The Leni Lenape, or Delaware (as the English called them, after the river that ran through the territory), once were a very important and respected tribe. Many other Algonkian tribes called members of the Lenape tribe "grandfather," a title of honor; the Shawnee and Mahican believed that they were descended from Lenape. In the early eighteenth century the Iroquois assumed control over the Lenape, then both Iroquois and white pressure pushed the Lenape out of their traditional lands. They settled in Ohio and Indiana and eventually lost all cohesiveness, some groups ending up in Arkansas, Texas, Kansas, and Oklahoma.

The Mahicans. The Mahican or Mohegan confederation extended from the Hudson River valley in New York as far north as Lake Champlain, and east into Massachusetts and Connecticut. Conflict with the Iroquoian Mohawk to the west, coupled with inroads by settlers, forced them to the south. They joined with the Lenape, finally losing their identity in the emigration to lands west of the Mississippi River. One of the tribelets of the Mohegan, the Stockbridge (named after the village in Massachusetts), moved to Wisconsin, where their descendants still live near Lake Winnebago. One of the Lenape groups, the Munsee, also set up a home there.

All these peoples seem to have lived much like the Northeastern Algonkians. Their clothing was of deerskin, with leggings, shirts, dresses, and robes in cool weather, and loincloths alone for men in warm weather. Leggings were often worn as much for protection against underbrush as for warmth.

Resources in the Northeast. A settler in the mid-seventeenth century described Northeastern food as a stew of maize and kidney beans boiled with fish or game. The fish included eels, shad, herring, and alewives, and the game was beaver, bear, venison, moose, raccoon, or otter. Other wild foods that might be boiled with meat were groundnuts, Jerusalem artichokes, and several kinds of nuts: acorns, walnuts, and chestnuts. Algonkians also ground nuts into flour, which they used to thicken their stews and soups. Corn was ground into meal and made into johnnycakes or porridge cooked in clay pots and spooned out with a wooden ladle. They made containers of bark and basketry as well as pottery.

Leaders, In Peace and War. Eastern Algonkian leaders are often called *sagamores* or *sachems*, English versions of two Algonkian words for "chief." Generally the position ran in families, though competence was always considered. Leaders served only with the people's consent and were guided by a council of respected elders. Some of the leaders were quite autocratic, but generally the tribal council tempered such tendencies. Sagamores were not monarchs, although the colonists, used to kings where they came from, often referred to Indian leaders as kings, princes, and so on.

Older men were honored for their wisdom, but war was the young man's way to prestige. War took the form of raids and ambushes, not large-scale battles. Tomahawks, shields, and scalping knives were used, along with the bow and arrow. It is from the New England Algonkians that we got the expressions "to bury the hatchet" and "to take up the tomahawk."

Warfare increased as conflicts arose with the English settlers. Tribes often broke up, and new groups might contain members of several tribes. Others fled west or into Canada, where the French were friendly. Refugees made new alliances with the tribes in the areas they fled to. All this changed the aboriginal political picture so rapidly that it is now impossible to know how formal the alliances were before Europeans arrived and how much the European onslaught forced the Indians into confederation in the face of a common enemy.

The Iroquois League

Iroquois speakers spread as a block across the Lower or Eastern Great Lakes territory and the southeastern shores of Lake Huron, wedging into the Eastern Algonkian territory. The major Iroquois tribes were the Huron, Erie, Tobacco, Neutral, and a group that came to be known as the League of the Iroquois: Seneca, Cayuga, Onondaga, Oneida, and Mohawk. These latter five were often called "the Iroquois," but Iroquois is *not* the name of a tribe or political unit; it is a *language*. We shall refer to the five nations collectively as "the League."

The Legend of Deganawidah. How the League got started as a federation is not clear. Some have claimed it really was an aboriginal development, while others believe it was formed because of European pressures. A legendary tradition involves a folk hero, Deganawidah, who lived in the sixteenth century and may have been a shaman. Deganawidah was distressed because the five tribes fought so much among themselves when they were all oppressed by the Huron, who were far more powerful at that time. (Deganawidah probably was a Huron by birth but a Mohawk by adoption.) He persuaded Hiawatha, a Mohawk chief (not the fictitious Chippewa Hiawatha of Longfellow's poem), to help him create an alliance among the five tribes. This alliance became the League of the Iroquois, whose object was to end intertribal war and promote peace and well-being among the five tribes and any others who chose to join them. The legend varies depending on when it was recorded and which tribe was telling it.

For decades after the League was formed, the five nations were greatly feared as aggressors by the Huron and by the Algonkians as well. The League never did really halt internal strife. In 1722, one group of southern Iroquoian speakers, the Tuscarora, joined the League, which became known as the Six Nations. Eventually some tribes of the League joined the colonists while others allied with the English during the Revolutionary War.

Iroquois Village Life. All Iroquoian speakers had a subsistence similar to the Algonkian. Their foods were cultivated crops, game, and wild plants. Farming and wild-plant gathering were women's tasks, while men took care of fishing, hunting, and warfare. Material culture too was much like the Algonkian in weapons, tools, and utensils. Like the Algonkians, the Iroquoians lived in villages, usually behind *palisades*, fences of sharp, pointed poles, but their homes were multifamily longhouses, not the wigwams of the New England Algonkians or the Quonset-shaped houses of some other Algonkian tribes. An Iroquois village might have several hundred people or as many as 2,000 to 3,000.

All tribes of the League used the *longhouse*, a building fifty to one hundred feet long and about twenty feet wide, which housed several related families. It had a door at each end and was gabled or vaulted, rather like a long, narrow barn. Down the center ran a corridor, in which each longhouse family had its fire. The families lived in separate compartments on either side of the corridor. Platforms against the walls were both beds and seats. The League symbolized itself as a vast longhouse, stretching from west to east. The Seneca were "Keepers of the Western Door," and the Mohawk "Keepers of the Eastern Door." In the center were the Onondaga, "Keepers of the Council Fire" and "Keepers of the Wampum Belts."

Wampum. Both Algonkians and Iroquois of the Northeast made beads of white and purple shells, stringing them into strands and weaving them into belts. Those beads were called *wampum*, an Algonkian word. Strung beads were sometimes used as adornment, but the woven belts took on greater importance, their symbolic white and purple designs representing treaties and agreements, records of events, and public accounts. One Onondaga sachem kept the treaty wampum for the five tribes; he had to remember what all the symbols meant and interpret them when necessary. Eventually wampum came to be a medium of exchange, a sort of money, after Europeans began using it. The beads were hard to make, and wampum disappeared when trade beads from Europe became available.

Warfare. The almost constant warfare among the Eastern tribes was broken by peace only for practical, beneficial reasons, such as trade. All the people of the area were aggressive, but the Iroquois got a reputation as particularly bellicose, even vicious, warriors.

Iroquois generally went to war for one of three reasons. First, warfare could bring a young man personal recognition, because the highest ideal

Iroquois Longhouse. The framework of logs and poles was covered with sheets of bark, and poles were also placed on the outside to help fasten down the bark. Fireplaces were located in the center under each opening.

of manhood was the warrior's life. Second, it was the way to avenge someone killed in battle or taken prisoner and tortured to death, a habit among all Iroquoian tribes of the Northeast. Third, warfare supplied prisoners for sacrifice to the supernatural.

Most captured males were taken to the home village to be tortured to death. Women and children might be killed at once, but often they were taken back to be adopted by a family that had lost a member in warfare. Such adopted prisoners apparently received emotional as well as physical welcome, and they seem to have accepted their new positions faithfully.

Male captives also might be adopted, but not until they had been tortured. Algonkians also tortured captives, but Iroquois torture was more severe. Sometimes the Iroquois stopped short of death, either adopting or enslaving the captive. It was the Iroquois women who made that decision. Women often were the principal torturers, too, perhaps an indication of their importance among the Iroquois. Many dead captives were eaten, the heart usually by a privileged person and the rest shared by all. Cannibalism, torture, and killing were looked upon as a form of sacrifice. They also have been explained as psychological release for people under tension from much warfare and many deaths among their own people. Whatever the explanation, these practices made the Iroquois not only feared but hated.

Social Order. The Iroquois diverged most from the Northeastern Algonkians in social organization. They were matrilineal; children belonged to their mother's clan. Iroquois life centered on the longhouse group, a subdivision of the matrilineal clan, sisters with their husbands and children living in a common dwelling. The women owned the fields and the houses and worked together farming and doing domestic chores. Husbands moved into the longhouses of their wives and returned to their mothers' homes if divorced.

Political Structure. Women were important not only because they were cultivators and property owners, but also because they nominated the leader who represented their clan in the tribal political structure and could recall him if he were unsatisfactory. Each tribe was governed by a council of chiefs, usually called sachems. Families within the clans held the rights to clan leadership positions, but competence settled which man would become a sachem. When an old sachem died, the women of his clan nominated his successor. The tribal council and the rest of the tribe had to approve the selection, but approval was almost automatic.

The League had nothing to do with internal affairs within each of the five tribes, but dealt with intertribal, external problems. The League was led by a council of fifty leaders, all sachems of the member tribes. Their titles were taken from the names of the first fifty leaders, except for Deganawidah. In his honor, a title in the League council was replaced by an honorary position called the Pine Tree Chief, which could be held by any distinguished person, male or female (sachems were always male). There was no set number of Pine Tree Chiefs. New League sachems were installed in winter, and the League met during the summer in Onondaga territory. One of the Onondaga sachems was chairman of the League.

The League council made decisions on common defense and offense, arbitrated disputes among the member tribes, and discussed common problems. For its members the League meant internal peace, but for its neighbors it usually meant war. Pine Tree Chiefs often tried to push the League council into hostilities, frequently with success. Most Pine Trees were young warriors, who gained power as conflict with Europeans increased.

All Iroquois might attend League meetings and listen to the deliberations. If they wished to express an opinion, they asked their sachem to speak for them, though Pine Trees spoke for themselves, Only sachems voted, each tribal group voting as a block; that is, though the Onondaga had fourteen sachems and the Seneca only eight, each tribe had just one vote. Only unanimous decisions were considered passed, so it might take many votes, interspersed with debate, for a measure to pass.

Ceremonies and Societies. The Iroquois observed agricultural ceremonies throughout the year, each one usually lasting four days. In the early spring, a maple syrup ceremony was followed by other rituals like the planting ceremony, wild strawberry ceremony, and green corn, green bean, and harvest ceremonies. Most important was the midwinter festival, which was a new year ceremony, a time of ritual cleansing and new beginning. The Iroquois celebrated many lesser rites, dances, and small ceremonies of thanksgiving. Religious officials (both men and women), called Keepers of the Faith, organized and managed these ceremonials.

Another organization of religious practitioners was the False Face Society, a group of curers who wore masks carved into grotesque grimaces as part of their curing ritual. A man became a member by dreaming that he had joined the society. All False Face members were men except one woman, who was Keeper of the False Faces. Anyone who was ill reported to the Keeper, who sent the masked dancers to that person's house. There they danced, shaking turtleshell rattles and sprinkling ashes to effect a cure. Anyone who dreamed he had joined the society also went to the woman, who directed him to carve a mask for himself. The initiate always carved his mask from a living tree, for that was more powerful than one carved from a block of dead wood. False Face Society members also performed spring and fall ceremonies to frighten evil spirits away from the villages. Another curing group was the Huskface Society, whose members wore cornhusk masks to represent harvest spirits. The Huskface Society performed at the midwinter ceremony and the green corn festival.

Many Iroquois sought out shamans for help when all else failed or to be sure they had skipped no possibility of spiritual help. Shamans were less important among the Iroquois than in tribes without organized religious societies.

Supernatural Power and Spirits. The Iroquois believed that all supernatural power came from *orenda*, an invisible power that flowed through nature and could be tapped or drawn upon through dreams. Orenda was a great impersonal force that filled the world, the sky, and all of life; it was not a spirit or deity. It is like the Polynesian concept of *mana*, and also has been compared to electricity. It exists in the natural world, but must be captured and harnessed to be useful for humans. Some other Indian groups had an idea similar to *orenda*; the Algonkians called it *manitu* and the Siouans, *wakonda*.

In addition to this general power, the Iroquois believed in animal spirits and other supernaturals, one of which was called the Master of Life. Europeans, especially church leaders, seized upon the concept of Master of Life and transformed it into a great single god. But the precontact Iroquois had no such religious classification; the Master of Life was merely one among many supernatural entities.

Chippewa Legend

Before there were human beings on the earth, the animal fathers lived there. They were kept busy making parts of the world; different animals created different parts. Beaver and his family made the Great Water (Lake Superior) by building a dam at the eastern end. Manabozho, the Great Hare, saw what they had done and he said, "That is not what I wanted. I do not want a dam there." So he stamped on the dam. But Great Hare did not stamp hard enough. He did not destroy the dam completely, but left rapids, waterfalls, and whirlpools.

Great Hare lived in land called Michilimackinak, with islands, rippling water, wide-spreading shade trees, and leaping fish. Manabozho made the first fish net after watching Spider weave her web. He knew that nets could help catch fish. Wild rice grew in the land of the Great Hare. He discovered it, and taught the Indians how to use it. Manabozho showed the Chippewa the islands of wild rice in the lake, and he showed them how to cut paths through the wild rice beds, and how to beat ripe heads of grain into their canoes. The Indians then taught the white man about wild rice.

The Western Great Lakes

Early Life around the Great Lakes

The subarea called Western or Upper Great Lakes covers roughly what we now call the Midwest. It stretched from the eastern borders of Lake Huron to the western edge of today's Minnesota, and from about one hundred miles north of Lake Superior to where the Missouri and Mississippi rivers meet.

The Western or Upper Great Lakes (Superior, Michigan, and Huron) are connected by many smaller lakes and rivers, either directly or by short overland trails called *portages*. Cultures around the Western Great Lakes were very similar because communication and transportation among them was easy, and the same natural resources were plentiful everywhere. All the Upper Great Lakes tribes were Algonkian speakers except for the Siouan Winnebago and the Iroquoian Huron.

Indians of the Upper Great Lakes lived in a region where woodland alternated with areas of prairie. All were cultivators, but the grass that today is called wild rice gave them a nutritious and plentiful substitute for maize. It grew on the shores of the Great Lakes and throughout the lake regions of Minnesota, Wisconsin, Illinois, and northern Michigan. There it was so abundant and so greatly used by the people that some authorities make a special culture area of the wild rice region. In addition to gathering wild-plant foods, the Indians also hunted woodland animals and even the bison that came into the nearby prairie.

Migrations and Changes

Tribes must have moved around the Great Lakes in prehistoric times, but gradually and apparently without much disruption. Shortly before European contact, some prehistoric Oneota populations appear to have moved westward into the prairie from the Western Great Lakes and the Upper Mississippi Valley, apparently in pursuit of the increasing quantities of bison to be found there. Among them were the ancestors of the Ioway, Oto, and probably Missouri.

However, change speeded up when Europeans in the East began pressing westward. As Eastern tribes shifted under European pressure, the less powerful were driven from their lands. Several Woodland groups moved westward to avoid the predations of specific groups as was the case during the Iroquois wars. The eastern Dakota once inhabited areas on and near the western and southern shores of Lake Superior, as well as the lakes region in eastern Minnesota and northwest Wisconsin. Between the late 1600s and middle 1800s they were pushed out of this region by the Chippewa, and relocated further to the southwest. Some Woodland tribes ended up in the prairie grasslands of the Midwest, others where their tribal range included both woodland and grassland environments.

Naturally, those changes forced adjustments in traditional ways of life. Where birch trees were scarce or altogether missing, people had to use something besides bark for housing or equipment like canoes. Consequently, dugouts were the water transportation through the prairie area. But life on the prairie had advantages, too, for the growing season there was longer and the winters were less severe.

Woodland tribes of the Western Great Lakes were the Menominee, Chippewa, Potawatomi, Huron, and Ottowa; the Great Lakes tribes of the prairies were the Winnebago, Sauk, Fox, Miami, Illinois, and the Prairie Potawatomi (sometimes called Mascouten). Tribes of the two ecological niches, woodland and prairie, traded and interacted regularly. Rivers and lakes made transportation easy, and most tribes spoke languages within the Algonkian family, so communication generally was not difficult. Differences that we can see in looking back at these groups probably were not noticeable to the people themselves.

Food and Technology. The peoples of the Upper Great Lakes grew maize, did much hunting and gathering, and made rice an especially large part of their diet. Except for wild rice, the culture of the Western Lakes was not very different from that of the Eastern Algonkians. Tools, equipment, and clothing were similar, and the houses were barrel-vaulted rectangular buildings or domed mat- or bark-covered wigwams. People used bark canoes on the lakes, and dugouts to travel the prairie streams where trees with suitable bark did not grow. East was like west, probably because the Lakes tribes had come from the north and east where most of their Algonkian relatives lived. When they moved into the Midwest, they did not need to make much change, since the new environment differed only in degree from their old homes.

Kinnikinnik. Men grew tobacco in the Lakes region, but more often smoked a substance called *kinnikinnik* (an Algonkian word meaning "mixture"). This was made from several plants, usually sumac, dogwood, and willow bark, and often tobacco too. Kinnikinnik was smoked in pipes, some of them very elaborate. Bowls were carved from an easily worked red stone called *catlinite*, quarried in Minnesota, and were fitted to long, often fancy stems. We call such pipes *calumets* or peace pipes, although men smoked them before going to war or on trading expeditions as well as at peace councils. Calumets were also used to burn tobacco as an offering to the supernatural. Travelers going through foreign or hostile territory carried them to prove their peaceful intentions. The calumet of historic times may have evolved from the platform pipes of the Hopewellians, and spread into the prairies, Plains, and the lower Mississippi Valley. Men who smoked a calumet together were bound together for a purpose (not necessarily peaceful); to break faith with fellow smokers, whatever the endeavor, was a serious breach of trust.

Social and Religious Organization. Algonkian kinship organization was somewhat different among these midwestern tribes. Most of the Western Great Lakes peoples developed a clan system tracing relationship patrilineally through males, whereas the New England and Middle Atlantic Algonkians traced their descent bilaterally, through both parents.

The northern Ojibwa Midewiwin or Grand Medicine Society penetrated south around the Lakes and into the middle Mississippi River area. This association of curers performed its most important rite, the Medicine

Canadian artist Paul Kane depicts a daily scene in an Indian encampment on Lake Huron, circa 1845–1850.

Dance, once or twice a year. The dance or ceremony varied from tribe to tribe, but it always included curing and initiation rituals and entertainment.

Like other peoples with ceremonial organizations, the Great Lakes tribes occasionally found that they needed a shaman to cure some difficult illness. Shamans had special power from the supernatural, which they demonstrated in their ritual tent-shaking performances. They would retire to a small skin- or bark-covered structure to contact the spirits. Observers on the outside would hear voices coming from the tent, and could see the tent move or shake, clearly indicating to the faithful that the spirits had come. A shaman's spirits helped him cure disease and bring good fortune to those who consulted him. Some people, however, felt that shamans were practitioners of evil because they had such power; shamans were respected, but they were often feared as well. Men of middle age or older were almost always the shamans in the Lakes region. For success in life, each young man expected to find his own guardian spirit.

The Prairie People

Midwest prairie Algonkians shared most of the Lake people's customs, though in some areas they may have traded for wild rice, which did not grow as abundantly in the prairie lands. Their housing, clothing, and equipment were different only in emphasis. In fact, some people, like the Potawatomi, extended into both environments. This group is believed to be represented prehistorically by the Dumaw Creek culture, a Woodland culture in western Michigan. This group apparently migrated from the northeast Atlantic coast, according to their oral tradition. Some Potawatomi eventually moved around to the western side of Lake Michigan, occupying settlements from Washington Island at the tip of the Door Peninsula in northeastern Wisconsin to the spot where Chicago later grew up. Other Potawatomi groups moved into the prairie lands, mostly to the west and south of Lake Michigan.

Other Midwest prairie tribes, the Sauk and closely associated Fox, probably were pushed there by aggressive Iroquois and Eastern Algonkians around the time of European contact. The Sauk and Fox were among a number of groups who sought refuge on the western side of Lake Michigan, trying to distance themselves from the eastern raiders, especially the Iroquois. They apparently lived in the wild rice area of Wisconsin for a while before being driven out by Menominee and Chippewa. Conflicts with the French, too, were responsible for the Fox moving away from the wild rice country. The Sauk and Fox settled in Illinois near the association of tribes known as the Illinois (Cahokia, Kaskaskia, and Peoria, among others).

These prairie tribes cultivated corn extensively, besides growing squash, beans, and tobacco. They conducted communal buffalo hunts that involved entire villages or even tribes moving around the prairies in search of bison herds for weeks at a time, normally while the corn was growing at their summer villages. Around 1800 they obtained the horse, and after that their subsistence was like that of the Plains Villagers in most ways.

The Menominee

When Europeans first met the Menominee in the seventeenth century, their territory was the land of forest and lakes around the Menominee River, the boundary between today's Wisconsin and Michigan. Menominee now live on the Wolf River in central Wisconsin.

Menominee society was divided into patrilineal clans that formed moieties of Earth People and Sky People. Moiety division here had little function except to regulate marriage (one married outside one's moiety) and to act as undertakers and mourners for each other. It was an egalitarian society, though Menominee chiefs all came from the Great Mythical Bear clan. As usual, however, only men who proved their ability became chiefs. The chief, a civil figure, was mainly responsible for keeping peace and order and taking action necessary for the tribe's welfare. A tribal council aided him in his deliberations. Shamans or members of the Medicine Society (the Midewiwin) often had greater influence than the chief, because they had supernatural power behind them.

War Customs. War leaders directed hostilities, holding their leadership only as long as the conflict lasted. To gather followers, they relied on their reputations as warriors and their charismatic personalities. Menominee war leaders owned war bundles believed to have supernatural powers that would lead their owners to successful exploits. Gathering for a pre-raid ritual, the war party watched the leader display what was in his war bundle. They did a war dance and sacrificed, then ate a dog (a practice probably taken over from the Huron). Then all went off toward their objective. Just before the attack, the leader distributed items from his war bundle to the rest, covering them all with spirit protection.

Warriors fought with clubs and bows, wearing no protective armor. Any warrior who killed an enemy won the right to wear an eagle feather, and the first to kill on a raid got a wampum belt. Warriors scalped the fallen, stretching the piece of flesh with its hair on a small hoop. In the victory dance the warriors displayed their scalps on poles, then gave them to female relatives. Menominee warfare usually stopped short of the extremes reached by the Plains or more easterly tribes.

Religion. Besides their simple shamanistic practices and the ceremonials performed by the Midewiwin Society, Menominee had other society and cult observances. With the Chippewa, the Ottawa, and the Potawatomi, they practiced bear ceremonialism. They regarded bears with special respect; whenever a man killed a bear, he treated the body reverentially. It was carefully disjointed, not hacked apart, and the hunter and his family gave a feast for invited guests. With the food he served the people, including the bear meat, the host spread out food that bears enjoyed, like maple sugar. The bear's head was decorated with ribbons and beads, and the skin was spread out on a mat. A speaker called upon the spirits of all bears, saying that they were respected by the Menominee, who always treated them well, and inviting other bears to come. After the meal, the host carefully gathered and disposed of the bear's bones, never leaving them thrown about for dogs to gnaw.

The Menominee believed in forces unfriendly and dangerous to people as well as in well-disposed supernaturals. They shared most of the beliefs of other Algonkians, though apparently not the Windigo phenomenon, perhaps because the Menominee had no fear of famine. The tribal culture hero was Manabush, their version of the Chippewa Manabozho. He was the Earth Maker who created the world and its beings and taught the Indians how to live. His earthly home was Mackinac Island. Stories about Manabush livened up long winter evenings and taught the children tribal lore.

Wild Rice. Though the Menominee practiced agriculture, it was largely the abundant wild rice around the Great Lakes that allowed their population to grow so dense that many European explorers remarked on it. Rice even gave them a name—*Menominee* means "wild-rice people." Today that same wild rice is popular as a luxury food. It is still harvested by Indians, now mostly for commerce.

Wild rice is hard to reap because the grains scatter at a touch. The harvester has to catch the grain as soon as it matures, for it quickly falls into the water and is lost. The Menominee reaped the grain from canoes, usually with one person guiding the boat and another bending the stalks over the gunwales, lightly beating the grain heads so the ripe kernels would fall into the canoe. The prickly hulls irritate the skin, forcing the gatherers to wear protective clothing.

To separate the edible grain from the hulls, the Menominee first parched or toasted the kernels, then trod on them in hide-lined pits in the ground or, in later times, in big containers. This "dancing the rice" was done by huskers wearing high moccasins in historic times, though it is said that long ago they danced barefoot. Men, women, and children danced the rice, separating the grain from the shucks, then winnowing the inedible portion by throwing the grain in the air and fanning the hulls away. The edible grain, heavier than the hulls, fell to the ground. After all the work was done, everyone joined for a big feast.

Muskogean Trickster Tale

Wildcat Elder tried for many days to creep up on Wild Turkey to catch him for his dinner. He tried and tried, but he was not successful. Then Wildcat got a bag, crawled into it, and rolled himself along. He rolled right up to Wild Turkey.

Wildcat said, "I'm having fun. See me roll around. If you would like to roll around, you can get into my bag."

Wild Turkey crawled into the bag. Wildcat quickly tied up the end and rolled the bag for some time. After a while, he stopped and untied the bag. "Yes, that was fun," said Wild Turkey. "But I don't want to have all the fun. Let me out so those young turkeys over there can have some fun." Wildcat let Turkey out of the bag, and Wild Turkey ran away. Wildcat was angry because he had

An engraving from 1884 showing Indians reaping wild rice.

planned to have Wild Turkey for dinner. So he said to the young turkeys, "Elder Turkey had a good time rolling in the bag. Would you like to try?" One young turkey got in, but he could not roll. Wildcat said, "It won't roll because it's too light. There is only one small turkey in it. Let some other young turkeys get in."

Finally some other young turkeys stepped in, and Wildcat tied the bag, threw it over his shoulder, and ran home. At home he gave the bag to his mother and said, "I have brought something home for dinner. Be careful how you untie the bag." His mother was curious, and she untied the bag too quickly. One young turkey flew out, but she managed to keep the others. Though Wildcat scolded his mother, they had enough for a feast.

The Southeast

Running from Virginia and Kentucky south, the Southeast subarea includes the territory we generally speak of as "the South." Along the coast is a low plain of barren soil, sand dunes, and saltwater marsh and grasses. Stands of cypress thrive with aerial roots that allow growth in the stagnant, oxygen-poor water. Many rivers and streams cross the plain, but they flow slowly and are filled with disintegrated rock and silts that build up soil deposits at the river mouths.

To the west of the coastal plain is the Piedmont, a plateau 100 to 150 miles wide, edged by the southern Appalachians. Like the North, the Piedmont and Appalachian areas are forested with deciduous and evergreen trees that shelter many kinds of forest animals. Beyond the mountains is an area of deep, fertile soil stretching to the Mississippi River, almost entirely occupied by the Muskogean-speaking tribes. Throughout the Southeast the climate is mild, in some places approaching subtropical, though snow falls in the higher elevations and frosts have been known as far south as middle Florida.

Early Southeastern Culture

The Muskogean-speaking peoples of the Southeast had distinctive traits which they shared with the Cherokee (Iroquoian), Southeastern Siouans like the Yuchi and the Catawba, and the Central Atlantic Algonkians. Many of the Southeastern Indians descended from the Mississippians and other prehistoric mound-building cultures. A few groups may have arrived in the Southeast closer to the time of contact. Connecting specific historic tribes with archaeological sites is difficult and often impossible, because tribes moved so much even before contact; after that, movement increased immensely. Some tribes, like the Shawnee, moved all over the East, from Pennsylvania and the Ohio River valley through the South, ending up in Indian Territory—today's Oklahoma. The Seminole tribe did not even exist until the middle of the eighteenth century, when it was formed by refugees of half a dozen Muskogean-speaking groups.

Southeastern Customs. From the accounts of early French explorers, we know that the most complex social development in the Southeast arose among the Natchez of the lower Mississippi Valley. The Natchez had a society that was unusually stratified, Their practices included torture of war captives, ritual cannibalism, the Green Corn Dance, and keeping perpetual fires burning in sacred buildings. From these traits, it is easy to see cultural connections between the Southeast and the Iroquois in the North.

Most Southeasterners shared in the customs of the Black Drink, an emetic brewed from a shrub, *Ilex cassine*, which caused vomiting. Men drank it to purify themselves during ceremonies, before going on a raid, or before a council meeting.

Towns in the Southeast. Almost all Southeastern people lived in towns along rivers or streams. The towns were arranged in much the same way: residences and public buildings around a plaza, with farmlands in all directions on the outskirts. Their sturdy thatched-roof houses had mud-plaster walls over poles interwoven with reeds or branches. Some houses were circular, some rectangular. Summer structures were open-sided to let cooling breezes through. Stockades of upright posts surrounded many towns, and moats or earthworks often added protection.

As elsewhere in the East, women were the farmers, but men helped clear the fields. Men hunted woodland animals and also alligators. Nearly all Southeastern people counted descent through women; after marriage, couples generally moved to the wife's village. Polygyny was allowed, but only wealthy men and chiefs had many wives.

Some Southeastern tribes had centralized political structures and definite social classes. Some even had a nobility formed of war leaders, priests, civil chiefs, and their families, and chiefs often wielded considerable authority. Such people expected and got special treatment. They wore clothing exclusive to their rank, and servants or slaves carried them around in litters, protecting them from the sun with sunshades.

Warriors. Warfare was the path to prestige and success. A warrior's adornment—feathers, body paint, and tattoos—told his feats in battle. As in the North, tribes were in a constant state of hostility with one another. Men about to go on the warpath fasted, danced, and smoked ritually. The warriors brought back scalps of the enemy, but scalping in precontact times was apparently far less frequent than later, when Europeans paid a bounty for Indian scalps. Warriors protected themselves with wicker armor and bark shields, but wore little else: only breechclouts and moccasins.

Religion. Warriors performed their own religious rites for success in war, but the major religious observances in the South were for planting and harvest. The new year started when the first crops ripened and was celebrated by a festival called the *busk* or Green Corn Dance. People threw out old goods and put out old fires. A new fire was ritually kindled by a priest, and women took flames or coals from it to light the new year's fires in their homes. A highlight of the festival was the Black Drink, which cleaned out the drinkers as they had cleaned out their houses. Toward the end of the busk, the first corn of the season was gathered, cooked, and eaten. The new year had started, and the people forgave every crime and misdeed of the past season, short of murder.

Only the Calusa, an alliance of small tribes in south Florida, differed from the Southeast subsistence pattern of agriculture. They were a hunting and gathering group, using a starchy tuber (kunti) which grew abundantly in their tropical land instead of corn.

The Central Atlantic Algonkians

In 1607, English settlers established a colony on the river they named the James in Virginia. Those colonists were in intimate contact with a now famous group of Indians, the Powhatan, whose chief was also known as Powhatan. The group's fame stems from the daughter of Powhatan and her part in colonial history: she was Pocahontas, the woman who, according to legend, saved Captain John Smith's life.

Powhatan, whose personal name was Wahunsonacock, was chief of six tribelets, a position he inherited from his father. Under his leadership at least two dozen others were added to the group. Consequently the Powhatan usually are considered a confederacy, although, once again, the alliance depended on one man's control and organizational ability, not a tradition of federation. Some of the tribelets in the confederacy were Pamunkey, Potomac, Rappahannock, and Chickahominy, whose names have been given to rivers in Virginia. South of the Powhatan, in what is now North Carolina, were other Algonkians, the most prominent being the Pamlico. The North Carolina Algonkians are not very well known, though they were recorded in pictures by John White and in writing by Thomas Hariot, an early colonist. We know the Powhatan from the writings of Captain John Smith, William Strachey, and some later authors.

Village Life. The Central Atlantic Algonkians lived in villages. Some groups, like the Pomeioc, are known only by the names of their towns instead of by tribal affiliations, because they became extinct as cohesive cultural units before much information had been gathered about them. However, we can use accounts written by the early explorers and settlers to recreate something of the life of those southern Algonkians.

Villages contained up to fifty multiple-family dwellings scattered among gardens of corn, tobacco, and other common crops. The people created their fields out of the forest by felling and burning the trees. Some of the towns were protected by palisades; others were open. A typical house was domed and rectangular, with removable matting over the framework, not unlike a longhouse. During hot weather, sections of the wall-covering were removed to keep air circulating. Rivers and streams were favorite sites for villages, which may explain why so many of the area's rivers came to be named after Indian tribes. The waterways allowed communication and transportation into the Piedmont by dugout canoe. They also provided drinking water.

The Temples. Within the towns were structures the early colonists called temples. These were no different from other village buildings except that they were used for mortuary, storage, and religious functions.

They contained wooden posts carved at the upper end in a likeness of a human face and sometimes draped with shell and copper beads. What these images meant to the villagers we do not know because the early records are inadequate. Presumably they were idols representing spirits.

The temples also held surplus produce, the chief's wealth in foodstuffs, furs, and other goods stored for hard times. But their most exotic function was to hold the mortal remains of chiefs. Most bodies of the villagers were buried, but those of chieftains were disemboweled and skinned; the flesh was sun dried, and the skin was cured. Then the skeleton, clothed in its own treated skin, was placed inside the temple beside those of other chiefs on scaffolds near the idols or images. The flesh or muscle tissue was wrapped in mats and placed at the mummy's feet. A religious official, living under the mortuary platform, watched over the remains. What all this meant to the inhabitants must forever remain a mystery to us. All we have to go on is interpretations by European observers, who were hardly unbiased scientific investigators.

Shamans. We do know that the Central Atlantic Algonkians had a class of religious practitioners, priests or shamans. They performed cures with herbs, emetics, and laxatives, as well as by bloodletting and scratching. They must have practiced in much the same way as Algonkian shamans of the North. People in this area seem to have taken sweatbaths for spiritual and physical purification, and shamans too purified themselves by sweating. They doubtless performed other purification rituals as well which we know nothing about. Shamans distinguished themselves from other people by shaving their hair into unusual patterns, painting their scalps, and rubbing the uncut hair with fat to make it stand up. They also sported hair decorations of snake or other animal skins, or even whole stuffed birds.

Clothing. Here on the coast (from Virginia to Carolina) the climate was generally mild the year round, and clothing was usually deerskin loincloths for men and aprons for women. Some apron-skirts left the buttocks exposed; others dipped down front and back. If the weather turned cool, both sexes wore robes of hide or fur or sometimes of feathers, perhaps decorated with beads or painted designs. Body and facial tattooing was common on women, less so on men, who usually adorned themselves with body paint, necklaces, and earrings.

The Chief. Tribes were warring all the time when the Europeans first arrived. That hostility may have been normal, but many experts believe Chief Powhatan aggravated it as he conquered neighboring tribelets and brought them under his dominion. He was an unusually powerful chief, a true autocrat, collecting tribute from subject tribes and keeping his

A Cherokee chief. This photo was taken in 1869, after the Cherokee were moved to Oklahoma.

wealth in special storehouses. He had several wives, though polygyny was not common, and the English reported that he had a sort of bodyguard of fifty select warriors. Such authority and centralization of power were far from usual among Algonkians and probably came from Powhatan's own qualities and charisma. The only power equal to his was found far away among the Natchez in the lower Mississippi Valley. But for the Powhatan group it was an innovation rather than tradition, the product of conquest by a powerful chief rather than voluntary confederation.

Chiefs generally had their land prepared, cultivated, and harvested by the people. Women did most of the farming, but men helped them clear the land. The chieftain's harvest was stored not only for his personal use, but for times of public need and for trade.

Food. Along with crops, shellfish of the coastal flats contributed to the diet; they also yielded shells that could be traded or made into beads and utensils. Plant foods included wild tubers, seeds, nuts, and greens. Central Atlantic Algonkians also caught fish with snares and weirs, spears, hooks and lines, and even by shooting them with bow and arrow. Meat, too, was a part of the diet. Hunters went after game individually or in group hunts, in which women and children joined to drive elk and deer into rivers or surrounds where the hunters could kill them in quantity. Then women roasted, boiled, and dried the meat for storage.

Initiation Rites. The practice the English settlers completely misunderstood was the boys' initiation ceremony. We do not have a good description of it, but it seems to have been a rite of symbolic death for the child, who was then reborn as an adult. Captain John Smith called the custom child sacrifice, believing the boys actually were put to death. The initiation appears to have been a ritual beating of the boys by adult men while the mothers wept and mourned as though the boys were really being killed. The boys, painted white, then lay in a depression or pit in the ground as though interred and spent the night there while some ritual was performed. Then they stayed in the woods, probably with an elder or shaman who taught them the tribe's sacred customs. When the boys returned, they were accepted as adult males. It is easy to understand why the English were mystified, especially since the boys surely could not reveal the secrets of initiation to the colonists or anyone else. It probably seemed another of the "savage ways."

The Natchez

The Great Sun. When French explorers came upon the Natchez in the lower Mississippi River valley, they were particularly struck by the

Natchez Indian in winter costume.

strongly centralized Natchez government and the stratified social classes. There was nothing else like the Natchez society north of Mexico. Their hereditary ruler, the Great Sun, was a monarch in the European style. He was in charge of the chiefs of Natchez villages, and his word was law. He was assisted by a council, however, so that other members of the nobility and the town chiefs limited his despotism somewhat. He was treated with reverence, his subjects remaining some distance from him and walking backward when leaving his presence. He and his representatives and close relatives were carried in litters on the shoulders of warriors or slaves. Small wonder the French were impressed! Unlike the Central Atlantic Algonkians, the Natchez political and social complexity could only have been built over many years, not put together by one unusually powerful personality.

The Great Sun lived in a large house facing a plaza in the main town of the Natchez. On the other side of the plaza was a temple which, like the Sun's house, stood on a mound. Also facing the town square was the house of the Head War Chief, a brother of the Sun. The plaza was a ceremonial center, and the rest of the villagers lived in houses scattered some distance away. Other Natchez towns also followed this pattern of plaza and temple, surrounded by dispersed dwellings of the townspeople, with the farmlands beyond. When a Great Sun died, his house and its mound were destroyed, and new structures were built for his successor.

White Woman. The Great Sun's mother held the title of White Woman. She too was very powerful. At her death her title seems to have fallen to her oldest daughter, but the early accounts are ambiguous and contradictory. In any event, the White Woman was never a wife of the Great Sun. Since the descent system was matrilineal, the successor to a Great Sun was never his son, but his sister's son. An early French explorer described the succession: "At [the Great Sun's] death his children are only nobles. . . . On the other hand, of the sons of his sister, who was herself white woman or female Sun, the eldest will be great chief or Great Sun, the second little Sun, chief of war. . . ."

The Natchez Class System. All Natchez filled some position in a system of social stratification that has been called both a class and a caste system. It included two major social divisions, the nobility and the commoners. The nobility too had gradations, from the Suns through the Nobles to the Honored People. The commoners have come to be known as Stinkards from the French name for them, *Puants*.

Marriage customs required that members of the highest class marry common people. Suns were children of Sun mothers and Stinkard fathers; Nobles were children of Noble mothers or of Sun fathers and Stinkard mothers. Honored People were offspring of Honored Women or of Noble fathers and Stinkard mothers, and Stinkards were produced by marriage between two Stinkards or between Honored Men and Stinkard mothers. In other words, children of women of the upper three classes took the rank of their mothers, but children of Stinkard mothers were one rank below their fathers unless their fathers were Stinkards. The Great Sun, of course, was from the Sun class, the child of a Sun mother and a Stinkard father.

People could move up in the ranks by meritorious service or war exploits. The important political and religious positions went to males of the Great Sun's matrilineage, his brothers and maternal uncles. At his death, the Great Sun's wives were expected to sacrifice their lives, and parents often offered their children for sacrifice, thereby raising their own rank. Sacrificial victims were strangled, but they first swallowed pills of strong tobacco, which made them unconscious.

Other Customs. As agriculturalists the Natchez grew the crops common to all American Indian cultivators: corn, beans, and squash. The women also gathered wild-plant foods, berries, nuts, and greens. Men helped with harvest and field preparation, and their hunting and fishing added animal protein to the diet. Domesticated dogs helped in hunting, and occasionally they were eaten.

As in other Southeastern societies, shamans performed cures and were also responsible for weather control, making rain or bringing fair weather. They did not manage public religious activities; those were the responsibility of the Great Sun and his officials. The Great Sun was in fact the tribal high priest as well as the ruler, and the government was thus a sort of theocracy.

Temples in each village held relics and holy images. They were sacred places before which a fire was always kept burning. The Great Temple of the tribe stood in the town of the Great Sun, and in it the bones of former Great Suns were preserved. Only White Women, Great Suns, and a few other special individuals might enter that temple. The Great Sun and White Woman performed rites there daily, people made offerings in front of the temple, and at the first-fruits ceremony each year, everyone presented seeds as an offering before planting. Produce was offered at harvest. The Natchez also had an annual cycle of agricultural rituals, thanksgiving and harvest ceremonies, and feasts of the hunt. The Great Sun presided over all these.

Our information about the Natchez is unusually good all the way back to early contact times, thanks to the records left us by many interested French explorers. We know less about neighboring tribes, yet we have good reason to believe that the Natchez social stratification was not unique; other tribes of the area probably had similar social classes. We have no indication, though, that any other group had marriage customs like theirs. Those practices set them off from tribes like the Tunica, Chitimacha, and Timucua, who appear to have shared many features of a social class system.

The Seminole

Throughout the East, Europeans caused dislocation, fragmentation, and realignment of Indian societies. In the Southeast most of the disruptions ended with the Indian peoples being pushed westward, but some groups of Creek found refuge in Florida. There they were joined by remnants of other tribes, mostly Yuchi, Apalachee, and Yamasee. Together they became known by the Muskogean title Seminole, which means "separatist" or "wild," implying that those people refused to be pushed around and broke away from the main body of Creek.

It was in the 1700s that the Seminole became recognized as a unit. Most of them came from two Creek segments, often called Upper and Lower Creek. Both were Muskogean speakers, but they spoke different languages within that family, Muskogee (Upper Creek) and Mikasuki (Lower Creek). They still have that linguistic duality today. The Creek remained dominant among the Seminole, and all other members learned to speak one Creek tongue or the other.

This mixture of people moved into Florida while it was under Spanish control. The Spanish had established missions in northern Florida, and enthusiastically tried to convert the Indians, but they were not colonizing as the English were doing in the North. Consequently the Florida tribes did not have to defend their lands.

Timucua and Calusa. The major tribes at the time of contact in the sixteenth century were the Timucua in northern Florida and the Calusa in the south. About the Calusa we know little more than that they were nonagricultural hunters and gatherers. Our information about the Timucua is better because a cartographer, Jacques le Moyne, left sketches of them. Le Moyne was in Florida in 1564 and 1565 during the French Hugenots' brief attempt to settle there. The French colony was destroyed by the Spanish in 1565, but Le Moyne escaped with his art. He pictured the Timucua as typical of the Southeastern Muskogeans: agricultural, sedentary, and well organized under a stratified, centralized government. Their houses were circular, not rectangular, but in other ways their material culture resembled the Natchez. Le Moyne probably did most of his sketches from memory when he returned to Europe, though he may well have made notations while he was still in Florida. His finished engravings made the Indians look like the exotic savages European expected.

Refugees Rebuilding. At the time the Seminole mixture came to be considered a distinct unit, there were few if any Timucua left. Both they and the Calusa had been ravaged by European disease, against which they had no immunity. Any people from either tribe still alive must have joined the Seminole, who settled in north Florida and quickly reestablished their old way of life. The hybrid character of the Seminole group made little cultural difference because the people all had similar backgrounds.

The new union was successful, and the Seminole, now free of English aggression, built villages and started anew. Some escaped plantation slaves fled into Spanish Florida as well, and they were either absorbed by the Seminole or established villages near them, following much the

CHARACTERISTICS OF THE EASTERN TRIBES

Clothing	Food production	Equipment	Shelter	Social and political organization	Religion	Warfare
Fitted skin clothing	Cultivation (corn, beans, and squash)	Bows and arrows	Some skin or bark tipis	Nuclear families	Shamans	Warfare continuous in Northeast and Southeast
Dresses	Hunting	Traps	Wigwams (Northeast and Great Lakes)	Patrilineal clans (Great Lakes)	Spirits	Raids
Skirts	Fishing	Weirs	Longhouses (Iroquois)	Matrilineal clans (Northeast and Southeast)	Guardian spirits	Ambushes
Aprons	Gathering (plants and shellfish)	Tomahawks	Barrel-vaulted, rectangular or round buildings (Southeast)	Bilateral groups (Northeast and Central)	Medicine societies	
Breechcloths		Shields	Sweathouses	Moieties (Menominee)	Agricultural ceremonies	
Shirts		Stone and bone knives		Village and tribal councils	False Face Society (Iroquois)	
Coats		Canoes		Tribal chiefs	Orenda (Iroquois source of supernatural power)	
Leggings		Bark containers		Confederacies	Temples (Southeast)	
Deerskin robes		Basketry		Social classes (Southeast)		
Moccasins		Pottery		Centralized government (Southeast)		
		Hoes		The League of the Iroquois		
		Wicker armor and bark shields (Southeast)				
		Spoons, cups, cutters, and scrapers of shell				

same subsistence practices. From the Spanish the Seminole acquired some new plants, like fruit trees, which they cultivated along with the traditional corn, beans, and squash, and they also began to raise horses and cattle. Their life was not very different from that of the English settlers north of Spanish territory. Recognizing their "civilized" way of life, Europeans began to refer to them, along with the Cherokee, Creek, Choctaw, and Chickasaw, as the Five Civilized Tribes.

The Seminole War. But the new nation, the United States, cast envious eyes on the peninsula. In 1817, Andrew Jackson entered Florida, supposedly to recover runaway slaves. In 1821, the United States annexed the territory. At that time, all the Indians in Florida were called Seminole, and once again they became the objects of military aggression as European settlers found their lands appealing. Then came the Seminole War of 1835 to 1843, after which most Seminole were removed to Indian Territory in Oklahoma. A few hundred, however, fled down the peninsula to the sawgrass everglades and cypress swamp region where soldiers and guns could not follow. There they established a new home in former Calusa territory. Unlike the Calusa, the Seminole remained agriculturalists, cultivating crops on high, drier areas in the swamp.

Displaced People. South Florida's environment was quite different from the Alabama and Georgia Creek territory or even the north Florida country, and the Seminole had to abandon many traditional ways when they moved into it. They did keep their matrilineal clans, their two languages (Muskogee and Mikasuki), and their housing, which they modified by leaving off the walls to keep air moving in the tropical climate, and by building the flooring as a platform about three feet off the swampy land. Dugout canoes became more popular in that area of high ground water. But the complex political organization typical of the Southeast was forgotten, and they could not pasture their herds of cattle in that undrained region. The Seminole groups became small autonomous camps without any political centralization or overall leadership, and slowly their observances of community religious ceremonials like the Green Corn Dance deteriorated, leaving all religious practices in the hands of the shamans.

Suggestions for Further Study

Bibliography

Lurie, Nancy O. 1966. *Mountain Wolf Woman.*

The life of a Winnebago woman in Wisconsin during the period of culture change after European contact, giving the so often ignored woman's point of view.

Morgan, Lewis H. 1851. *League of the Ho-De-No-Sau-Nee or Iroquois.* (Several editions.) A classic ethnography by one of the first American scholars who studied Indians.

Ritzenthaler, Robert E., and Pat Ritzenthaler. 1970. *The Woodland Indians of the Western Great Lakes.*

A very readable and informative survey of Midwestern Indian cultures.

Swanton, John R. 1946. *The Indians of the Southeastern United States.*

This encyclopedic compendium of the Indian societies of the Southeast gives a list of tribes from the mid-Atlantic states south as well as general aspects of Southeastern culture.

Thwaites, Reuben G., ed. 1896–1901. *The Jesuit Relations and Allied Documents.*

Seventy-three volumes of priceless information recorded by the first literate Europeans to come in contact with many Northeastern tribes, from 1611.

Other Pertinent Works

Garbarino, Merwyn S. 1972. *Big Cypress, a Changing Seminole Community.*

Gearing, Fred. 1962. *Priests and Warriors: Social Structure of Cherokee Politics in the 18th Century.*

______. 1970. *The Face of the Fox.*

Hickerson, Harold. 1970. *The Chippewa and Their Neighbors.*

Hoffman, W. J. 1893. *The Menomini Indians.*

Hudson, Charles. 1980. *The Southeastern Indians.*

Landes, Ruth 1970. *The Prairie Potawatomi.*

Price, John. 1979. *Indians of Canada.* Scarborough, Ontario: Prentice Hall of Canada, Ltd.

Radin, Paul. 1926. *Crashing Thunder, the Autobiography of a Winnebago Indian.*

Trigger, Bruce G. 1990. *The Huron, Farmers of the North*, 2nd ed.

MAJOR GROUPS AND LANGUAGES OF THE EAST

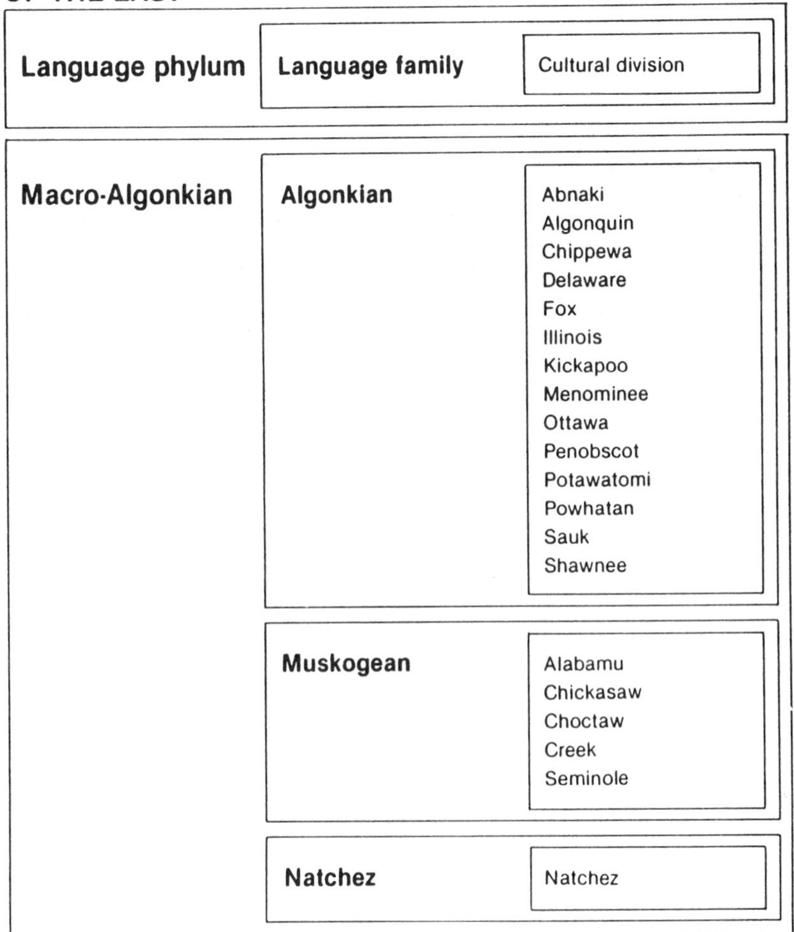

Language phylum	Language family	Cultural division
Macro-Algonkian	Algonkian	Abnaki Algonquin Chippewa Delaware Fox Illinois Kickapoo Menominee Ottawa Penobscot Potawatomi Powhatan Sauk Shawnee
	Muskogean	Alabamu Chickasaw Choctaw Creek Seminole
	Natchez	Natchez

MAJOR GROUPS AND LANGUAGES (continued)

Language phylum	Language family	Cultural division

EAST (continued)

Language phylum	Language family	Cultural division
Macro-Siouan	Catawba	Catawba
	Iroquoian	Cayuga Cherokee Huron Mohawk Oneida Onondaga Seneca Tuscarora
	Siouan	Winnebago
	Yuchi	Yuchi

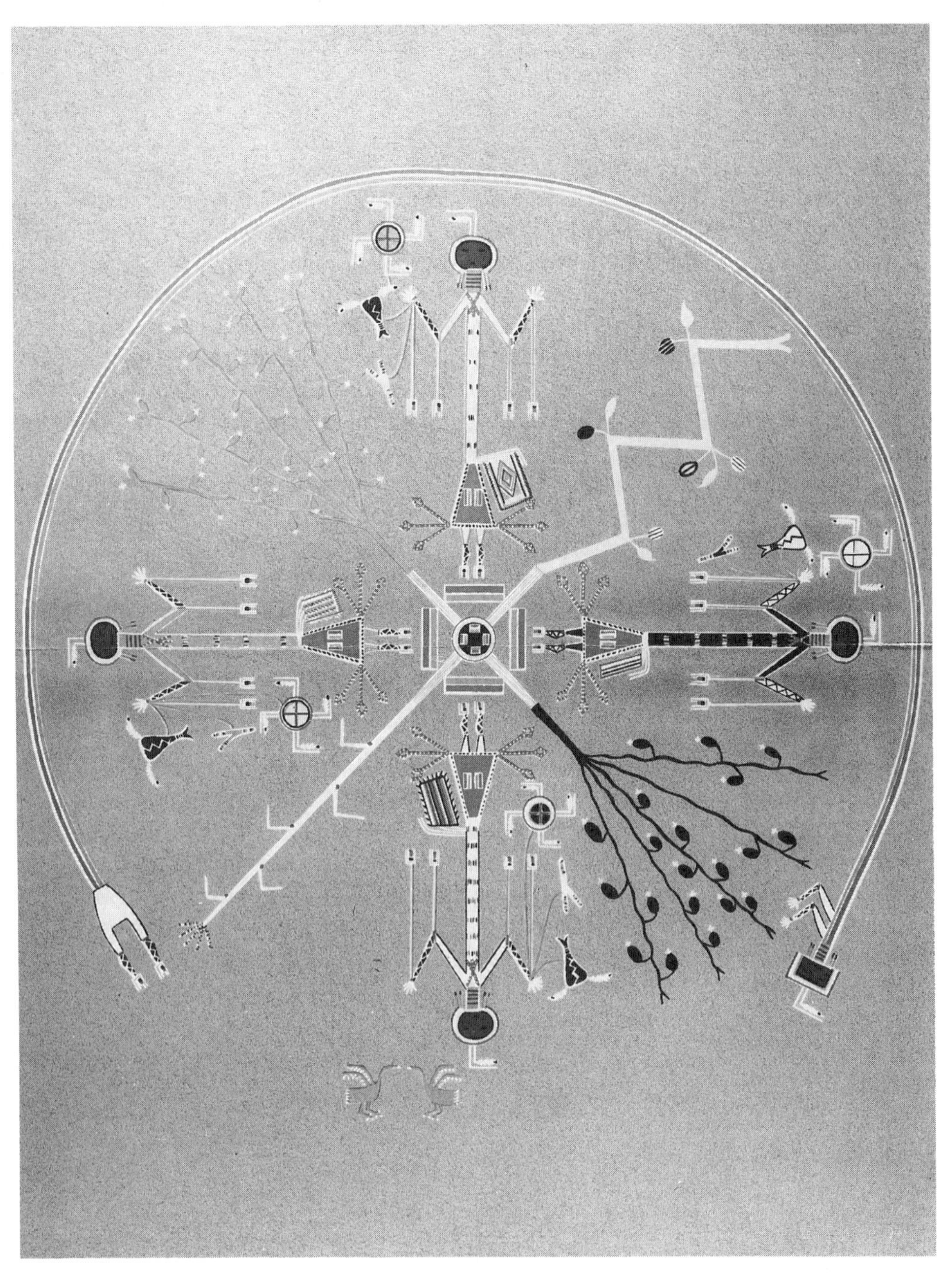

Part III

NATIVE AMERICAN CULTURE

In Part II we have examined native American societies in a geographic framework, noting similarities and particularly contrasts from one area to another. We have seen that even within a fairly small region, groups often adapted to their environment in quite different ways. Now we will approach Indian cultures from another point of view by looking at general aspects of native American life as a whole—technology, art, religion, political and social organization, economics and trade, and warfare. For in spite of the tremendous regional variations, in many ways Indian societies followed the same basic pattern, one much different from our own.

Incredible as it may seem, as recently as the nineteenth century some European social scientists still denied that tribal peoples had the institution we call marriage, or that they followed any ethical or religious precepts at all. Europeans were fond of describing non-Europeans as childlike and emotional and themselves as rational and scientific. Stereotypes born of misconceptions like these can best be laid to rest by information organized topically. This arrangement makes it easier to see the real differences between European and Indian ways, and also to see the many similarities.

Even today, people tend to ask for general information about Indian life rather than about Indians of specific areas. What kind of marriage customs did Indians have? What was their religion like? How did they rear their children? How did they make political decisions? What kinds of tools did they use? While answers to these and other questions must vary from area to area, there are, nevertheless, many general statements we can make about Indian life. Though some of the data of this section may repeat information in earlier chapters, Part III is included to make cross-cultural comparisons and contrasts clearer and more precise.

Suggestions for Further Study

Bibliography

Astrov, Margot, ed. 1946. *American Indian Prose and Poetry.*

Songs and stories from the major culture areas.

Bandelier, Adolf. 1890. *The Delight Makers.*

A fictional account of precontact Pueblo Indians. Gives a real feeling for the fear of witches and witchcraft.

Driver, Harold E. 1969. *Indians of North America.* 2nd ed.

A major textbook, the only one arranged by topics of culture. Every student should be acquainted with this work.

Furst, Peter T. and Jill L. Furst. 1982. *North American Indian Art.* Good illustrations of art by culture area.

Other Pertinent Works

Adair, John. 1944. *The Navajo and Pueblo Silversmiths.*

Benedict, Ruth. 1923. *The Concept of the Guardian Spirit in North America.*

Densmore, Frances. 1926. *The American Indians and Their Music.*

Douglas, Frederick H., and Rene D'Harnoncourt. 1941. *Indian Art of the United States.*

Feder, Norman. 1965. *American Indian Art.*

Gifford, Edward W. 1928. *Pottery Making in the Southwest.*

Huyltkranz, Ake. 1987. *Native Religions of North America.*

Morgan, Lewis H. 1965. *Houses and House-life of the American Aborigines.*

Radin, Paul. 1956. *The Trickster: A Study in American Indian Mythology.*

Speck, Frank G. 1919. *Functions of Wampum among the Eastern Algonkian.*

Spier, Leslie. 1921. *The Sundance of the Plains Indians.*

Thompson, Stith. 1971. *Tales of the North American Indians.*

9

TECHNOLOGY, ART, AND RELIGION

Potawatomi beadwork.

A society's practical arts—the way its people make and use the tools they need to sustain and reproduce life—constitute its technology. A human group provides itself with food, shelter, and protection with its technology. And beyond simply satisfying those physical needs, technology includes the means to satisfy intellectual and aesthetic needs: the performing arts, such as music and dance, as well as the graphic arts, such as sculpture and painting.

Throughout the New World, people created all the tools and utensils they needed from the natural materials of their environment. Though archaeologists have shown that long-distance trade existed long before European contact, that trade was highly specialized in luxury or exotic goods such as mica, obsidian, and shells. Implements of daily living, the common household tools and building materials, had to come from the immediate vicinity. Thus, as we examine native technology, we find that the major variations in housing, transportation, weapons, and clothing arise naturally from the environmental differences and the availability of various resources. Still, many raw materials were available over nearly all of the continent—stone and bone, for example—so we can generalize about the manufacture and use of many implements.

The Food Quest

The food any human society eats depends upon what is available. We have already pointed out the abundance of food in the Northwest Coast culture area and the scarcity in the Subarctic. But no society can eat without first doing some work to obtain food. The kinds of food-getting work American Indian societies did were hunting, gathering, fishing, and cultivating. Later, after the Europeans introduced domesticated animals, Indians added stockraising.

Gathering

In the Great Basin and California, people ate more wild plants than any other food. Everywhere else except for the Arctic, wild plants were important even where the cultural emphasis was on hunting or agriculture. American Indians ate a vast variety of wild vegetal foods, from roots and tubers to greens, fruits, seeds, and nuts. Even fungi added to the diet: Indians of the Southeast made one fungus, tuckaho, into bread.

Everywhere the primary gatherers were women, often aided by their children and in some instances, by men. For most gathering they needed no implement other than containers; going to pick berries or greens, they usually carried baskets. To reach tubers and roots, they used digging sticks, and for seeds, simple beaters to knock the ripe grain into containers. They knocked down nuts too, reaching into the trees with long poles. To gather the hard-to-reach fruit of the prickly pear cactus, which was protected by sharp spines, women made tongs. Most of these looked like large clothes-pins, a piece of wood with a slit, but sometimes they were two pieces held together like chopsticks or paddles. Tongs also were used to handle hot stones for stone boiling or sweatbaths.

Although there is no direct proof archaeologically or historically, it seems reasonable that any people aware of every consumable source the environment had to offer would have recognized and enjoyed the sweet sap of the sugar maple tree. There is every reason to question, however, whether Indians made the sap into sugar in pre-contact times. Some reports tell of Indians in areas where the sugar maples grew tapping the trees and catching the sweet sap that oozed from the wound, then cooking the sap both by direct heat and by stone boiling. But that was more than a century after European contact, and it appears that sugar making was definitely a post-European activity. In the eighteenth century Indians used iron kettles obtained in trade, and maple sugar production had by then become a commercial venture by Indians and whites.

Hunting

Though much of their diet came from wild plants, Indians considered the hunt more important. People of the Plains gave so much prestige to hunters that other food resources got little attention, even though it was plant food that often staved off starvation in lean seasons. Game was the favored food almost everywhere. Through the years, Indian hunters developed many ways of trapping, disabling, and killing animals. They studied each animal's ways and learned how to get close to it without warning, stalking against the wind, wearing disguises of animal skins, and waiting for prey at water holes.

The large game animals Indians hunted were bison, moose, caribou, elk, antelope, deer, and bear. Deer were the most widely hunted, but the Plains Indians preferred bison, and the Subarctic people went mostly after caribou. The Eskimo and Indians of the Northwest Coast hunted sea mammals as well as land animals.

The people generally preferred hunting large game animals over small animals, simply because they had more meat on them, though small animals filled many a stomach when larger game was not to be had. One bison meant at least half a ton of meat, one deer a hundred pounds, and a large rabbit ten pounds or less. The many by-products made the big animals even more desirable; hides for clothing and shelter, hair for embroidery and padding, antlers for handles and projectile points, hooves and horns for glue, sinew for thread and string, bones for needles and other tools and for ornaments, and guts for containers.

Deadfalls (traps with heavy weights that fell on animals, disabling them), surrounds, and *impounds* (the confined areas where animals were driven and killed), used in ancient times, remained important in hunting herd animals. Antelopes' great speed might have kept them safe from hunters except for the animals' great inquisitiveness. Indians knew how to attract their curiosity by waving strips of hide or feathers from long poles. As the antelopes went to investigate the flapping objects, the men could get close enough to shoot them. Dogs often went along to hold animals at bay while hunters closed in for the kill, and hunters sometimes would try to lure the animals by imitating mating calls.

Hunting Weapons. Indians depended on two basic devices for killing: spears and bows. Spears, as we know from archaeology, were the oldest implements of the hunt. With the spear thrower or *atlatl*, hunters gave their spears added thrust and accuracy, but because atlatls were unwieldy on horseback, mounted Plainsmen rarely used them. Hunters of the Big Game period in American prehistory used spears, but we still have not determined the earliest use of the bow and arrow in North America. Nor do we know whether Indians invented bows here independently or ancient hunters brought them across the Bering Strait from the Old World. Sure evidence—preserved prehistoric bows—demonstrates their existence by A.D. 500, but many archaeologists believe that hunters used bows far earlier, by 1500 B.C. Bows and arrow shafts decay rapidly, of course, so we do not have any very ancient remains. Stone arrowheads might seem likely to show the date of introduction conclusively, but they do not because many stone points small enough to be used on arrows might also have been points for small spears, such as fishing spears. We know too that arrows for small game such as birds and squirrels usually did not have stone tips. By the time of European contact, though, all Indians and Eskimo used bows.

Hunters made four basic kinds of bows: the self-bow, the sinew-backed bow, the sinew-wrapped bow, and the compound bow. Indians chose springy wood, bone, or horn for the compound bow, put together in several layers and glued and lashed together. Plains Indians favored this style. In the Eastern woodlands the self-bow was the popular form, made of a single length of wood, often four feet long or more. The sinew-wrapped bow was an Alaskan form, brittle wood wrapped with sinew. Hunters made sinew-backed bows from self-bows by backing them with sinew to give extra spring. Some Eskimo made their compound bows

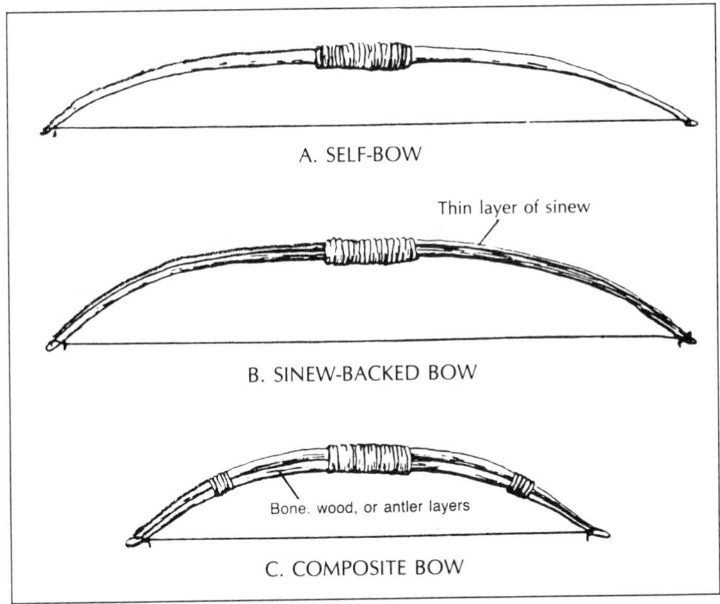

Three kinds of bows used by hunters: the self-bow (A); the sinew-backed bow (B); and the compound bow (C).

of whale ribs, with a wooden grip. Plains bows were usually short for easier shooting on horseback.

Indians selected reeds, canes, or light wooden boughs with great care for arrow shafts. They dried them to season the wood and straightened and smoothed them with stone or bone implements. Feathers for arrows came primarily from hawks, eagles, and turkeys. Properly attached, the feathers made the arrow twist or spiral in flight. Indians usually split the feather before attaching it with glue, but Eskimo usually used the whole feather.

The men made bowstrings from rawhide, sinew, or twisted fibers. Glue came from animal tissues, hooves, sinew, or horn, boiled for several days to produce a jelly-like substance that was a very effective adhesive. Indians also used gum resins or pitch from some trees and shrubs.

Indians formed arrowheads not only of stone but of bone, horn, antler, shell, wood, and copper, and in many styles and shapes. Some arrows had points loosely attached so the point would stay embedded in the flesh when the shaft was withdrawn, but most hunters bound their arrowheads firmly to the shafts to that they could recover both. The heads were attached with sinew, cording, or rawhide slipped around the notches, or lashed firmly in an over-and-under pattern if they had no notches. Hunters used the same techniques to attach spear and knife blades to shafts.

Hunting Methods. Often, when an animal had been wounded but not killed, hunters clubbed it to death with anything from a simple knobbed stick to carved stone or wooden implements to clubs set with spikes, stone heads, or copper blades. Pueblo hunters used missile clubs, called rabbit sticks, which were thrown to bring down rabbits.

Hunters of the Southeast and the Iroquois in the Northeast used blowguns to kill small animals and birds. They hollowed long stalks of cane or straight pieces of wood, then fashioned a projectile or dart from a splinter of cane or wood, padding it with thistledown, cotton, or other soft material at one end. The other end of the dart was sharp. The padding provided resistance which the hunter blew against. With practice, a hunter became skillful in bringing down small game with a blowgun.

Indians caught many smaller game animals such as foxes in traps. Some traps killed the animals, while others imprisoned them alive. One simple trap used a morsel of food as bait. One end of a heavy stone was propped up by a stick above the food. When the animal tried to take the food, the stone fell, stunning or killing the animal. Another trap was a pit in the ground, covered with branches. When the animal stepped onto the branches, it fell through into the pit. Some pits had a sharp stake at the bottom to impale the animal; others merely imprisoned the animal until the hunter killed it.

A clever way of catching eagles and hawks, which were prized for feathers, was for one man to lie concealed in a pit over which brush had been laid. On the brush another man would put a dead squirrel or rabbit. When the bird, attracted by the prey, alighted, the hunter in the pit would grasp its feet, then crush or strangle it.

Hunters set snares for rabbits, birds, and other small game. Along animal paths to watering places or feeding grounds, a trapper suspended a loop of sinew or hide from the tip of a springy sapling bent over and lightly set into a notch on another tree. An animal stepping on the loop released the bent sapling, which sprang up, catching the animal in the noose.

To butcher and skin animals, Indians used knives of stone or almost any material that would take and hold an edge: wood, reed, antler, shell, bone, and copper. Beaver teeth made very good cutting implements. Indians usually hafted the knife point to a shaft exactly as though they were fashioning a spear or arrow, but the knife shafts were much shorter, only four to six inches long.

Fishing

In much of native America, fishing was not very important. People of some tribes (notably in the Plains and the Southwest) even thought fish were not fit to eat. But fish was the most important item in Northwest Coast and Plateau diets and was also vital to the Arctic and Subarctic folk.

Aboriginal fishing implements included nets, weirs, hooks, spears, and traps of many styles and designs. All across the continent Indians built the traps called weirs, wickerwork dams that let water flow through but trapped the fish. Indians constructed many other styles of fish traps, but the principle was the same: fish entered an enclosure in which they could not turn around to swim back out. The people fished with hooks and lines as well as spears, and especially in the Southeast and California they used fish poisons. These worked only in still water, diluting too rapidly in moving streams. The poison, made from plants like crushed walnut bark or soap root, caused temporary paralysis of the fish's breathing mechanism, but was harmless to anyone who ate the fish.

Fishers dipped nets lashed to poles into water where fish were plentiful and also stretched large nets all the way across streams. A group of Indians working together could sweep a lake or pond with a large net, holding the lower edge of the net on the bottom with sinkers.

Fishhooks were made of bone, shell, ivory, wood, or copper. The gorge, much like the hook except in shape, was a straight sharp pin at the end of a line. When a fish swallowed a gorge, it stuck in its throat, and the fisher could haul the catch from the water. People also shot fish with bows and arrows and caught them with pronged spears. In northern areas, the men chopped holes in ice to fish in winter with hooks, gorges, spears, or bows. People of the Northwest Coast caught large fish with harpoons.

Along the north Pacific coast, the Indians relished fish eggs, collecting them on evergreen branches held down with weights in water where fish spawned. Once the eggs were deposited, the branches were removed and the eggs dried for storage. Around lakes and ponds, men learned to attract fish at night with torchlights and then spear or shoot them with arrows. Wherever shellfish could be found, women dug them from the sand.

Cultivation

Native peoples of Mexico and South America developed many domesticated plants, but Indian north of Mexico cultivated only three in quantity—corn, beans, and squashes—though they grew many varieties of each. Some societies used sunflowers and amaranths, which we consider weeds today; those "weeds" added important amounts to the food stock.

Everywhere except among the Pueblo Indians, women were the cultivators of everything but tobacco, which was the other major cultigen north of Mexico. Men grew tobacco to smoke for ritual purposes as well as for pleasure, planting it even where nothing else was cultivated, as in the northern Plains. All the cultivated plants except the "weeds" had originated in Mexico or farther south in prehistoric times, and much archaeological investigation today is aimed at pinpointing where they started and by which routes agriculture diffused to tribes north of Mexico.

Planting and cultivating were simple throughout North America, involving digging sticks, hoes, and rakes. Farmers punched holes in the ground with the digging sticks and dropped seeds into the holes. They usually planted corn, beans, and squash in the same field, often using cornstalks as supports for the squash vines. Indians had no draft animals or ploughs, but fields for the native plants did not require or get the kind of preparation associated with the Old World plants like wheat.

Some digging sticks were no more than pointed branches, but others were made with a toe rest and one end broader and flatter than the other, like a narrow spade. Occasionally the cultivator slipped a ring of stone over the stick as a weight to give more thrust. Hoes had heads of flaked stone, wood, and also bone; the scapula or shoulder blade of a bison made an excellent hoe. People also made rakes of wooden prongs attached to a handle, but just as often used an unmodified antler. Both rakes and hoes were used for weeding and breaking up the ground, though nowhere was much weeding done. In fact, Indians did not look after their gardens very diligently, putting most of the effort into planting and harvesting. Where fields were rocky, they just planted around the rocks.

Indians did not need to design special tools for harvesting, for corn, beans, and squash required no implements not already in use for gathering. The men picked rather than cut tobacco leaves, and the harvesters moved the produce from field to home or storage in large baskets.

Preparing Food

People have always eaten some foods without preparing them in any way, but other foods have to be treated before they are eaten. Most grains or seeds are easier to digest as flour or meal, and people generally prefer cooked meats to raw. Cooking food also makes it easier to preserve and store for the future.

Grinding and Pounding

With stone or wooden equipment, Indian women of North America pounded and ground maize, acorns, other seeds and nuts, leaves, stalks, and dried meats, making them more edible or preparing them for storage. Grinding was the main technique for turning nuts and seeds of all species into flour for gruels and breads. In the West, women usually used stone grinding equipment, while wood was more popular in the East, but both were distributed widely.

A woman ground grain by rubbing it between two stones, using the larger as a base and holding the smaller in her hand. Today, the smaller stone is called a mano (especially by Spanish-speaking people) or *pestle*, and the larger stones are termed metates or *mortars*. Anthropologists often speak of this equipment as milling stones or grinding stones. Grinding stones might be oblong, round, or irregularly shaped. Usually the metate is an oblong stone; the pestle is shaped like a rolling pin, while a mano usually is rectangular.

Women of the East did their grinding by pounding rather than rubbing, and they used wooden equipment. Their mortars were sections of tree trunks about eighteen inches in diameter, hollowed to a depth of about two feet. Into the mortar they poured the grain, then pulverized it with a wooden pestle, a large pole with thickened ends. Women stood while using a tree-trunk mortar.

Food Preservation and Storage

Indians dried both animal and plant foods in strong sunlight, or by the fire in regions that had cloudy weather. Strips of dried meat called *jerky* might be stored in containers without further processing, but often women pulverized jerky into pemmican by mixing it with mashed berries and suet, then packed it away. Women made many varieties of pemmican with different meats and berries, occasionally adding bone marrow, and in some places using dried fish for the base.

People had many ways of storing dried meat, fish, plant foods, and pemmican, always choosing storage places where the foods would stay dry and safe from animal scavengers and vermin. To keep food from predators, they hung it from tree branches in hide or basketry containers or hid the filled containers in cache pits. Some people, like the Mandan, dug these pits in the floor of their lodges, but many pits were outside and unprotected, covered only with stones to keep animals out. In the Arctic, it was impossible to dig into the permanently frozen ground, so food was simply left on the surface. Covered with a pile of stones, it kept very well in this natural deep-freeze. The Mandan and many others lined their large pits with clay, rawhide, and grasses to keep out burrowing beasts and insects. To conceal caches from enemies, Indians often built fires over them so that the ashes would hide the traces of digging, or else they carefully removed and replaced the sod or poured water over the soil to even out any evidence that something had been buried there.

For more immediate use, people braided shucks of corn together and suspended them from the roof poles of the house. Southeast people built small corncribs near their houses, plastering the insides to discourage vermin and animals. Women might store full ears of corn in the cribs, or just grain. Inside their homes they kept daily food on shelves or ledges in containers of natural materials like bark, pottery, basketry, skin, or wood.

Cooking

Women did all the cooking: roasting, broiling, boiling, and baking. The only cooking technique common today that the Indian women did not use was frying.

To boil foods, women used fireproof containers of pottery, or even bark that could be hung close enough to the fire to bring water to a boil without burning through. Or they might drop very hot stones into liquid in containers of skin, basketry, wood, or viscera (like stomach pouches). Heat from the stones would eventually bring the liquid to a boil, but stone boiling was much slower than direct boiling.

Women roasted or broiled meats and some vegetables, especially ears of corn in their own husks. In the Southeast they broiled fish on a grill of green sticks over the fire; elsewhere meat or fish was put on a long stick stuck in the ground at an angle toward the fire. Often people roasted meat and whole small game in the coals and hot ashes, first encasing the food in clay or leaves. In addition they cooked many foods in earth ovens, which were holes in the ground with hot coals or stones at the bottom. The cook put wrapped foods on top of the stones or coals, covering everything with soil to keep the heat in long enough to cook the food. The New England clambake is a direct descendant of these earth ovens.

The women baked breads directly in warm ashes or by laying the dough on "baking stones" over a flame or coals. In very early Spanish times, the Pueblo began to use simple beehive ovens with draft holes, probably copied from the newcomers. Pueblo women baked their corn bread, something like tortillas, on flat hot stones.

Fire-making

Indians used fire not only for cooking, but also for warmth and protection from wild animals. Fire-making was important in many ceremonies we have discussed, such as the Creek Busk and other new-fire and world-renewal rituals.

Indians had two techniques for starting fires. Striking a spark with flint and pyrites (iron-containing rocks) was common in the Arctic, Subarctic, Northwest Coast, and New England areas. The other way was to produce heat by rubbing wood on wood. The firedrill was a favorite way of creating friction: spun rapidly, it heated tinder or wood powder at the point of contact to combustion temperature. The Onondaga appear to have been the only group to create friction by rubbing a stick over a wooden plane surface, sometimes called a *fire plough*. Keeping coals alive was a necessity everywhere because it was quite difficult to start a fire.

Housing

All over the continent people needed shelter from cold, rain, or heat. Some types of house were specific to tribes or regions: hogans, pueblos, and plank houses. General structures appeared in several areas, including wigwams, wickiups, tipis, and earth lodges. Indians also built cruder structures for temporary shelter. No one name covers such buildings, but we would call them huts, lean-tos, or shacks.

General Forms of Housing

Wigwams and Wickiups. The word *wigwam* is Algonkian for "dwelling," but Algonkian speakers built other house types too, including the barnlike structures of the Central Atlantic people. We have no word for these houses, but they were much like the Iroquois longhouse. Wigwams had circular or oval floor plans and domed roofs; they were covered with sheets of bark, woven mats, or skins. The framework was of saplings imbedded in holes about two feet apart with tops bent over and bound to make the arched roof. Some wigwams housed only one family; others were much larger.

Wickiups looked something like wigwams, and people often have confused the two, but there were differences. Wickiups housed Apache, Basin, and California peoples, while wigwams were Algonkian. The wickiup floor plan was often irregular, though sometimes oval. Wickiups were less permanent than wigwams, and generally cruder. Instead of hides or sheets of bark, they were covered with brush. They were favored by nomadic people unwilling to spend much time on buildings they would soon abandon.

Tipis. Tipis appeared in the Subarctic, Northeast, and Plains areas, small conical structures covered with hides or bark. In the Northeast and Subarctic, the buildings never were very large, but after horses appeared on the Plains, tipis there became much larger.

Women put up and took down the big Plains tipis and made the buffalo hide covers for them. Men cut the poles for the framework. Once all materials were gathered, two women could erect a tipi in an hour.

Most tribes used a tripod of especially strong poles for the tipi's main support, but some tribes used four poles. The women tied these poles together at the top and raised them, planting the untied ends firmly on the ground. Then they leaned more poles against the original group and tied them in place. The frame was not a true cone but was tilted slightly to give more room at the rear and better ventilation through an off-center smokehole.

When the poles were all in place, the women fastened the hide cover to another pole, hoisted it over the frame, draped it around the poles, pegged the bottom edge down, and closed the open seam with large wooden pins like skewers. They attached a door flap that could be adjusted for ventilation. Finally, they inserted two lighter poles outside the tipi in the smoke flaps at the top of the cover. By moving the poles, the women could adjust the flaps to compensate for changes in wind direction or close them completely in rain or snow. When finished, the average Plains tipi was about fifteen feet in diameter at the base, providing ample room for a family and their equipment.

Good poles were hard to find on the grasslands, so people took along the framework of the tipi as well as the cover when they moved. Often the poles formed part of the horse travois.

Earth Lodges. Earth lodges were permanent homes for semisettled people, most common among Plains villagers, in the Plateau, and in southwest Alaska. They varied somewhat in floor plan, but most were circular, and almost all were dug two or three feet below the surface of the ground before the framing was put up. Lodges were large, some having room for prized horses as well as several families.

The earth lodge is named for its insulating covering of soil or sod that kept the interior warm in winter and cool in summer. Indians constructed the lodge framing with sturdy posts, for it had to support not only the heavy soil on top, but the pressure of its own size as well.

Many of the Plateau lodges were entered at the top, with a ladder through the central smokehole, but the Plains villagers built their lodges with tunnel-like vestibules and entries large enough for horses to pass through. Dwellings of the Pima and some California tribes were like the earth lodge, but smaller, less sturdy, and relatively impermanent. The Navajo hogan was like an earth lodge in that it was slightly underground and often covered with a layer of soil, but it too was much smaller.

The Wattle and Daub House. In the Southeast, rectangular and also circular houses were made of pole frameworks intertwined with tough vines or flexible branches. The Southeasterners then covered the framework with a mud plaster called daub. Most such houses had peaked or gabled roofs. In hot weather, the people built similar shelters from the sun, leaving off the siding of branches and daub to improve air circulation. Such structures were found in all hot regions, with minor differences in style.

Specialized Forms of Housing

Pueblos. The pueblo structure evolved from the early Anasazi pit house. The early domed houses, built over saucer-shaped depressions, developed into straight-sided buildings with upright posts supporting a flat roof. People entered these either through the smokehole or through a side passageway. It was during this early transition period that the residents also began to build rooms side by side. The pit house continued on as a ceremonial room (kiva), while the above-ground rooms were built up of wood and stones, often with an adobe clay plastered over the stone, into the pueblo of several stories. Logs spanned the pueblo walls, creating a flat roof; over these, the builders laid brush and poles, plastering them with more clay. In time, they built more rooms over the first, and the roof of each room became the floor of the room above.

In later times, probably because of Spanish influence, people began to make the adobe clay into sun-dried brick, which they used in place of stone. From the Spanish, Indians also learned to build indoor fireplaces with chimneys, and to build more doors and windows into the pueblos. Taos, a pueblo still occupied today, shows not only these additions, but television antennas on the roofs.

Hogans. The Navajo house, the hogan, gradually changed in floor plan and construction. The early form was cone-shaped, with forked logs as its main structural support. The builders set the logs upright and placed poles or branches crosswise, supported by the forked ends of the logs. Over this basic framework they laid brush, and covered the whole with earth, leaving a smokehole in the center roof and a doorway on the east. The later form of the hogan was six- or eight-sided, made of horizontal timbers, and was usually much larger than the earlier.

Plank Houses of the Northwest. Woodworkers felled tall, straight cedar trees, trimmed off branches, then split planks from the trunk by driving wedges in a straight line from end to end. They used the planks for both siding and roofing over a framework of heavy cedar posts with rafters or crossbeams also of cedar. Entryways into homes of high-ranking individuals were elaborate, many with totem poles in front. Sometimes the carved pole formed the doorway. A post with a hole large enough for an adult to pass through was set flush against the front of the house. Often woodworkers carved the crest of the owner on the major structural house supports as well.

Iroquois Longhouses. Upright posts formed the main supports for the longhouse, and horizontal poles lashed to the vertical posts created rafters. Though the longhouse roof was peaked, it had no ridgepole. Instead, the builders slanted roof supports toward each other from the two sides, crossing the ends at the top and lashing them together.

Large slabs of bark covered the framework. Often women prepared strips of bark by laying them on the ground, slightly overlapping, and lacing them together with cords of plant fiber. Then the men lashed the sheets to the sides and roof of the building. Single slabs of bark were often lashed directly to the structure.

Sweathouses. Sweathouses of one sort or another appeared in pre-Columbian America from the Arctic to Mexico. The most common form was a small wigwam, its framework of flexible poles bent and fastened into a domed structure and covered with skins, bark, or matting. Inside, a shallow firepit contained hot stones on which people sprinkled water to make steam. Ordinarily one person at a time used this small sweathouse, though once in a while two might use it together.

Some areas, like Alaska, had large, fairly permanent sweathouses dug into the ground. Such buildings almost always doubled as men's clubhouses when they were not being used for sweating. In the large structure, men built fires inside and sweated from the direct heat. Everywhere, a dip in a stream followed sweating.

Building either kind of sweathouse usually involved ceremonial observances, for sweating had to do with ritual purification. In some areas women availed themselves of the sweathouse, but never at the same time as men.

Housing is an interesting example of the impact of environment on culture. But it is also excellent evidence of people's inventiveness and creativity. Natural resources determine the building materials, but people turn those materials into many varied styles. Clearly, environment is never deterministic. Even in the two most difficult regions, the arctic and the desert, human choice and creativity led to many and diverse results.

Transportation

It may seem surprising that although many Indian groups were constantly moving themselves and their possessions from place to place, they had no knowledge of the wheel. Actually, wheeled transport would not have been much use to them, for they had no draft animals to pull vehicles. They did need transportation for such daily tasks as moving food and materials, and larger jobs like hauling raw materials and goods long distances for trade, and transporting the young, aged, and sick to new homes or village sites. Before Indians had horses, their transportation depended almost entirely on human endurance; they had only dogs to help with light loads.

Water Transportation

Though Indians made other kinds of boats as well, canoes were their most common means of water travel. The bark canoe was broad and sat high in the water, so that it could be paddled in very shallow places. Tribes developed their own styles, but most bark canoes had similar framework: lightweight wood sheathed with bark, preferably birch. Where birch did not grow, people learned to use other barks, especially elm. Men sewed sections of bark together with root fibers and waterproofed seams with melted pitch or tar. These light boats were fairly easy to carry overland between waterways.

Dugout canoes, differing only in style, had wide distribution, from the Northwest Coast to the Southeast. To make one, men set fire to a suitable tree, carefully limiting the blaze, and then cut it with stone axes; charred wood cut more easily than green wood. With adzes and gouges, the canoe maker removed wood, making a depression in the log, which he filled with water. By dropping hot stones in the water, he softened the wood enough to spread the sides, which were propped apart with boards. He then emptied the water, and when the dugout dried, the spread was permanent. With more trimming and perhaps separate pieces added on for prow and stern, the canoe was ready to try out. Because dugouts were carved from such large trees, they were rarely portable.

Eskimo boats, the kayaks and umiaks, were skin covered, and so was the *bull boat* made by villagers of the Upper Missouri. The bull boat was like a cup, with a framework of saplings; it had no prow or stern. Villagers used it only to cross rivers, not for travel, for its circular construction made it very inefficient for speed. Peoples of the California area made boats with bundles of reeds, and the Chumash of California made plank canoes. Indians propelled all types of canoes with paddles. Whether people of the Northwest Coast used sails before European arrival is not certain, but they were reported to be sailing shortly after European contact, the only Indians known to have done so. Only the whaling Northwest Coast peoples went out to deep ocean waters. Others kept to inland waters or ventured not far off the coast.

Land Transportation

Human backs carried most of the loads on land, over the network of trails that covered the continent. Backpacking moved items of trade, personal belongings, food, and babies. To ease the burden, Indians often placed a strap called a *tumpline* across their brows and connected it to the bundles on their backs. Mothers often carried their babies on their backs in cradle boards suspended from tumplines or straps over their shoulders. In the Arctic, women carried babies in their hoods or pouches in their clothes.

Before horses arrived in America, the dog-drawn travois carried many goods. Once they had horses, Indians enlarged the travois. Horse travois held household goods, and often old people and infants, too. Sometimes a simple top or shade was added to keep off sun and rain, and some Plains Indians even made a cage travois for transporting puppies.

Travel over snow required sleds and snowshoes. Eskimo and Indians of the North used sleds drawn by dogs and by people, made in many shapes and styles depending on the materials available and the use they were meant for. Sleds had runners, with a deck or platform. Subarctic people invented toboggans without runners, the bed or deck running directly on the snow.

With snowshoes people could walk over snow without sinking, moving much faster than without them and cutting fatigue. Indians made more styles of snowshoes than sleds, all with the same basic parts: a wooden rim with toe and heel crossbars of wood or rawhide, netting across the framework for the feet to rest upon, and thongs to attach over the instep. On snowshoes the traveler walked with long strides, raising his toe at each step and letting his heel drag. Indians did not have skis.

Clothing

Indians wore clothes as climate dictated, not for modesty or to conceal their bodies, for the nude human body aroused no shame or embarrassment. In fact, Eskimo, who wore far more clothing than any other North American natives, went about entirely or nearly naked in their homes. Clothing was worn for more than protection, though: Indians decorated themselves with objects and paints they found pleasing, and some groups indicated social position or religious office by the clothing or ornamentation they wore. Men generally dressed differently from women.

Kinds of Apparel

Of all the people on this continent, the Eskimo stand out as skillful makers of protective garments for cold weather. They tailored their clothing fully and knew how to make waterproof seams. Their garments were tight at the wrists, neck, and ankles, but loose over the rest of the body. Clothes had two layers, creating a dead air space between the inner and outer layers that kept body heat in and arctic cold out. Eskimo used both furs and dehaired hides of sea mammals, caribou, polar bears, and foxes for their apparel, and insulated their mittens and boots with feathers, down, and moss. The women sewed with sinew thread and needles and awls of bone.

Much of America's aboriginal population dressed in animal skins, though people in warmer climates made fabrics of plant fibers. For most of the continent, people favored deerskin. Where buffalo were available, people used their skins for robes and blankets; but whatever animals the hunters brought home contributed furs or hides for clothing. For the most part women made the clothing, though in a few California and Basin tribes, men and women each made their own.

Clothing Styles. Men usually wore breechclouts (loincloths or breechcloths), with shirts and leggings for more protection. Northeast and Plains women wore skin shirt dresses, and in the Northwest and Plateau they had woven plant-fiber skirts. In California and the Southeast, women wore only fiber or skin aprons. Both men and women added robes of fur (buffalo, wolf, rabbit—the animals of their environment) in cold weather.

Pueblo Indians grew cotton, spun it into yarn, and made their clothes from cotton cloth into which the yarn was woven. Pueblo men wore a kiltlike garment, and the women draped dresses over their right shoulders and under their left.

The rainy, foggy Northwest Coast climate made some rain garment useful there. Indians of that area made basketry hats (much like Chinese coolie hats) and a kind of poncho of basketry matting. Despite the rain, however, the coast was not cold; the Indians often wore nothing, which was better than keeping on clothing that got wet and stayed wet.

Footwear. Footwear of leather appeared everywhere except among some prehistoric Southwestern groups, who wove or braided plant-fiber sandals. People of the Southeast usually went barefoot. In the rainy Northwest, people found footwear a nuisance much of the time. Leather becomes stiff when it get wet and then dries; bare feet were far more comfortable.

Indians made two types of moccasins: those with rawhide soles separate from the soft upper leather parts, and those made of a single piece of soft leather. The two-piece moccasins were favored by Plains and western Indians and the one-piece style by Northeast and Great Lakes peoples. Some groups also made long or "boot" moccasins. The Pueblo women wore these with strips of leather wound around the calves of their legs like bandages.

Body Decoration

Hair. Indians had little body hair and scanty beards. While a few Indian men were reported with mustaches, most carefully removed facial hairs with tweezers made of bivalve shells or two small pieces of bone, shell, or wood. They decorated the hair of their heads in enormously varied ways, even within one culture area or tribe. Men and women decided for themselves how they would wear their hair. Some men shaved their scalps, leaving a ridge of hair, called a roach, from forehead to the nape of the neck. Men of many areas also made artificial roaches from animal hair, especially from stiff deer hair, and wore them to pad out their own hair or placed them over their unshaven heads as a kind of headdress, tied under the chin, or under braids, or pinned on. Braids were popular all over the continent for both men and women, and people of all areas also allowed their hair to flow loose. Among the Pueblo, many men and women cut their front hair into bangs. A Pueblo woman's hair style told whether she was married: elaborate buns of hair over each ear meant she was single. To groom their hair, Indians made combs of wood, bone, horn, and stiff straw, and porcupine tails were their brushes.

In many tribes a baby's first haircut was an important event, and parents often saved the hair from that first cut to give the child later. Hair was important; it was connected with life. Many believed that an enemy who got hold of hair clippings would have power over the one the hair belonged to, so hair clippings were disposed of carefully and secretly.

Where it was available, bear fat was a favorite hairdressing, sometimes mixed with pigments to color the hair—soot to make it blacker or ground red ochre to make it red. Many Indians also padded out their braids, not just their roaches, with animal hair. After European contact, horse hair became very popular for false hair. Indians often used animal fats and oils to groom their hair, and in the Southwest the Pueblo made shampoo suds from the pounded root of yucca.

Paint and Tattoos. People sometimes painted their faces and bodies with symbols of clan relationship, bereavement, or intent to make war. They also decorated their bodies with paints to protect against sun and wind, or just because body paint seemed attractive. In warm areas where clothing was scant, Indians were particularly fond of body paint for decoration.

Indians of the Southeast used body paint lavishly, and tattooed their bodies too. Someone skilled in tattoo design perforated the skin with sharpened shells, stones, or bones, and rubbed in soot to make the design permanent. We have sixteenth-century paintings by Europeans of Southeastern Indians, showing people with every inch of exposed skin covered with tattooing.

Jewelry. All across the land men and women enjoyed wearing earrings. Mothers usually pierced babies' ears when they were one or two years old. Earrings might be quite elaborate, made of bones, colored stones (like turquoise), and copper. People of the mound builders' period often inserted large copper spools in their pierced earlobes, stretching the lobes by inserting bigger and bigger ones until they could fit spools two or more inches in diameter.

Earrings were just one form of jewelry that Indians everywhere liked. From bone, claws, colored stones, shells, and indeed any attractive material they made necklaces, headbands, and armbands. Hair decorations of feathers, down, and other colorful items were universally popular too. On the Plains, a necklace of bear claws was a sign that the wearer was very important, and women sewed elk teeth onto clothing for another impressive type of decoration. Plains warriors strung long tubular bones called *hair pipes* into breastplates. After contact, Indians sought imported glass and china beads to sew onto garments or to weave into belts or necklaces. The period of great beadwork was the last half of the nineteenth century.

Arts and Crafts

Indian art is applied art, a practical thing, not a purely aesthetic exercise done for enjoyment. We do have some sculptures with no known function: ivory carvings from the Eskimo, a deer head from Key West, stone images by the mound builders. Perhaps their creators intended them as hunting or health charms, but they might also have carved them just from artistic impulse. Most often it is impossible to separate Indian art from craft. Probably the artists themselves thought of their work as decoration rather than art. But we do not have to distinguish between art and craft to appreciate the results.

The Indian artist was essentially a conservator, not an innovator, trying to preserve cultural traditions and values through art. Even when Indians used a new material, like glass beads, they applied it in culturally established ways. However, new ideas and new materials brought change over the years. Some elements of prehistoric art still appear today, but contemporary Indian art is quite different even from that of the generation just before it.

Indians decorated both utilitarian and ceremonial objects: containers, weapons, clothing, masks, ritual headdresses. Styles varied from one culture area to another—it does not take a specialist to spot a mask or totem pole from the Northwest Coast or a katcina mask or doll from the Southwest. However, neither portraits nor the use of perspective appeared anywhere in the art of native North America.

Woodworking

Indians in forested areas were skilled woodcrafters, and Northwest Coast woodworking was the highest development in carving north of Mexico. In pre-European times Indian carvers used adzes and knives of shell, stone, copper, and animal teeth. They chopped down trees that were not too large with axes and set fire to the base of larger ones, charring them for easier cutting. They also used drills, chisels, scrapers, and sanders or smoothers. Pueblo people made dolls, figurines, and other objects of wood so soft that they could shape it entirely by rubbing or sanding it with coarse rock. After iron knives became available, woodcarving flourished, especially on the Northwest Coast.

Indians bent or straightened wood by steaming or soaking it. They carved knots of trees into dishes and small bowls by gouging and scraping them, and fashioned some spoons and ladles of wood.

Bone and Horn

Surrounded by artificial materials as we are today, few of us think of bone and horn as useful raw materials. To the Indians, though, they were a valuable source of spoons, cups, ladles, and other utensils. To work horn, the craftsworkers first rid it of fatty deposits by heating it. Then they boiled it in water until it was pliable and could be worked with stone or bone knives or bent to the desired shape. After the horn was formed into the desired utensil, it was left to cool and harden. It would then hold its shape permanently, needing only to be polished with sand or sandstone, and perhaps rubbed to a gloss with animal fat or oil.

To work bone, the Indians followed much the same procedure. After heating or boiling it, they let it lie in sunlight to dry and bleach, then fashioned it into beads or pendants or even combs.

Pottery

The Eskimo, northern Indians, and those of the Pacific Coast and Basin had little pottery, and the mounted Plains Indians abandoned pottery because it was too fragile to transport. All other groups gathered, mixed, and tempered clay to form pottery, a women's craft throughout North

America. Each region showed its own style, but the major technique was the same across the continent.

First the potter obtained a clay and fine sand. She washed the sand and ground the clay to a fine powder, carefully removing any foreign matter, and mixed them in just the right proportions. Sand acted as a temper, keeping the pot from cracking while it was being fired. But if there was too much sand, the pot became crumbly. Sand was the most common temper, but some women used crushed shell, crushed pieces of old pots, or plant fibers instead.

After mixing the clay with the temper, the potter added water until she could work the paste and form it into a roll or patty. She shaped the base of a pot using the bottom of an old pot as a mold, shaping the clay around it, or she might press out a disk of clay paste with her fingers. Once she was satisfied with the base, she made rolls of clay a foot or so long and about an inch in diameter. She built up the side of the pot by spiraling these rolls of clay around the base, higher and higher, thinning the sides as she built them up. As she added each new coil, she pressed it in place and smoothed it with a bit of shell or stone, or a piece of dried gourd.

When the shape and size were right, the potter put the pot aside to dry. After it was dry, she smoothed it once more and added a thin mixture of sand and clay and water to the outer surface to create a finish called a *slip*. This gave a background for painting a design or for a polished surface. If there was to be a design, she painted it on freehand before she fired the pot; designs painted after firing were not permanent. Some potters cut designs into the paste with a sharp tool, pressed them on with a serrated shell, or stamped them with a carved paddle.

When the paint had dried, the potter put her pot, upside down, on stones over hot coals, with any other pottery that needed firing. She covered the pottery with old broken pots to keep the heat even. If flames or smoke touched it, they would leave black smudges. The temperature of the fire was about 1,200 degrees Fahrenheit, and the pottery remained on the fire for two or three hours. With tongs or sticks, the potter removed her pots after firing and let them cool.

Stone Working

For cutting and piercing implements, projectile points, axes, and knives, stone was the Indians' most important material. Stone that was easy to carve, like catlinite or soapstone, made excellent dishes and containers as well as pipe bowls. In fact, catlinite (named after the famous painter of Indian life, George Catlin) is often called *pipestone*. The Indians drilled colorful rocks like turquoise for beads to string into necklaces.

Making Stone Tools. Men worked stone by flaking, grinding, and polishing, matching the technique to the kind of stone. Flint is easy to chip or flake, but a granular stone like quartzite is less easy to control. Some stone, like slate, takes a very high polish. The earliest people to cross the Bering Strait undoubtedly knew simple stone-working techniques; later people developed their own in the New World.

Tools to work stone were other stones, bone, antler, wood, and copper. To make a projectile point, a man chose a suitable pebble or nodule of stone, and struck it to chip off some flakes and rough out a leaf-shaped blade. This usually was done with another stone called the *hammer stone*. Then with a more refined tool like a piece of bone or antler he put pressure first on one side, then on the other, detaching flakes to leave a sharp edge and the notches or stem required. Taking time and care, an expert flint knapper could work very fine large or small points. Yurok stone workers made great ceremonial blades of *obsidian* (volcanic glass).

Drilling. Stone was polished and ground with an abrasive, usually sand, moistened and held on leather or a wad of plant fiber, or with a block of sandstone, pumice, or other abrasive rock. Workers also drilled stone and shell, bone, ivory, and pottery with an abrasive. Drills were twirled by hand, with dry or wet sand at the point of contact to increase the friction. Drill heads were copper, stone, bone, and wood. Men also used slender, hollow cane filled with sand as drills. More complex drills rotated faster and cut more quickly. The strap drill was kept upright and in position by a wooden head that the driller held in his teeth. The driller wound a strap once around the shaft, then pulled it from side to side. The *bow drill* was similar except that the driller pulled the bow that held the strap from side to side with one hand, holding the shaft in the other. The more complex pump drill made the shaft revolve faster than the others did by a pumping motion which the driller gave to attachments slipped over the shaft. These drills could perforate even the hardest substances, like granite.

Leather Work

Women usually did all the skin dressing; only Pueblo men and a few in California processed hides. Except for some regional variations, the treatment for curing hides was the same in all areas. Nowhere did Indians apply the chemical most used for tanning hides today, tannic acid; instead they softened skins by physical manipulation.

First the woman skinned the carcass, and while the hide was still soft she staked it out, flesh side up, or stretched it in a frame. Then she scraped all fat and flesh from the skin. If she wanted fur, she left the hair on; if not, she scraped both sides with stone or bone implements. She then treated the hide with a skin-dressing mixture, usually a paste of mashed brains from the animal that supplied the hide, sometimes with a bit of the liver or marrow added. Human urine was another common skin-dressing material. After this treatment, she manipulated the hide to make it supple, sometimes by pulling it around the trunk of a rough tree, or over a stretched rope or a smooth rounded stake driven into the ground. Eskimo women often chewed skins to soften them. For a tan or buff color, the hide worker smoked her hides by suspending them over a low fire in a pit.

Indians also made rawhide, which is untanned or uncured leather, remarkable for its toughness and durability. Fresh hide was stretched on a frame or pegged to the ground just like hides being cured, but it was allowed to dry for several days without chemicals or manipulation. Plains Indians made their parfleche containers of rawhide, which, made into rawhide shields, also was excellent protection against arrows.

Metal Work

In pre-Columbian times, Indians north of Mexico did not know how to extract metal from ore by smelting. Around Lake Superior and the Copper River in Alaska, though, copper appeared naturally in pure form, and the Indians mined it. They shaped the nuggets of copper by hammering and grinding them, sometimes heating the copper early in the hammering, but not hot enough to melt the metal.

In the Midwest and Northeast where Indians traded Lake Superior copper, metalworkers hammered copper into breastplates, earrings, pendants, and other decorative and ritual items. They also made copper knives, projectile points, drills, and awls, but copper was too soft to replace stone for most utilitarian objects.

The Northwest Coast people got copper from the Alaskan source and hammered it into the ornamental shields known as coppers. With stones they pounded the metal flat, occasionally heating it to make it less brittle. To decorate the coppers, craftsworkers hammered raised patterns into the copper from the back or incised designs on the front.

There is evidence that Indians used iron from meteorites when they were lucky enough to find it. They treated it too by hammering.

In the middle nineteenth century some Spanish-Mexican itinerant craftsworkers taught a few Navajo men to hammer silver ornaments from coins, cutting the thin metal with shears and incising some designs. The Navajo copied Spanish motifs and items, and through the years elaborated and refined their artistry to produce beautiful squash blossom necklaces and concha belts. Traders made silver available in ingot and sheet form, and also acted as intermediaries to sell the finished products. At no time did Indians mine silver ore. Silversmithing spread to the Pueblo who further enhanced the art with settings of turquoise, shell, and other materials. The old hammerwork yielded place to sandcast silver made with a mold of *tufa* or volcanic pumice. The silversmith then filed and polished the casting. Today many other techniques are used in response to burgeoning commercial demands.

Basketry

Basketmaking is a very old craft in America. Archaeologists have found remains of baskets dating to around 8000 B.C. in the Basin. Natives of North America wove basketry everywhere, though it was rare in the Arctic. From it they made containers, mats, fish traps, hats, rainwear, and cradles. Women were the basketmakers, though men made fish traps and cradles in some areas.

Basket weavers used a variety of materials, depending on what grew nearby. Indians of the Northwest Coast made much of their work from spruce roots, and Southeastern people chose cane, reeds, and palmetto fronds. Other important materials were vines, grasses, and slender strips or twigs of wood. The two techniques in this craft were coiling and weaving. Woven baskets had a background of one set of parallel fibers, through which the craftsworkers wove other fibers crosswise. The coiled basket was built up in a spiral.

Indians made some containers large enough to hold an adult and some so small that the weave was almost invisible. The latter probably were toys. Some basketmakers left their materials a natural color; others dyed theirs. To make a pattern, women wove in dyed or naturally colored fibers. Northwest Coast weavers painted some of their designs. Pomo basketmakers were famous for their work decorated with bird feathers and tiny shells or beads. Though experts give the Pomo credit for the most intricate and skillful work, other people of California, the Great Basin, and the Southwest produced very fine basket work.

Western basketmakers often used their baskets for stone boiling, which required very tightly woven containers. Some of these could hold water even without further treatment, but for better waterproofing the women often coated their cooking baskets with pitch and asphaltum where they could get it.

Painting, Dyes, and Pigments

Indians applied color and designs to their persons, their clothes, their homes and their tools. On their bodies, paint was both decorative and functional; it might indicate social connections, warlike intent, or great deeds. Men painted their shields with symbols of their guardian spirits and their tipis with designs telling of their success in hunting and warfare. In the Pacific Northwest, the painted and carved crest figures usually described family connections. Painting on pottery, katcina masks, and dolls in the Southwest often represented rain, clouds, and sun.

Indians applied paint with their hands or fingers, with sticks, and with crude brushes made of twigs or fibrous material chewed or pounded at one end until pliable. Sometimes they took paint in their mouths and sprayed it on. Plains people often used a piece of bone spongy enough to hold paint and sharpened to make a fine line. For paint containers, people often used shells, where they could find them, and the Pueblo made little clay pots.

Indians made their colors from plants and minerals. For paint pigments, they used inorganic materials. They got red, yellow, and browns from earth containing iron ore, black from soot or graphite, white from clay, limestone, and gypsum, and green and blue from copper ore. The artist ground the pigments on mortars and mixed them with grease or saliva. Dyes came from organic sources: brown and red from roots and barks, white and yellow from grasses and rushes, and others from berries and lichens. They used dyes to color quills, basket materials, yarns, and fabrics.

Textiles

In addition to hides and furs, people in some areas wore clothing made of woven fabrics. Indians made yarn for weaving from plant fibers like the inner bark of cedar and other trees, or, in the Southwest, cotton. They also used wool from buffalo, mountain goats, dogs, and other animals. Women did most of the weaving, though Pueblo men also wove. Only the Pueblo had a real loom; the other weavers merely suspended threads from a horizontal bar (perhaps stretched between two trees) and twined other yarns over and under. The foundation yarns (those hanging vertically from the bar) are called the *warp* yarns; the weaving yarns are called the *weft* yarns. Often the two were of the same material. Chilkat weavers on the Northwest Coast used warp yarns of cedar bark and weft yarns of mountain goat hair; the Great Basin people used warp of plant fiber and weft of strips of rabbit skin to make their rabbit blankets.

Weavers created patterns in their weaving by using dyed yarns rather than by changing the weave, which varied little in their woven products. In the Southeast, people sometimes used bird feathers to decorate their cloth of *bast* (inner bark). Chilkat blankets and skirts were woven work

A group of Navajo women spinning and weaving outside a traditional hogan.

of great beauty, worn only by high-ranking individuals on special occasions. Pueblo Indians alone wore woven fabrics as their daily clothing. The Navajo learned weaving from the Pueblo. After they acquired sheep from the Spaniards, Navajo women began to spin sheep wool and weave their well-known blankets.

Toys

To amuse and quiet infants, parents made toys like rattles and objects hung from the cradle. Older children played with miniature copies of adult implements—bows, dolls, and sleds. Today these toys might be classified as educational, for the children learned some adult practices by playing. Even the toy katcina doll taught the children about the kinds of katcina spirits. Of course, like all children, the young Indians also invented their own toys.

The Eskimo, with their long winter isolation, made more toys than any other native Americans. Their children played with toy boats, sleds, weapons, carved dolls and animals, and household utensils. Eskimo carved dolls and animals from wood, ivory, bone, and stone, often clothing dolls in furs and making beds, lamps, and other doll furniture. Children in all areas also played with toys like building blocks, balls, and tops, made from the native materials of their region.

Dramatic Arts

Every ceremonial presentation had its dramatic aspects. It is nearly impossible to separate what we would call the performing arts from the rituals in which they were imbedded. Regular patterns of movement, music, and recitation appeared in many ceremonies, but nonreligious drama, like plays, pantomimes, or operas, did not exist in pre-Columbian times, and neither did professional actors. Perhaps the closest any Indian groups came to our theater was the winter performances on the Northwest Coast, re-creations of clan and tribal legends in song and dance, with some spoken parts. These also included elaborate costumes greatly valued by their owners. Pueblo ceremonies in the open plaza also had expressive episodes, with dancers representing spirits, clowns, and heroes. Here too the dramatic effects were heightened by costumes, paint, and masks. Many Southwestern societies performed dances in public, including the very popular clowns or "delight makers."

Dance and Music

Like drama, dancing and music were an inseparable part of the military, religious, or social activities directed toward community welfare or personal glory. Unlike European dances, which are often a means of personal expression and social interaction, Indian dances were dictated by tradition and were mainly symbolic. Group dances, performed in a circle or oval, were the most common form in the Southwest, prairies, and woodlands, and straight-line dancing was popular in the Plains, Basin, and Plateau. The rhythmic gestures and movements of dancing varied from Pueblo dancing, which was slow, almost hypnotic, to the Plains kind, which sometimes approached frenzy. Some dances were only for one sex, and some were performed by just one dancer. Sometimes special clothing or costumes were required.

Dancing was usually accompanied by percussion instruments and chanting, the main form of Indian music. There were no purely instrumental performances, and no harmony singing or playing. Drums, rasps, rattles, and clappers were common, but the only Indian instrument that could play a melody was the flute or flageolet. This was used mostly for courting: a young man played love songs on it when he went wooing by blowing into one end and controlling the tones with finger holes.

Folklore

Indians had no written literature; their myths, legends, tales, and fables were passed down orally by each generation. Like the other arts, folklore

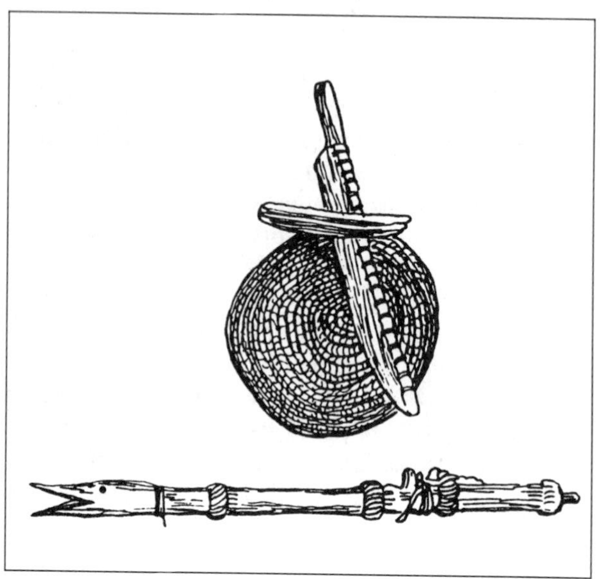

A rasp and a flute. To play the rasp a musician dug a small hole in the ground and placed the circular basket upside down over it. The pointed end of the rasp was placed top-center on the basket; the cylinder end was held in the musician's left hand. Sound was produced by running the scraper back and forth over the notched surface of the rasp. The basket and hole acted as an amplifer-resonator.

played an important part in daily existence, reflecting the people's concerns and problems. In the absence of science as we know it, folklore explained the mysteries of life: why people die, why evil exists, and how nature works. It described the beginnings of the world and the creation of people and animals. It told about a tribe's origin and history, and the great deeds of their people. In addition, some tales had morals that showed what happened when someone did not observe the proper ways of the tribe. Such tales performed part of the function we call *socialization*, teaching children the traditional, proper behavior. And of course many stories were just entertainment, humorous tales to make people laugh, or adventure stories about some culture hero.

Characters In Folklore. While some folklore themes or characters stayed within one language group or culture area, many crossed cultural and linguistic boundaries, and some were almost universal. People everywhere told stories about animals, wise and powerful or weak and foolish. Most Indian societies also handed down fables about giants, little people, and witches. A common character was the trickster, who deflated the pompous and did many things forbidden to human beings. He provided not only comic relief from life's trials but a chance for vicarious enjoyment; listeners naturally sympathized with the way the trickster flouted social conventions. Often tricksters were animals: Coyote, Bluejay, Raven, Hare, and Mink were among the most prominent. Bodies of legends about these beings are called "trickster tales." In the legends beginning the chapters of Part II, you have read of some tricksters: Coyote, Inktomi, and Manabozho (Chippewa) or Manabush (Menominee). In New England, the trickster was Gluskap or Kluskabe; and the Cree trickster was Wisagatcak, which Europeans mispronounced Whiskey Jack. Probably the popularity of trickster tales is the most characteristic feature of Indian oral tradition.

Another common figure was the Earth Diver, an animal (usually) who helped create the world. Earth Diver legends told about how the world began as a piece of earth or mud brought up from an endless sea that was all of existence. Usually Earth Divers gave their soil or mud to the culture hero, sometimes called Creator, sometimes Earth Maker. Occasionally Earth Divers themselves created the world.

In many legends, Indians portrayed the culture hero not as an animal but as a human figure, a demigod or superhuman who put the world in its present state. Often Indian tales blended the hero with the trickster, shown sometimes as human, sometimes as animal. Manabozho, Gluskap, and others appeared both wise and foolish, just as humans do, at different times.

Folklore Themes. Parts of native American folklore were common to many areas, but culture areas did have their own typical themes and figures. Eskimo tales were less varied than those of most other peoples. The tale of the goddess Sedna, who created the sea mammals from her fingers, was told by most Eskimo groups, but there were few other Eskimo stories. Plateau people emphasized trickster pranks and mischief in their folklore—coyote was trickster throughout the Plateau—and as you might guess, Northwest tales had much to say about social rank and proper behavior. The trickster theme also was popular there, and so were stories about sea mammals and salmon. Gluttony was a popular trickster motif along the Pacific Coast. The long winters and normally adequate food supply gave time for not only the clan dramas and winter ceremonials, but also much storytelling. California folklore was meager, like the Eskimo's, and focused on trickster and creation mythology, especially the Earth Diver theme.

All types of stories were told in the Plains, probably because of the people's varied backgrounds, and also in the Eastern woodlands, both north and south. Iroquois tales often dealt with cruel relatives, cannibalism, and monsters, as well as with creation. Twins, one good and one bad, were the Iroquois culture heroes. The Southeastern people emphasized animal tales of the Uncle Remus sort, with animals that behaved like people and plots with a moral. Southwestern people told many long and complicated stories of creation with many characters rising from lower worlds. The Subarctic Algonkians shared the legends of the other Algonkians, and the Subarctic Athabaskans tended to borrow their folklore from whatever cultures were nearest. Among the agriculturalists, stories about how Indians got corn, beans, and squash were very common, and hunting peoples leaned toward story plots involving the dangers and problems of the hunt.

Religious Beliefs

Ideas about the supernatural were part of every aspect of Indian life. People looked for supernatural assistance in everyday doings as well as in life's crises. Hunters wanted spirit aid for success in hunting, agriculturalists for good crops, warriors for victory in battle. That much we know. But we have difficulty reconstructing pre-Columbian beliefs and practices, and the earliest written material comes to us from people who misconstrued what they saw and heard. For example, the idea of a sole god or "The Great Spirit" was simply incorrect interpretation on the part of observers. No groups in America north of the Rio Grande had such a monotheistic belief system. "The Happy Hunting Ground" was another popular fallacy Europeans ascribed to Indians.

Supernaturals of many sorts filled the Indian world. Some, like Sedna of the Eskimo, were gods and goddesses. Others were semidivines or demigods, culture heroes like Manabozho of the Algonkians. And then there were spirits of fields, trees, lakes, and other aspects of nature. Some Indians named these spirits, some did not. It is difficult for us to grasp how people felt in societies where every act and event had supernatural significance. To the Indians, the world of nature was alive with spirits, and generally superior to the human world. Spirits could withhold food and goods if people behaved badly, and could reward them for patience and perseverance.

Supernatural Power

Almost all Indian peoples believed in a general power beyond the spirits, a force in the universe that has been likened to electricity. It was impersonal; it ran throughout nature; and it could be tapped if one had the right knowledge and equipment. This was the force or power that the individual usually sought on the vision quest. But rarely is it clear exactly what difference Indians saw between this natural force and specific spirits. Perhaps they were never clear about it themselves, for they were quite practical and sought help from all sources. And they had no way of recording ideas of any tribal philosophers who may have thought about the nature of the supernatural. The Indian attitude toward supernatural aid seems to have been that if one type was good, more were better, and there were no hard and fast categories.

Though people throughout native America believed in a generalized world force, the words for it varied: Algonkians called it *manitu*, the Siouan, *wakonda*, and the Iroquoian, *orenda*. Other linguistic groups had their own terms, but the idea was the same: there was general power more potent than humankind. Some groups may have believed in power, spirit, and deity condensed into one being that early European observers recorded as the Great Manitu, but we really do not know how much of that was Indian and how much came from Europeans hoping to find Indian parallels to Christian beliefs.

Although we find no evidence of monotheism, some tribes seem to have had high gods or more important gods as well as lesser beings and the idea of a general world force. The Pawnee deity, Tirawa, lived in the upper sky above the Winds, the Sun, and the Stars, all of which were spirits. Tirawa had given everything necessary to humans when he created the earth with the help of his fellow spirits, the four Air Powers: Wind, Cloud, Lightning, and Thunder. Stars looked after humans and each was a patron of a Pawnee village. The Pawnee believed the offspring of the union between the warrior Morning Star and his mate, Evening Star, was a human girl, and the offspring of the Sun and the Moon was a human boy. They were the first human beings. The Pawnee thus believed in many supernatural beings besides Tirawa; they clearly were not monotheistic.

Another body of religious beliefs found throughout native American societies concerned physical and psychological conditions of human beings. Indians recognized that some kinds of disability, like broken bones and wounds, had natural causes, but they believed that many of the body's ills came from either the spirit world or witchcraft. Individuals could do little to prevent illness caused by witchcraft, but the right observances could keep them in good grace with the supernatural and prevent disease from that source. Therefore Indians carefully observed the tribal taboos, of which those associated with food and sex were most common; probably every tribe had some kind of food that was taboo. Witchcraft explained the inexplicable. It answered the question, "Why me?" In a world that had no concept of random chance, people wanted to know why a particular person suffered misfortune rather than someone else. The only answers, it seemed to them, were either that the supernaturals were angry or else it was magic. If one had observed the taboos and lived properly, it must then be magic, witchcraft.

Souls

Indians also believed in soul sickness, arising from loss or theft of the soul. If the soul was not recovered, the victim died. After death, according to some groups, the soul went to a western land or land of the ancestors. This afterworld was a dull place, a pallid copy of life, or a reverse image of life—by no means a "Happy Hunting Ground."

Algonkians conceived of the soul as a shadow; the Shasta thought it was invisible but could leave a trail and footprints. Omaha believed it glided through the air, and Bella Coola and Tsimshian thought of it as a bird or butterfly. Belief that the souls of the dead appeared as owls was fairly widespread. And many tribes believed in two souls, one that died when the body died, and one that might wander on, though it too might die. Some groups, like the Eskimo, believed in multiple souls. In some areas the soul of a dead person—the ghost—was greatly feared, for it tried to seek out the living, for whom it was lonely, and take them away. Even while they mourned for their dead, those people pleaded with the ghosts to go and stay away.

Religious Behavior

In almost all areas of America, Indian men and some women sought individual power. This was true regardless of what religious specialists their community might have, for personal power was essential for almost every endeavor. At the mercy of capricious nature, people knew that death from hunger, disease, or enemies was never far away; to survive, they felt a need for some powerful assistance. Calling the search for this help the vision quest may be misleading; in many culture areas, people could get power without having a vision. Most often, though, power did come through a vision.

Visions and Personal Power

Visions came usually in the form of animals, but occasionally as sun, stars, or other natural objects. The vision indicated that one had gained power through a personal protector, a guardian spirit that would protect the seeker and impart spiritual power. Usually one made contact with a spirit by acts of purification—bathing, sweating, fasting, vomiting—

until the body and mind were clean and acceptable to the supernatural. Adolescent boys sometimes worked physically to make themselves receptive to a guardian spirit by dancing, self-flagellation, mutilation, or swallowing or inhaling drugs. At important times or crises in adulthood, people used the same ways of getting in touch with the spirit world. The power they received gave them special abilities in hunting, warfare, acquiring wealth, or reaching any goals they might desire.

The vision quest was by far the most popular way of getting power, but not the only one. The Blackfoot bought power in medicine bundles that contained powerful medicine (that is, sacred objects and charms), and sometimes charms and incantations were enough to bend the supernatural to one's will. Incantations acted upon the spirit world with compulsive force, if one adhered rigidly to the proper form. When incantations did not work, Indians blamed a lapse of memory or slip of the tongue. Beseeching the deities with prayer and pleas was another way of communicating. Prayers were more commonly addressed to animal, weather, and general spirits and deities than to the impersonal power, though one might approach it too in that way.

Religious Specialists

When one could not get results by personal contacts, it was time to call in religious specialists. Everywhere in native America there were shamans who could communicate with the supernatural easily and who usually had several personal spirits or ''familiars.'' Along with shamans, the Pueblo and some other groups had priests. Whereas shamans got their power by direct contact with the supernatural, priests' powers came from formal training. Shamans might have some training as apprentices to old shamans, and priests might have visions, but the priests got their power from education rather than the personal religious experiences that were the essence of the shaman's power.

Shamans. The word *shaman* comes from Tungus, the language of the Tungus, a Siberian tribe well known for its shamanism. Both men and women were shamans, though in most societies women were not eligible until after menopause. The other names we use for shamans—medicine men, witch doctors, rainmakers, curers—indicate the wide range of shamanistic duties. The shaman's general ability to contact the spirit world meant that he was important and powerful almost everywhere, because people needed him and sought his advice. And since he could manipulate the supernatural, the shaman was often feared. The line between using the spirit world to benefit society and using it for selfish or antisocial purposes was narrow, and shamans often were suspected of witchcraft.

The shaman's greatest responsibility probably was curing. It was mainly the diseases thought to have supernatural causes that shamans treated, though most shamans had good knowledge of medicinal herbs and often treated problems like constipation and nausea as well. Supernatural disease had two causes: either it had been put into the body in the form of some object like a stone or stick by the supernatural or by a witch, or the soul had been lost or stolen. The shaman had to remove the object causing the illness or retrieve the soul. Sucking, through a straw or other implement or by placing the lips directly on the body, was the usual technique for removing the foreign object that brought sickness. The shaman usually concealed something in his mouth to spit out at the end of his performance, showing that the cure had been effective. Sometimes he bit his tongue and spit out a little blood too. To bring back a soul, people believed the shaman somehow sent his own soul or one of his spirits to recover it. Shamans performed these cures accompanied by chanting, drumming, dancing, tobacco smoking, and the like, usually with a number of people watching. The shaman often called for confessions from the patient, which would not cure germ-produced disease or organic disabilities but was very effective on psychosomatic disorders, because it reduced tension and relieved anxiety.

Among all the curers, perhaps none was more aptly called a medicine man than the Navajo shaman. His cures took days and involved not only the usual activities but also preparing elaborate dry paintings. Navajo were more interested in bodily states than most other native peoples, and a curing ceremony always drew a large crowd of spectators.

In larger tribes, shamans tended to specialize: some treated with dreams, some sucked out disease, and some did little curing but emphasized weather control and predicting the future. In the small groups, one or two shamans took care of all needs including treatment with herbal remedies, setting broken bones, and cleaning wounds.

Payments for shamanistic services varied, and they were usually returned if the treatment did not work. Occasionally shamans were killed when a patient failed to recover.

Shamans often required the patient to appease the supernatural or make amends for bad behavior, since much sickness was the patient's own fault for not observing taboos. Offenders atoned with both confession and punishment, appeasing the spirits with body mutilation and dietary restrictions. Confession of guilt, usually in public, was common among the Eskimo and Iroquois, and was often followed by mild punishments such as fasting or purging. On the Plains, making a vow to perform a ceremony was an accepted way of atoning for transgressions.

Shamanistic practices on the North American continent probably

A Blackfoot medicine man. The painting on his face, his necklace, and the decorations on his fur hat all relate to his magical power.

varied less than almost any other aspect of religion, but there were a few regional differences. In the Northwest, where rank was so important, some shamans inherited their power and combined religious functions with civil power by being house or town chiefs. The Hupa of California had a dancing shaman who located the cause of disease and a sucking shaman who cured it. Mojave shamans received their power by dreaming, as did many in California, and the Delaware also had dreamers who foretold the future. Eskimo shamans, besides curing, foretold weather conditions and located whales, seals, and other food animals. Shamans often went along on war parties even though war leaders were always expected to have their own power. Shamans were also very important politically in most tribes, partly because they were feared as well as respected. Shamans were least important among the Pueblo, where any undue individualism was suspect, and they were relatively unimportant in the Plains and the Plateau, where every man—and many women in the Plateau—sought spirit power and communicated often with the supernatural.

Priests. Priests are specialists in group ritual, and priests in Indian societies organized and directed major tribal ceremonies. They acted not as individuals, like shamans, but as representatives of the tribe. Priests were most common in larger societies with elaborate religious systems. The Iroquois Keepers of the Faith, who were responsible for six major ceremonies each year, were typical priests. The most highly organized priesthoods developed among the Pueblo, but healing associations such as the Algonkian Midewiwin can be classified as priesthoods, and on the Northwest Coast the town or tribal chiefs performed priestly functions in the ceremonials. The Creek of the Southeast had town priests influential in civil and military affairs, and the Great Sun of the Natchez was considered a divinity, high priest of the tribe, and a descendant of the sun. The priesthoods actually controlled civil and military affairs among the Pueblo, whose government may be considered a theocracy.

It was their formal training in religious duties and ceremonial roles that separated priests from shamans. Also, priests often did not have personal contact with the supernatural. The length of training for ritual performances varied. The Midewiwin organization of the Western Great Lakes tribes was set up in degrees, and only a few ever attained the fourth degree in the Midewiwin hierarchy. Creek priests attended a school where they were trained in the necessary lore and sent out for direct contact with the spirit world. The Creek had three degrees of proficiency, and the war leaders and high priests for town ceremonies were chosen only from those who had reached the third degree.

All these ways of reaching the spirit world may seem ambiguous, and the many categories of spirit beings and types of religious behavior may look contradictory and overlapping, but Indians saw no inconsistency. They thought it only sensible to try every possible way of getting help.

Religious Ceremonies

The ceremonies in North America that we will consider are those that lasted for a day or more and had to do with the supernatural—not social ceremonies such as athletic events and puberty rituals or short medical ceremonies. Hunters and gatherers held ceremonies mostly for success in the hunt, plentiful wild-plant foods, and fertile game animals. Agriculturalists celebrated the crops, particularly corn, and controlled the weather. The famous rain dance was not one but many dances performed by Indians of dry lands to bring rain. In the Southeast, controlling weather meant more than bringing rain, for flood control was also important. Major ceremonies generally had something to do with the most important source of food. Most areas also had ceremonies for general well-being, world renewal, and thanksgiving, many of which were incorporated in the longer tribal ceremonials.

The whole tribe took part in some ceremonies; others belonged to an association or secret society. Some too were part public and part private. Many dances were performed for the entire community and were followed by private rites for members of the society sponsoring the affair, or for men of special rank or social status like chiefs and shamans. Almost always combinations of activities went on simultaneously—dancing, drumming, singing, prayer, recitation. Most ceremonies took place outdoors, but the Pueblo held many in the kiva, their ceremonial chamber. In other areas, special structures were raised for the occasion, like the lodge for the Sun Dance on the Plains. Many ceremonies called for long purification of those taking part before and after as well as during performances. Some ceremonies were held regularly at appointed times, like the solstice ceremonies of the Hopi, but others were held only when an individual vowed to give a performance—the Cheyenne Sun Dance, for instance. Others were held any time a contact with the supernatural seemed advisable.

Regional Rituals

The Arctic, Subarctic, Plateau, and Basin lacked the formal, lengthy ritual life that is truly ceremonial. There populations were sparse, and rites focused on individual rather than community occasions. Plains people had many ceremonies for tribal and personal well-being and to celebrate the life of the hunter, the most spectacular and widely performed being the Sun Dance. Some tribes gave an annual performance during the summer hunt when all the bands had assembled, while others held it only to fulfill a vow. The Sun Dance had common features everywhere: special preparation of the lodge or tipi, its ceremonial raising, dancing lasting one to four days. For almost all who observed it, the total period of the Sun Dance was eight days. Dancers blew whistles in many performances, and voluntary self-laceration was common in some groups. Other Plains ceremonies were held by the warrior or men's societies or, in a few tribes, women's societies.

In the Southwest, the Pueblo had almost endless ceremonial life—more than a hundred days out of each year, by one estimate. Part of almost every Pueblo ceremony took place in private in the kiva of the religious society officiating. Initiation into the societies was an important

Hopi life was intimately tied to ceremony and religion. Among this group of costumed performers are the young women in the foreground, whose "squash blossom" hairstyle indicates marriageablity.

part of Pueblo ceremonial life. Pueblo ceremonials were rich in symbols of rain, clouds, and thunder.

The Navajo and Apache had extended curing ceremonies directed by shamans, and elaborate public girls' puberty ceremonies attended by masked dancers. These rituals were complicated and elaborate, with dry paintings, chanting, masks, and dancing, but they were not held with seasonal regularity like the great Plains or Pueblo ceremonials, and they were directed more toward individual health and well-being than the food quest or tribal life.

In California, extended ceremonies were tribal mourning observances or initiations into shamans' cults, first-fruit celebrations, world-renewal ceremonies, or performances for general well-being.

Northwest Coast peoples had many long, elaborate ceremonies, generally performed by cults or societies. One very important winter presentation, which re-created myths in song and dance, was a chance for high-ranking individuals to prove their rights to social status. Almost all Northwest Coast performances had something to do with social rank. People there used more costumes than most others and carved very elaborate masks.

Major ceremonials in the East were for agriculture, good crops, good weather, and thankfulness for bounty from the spirit world. The Busk or Green Corn Dance was widely performed.

Sacrifice

Indians sacrificed to all kinds of supernaturals—spirits, deities, the sky, the sun, the four (or six) cardinal points, and the stars. They also sacrificed to the winds, thunder, mountains, various manitu, and personal medicine bundles and guardian spirits. Dead ancestors and relatives often were presented with gifts. In return for their sacrifice people expected to receive benefits and escape evils. Sacrifice pleased the supernatural, which responded by giving people food and good health, good weather, and success in war. Most sacrifices were individual: they might involve tossing bits of food into fires for the spirits, adding rocks to piles, or offering first fruits. War leaders made sacrifices before an expedition, throwing food in the fire or blowing tobacco smoke into the air. Shamans prescribed sacrifice to cure illness. However, there were some tribal sacrifices in which many people took part, such as the Iroquois communal White Dog Ceremony, in which a white dog was sacrificed.

Tobacco was by far the most common sacrificial offering. People smoked it in pipes or tubes and also offered it loose. The smoke was considered a gift to the supernatural. Food, clothing, and adornment were also sacrificed, and, less often, hunting and fishing equipment. Like the Iroquois, the Illinois, Cree, Ottawa, and others sacrificed dogs; in buffalo country, the skin of a white buffalo was an acceptable offering. Skins of bears, too, were offered, and sometimes game animals like deer, elk, and moose. In the Southwest, the Pueblo, Navajo, and Apache sprinkled corn meal on the ground.

A warrior's self-mutilation was a kind of sacrifice—giving a piece of himself such as a finger or a strip of skin—but the only regular human sacrifice was offered by the Pawnee to the Morning Star. They tied up a captive woman and slew her with arrows, sending the symbolic Evening Star (the victim) to seek her husband, the Morning Star. Perhaps the Iroquois' torture and killing of war captives was a kind of sacrifice, for those victims often were dedicated to the supernatural, but revenge really was a stronger motive there. Wives of the Great Sun and some of his servants were killed when he died, which might also be considered a kind of sacrifice.

To sacrifice a game animal, people killed it, then burned it on a fire, often removing it partially burned to eat the remains. People also made sacrifices by putting objects like foods and gifts on poles, in trees, or on rocks. A gift of that sort might calm any supernatural who was angry with human behavior.

Religious Paraphernalia

Tobacco. Though Indians smoked tobacco for enjoyment, it was primarily a ritual item. Besides smoking it, they often burned it like incense, or blew powdered tobacco into the air as an offering. Sometimes they blew puffs of smoke specifically toward the supernatural; sometimes they offered the stem of the pipe to the four cardinal points and up and down. Tobacco was in many ways a sacred plant, grown by hunters and gatherers who cultivated no other crops and grown only by men where women were farmers. In one form or another it was essential in many curing ceremonies; Indians believed it would cure disease and wounds, prevent hunger and thirst, and stimulate the weary. Sometimes they ate it as an anesthetic, as the Great Sun's wives and servants did before being sacrificed.

Sacred Objects. From wing bones men fashioned the whistles they blew during the Sun Dance, and they considered eagle and bear claws to be powerful charms. Eagles and bears symbolized nature's power, mystery, and majesty, and Indians worshiped them across the continent. Bones and claws were useful, but feathers and down were most important. They symbolized a warrior's deeds or coups; they were attached to masks, rattles, and prayer sticks for ceremonial occasions; and down was scattered in the air or sprinkled on costumes in ceremonies.

Many tribes had their own sacred objects in addition to the sacred items common to many. The Pueblo and some other groups used *prayer sticks* to honor or appeal to spirits. These were decked with feathers, plumes, or down to convey prayers to the supernatural, and with small packets of food or tobacco as offerings. The Kiowa of the southern Plains had a small stone image called *taime*, which vaguely resembled the head and shoulders of a man and was decorated with down, feathers, and images of the sun and moon. They kept it in a parfleche and exposed it only once a year at the Sun Dance. The four Medicine Arrows of the Cheyenne were sacred, and the Arapaho had a special flat pipe that was kept by a priest with an ear of corn and a stone turtle in a bundle opened only on special occasions. Warriors' own medicine bundles held supernatural power and symbols of their guardian spirits.

Charms or fetishes were objects that possessed power and brought luck and success. Like rabbits' feet and four-leaf clovers, they were thought to enable their owners to accomplish more than they would otherwise. Some peoples, like the Zuni and Eskimo, manufactured them, carving animal forms of wood, rock, or ivory. Other charms were natural objects such as bear claws and eagle feathers. Charms found at the site of a vision were thought to have been given by the guardian spirit. Some were gifts, others were taken from a slain enemy, but in the owners' minds, fetishes had some connection with supernatural power.

Masks. Masks were worn in many religious ceremonies, sometimes only by priests and shamans, sometimes by all participants, because they were supposed to intensify the presence of the supernatural. Some masks were merely prepared heads of buffalo, deer, or other animals, and some were very complex with movable parts, of which the finest were made on the Northwest Coast. A mask gave its wearer the qualities of the thing it represented, and it was usually sacred in its own right. Masks were made only after the artist had attended to purification and other rituals, and they were put away carefully after use. Hopi and Apache were renowned for their masks in the Southwest, and the Iroquois for their false faces and cornhusk masks in the East.

In most areas, the mask was made by its wearer, though Pueblo masks were clan property. Pueblo passed their masks and other ceremonial paraphernalia from generation to generation, making new ones only when the old wore out. But the Northwest Coast was an area of specialists, and there craftsworkers made masks for others.

10

SOCIAL AND POLITICAL SYSTEMS

Hiawatha Belt, which records the formation of the Iroquois League.

Everywhere human beings organize into groups, for human survival depends on cooperation with others. From the moment of birth, which places us in our first kinship group, we live our lives in social groups. In Indian societies, as in ours, social groups got the work done, devised and carried out ways to exploit the environment, supplied new members to society, taught those new members the traditional ways of doing things, and protected and fed all members. Kinship was the tie that formed the most important Indian groups, but these were supplemented by organizations based on common interests, occupation, social status, sex, age, and neighborhood or locality. Sometimes Indians ranked their social groups, like the Natchez classes and the Northwest Coast kin groups.

Marriage

Marriage was the beginning of a new family, and it also formed or cemented alliances between families because it bound kinfolk as much as it did the man and woman. Always some people were kept apart by the incest taboo: the society banned their sexual union because of their kinship. Parents, children, and *siblings* (that is, brothers and sisters) could not marry each other, nor could any cousins who called each other "brother" and "sister." In addition, wherever people had clans, they almost always observed clan *exogamy*—no one could marry anyone in his or her own clan. Tribes that were divided into two moieties usually practiced moiety exogamy. In a very few cases, residents observed village exogamy.

Most societies were very permissive about premarital sexual experiences, with a few exceptions. The Cheyenne prized female virginity and marital faithfulness, and the Northwest Coast people, especially those in the higher ranks, carefully guarded marriageable females to ensure their virginity at marriage. By far the greater number of peoples considered premarital sexual relations a normal and expectable experience.

Arranging a Marriage

Guided by the group's prohibitions, one chose a spouse, usually in consultation with parents and other kinfolk, who helped make a wise decision. If kin opposed the choice too vigorously, the couple could elope, but apparently that seldom happened.

Throughout pre-Columbian America, marriage was a civil matter, not a religious one. It rarely involved any ceremony, except for the upper ranks of the Northwest Coast and the chieftains of the Southeast. In most areas the couple, with family approval, decided to live together, and the rest of the people recognized them as married, though people did not always consider the marriage truly established until a child was born.

Bridewealth. In the Plains and the Northwest, a marriage was not completed until the man presented a gift to the parents of the woman he wished to marry. That gift, called bridewealth or brideprice, was not a way of buying a wife but an acknowledgment that the parents were losing a daughter's services and should be compensated for that loss and for their time and effort in raising her. Bridewealth also established the rights of the man's kin line to the children of the marriage. Girls of high-ranking families brought the best bridewealth. As you would expect, horses were the bridewealth on the Plains, while cedar blankets, carved boxes, dentalia, and other goods were given on the Northwest Coast.

Elsewhere a man might make gifts to his wife's parents, but bridewealth was not so well defined or strictly required as in the Plains and Northwest. A Comanche woman expected her son-in-law to bring her a good portion of his game, and while there were no formal rules about it, people would have looked down upon any young man who did not fulfill this obligation.

Marriage was economically important for more than bridewealth and service; it joined the production efforts of man and woman. One person alone could not hunt, gather, cook, make clothing and tools, and protect himself, and without paid help, marriage was the best way of binding people for exchange of labor and mutual protection.

Residence. After marriage, the couple had to set up a home, sometimes moving into or near an existing household. The Iroquois man moved into his wife's longhouse; Hopi men and other Western Pueblo also moved in with their wives. Many times, women moved to join their husbands' households, or the couple might set up a new residence, though always in a community where one or the other had relatives. It was very unusual for a couple not to have some kinfolk nearby. Many families moved over the years, sometimes living with or near the man's kin, sometimes the woman's. No culture area had an unvarying residence pattern.

Affection and Divorce. Love had little to do with marriage, but husbands and wives expected that years of raising children and facing domestic problems together would make them fond of each other even if they felt little affection at the beginning. If a marriage proved unworkable, divorce was an acceptable way out, and in most areas one or the other spouse easily began the divorce simply by moving out of their common home. People separated for such reasons as sterility, laziness, lack of support, physical abuse, or incompatibility. Some groups, such as the Cheyenne, considered adultery immediate grounds for divorce, but others did not unless the adultery was frequent and flagrant. Bridewealth made divorce more complicated, because the girl's parents had to return the gifts unless the husband was obviously at fault. Among some matrilineal people, any woman who no longer wished to be married made a bundle of her husband's possessions and placed it outside the home. Seeing what she had done, he would take his things and return to his mother's home. Divorces usually required no more formality than marriage, and children of the marriage almost always stayed with their mother.

Polygamy

Most societies allowed *polygamy* (multiple marriage), though monogamy predominated everywhere. *Polygyny* (having more than one wife) occurred among all peoples except the Iroquois and the Western Pueblo, but few men could afford more than one wife even where custom allowed it. Even on the Plains after the horse came, where polygyny was most common, few men had more than four or five wives. *Polyandry* (having more than one husband) was very rare, occurring mostly among Eskimo and Basin people, where a woman might be married to two brothers. Some experts believe that even the Eskimo did not have true polyandry; they think that occasionally an older man would allow his younger brother sexual access to his wife, but only the older brother was married to her.

Sometimes polygyny followed the death of a spouse. Among all societies except those prohibiting polygyny, the practice of wife inheritance might lead to multiple marriage: a widow married her dead husband's brother, even if he already had a wife. In some places this practice was optional, in others it was mandatory. Another marriage custom in almost all tribes was somewhat similar, though it did not lead to multiple marriage: a widower often expected to receive a sister of his dead wife as a spouse. Both of these customs protected the single person, especially in environments where living alone meant almost certain death. When a dead spouse had no brothers or sisters, cousins took these roles. These practices emphasize how economically vital marriage was; the two sexes needed each other for much more than just sexual gratification.

It was not at all unusual among the Plains tribes for men to get wives by capturing them in warfare. Women captives were generally married by their captors, but most warriors married women of their own tribe first. Captives thus became secondary wives with low status, often no more than servants for the first or head wife.

The Family

Among the American Indians the family did most of the educating of the young and held the main responsibility for child rearing and welfare. In the very few societies that had formal schools, the schools provided training only for ritual positions. Within the family children learned to talk and to behave in approved ways; family life socialized children into adulthood. Parents, older siblings, and other relatives taught children etiquette, domestic duties, ceremonial behavior, artisanship, ways of getting food, and how to use weapons. Grandparents usually passed on folklore and tribal tradition.

The economic functions of marriage included the family as well; members pooled their labor and shared economic responsibility. Adults took care of the young, women by providing domestic care and men through hunting and defense. The extended family sheltered the aged, who in turn helped with child care and education.

The Indian family took several forms. The basic unit was the *nuclear family*, a man and woman and their children. Larger than the nuclear family was the *extended family*, which included another generation (that is, grandparents) or more wives. Another form was a group of sisters or brothers living together with their spouses and children, like the Iroquois longhouse family, with sisters and their husbands and children living in the same building. A true extended family was permanent; the people all lived together as a regular thing. All these types of family were found in aboriginal America, and almost all communities had some form of extended family.

Adoption

Children who had lost one or both parents and illegitimate children usually found a home with kinfolk who raised them as their own. War captives, particularly women and children, were often adopted too. Even adult male captives might be adopted to replace a dead family member, becoming faithful sons to their new parents though formerly they had been enemies.

Some tribes adopted members not only into families but into clans. A child or an adult adopted by a Iroquois family assumed not only the family connection but also the clan affiliation. On the other hand, among the Seminole, a child adopted into a family kept his biological mother's clan affiliation (Seminole were matrilineal).

Occasionally, whole groups were adopted. When the Tuscarora tribe moved north, the Oneida suggested to the League of the Iroquois that the whole tribe be adopted. The council agreed, creating the Six Nations where formerly there had been five.

Childhood

Children were universally desired, and were one reason a couple married. Infant mortality was high, and a child's death was considered a great tragedy. Few families had more than three children who lived to adulthood. Yet in spite of their love for children people sometimes practiced *infanticide*, deliberately killing a baby, usually because of famine and inability to feed the child. Infanticide—like killing or abandoning the aged—was practiced only in extreme circumstances. If a woman died in childbirth (and this was the most common cause of death among women of childbearing age), her baby might be buried with her even though it was alive. There was no way of caring for it unless another lactating woman could feed it, for Indians had no dairy animals in the days before Columbus. People also killed twins at birth in some areas where they were thought to be unlucky or evil, and many deformed children were not allowed to live. Infanticide was a decision to be made by the parents and was not criminal or illegal. It was a civic matter only if the child was older, when the clans or other kin groups might have some say in the matter.

The mothers's kin group usually raised illegitimate babies, though illegitimacy was apparently not always accepted. A few reports from the various culture areas indicate some killing of illegitimate newborns, and a few abortions as well, though information is scant on that subject.

Children were taught to behave by various forms of reward and punishment. Very young babies were treated with great permissiveness in most societies; they were hardly ever severely punished, but were loved, praised, and cajoled into proper behavior. As the children grew and learned to walk, their parents, older siblings, and others ridiculed them for misbehavior. In some societies, ridicule was the strongest punishment, but spanking and other physical punishment were administered too. Muskogeans of the Southeast scratched a child's arms and back with the teeth of garfish as punishment. The scratches showed for several days and publicly shamed the offender. In matrilineal societies, the maternal uncle disciplined older children, but the younger ones were chastised by their parents. Grandparents were less agents of discipline than figures of affection and tenderness.

Parents set small tasks for their young children, initiating them into the work they would do as adults. Girls learned sewing, cooking, gathering, and other women's tasks, and boys patterned their ways after their father, uncles, and older brothers. Older adults taught tribal ethics, codes of conduct, and religious customs by oral instruction and by personal example.

Indian children shared with each other. There was little private property even in adult society, and children rarely quarreled over toys. Older children helped care for their younger brothers and sisters, and sibling rivalry too is not recorded as common. Because of high infant mortality, few Indian families had many children. Some, like the Cheyenne, spaced their children widely. Older children were taught that the arrival of a new baby was a joyous event that reflected well on the whole family.

Rites of Passage

Every known society recognizes periods of change or crisis when the individual leaves one social status and enters another. Often these periods are celebrated with rituals: the Hebrew bar mitzvah, for example, marks the transition from childhood to adulthood. Such a transition is called a *rite of passage*.

All Indian groups celebrated rites of passage, some observing more than others. Northwest Coast people of high rank observed a child's first teeth or first steps by giving a potlatch. In some Indian societies, initiation into an age-grade or warrior association was an important rite of passage.

These rites generally separate people from their old status and incorporate them into new ones, and many such rites take the form of symbolic death. The Central Atlantic Algonkian initiation rite witnessed by the English settlers was a ritual of this sort. The "death" destroyed the boy or girl as a child, to be reborn into the new status of adult. At transition times, especially at childbirth or when the child becomes an adult, Indians believed that individuals were in a state dangerous to themselves and to society. Society usually avoided the danger by segregating the individuals. Almost all Indian groups acknowledged four passages in one way or another: birth, naming, puberty, and death. Some tribes, especially on the Northwest Coast, celebrated many more changes of status, but these four are the most common.

Birth

Though Indians wanted babies, they attached less importance to the baby at birth than to its mother. In many societies she was believed to be in

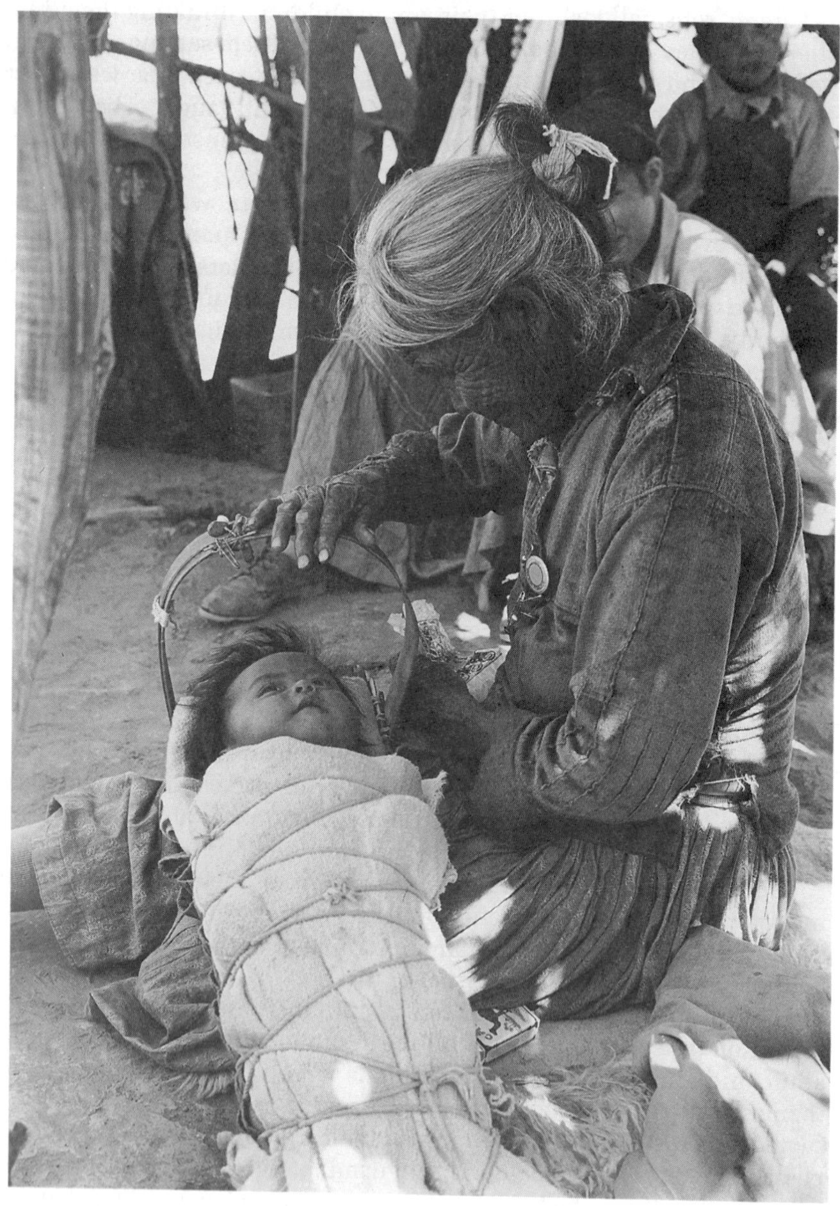

Navajo woman with her tightly swaddled grandchild on a cradle board.

a state of supernatural danger, not to herself but to the males of the community and to their hunting equipment and spiritual well-being. The danger covered her entire pregnancy, so many Indian societies secluded pregnant women not only at delivery but also for the full nine months. During that time women observed food and activity taboos. Delivery usually took place in a special hut with one or more women in attendance. Usually the umbilical cord was put away until the child was older and the afterbirth was buried. In the Basin and in a few societies in California, fathers too observed taboos, staying in bed for a time after the birth and following a restricted diet. At the end of her seclusion, the new mother bathed, then she and the baby made a public appearance at a feast or some other celebration, where the baby was presented formally to the sun, the moon, or the supernaturals.

Mothers kept their babies in cradles of many styles, strapping the cradles to their backs for transportation, standing them upright, or hanging them from a tree. It is said that the lullaby "Rockabye Baby" was an Indian song and referred to the cradleboard hanging on a tree. Among the Seminole the baby stayed in a hammock, and in the Northwest the cradle was a wooden box.

Naming

Male and female names were often but not always different. Babies usually received a name when they were first presented to their father, clan, band, or community, but some groups called the infant "baby" or "boy" or "girl" until the child exhibited some characteristic suggesting a name. In clan systems, clan names often were used for new members, and in some groups, names came from mothers' or fathers' dreams. Sometimes names were given in memory of an ancestor, although among some people names of the dead were never reused or even mentioned. For a child of high rank on the Northwest Coast, the naming and presentation ceremony was a lavish potlatch at which the parents gave gifts to all guests.

Indian naming practices seem confusing because Indians often changed their names as they grew older. Though sometimes the childhood name was the only name for life, except for nicknames, children in many tribes got new names at puberty—at the first menstruation for girls, and at initiation for boys. In addition, a boy might take a new name after finding a guardian spirit or after his first war party. If a Natchez rose in rank from Stinkard to Honored Man by bravery in war, he took a new name. Boys might also take clan names after distinguishing themselves. On the Northwest Coast, the successor to a chief took the chief's titles and names, but he had to validate his rights to them by giving a potlatch.

Such naming practices bewildered the Europeans, who had no parallel custom. If an Indian dropped a childhood name upon receipt of a new name at puberty, and many did, European record-keeping became very difficult—particularly when, over a valorous and long life, a person assumed ten or more names. Names were precious to their owners; assuming a name as a sign of honor or accomplishment was a very important occasion, marked with solemn rites.

In many societies it was considered bad manners to address someone directly by his or her personal name, which was thought of as private and sacred. Nicknames were used instead. In other societies, names could be purchased or loaned. All in all, names and the rites of naming were far more significant in Indian society than in Europe or in America today.

Puberty

Almost all North American people had special rites for a girl at menarche, her first menstruation, and many women went through similar but less rigorous observances during every menstrual period. Indians had two reasons for those rites: they believed that anything a girl did during her menarche influenced her whole life, and that menstrual blood was dangerous to hunters, game, and the supernatural. For these reasons girls were isolated and required to behave in certain ways. They were set tasks so that they would not be lazy, and they observed restricted diets so they would not be greedy. They used drinking straws and scratching sticks to keep from touching their heads, where supernatural influences were concentrated. While menstruating, they were careful not to pollute men's hunting equipment by touching it. On the Northwest Coast, where people coveted wealth, a pubescent girl did not work during her isolation, so that she might marry a chief and be waited on by slaves. Isolation and restriction usually ended with a feast at which it was announced publicly that the girl was ready to marry. Not all tribes had elaborate rituals, though; Hopi girls did not observe the taboos common elsewhere, but merely changed their style of hair dressing to show that they were marriageable.

Boys' puberty rites were not so directly connected with biological changes, but initiation ceremonies ending childhood were common: and some of them were true ordeals. Among the more severe trials were isolation and fasting, taking drugs, and body mutilation. Less severe practices included sweatbaths and taking part in a successful hunt. These exercises, like the girls' rites, were thought to influence the boy's future. On the Plains and elsewhere, some boys were initiated into associations at about the time of puberty, and the association's secrets were revealed to them by older members. Often several boys were initiated at the same time, especially in age-graded associations. The vision quest ordeal, on the other hand, was a solitary search for supernatural help. In southern California, visions were not left to chance. Boys were given a drink or infusion that induced hallucination. In some areas boys drank emetics and laxatives, symbolically wiping out the past and making a new, clean start.

Not all peoples held public ceremonies for girls and boys at puberty. Sometimes, as among the Hopi, girls were instructed by an older woman about the biological change and how to care for themselves. Boys sought a spirit helper, but without public recognition of their change from child to adult. There was some tendency for boys' puberty or initiation ceremonies to be dramatic where girls' rites were largely ignored, and vice versa, but this was by no means always true. In southern California, both girls and boys had elaborate public initiation ceremonies.

Death

The most common cause of death among women was childbirth; among men, it was warfare. The time of highest mortality for both sexes was infancy. Other causes of death were *geronticide* (killing or abandoning the aged) and suicide, which was not uncommon but about which we have very few data. Of course, many people died of disease and old age. After European germs spread through Indian communities, death rates leaped and disease became the major killer, far exceeding warfare.

Disposal of Bodies. Indians disposed of their dead in ways as simple as leaving the corpse on the ground or as elaborate as mortuary rites observed on and off for a year or more. Eskimo left their dead on the ground because they could not dig into permafrost, though they sometimes covered the bodies with stones. Disposal by burial was common, but Indians followed many other customs: cremating the corpse, embalming or mummifying it, disposing of bones in urns, and entombing bodies in trees or on scaffolds.

Most burials were in pits or graves in the ground, though some were in mounds or beneath houses. Many of the bodies were flexed, with knees drawn up, probably because that took less space—which was something to consider where people had only hoes and digging sticks. In the Southeast, secondary bone burial was common. Mourners buried the corpse, then exhumed it after most of the flesh had decayed. They called on a bone-picker, a ritual specialist unique to the Southeast, to remove all that was left of the tissues. Known as a Buzzard Man, he kept his fingernails very long to clean the bones efficiently, which he did in the presence of the mourners. Then the bones were either reburied or placed in a mortuary house. Sometimes bones were buried in communal pits called *ossuaries*, either individually or in urns.

In the Basin, human remains were often deposited in caves or fissures in rocks. Embalming and mummification apparently were used only in the central and south Atlantic coastal area. Tree or scaffold burials were widespread on the Plains: the bodies were wrapped in skins, then laid on a platform or scaffolding or in the crotch of a tree. On the Northwest Coast, the dead were placed in wooden mortuary cabins or in boxes or canoes raised on posts, which were decorated with the crests of the family line if the deceased was important. Cremation was a common means of disposal in California.

Mourning. Mourning rites varied. Many people placed food and possessions of the dead person in or near the grave, which relatives might visit for a time with other offerings. On the Plains, a man's favorite horse was usually sacrificed at his death; slaves occasionally were killed in the Northwest, and often a wife among the Natchez. In some tribes, relatives mourned for a set time and many cut their hair, especially the widow. California tribelets mourned with much wailing and overt grief, with long ceremonies and an anniversary mourning ritual after one year, and sometimes again after another had passed. Among the Hopi, too, mourning meant wailing on the day of the death, and more crying a year later. Many people discarded personal ornaments or blackened their faces, and some gashed their arms and legs to shed blood as a sign of great sorrow. Navajo and Apache greatly feared the dead, or rather the ghost of the dead, no matter how well loved the individual might have been in life. They buried the corpse quickly and observed a mourning period of four days. If the death occurred in a dwelling, it was burned or abandoned.

Clans and Other Large Groupings

A clan is a unilineal descent group whose members consider themselves related, having descended from a common ancestor. Often the ancestor's name has long been forgotten, and clan members have come to believe that it was an animal or a spirit being. Clan names often refer to this supposed ancestor. The *unilineal* aspect of a clan means that membership passes through either the male or female line, but not both. To say a clan is *matrilineal* or *patrilineal* tells through which line descent is reckoned. In a matrilineal system, all children belong to their mother's clan. Because clans are almost always exogamous (meaning that marriage within the clan is forbidden), husbands and wives will never be of the same descent groups. In matrilineal systems, then, children will never

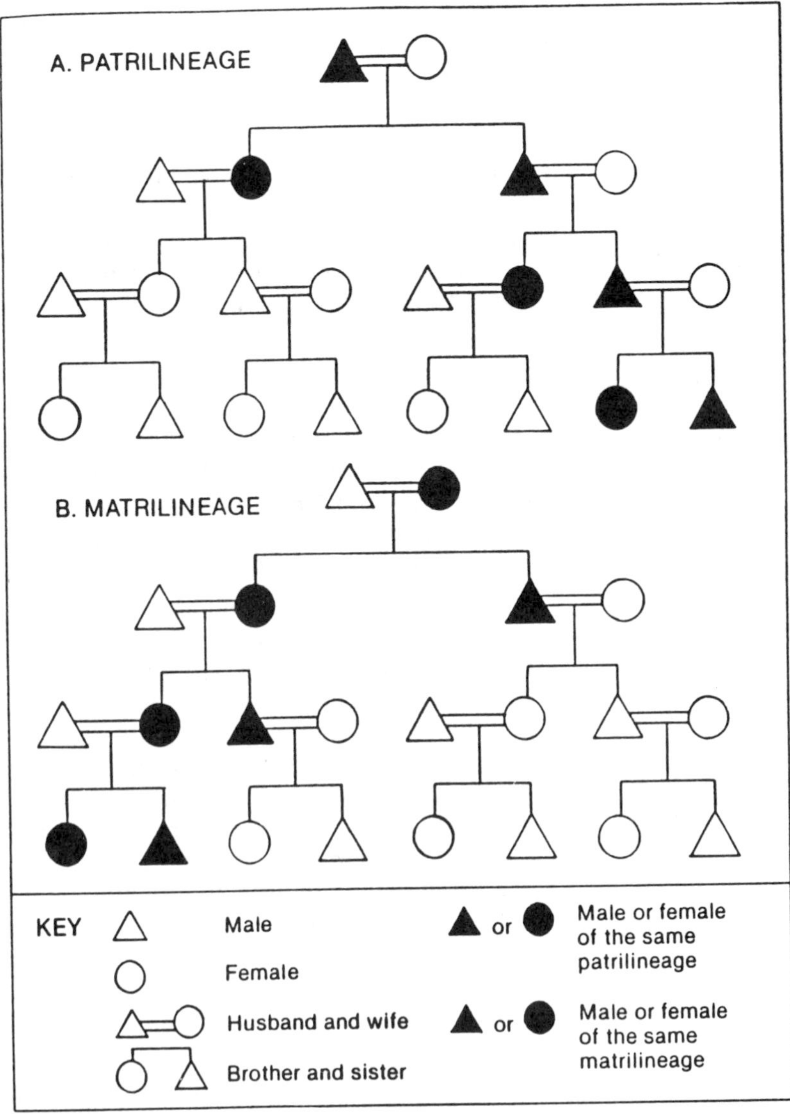

In patrilineal reckoning (A), descent group membership is passed from the father to his children, both male and female, but only males can pass on membership. In matrilineal reckoning (B), group membership goes from the mother to her children, both male and female, and only women can pass on membership.

belong to their father's clan; boys as well as girls belong to their mother's clan. Likewise, in a patrilineal system children belong to the fathers' clan, and patrilineal clan membership includes girls but is not passed on by girls.

Most Indian groups did not have clans. The Iroquois, Haida, Tlingit, Southeastern Indians, Western Pueblo, some Athabaskans, and Plains villagers of the upper Missouri were matrilineal. Some Plains villagers, the Upper Great Lakes people, and some California tribelets were patrilineal. All the rest of North America figured descent *bilaterally*, through both maternal and paternal sides.

Clan Rights and Duties

Being in a clan did not mean that children thought they were related to only one parent. Where they had clans, people still recognized relatives not in their own clan. The significance of clans was that they were responsible for property inheritance, rights to certain offices, and social control. In matrilineal societies, since the father was not a member of his children's clan, he had no authority over certain areas of their lives. The older male in his children's clan was their maternal uncle (mother's brother), who was responsible for some types of training that would have been left to the father in patrilineal or clanless systems.

Clan members often held their land in common. Iroquois clans held title to the longhouses and cultivated fields and also owned clan burial grounds. In the Northwest, clans controlled sections of the coast, fishing stations or strips of land along streams, and entire valleys for hunting. Pueblo clans too owned land, and also ceremonies and the masks, songs, medicine bundles, and dances that went with them.

Much tribal political and legal structure had to do with clan membership. Clans often had rights to chieftainships and council membership. The women of Iroquois clans selected members of the tribal council, who formed the League council, and Omaha clans also nominated council members.

Clan members had individual duties and responsibilities as well. Clans regulated marriage, in that members had to observe clan exogamy. Each member also was obliged to support and defend other members and to observe clan taboos and rules.

Other Kin Groups

Some clan systems were further organized into *phratries* or associations of clans. Clans belonging to the same phratry usually observed phratry exogamy: one could marry neither a member of his own clan nor a member of the other clan or clans in the phratry. Phratries were most common in the Southeast, the Northwest, and the prairies.

Some tribes were divided into two segments called moieties, from the French word for "half." Indian moieties were usually, though not always, exogamous. Membership in moieties was inherited matrilineally or patrilineally. Moiety functions usually were less important and less clearly defined than those of clans, except for exogamy, which was always clear wherever it existed. But moiety organization did have some common characteristics. It was customary for members of one moiety to perform the mortuary rites, conduct mourning observances, and offer comfort to those bereaved in the opposite moiety. In the Southeast, sports competitions usually pitted members of the two moieties against each other. And moieties often had important functions on ceremonial occasions. Each Creek moiety had specific parts to play in the Busk. Moiety divisions occurred among peoples with and without clan organization: a society could have a dual organization without being further divided into clans.

Pseudo-kinship

We saw in chapter 3 how Eskimo trading partners and members of hunting parties entered into special relationships. Those men had no biological or marital connections but called each other by a kin name, putting each other into a special status anthropologists call *fictive kinship*. In many Indian societies, good friends might pledge themselves to lifelong blood-brotherhood or comradeship, a custom popular among Cree men. Two Cree boys would vow blood- brotherhood and thereafter call each other "brother" and each other's parents "mother" and "father." Hopi children had ceremonial parents (something like godparents), a "mother" for a girl and a "father" for a boy, who sponsored them for initiation into the Katcina Cult. Hopi ceremonial parents could not belong to the phratry of the children's real mothers or fathers.

In native American societies where all rights and status came only through kinship connections, people might extend fictive kinship to traders or other outsiders to give them rights in society. Fictive kinfolk had mutual duties and obligations like real kinfolk. If one died, the survivor might be held responsible for the other's family.

Associations

Associations are organizations built on some principle other than kinship. American Indian associations formed around mutual interest (military societies), religion (ceremonial societies), sex (men's and women's clubs), and age (age-graded association). All provided mutual aid to members, and also education, recreation, and social control. On the Plains, the military societies provided comradeship and mutual aid. They also handled policing when large numbers of people assembled for hunts and tribal ceremonies, and they trained young men in the military arts. Usually they were not fighting units; members were or had been fighting men, but raiding parties assembled independently of the military associations.

Five Plains tribes had age-graded associations: Blackfoot, Hidatsa, Atsina, Mandan, and Arapaho. Members belonged to levels or grades according to their approximate ages, purchasing the rights and paraphernalia of each grade as they entered it. Though it was possible to skip grades, the membership of each group remained much the same as they advanced. Those age-graded groups functioned like the nongraded military societies of the Plains.

Associations, age-graded or not, were not exclusively for males. Women had societies too, age-graded among the Hidatsa and Mandan. These often formed as organizations of mutual interest or occupation—hide workers, beaders, or cultivators—but women sometimes joined curing or ceremonial societies with men.

The Hopi Katcina Cult was a religious association that included all members of the tribe. It bound even non-kin Hopi together in ceremonial observances and common supernatural belief. Hopi men and women also entered other ceremonial societies limited to one sex. Most activities of Hopi cults or associations concerned the agricultural cycle and fertility. Other cult societies were the Kuksu Cult in California, and the Iroquois False Face Society. Associations on the Northwest Coast often have been called "secret societies," though membership was actually more exclusive than secret.

Among the Kwakiutl, nonmembers deeply feared the Cannibal Dancers, who were thought to be possessed by a cannibal spirit that could make them eat other Kwakiutl. During performances, Cannibal Dancers ate smoked carcasses of bears that looked enough like human cadavers to convince onlookers that the dancers really were eating human flesh. The Cannibal Society was powerful as well as feared; its members were high-ranking individuals who held significant political positions in Kwakiutl society.

The Midewiwin or Grand Medicine Society of the Great Lakes Algonkians was based on occupation. Entrance and advancement through its four grades were open to both men and women curers and required both payment and hard study. Members became wealthy and powerful as they passed through the levels because people respected them and feared their powers, and because many curers charged very high prices. Though some associations included women, and a few were exclusively for women, associations were mostly male in pre-Columbian times. Domestic demands in primitive society left women little time to devote to club life, and the few women's associations usually were auxiliaries to men's groups or specialized in craft production.

Most associations in Indian societies were found in larger and richer groups. The Arctic, Subarctic, Basin, and Plateau had few non-kin organizations.

Games and Recreation

Moiety divisions generally meant ready-made athletic opponents, for one of the functions of moieties was to oppose each other in athletic events. In the Southeast, recreation between the two moieties was an important training exercise for warfare; the Indians there even called sports "little brother of war." Where people had no moiety divisions, competition was on a temporary basis, changing from game to game or from time to time. Except for this structuring of rivalry into the social system, games were surprisingly similar from coast to coast, regardless of culture area or linguistic affiliation.

Indian games were of two types: games of chance or gambling games, and games of skill or dexterity. Indians gambled with objects like dice or marked sticks, thrown at random to give a count or number, much like shooting craps. They also had guessing games, on which they bet a sum. An item, usually a special stick, was concealed in a team member's hand, and the opposing team tried to guess who held it. Probably the best-known Indian game of chance, this is usually called "the hand game," and was accompanied by songs or chants.

Games of skill often required athletic prowess: archery, javelin throwing, racing, chunkey, and snow snake, for example. Chunkey, played in the Southeast, was an attempt to throw a pole at a moving stone ring or disk. Another version was called hoop and pole, which was played with a hoop covered with netting, rolled on the ground. Players shot at it with arrows or threw javelins at it. In snow snake, opponents slid a lance on snow or ice to see whose projectile would travel farthest. They also had team games: lacrosse, an Indian invention, was played by men, and women played shinny, something like field hockey, with a ball and stick. Children played games too, some of them much like their parents' games, and women as well as men took part in most games and sports. For men, though, these activities were more than just fun and recreation; these workouts hardened the players and made them more skillful warriors.

Crow women gather for a game of dice.

Women's Status

Women held a respected place in nearly all communities, with a very few exceptions like the Chipewyan and some other western Subarctic people. Europeans once believed that Indian women were menials, hardly more than slaves to Indian men, but they had misinterpreted the division of labor in native American society. When bands or communities moved, it was usually to search for food or to escape pressure from aggressive neighbors. Either way, men could not travel burdened with goods, utensils, or children, for they had to be free to use their weapons in hunting or warfare. Consequently, women seemed to Europeans like beasts of burden, since they carried all the family possessions on their backs. Early European arrivals were shocked to see women laboring in the fields, for European tradition said that farming was men's work. Measuring Indian customs by European standards caused many erroneous conclusions.

Indian women never were major political figures in any tribe (in fact, women have rarely been political officials anywhere in the world until recent times), but though they did not make community-binding decisions, their opinions and suggestions were highly regarded. Among the Iroquois particularly, women's right to nominate and depose the sachems gave them much political power. Men were very conscious of women's part in agriculture, too, for except among the Western Pueblo, women were the primary cultivators. In gathering wild-plant foods, women did nearly all the work. Even in the hunting societies like the Plains tribes, women's economic contributions were extremely important; no matter how many buffalo a man might kill, he could sell only as many hides as his wife or wives could cure. And, of course, everywhere women were responsible for nurturing new members of society.

Women were forbidden to take part in many male ceremonial activities, but in some areas they had associations and ritual observances of their own. In many matrilineal societies, women owned the family dwelling and the fields and they cared for the clan property. With men away from home hunting, fishing or at war for days or even months, women had to be responsible for domestic economics, and they learned in childhood how to be self-reliant. Men made their own equipment and commonly supplied heavy materials for housing, but women had to do most of the craftwork like pottery, weaving, basketry, and skin dressing. Only in the Southeast and a few other areas where they were rarely away from home long did men take a hand in such manufactures. Labor in the home naturally fell to women because of the human reproductive cycle and the period of lactation, but just as women recognized men's importance in protection and subsistence, men were aware that women's contributions were indispensable.

Slavery

It is unfortunate that there are not more words in English for the varying degrees of servitude, because slavery in our society has implications that it rarely had among Indians. Except in a few cases, Indian slavery did not mean ownership of a human being as a chattel or possession. Only among the Northwest Coast people did it approach total bondage and power over life and death. The only hereditary slaves were in the Northwest, where children of slaves automatically became slaves, producing a permanent slave class. Even the Iroquois and Natchez, who rank after the Northwest Coast people as slaveholders and who tortured and sacrificed enslaved war captives, had no slave class, for children of slaves were free citizens. Slaves almost always were treated as members of households, and not infrequently they married into the family.

Only on the Northwest Coast was commercial traffic in slaves common. Even there, slaves who had been captured in war might be ransomed by their kinfolk; in some tribes, they might purchase their own freedom if they could accumulate enough wealth. Women and children slaves in the Northwest were household drudges for high-ranking families, and male slaves helped with construction, canoe building, and the like. Most of their tasks were the same as those done by middle- and lower-class Northwest people. But slaves did live under definite restrictions in the Northwest. They were rigidly excluded from ceremonials, usually were prohibited from marrying free citizens, and occasionally were killed—Tlingit chiefs sacrificed slaves to be buried under the main posts of their houses at the time of construction. Of course, chiefs did not build houses often. Occasionally wealthy men sacrificed slaves at potlatches just to show how wealthy they were and gain prestige, but sometimes, for the same reason, wealthy men freed their slaves in a flamboyant gesture at a potlatch.

Outside the Northwest Coastal area, the words captive and slave were almost interchangeable, for most slaves were war captives. In some areas, like California, people were enslaved for debt. Life for most slaves probably was no harder or less pleasant than their captors' lives.

Political Organization

Among the functions of all human societies are maintaining internal order and making decisions that are binding on their members. In addition, most groups have some rules governing external relations or contacts with outsiders, like warfare and long-distance trade. We call the structures and relationships that perform these functions a society's political organization.

Unlike kinship structures, political structures are territorial—they occupy space. A group like a band, village, or a tribe is defined at least partly by the fact that its members share (or divide) common territory. Even nomadic groups are not totally free-wandering, for their activities too occur within a certain region. Members of a political unit recognize the territory that is their common land, and they recognize land outside their boundaries as belonging to other political units. Those who want to go through land not their own must either have some sort of safety pledge or risk being attacked.

Some native American societies had no specifically political structures. Among the Eskimo, political power and authority grew out of kinship or were vested in temporary leaders whom others followed out of respect for their competence. Other Indian groups, like the Natchez, had strongly centralized political organization. Most Indian societies lay somewhere between these two extremes. In many of them, groups such as clans made the important political decisions. A convenient and common way to classify the varying types and degrees of Indian political organization is as bands, tribes, and chiefdoms.

Bands

The simplest kind of political organization, the band, had between 50 and 150 people. It was made up of families who held territory in common for hunting, fishing, or gathering. A band was an egalitarian organization with no inherited power positions. Some sort of leader, often called a headman, acted for the group, but he had no power to enforce his decisions. People followed his suggestions because they respected his wisdom and had seen proof of his ability in the past.

Indian bands had little need for formal government, for social control was rarely a problem. Their population was small and homogeneous: everyone grew up with the same general experiences and about the same expectations. People held very little private property, and all shared food and supplies equally. The Paiute of the Basin were hunters and gatherers who recognized no political unit larger than the band, though several bands joined together each summer for rabbit or antelope hunts. Indian bands were commonly exogamous, and the Paiute arranged marriages too during this annual gathering.

Not all Indian bands were so nomadic as the Great Basin peoples. Where food resources were more plentiful and regular, people moved less often, following the seasons. Groups like the Klamath bands were really village groups, sedentary for the winter months and dispersed during the summer. The villages were close enough to do things together throughout the year, not just during an annual hunt. But since the Klamath units recognized no authority beyond their own community, we can consider them, too, as a band-level society.

Tribes

The tribe is difficult to define. Its members recognized that they belonged together; they spoke the same language, had the same customs, and married each other. They were often made up of bands, like the Plains tribes that gathered during the big buffalo hunts. Other tribes, like the agricultural Plains Indians and the Iroquois, were composed of villages rather than bands. Tribes in North America were much larger than bands, but even so they rarely exceeded 5,000 people.

The convenient and traditional way of referring to American Indian societies is to call them *tribes*, as we do throughout this book. Here, however, as we discuss political units, we need a more precise differentiation. In this section, the word *tribe* is meant as defined above. Elsewhere we will continue to use it in its more casual sense. *Nation* too can be confusing, especially the expression *Indian nation* as used in the popular press. *Nation* is not an appropriate term for societies north of Mexico; it implies a political complexity never found north of the Rio Grande in aboriginal times. None of these categories is absolute; they grade into each other, forcing us to be fairly arbitrary, for instance, when we distinguish a tribe from a chiefdom.

Tribes were usually much larger than bands, and had associations within them that took members from each of the component bands or villages. Warrior societies in the Plains had members from all the various bands, and medicine societies among the village tribes drew members from more than one village. Clans also integrated tribes in that clan members were scattered through bands and villages. These pan-tribal associations and kin groups helped bond the units together and built tribal identity and unity. Without some such unifying device, tribes might have developed serious rifts between bands or villages.

Tribes, like bands, are egalitarian, in spite of the Europeans' habit of applying the word *chief* to leaders. Tribal leaders had little coercive power, for the chief's position rested entirely on the people's willingness to follow. Tribal chiefs governed with advice from a council, usually elders or headmen from the families, clans, or bands. Any policing was done by the associations and the tribal council, both of which had members representing all the bands or villages; their decisions helped avoid charges of favoritism or discrimination.

Chiefdoms

Chiefdoms have centralized authority, and they are not egalitarian. The political leader of a chiefdom has the socially recognized right to mobilize people and goods, and the society under him is stratified or ranked, with some social classes, individuals, or family lines considered higher, superior, or more prestigious than others, because of birth rather than achievement. The Natchez and the Powhatan were in this political category. The population of chiefdoms varied in North America, but most of them had fewer than 5,000 people.

The title *chief*, when it was used of someone like Powhatan, Pocahontas' father, meant a man of power who had force to carry out his orders. Plains chiefs usually were respected leaders, but they never had authority so absolute as Powhatan's. Plains chiefs were advisors.

Both tribes and chiefdoms usually had different chiefs for different purposes—military, religious, and civil. Even the Great Sun of the Natchez had a war chief. Civil or peace chiefs were usually older men, once renowned warriors but now beyond youthful rashness, men who could be counted on to keep cool. The ceremonial or religious chief's position often was not clearly separated from shaman or priest, especially among the Pueblo. The war chief was of course a great warrior, a man others would follow. Some of these positions might be reserved for a family line or clan, but proven ability settled the choice even in chiefdoms. Rarely would one man act as two kinds of chief.

Other Political Classifications

Some Indian groups are hard to place in the categories we have been using. California peoples were organized in groups of autonomous villages called tribelets. Some of these lacked any tribal organization, having no overall leadership, and their only unifying force was their common language. Others had more definite political structure, with local units in villages led by headmen and chiefs who served as ceremonial and civil officials. These tribelets had strikingly large populations for hunters and gatherers with little political unity.

Because Pueblo religious societies ran the government, with religious officials also serving as political officials, their organization may be considered a theocracy. The Hopi lived in several villages on adjacent mesas, each village having its own religious or ceremonial associations. We would classify the Hopi as a tribe, even though the villages were mostly autonomous. Clan heads were leaders of the ceremonial societies and formed a council that considered village problems.

Some of the Southeastern people would be classified between tribe and chiefdom, showing characteristics of each. The Natchez may have been developing into a state, a politically organized body of people, when they were disrupted by Europeans; they certainly came closer to it than any other recorded group.

Councils

In all political groups larger than bands, the council was very important. Even the Great Sun of the Natchez had to listen to his council.

Sometimes Indian councils were groups of former warriors who had gained the community's respect for their bravery and military exploits. Other councils were clan elders representing all the tribal clans. The Pueblo councils included clan heads and leaders of ceremonial societies. Membership in the council could be based on kinship (leaders of clans), or territoriality (headmen of bands), and sometimes council members came only from specific families within clans. In some tribes council members held their position for life; others had limited terms of office.

Some councils, like the League of the Iroquois, had as many as fifty members; the Cheyenne tribal council had forty-four. Others had a dozen or fewer. In some tribes the council governed alone, while in others it acted as an advisory body for a ruler, like the Natchez Great Sun.

Councils acted as deliberative and legislative bodies. They discussed issues, and since the council members represented the bands, clans, and villages, they were a sounding board for the community's sentiments. In tribal organizations, council decisions were almost always unanimous. If the members could not reach unanimity, they kept deliberating. Most tribal government was democratic, but in a chiefdom the ruler could override his council. Only a very secure and personally powerful leader like Powhatan would have done so, however, and even he, we may be sure, listened to his council.

Social Control

As in all human societies, the most fundamental social control among American Indians was the socialization common to every member of the group. Adult Indians behaved properly most of the time because they had leaned in childhood what the tribe considered right and wrong. Adults rewarded the child's proper behavior with praise, and punished improper or socially disruptive behavior with ridicule and shame. As children grew up, prestige and gifts were added to the rewards, while punishment became more severe, including locking up, restraint, or whipping. In the bands very little physical punishment was necessary.

Supernatural Control

Indians believed that the spirit world kept watch over human behavior, and that by withholding favors or protection the supernatural would punish those who neglected taboos. Some misbehavior, such as incest, was so dreadful that only the spirits could punish the wrongdoer by making him sick. In band societies, social control by these means was adequate; judges, courts, and policing officials were not needed.

Indians in some areas felt that wrongs would be avenged by witchcraft. If belief in it was strong, that could be a very effective way of dealing with social disorder. Pueblo Indians feared being accused of witchcraft as much as they did the results of witchcraft. Such fears were strong incentive to conform to social norms, for others might blame any abnormal behavior on the practice of witchcraft.

Control of Adults

Many of the ways of training children in proper behavior carried over as social controls for adults. Ridicule, gossip, and shame embarrassed violators of social convention enough to stop their socially disapproved behavior. Years of being socialized into culturally proper ways also made people feel guilty about misdeeds, and public comment and avoidance also kept people in line. And of course rewards such as prestige, gifts, and praise kept reinforcing good behavior all through life.

However, such informal controls were not always enough. Warrior societies could take coercive actions during tribal buffalo hunts on the Plains. They might take away a man's weapons, banish him from the hunt, or confine him to camp or even to his tipi. Occasionally the military societies could even impose capital punishment, for acts like premature hunting or stampeding the buffalo endangered the whole tribe's food supply. Such behavior was a crime against society itself.

Capital punishment, the ultimate social control, was rare among American Indians, and such extreme measures were used only for extreme provocation. Occasionally, though, it was the only way of preserving social order. Among the Eskimo, when a man had murdered several times, it was customary for the community to condemn him to death. With the community's sanction, one man executed the murderer. When social approval backed up this capital punishment, the kinfolk of the condemned man made no attempt to avenge him. Like the rest of the community, they recognized that this punishment was the only way of maintaining social order, and they accepted the verdict.

The one serious and largely uncontrollable disturbance was feuding, that is, aggression between two kin groups in the same society. It was dangerous because no one had a way of settling the feud, which perpetuated itself. For a murder within a tribe the victims's family sought revenge by murdering someone in the killer's kin group, who then sought revenge in their turn. On the Northwest Coast and in northern California, blood-money payments could resolve the feud, but in many places nothing could settle it once it got underway unless both groups accepted a peace chief or some other respected individual as a mediator. Otherwise the feuding could destroy the band or village. The Eskimo were the one group to settle private quarrels and disputes with a remarkable sort of word duel in the form of song.

Economic Systems

The word "economics" covers all the ways in which people produce, distribute, and consume goods and services, including the items their technology produces and their ways of obtaining the raw materials they need to manufacture those items. We discussed the material bases of life in chapter 9; here we will examine Indian ways of exchanging or distributing goods, and their ideas about property.

Property Rights and Land Tenure

Most Indian property was personal, like clothing, weapons, ceremonial apparatus, and subsistence and craft implements. The Plains giveaway and the Northwest potlatch customs tell us that some property was owned outright and could be disposed of according to the owner's wishes, even destroyed if he chose. Land, however, was almost never owned by individuals. Kin groups or communities had the rights to land, and Indians had no such concept as private ownership of real estate. This one difference of ideas caused great misunderstanding and hard feelings when Europeans arrived and tried to purchase Indian lands.

Agriculturalists by custom assigned garden areas to individuals or groups of kinfolk for cultivation. Where women were the gardeners (in all the agricultural societies except for the Pueblo), the produce was usually looked upon as theirs, but they always shared it. Families almost everywhere had the right to gather and fish at will within the tribe's or band's territory, and hunting land too was open to all in the local group. Along the Pacific coast and in the Subarctic, rights to fishing stations belonged to families, but only among the Yurok were fishing areas private property that could be sold. In the Western Great Lakes region, Indians recognized wild rice areas as belonging to families, who marked their territory by bending and tying off clumps of the grain. Still, all rights to land were rights to use it, not to destroy it, or let it lie unused. Any garden, fishing, or gathering areas that were not used for some time could be allotted to others if tribal or kin group authorities approved.

Communal housing too was kin group property, though in Plains tribes the skins and poles of a tipi belonged to the woman who cured the skins and raised and took down the tipi when the family moved.

Agricultural land was more uniformly controlled or owned by kin groups than hunting, fishing, or gathering territory, but every member of a band or tribe had rights to the produce of its land, whether those rights came from kinship connections or citizenship. And even in the few cases where property was clearly defined as belonging to an individual, he had to recognize claims coming from one group or another: the owner always let some groups of people, like his family, exploit his property.

Indians had intangible property too, like names, titles, songs, magical chants, and incantations. These almost always were privately owned and usually could be sold or given away, but on the Northwest Coast names and titles belonged to the kin group.

Inheritance

All peoples have ways of distributing property and rights from the dead to the living, a flow of belongings from generation to generation that is called inheritance. Communal or kin group property always remained with the group. No one person had the right to dispose of it or prevent another member of the group from using it.

A person could leave personal property to another, though. If he did not choose his own heir, a man's sons got his personal possessions and a woman's daughters got hers, where possessions did pass to the next generation. However, in some areas they were not passed on. In southern California, relatives burned the deceased's private belongings at the mourning ceremonies, and in the Plains, relatives often killed a dead warrior's favorite horse, though they might distribute others among the community. Distributing or destroying personal property was part of funeral ceremonies everywhere. One-family houses sometimes were inherited, but the Navajo and Apache burned or abandoned them after a death.

Trade and Commerce

Because natural resources are unequally distributed on this earth, some Indian societies had minerals, plants, and animals not available to others. Needing some kind of mutual exchange system, Indians built long-distance trading routes centuries before Columbus. Though actual routes are not known, we have plenty of evidence from burials and archaeological sites that mica and conch shells from the South, copper from Lake Superior, obsidian from the Rocky Mountains, and flint from Ohio circulated in some kind of regular trading network. Many other items probably were traded over shorter distances, but naturally we have no record of perishable items like foodstuffs. We know tobacco was traded after European arrival, but tracing it to prehistoric times is a problem because, though we have found pipes and other smoking devices, people must have used many of them to smoke kinnikinnik, not tobacco. Specialization in craft also brought trade in both raw materials and finished products. After contact, European guns, metal objects, glass beads, cloth, and horses entered the exchange systems.

Some tribes became famous as intermediaries or traders. The Chinook controlled an important part of the Columbia River down which much trade passed. Huron territory was the heart of the early fur trade, and the Tobacco tribe even got its name from the part it played trading that plant.

Trade Routes. When most goods had to be carried on the human back, trade followed rivers wherever possible so that boats could be used. The Mississippi River and the Great Lakes were important tradeways. Overland trails that may have been made originally by seasonally migrating animals covered the continent.

Long trade routes were bound to lead through alien territory, and that called for ways of showing that the traveler's purpose was peaceful. Carrying the calumet or peace pipe was one of these. Even the trails heavily traveled by traders, migrating bands, and war parties were only wide enough to accommodate one person, because Indians preferred to move in single file. Where they could, they chose routes to avoid hard, stony ground that wore out moccasins and dense undergrowth that slowed them down. In the North many trails crossed frozen rivers or lakes in the winter. The Santa Fe Trail and the Oregon Trail followed by frontiersmen were originally Indian routes, and maps drawn by the European colonists showed Indian trails like the one through the Cumberland gap in Tennessee. Many trails later became paved roads and railroad tracks.

Media of Exchange. Indians had no general-purpose medium of exchange or commodity like money before European contact, but some items were used locally as standards of value and media of exchange. These things were not true money, though wampum has often been called that. It was valuable, but it was not currency. On the Atlantic coast, wampum became a medium of exchange after Europeans began using it; roanoke was another kind of shell the Indians used for both adornment and exchange. Both got their value from scarcity. The shells used for wampum, particularly the black or purple variety, were rare. One purple bead equalled two white ones in early times. The strung shell beads were convenient to carry as necklaces or belts. European glass beads later came in such quantity that the native shell lost its value. On the Pacific coast, dentalia were very valuable shells, and Indians used them for exchange. The value of each shell in this case depended on its length, not its color.

Away from the coasts, in the interior, pelts (especially beaver) were used for exchange and as a standard of value. Like wampum, they continued in use for a time after Europeans came. The Hupa of northern

California used woodpecker scalps, and eagle feathers may have had a value for exchange among the Pueblo, who also used turquoise and shell beads. Many other items were used locally, but however prized they were, people still conducted most trade directly, by bartering goods, foods, and raw materials for each other.

Gift-giving. Most exchanges went on either within the tribe or with close neighbors, far more than occurred through long-distance trade. Within the group, gift-giving and sharing were the most common form of exchange. Indians gave presents at specified times such as weddings, when the two families exchanged gifts. Potlatches and giveaways were ways that wealthy men allocated food and goods on special occasions, described in previous chapters. These were actually leveling mechanisms, distributing wealth to many people instead of allowing it to accumulate in the hands of a few.

Most of these exchanges within the group or community were reciprocal, as most gift-giving is; even though no one says so, people generally expect a gift or action in return. Thus, gift-giving was more than a way of distributing goods and services; it was like social security. Reciprocity meant that one could always count on receiving in times of need if one shared in times of plenty.

Warfare

Indians settled their internal disputes according to regular patterns most of the time, but no group had any standard ways of solving intertribal conflict. The common solution was war. Wars for expansion of an imperialist sort did not occur in the areas covered in this book, and such wars were rare north of Mexico. However, wars did arise from economic causes. Hunters who pursued game into alien territory might be attacked, and offensive wars were fought to win control of food and perhaps mineral resources. After European contact, economic motives greatly increased tribal aggressions, as in the struggles to control territory for the fur trade. Defensive warfare too was necessary to protect homes, villages, women, and children.

In the East and on the Plains, raiding for captives, horses, and glory accounted for much aggression. But even there and on the Northwest Coast, where wars were fought mostly for captives, prestige, and revenge, there were no true military specialists. Even the warriors and the war chiefs were still hunters, not full-time warmakers.

Some areas, including the Arctic, Subarctic, and Great Basin, had no organized warfare. Other groups became much more warlike after they acquired horses, especially the Plains people and also those in the

Plateau. Californians were not very aggressive except for some raiding. The Pueblo, on the other hand, though often described as very peaceful, had a fighting force of leaders and warriors to protect themselves against the nomadic Athabaskan raiders, and they had a priesthood in charge of war rites. However, they placed no high value on the warrior's way of life; anyone who killed had to go through long purification rituals. The very aggressive groups were in the East, the Plains, and the Northwest, and the Athabaskans in the Southwest.

Going to War

Preparation. Where warfare was frequent, physical training prepared young men to endure physical hardship. They learned to refrain from personal indulgence and to accept the decisions of their war leader. Prestige in warfare came from valorous achievement, and rights to insignia such as eagle feathers had to be publicly bestowed in religious ceremonies. Anyone who claimed war achievements he did not deserve was publicly humiliated, scorned not only by other warriors but also by the women and children of the tribe.

The war leader prepared by fasting and sexual abstinence and observed all the rites by which he could appeal to the supernatural. Followers joined him because they believed in his ability and his chances for success. During the conflict his leadership was autocratic; if a man in the war party was disobedient, the leader might order him whipped or send him home. Leaders usually appointed an alternate or two to take over if they were killed. Each man fought independently for most of the time, but tried to save any comrade in danger and to keep fallen tribesmen's bodies from being mutilated. Each was free to win as much prestige as he could. The leader had no rights over the glory gained by others, though he had the right to distribute the spoils of battle.

The Battle. The Plains Indians rode horses if they had to travel far to attack an enemy, but almost all their fighting, as in other areas, was hand-to-hand and on foot. In the Plains the leader would carry a war standard into battle, a ceremonial lance which he thrust into the ground and fought beside until victory or death. He was under honor not to leave unless a member of his own party pulled up the lance. To us, an act like that may seem the height of vainglory, but for the warrior it won praise and renown.

In a defensive fight, warriors tried to engage the enemy somewhere beyond the village limits to give women, children, and the elderly time to build breastworks or other physical shields and remove the young and incapacitated beyond the range of enemy fire. Women took part in defensive battle at close range, and in rare cases went into battle and fought as equals with the men. Most women who went with the war party were there to serve the men; often they were given a share of the loot.

Scalping

Mutilation of enemy dead was not universal, but scalping and beheading occurred in widely separated regions. Contrary to the common belief, scalping did not usually cause death, nor did it break or crush the skull. Probably the idea that it was always fatal resulted from the fact that the dead usually were scalped by their enemies. In fact, scalping was simply removing a piece of skin with hair attached, most often a patch about the size of a half dollar, from the crown of the head. If a living person was scalped, skin grew back over the wound but hair did not, leaving a small bald spot.

Warriors kept scalps they had taken as trophies and war insignia. Occasionally a warrior removed the whole top skin of the scalp, later dividing it into smaller pieces to decorate garments or horse trappings. If the fallen enemy was not dead, removing the entire scalp did kill him. Some Plains warriors stretched the scalp on a small hoop and carried it as a sort of banner at the end of a pole. Sometimes women carried the pole while they did a triumphal scalp dance when the war party returned. Some fighters wore a scalp lock, a small lock or braid of hair, in defiance of any enemy.

Scalping was not unique to American Indians. Herodotus, Greek historian of the fifth century B.C., reported it among the Scythians in his time. And not all people of North America took scalps. As nearly as we can tell, it was mostly an Eastern war practice that spread into the Plains. Even there, however, counting coup—rather than scalping—was the usual measure of a warrior's prowess. Along the Northwest Coast, the trophy was the head itself; after beheading an enemy, the warrior might on the way home remove a scalplock from the head. In general, scalping increased after European arrival because colonists offered bounties for scalps of Indians fighting against them, but the practice itself appears to have been aboriginal.

Part IV

CONFLICT BETWEEN CULTURES

The glimpses we have had of Europeans as they came upon various Indian cultures have readied us for a historical look at the encounter and the results of their meeting. Overwhelming the native people, these invaders took control not only of the Indians' lands, but often of their very lives. While the European discovery of the New World brought change to Europe, it meant even greater change for the Indians. In spite of the many Europeans who tried to understand the Indians' ways of life and treat them fairly, there were many others who cheated the native peoples and took away their land.

Europeans also brought in diseases to which the Indians had no resistance, and thousands of Indians and Eskimo died in epidemics of smallpox, tuberculosis, and measles, among others. Many thousands more died in warfare with the Europeans, who met the Indians' bows and arrows and spears with guns. Sheer weight of numbers guaranteed that the advancing white population would overcome the native people. People began to refer to Indians as the vanishing Americans.

Today, however, they are anything but vanishing; their birth rate is higher than that of non-Indians. In all that time many have not been assimilated, though absorption into the dominant culture has been the goal of most government policies. Earlier in their history, massive destruction nearly finished them as a people. More recently their story has been one of advances in education, employment, and self-determination. It is with the successes and problems of Indians and Eskimo today that we shall close Part IV.

Suggestions for Further Study

Bibliography

Andrist, Ralph K. 1964. *The Long Death: The Last Days of the Plains Indians.*

An account of the U.S. Army's final and decisive victory over the Plains Indians from a description of the Indian frontier of the 1840s to the Massacre at Wounded Knee in 1890.

Brophy, William, and Sophie D. Aberle. 1966. *The Indian, America's Unfinished Business.*

The report of the Commission of Rights, Liberties and Responsibilities of the American Indian. Discussed are laws, values, political affairs, health, education, and economic development.

Brown, Dee. 1970. *Bury My Heart at Wounded Knee.*

A detailed account of the wars against the Indians from 1860 to 1890. An attempt to tell the Indian side of history.

Catlin, George. 1841. *Letters and Notes on the Manners, Customs, and Conditions of the North American Indians.*

Diaries and letters from a famous painter of Indian subjects. Fascinating accounts of culture change and the tragedy of disease.

DeLoria, Vine, Jr. 1969. *Custer Died for Your Sins.*

The opinions of a Sioux Indian concerning the position and problems of contemporary Indians.

Dorris, Michael. 1989. *The Broken Cord.*

A discussion of Indian health problems.

Forbes, Jack D., ed. 1964. *The Indian in America's Past.*

Includes speeches of Indian leaders, descriptions of U.S. policy toward Indians, and a section on contemporary Indians.

Greenway, John. 1969. "Will the Indians Get Whitey?" *National Review*, March 11.

A minority opinion about Indian history and contemporary Indians, one of which many will disapprove, but students should be aware that such attitudes exist.

LaFlesche, Francis. 1963. *The Middle Five.*

Written by an Omaha Indian who became a professional anthropologist, this book tells of his life in a boarding school at the turn of the century. Gives an immediacy that accounts written by outsiders cannot attain.

Levine, Stuart, and Nancy O. Lurie, eds. 1970. *The American Indian Today.*

Readings on culture change, Pan-Indianism, contemporary Indian tribalism, and legal problems of Indians.

Mooney, James. 1965. *The Ghost Dance Religion.*

An edited edition of Mooney's original work on the Ghost Dance and the Sioux uprising of 1890, eliminating the more technical parts and retaining a detailed account of the history of the Ghost Dance and a description of the ceremonies.

Washburn, Wilcomb E., ed. 1964. *The Indian and the White Man.*

Collection of documents like treaties, letters, and statements by and about Indians.

White, Robert H. 1991. *Tribal Assets, The Rebirth of Native America.*

A discussion of economic development.

Wilson, Edmund. 1960. *Apologies to the Iroquois.*
Fascinating study of contemporary Iroquois visited by the writer. The book includes Joseph Mitchell's article, "The Mohawks in High Steel," which relates the success some Mohawk have found in high-steel work.

Other Pertinent Works

Barnett, Homer G. 1957. *Indian Shakers.*

Brody, Hugh. 1981. *Maps and Dreams: Indians and the British Columbia Frontier.*

Cohen, Felix. 1942. *Handbook of Federal Indian Law.*

Crowe, Keith. 1974. *A History of the Original Peoples of Northern Canada.*

Deardorff, Merle. 1951. *The Religion of Handsome Lake.*

Innis, H. A. 1976. *The Fur Trade in Canada.*

Leacock, Eleanor, and Nancy O. Lurie. 1971. *North American Indians in Historical Perspective.*

O'Brien, Sharon. 1989. *American Indian Tribal Governments.*

O'Donnell, Janet. 1991. *The Dispossession of the American Indian, 1887–1934.*

Patterson, E. Palmer. 1972. *The Canadian Indian: A History Since 1500.*

Prucha, Francis P. 1962. *American Indian Policy in the Formative Years.*

______. 1971. *The Indian in American History.*

______. 1984. *The Great Father: The United States and the American Indians.*

Spicer, Edward H. 1962. *Cycles of Conquest.*

Van Stone, James W. 1962. *Point Hope: An Eskimo Village in Transition.*

______. 1967. *Eskimos of the Nushagak River.*

11

INDIAN-WHITE RELATIONS

Arapaho "ghost shirt," worn by participants in the Ghost Dance.

Early in the eleventh century, Leif Ericson, a Norwegian, and Thorfinn Kerlsefni, an Icelander, discovered a territory they called Vinland. We still do not know whether that was Labrador or the New England coast, but it was the first European landing in North America that we know of. The Norsemen called the people they met *Skraellings*, which was their word for "natives." Probably the Skraellings were northern Algonkians or possibly Eskimo, but their contact with the European explorers was so brief that no trace of it has come down in Indian or Eskimo legend.

Other European voyagers might have reached the shores of North America, blown there by storms or even venturing there deliberately, but if they did, they left no record. It took almost 500 years for another European to reach mainland North America. John Cabot landed in 1497 somewhere in what is now Canada, probably on the coast of Labrador or Newfoundland, and he claimed North America for King Henry VII of England.

Columbus, with his crews on the *Nina*, *Pinta*, and *Santa Maria*, is the European given credit for discovering the New World, and in terms of the far-reaching results of his landing in the West Indies, he deserves it. Floods of Europeans soon swept North and South America, coming face-to-face everywhere with the native Americans.

European powers were fascinated by North America's commercial possibilities. Ponce de Leon sailed around a southeastern projection of the mainland, named it Florida, and claimed it for Spain in 1513. He found the natives hostile and did not venture inland. The middle part of North America's eastern seaboard was still largely unknown to European mariners in the early 1520s, but Newfoundland and Nova Scotia, called Codfish Land because fishing was so productive along their coasts, were familiar to crews of many European vessels who put into the bays for water, fresh food, and repairs. They must have had some contact with the natives though they left no record of it. Between Codfish Land and Florida even the coast was unknown territory.

Early European Exploration

Between 1492 and 1763, no one European power was dominant in North America. France, England, and Spain were engaged in a physical and diplomatic power struggle for control, while colonists from a few other nations such as Holland hacked homes out of the forests.

Areas of Investigation

France, concerned for its fishing enterprises off the North American coast and hoping to find a northern waterway to the Orient, sent Jacques Cartier on exploratory voyages into the Gulf of St. Lawrence. There he made friendly contacts with the Algonquin (not to be confused with the Algonkian language) and Huron tribes. He went as far as 900 miles inland from the Atlantic by 1541, thus laying the basis for later French claims in North America. Some French settled far to the south in Florida, only to be destroyed by the Spanish in 1565. Religious wars in France kept its voyagers home for the next two generations.

Spanish troops, after destroying the French Florida settlement, built a frontier fort, St. Augustine, which grew into the first European town in North America. The Spanish set out for the interior from the Florida territory in 1539 under Hernando de Soto. At about the same time, Spanish explorers and troops under Francisco de Coronado entered the Southwest from Mexico. They were seeking Cibola, the legendary Seven Cities of Gold reported by survivors of an earlier expedition. The Spanish were in the New World mostly for wealth, especially gold, and legends sprang up throughout their territory about cities of gold. In 1539 a priest decided that the Zuni Pueblo must be Cibola. De Soto and his men marched westward from Florida across the South to the Mississippi River and then north. Coronado reached the Pueblo Indians, and his soldiers were the first Europeans to see the Grand Canyon of the Colorado. He then turned east to what is now Kansas, where he almost met de Soto. Both parties ran into many tribes of Indians along their way.

Following up late on Cabot's 1497 claim, the English, barred from the southern seas by Spanish sea power, turned north. In 1583, Humphrey Gilbert tried to start a colony in Newfoundland, and in 1587, Walter Raleigh did the same far to the south on Roanoke Island off the coast of today's North Carolina. But the first lasting English settlements in North America and the beginning of long-term contact with Indians were at Jamestown in Virginia and the Pilgrim colony in Massachusetts. These people were far more interested in Europe than in seeing the interior of the American continent, and generations passed before they went west of the Appalachians.

The French explored the Mississippi basin, their way made easy by the connecting waters of the St. Lawrence River, the Great Lakes, and the Mississippi. Jacques Marquette and Louis Joliet sailed down the Mississippi almost to the mouth of the Arkansas in 1673, charting the territory. Thus the general geography of the eastern third of the continent was mapped through the combined knowledge of Spanish, English, and French explorers.

Struggle in the East. Until the Revolutionary War, the English settled along the coast—east of the Alleghenies, all the way from Canada to Spanish Florida. Scattered among the British population were small groups of Dutch settlers, and Africans in the South, and a few French, Germans, and Swedes.

After the French and Indian War (1755–1763), in which England, France, and Spain fought each other for control of North America, England became the sole power east of the Mississippi, although France still held the Louisiana territory to the west. All three major European powers in colonial America needed and used Indian allies to supplement their forces in military campaigns. The Indians, long accustomed to hostilities between tribes, took sides against traditional enemies: some Iroquois tribes and some Algonkian speakers, for example, joined the Europeans to fight each other.

That conflict of Indian against Indian led Tecumseh, Pontiac, and some others to try to unite the Indians and drive out the Europeans. Perhaps there was a time early in the colonization when the combined efforts of the tribes could have expelled the invaders. But soon the Europeans came in such great numbers and their technology was so superior that Indian defeat was inevitable; and the Europeans turned on their Indian allies and drove them from their own territory.

Ten years before the American Revolution, Spain dominated the Southwest. France, forced out of the East by the Treaty of Paris, gave up to Britain all of Canada and Louisiana east of the Mississippi River, except New Orleans; thus the Eastern Indians suddenly became British subjects. Great Britain also acquired Florida from Spain, holding it for only two decades, from 1763 to 1783. Spain, meanwhile, took over Louisiana west of the Mississippi as well as New Orleans, only to agree in 1800 to transfer them back to France.

Exploration of the Northwest Coast. With the Spanish established in Mexico, which then included much of California and the American Southwest, most of North America was known to Europeans. The last area to come under European scrutiny was the Northwest Coast. Gold and fur seekers from imperial Russia followed fishermen to the Aleutian Island chain. Then in 1741 Vitus Bering, a Dane sailing under the Russian flag, discovered the strait now named after him which separates Asia from the New World. From that moment, fur traders from Russia poured into Alaska seeking valuable pelts and advanced down the coast. Traders and explorers from other countries followed, among them James Cook and George Vancouver from England, and by 1793 all the coasts of North America were mapped.

European Goals

Indians thus met many different groups of Europeans, each with a different goal. In general, the English came to the New World to settle, build homes, own land, and raise families. The French came for commercial reasons, the fur trade primarily, and with the traders or immediately behind them came French priests to convert the natives. The Spanish came after gold, though their priests too came for converts. Like all generalizations, these statements tend to break down in the particular, but they are some help in understanding the different attitudes of people from the three most involved nations toward the American Indians. Because these goals and attitudes made the interactions and relationships among the many European and Indian groups very complicated, they are worth describing in greater detail.

The Spanish. In the sixteenth and seventeenth centuries, the Spanish occupied strategic points along the Florida shoreline for military purposes. English privateers preyed on Spanish gold and silver bullion ships traveling with their cargoes from Mexico to Spain through the Straits of Florida between the mainland and Cuba. The Spanish used their forts as supply depots and ports of refuge for their ships. They were not interested in taking land from the Florida Indians or permanently settling there. Spanish priests came over, though, dedicated to saving souls, beginning a remarkably friendly and lasting contact between priests and natives.

In the Southwest the search for gold proved fruitless; Spanish commercial interest there waned, but again the secondary goal of conversion to Christianity remained strong. In fact, when the Rio Grande Pueblo resisted conversion and insisted on keeping their traditional religious practices, the clergy called upon the Spanish military to force Christianity upon the Indians. That destroyed peaceful relationships in that area. In California, the Spanish established missions backed by military might, but the California natives were less resistant to the clergy's appeals and did not fight for their traditional ways. Consequently Spanish rule there was gentler than in the Southwest, though they did punish Indians caught in their traditional religious practices, which the Spanish priests considered idolatrous, and forced them into an alien way of life. But the California fathers were generally kind in a paternalistic way and genuinely wanted to better Indian life, at least by Spanish Catholic standards.

The English. English explorers and settlers landed all along the Atlantic coast, from Canada to the Carolinas. English and Indians were at peace and generally friendly at first, but the cordiality did not last. There were two basic reasons for the increasing conflict and distrust that soon separated them: religion and economics.

Puritan English settlers saw the Indians as heathens (non-Puritan and non-English) and devil worshipers, but more than that, many of them often believed the Indians to be less than human. While official Catholic doctrine proclaimed Indians to be human beings and therefore candidates for conversion, Protestantism, at least in its more rigidly Puritanical forms, denied their humanity.

Many English did not bother to understand or even learn about native values and beliefs. Most of them treated the Indians as heathens, inferiors, and undesirables, although there were a few notable exceptions like Roger Williams of Rhode Island Colony and William Penn and other English Quakers. Even when they managed to convert the natives, many English looked down on them and insulted Indian pride. Some theologians (Cotton Mather was the prize example) thought that Indians were too savage and too inferior even to profit from conversion. Naturally people with attitudes like those saw nothing but sin and horror in the idea of marriage between Europeans and Indians, so that intermarriage in the English-dominated area was rare.

One economic fact inevitably brought strife between Indians and English—and indeed between Indians and all Europeans: their difference in attitude toward land ownership. To the Indian, land was a free good, to be used but not owned. But for the English, owning their very own land was the goal that drew many, perhaps most, across the ocean. Most of the British immigrants were the poor, the dispossessed, and the younger sons of nobility who had no rights in land back home. They had dreamed of finding cheap real estate subject to complete private ownership, and that was what they came after. When an Indian gave up rights to land in exchange for goods, the English took it to mean sale of land into private ownership. They did pay for the land they took but the Indians did not understand what the English meant by the transfer of property rights.

Such differences of opinion over land could lead only to conflict. Defending private ownership of land always brought political confrontation, and when that failed, warfare. Military activities were justified by religion. If Indians were heathen, inferior, perhaps not even human, it was perfectly all right to take their land, and if they resisted, it was all right to kill them. Thus religion was called on as an excuse for human destruction. In the Northeast, the English moved in and the Indians moved out.

Not all British were of this turn of mind, however. Many Scots who came to the New World were more sympathetic than the English to Indian ideas and ideals. Scottish colonists, descendants of Scots who had lived for a century in Ulster, Northern Ireland, settled down in the

Southeast. Unlike the English farther north, many of the Scots were single men, and they often married Indian women and set up homes and families. A fairly large population of mixed Scots-Indian descent grew in North Carolina, Tennessee, and Georgia. From that group came famed Indian leaders like Alexander McGillivray and Chilly and William MacIntosh of the Creek, and John Ross of the Cherokee. Scots who settled in Canada also became friendly with the Indians. Scottish fur trappers settled in the Athabaskan Subarctic, married Indian women, and produced a group of mixed-blood descendants.

The British established some schools to civilize and Christianize Indians. Dartmouth College was specifically set up in 1769 as an institution for Indian youths, and Harvard College and the College of William and Mary also were supposed to offer educational opportunities for Indians. Few Indians attended those schools, and before long their student bodies contained no one of Indian descent at all.

Trade goods were a far more powerful English influence than education. Guns and gunpowder, metal goods, and liquor were most important in commerce between English and Indians. The English also introduced domestic animals—horses, cattle, pigs, chickens—and appliances like the spinning wheel, loom, and plow. Indians of the East were using all these items in colonial times, before the Revolutionary War, and they also became accustomed to European household furniture, such as beds, and to English-style clothing. Pictures we have from colonial days show Indians not in buckskin but in calico, with cloth turbans on their heads.

The French. French missionaries were at work from early times. In 1615, Champlain sent missionaries into the St. Lawrence area; first Franciscans, then Jesuits came. Some of the best information we have about Northeastern Indians comes from the Jesuits' careful study and recording of Indian customs. The Montagnais and Huron were particular targets for conversion. Working strenuously to halt the sale of liquor to Indians and to counteract its effects, the French clergy managed to get laws passed banning its sale, but when the Indians turned to the Dutch and English for supplies, the government reversed itself and again allowed alcohol to be sold in French territory. The missionaries kept trying to halt the traffic; they were out to help the people, not the government.

French contact with the northern Algonkian-speaking people was mostly sympathetic and friendly. French forces considered the Algonkians allies, and the French in general looked on Indians as human beings. Their Catholic doctrine was quite unlike Calvinist Protestantism: Indians were to be converted and then received as equals. European and Indian blood thus was mixed far more in French territory than anywhere else north of Mexico. The French respected most Indian institutions and even tried to learn Indian languages. Mixed-bloods spoke both French and Indian tongues, a political and economic advantage to the French.

French trade in guns gave their Indian allies an advantage over the other tribes and helped the French gain control over territory in the fur trade. The French also saw that Indian alliances would be bulwarks against the English threat. However opportunistic the French may have been, though, they usually treated the Indians as human and equal.

The French lost their hold on the New World largely because the Indians with whom they allied themselves were weaker than those allied with England. The League of the Iroquois was hostile to the French mostly because the League members were hereditary enemies of the French Indian allies, the Algonkian speakers and the Huron. Earlier, alliances with the Algonkians had helped France win a stronghold in the Northeast, but it was largely the Iroquois alliance with England that drove the French out. The Iroquois were better military strategists than the Algonkians, and the French had allied themselves with the weaker side.

Consequences of Contact

Religious Reaction

In spite of the determination of missionaries of many faiths, Indians did not change their religious beliefs and practices easily. Many Indians were perfectly willing to add Christian dogma to their religious system—the more gods and spirits the better. But few were willing to abandon the old ways for the new.

Like their ideas about land ownership, Europeans and Indian approaches to the supernatural were irreconcilably different. Indians did not mix ethics with religion, and Christian morality was alien to Indian thought. Missionaries deplored dream and vision seeking, particularly when it involved drugs, and they tried to stop such practices. Whereas missionaries preached moral behavior as preparation for a future life, Indian philosophy was practical and immediate. Indians used religion to persuade the supernatural to help in the problems of living, not to attain future bliss. Indians pacified spirits with offerings and observed many taboos to compel the spirits to help them. Missionaries usually saw such practices as devil worship.

Indians believed too that the natural world had a dual existence: animals, plants, and places had spiritual as well as physical being, and proper ritual could compel them to help human beings. Missionaries, on the other hand, were horrified at the idea of many gods and of merely adding Christian practices to old beliefs. They wanted Indians to change completely, to abandon the traditional ways and the traditional gods—anything less was unacceptable.

The Spread of Diseases

Germs, which could cross all cultural boundaries, caused far worse devastation than any military action. Diseases to which Europeans had developed immunities spread among New World natives with immediate and disastrous results. Isolated for 20,000 years or more, Indians had no protection against the microbes of the Old World. Whole societies perished: within a hundred years of contact, disease had left no Indians in the West Indies, and it had cut down population in some other areas to one-tenth the numbers at contact. The Indians were helpless, and so were the agents of transmission, the newcomers, who could not halt the destruction they had unleashed on unresistant peoples. Scientific medicine had little to offer before the nineteenth century.

We do not know how many Indians died from disease. Mortality figures are no better documented than those on Indian population in general. Seven-eighths of California's population at the time of contact may have died of disease, while overall mortality has been estimated at 90 percent. But these are estimates based on estimates. We do know that far more Indians died of disease than by European aggression.

Some diseases, like smallpox, flared up in sporadic epidemics or outbreaks. George Catlin, the artist who painted many Indians in the nineteenth century, described a smallpox outbreak that virtually wiped out the Mandan on the upper Missouri River. Fur traders visiting a Mandan village in 1838 had accidentally introduced the disease. All the wives and children of a man Catlin had painted died of smallpox; the man lost all interest in life, refused to eat, and died of starvation. Only thirty or forty Mandan remained alive after the epidemic, and they were enslaved by their enemies, the Arikara.

About 1800, Edward Jenner invented a vaccination against smallpox, a disease as much dreaded in Europe as in America. Doctors tried to vaccinate Indian populations as the disease spread in the nineteenth century, but failed because there were few doctors in areas of high Indian concentration, and Indians who had not seen what smallpox could do resisted attempts to vaccinate them, believing their shamans' skill would protect them.

The Spread of New World Cultigens

Plants domesticated by New World people were botanically very different from Old World crops. Many of them became important in parts of the Old World where the traditional domesticates did not grow well. Old World cultigens like wheat, barley, and rice are not suitable crops in many areas where New World domesticates, especially maize and white and sweet potatoes, can flourish. Corn spread to Africa and southern Europe, the sweet potato to China, and the white potato to northern Europe, where it became known as the Irish potato because it became so important to the Irish diet.

Tobacco cultivation also spread around the world. Carib Indians in the West Indies smoked tobacco, as Columbus discovered when he landed there. They rolled the leaves to smoke them as cigars and also burned dried leaves, inhaling the smoke through hollow reeds. Spaniards introduced cigars into Spain in 1519, and Sir John Hawkins brought tobacco to England in 1573. Tobacco used as snuff and for chewing as well as smoking became popular in the Middle East before the end of the sixteenth century. Virginia Colony virtually pinned its life on its tobacco exports in the early seventeenth century. In the early years, colonists even used tobacco leaves as a medium of exchange.

Government Policies toward Indians

The Colonial Period

During the American colonial period, from about 1620 to 1756, England left relations between the colonies and the Indians to the local governments, for the most part. The only requirements were that settlers or colonies should pay for any Indian lands they acquired, and individuals could purchase Indian lands only with permission from the government. In 1756, the king centralized control of Indian affairs by appointing two superintendents, one for northern affairs and one for southern, to negotiate with Indians and regulate trade.

Contrary to popular belief, the official British policy was to compensate Indians for their lands. Though that compensation may seem to have been pitifully inadequate, Indians had no other way of obtaining the European metal implements, mirrors, glass beads, and even firearms they wanted, and they were quite willing to exchange rights in land for these treasures. Knowing no such thing as private ownership of land, Indians probably did not realize that they were actually surrendering their property. And the English did not realize that the Indians did not share their idea of the exchange.

Treaties. Colonists considered Indians independent sovereign nations and treated them as they would any nation, under international law. Accustomed to centralized political power, the English assumed that each tribe had a chief who had the right to sign for his tribe as the reigning official. In a few cases that was so: the chief of the Powhatan and the Great Sun of the Natchez did have such power. But most groups had no person with authority to sign away tribal lands, though colonists rarely realized that.

As the colonists signed treaties which ceded tribal land to them, they were, in effect, pushing the tribes out of their traditional regions. In some colonies, tax-free land was set aside by treaty for the Indians within the colony's territory, and the colonists further promised regular payments of goods and food to the Indians who moved onto that land. Thus in a small way the *reservation* system began.

The Reservation System. The idea of reservations was not new. It had a respected place in English history. Under James I in 1603, English colonists trying to take over a section of Celtic Scotland moved the native Celts onto reservations—those Celts whom they did not exterminate. The "removal" worked so well that they used it in Ireland a few years later, justifying the move on the grounds that the Celts of both Scotland and Ireland were wild and primitive folk, and civilized English would make better use of the land. Native languages were suppressed and tribal customs were banned. Scottish and Irish children were sent away to English schools to be "civilized." Change the names "Celts, Scots, Irish" to "Indian" and you have described the reservation policy in North America, a heritage from British colonialism to the United States.

After Independence. After the Revolutionary War, eastern pioneers continued to press westward, forcing still more Indians from their land. The new federal government, still treating the tribes as independent sovereign states, worked out a program by which Indians exchanged their lands east of the Mississippi River for territory to the west. Population in the West was light, and few whites sought western lands in early federal days, though some eastern residents and government officials began to see a surge of white population to the Pacific Ocean as the nation's "manifest destiny." Those few recognized that sooner or later conflict with the western Indians had to come, and it did. Between the time of independence from Britain and the end of the nineteenth century, both Indians and whites did many cruel and treacherous things. The Indians, of course, were trying to save what was left of their lands and homes; the whites wanted more land rights.

The Bureau of Indian Affairs. Indian removal from the East was accompanied by payments and promises from Washington of annual funds, goods, and food, plus guarantees that the new lands would not be taken from the Indians for "as long as the grasses shall grow and the waters run."

In 1824 the federal government established a Bureau of Indian Affairs in the War Department, a clear sign of the official attitude in Indian-federal relations: hostile. Although in 1849 the Bureau of Indian Affairs was transferred to the Department of the Interior, Indians had few contacts with white Americans that were not hostile.

Indian Removal. By the Indian Removal Act of 1830, President Jackson and Congress specified the removal of all eastern tribes to west of the Mississippi River. Most eastern seaboard tribes had already fled west of the Alleghenies which made removal easier than it might have been for both the government and the tribes. However, some southeastern tribes, especially the Five Civilized Tribes (see chapter 8), resisted and suffered greatly when with few exceptions they were forced to leave.

By this time, Congress had designated part of the land received from France in the Louisiana Purchase (1803) Indian Territory; it would later become the state of Oklahoma. Some eastern Indians had already moved there, but now all tribes in the East were forced to abandon their old homes and resettle within the area which was the traditional home of nomadic Indians of the south Plains like the Comanche and the Kiowa or the more sedentary river agriculturalists like the Wichita and Quapaw. The government signed removal treaties assigning acreage to each tribe.

Homestead Act. In 1862, the Homestead Act opened up Indian land in Kansas and Nebraska to white homesteaders. After the Civil War, ex-soldiers flooded the plains seeking homesteads. By the 1870s, the Indian tribes were no longer treated as independent sovereign states, but as domestic dependencies. Almost all Indians in Canada and the United States were by then living on reservations, though many tried to resist confinement. The reservations became prison camps, federal soldiers seeing to it that Indians stayed in their allotted areas. The government established reservation schools and boarding schools in an attempt to Anglicize Indian children. Agents were put in charge of the reservations, and though many of them were genuinely sympathetic toward the tribes, they could do little, for they did not set policy. Many agents were very poor administrators; worse yet, some were dishonest, keeping supplies and embezzling money intended for Indian welfare.

Allotment. In 1887, the Allotment Act permitted individual Indians to own parcels of reservation land outright, in hopes that the new owners would take to farming and ranching and turn into farmers on the European model. It did not work that way; individual Indians leased or sold their lands to whites. Also, the government sold to whites reservation lands that were not allotted to Indians, further decreasing Indian territory. By the turn of the century, the living conditions and psychological states of reservation dwellers were hopelessly low. Strict, supervised reservation life had not "civilized" the Indians, private ownership of land had not turned them into proud farmers and ranchers, nor had forced schooling "civilized" them.

No matter how hard lawmakers in Washington tried to enact legislation to relieve the Indians' most severe problems, no matter how interested they were in fairness, they could not control the frontier and reservation territory. Far from the nation's capital, men took law into their own hands or ignored it altogether. Supplies were sent to help the Indians adjust to reservation life, schools were set up, but more often than not the Indians never got the supplies or heard of the benefits they were entitled to. Crooked agents were legion. They became wealthy profiteering while Indians were inadequately housed, clothed, and fed. Substandard living conditions, coupled with disease, kept mortality high. Many who lived felt they had nothing to live for. Their lands were gone and the governmental authorities refused to let them follow traditional ways. A change so great in so short a time, loss of both land and freedom to wander, could only be destructive. It was forced on an unwilling people who had no part in the planning, and few of those who did plan had any real knowledge of conditions or desires among the people whose very lives were involved.

It seemed logical to planners who knew little about the diversity of Indian life that if they had land and an opportunity to farm, all Indians would settle down happily to an agricultural life. Many Indians, of course, had long histories as farmers, but many others did not. Besides, only the Pueblo men among all the Indians had done actual cultivation; the others considered farming women's work. Former warriors and hunters were emasculated psychologically when they were forced to turn to farming. With proper preparation a change like that probably could have been made over several decades or generations, but not all at once. And no one consulted with Indians or asked them to take part in decisions. Administrations changed in Washington; many social, religious, and government groups were sincerely interested; but too few really knew what they were doing.

Citizenship and the Vote. Although some individual Indians had been made citizens of the United States in the nineteenth century, Indians in general were not citizens, could not vote, and had little say in their own affairs. In 1924, Congress made all Indians who were twenty-one and older, on reservations or not, citizens of the country and enfranchised them for federal elections. Most states soon thereafter gave Indians the vote, though they still could not vote in New Mexico and

Arizona until after World War II.

In 1934, Congress passed the Indian Reorganization Act, giving reservation Indians the right to establish tribal governments. The act also made funds available for loans to duly elected Indian councils to improve conditions on reservations and to undertake self-government. It had provisions for education and for agricultural and industrial credit. Allotment was discontinued, making it impossible for outsiders to buy any more reservation land. The federal government ceased making treaties with the tribes in 1871, and since that date the vehicles of interaction have been Congressional Acts, Executive Orders, and Executive Agreements.

Local Culture Contact and Change

Indian societies were not all alike, nor were all the Europeans who came to the New World the same. In general, European reactions to Indians varied according to the newcomers' nationality, goals, and philosophies. Now let us see how European contact affected the native American people region by region.

The Northeast

Early in the sixteenth century, French and Basque fishermen and some from other nations fished for the rich schools of cod swarming off the Newfoundland banks. The set up small depots in natural harbors to dry their catch, and while ashore they traded European goods with Indians for fresh food. Along with the goods they passed on European diseases, which moved into the continental interior far more quickly than the explorers.

Fishermen soon saw how plentiful fur-bearing animals were in the North Atlantic area, and interest turned from fish to furs. Indians swiftly took advantage of the European desire for pelts and brought fox, mink, muskrat, and, above all, beaver to the coast to trade. French traders and fur trappers moved toward the interior along with Catholic clergy, who started small settlements. The priests and nuns were there for conversions, not furs, and they made close and friendly contact with Algonkian tribes on both sides of the St. Lawrence River. French traders built Quebec as a fur depot where Indians could bring pelts to exchange for firearms, kettles, cloth, and other European imports.

The Huron Indians, Iroquoian speakers, became the intermediaries in the extensive fur trade of the north. They were friendly to France and to Indians west of them, but enemies of the other Iroquoian speakers, members of the League. The Huron, on the shores of the lake of that name, charged toll to other Indians bringing furs for trade. Making use of their friendship with the Huron, the French had the advantage in the first part of the seventeenth century. The English were struggling to stay alive in settlements farther south, so that the only problem the French faced was tribal warfare between friendly Indians and their enemies. In those fights, France was forced to take sides to keep the Huron loyal, making France the enemy of the League of the Iroquois.

As fur trade expanded, trappers moved farther west seeking new supplies of the fur-bearing animals, for unrestricted trapping was rapidly bringing some species in the East near extinction. The French penetration into the Algonkian Subarctic was swift, and with the accompanying disease it was deadly. Not only were animals being hunted to extinction; whole tribes, like the Beothuk, were dying out. Though French and Indians were friendly and each got desirable items from the other, Indian life as it had been before contact was destroyed, with disease killing vast numbers. Indian ways changed as their old hunting and gathering habits gave way to fur trapping, and they learned to depend on trade goods.

The Atlantic Seaboard

The land from southeastern Canada to the border of Spanish Florida was settled by the English. Dutch forces briefly held the Hudson River valley, but their impact was slight. English settlements sprang up rapidly on the coast and more slowly in the interior. The area was not good for furs; besides, the English had come to build homes, not trade. Indians helped the English settlers at first, teaching the colonists how to grow the New World plants and how to cook the new foods. A few interracial marriages took place; Pocahontas married John Rolfe and went to England. But soon the friendliness disintegrated, and acts of aggression, some quite frightful, came from both sides.

Before the Eastern Indians were driven out, killed, or destroyed by disease, they received European goods that changed many of their traditional ways. By the mid-1600s, Eastern Indians were wearing garments of European cloth, cooking with pots and pans, and hunting with guns. As the English learned about North American crops, the Indians began to raise chickens, horses, dairy cattle, and fruits such as peaches and apples. The Algonkian tribes took up European styles of embroidery, in the Subarctic and Great Lakes region as well as on the coast, and with imported threads and beads combined those styles with their traditional curvilinear designs to produce attractive work on buckskin and cloth, on belts, moccasins, hats, and other clothing. People are often surprised to see how similar Algonkian design is to European peasant design. They are related through the combination of the needlework that the nuns taught the Indians in French territory and the traditional vine and leaf patterns of the Eastern Indians.

The Southeast

In the Southeast the Spanish held Florida, except for a brief period of British rule, until they ceded it to the United States in 1821. When Spanish priests arrived in Florida, they turned their attention to the Florida Indians, especially the Timucua in the northern half of the peninsula. Spanish military leaders looked on these northern Indians as buffers against English settlers and soldiers threatening from the Carolinas and Georgia. In the Southeast as in the North, the Indians fought each other as allies of warring European powers. And they suffered from fast-spreading European disease.

The Creek Indians sided with the English, the Timucua and Yamassee with the Spanish, and the French had allies in the Natchez and Choctaw along the lower Mississippi River. It was during the English-Spanish conflict in the early eighteenth century that the first groups of Creek separated from the main body and moved to Florida, where they became known as Seminole.

As in other Eastern areas, Indians rapidly acquired European material culture, and their traditional clothing, equipment, and furnishings disappeared. The Spanish introduced citrus crops as well as cattle in Florida, and the northern Florida Indians and the Seminole separatists put in orchards and raised herds of cattle. The Spanish word for cattle, *vaca*, remains in the Mikasuki (Seminole) vocabulary in the south Florida swampland as *waki*.

The Spanish made no effort to settle Florida with colonists or to take land from the Indians. Spanish soldiers were there only to protect Spanish trade routes; once the Florida Indians had been converted to Catholicism, no further interference came from Spanish sources. The Florida Indians lived in peace until the American Revolution, except for the disease that, as everywhere, decimated the population.

After the Revolution, military forces under Andrew Jackson invaded Florida and forced out the Spanish. In the brutal wars that followed—with federal losses higher than in any other Indian wars—Indians were all but eliminated from Florida and the rest of the Southeast. They were moved onto land west of the Mississippi, leaving only small and isolated settlements in the East, the Cherokee in North Carolina, the Choctaw in Mississippi, and the Seminole in south Florida. The rest were forcibly settled in the lands Congress called Indian Territory, now Oklahoma. The Indians took with them little but their knowledge and skills, and started a new life far from their homelands.

The Midwest

As trapping depleted the supply of animals in the East, Indian and European trappers pushed on to the Western Great Lakes, following the chain of lakes and streams to the Mississippi River. As in earlier colonial times, those most involved with the fur trade were the French. Until the middle of the seventeenth century, few Frenchmen did the actual trapping in the Western Lakes area because the Huron kept the sources of supply for themselves. However, the Huron were defeated by their traditional enemies, the League members, and after 1650 the French and other Indians moved into the rich Huron fur lands of the Upper Great Lakes.

Contact between the Europeans and Indians of the Lakes and prairie went as it had in the East. Trade boomed and disease spread. Eastern tribes, pushed off their lands by settlers, moved into the Lakes territory and in turn pressed against the tribes there. The Midwest was the scene of jockeying for territory and favorable trade positions during the 150 years before the Revolutionary War.

Many French trappers settled down and married Indian women. Trade goods supplanted traditional Indian materials; steel and iron tools as well as firearms became common Indian possessions. Like the Scottish population of the Southeast, mixed-blood families often produced political leaders. Many of the Winnebago, Ojibwa, and Ottawa came to have French names. Catholic missionaries tried to convert Indians and also to keep the French traders from undoing the conversions, for the traders paid slight attention to religion.

Stimulated by new ideas from contact with Europeans, arts and crafts among the Lakes and prairie tribes literally blossomed. Women reproduced their traditional curved designs of flowers and vines with the imported beads and silk ribbons the French introduced. The Menominee, Potawatomi, and Winnebago developed an appliqué ribbon work to adorn the cloth clothing they now wore instead of buckskin.

English pressures began to change life for Lakes Indians. The English dispossessed the tribes in the East, who began to move into the Midwest, creating pressures on the tribes there. English trade goods, often more plentiful and of better quality than the French could supply, filtered in from the East to tempt the Indians. French and English confronted each other all across the Northeast and Midwest, and the English won.

The prosperity the Indians had achieved under the French was lost as England became the sole European power. As in the East, English settlers eyed Indian land for home sites. Indians fought desperately under Pontiac, an Ottawa, to drive back the English in 1763. They failed, as they would under the Shawnee, Tecumseh, fifty years later.

England controlled the Great Lakes area only until 1776, when forced by the War for Independence to give it up to the new United States. After that, Indians had no chance to stay and rebuild. The new nation planned expansion into Indian territory; Indians lost their land and their traditional ways, and had to abandon the new life they had become accustomed to under the French. The disease that broke out again, and alcohol, the one item of trade they always managed to get, further disorganized their lives. Sadly, as wards of the government, they moved onto reservations.

Handsome Lake. Throughout history, in times of cultural stress, societies have turned to the types of religion often called *revitalization movements*. These have been especially common in situations of oppression and deprivation, and a number of them developed among Indians as they were defeated and driven off their lands by Europeans. The earliest and most enduring Indian religious response to economic and social threat was the Handsome Lake religion, which started in the very early 1800s.

Handsome Lake was a Seneca Indian, a tribal official (the name Handsome Lake is actually a sachem's or chief's title). He was not renowned as a warrior; before his religious awakening he had been something of an invalid, a heavy drinker, and subject to visions and trances. About 1800 his dreams and visions took a new direction. He believed that he was in communication with the spirit world and that the spirits gave him a message to preach to his people, the League of the Iroquois, who were sadly disunited by the Revolutionary War. Some had sided with the British, some with the colonists, and the League had disintegrated.

Handsome Lake had had some experience with different forms of Christianity. He had some Quaker friends, and he had probably been to some of the evangelical revival meetings that were popular among frontier folk of New York. Those camp meetings were held in tents where preachers roused congregations to religious frenzy. Handsome Lake's message combined Christianity and cultural revitalization. He preached that there was a god and a heaven, and that George Washington was there too. He combined traditional Iroquois beliefs with these new doctrines, not rejecting the old ways but emphasizing changed behavior and hard work. He taught that Indians should give up alcohol and turn to farming and animal husbandry. But he did not want them to be just like the whites. He urged his people to observe their kin obligations, to avoid divorce, and to take better care of Indian children. He thought Indians should remain neutral in all wars between the whites, but he wanted them to learn some white ways. Two boys from each tribe should attend white schools, he said, but all Indian children should not go to school.

Handsome Lake died in 1815, but his doctrine was taken up and memorized by followers. By mid-century it had been recorded in writing as the Code of Handsome Lake. It spread widely as a doctrine of reform while preserving Indian identity. The Code, originally quite revolutionary, came to stand for traditional ways, and today it still has many adherents, who are considered the conservatives among the Iroquois.

The Plains

Life on the Plains changed radically when the Indians acquired horses; in fact, the area's culture climax was the result of European contact. The Indians could cover two or three times as much ground as they had on foot, and as mounted nomads they could follow the buffalo herds. They also could accumulate more property now that they had horses to carry it. The horse totally changed their economy, and in so doing changed their social structure.

The period of cultural climax with the horse was as brief as it was dramatic: by 1850 the heyday was over. While it lasted it was so satisfying that the Indians forgot their old traditions and began to think they had always been equestrians. When the days of mounted freedom were over, nothing remained to take their place. The Plains people had no desire to return to old hunting and gathering ways or to turn to agriculture, even if they remembered such activities. Never had the men of the Plains tribes been farmers. Even in the groups with farming traditions women had been the cultivators. Farming was women's work, not fit for the hunter and warrior.

Because they had kept up cultivation in their new equestrian life, the Plains Village tribes did not lose quite as much as the mounted nomads. They went back to agriculture, though they too felt that farming was degrading work for a man. And it was a severe indignity to be confined to reservations.

The Fading of the Plains Tradition. How did the flamboyant way of the Plains nomad end? It had begun while England and France were fighting in the East for control of North America, so that neither nation had time to interfere with the Plains development. After independence, the new United States was preoccupied with unity and federation; it too, for several decades at least, was too busy to consider expanding beyond the Mississippi. In fact, through the first part of the nineteenth century, the government saw the Plains Indians as a buffer protecting the United States from Spain and Mexico in the Southwest. The United States needed time to organize and develop a strong federal government, and for a while it had enough territory east of the Mississippi to contain its attentions. The nomads of the Plains flourished in their dramatic new life without interference from Washington.

By 1850 the country was united and strong with nothing to fear from European powers. The fur trade, having wiped out much of the animal population of the East, was expanding into the Northwest. In 1848, gold was discovered in California. Settlers were beginning to agitate for homesteads in the West, and in 1862 the Homestead Act set up inexpensive 160-acre plots of land to meet this demand. All these events produced a new interest in the Plains and put pressure on the federal government to expand into that territory. Lewis and Clark had made their long journey through the Northwest, and people expressed interest in settling there, as far off as Oregon territory. The government began planning to confine the Plains tribes to specific areas.

The End of the Buffalo. As the horse had spread into the Plains from the Spaniards in the Southwest, so firearms came in from the French in the north. Mounted Indians with guns, especially after the repeating rifle was available, began to kill far more buffalo than bows and arrows ever had. White hunters, too, pursued the buffalo. In the old days Indians had used all parts of the buffalo—hooves, horns, sinew, even stomachs had been washed out and used as containers. But with their new killing power and the demand for buffalo hides, the hunters skinned the buffalo and took the hide, leaving the carcass to rot. Such waste had never been known before. Even when herds of buffalo had been stampeded over deadfalls—which was not frequent—the waste had not been that great. Buffalo began to disappear, hunted out as the fur-bearing animals had been a century before in the eastern Subarctic and Great Lakes regions.

Inevitably, the government responded to complaints and demands from its citizens by trying to confine the Plains Indians, preventing their free-wandering movements following the seasonal cycle of the buffalo. At first Washington or its agents tried to set boundaries for each tribe—not reservations, but borders within which the Indians were to be free to follow their accustomed way of life. But there was never enough territory within those boundaries. To pursue the buffalo, the tribes had to move over greater distances. The next federal move was to create reservations, none of which was large enough for the old hunting practices. By then the old wandering would have come to an end anyway, for the gun had done the trick; the buffalo were gone—almost overnight, it seemed. Those great herds of thundering animals, seemingly an inexhaustible source of food, clothing, shelter, and equipment, had vanished. Government agents reasoned that it was time for the Indians to settle down, to become farmers and livestock raisers. Of course, many of the lands appropriated for Indian occupation could not support agriculture; but the Plains warriors were not interested in farming anyhow.

Desperation of the Plains. Meanwhile, railway lawyers got Indians to sign over rights-of-way through Indian territory so that railways could be built. Many deeds were signed by Indians whom the whites considered chiefs but who had no right to sign away tribal lands or to make decisions for the tribes. The plains were crisscrossed with trails and railroads and invaded by Easterners who had no right to be there but who expected protection from the federal government.

Psychological blows fell one after another on the Plains people. Their source of food gone, little aggravations piling up broke the Indian spirit, leaving despair and a sense of futility. Under pressure from church groups, the government banned the Sun Dance as brutal and uncivilized. Missionaries tried to undermine the old religions and to prevent the vision quest, calling them barbaric, superstitious, and ignorant. Alcohol too was banned, but it was always available, and from it came solace, a way of forgetting and of achieving a new kind of vision. While Indians tried to forget by using intoxicants, whites used liquor to cheat Indians, to get them to sign away property or rights while drunk.

Desperate, a few men tried to do what no other Indians had been able to do: rally men of different bands and tribes to unite and fight back. But even at that late date, Indians had not learned to stand together. Unused to long-term military discipline, cooperation on a large scale, or integrated tactics, they made few successful forays, winning a few battles here and there but losing the war. After General George Custer was defeated at the battle of Little Bighorn in 1876, the Indian troops disbanded. The federal troops, though defeated in battle, replaced their losses and returned to destroy another day. Indians fought well in commando-like raids or ambushes on wagon trains of supplies, and finally in isolated attacks on travelers and homesteads. But the army always came back at them, organized, united, with supplies, personnel, and replacements the Indians could not muster. The end was bound to be in favor of the federal troops.

The Ghost Dance and Wounded Knee. Living a cramped and meaningless life on rations allotted by the federal government, the once free and proud Plains Indians turned to mystical comfort. Wovoka, a Paiute, claimed to have received a vision that directed him to journey from tribe to tribe and teach a new way of life, a new doctrine. His message was to give up European ways, to return to old customs that had been practiced before the Europeans arrived, to go back to the simple life, with no guns, no alcohol, no trade goods. Give all that up, and dance. Dance, and the Europeans would depart, leaving the land once more

Wovoka, a Paiute, devised the Ghost Dance based on a vision he had received. The dance was intended to lead the Indians away from conflict with their white oppressors, but nevertheless ended in the massacre at Wounded Knee.

to the Indian peoples. Dance, and the great warriors of old—all the departed Indians—would return.

Some tribes took this as a message to return to the simple life; others saw it as aggressively antiwhite; but everywhere the people believed that the dancing would bring back the Indian dead. For that reason, this religious or revitalization movement came to be known as the Ghost Dance. Throughout the West, even into California, tribes laid down their arms. Wearily they turned away from conflict, and they danced. A slow, hypnotic dance it was, not anything wild and frenzied. Some groups wore shirts, called Ghost shirts, which were supposed to give magic protection against bullets.

Federal troops were everywhere, guarding against insurrection, and this strange behavior made them nervous. The troops were on edge, always expecting some attack, some ambush, remembering the battle of Little Bighorn and Custer's defeat; they could not believe that the Indians had given up. The Indian turn to the mystical, together with the soldiers' skepticism, led to perhaps the saddest confrontation ever between Indian and white. A band of Indians were camped under guard

After the massacre at Wounded Knee, federal troops shoveled the bodies of the Native Americans, frozen stiff, into a mass grave.

by the federal troops at Wounded Knee, South Dakota. On December 29, 1890, they assembled and began to dance. An army officer ordered them to stop. Someone, it is not known who, Indian or white, fired a shot, and the cavalry guard opened fire. Two hundred Indians and sixty soldiers soon lay dead. That was the battle of Wounded Knee, the last open confrontation between Plains Indians and the dominant society.

The Southwest

Spanish explorers under Coronado's leadership were the first Europeans to set eyes on the Pueblo Indians. Seeking the fabled Seven Cities of Gold, Coronado may have thought he had found them when he saw the Pueblo dwellings along the Rio Grande in 1540. But there was no gold, and the Spaniards claimed the land for Spain, stripped the Pueblo people of their food supplies, and moved on, leaving behind only the memory of pillage. Later, in 1598, Spaniards established a colony at Santa Fe as an administrative center for Spanish territory. The Pueblo people made no resistance and were easily dominated by the Spaniards. The Rio Grande settlements had never had any unity, and no one pueblo could stand alone against Spain's military might. The Spaniards did not strike out farther west into Hopi territory, but concentrated on the pueblos clustered along the river, where they easily imposed Spanish political and religious ways.

The traditional independence of each pueblo kept the Indians from uniting for nearly eighty years, but finally interference in their religious practices by Spanish priests goaded the Pueblo people into active resistance. They had borne Spanish military and political rule with little complaint, but the missionaries' determination to destroy "idolatrous practices" angered the people beyond endurance. The missionaries banned Pueblo dancers' masks, and when some Indians protested, the Spanish seized and hung them. By 1670, secret efforts were organized to unite the Pueblo.

Popé Uprising. The resistance was led by a man named Popé, who had been a medicine man or shaman, imprisoned by the Spanish for sorcery. Released after being whipped—a great humiliation—he began to preach revolt, claiming that the spirits would side with the Pueblo to overthrow the Spanish. He promised too that if the Pueblo united and drove out the foreigners, not only would the Indians be able to practice their old religion, but they also could keep all the booty—the Spaniards' equipment and goods.

The schedule for the uprising was kept very secret. Only Popé and a few trusted individuals who also had been flogged by the Spanish knew the details of the plot. Every pueblo had a leader in touch with Popé, who was to send a message to each leader to start the uprising in his town. The secret plans were leaked to the Spanish governor by a few Indians who refused to revolt. No one knew the date, however, and the Spanish mistakenly thought it was August 13. Tesuque pueblo started their revolt on August 11, 1680, and the others followed. The Spanish, taken by surprise, were driven out after much bloodshed and returned to Mexico.

Between 1680 and 1682, Spanish forces made some unsuccessful attempts to retake the Pueblo. For a while, Popé acted as a leader for all Rio Grande Pueblo, but the Indians faced unexpected problems. The food supply ran out, and marauding Apache attacked them. When Popé died around 1688, the Indians discovered that they were now dependent on Spanish trade. The Indians had equipment and firearms, but when something broke or wore out, they could not replace or repair it, nor could they make bullets. Famine, lack of central leadership, and the need for goods all created discontent among the Pueblo. In 1692, the Spanish made a stronger attempt to return and met little resistance. By 1696, all the Rio Grande pueblos were again under Spanish control. One group of the Rio Grande people fled to the Hopi, who had remained free of Spanish domination, and there built the town of Hano on the first mesa, where it still stands. The Pueblo never again revolted against European conquerors. In fact, in the nineteenth century, they joined with the Spanish in military forays against the Athabaskan raiders who plagued them.

Pueblo religion went underground after the Spanish reconquest. The Indians paid lip service to Catholic observance, but they continued their traditional religious practices privately in their kivas. The Spanish had less impact on other aspects of Pueblo culture, and life generally continued as in past ages, though the Pueblo accepted Spanish goods and learned to speak Spanish as well as their own tongues. The Spanish influence can be seen today in interior decoration and Spanish surnames as well as in Catholic ritual.

Athabaskan Reaction. Unlike the Pueblo, the other tribes of the Southwest were greatly changed by Spanish conquest. The Navajo acquired herds of sheep, and sheepherding became an important part of their economy. The Apache, some Navajo, and some tribes on the boundary of the plains, like the Kiowa Apache, took to a life on horseback more typical of the plains than of the Southwest. They concentrated on buffalo hunts and warfare, raiding not only the Pueblo but also Spanish settlements for metal tools, guns, and horses.

By the time the Spanish Southwest became United States territory in 1848, the Athabaskans had lived as they pleased for many years. They had acquired horses and equipment from the Spanish, but the Spanish or Mexicans had not tried to settle colonists on the land or tried to take land from the Indians. However, the United States, especially after the Civil War, began to move troops into the area, and it suddenly became clear to the Navajo and Apache that the Americans were something new to contend with. The Americans offered the Athabaskans treaties, but the Indians were too divided to sign them.

The Navajo are a case in point. In 1846, the American army signed a treaty with one Navajo band, assuming that the provisions would cover the entire tribe. Other Navajo bands did not agree, and hostilities continued. Finally the government ordered removal of all Navajo from Arizona territory to Ft. Sumner in New Mexico, 250 miles away. To force compliance, the military under Colonel Kit Carson rounded up and slaughtered the Navajo livestock. The starving Navajo were finally captured band by band and sent to the fort where they were kept for almost four years in an attempt to teach them to become farmers. The trek is remembered by the Navajo as the "Long Walk."

When it became apparent that the incarceration was a failure and a

Indian scouts, along with an interpreter and an officer, crouch for battle in Arizona's desert country.

cruelty, the government concluded a treaty establishing a Navajo reservation in northeastern Arizona, their old territory. However, the new reservation surrounded Hopi traditional lands and led inevitably to confrontation between the Navajo and the Hopi (see chapter 12). In compensation for the earlier destruction of flocks, the government restocked the sheep. It was following their return that Navajo women began to trade blankets woven from wool they had spun and dyed for cash income. The blankets—sometimes referred to as rugs—are today some of the best known and admired Indian art.

The Apache were trained fighters who knew the rugged land far better than the American troops sent to control them. They were fierce warriors led by fighters like Cochise and Geronimo. When placed on reservations, the Apache often refused to remain. It took many campaigns to subdue them, but the job was complete by the end of the nineteenth century. Agents encouraged the Apache to take up farming, but it appealed to them no more than to the Plains Indians. They too suffered despair and economic hardship, but eventually turned to ranching, and the western groups began to farm. The Ghost Dance found no converts among the Athabaskans because they feared the dead; the last thing they wanted was to have the dead return.

California

In 1542, hoping to find a waterway connecting the Pacific and Atlantic oceans, a cross-continent passage to the Orient, Juan Rodrigues Cabrillo sailed up the coast of California and into bays that looked as though they might lead inland. The first European to appear on the shores of California, he claimed the land for the Spanish crown. No other Spaniards followed him until the middle of the eighteenth century, when Spain began to fear encroachment by the Russians, who were then moving down the west coast from Alaska.

No one ever found a waterway between the oceans, for none existed, but the Spanish stayed to build missions and convert Indians. The first mission, San Diego, was established in 1769 where the city is today. Indians soon learned that they could get valuable trade goods at the missions, and they began to assemble and sometimes to live near the missions. Eventually Indians became virtual prisoners of the missionaries, who kept them at the missions by calling Spanish soldiers for help. Runaways were tracked down and whipped. Some offenders were even shot, and uprisings were quickly put down. The priests halted all the Indian ceremonies and refused to allow Indians access to shamans, or to cremate their dead. The Spanish fathers were determined to civilize the Indians, to teach them to work regular hours tilling the land and raising livestock.

The priests also taught the Indians to make adobe bricks for the mission buildings, which were almost like forts. The thick walls surrounding them had only one entrance, and the buildings themselves had thick walls with very small windows. Most missions had dormitories for unmarried Indians, one for men, one for women. Married couples and their children lived outside the mission walls, but they were not free to move away. After a generation or two, they no longer wanted to move away; having forgotten their old ways, they knew only how to live under the fathers' guidance.

Each mission aimed to be self-supporting. The Indians planted corn and European crops like wheat, fruit trees, and melons; wheat bread took the place of acorn bread. Women learned to weave cloth. Some Indians became sheepherders; they had freedom denied those working the mission fields because sheep had to move from pasture to pasture, and whole families went with them. While away from the mission herding sheep, the women gathered seeds and acorns and prepared food as in the past. But even the herders were kept under mission control. Soon all Mission Indians dressed and ate like Spaniards.

The fathers taught blacksmithing to the Indians but never allowed them to own horses: they could escape too easily on horseback. Many Indians did escape, but most discovered that they no longer knew how to live in the wilderness and went back to the missions for food. They had become dependent upon European technology, agriculture, livestock, and tools such as metal axes and saws.

When the United States took over California from Mexico in 1846, the Indians ran into active persecution by whites. The newcomers who came from the East to live and farm had no knowledge of Indians and did not want them on the land. Justice for Indians was so rare that few Mission Indians were left by the twentieth century.

California Indians north of the mission areas were not troubled by whites until the gold rush of 1849. After that their story was one of continuous loss of territory and general destruction. Some reservations were set up by the federal and state governments, and some Indians began working for the new arrivals on the ranches and farms. But of California's dense aboriginal population only a few remain today.

Under the Mission Relief Act of 1881, remnants of the Mission Indians received some acreage of generally poor lands which they still hold today. Though most of these small holdings have remained economically unproductive, and indeed, some are not even inhabited, one of them, the Agua Caliente Reservation, is now extremely valuable: the city of Palm Springs lies within it. Other small tracts of land passed to the native people of central and northern California under treaties of 1851, not acted upon until 1906 to 1910. These parcels represent the bulk of Indian land in California and are known as "rancherias." Total Indian holdings range in size from the Hoopa Valley Reservation of 87,000 acres to rancherias of less than 100 acres. In 1958, the Rancheria Termination Act provided for the gradual withdrawal of these small tracts from government supervision. Under management by the BIA, land and assets have passed to individual Indians.

The Plateau and the Basin

People of the Plateau felt the European presence in North America long before any came to their area. Trade goods had entered the Plateau in exchange for furs, and the tribes in the eastern part of the area had horses by the middle of the eighteenth century. The eastern Plateau and mountain slopes provided good grassland for pasturage, and some tribes of that area began to live a mounted life and became able horse raisers. The Nez Perce were noted for their fine horses, which Plains Indians often sought in trade. The Cayuse horse herds were so well known that the word *cayuse* entered the English language as slang for horse.

Life changed for the Plateau people who raised horses much as it did for the Plains people, though less drastically. War and war honors became important for the men, and war chiefs had high prestige. Of course, horse raising brought about many changes in clothing, equipment, and even housing. The movable tipi became the common shelter while men were hunting. Some of the Plateau warriors even began to wear feathered warbonnets.

Almost identical changes occurred in the Basin close to the Plains, though the dry lands in most of the region made horse raising impossible. The easternmost Basin people moved out into the grasslands and lived as nomadic hunters. The Shoshoni, above all, became true mounted warriors, and the Comanche, once merely a band of Shoshoni, became the terrors of the southern Plains. All these changes happened before Indians and whites actually met.

Contacts and Changes. The Lewis and Clark expedition was the first intimate contact between the Plateau and Basin Indians and whites. The interpreter for that journey was a Shoshoni woman, Sacajawea, who was married to a French fur trapper. They were living among the Mandan Indians when Lewis and Clark came through. She said she would like to go with them when she heard that they were heading for the Pacific Ocean, explaining that she had wanted to see that great body of water ever since she first heard of it. So she went along, and gave birth to her first child while on the march. She made the journey easier by serving as an interpreter, and several times prevented aggression by suspicious tribes. Both leaders expressed their gratitude and spoke of their debt to her.

Traders and fur trappers followed through the Northwest, many with Indian wives. As in the East, trapping soon became big business, for the demand for fine furs in Europe and Asia never ceased. Traders and trappers never caused Indians much worry, except for the germs they carried, but the settlers from the East who eyed the Northwest for homesteads and farmlands were another story. The Basin land was not desirable for agriculture, but both Basin and Plateau people felt the loss when the buffalo herds began to vanish; tribes like the Nez Perce and Shoshoni suffered as keenly as the true Plains tribes. The Basin and Plateau folk were also targets for missionaries who considered Indian religious practices devil worship, worse than heathenism. The clerics, the settlers, the loss of the buffalo, and the high incidence of disease produced despair, disorganization, and finally apathy.

The Nez Perce under Chief Joseph had befriended settlers and explorers, but felt betrayed when the government refused to respect a treaty of 1855 establishing tribal grounds and called instead for new discussions. The two parties went to war, and Chief Joseph carried on masterfully but futilely. In defeat he made a poignant speech, saying in part, "It is cold and we have no blankets. The little children are freezing to death. I want to look for my children. . . . Maybe I shall find them among the dead. Hear me my chiefs, I am tired. My heart is sick and sad. From where the sun now stands I will fight no more forever." That ended the Nez Perce War of 1877, a final dramatic attempt to drive the enemy away and the last resistance in the Plateau. The Nez Perce were confined to the reservation that had been established for them two decades earlier.

The outcome of white encroachment was much the same for the Ute, Paiute, and other Basin tribes, though their lands were less desirable and the white pressures came later than elsewhere. The Basin people rarely saw whites until after the middle of the nineteenth century. Then the discovery of gold in California, and silver in Nevada, brought outsiders into the Basin. The men who came searching for precious metals were rough and cruel, few having families or social ethics to modify their behavior. In many ways they were the outcasts of white society, the most lawless sort of frontiersmen. The atrocities they inflicted on the peaceful small bands of Indians are almost unbelievable—it can even be said that the miners exterminated Indians deliberately. So it is not surprising that the man who originated the Ghost Dance was a Paiute. The dance itself was probably a traditional Basin dance with the new message added. But of course the Ghost Dance produced no more miracles for the Basin people than it did for the Plains. Miners and ranchers took over their land, and the few Indians who survived were placed on small reservations.

The Cult of Smohalla. In the Plateau a religious movement with some aspects of the traditional vision quest taught that Indians should ignore the intruders, give up new ways, and return to the old life. An Indian known as Smohalla (the name is really a title meaning preacher), born about 1815, visited a Catholic mission as a boy. He acquired some ideas about ritual from his experiences at the mission, and after distinguishing himself as warrior, he turned to a life of preaching in about 1850. He traveled a great deal, once as far as Mexico, and visited many tribes. He claimed to have lived in the spirit world, where the Master Spirit told him that Indians should return to their primitive life. He held services on Sundays with ritual that combined Catholicism and the Ghost Dance. The cult had its own flag, and the congregation sang songs and did simple dancing to drumming. They also practiced confession. An important part of the doctrine was that dreams helped people to get religion; people reported their dreams at the services. Smohalla preached that the earth should not be plowed and that the land should not be sold. The Nez Perce in particular followed his doctrine.

The Northwest Coast

In the years after Bering's voyage to the Aleutian Islands and Alaska, Russian traders set up an outpost near Sitka and systematically hunted otters, seals, and other sea mammals almost to extinction. The Russian fur trade was a monopoly along the coast until 1867, when the United States bought Alaska. Though most of the Indians were not actually under Russian rule, they became dependent on Russians for the highly desired trade goods, especially metal implements. Some Spanish and British ships also touched the coast at a few points, and the Chinook traders on the Columbia River added European goods to their trade inventory.

With their new tools, especially metal woodworking tools, the Northwest Indians had a brief burst of creative activity similar to the artistic reaction in the East to ribbons and glass beads. Indian woodworking became larger and more elaborate, and the very large totem poles date from the period of metal tools. Among the items the Indians eagerly sought were metal pots and kettles and Hudson Bay blankets. Both Indians of the Northwest culture area and Athabaskans of the interior exchanged furs for these goods at traders' stores or traded them through the Chinook agents. Furs were so plentiful that Indians built up great wealth in trade goods.

Potlaching Explodes. As in other areas, Europeans brought not only goods but disease, causing so many deaths that many positions of high rank were left vacant as legitimate heirs died out. The combination of new wealth and a high mortality rate directly affected potlatching. Wealthy people with no rights to high rank gave wildly extravagant potlatches to rouse support for their attempts to claim titles. In the late nineteenth century, potlatching became a chaos of consumption and waste, with commoners amassing goods to give away and even destroy as they rushed to outdo all rivals. The whole rank system began to crumble.

In Canada in 1884, missionaries persuaded Parliament to ban potlatching, thus abolishing the major means of recognizing new chiefs, honoring the dead, and marking social events. The missionaries saw the ceremony as pagan and a threat to morality. It was not until 1951 that the Canadian government lifted the ban.

Eventually settlers moved into the area, and Indians began to feel pressure from white rule. Many Indians were kept off their old fishing, gathering, and hunting territory. Not long after 1850, Canada and the United States began moving Northwest and Western Subarctic Indians onto reservations. Economic and social disorganization asserted itself here as elsewhere. Alcoholism increasingly caused more and more of a problem. And as elsewhere, some of the people turned to a religious movement in an attempt to come to grips with the white intrusion and economic threats.

The Shakers. Indians of the Northwest found solace in the Shaker Church, founded by a Puget Sound Indian named John Slocum. (This church is not to be confused with the German Shakers of the East.) Slocum believed that he had died and then returned to life, and that during his death he had been told by an angel that he was too wicked to enter heaven. The angel sent him back to set up a mission among Indians. His doctrine was not antiwhite. He was to build a church and preach against drinking, gambling, and betting on horse races. His message was that the dead would come alive and the ocean would disappear to make room for all the people. He preached curing by laying on of hands and believed that he was the medium of communication with God. Some time later, shaking was added to the curing practice when Slocum became sick and believed he had been cured by his wife's hysterics, which included shaking; thus the sect became known as the Shakers.

The Arctic

Eskimo-white contact was infrequent until the end of the nineteenth century, and very little culture change occurred until after World War II. In Canada, trading posts and missions appeared, stimulating the development of permanent Eskimo settlements like those that had been common in Alaska but traditionally lacking in the Canadian Arctic. These small settlements were clustered around the European outposts where new goods were available. The greater density of population (though the settlements rarely had more than a hundred people) spread disease as well as trade goods, and as in areas to the south, mortality from smallpox, measles, tuberculosis, and other diseases was high.

Imported rifles made hunting more efficient, and demands for furs, especially of the arctic fox, made trapping a new commercial pursuit. Many Eskimo hunters gave up seeking game and turned to fur trapping to get furs to trade for European equipment. Some took jobs for wages. With less time left to hunt, many Eskimo came to depend on imported foods. Besides, game resources, especially caribou, had been depleted by disease, scarcity of lichen forests (the caribou's main food source), and above all, overkill with guns.

Jobs for money as well as trade goods could be found at trading posts, missions, and, later, government and defense installations. Settling around these, Eskimo gave up not only traditional subsistence pursuits, but their housing and other material culture, for European types.

Canadian Eskimo no longer lived so widely dispersed, and some groups, like the Caribou Eskimo, disappeared as a distinct group because of disease, famine, and movement away from the Barren Grounds.

In Alaska, even more people moved to towns and into wage labor than in Canada. Intensive commercial whaling by Europeans, Japanese, and Americans depleted that resource for the Alaskan Eskimo, and with the whalers came disease and alcohol. As in Canada, game became scarce as repeating rifles made killing more efficient. The Alaskans changed from hunting subsistence to a money economy, selling furs, ivory, and whalebone to traders. As towns, missions, and government posts increased, some people began to work for salaries or wages, completely abandoning hunting. Settlements in Alaska changed from native villages of one hundred or so people to concentrations in larger towns and even cities.

For aboriginal people the international boundary between the United States and Canada did not exist, of course. However, to understand some differences in the history of Indian-European interaction in the two countries and especially differences in law, we have to take that border into consideration because political conditions have varied over the years.

Canadian Government Policy

Brief History of Canadian Nationhood

Canadians regard Jacques Cartier as the founder of Canada. In 1534, he sailed into Chaleur Bay, and the following year he went up the St. Lawrence River guided by two Iroquois. From then on, settlement in Canada was pioneered by the French who founded a colony, New France, in 1663. Britain, expanding from its American colonies on the south and from fishing settlements on the coast, fought France, captured Quebec, and took control over the territory in the Royal Proclamation of 1763.

In 1867, the British North America Act created the Dominion of Canada under the British Crown. That act became the country's constitution, establishing a parliament on the model of England's. The Canadians severed the last formal political ties with Britain in 1982.

Relations With the Native Peoples

Canada's basic policy for dealing with Canadian Indians was spelled out in the Proclamation of 1763, which provided that native peoples would be removed from land only with their consent and the approval of the Crown. Title to land was vested in the Crown, and the aboriginal people had the underlying right to use and occupy the land. At first cash payments were made for land surrendered, but later the government set aside reservations, called *reserves* in Canada, and provided annuities for those giving up title.

Assuming that Indians, who were hunters and gatherers, placed no value on land, the agricultural Europeans showed a complete lack of understanding of native culture and values, and their advance destroyed traditional plant gathering areas. In addition, as Indians acquired guns, they became more successful hunters, and intensive hunting and trapping resulted in wanton slaughter of game. Furthermore, alcohol was a favored item of trade—causing greater demoralization of the native people.

The story followed predictable patterns. Settlers pushed Indians into inferior environments where game was scarce, and population movement from the east caused dislocation across the Great Lakes. As people moved west, so did disease. Disease—typhoid, tuberculosis, smallpox, and others—killed thousands, the same old story. On the Canadian plains people saw similar cultural changes to those on the American plains, with the same sad conclusion.

The government did not make treaties with Indians until the 1850s. The treaties involved various things: setting aside land for Indian use exclusively, trusteeship by the government, control of liquor, and establishing schools, among other provisions. Lands that the French had set aside for Indians when under French control remained Indian land after the British took over. Reserves were established on lands already occupied by Indians or in nearby, similar environments. Canadian Indians were never removed in large numbers from their original lands to distant territory as they were in the United States.

Enfranchisement. Underlying all government dealings with the native peoples was the goal of assimilation. In 1857, a specific act toward assimilation was passed, aimed at "enfranchisement." This was a mechanism whereby an individual would no longer be considered legally an Indian, but rather would enter into full citizenship. The act provided that any male over the age of 21 who was literate in French or English and of good moral character would be "enfranchised" or no longer deemed to be an Indian. He would then receive title to some reserve land plus his share of his band's trust fund. Any Indian who decided to become enfranchised gave up all rights as an Indian. While bands might apply for enfranchisement and division of trust funds, the government approved enfranchisement only when the person was considered able to assume the duties and responsibilities of citizenship and to support himself and his dependents. Under later amendments to the act, any Indian woman marrying a non-Indian was automatically enfranchised. When people were enfranchised their names were taken from the Band List and the General List, and Indian statutes no longer applied to them. They relinquished their claims to reserve land.

The Indian Act of 1876. When Canada became a Dominion, it inherited from Britain all previous Indian legislation which it tried to consolidate and expand in the Indian Act of 1876. The act formulated the difference between a "status" and a "non-status" Indian. A status Indian was registered with the government and his or her band, and a non-status Indian was not. Indians who were entitled to be registered were direct descendants in the male line of those who were registered in 1874 and their wives and children. Furthermore, a non-Indian woman marrying a status Indian man actually gained status, while any Indian woman marrying a non-Indian lost status, clearly sex discrimination. These practices were not changed until 1985. In addition, in 1880 an amendment to the act expanded enfranchisement by decreeing that any Indian with a college degree or any member of the clergy was automatically enfranchised.

The Métis. Not classified as Indians under the Indian Act, descendants of fur traders and Indian women are called Métis, one of the three groups of native peoples of Canada, Indians and Inuit being the other two. (*Inuit* is the name chosen by the Canadian Eskimo. It means "the people" in their language. There is nothing derogatory about the word "Eskimo," but the Canadians prefer Inuit.)

The Métis developed their own frontier life-style, a combination of European and Indian customs and practices. They suffered all the disabilities enumerated earlier: disease, loss of land, diminishing game. The Métis sought land settlements similar to those granted Indians, but problems arose, and by 1885 the Métis were still without federally recognized territory. There was a rising of the Métis in 1870 and another in 1885. The rebellions were crushed, and the leaders were sentenced to death.

Though Métis were clearly a Canadian ethnic group, by constitutional definition they were not Indians since they were descended through women. Many of their descendants live in Quebec today where they know of their racial ancestry but identify as French-Canadians, which they are culturally. Communities of Métis in the Northwest Territories have joined with the Dene (Athabaskan-speaking Indians) to initiate a land claim which is yet to be settled.

Later Legislation. In 1961, the native peoples became eligible to vote in federal elections, and now they participate at all levels of government. Elected band councils are the decision makers for internal band affairs, and some bands have established self-governments outside the Indian Act. Indians can choose to live on or off their band territories.

In 1985, an amendment to the Indian Act removed sex discrimination and restored status and band membership rights. Bands were given control over their own membership rules, and the concept of enfranchisement was abolished. The term "status" was kept, but it was widened to treat men and women equally and prevent anyone from gaining or losing status through marriage. A department of the federal government keeps the Indian Register, which is a centralized record of all individuals registered under the Indian Act. Those newly eligible for membership—those previously excluded by descent through women—may now apply for status.

The Department of Indian Affairs and Northern Development (DIAND). Indian affairs were under military jurisdiction in early years, but now they are under civilian guidance through the Department of Indian Affairs and Northern Development. DIAND is to Canada what the Bureau of Indian Affairs (BIA) is to the United States (see chapter 12). DIAND is the branch of the federal government responsible for fulfilling the federal obligations arising from treaties and the Indian Act and its amendments. It provides basic services to status Indians and to Inuit communities and aids in economic development of their lands. Additional responsibility is to negotiate settlement of aboriginal claims. Most federal expenditure on aboriginal programs is made through the department. Such things as resource development, housing, education, social development, and so on are provided by divisions of DIAND; and it is DIAND that processes applications for Indian status and keeps the Indian Register.

Population in 1990. There were 490,178 status Indians registered in 1990, approximately 60 percent living on reserves. That population was expected to reach over 530,000 by 1992 as more people registered who had formerly been ineligible under discriminatory clauses in the Indian Act. The Inuit population in 1990 was estimated at 32,620, and there were 601 Indian bands. The 1990 census showed 892,000 self-identified Indians, obviously including many either not qualified for status or not yet having received status. As in the United States, racial categories in the Canadian census are left to self-identification.

12

CONTEMPORARY INDIANS

Navajo silver work of the 20th century.

More than 1,960,000 self-identified Indians and Eskimo live in the United States today, fewer than half of them on reservations. In the East scattered groups of Indians are mixed in the general population, speaking no language but English and living and working exactly like their non-Indian neighbors. Only on special occasions or holidays do they gather for ethnic activities, as Italian-Americans may hold a parade to celebrate Columbus Day. In Rhode Island, for instance, people who consider themselves Narragansett Indians still hold "tribal" meetings. Biologically, these people are very little Indian—no one could distinguish them from the rest of Rhode Island's population. Yet they hold yearly festivals and support an "Indian" church. In most of their living habits, there is little to remind us of the former large tribes in the East.

California too has small groups who do not live on reservations. Most of those Indians are rural, and usually they work for wages in agriculture. They appear to be less assimilated into the general population than the Eastern nonreservation Indians, but their employment, schooling, and marketing often put them in contact with non-Indians. Their cultural distinctiveness seems to be decreasing.

Oklahoma has the largest Indian population; Arizona and California also have more than 200,000 Indians. In the early 1800s, Congress designated Oklahoma "Indian Territory," where Eastern Indians were settled after being removed from their lands. Reservation lands once covered 30,000,000 acres. By about 1910, all except for the Osage reservation was allotted to individual Indians or sold to non-Indians. This reservation became a county. Today, descendants of people of many tribal affiliations live in Oklahoma, among them Creek, Cherokee, Seminole, and Osage, but there are no longer any reservations, only tribal trust lands and individual allotted lands held in trust by the federal government. Many Oklahoma Indians live in rural areas where they often control or actively participate in county government; others have settled in Tulsa and Oklahoma City.

All these people think of themselves to some degree as Indians, though their amount of Indian genetic inheritance may be as little as a sixteenth or less. Yet most are not federally recognized as Indians: they are not covered by federal Indian law or eligible for the services offered by the Bureau of Indian Affairs. Hundreds of thousands of others who are part Indian, an eighth or more, do not think of themselves as Indian or count themselves Indian in the United States Census. Being Indian, then, is a matter of culture and, to some extent, choice—not just blood or biology.

Since World War II, more and more Indians have moved from rural areas and towns and from reservations into cities. Los Angeles has more than 70,000 Indian residents, almost all from out of state, and other

American Indian, Eskimo or Aleut Resident Population by State: 1990 and 1980

Rank	State	1990 American Indian, Eskimo or Aleut Population	1990 Percent of State	1980 American Indian, Eskimo or Aleut Population	1980 Percent of State
1	Oklahoma	252,420	8.0	169,459	5.6
2	California	242,164	0.8	201,369	0.9
3	Arizona	203,527	5.6	152,745	5.6
4	New Mexico	136,355	8.9	106,119	8.1
5	Alaska	85,698	15.6	64,103	16.0
6	Washington	81,483	1.7	60,804	1.5
7	North Carolina	80,155	1.2	64,652	1.1
8	Texas	65,877	0.4	40,075	0.3
9	New York	62,651	0.3	39,582	0.2
10	Michigan	55,638	0.6	40,050	0.4
11	South Dakota	50,575	7.3	44,968	6.5
12	Minnesota	49,909	1.1	33,016	0.9
13	Montana	47,679	6.0	37,270	4.7
14	Wisconsin	39,387	0.8	29,499	0.6
15	Oregon	38,496	1.4	27,314	1.0
16	Florida	36,335	0.3	19,257	0.2
17	Colorado	27,776	0.8	18,068	0.6
18	North Dakota	25,917	4.1	20,158	3.1
19	Utah	24,283	1.4	19,256	1.3
20	Kansas	21,965	0.9	15,373	0.7
21	Illinois	21,836	0.2	16,283	0.1
22	Ohio	20,338	0.2	12,239	0.1
23	Missouri	19,835	0.4	12,321	0.3
24	Nevada	19,637	1.6	13,308	1.7
25	Louisiana	18,341	0.4	12,065	0.3
26	Alabama	16,506	0.4	7,583	0.2
27	Virginia	15,282	0.2	9,454	0.2
28	New Jersey	14,970	0.2	8,394	0.1
29	Pennsylvania	14,733	0.1	9,463	0.1
30	Idaho	13,780	1.4	10,521	1.1
31	Georgia	13,348	0.2	7,616	0.1
32	Maryland	12,972	0.3	8,021	0.2
33	Arkansas	12,773	0.5	9,428	0.4
34	Indiana	12,720	0.2	7,836	0.1
35	Nebraska	12,410	0.8	9.195	0.6
36	Massachusetts	12,241	0.2	7,743	0.1
37	Tennessee	10,039	0.2	5,104	0.1
38	Wyoming	9,479	2.1	7,094	1.5
39	Mississippi	8,525	0.3	6,180	0.2
40	South Carolina	8,246	0.2	5,757	0.2
41	Iowa	7,349	0.3	5,455	0.2
42	Connecticut	6,634	0.2	4,533	0.1
43	Maine	5,998	0.5	4,087	0.4
44	Kentucky	5,769	0.2	3,610	0.1

45	Hawaii	5,099	0.5	2,768	0.3
46	Rhode Island	4,071	0.4	2,898	0.3
47	West Virginia	2,458	0.1	1,610	0.1
48	New Hampshire	2,136	0.2	1,352	0.1
49	Delaware	2,019	0.3	1,328	0.2
50	Vermont	1,696	0.3	984	0.2
51	District of Columbia	1,466	0.2	1,031	0.2
	Total	**1,960,996**	**Total**	**1,418,398**	

Source: Department of Commerce, Bureau of the Census.

western and midwestern cities also have thousands of Indian residents. Of the Indians age sixteen and over who are employed, 50 percent work in urban areas.

Reservations

Reservations are the 278 hundred tracts of land set aside by the United States government in treaty, statute, or executive order for the use and benefit of Indian tribes. Some reservations are solid blocks of tribal land; others are interspersed with sections of land belonging to non-Indians. Some reservations are restricted to one tribe, though many are home to several tribes. The federal government recognizes 510 tribes and Alaskan village groups. Membership in a tribe or rights to a place on a reservation are determined by requirements set by the tribe or its governing body. How much Indian blood one must have to claim tribal membership varies from tribe to tribe.

Reservations fall under two different jurisdictions. Most are federal trusts controlled by the federal government, but others are state reservations, especially in New York, Pennsylvania, and Maine—and in California, where they are often called rancherias. The only federal reservations east of the Mississippi are in the Western Great Lakes area and in New York state, and those of the Cherokee in North Carolina, the Seminole in Florida, and the Choctaw in Mississippi. Largest of all is the Navajo reservation; with more than 14,000,000 acres, mostly in Arizona, it completely encloses the Hopi reservation. Navajo population is also largest.

Indian Rights on Reservations

Indians who live on reservations are free to come and go or to live anywhere else they choose and can afford. The government is the trustee

SOME FEDERAL INDIAN RESERVATIONS

ARIZONA
- Ak-Chin
- Camp Verde
- Cocopah
- Colorado River
- Fort Apache
- Fort McDowell
- Gila Bend Papago
- Gila River
- Havasupai
- Hopi
- Hualapai
- Kaibab
- Maricopa
- Navajo
- Papago
- Salt River
- San Xavier Papago
- Yavapai

CALIFORNIA*
- Agua Caliente
- Alpine Washoe
- Big Pine
- Bishop
- Cabazon
- Cahuilla
- Campo
- Capitan Grande
- Chemeheuvi
- Colorado River
- Fort Independence
- Fort Mojave
- Fort Yuma
- Hoopa Valley
- Hoopa Valley Extension
- Inaja Cosmit
- La Jolla
- La Posta
- Lone Pine
- Los Coyotes
- Manzanita
- Mesa Grande
- Morongo
- Pala
- Pauma
- Pechanga
- Ramona
- Rincon
- Round Valley
- San Manuel
- San Pasqual
- Santa Rosa
- Santa Ynez
- Santa Ysabel
- Soboba
- Sycuan
- Torres Martinez
- Tule River
- Twenty-Nine Palms
- X L Ranch

COLORADO
- Southern Ute
- Ute Mountain

FLORIDA
- Big Cypress
- Brighton
- Hollywood

IDAHO
- Coeur D'Alene
- Duck Valley
- Fort Hall
- Nez Perce

IOWA
- Sac and Fox

KANSAS
- Kickapoo
- Potawatomi

LOUISIANA
- Chitimacha

MICHIGAN
- Bay Mills
- Hannahville
- Isabella
- Keweenaw Bay
- L'Anse
- Ontonagon

MINNESOTA
- Deer Creek
- Fond du Lac
- Grand Portage
- Greater Leech Lake
- Lower Sioux
- Nett Lake
- Prairie Island
- Prior Lake
- Red Lake
- Upper Sioux
- White Earth

MISSISSIPPI
- Choctaw

MONTANA
- Blackfeet
- Crow
- Flathead
- Fort Belknap
- Fort Peck
- Kootenai
- Northern Cheyenne
- Rocky Boys

*Only major reservations listed. California also has many rancherias—very small land trust areas.

SOME FEDERAL INDIAN RESERVATIONS (continued)

NEBRASKA
- Omaha
- Santee
- Winnebago

NEVADA
- Battle Mountain
- Carson
- Duck Valley
- Duckwater
- Elko
- Ely
- Goshute
- Las Vegas
- Lovelock
- Moapa River
- Odgers Ranch
- Pyramid Lake
- Reno Sparks
- Ruby Valley
- South Fork
- Stewart School
- Summit Lake
- Walker River
- Washoe
- Winnemucca
- Yerington

NEW MEXICO
- Acoma
- Alamo Navajo
- Canoncito Navajo
- Cochiti
- Isleta
- Jacarilla
- Jemez
- Laguna
- Mescalero
- Nambe
- Navajo
- Picuris
- Pojoaque
- Sandia
- San Felipe
- San Ildefonso
- San Juan
- Santa Ana
- Santa Clara
- Santo Dominto
- Tesuque
- Taos
- Ute Mountain
- Zia
- Zuni

NEW YORK
- Allegany
- Cattaraugus
- St. Regis
- Tonawanda

NORTH CAROLINA
- Cherokee

NORTH DAKOTA
- Devil's Lake
- Fort Berthold
- Sisseton
- Standing Rock
- Turtle Mountain

OKLAHOMA
- Osage

OREGON
- Fort McDermitt
- Umatilla
- Warm Springs

SOUTH DAKOTA
- Cheyenne River
- Crow Creek
- Flandreau
- Lower Brule
- Pine Ridge
- Rosebud
- Sisseton
- Standing Rock
- Yankton

UTAH
- Goshute
- Navajo
- Skull Valley
- Unitah and Ouray

WASHINGTON
- Chehalis
- Coleville
- Hoh
- Lower Elwha
- Lummi
- Makah
- Muckleshoot
- Nisqually
- Ozette
- Port Gamble
- Port Madison
- Puyallup
- Quileute
- Quinault
- Skokomish
- Spokane
- Squaxon Island
- Swinomish
- Tulalip
- Yakima

WISCONSIN
- Bad River
- Lac Corte Oreille
- Lac du Flambeau
- Menominee
- Oneida
- St. Croix
- Stockbridge Munsee

WYOMING
- Wind River

of Indian land, not the master of individual Indians any more than it is of other citizens. At one time, some Indians were considered "wards" of the government, but no longer. The reservations are not prison camps; they are not enclosed. Many major highways run through reservation lands, and outsiders frequently travel them, often without realizing that they are on a reservation.

Reservation Indians have rights in their land and can live on it without paying land taxes. They share in sales of mineral wealth, land rentals, and agricultural produce from the land. Each individual's share may be a cash payment, or it may be a share in investment or improvements made for all the tribe, such as housing, recreation facilities, or college scholarships. Indians do pay the other taxes that are levied on the general citizens—income tax, sales tax, and even real estate tax if they buy land outside the reservation. No Indian can sell his or her share of reservation land, though it can usually be bequeathed to heirs if they are tribal members.

Indians have the same voting rights as all other citizens. For federal, state, and county elections they vote in their districts, wards, or precincts, and all are enfranchised at the age of eighteen. Eligibility to vote in tribal elections is determined by the tribe. Non-Indians living on reservations usually are not allowed to vote in tribal elections, though of course they can vote in the other elections. Indians also can run for office in general as well as tribal elections. Many have held state and federal office in the western states where Indian populations are large. Ben Whitehorse Campbell, a Northern Cheyenne, was elected United States senator from Colorado in 1992.

Reservation Facilities

Reservations are not totally rural; they usually have towns or villages, and a few include small cities. In recent years industry has developed on a few reservations, but most Indian territory is far from major transportation centers and skilled work forces, so that industrial development has been slow. The lack of industry and other job opportunities has been a major reason for the movement to cities. Most reservations do, however, have small shopping centers or a few stores.

On the Navajo reservation there are still more than two hundred trading posts, even though towns have grown up there as well. The relationship between Navajo and traders benefits both. Set up in remote areas, the posts are stocked with thousands of items of food and merchandise, many of which the people would have to travel far to get otherwise. Traders often provide services as well, like burying the dead, a task the Navajo are most reluctant to undertake. Navajo also can pawn jewelry with traders or get credit from them when they are in financial straits. The trader, of course, makes a profit. At one time many traders were unfair because they had a monopoly on trade, but today laws regulate trading practices, and the Navajo are better educated and too sophisticated to be cheated easily.

At one time both state and federal laws prohibited sale of alcoholic beverages to Indians. In 1953, Congress gave Indians the right to buy liquor off reservations under the same conditions and regulations as non-Indians. However, the ban against selling liquor on reservations has remained in effect unless the tribal government voted for legalization. Now some tribes allow sales on their reservations and some do not.

The Bureau of Indian Affairs

Administration of federal Indian reservations is supervised by the Bureau of Indian Affairs (BIA) with its central office at 1951 Constitution Avenue N.W., Washington, D.C. 20245. The Bureau, sometimes called the Indian Service, was created within the War Department by Secretary of War John C. Calhoun in 1824. In 1832, the post of Commissioner of Indian Affairs was established to head the BIA, and in 1834, the Bureau received official recognition from Congress. In 1849, it was transferred to the new Home Department of the Interior.

The Bureau is the designated trustee for lands and moneys held in trust by the United States government for Indian tribes, and over the years, the official objectives of the Bureau have turned toward supporting the relationship between tribal government and federal government rather than attempting to manage tribal affairs. Today the Bureau publicizes its policy of support of efforts by Indians and Alaskan Natives toward self-sufficiency, self-determination, and development of their natural resources and human potential. Nevertheless, in the early years, the BIA, if not despotic, was clearly paternalistic and maintained strong control over decision making on reservations.

The Indian Reorganization Act of 1934 and the Indian Self-Determination Act of 1975 were promulgated to give Indians more control over their own lives and opportunity for greater participation in community decisions on reservations. The act of 1934 aimed at reviving or restoring Indian uniqueness and identity, encouraged Indian art and customs, and set up the mechanism for tribal government on reservations. Tribes forming governments under the provisions of the act have been able to take a large part in internal planning and decision making though supervision by local representatives of the BIA has continued.

Where reservation residents are well educated, the tribal government has more to say in making decisions. When there are fewer educated

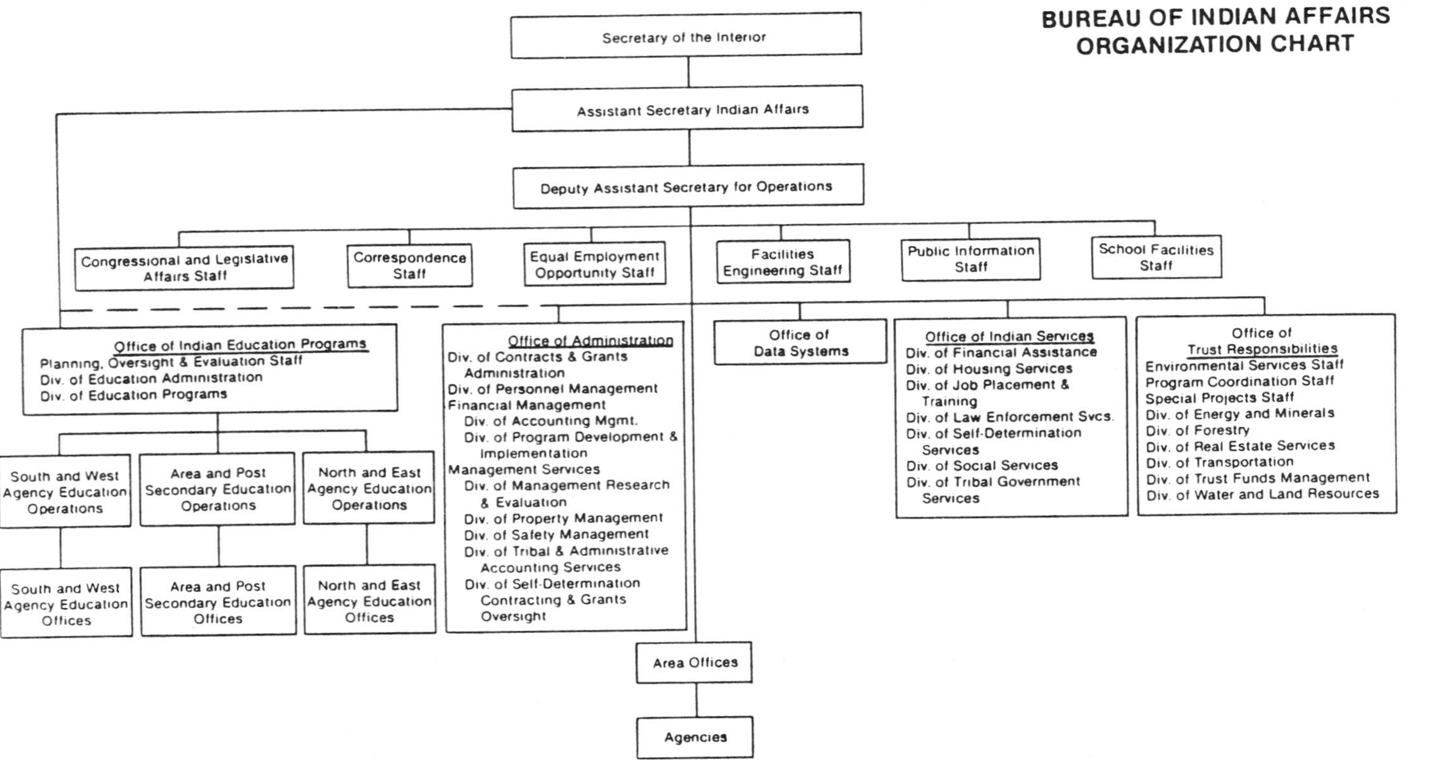
BUREAU OF INDIAN AFFAIRS
ORGANIZATION CHART
Secretary of the Interior
Assistant Secretary Indian Affairs
Deputy Assistant Secretary for Operations
Congressional and Legislative Affairs Staff
Correspondence Staff
Equal Employment Opportunity Staff
Facilities Engineering Staff
Public Information Staff
School Facilities Staff
Office of Indian Education Programs
Planning, Oversight & Evaluation Staff
Div. of Education Administration
Div. of Education Programs
Office of Administration
Div. of Contracts & Grants Administration
Div. of Personnel Management
Financial Management
Div. of Accounting Mgmt.
Div. of Program Development & Implementation
Management Services
Div. of Management Research & Evaluation
Div. of Property Management
Div. of Safety Management
Div. of Tribal & Administrative Accounting Services
Div. of Self-Determination Contracting & Grants Oversight
Office of Data Systems
Office of Indian Services
Div. of Financial Assistance
Div. of Housing Services
Div. of Job Placement & Training
Div. of Law Enforcement Svcs.
Div. of Self-Determination Services
Div. of Social Services
Div. of Tribal Government Services
Office of Trust Responsibilities
Environmental Services Staff
Program Coordination Staff
Special Projects Staff
Div. of Energy and Minerals
Div. of Forestry
Div. of Real Estate Services
Div. of Transportation
Div. of Trust Funds Management
Div. of Water and Land Resources
South and West Agency Education Operations
Area and Post Secondary Education Operations
North and East Agency Education Operations
South and West Agency Education Offices
Area and Post Secondary Education Offices
North and East Agency Education Offices
Area Offices
Agencies

people the superintendent (frequently an Indian but usually of different tribe) has to handle more decisions because the Indians feel inadequately prepared to make judgments. The superintendent and his or her aides are supposed to be advisory; still friction often builds between the superintendent, representing the federal government, and the Indian tribal government, even though Indian residents may like individual superintendents very much.

An important function of the BIA is to assist Indians in gaining educational access either through public educational systems or the development of educational systems of their own. The passage of the Indian Self-Determination and Education Assistance Act in 1975 facilitated contracting for the operation of educational programs by tribal groups, and the passage of Public Law 95–561 and its implementation resulted in decision-making power for Indian school boards to direct funding for schools and to hire teachers.

Under the Johnson-O'Malley Act of 1934, the BIA provides funds to meet special needs of Indian students in public schools. These funds are largely administered through contracts with tribal organizations, and in 1990–91 about 225,800 Indian students in public schools received assistance.

During the administration of President Gerald Ford, the BIA underwent organizational restructuring to make it compatible with other units of the Department of the Interior. Today, chief executive of the BIA is the Assistant Secretary for Indian Affairs, appointed by the President and confirmed by the Senate, who is aided by a Deputy Assistant Secretary for Operations. The Deputy Assistant Secretary is responsible for the general functioning that had been the job of the former Commissioner. Currently the BIA interacts with 510 federally recognized tribes and Alaskan village groups through 12 Area Offices. Area directors are in charge of regional offices that supervise the agencies for the reservations. Superintendents (sometimes referred to as agents) are in charge of the agencies.

By the beginning of 1985, the BIA had over 15,000 employees throughout the nation, and Indians composed more than 75 percent of that workforce. The BIA gives preference in hiring to individuals who are members of federally recognized tribes or are one-half or more Indian blood. Indians hold most of the top level positions within the BIA, and most of the positions in the Bureau's schools are staffed by Indians.

Indian people reveal ambivalent reactions to the Bureau, some believing that it has failed to protect Indian interests, others feeling that the Bureau still interferes with Indian self-determination. Other charges against the BIA are that it spends more money on its own bureaucratic structure than on help for Indian people and that BIA attempts at industrial and commercial development on reservations have been indifferent and more of benefit to outsiders than to the Indian residents. Though this ambiguous relationship will doubtless continue, it is hard to find any agitation with wide support among Indians for the abolition of the BIA.

The Navajo-Hopi Land Settlement. Not all land disputes have been between Indians and non-Indians. In the 1860s, after their release from Ft. Sumner, Navajo began to return to their traditional lands in northeastern Arizona. A reservation established there for them surrounded Hopi territory, and both Navajo and Hopi disputed the right of the other to some of that land, initiating a bitter quarrel that has festered for more than 100 years.

In the 1940s, Congress set aside land within the Navajo reservation for Hopi use, but Hopi claimed that some land given to Navajo contained spots sacred to the Hopi tribe, and that Navajo were living on what had become the Hopi reservation. The Navajo in turn contended that Hopi settlement violated ancestral claims of the Navajo people. Feelings were high. Finally in 1992, the two tribal councils voted their agreement in principal to a solution that would involve ceding about 500,000 acres

Navajo veterans and supporters marched in 1986 to protest giving up any of their land to the Hopi Indians.

of public and private land to the Hopi in compensation for their loss of land to the Navajo. Under the proposal, Hopi will lease land to Navajo who have been living on it, the lease to expire in 75 years. Some non-Indian Arizonans object to loss of public land, but others point out that it was the Indians' land in the first place. Resolution of the issue will require approval by Congress.

Reservation Land

Although it might seem as though Indians have much reservation land—altogether some 50,000,000 acres, or a little less than the state of Minnesota—much of it is unproductive. Many parts are useless for agriculture or stock raising, and too far from centers of population and transportation to be useful for industrial development. Nevertheless, some is good agricultural land, some is good for grazing, some is well timbered, and a few places are rich with mineral resources. The Osage territory, now the largest county in Oklahoma, for example, has rich oil fields. A major aim of both the federal government and Indian residents is to develop the land for economic return, raising the standard of living while preserving the territory's beauty and productive potential. Thus Indian timberland is reforested under contract with lumber companies or by Indians themselves so that lumber resources will not be depleted. Land management is an important job of the Bureau of Indian Affairs and its local representatives. Still, so much Indian land is not productive that lack of opportunity has drained population to other areas where employment is better.

Reservation Housing

Very few Indians still live in traditional structures. Tipis appear only for summer celebrations of a few tribes on the Plains. Although some Navajo continue to live in hogans, and many others have built hogans for ceremonial purposes or storage, more and more Navajo have moved into cabins or ranch houses. Even the hogans that remain have changed. The ancient pointed wooden structure covered with earth is rarely seen on the reservation today. The common hogan form now is six- or eight-sided, made of horizontally laid logs, plastered with mud or even entirely covered with earth for insulation.

On the plains, a few Indians live in sod houses or cabins very much like those that housed nineteenth-century pioneers. No one lives in tipis, and most of the population have ranch-style homes or western farmhouses. In the towns on reservations, Indians may live in flats above stores, and the towns also have housing developments as well as individually built homes just like those of western towns off the reservation.

Perhaps more traditional housing is still used by the Pueblo Indians and Florida Seminole than any other Indian communities, but even in these places new styles are catching on. The traditional open-sided, palmetto-thatched *chickee* still stands on Big Cypress Seminole Reservation in Florida. It is good shelter for the tropics, letting air flow freely. But the Seminole also have two other types of buildings, concrete-block ranch houses and wooden housing built on a poured cement slab. The block houses, despite their unattractive name, are typical of Florida construction. Florida state law specifies that type of structure, even for the most elegant housing, because of its greater ability to withstand hurricanes. The wooden buildings were started in the late 1960s as part of a mutual-help home building program on many reservations. The wooden buildings are partially open-walled like the *chickees*, but they are screened and have complete plumbing and electrical wiring.

Although Indians have abandoned most traditional house forms for ranch and farmhouse types and wooden cabins, some of this reservation housing is sadly substandard. Many homes are still little more than tarpaper shacks, without hot and cold running water, electricity, screening, and reasonable sanitation. Recognizing these inadequacies, federal and tribal governments have tried to improve Indian housing with mortgage loans and mutual-help building programs. These programs include professional plumbing and electrical work, but much of the carpentry and other labor is done by people of the community, helping each other.

Though much remains to be done to improve reservation housing, it is not all inadequate. Homes on reservations range as widely in appearance, sanitation, and maintenance as they do anywhere else. A lot of reservation housing is attractive, with modern facilities, and clean. The worst is very bad indeed, but many homes compare very favorably to housing in the rural white communities near the reservations. Almost all reservation dwellings have electricity, even the few traditional structures still in use.

Reservation Life

Just as there is no typical Indian tribe, there is no typical Indian reservation. Reservation lands vary from saw grass and cypress swamplands in south Florida to plains in northern Montana and deserts in Arizona. Some reservations are large—the Navajo is nearly 25,000 square miles; some are small—rancherias in California may be only a few acres. Some reservations have towns and others are totally rural.

Work and Recreation. Daily life on a reservation involves the same kind of activities other rural Americans engage tn. The children go to school, walking if it is nearby or taking buses if it is at some distance. Women do housework and wage work. Many Indians work for their agency or tribe as clerks and secretaries, nurses and nursing aids, social workers, or teachers and teacher aides in the schools. Where there is industry, both men and women may do wage work. Men also do many kinds of work for the agency or tribe, from administration to work on road crews and general maintenance, and often cattle ranching and farm work. Men and women may continue traditional crafts, though usually to sell their products rather than to use them. Adults and children go to town for shopping and entertainment, watch television, and take part in sports like baseball, basketball, swimming, or, especially in the West, horseback riding competitions or rodeo performances. Reservation life in general is much like that of neighboring non-Indian areas.

Many reservations, particularly the larger ones, have their own police force with Indian personnel. Other reservation people have voted to accept the county or state police. On Sundays, the people may go to one of the churches on the reservation or in neighboring towns. Missionaries from many denominations or Indian ministers may lead the churches, which may include Indian religious groups like the Native American Church or the Longhouse People.

Indians and Whites. Relations between reservation Indians and whites vary a good deal. In many places white people living close to reservations dislike and discriminate against Indians, often fearing competition for jobs. The only contact between Indians and whites of the area may be of the most unfortunate sort. Whites may know only the Indians who have gotten into trouble for drunkenness, theft, or other undesirable behavior while in town. The whites rarely meet Indians socially as equals. Prejudice among small-town whites toward neighboring Indians prevents meetings that might create real understanding and friendship. Whites who live some distance from reservations, on the other hand, often are more tolerant and interested in Indian life and problems. Yet their image of Indian life may be romantic and equally erroneous: they see the Indian as a noble but vanishing savage, someone it may be fashionable to know.

Tourists visiting Indian reservations are often insultingly naive. Many expect Indians to be primitive, unable to read, write, or even speak English. Tourists are often incredibly rude without realizing it when they take photographs without permission and make derogatory or unpleasant remarks in front of Indians as though the Indians were unable to understand. Without knowing it, such visitors increase reservation people's suspicion and animosity toward non-Indians.

Reservation Culture

Little of the great variety of cultures that Indians had when Europeans first landed on this continent remains on reservations today. A veneer still distinguishes Hopi from Seminole from Chippewa, but on all reservations many patterns of life are similar. Visitors going from reservation to reservation get the feeling that they have seen it all before. The life-styles all seem very much alike, regardless of the people's cultural traditions. And those life-styles seem much like those of the rural white communities of America, especially the poorer ones. All over the continent Indian people have adapted to reservations in similar ways, to the point that some anthropologists have begun to talk of a *reservation culture*.

Reservation culture, the various tribes' common response to outside pressure and stress, has been described as sterile, depressing, and above all, boring. It is the primary reason that the ambitious and educated leave the reservations and return only to visit. Cultural vitality and variety seem to have been washed out by the overriding similarity all reservation people have experienced in isolation and overdependence on the BIA. Reservations look to many like an intellectual, cultural, and economic backwater, housing the inept and unambitious.

Changes after World War II

Two significant programs for Indians were launched by Congress in the 1950s. Behind each one was the idea that Indians should no longer live in a special relationship to the government, that opportunities should be created to put Indians still on reservation lands back into general American society. One plan became known as *relocation*, and the other as *termination*. Before we discuss these two plans, let us look at the ideas behind them.

The Development of Indian Policies

Early in its history, the United States gathered in immigrants from many nations, making the idea of national integration or the "melting pot" theory popular, as it has been ever since. Although ethnic, racial, and religious enclaves did form in the United States, and majority populations throughout history have discriminated in one way or another against the minorities, the general melting-pot philosophy has always been strong. Most people, whether government workers or scholars, assumed that Indians would be absorbed into American society if they were given a chance. And many were—perhaps more than were not.

But some continued to think of themselves as Indian and refused to integrate with the dominant community. Except for legislation designed to remove Indians to western territory, most government acts aimed at assimilation. The Allotment Act was passed with the idea that private ownership of land would stimulate assimilation.

One major piece of legislation stopped the trend toward assimilation—the Indian Reorganization Act of 1934. However, after World War II, the mood of Congress and of influential people connected with Indian affairs reverted to the feeling that Indians really should be assimilated.

Many thought that Indians were kept from assimilation by poor education, poverty, and especially isolation from the American mainstream. It seemed that Indians had simply become so dependent upon the BIA that they no longer could make their own decisions or lead their own lives. It was a vicious circle. The BIA controlled the Indians both directly and subtly, because government officials thought Indians could not manage their own affairs, and the more the Bureau made decisions, the less the Indians could do so, for they never got any practical experience.

Termination

In the 1950s, the idea spread that in spite of such deadening dependence on the government, some Indians had the economic understanding, stability, and education to break away. Several members of Congress thought that the Klamath and Menominee reservations, with their wealth of marketable lumber and people who were trained and competent in logging and milling, were ready to stand without government support. Seconding that position were others who questioned whether some citizens should have a relationship to the federal government denied to other citizens. After the war the feeling grew in the dominant population that ethnic and racial minorities should have the same rights as the majority, and that special treatment for one group was really discrimination against others. Indians, on the other hand, saw attempts at assimilation as just another move by whites to take away Indian land. The problem of assimilation and its solution were hotly debated and very difficult to handle because they touched off so much emotion on both sides.

In 1953, Congress passed a resolution that came to be known as termination. It severed the special relationship between the government and the Menominee, Klamath, and some smaller groups; those reservations were declared terminated. A cash settlement was paid for the land, which in some cases was distributed to individuals and in others was invested for tribal members. Perhaps the large amount of money persuaded many Indians to vote for termination.

Although the majority vote on the reservations affected by this resolution was for termination, some voted against it, and some did not vote at all; and after termination, many of those who voted for it regretted their act. For the Menominee, the settlement was tied to a possibility that government funds due the tribe would be withheld if they refused to vote for termination, or so many Menominee believed. Wisconsin created a county out of the Menominee reservation, and the new county residents had to pay real estate taxes. Many could not pay taxes nor could they pay for the county services that formerly were supplied free by the federal government. The Klamath managed somewhat better, but they too suffered financially. It was soon apparent that many Menominee and Klamath were not as ready for independence from the Bureau as had been thought. Once again, the years of government control had encouraged dependence; no one was properly prepared for freedom from supervision.

In December 1973, under much pressure from Menominee and some others, Congress voted to reverse Menominee termination. It is too soon to assess this legislation. Wisconsin favored restoring federal supervision so that the state would not have to try to cover services formerly paid for by the federal government. The other terminated areas have remained terminated, and they are now under the jurisdiction of their states. In 1983 in a statement of his American Indian policy, President Reagan expressly repudiated termination.

Relocation

Reservation populations began to rise after World War II, and there were few job opportunities on most reservations. Some Indians had moved to cities before and during the war because of the boom in war-related jobs. Many of those people stayed in cities, returning to reservations or the rural areas of their childhood only for visits.

In 1951, the BIA launched an employment assistance program popularly known as relocation; because areas with high employment were all urban, the employment program necessarily moved people to cities. Relocation started in a small way, operating in only a few cities. By the 1960s, however, relocation placement centers had been established in many others. The cities most prominently involved early in the program were Chicago, Denver, Los Angeles, and Oakland, California.

Under this program, the move to the city started on the reservation. Interested Indians, both men and women, applied there for training or jobs. Counseling was provided to prepare the relocated people for their city experience, and through it the local BIA personnel tried to eliminate anyone they believed obviously unable to cope with city living. Many of the young Indians just after the war already knew quite a bit about city life from their education, television, time in military service, or visits to family and friends living in a city. Adjustment was harder for older people. Certainly in the first years of the program both Indians and government officials had hopes that were not always realistic.

In the city, the BIA city office helped find housing and periodically talked with the new arrivals to help them adjust. A relocated individual might go into an education program leading to a degree or diploma, or into on-the-job training. After the period of training and adjustment, specialized government services ceased, and the new city Indian was on his or her own.

Relocatees almost always changed living quarters and often jobs after they came to know their new surroundings. In some cities Indians concentrated in one section; in others, they dispersed. After government contacts were severed, any Indian who needed help from public agencies had to go to those serving all residents of the city, not just Indians.

Success of Relocation. Even though many of the people settled in cities by the program later returned to reservation living, it must be judged successful in terms of numbers resettled. Well over 100,000 Indians have entered cities as relocatees, and many others have come on their own without BIA assistance. Most Indians think it has been a good program—at least the goals are good. Usually any dissatisfaction arises from breakdowns in help, information, or counseling either in the city or on the reservation before the move.

How well individual Indians react to city life has depended too on the sophistication of their home reservation. People from the Great Lakes and northern Plains reservations usually have been to public schools with non-Indians. Most of them speak English, and they are quite familiar with such things as public transportation. Indians from more isolated reservations, especially where English, if it is spoken at all, is a second language and where many traditional customs are still common, find it harder to adjust to city life. More sophisticated Indians may not like the city, but their reasons are the same as those of the general population: noise, dirt, traffic, and crowding. The more traditional relocatees feel alienated, lonely, and perhaps frightened. For them adjustment is very much more difficult, sometimes impossible. They probably will not stay long in the city regardless of job opportunities.

One of the relocation program's goals was to train people who planned to go back to reservations to use their new knowledge. Unfortunately, many of the educated have not gone back because they can find few ways of using their new skills there. This and other programs such as college training thus have caused a "brain drain" from the reservations. Young, educated Indians are on reservations as visitors, not residents.

Adjustment to Urban Life. Happiness in city life seems to depend most on adequate preparation and realistic expectations. Membership in a stable group, usually one's family, also makes adjustment easier. If the family group is not stable, divorce, drunkenness, or abandonment will affect the whole family and may make city life worse than reservation life. Back on the reservation, people with family problems still can find other relatives and long-time friends to turn to. Personal characteristics also contribute to adjustment to city life. The ability to be flexible and take misfortune and new situations in stride makes life less stressful in the city or anywhere else.

Having a place for meetings and recreation also eases newcomers into the unfamiliar and busy rounds of urban living. As city Indian populations have grown, Indian centers have been established to meet this need. The first, started in 1952, was the Chicago American Indian Center. These centers generally try to support an Indian way of life in the city and to help solve problems of urban life by providing a social outlet. Originally they specialized in recreation because many city entertainments were beyond the means of Indians. Since the relocation program began operating, some centers have grown to provide social welfare, psychological and legal counseling, and education programs ranging from Headstart preschool to high school classes or adult education classes leading to the GED (a general education certificate of high school equivalence).

With more Indians living in cities, some perhaps inevitable conflicts have come up between reservation and nonreservation Indians. Because so many Indians live off the reservations, some reservation governments have changed voting regulations. Some tribes have refused to allow off-reservation voting because those left on the reservation believed the others were opposed to their interests. Off-reservation members of the Colville tribe in Washington tried to have tribal status terminated and the reservation assets sold and distributed to tribal members. Those living on the reservation were able to vote down the attempt at termination, but such differences are bound to continue as the move to cities continues.

Education

Very early in the history of European-Indian contact, Europeans decided that one way to transform Indians into "civilized" people was through education on the European model. Although some early colonists did think the difference between Europeans and Indians was biological and unchangeable, many others believed that the distinction arose from experience and tradition. They reasoned that proper schooling would erase the differences if enough young Indians could be persuaded to go to school.

In the East in colonial times, some private organizations, usually religious, set up schools either specifically for Indians or with programs for Indians. The United States government entered the field of Indian education in the early nineteenth century. However, it had neither the personnel, facilities, nor skills to get directly into education, so Congress appropriated money, called the Civilization Fund, to be used by churches and other private institutions to educate Indians. Many treaties required that the federal government arrange for the education of Indian children; in those early days, many tribes were eager to learn to read and write so that they could compete with whites for jobs. The Cherokee refused to let missionaries work in Cherokee territory unless the sponsoring church set up schools. Federal funds also supported occupational training programs or manual labor schools.

Sequoyah

One man did not wait for Europeans to educate him. The son of a Cherokee mother and British father, Sequoyah took part in both Indian and European traditions. He was a silversmith and blacksmith as well as a fairly prosperous farmer. During his lifetime (about 1770 to about 1843), the Cherokee were losing territory to white settlers year by year. Though he could neither read nor write and knew no language but Cherokee, he was convinced that literacy was the secret of white power. He was sure that his language could be written, and when he was about thirty, he set out to invent a system of writing for Cherokee.

He first tried to create a symbol for each word—a method too elaborate to work, for even he could not remember what all his symbols meant. Eventually he realized that he could represent each Cherokee *syllable* by a symbol, calculating that the language had eighty-six syllables. He then invented a syllabary of Cherokee characters, composed of capital and lower-case letters of the English alphabet, some turned upside down, and some original symbols of his own. He taught his daughter his system, showing all doubters that she could read anything he wrote. Cherokee back in the East as well as Sequoyah's neighbors in Arkansas accepted his system. In 1828, the Cherokee published a newspaper, *The Cherokee Phoenix*, running news in English and in Cherokee. Sequoyah is the first known person who, though illiterate, created a whole system of writing. The sequoia tree and Sequoia National Park memorialize his name.

Early Indian Schools

The privately operated schools of the early years were set up on reservations or in Indian territory. The first one off the reservation, Carlisle Indian School, was established in Carlisle, Pennsylvania in 1879, and continued there until 1918. It was more famous for football teams than for academic excellence. Jim Thorpe, the famous Sauk-Fox Indian football and track star, got his start at Carlisle. During World War I, Carlisle was turned over to the army and permanently closed as a school because it was too far away from the centers of Indian population.

During the last quarter of the nineteenth century, the government began to build federally administered Indian schools close to Indian populations. In the late 1800s, most Indian schools were boarding schools where the children lived, returning to their kinfolk only during holidays. Behind the boarding schools were two theories of Indian education. One was that the only way to educate young Indians for assimilation into white society was to remove them completely from tribal influences. The other was that setting up as many separate day schools as it would take to cover all reservation groups would weaken academic quality and overstretch the educational budget.

Probably few of the children taken from their families—sometimes by force—thought of Indian boarding schools as an opportunity. But being children, they were flexible enough to live through separation from their families, and many went on to graduate from those schools with a sense of accomplishment. Nevertheless, many people, non-Indians and Indians, saw the cruelty in a program that took children, some hardly more than infants, from their homes and forced on them an alien and generally authoritarian way of life. Eventually the outcry against such practices resulted in the establishment of more day schools on Indian lands. Still, where populations were sparse and settlements widely scattered, children could not go to day schools, so some boarding schools still operate. They are run by the Bureau of Indian Affairs not only for children far from public schools and Indian day schools, but also for those who need home care as well as education because of sickness, death, or broken families. In addition, schools operated by churches or other private institutions care for about 10 percent of Indian children in school today.

Education Today

Federal day schools and boarding schools cover kindergarten through twelfth grade. The government also offers vocational or technical training beyond the high school level in two schools operated by the BIA: Haskell Institute in Kansas, which grants a two-year associate's degree, and the

Fifth-graders at a boarding school run by the BIA on the Pine Ridge (Oglala Sioux) reservation in South Dakata, 1956.

Southwestern Polytechnic Institute in Albuquerque. Neither of these schools offers the equivalent of a four-year college education. For that academic level, Indians must enter schools that are also open to the general public. Approximately 15,000 Indians received scholarship grants from the BIA in 1990 to attend universities and colleges.

There are more than 20 two-year, tribally owned, community colleges open today. The oldest and largest is on the Navajo Reservation in Arizona: The Navajo Community College, with an enrollment of about 2,000. It was chartered by the tribe in 1968 and was housed temporarily in a BIA high school. Now it has its own campus at Tsaile. To emphasize that it is a Navajo institution, ten dormitories are shaped like hogans, and the new glass-sided administration building is also built in the shape of a hogan with the main entrance to the east. The college offers a two-year program of study leading to an associate of arts degree in academic studies or a certificate of proficiency in vocational fields. The curriculum also has courses on Navajo language and culture.

The college is operated under a ten-member board of regents appointed by the Navajo Tribal Council. About 70 percent of the administration is Navajo. Indians other than Navajo also attend, as well as a few non-Indians. The Navajo tribe appropriated a million dollars for the first phase of construction, and the federal government provides the operating funds and pays tuition, room and board, and book fees for all Indian students at the college.

Indian dropout rates at all levels are higher than those of the general population. Educators believe there are three reasons for this. First, where English is not the primary language, as in most Navajo settlements, the language handicap is great. Indian children who must learn English are much older than their classmates from the general population, a position which can embarrass or discourage them. Most Indians with major language handicaps fail to catch up to their age level. Second, many Indian children and their parents do not value scholastic achievement as much as members of other ethnic groups do, and thus they are not so highly motivated. Third, many Indians can see no benefit in the kind of education that is represented by the schools. School subjects used to seem very remote from Indian life. Today this view seems to be changing as most Indian parents realize that their children need certain basic skills to get desirable jobs and goods. More and more, parents are encouraging children to stay in school.

Most Indians of school age are not in government schools but in state public schools. When reservation Indian children attend these, the federal government pays the school district to compensate for the fact that Indians pay no state land tax to support the schools. Indian children in federal schools must meet the same educational requirements and standards as other public school students. Because BIA schools must meet the standards of the state in which they are located, Indian children also are subject to the state's compulsory attendance laws whether they are in state or federal schools. No children can grow up without attending some schools, so the literacy rates of Indian children today are almost as high as for children from the general society. However, Indian children more often drop out as soon as they have reached the age at which their state lets them leave school.

Health

Since 1955, health services for reservation Indians have been handled by the United States Public Health Service, Division of Indian Health Service, of the Department of Health and Human Services. Before that, the Bureau of Indian Affairs supplied health services. Off-reservation Indians use the same services as other citizens, public or private depending upon their means. Reservation health services are provided by the federal government because state services or private physicians are hard to reach from reservation areas far from population centers. Because Indians do not pay state property taxes on reservations, they do not have state coverage for many services, including health. The Indian Health Service has contractual arrangements with hospitals for surgical, gynecological, and in-patient care, and the bureau operates some hospitals itself. The federal government also helps with other health services, such as constructing sanitary facilities and sewage systems, and testing water.

American Indians have some special health problems, including high rates of trachoma (an eye disease), tuberculosis, and diabetes. Others are common infectious diseases and forms of dysentery and gastroenteritis that come from poor sanitation and diet. On the other hand, some disorders are only about half as common among Indians as in the general population, including cancer, heart disease, and strokes. The Indian birth rate is almost twice that of whites; the average life expectancy is about six years less than for members of the general population.

Indians who speak English as a second language or not at all often have trouble communicating with doctors and other health officers. Trained bilingual medical aides have bridged this gap in many cases. Relationships between patient and doctor are better when the doctor is an Indian, but many Indians who get a medical degree do not go back to reservations to practice. In fact, the doctor shortage is acute on some reservations. Of course, most of the problems Indians face in finding adequate health care are not unique, but are shared by all people in isolated areas or in lower socioeconomic classes where information is inadequate, misinformation is widespread, and shortages in medical personnel are constant.

Religious Change

In spite of unflagging efforts by Catholic and Protestant missionaries, Christianity did not make great strides among Indian peoples. It was too exclusive, requiring that they abandon old ways. Left to themselves, Indians preferred to combine elements of old and new.

Many Christian denominations claim Indian members today, and some traditional Indian practices and beliefs are still strong in areas with dense Indian populations. Religious organizations that Indians have found appealing combine old beliefs and Christianity. The religion of Handsome Lake, described earlier, still has followers among the Iroquois. The meeting place is a longhouse, and today the movement is usually called the Longhouse Religion. Shakerism too has continued as a local religion in the Northwest, also combining Christian and traditional Indian beliefs.

The Native American Church

The newest and most important religious movement among Indians today is the Native American Church, often called the Peyote Cult. (*Peyote* is a nonaddictive hallucinogenic drug.) This cult spread after the Ghost Dance declined in the Plains just before 1900, replacing the Ghost Dance in many tribes. After 1900, the Peyote Cult became popular in other areas, especially the Southwest and Midwest. It has never had much following in California, which some anthropologists say is explained by the common use there of another hallucinogen, *jimsonweed* (see chapter 5). The use of the two drugs seems to be mutually exclusive.

The Native American Church has about a quarter of a million members. It combines something of the vision quest and belief in general supernatural power with the Christian Trinity; its doctrine teaches that God is a great spirit and Jesus a guardian spirit. Christian morality is woven into its precepts: brotherly love, honor, trust, the golden rule, and some ethics derived from the Ten Commandments such as no adultery or divorce. Members believe especially in total abstinence from alcoholic beverages.

Though the doctrine or belief derives much from the Bible, peyote ceremonialism bears little resemblance to Christianity. The Peyote Cult uses many trappings from traditional Indian ritual: feathers and rattles, bone whistles, drumming, and eating peyote to achieve a vision. The ritual varies from group to group, but meetings usually begin at sundown with one man, the peyote chief, in charge. He is assisted by other officials in the church. Peyote, the bud of a cactus species, is chewed in its dry form and spit out, or made into a tea and drunk. The ritual chief administers the peyote to the congregation accompanied by drumming and singing. The songs, called peyote music, often deal with subjects from the Bible, but they can also be nonsense verses taken from a drug-induced hallucination. Sometimes peyote acts as an emetic, causing many novices to vomit. Peyote is used with careful control; it is regarded as a sacrament. At dawn a woman brings in drinking water because peyote makes one very thirsty; then the participants eat breakfast together.

Indians in Today's World

Indians hold about as many different jobs and enter as many professions as the general American population, but Indian unemployment is very much higher. Only a small percentage of employed Indians are in occupations requiring college degrees. One reason is, of course, that the percentage of Indians holding degrees is much smaller than in the general population. Also, many Indians entering the professions no longer identify themselves as Indians.

Indians on reservations generally have a higher rate of unemployment than nonreservation Indians because jobs on reservations still are scarce and usually call only for unskilled workers. Until recently these jobs depended mainly on farming, stock raising, and similar enterprises. Though efforts have been made to bring industry to reservations, wage work from such sources is still rare. In addition, reservations are overpopulated, reservation land is not productive, and competition is tremendous for whatever jobs do exist.

Poor education has been another great cause of Indian unemployment. As we have mentioned, the dropout rate of Indians at all educational levels is high. Reservation schools are employing teachers specially trained to handle Indian problems like language and motivation, and many school systems in cities with large Indian populations have special curricula to stimulate Indians to work for scholastic achievement and to correct deficiencies. Of course, one reason many Indians lack motivation to finish school is that even those who have diplomas find it hard to find work on reservations. Students educated elsewhere who had hoped to return to their home reservations to use their education to benefit the tribe often have found no suitable jobs.

Economic Success

It may seem that Indians either abandon Indian ways or live in poverty and ignorance, but that is not the case. Though no one can deny the economic and educational problems they face, many Indians have reached economic self-sufficiency without losing their Indian identity. Indians on some reservations have been outstandingly successful in developing resources. The Western Apache are an example that other Indians can point to with pride, for they have developed a cattle-ranching industry fully competitive in the general market. In fact, stock raising has turned into an important economic opportunity in unlikely places, such as Big Cypress Seminole Reservation in Florida. Big Cypress is a south Florida swamp area that seems completely unsuitable for cattle land, But the Seminole, with BIA and state aid, have drained large areas and turned them into pasture for herds of Angus cattle. For Seminole interested in raising cattle, this has been a great economic opportunity.

Mohawk Indians have received a great deal of publicity for their work in high steel construction for skyscrapers and bridges. Long ago in colonial times, English surveyors noticed how little fear of heights Mohawk displayed, and in 1886, when a railway bridge was built across the St. Lawrence River near a Mohawk village, some Mohawk men were employed. Engineers and company officials were impressed by the men's agility and confidence, and since that time, Mohawk have worked in high steel all over this continent. They have been involved in building most of the major bridges and skyscrapers, among them the Empire State Building and the George Washington Bridge. These Mohawk steel workers live today in several apartment buildings within one neighborhood in Brooklyn, New York, not on the Canadian or New York State Iroquois reservations, though they often visit there.

The Northwest Coast Indians have been quite successful in commercial salmon fishing, and also working in the fish canneries. Some of their success may come from the competitive personality their ancestors showed in the potlatch, but they have profited too because of the Alaska Native Brotherhood. During the second decade of this century, a group of Tlingit Indians organized the Alaska Native Brotherhood to oppose discrimination in employment, education, and citizenship rights. It has grown to include many Alaskan Eskimo and Indians as well as the Tlingit. The brotherhood became active in labor relations in the fishing industry and fought for nonsegregated schools in Alaska; a Canadian Indian organization with similar aims was formed in British Columbia. The primary goal of the brotherhood has been acculturation—the adoption by Indians of non-Indian ways—and it has always had strong Christian leanings though it is not connected with any denomination. In recent years the organization has been trying to encourage Indians to be more active in politics.

The Canadian Eskimo formed an organization, the Inuit Tapirisat, to speak on their behalf about major economic, environmental, and political issues concerning the Arctic, and they joined with Eskimo in Alaska, Greenland, and the Soviet Union to form the Circumpolar Conference to address the same issues internationally.

Economic Hope

Both Indians and BIA officials see recreational development on reservations as an important way to create jobs and income in the future. Some tribes have already built motels, camp grounds, restaurants, and the like on reservation territory. Also, because most tourists and visitors show interest in Indian traditions, the performance of dances, celebrations, and ceremonials would allow Indians to practice traditional ritual display and make money at the same time.

Selling arts and crafts to tourists already brings in supplementary income in many areas. Since the Indian Reorganization Act of 1934, federal officials as well as Indians themselves have promoted commercial sale of traditional Indian works, Public recognition of these productions has helped build pride in the Indian cultural heritage. Some artists and craftspeople have won national recognition for their skill and talent. One of the most famous is Maria Martinez, a potter of San Ildefonso Pueblo. Her pottery, known as black-on-black, is in some of our great art museums. Other Indian artists hold positions in art departments of universities or paint and teach privately. Basketry is going through a renaissance, especially in California and the Southwest, as is woodcarving in the Northwest. Also in the Northwest, argillite (often erroneously called slate) carved into bowls or statuary has become a new medium for expressing traditional motifs and styles.

After the Spanish introduced silver work to the Pueblo people, the Zuni became master silversmiths, and the Navajo too began to produce strikingly beautiful silver products using Spanish designs. The squash blossom necklace with the pendant called the *naja*, a Spanish gypsy symbol to ward off the evil eye, is treasured not only by Navajo and Pueblo, but by anyone fortunate enough to own one.

Navajo blankets, of wool homespun from Navajo sheep, are an important source of income to those who weave. Most colors used in these blankets today are modern aniline dyes, but some weavers still take the time to make and use the old natural dyes. Prices may seem high—a good blanket about 4 by 6 feet may cost a thousand dollars or more—but for the time that goes into making the blanket, the pay is low.

Ceremonial costumes of all tribes are much brighter now than traditionally, for they too are colored with aniline dyes. Most modern costumes combine items from many culture areas: Indians of the Great Lakes now perform dances wearing the feathered bustles and headdresses of Plains Indians. Beaded designs include patterns from widely separated tribes as well as from European peasant styles. Art styles today are truly pan-Indian, with the emphasis on being *Indian*, rather than of a particular tribe.

The Eskimo, traditionally skilled carvers in bone, ivory, and antler, have turned to soapstone, the material used long ago for oil lamps, to produce a sculptural art that has great appeal. The Canadian government helps retail these figurines, and some museums now have fine collections. The subjects are the people and animals of the Arctic: fat walruses and plump seals dozing on their flippers, gamboling polar bear cubs, chunky Eskimo mothers with babies on their backs. The animal figures are in the tradition of Eskimo good-luck charms or amulets, carved during times of famine as magical devices to bring the game or to appease the spirits.

Casino Gaming. In their search for economic opportunities on the various reservations and reserves, both American and Canadian Indians hope that casinos will be a way out of poverty and unemployment. More than one hundred reservations and reserves have tried some form of gambling, from 6,000-seat bingo parlors to full scale casino gaming. It all began with the Seminole Indians of Florida in 1979 when regular bingo parties brought in chartered bus-loads of tourists who not only played bingo but who bought food, drinks, and souvenirs. Unemployment, a constant among the Seminole, was greatly lessened as Seminole learned to manage not only the sales but also the bingo operation itself. Probably the most sophisticated operation by Indians is on the Sault Ste. Marie Chippewa Reservation in Michigan where an elaborate casino offers slot machines, blackjack tables, and roulette games. There is real hope that gaming might be a ticket out of poverty and financial dependence on the federal government.

Nevertheless there are problems. In the United States the most severe is the fear of organized crime taking over the operations. Crime worries state governments that are not legally able to interfere on tribal or federal land—Indian reservations are federal trust land—and threatens the continuation of some gambling operations. A new National Indian Gaming Commission decides which games and devices (like slot machines) must have state approval. Also, where management of the casinos has been

Sycuan gaming center on the Sycuan Indian reservation in Southern California. This center is the only one in the state to offer all five forms of legal gambling in the state under one roof.

turned over by the Indians to outside contractors, some tribes have paid 75 percent or even more of their net profit to the outsiders. There has been, consequently, an effort to train Indians and at the same time to put a limit on the amount outside management firms can charge. In addition, merchants close to reservations are frequently disgruntled because they must pay state liquor and sales taxes which Indians on reservations do not.

In Canada many similar concerns arise, but one problem seems paramount: the conflict of jurisdiction. If a reserve is within a province that does not allow gaming, people in the general population do not want it on the reserves. As of 1993 only four provinces—British Columbia, Alberta, Manitoba, and Ontario—allow gambling. Reserves in other provinces have not yet opened casinos, but many would like the option.

Political Movements

Indian organizations that have been active in national political and economic affairs are the National Congress of American Indians (NCAI), the National Indian Youth Council (NIYC), and the American Indian Movement, (AIM). NCAI is the oldest of the three. It was founded in 1944 "to protect, conserve and develop Indian land, mineral, timber and human resources; serve legislative interests of Indian tribes; improve health, education and economic conditions." It is composed of both tribes and individuals, and more than a hundred tribes are affiliated with it. NCAI conducts research on Indian problems as a service to Indian tribes, has a legal aid program for Indians, and runs a lobby in Washington to present Indian needs and wishes. In general, it appeals to industry and commerce for greater employment of Indians, and tries to promote legislation to improve Indian conditions and to secure Indian rights.

The National Indian Youth Council

The National Indian Youth Council was founded in 1961 by a group of young Indians during a conference of American Indians at the University of Chicago. It received some national recognition when members conducted a "fish-in" in the state of Washington in 1964: NIYC members and some others fished in the Nisqually and Puyallup rivers in Washington, defying state law. This effort through civil disobedience to preserve Indian rights to traditional fishing sites, and the resulting publicity, brought national attention to Indian economic problems.

The issue behind the fish-in was whether or not Indians were subject to state regulations on hunting and fishing. The Indians claimed that under the Medicine Creek Treaty of 1854 they were guaranteed fishing rights. The state of Washington contended that net fishing (the kind of fishing the Indians did) was against conservation laws. The State Fisheries personnel tried to remove the nets from the Puyallup River, and Indians shot at them. Police came in, subdued the Indians with tear gas, and arrested sixty. The case was eventually settled in favor of the tribes, however, allowing limited net fishing by Indians only.

The American Indian Movement

The American Indian Movement, founded in Cleveland in 1968, is generally thought to have radical leanings, and many Indians want no part of it. It was the moving force behind the confrontation between Indians and federal forces at Wounded Knee, South Dakota, in 1973. On February 28 of that year, Indians under the direction of AIM took at least ten Indian hostages at Wounded Knee and demanded concessions from the federal government: that the Senate Foreign Relations Committee hold hearings on treaties made with Indians; that the Senate begin full-scale investigation of government treatment of Indians; and that another inquiry be started into all Sioux reservations in South Dakota.

Members of AIM occupied a trading post and church at Wounded Knee, and federal police surrounded the town. Inhabitants of Pine Ridge Reservation, where Wounded Knee is, claimed that AIM was interfering in internal tribal affairs and did not represent the reservation. The chairman and council of Pine Ridge said the occupation was tied to the struggle for political control of the reservation. Through the next few months, the conflict grew, with AIM demanding that the tribal chairman step down, and the chairman insisting that the nonresidents (AIM people) be expelled. Gunfire exchanges became frequent, finally killing two people. The seventy-day occupation ended on May 8, with nothing really changed. Most reservation Indians were very upset and angry at the shooting and occupation and destruction by fire of their homes and other buildings. While most Indians disavowed tactics AIM used, others—most of whom are not on the reservation—believe that such measures are the only way to win justice. Support, membership, and leadership for AIM have come mostly from younger, nonreservation Indians.

Occupation of the BIA Building

In late October 1972, a group of activist Indians organized a protest which they called the Trail of Broken Treaties. They meant to dramatize Indian grievances, for they thought that Indians had too long been silent on Indian health, housing, education, and neglected treaties. Joined by some members of AIM, they went to Washington, D.C., to discuss Indian problems with BIA personnel. They planned a peaceful demonstration to gain social and economic benefits, but the Indian leaders of the protest came to feel that their talks with the BIA officials were without result and that the government was generally disinclined to discuss any serious matters with them.

On November 2, about five hundred Indians, AIM members and participants in the Trail of Broken Treaties, took over the BIA offices in protest. They scuffled with police inside and outside, but no arrests were made, and word came from high officials to let the Indians remain in the building, They held the offices until November 8, when they left after reaching an agreement with White House negotiators to hear Indian proposals for aid and solutions to their many problems.

During the occupation, the Indians did over a million dollars' worth of damage to furniture and equipment in the building, and when they left they took documents and records as well as Indian paintings and artifacts. Most of the militants were urban Indians; the government charged that they did not represent the Indian peoples. However, the government agreed not to prosecute those who seized the building, and allotted $60,000 in government funds to help them get home. Then some Indian members of the National Tribal Chairmen's Association inspected the damage and called for investigation and prosecution of the militants; their president blamed the government for letting militants occupy the building. Many Indians who had not been involved were particularly disturbed over the destruction and theft of treaty and land documents recording vital negotiations on Indian rights. They said that the acts of destruction were self-defeating, harmful only to Indians, not to government personnel.

Taken alone, this kind of action may be seen by many as either futile or merely an attempt at publicity for individuals. Yet it does prove that young Indians are politically aware and active. Many people, while deploring acts of destruction and violence, are encouraged that some Indians are beginning to take steps on their own rather than leaving planning and action to the BIA.

Preservation of Human Remains and Repatriation of Indian Property

Few controversies have raised more heat and ire than the ownership and preservation of Indian artifacts and human remains. During the last half of the twentieth century many states have passed laws regarding the disturbance of Indian burials. Prior to passage of these laws and increased awareness of Indian feeling on the subject, it was not unusual for highways, buildings, dams—construction of all sorts—to proceed even when human remains were uncovered in the way. In addition, archaeologists themselves have been charged with thoughtless disregard for Indian beliefs and opinions. And perhaps the most objectionable of all, burial sites have been pillaged for their grave goods by people just wanting Indian relics and artifacts for personal collections or for sale. Much of such despoiling has been carried on with no thought for the feelings of descendants of those buried. Indians quite rightly have felt that the resting places of their ancestors were being plundered, destroyed, and generally desecrated.

As a result of increasing awareness of these problems, individual states, especially those known to have Indian burial sites, have passed laws regarding intrusion or excavation. For example, the state of Iowa requires that anyone uncovering or discovering human remains for any reason whatsoever must notify the Office of the State Archaeologist at once and stop all excavation. The state will then examine and study the remains and consult with an Indian Advisory Committee. Results of any study will then be published and the remains will be re-interred in cemeteries designated for that purpose.

Most states have provisions of this sort. In some, the State Historical Society is the responsible agency, and there are ways of applying for permission to investigate a particular burial if there is a legitimate reason to do so, as for example a scientific or environmental purpose or to identify cultural or tribal affiliation or for a change in land use. These laws have been enacted to ensure that all human remains are treated equally. Indians have often expressed the opinion that their burials were not protected whereas no one would dream of invading a non-Indian cemetery. In fact, archaeologists have within recent years disinterred several colonial burials on the East Coast in an attempt to identify the remains. But it is true that in earlier years, Indian burials were *freely* disturbed, both by archaeologists and by others, with no attempt to seek permission either from state agencies or from possible descendants. Now the law protects all human burials, and one must seek and receive permission before engaging in any kind of exhumation.

One can question why anyone, even scientists, should be digging up human burials. The answer is that often old cemeteries and burial grounds cannot be avoided, and in that case reasonable people usually agree that careful and respectful reburial must follow. For scientists like archaeologists and forensic anthropologists, it is information for the study of ancient populations that is the important factor: mineral and protein deficiencies, diseases, skeletal anomalies like skull deformation, diet and tooth decay may all be identified. Even ancient DNA has been recovered. However important such research may be, it is imperative that it be done with sensitivity, recognizing that *those not in the scientific field may not find such goals acceptable*. Above all, careful re-interment should be the conclusion.

Another area of controversy, somewhat less heated, has been the question of collections, especially in museums, of Indian artifacts. Some such artifacts, though legitimately acquired in the sense that they were paid for, are regarded as sacred by some tribes. There has been a recent attempt to get many of the major museums of America to return items that are on display or in storage. The argument by Indians has been that artifacts were sold or given away years ago by Indians who did not understand what would be done with them or by those who had no right to dispose of tribal goods. In addition, there is no doubt that many Indian belongings were taken away unfairly or simply stolen. Museum curators have replied that if the items had been left on reservations they would not still be in existence, that they require special care and treatment for preservation which only a modern museum with heat and humidity controls can offer. Furthermore, say the curators, museums offer opportunities for many people to learn about American Indians in a very real, visually meaningful way. Some Indians have responded that they have a right to decide on the disposition of their own property or tribal remains, and that includes the right to destroy them or let them decay. Other Indians have built tribal museums and asked for the return of their tribal belongings. A federal law became effective in 1990 compelling the returns of sacred items. Some museums have, indeed, returned items where care is assured. However, the controversy continues as, unfortunately, does the looting of sites, especially those in inaccessible places where policing is minor or nonexistent.

Current Conditions in Canada

Land Claims

The Canadian government announced in 1973 that it would negotiate land claim settlements with all Inuit and Indians whose ancestors had never signed treaties. The goal was to establish ownership over land and resources based on evidence of aboriginal title and a clarification of the rights of natives and non-natives.

The James Bay and Northern Quebec Agreement. In 1971 Quebec announced a giant hydroelectric development to exploit the provincial resources. Indians and Inuit of the area applied for an injunction to halt all construction on the grounds that native land claims had not been resolved. Work was delayed, but agreements were reached in 1975 and 1978 that compensated the native peoples for loss of territory with cash payments, set aside some land for the exclusive use and benefit of the natives, and indicated other land for development and use under federal or provincial jurisdiction. This was the first modern claims agreement reached in Canada.

This particular settlement received much publicity because of the interest in the huge hydroelectric station at James Bay which when fully operative could send power as far as New York City.

The Inuit-Nunavut Settlement. No other disposition of land claims has been more interesting internationally than this, for other governments with restless, alienated minority peoples have watched closely, and when settled this will be the largest claim settlement in Canada.

Canada is composed of ten Provinces and two Territories. One of the latter, the Northwest Territories (NWT), is huge. It is thinly populated by Dene Indians, Métis, and Inuit. The Inuit live in the eastern part of the Territories where they comprise 80 percent of the population. Unlike the people of Quebec, the Inuit do not seek separation from Canada. They regard themselves as Canadians, but wish to have the traditional territory of the ancestors under their control with the same degree of political and economic sovereignty as people in the other areas. Under a Supreme Court decision that they still had aboriginal title to their land since no treaties had been signed, the Inuit proposed the creation of Nunavut, "Our Land" in their dialect, a new Territory, carved from the eastern part of the NWT with its own capital city.

After almost two decades of discussion, an agreement between the government and the Inuit created Nunavut and gave 18 percent of it exclusively to the Inuit, with rights to hunting and a share in oil, gas, and mineral royalties throughout the rest. Among other rights and benefits was a fund to train Inuit civil servants, important because the Inuit must learn how to operate the new territorial government.

Agreement in principle was signed by the negotiators in 1990, and it was ratified by vote of the Inuit in 1992. Legislation now awaits passage by Parliament, and the Inuit will become self-governing by 1999 within the nation of Canada.

More than two dozen other native claims still remain for negotiation.

Economic Development

The government has aided Indian and Inuit business through the Indian Economic Development Fund established in the 1970s by DIAND. The object has been to encourage community-based development because economic self-sufficiency is seen as the critical element in self-determination. The businesses supported here have included such things as motels, tourist resorts, grain farming, manufacturing, and so on. Agreements with petroleum companies to build plants on or near reserves will bring royalties to certain bands, and the federal and provincial governments and private organizations have helped develop mineral resources on reserves as well as to create business opportunities such as stores and gas stations. The federal government has especially encouraged Indians and Inuit to produce traditional arts and crafts. Items that sell well are moccasins, gloves, jackets and *mukluks* (the sealskin boots worn by Indians and Inuit of the Northwest Territories). In the Northwest Coast area, woodcarvings of totem poles and masks bring important supplementary income.

In the Subarctic, besides some wage work in towns, many Indians and Inuit continue to trap, hunt, and fish for a livelihood. They have increased the production of fur-bearing animals with new techniques and management developed in cooperation with the provincial governments. They are also going into the commercial fishing industry, and some Indians make their living as guides to sports enthusiasts. In addition, residents of some reserves hope for good income from casino gaming or other forms of gambling.

Hunting and Fishing Rights

Indians claim the traditional right to fish and hunt for food and for ceremonial reasons without regard to federal and provincial law. This position has resulted in some conflict between native people and the general population. Outsiders fear the danger to wildlife resources and endangered species. Indians feel that conservation laws discriminate against native rights.

There are several viewpoints. Animal rights groups have campaigned against all hunting and trapping and have tried to halt this part of the traditional life of native people. The government has tended to side with the natives since there are limited means of participating in a cash economy except through these activities. Believing that complete elimination of hunting and trapping would seriously affect native people, not only in their attempts for economic viability, but also by destroying an important source of food, DIAND has been an ardent advocate of humane and responsible trapping and has tried to increase public awareness that Indian and Inuit trapping and hunting are effective wildlife management mechanisms.

Fishing, like hunting and trapping, has been a significant tradition to the native peoples—many of whom have always been dependent on fish for food. The conflict in this case has arisen with non-native commercial fishing industries that oppose the sale of fish by Indians, especially along the Fraser River. The legal provision that allowed Indians an increase in the amount of their catch specified that the sale of fish was forbidden; the fish were to be solely for Indian consumption. Nevertheless, Indians have entered into some commercial deals. These controversies must be worked out to the satisfaction not only of natives and commercial fishers but also to satisfy environmentalists. All parties are working to solve the problem.

Education

The federal government is responsible for education of registered Indian children from age 5 to 17, living on reserves. (Those not living on reserves or not registered get their education from the province in which they live and pay taxes.) The government also contributes services and funds for post-secondary education through scholarships and grants with the result that today more Indian professionals are being trained to work in their communities and in the general Canadian society.

Until the 1970s the majority of Indian children received their education in residential schools, almost exclusively run by churches. At those schools the native languages and customs were discouraged and the children were isolated from family and friends. Many Indian groups demanded an end to this separation with the result that the government made major changes.

Today there are three types of schools. DIAND operates some federal schools for students from kindergarten through high school. About 15 percent of the native children attend these schools. Approximately half of the native students go to regular provincial schools. DIAND has made agreements with these schools and pays tuition and other costs that the province would otherwise get from taxation or provincial residents.

Probably the most creative new schools are those where the school boards are band managed and the schools are band operated. These schools offer an education equivalent to the provincial schools but they have additional contribution by band elders and some instruction in native language and culture. About 35 percent of the students go to band-operated schools.

Conclusion

Everywhere traditional native American ways are changing. Today's Indians are not like their ancestors of Columbus' time, and those people were not like the first who came across Beringia many thousands of years ago. Yet some traditions remain, and some tribes, especially the Pueblo, have kept many of their ancestors' customs. Other groups have revived old ways for festivals and ceremonies, both for commercial profit and from pride in their past.

Some of the old variety of Indian culture still exists, but socioeconomic and educational differences are far more important among Indians today. Indians have entered general North American society at every level including the learned professions, and they are as much affected by social and economic conditions in their country and in the world as any other member of society.

Since World War II, Indians have awakened to the idea that they can control their future. With their own political organizations, they have learned how to pressure the United States and Canadian governments to let them make their own decisions, and to persuade business and industry to employ more qualified Indian people. They have encouraged their young to seek more education. Indians are increasingly taking over Indian affairs, assuming the obligations and duties of citizenship as well as demanding the rights due them. They are making their own suggestions about what can be done to help their people and are insisting on the right to take part in pertinent decisions at all levels.

It seems likely that old traditions of art, mythology, and kinship responsibility will last or will be revived, but only as a veneer over industrial life. No Indian wants to live in a tipi or expects to subsist by hunting and gathering any more than whites want to live in log cabins. Indians recognize that the idea of holding onto a way of life that passed more than a hundred years ago is as unrealistic as it is insulting. It implies that Indians somehow cannot change—or can change only in degrading ways. Instead, Indians want to be able to make their own decisions and to keep up a private life as traditional as they may wish, while entering fully into public industrial life. In this they are no different from any other ethnic group.

GLOSSARY

aboriginal the population native to an area from the time of its earliest occupation.

adaptation a change in structure, function, or form that leaves an animal or plant better adjusted to its environment.

adobe a kind of clay used in building, either applied like plaster or made into sun-dried bricks. Adobe became a major building material in the Southwest after Spanish contact.

age grade a subdivision of a society in which membership is based on age. Members of an age grade form a social group and engage in various activities together.

association an organization built on some principle other than kinship. American Indian associations formed around mutual interest, religion, age, and sex, and provided aid, education, recreation, and social control.

atlatl a board or stick, 20 to 24 inches long, fitted with a handle on one end and a groove or peg at the other, used in throwing a dart or spear.

babiche rawhide strips for snowshoes, netting, thongs, and other uses.

band a simple level of social organization with groups of fifty to a hundred people in families or other kin groups, living and finding food together. A band night be composed of brothers with their wives and younger children.

bast the inner bark of a tree.

berdache a man who chose not to follow the ideal masculine ways of the Plains warrior, and instead led a woman's life. He was not necessarily a homosexual, and his way of life was considered socially acceptable.

Beringia the former region encompassing the area of the Bering Sea exposed as land due to lowering of sea level during the Pleistocene glaciation. It also included adjacent areas of northeastern Siberia and western Alaska.

bilateral descent tracing descent equally through the maternal and paternal sides of the family.

blood money material retribution paid for injury, loss of life, or loss of property.

bow drill a drill consisting of a straight stick that is rotated by a string looped around the stick and pulled rapidly back and forth.

bridewealth gifts given by the groom's family to the bride's family as compensation for the loss of her services.

buffalo chips buffalo dung, used as fuel by the Plains Indians and later by the European settlers.

bull boat a cup-shaped boat used only to cross rivers. It had a framework of saplings covered with skins.

burial mound a grave for one or several people covered with a hill of earth.

cacique the Spanish name for the head of a medicine society, who was also the head of the town.

calumet a pipe with a long stem, also known as a peace pipe. It was smoked before going to war, on trading expeditions, and at peace councils; in it tobacco was also burned as an offering to the spirits.

carnivore a meat-eating animal.

catlinite a soft, easy to carve stone, ideal for pipe bowls, dishes, and other containers; also called pipestone.

chert a type of flint-like rock found in many areas of North America that was frequently used to make stone tools.

chickee the traditional Seminole house, an open-sided palmetto-thatched structure.

chiefdom a stratified society, having centralized authority and a leader who was set apart from or considered superior to his followers.

chunkey an aboriginal game played by the Cherokee, Creek, and many other eastern groups usually involving rolling a stone disk and throwing a spear or stick to land near it.

clan a kinship group descended either through men or through women from a common ancestor.

Clovis point a spearhead specialized for mammoth hunting, lance-shaped, with a mildly concave base, larger than a Folsom point, and with fluting extending one-quarter to one-half the length of the base. Clovis points, found from coast to coast, are always associated with the Big Game Hunting tradition.

copper a one- to four-foot shield-shaped plaque made of copper, used as a symbol of prestige on the Northwest Coast.

coup stick a small stick carried into battle by Plains Indians to touch the enemy. Touching a live enemy in battle brought great glory; the act was recounted back home by striking a pole with a coup stick.

cultigen a plant capable of being cultivated.

cultural diffusion the transmission of cultural practices, ideals, values, and so on through contact between one society and another.

culture the collected ways of life led by a group of people, including all their knowledge, customs, institutions, and material goods.

culture area a geographically distinct region within which various groups developed similar ways of life.

deadfall a trap that lets a weight such as a heavy log fall on an animal thereby killing or disabling it.

dentalia long, pointed shellfish that became an important medium of exchange on the Northwest Coast.

earth lodge a type of house common to the cultures of the plains and prairies, constructed partly underground and having a log frame covered with an outer layer of sod or packed earth.

earth oven a shallow pit dug in the ground, used for cooking food. The food is wrapped and placed in the pit on top of hot stones or coals, and covered over with earth until cooked.

earthwork any of a variety of embankments or mounds constructed of earth.

Eastern Agricultural Complex the name given to a set of plants native to the Eastern Woodlands and Missouri Valley that were cultivated by Late Archaic, Woodland, and Mississippian peoples, starting approximately 4000 to 5000 years ago. Some of the plants were domesticated prehistorically, such as sunflower, marsh elder, and goosefoot. These were grown along with forms of gourds and possibly squashes that were either introduced from Mexico or domesticated in the East. Other plants cultivated but not domesticated included maygrass, lambs-quarter, knotweed, and little barley.

effigy mound an earthen mound constructed in the shape of animals, humans, or geometric designs.

epicanthic eye fold a small fold of skin covering the inner corner of the eye. It is the characteristic that creates the so-called slant eyes common to people of the Mongoloid race.

ethnographic analogy a comparison between the facts we have about prehistoric peoples and what we know about similar groups who live today or who lived in the recent past. Used carefully, information about living groups can be helpful in reconstructing a picture of ancient societies.

exogamy the practice of selecting your spouse from a group other than your own.

extended family a domestic group consisting of a nuclear family plus another generation (grandparents), or more wives. It could also be a group of brothers or sisters living together with their spouses and children.

family (linguistic) a major category for classifying languages. Two or more related linguistic families comprise a linguistic phylum.

fictive kinship a special relationship in which people accord each other the status of kin, such as blood brothers or ceremonial parents. Fictive kinfolk have mutual duties and obligations like real kinfolk.

first fruit ceremony a public activity celebrating the season's first catch of fish or animals or the first plants of the season.

flute a long rounded groove, such as those on the surface of Folsom and Clovis points.

Folsom point a spearhead specialized for bison hunting, with parallel edges, a concave base, and flutes or grooves extending the entire length of the point. Folsom points are always associated with the Big Game Hunting tradition, and are found only in the North American High Plains.

foraging food-getting practices dependent upon the acquisition of wild plant and animal foods, also known as food collection or hunting-gathering.

galena the bluish or silvery gray mineral comprised of lead sulfide that occurs naturally in cube form.

geronticide the abandonment of aged persons who could no longer make an economic contribution to their group. It was practiced only under extreme conditions, and for the benefit of the whole group.

gorge a double-pointed piece of bone with a line attached in the middle, used much like a fish hook. Swallowed by the fish, it lodged in the throat, and the catch could easily be hauled in.

gourd any of a variety of inedible, hard-rinded plants often used for vessels.

graver a type of tool having a chisel-like edge used to engrave or splinter materials such as bone, ivory, antler, wood, or stone.

guardian spirit a spirit, usually in the form of an animal, which acted as a personal helper for its possessor, helping him or her win success in life. Guardian spirits usually appeared to those who sought them in a vision quest.

haft the handle of a weapon or tool.

hair pipe a long tubular bone strung into a breastplate by Plains warriors.

hammer stone a hard stone used to strike another, chipping off pieces to be fashioned into tools, such as projectile points or flint blades.

headman a leader, somewhat like a chief, whose authority rests on consent of the group he leads.

hogan the traditional Navajo house, a circular log-framed, earth-covered structure, its doorway always on the east.

Homo sapiens the scientific name for the genus and species to which all human beings belong.

horticulture plant cultivation with hand tools like hoes and digging sticks.

impound the confined area into which animals are driven so that they can be killed easily.

infanticide the abandonment or killing of a newborn infant, who could not be fed because food was scarce or its mother ill or dead. Infanticide was practiced only under extreme conditions, and for the benefit of the whole group.

jerky a strip of dried meat.

katcina a good spirit, believed by the Hopi to bring rain. Katcinas were said to have come from the Underworld with the people; men were allowed to impersonate them and dance to make it rain.

katcina doll an image of a katcina, given to children to teach them about the many katcinas.

kayak an Arctic canoe made of skins stretched over a frame of wood, covering it completely except for the open space where the paddler sits.

kinnikinnik a substance consisting of sumac, dogwood, willow bark, and sometimes tobacco, smoked by men of the Great Lakes region. *Kinnikinnik* is an Algonkian word meaning "mixture."

kiva a chamber, often subterranean, used by some Southwestern tribes for ceremonial purposes.

labret an ornamental lip plug, inserted through a hole pierced in the lip.

leaching a process for removing harmful or bitter substances from a potential food item, commonly by the percolation of water. One example of leaching would be the use of water to remove tannic acid from acorns.

lean-to an open dwelling consisting of a single wall, supported at an angle.

Little Ice Age a period characterized by colder climate in the northern hemisphere, lasting from approximately A.D. 1500 to 1850.

longhouse an Iroquoian dwelling, 50 to 100 feet long and about 20 feet wide, which housed several related families. It had a door at each end and was gabled or vaulted, like a long, narrow barn.

maize corn.

mammoth an extinct Pleistocene elephant species of the New World, approximately fourteen feet tall and having a high-crowned skull, long curved tusks, and teeth well suited to shearing and grinding grassy vegetation.

manitu an Algonkian belief similar to the Iroquoian orenda and the Siouan wakonda, a great supernatural force flowing through the universe.

mano the upper stone used on a metate to grind corn and other grains. It is held in the hand and moved back and forth over the metate.

mastodon an extinct Pleistocene elephant species of the New World, stockier and somewhat shorter than its distant relative, the mammoth, and having teeth capable of processing a greater variety of vegetation, including leaves, branches, and roots.

matrilineage a descent group in which membership is inherited through mothers.

medicine bundle the sacred container in which a Plains warrior carried his "medicine," items that had a kind of supernatural power similar to good-luck pieces, sacred talismans, or religious relics. Strangely shaped stones, bones, or feathers symbolized the warrior's visions or the animals that sent him power; these were his "medicine."

metate the trough-shaped lower part of a grinding stone, used for milling corn and other grains.

mica a transparent, often silvery-appearing mineral that separates into thin layers or leaves.

microblade a small, narrow flake of stone with sharp edges. A microblade could be used for making toothed saws, or as the point of a spear or harpoon.

moiety a kin group consisting of half a tribe. The two moieties of a tribe might compete in sports or perform important rites for each other.

mother-in-law avoidance a behavior pattern, designed to reduce the usual tension between a man and his wife's mother, by eliminating almost all face-to-face interaction between the two.

mukluk a sealskin boot worn by Indians and Eskimo of the Northwest territories.

naja a Spanish gypsy symbol believed to ward off the evil eye. The naja design appears in Navajo squash-blossom necklaces.

nuclear family a domestic group consisting of a married couple and their offspring.

obsidian volcanic glass.

orenda for the Iroquois, the source of supernatural power. It was a great invisible force that flowed through all the world, and could be tapped through dreams. It is similar to the Algonkian manitu and the Siouan wakonda.

ossuary a communal pit where the bones of exhumed corpses were buried.

oulachon an oily fish known as the candlefish because it burns like a candle when a wick is run through its body.

outfit a Navajo group composed of matrilineally related extended families living fairly close together. Members of an outfit farmed together, held common land rights, and had a headman who represented the group in dealings with outsiders.

Paleo Indian the name given to the earliest known cultures of the New World, characterized by a nomadic hunting-gathering existence focused on the hunting of large game animals, and involving the use of stone tools.

Paleolithic the cultural stage of development in the Old World characterized by a nomadic hunting-gathering existence and the use of chipped-stone tools. Also known as the Old Stone Age.

palisade a tall fence of sharp, pointed poles.

panpipe a primitive musical wind instrument consisting of a series of short flutes of increasing size that are bound together with the mouthpieces in an even row.

parfleche a container used by Plains Indians, which was actually a giant rawhide envelope. When packed, it expanded to the size and shape of a small chest.

patrilineage a descent group in which membership is inherited through fathers.

patrilocal the residence pattern in which a married couple and their children live in or near the husband's father's home.

pectoral a large chestplate of bone worn by Plains warriors.

pemmican an Indian dish made of dried, pulverized meat and berries, mixed with suet or other fat. Pemmican remains edible after a year of storage.

permafrost permanently frozen subsoil.

phratry an association of clans. This social grouping was most common in the Southeast, the Northwest, and the prairies.

phylum (linguistic) a major category for classifying languages. A linguistic phylum contains divisions called families.

physical anthropology the study of humankind's animal origins and its genetically determined nature. Physical anthropology focuses on human evolution, using both the fossil remains of humans and their ancestors, and the distribution of hereditary variations in living peoples.

pipestone a soft easy to carve stone, ideal for making pipes, dishes, and other containers.

pithouse a semisubterranean dwelling constructed over a pit, made of a frame covered with dirt removed from the pit.

platform burial a method of burying the dead upon a platform or scaffold usually constructed of wood either on posts above the ground, or in some cases, within trees. Also referred to as a scaffold burial.

platform mound a mound usually having a flat upper surface to accommodate one or more structures, such as houses, temples, or other public buildings.

Pleistocene the last major geologic epoch, beginning more than two million years ago and ending about ten thousand years ago. In this period the great glaciers spread over much of North America.

polyandry the form of marriage in which a woman has more than one husband.

polygamy a form of marriage in which there is more than one husband or wife.

polygyny the form of marriage in which a man has more than one wife.

pot irrigation a method of irrigation involving the use of a pot or other vessel to water individual plants within an agricultural plot.

potlatch a large feast given by some Northwest Coast peoples, usually to validate a social title in public. The potlatch included singing, dancing, and giving away large amounts of valuables.

prayerstick a stick covered with feathers, plumes, or down, used by the Pueblo and some other groups to convey prayers to the supernatural. Also attached to it might be small packets of food or tobacco as offerings to the spirits.

pueblo an apartmentlike dwelling of clay, mud, or stone. *Pueblo* is a Spanish word meaning "town."

raptor any of various birds of prey, including eagles, hawks, or owls.

reservation a tract of land set aside by the United States government in treaty, statute, or executive order for the use and benefit of Indian tribes.

reserve the Canadian term for an Indian reservation.

revitalization movement a special kind of religion, usually occurring where people are oppressed and deprived. A main element in movements is an attempt to recreate the happier times of the past.

rite of passage a ceremony marking an important event in the life cycle, such as puberty rites, marriage, or death rites.

roach a stiff ridge of hair two or three inches high, running from the forehead to the back of the neck, and sometimes padded out with red-dyed deer hair. The roach was a common male hair style in the East.

sachem an English version of an Algonkian word for "chief," synonymous with a sagamore.

sagamore a sachem.

sand painting a picture made by dribbling colored sands, minerals, pollen, or other fine material into designs 3 to 12 feet in diameter. The paintings had elements that stood for serpents, stars, mountains, and other natural features. Sand paintings were used in rituals by Pueblo, Navajo, and some Mission Indians. Also called dry paintings.

scalp lock a lock of long hair grown on an otherwise bare head by men in the East as a challenge to enemies.

scraper a stone implement used to scrape leather, smooth wood, or remove fat from the underside of a skin.

secondary burial a burial that has been removed from one mortuary context and moved to another for final disposition, often after the flesh has decomposed or been removed, leaving only the skeletal remains.

sedentism the tendency to remain in a given place or area permanently or for a relatively long period of time.

shade a four-posted, brush-roofed shelter without walls that allowed air to circulate freely while protecting against the sun's searing rays.

shaman a religious specialist, such as a medicine man or a ritualist.

shovel-tooth a physical trait occurring in Asian and North American Indian populations. The inner sides of the upper central incisor teeth are hollowed out, giving them a scoop or shovel shape.

sibling a brother or sister.

slash-and-burn agriculture a method of preparing fields for farming by cutting and then burning the trees on the field to be planted.

socialization teaching children the traditional, proper behavior expected in their culture.

subsistence pattern the way in which a group of people obtains its food, as by hunting or gathering, herding, or agriculture.

sweathouse a small building in which people gather to sweat, as in a steam bath, often for ritual purification or to socialize.

temper fine bits of stone, shell, or fiber mixed with clay in making pottery, to keep the clay paste from splitting and cracking as it is heated.

teosinte a grass representing the wild ancestor of domesticated maize, native to Mexico and Central America.

totem pole an elaborately carved cedar log, usually depicting animals and supernatural beings. This Northwest Coast art form honored dead chiefs, marked the graves of important people, served as portals to houses, and in general was a sort of coat of arms indicating owner's rank and title.

travois an A-shaped sled consisting of a platform or net and two supporting poles. The narrow end was placed over a horse's or dog's shoulders, and the broader end dragged behind.

tuber a fleshy underground stem, root, or bulb.

tumpline a strap placed across the brow and connected to a bundle carried on the back, easing the burden.

tundra the level, treeless plains of the Arctic region.

umiak an open boat used in the Arctic, made of hide stretched over a framework of lashed wood.

unilineal descent kinship traced solely through males or females. If descent is traced through males, it is patrilineal; if traced through females, it is matrilineal. A clan is a unilineal descent group.

waconda a Siouan belief similar to the Iroquoian orenda and the Algonkian manitu, a great supernatural force flowing through the universe.

wampum strings of white and purple shell beads woven into belts by the Algonkians and the Iroquois. They could be used for adornment, but more important, wampum designs represented treaties, agreements, and records of events. After European contact, wampum became a medium of exchange.

weeping-eye motif a Mississippian symbol comprised of an eye with a downward-facing arc or angle, believed to represent the facial patterning of a peregrine falcon.

weir a fish trap that allows water to pass through but obstructs the way for fish; the fish are confined and easily caught.

wickiup a conical or domed hut of poles covered with brush, matting, or bark strips, with a center fire pit and a smoke hole in the roof.

windbreak a simple, usually roofless, structure or fence constructed of any of a variety of materials (brush, wood, stone, skins, bark, etc.) particularly for providing shelter from the wind.

wigwam a domed dwelling made of bent poles or saplings, tied together and covered with sheets of bark, hide, or woven matting.

BIBLIOGRAPHY

This bibliography contains fuller citations for the works listed in the bibliographies appearing in the text, along with other suggested references.

Abbreviations used:

APAMNH Anthropological Papers of the American Museum of Natural History. New York.

ARBAE Annual Reports of the Bureau of American Ethnology. Washington, D.C.

BBAE Bulletin of the Bureau of American Ethnology. Washington, D.C.

MAAA Memoir of the American Anthropological Association.

MAES Monograph of the American Ethnological Society. Seattle: University of Washington Press.

UCPAA University of California Publications in American Archaeology and Ethnology. Berkeley and Los Angeles.

UPMAP University of Pennsylvania Museum Anthropological Publications. Philadelphia.

YUPA Yale University Publications in Anthropology. New Haven.

Aberle, David F. 1966. *The Peyote Religion among the Navaho*. Chicago: Aldine.

Adair, John. 1944. *The Navajo and Pueblo Silversmiths*. Norman: University of Oklahoma Press.

Andrist, Ralph K. 1964. *The Long Death: The Last Days of the Plains Indians*. New York: Collier Books.

Astrov, Margot, ed. 1946. *American Indian Prose and Poetry*. New York: Capricorn Books. Also published as *The Winged Serpent*. New York: John Day, 1946.

Balikci, Asen. 1970. *The Netsilik Eskimo* (reissued 1989). Prospect Heights, IL: Waveland Press.

Bandelier, Adolf. 1890. *The Delight Makers*. New York: Dodd, Mead & Co.

Barnett, H. G. 1957. *Indian Shakers*. Carbondale: University of Southern Illinois Press.

Basso, Keith. 1970. *The Cibecue Apache* (reissued 1986). Prospect Heights, IL: Waveland Press.

Beaglehole, Ernest. 1935. *Hopi of the Second Mesa*. MAAA 44.

Bell, Robert E., ed. 1983. *Prehistory of Oklahoma*. New York: Academic Press.

Benedict, Ruth. 1923. *The Concept of the Guardian Spirit in North America*. MAAA 29.

Birket-Smith, Kai. 1958. *The Eskimos*. 2nd ed. New York: Humanities Press.

Boas, Franz. 1888. *The Central Eskimo*. ARBAE 6:390–669.

———. 1966. *Kwakiutl Ethnography*. Helen Codere, ed. Chicago: University of Chicago Press.

Brinton, Daniel G. 1876. *The Myths of the New World*. 2nd ed. New York: Henry Holt & Co.

Brody, Hugh. 1981. *Maps and Dreams: Indians of the British Columbia Frontier*. Vancouver: Douglas and McIntyre.

Brophy, William, and Sophie D. Aberle. 1966. *The Indian, America's Unfinished Business*. Norman: University of Oklahoma Press.

Brown, Dee. 1970. *Bury My Heart at Wounded Knee*. New York: Holt, Rinehart and Winston.

Bunzel, Ruth. 1932. *Introduction to Zuni Ceremonialism*. ARBAE 47:467–544.

Catlin, George. 1841. *Letters and Notes on the Manners, Customs, and Conditions of the North American Indians*. Reprint. New York: Dover Publications, 1973.

Codere, Helen. 1966. *Fighting with Property*. MAES 18.

Cohen, Felix. 1942. *Handbook of Federal Indian Law*. Washington, D.C.: U.S. Government Printing Office.

Cordell, Linda S. 1984. *Prehistory of the Southwest*. New York: Academic Press.

Cordell, Linda S., and George J. Gumerman, eds. 1989. *Dynamics of Southwest Prehistory*. Washington, D.C.: Smithsonian Institution Press.

Crowe, Keith. 1974. *A History of the Original Peoples of Northern Canada*. Montreal: McGill-Queens University Press.

Deardorff, Merle. 1951. *The Religion of Handsome Lake*. BBAE 149.

de Laguna, Frederica. 1960. *The Story of a Tlingit Community*. BBAE 172.

Deloria, Vine, Jr. 1969. *Custer Died for Your Sins*. New York: Macmillan.

Densmore, Frances. 1926. *The American Indians and Their Music*. New York: The Women's Press.

Dillehay, Thomas D., and David J. Meltzer. 1991. *The First Americans: Search and Research*. Boca Raton, FL: CRC Press.

Dobyns, Henry F. 1966. Estimating Aboriginal American Population. *Current Anthropology* 7:395–449.

Dorris, Michael. 1989. *The Broken Cord*. New York: Harper and Row.

Douglas, Frederick H., and Rene D'Harnoncourt. 1941. *Indian Art of the United States*. New York: Museum of Modern Art.

Downs, James. 1966. *Two Worlds of the Washo*. New York: Holt, Rinehart and Winston.

______. 1972. *The Navajo* (reissued 1984). Prospect Heights, IL: Waveland Press.

Dozier, Edward. 1966. *Hano, A Tewa Indian Community in Arizona*. New York: Holt, Rinehart and Winston.

______. 1970. *The Pueblo Indians of North America* (reissued 1983). Prospect Heights, IL: Waveland Press.

Driver, Harold E. 1969. *Indians of North America*. 2nd ed. Chicago: University of Chicago Press.

Drucker, Philip. 1951. *The Northern and Central Nootkan Tribes*. BBAE 144.

______. 1955. *Indians of the Northwest Coast*. New York: McGraw-Hill.

______. 1958. *The Native Brotherhoods*. BBAE 168.

______. 1966. *Culture of the North Pacific Coast*. San Francisco: Chandler Press.

Duke, Philip. 1991. *Points in Time, Structure and Event in a Late Prehistoric Northern Plains Hunting Society*. Niwot: University Press of Colorado.

Dunn, Dorothy. 1968. *American Indian Painting*. Albuquerque: University of New Mexico Press.

Eggan, Fred. 1937. *Social Anthropology of North American Tribes*. Chicago: University of Chicago Press.

______. 1950. *Social Organization of the Western Pueblos*. Chicago: University of Chicago Press.

______. 1966. *The American Indian*. Chicago: Aldine.

Emerson, Thomas E., and R. Barry Lewis, eds. 1991. *Cahokia and the Hinterlands: Middle Mississippian Cultures of the Midwest*. Urbana: University of Illinois Press.

Ewers, John. 1955. *The Horse in Blackfoot Indian Culture*. BBAE 159.

______. 1958. *The Blackfeet*. Norman: University of Oklahoma Press.

Fagan, Brian M. 1987. *The Great Journey: The Peopling of Ancient America*. New York: Thames and Hudson.

______. 1991. *Ancient North America: The Archaeology of a Continent*. New York: Thames and Hudson.

Farb, Peter. 1968. *Man's Rise to Civilization as Shown by the Indians of North America from Primeval Times to the Coming of the Industrial State*. New York: Dutton.

Feder, Norman. 1965. *American Indian Art*. New York: Harry N. Abrams.

Fiedel, Stuart J. 1992. *Prehistory of the Americas*. 2d ed. New York: Cambridge University Press.

Fletcher, Alice, and Francis LaFlesche. 1906. *The Omaha Tribe*. ARBAE 27.

Forbes, Jack D., ed. 1964. *The Indian in America's Past*. Englewood Cliffs, NJ: Prentice-Hall.

Ford, C. S. 1941. *Smoke from Their Fires*. New Haven: Yale University Press.

Ford, Richard I. 1981. Gardening and Farming Before A.D. 1000: Patterns of Prehistoric Cultivation North of Mexico. *Journal of Ethnobiology* 1 (1): 6–27.

Fowler, Melvin L. 1969. *Explorations into Cahokia Archaeology*. Illinois Archaeological Survey.

Frison, George C. 1978. *Prehistoric Hunters of the High Plains*. New York: Academic Press.

Furst, Peter T., and Jill L. Furst. 1982. *North American Indian Art*. New York: Rizzoli International Publications.

Garbarino, Merwyn S. 1972. *Big Cypress: A Changing Seminole Community* (reissued 1986). Prospect Heights, IL: Waveland Press.

Gearing, Fred. 1962. *Priests and Warriors: Social Structure of Cherokee Politics in the 18th Century*. MAAA 93.

———. 1970. *The Face of the Fox* (reissued 1988). Salem, WI: Sheffield Publishing Co.

Gifford, Edward W. 1928. *Pottery-Making in the Southwest*. UCPAA 23:353–73.

Greenberg, Joseph H., Christy G. Turner II, and Steven L. Zegura. 1986. The Settlement of the Americas: A Comparison of the Linguistic, Dental, and Genetic Evidence. *Current Anthropology* 27(5): 477–497.

Greenway, John. 1969. Will the Indians Get Whitey? *National Review* 21 (March 11).

Griffin, James B. 1967. Eastern North American Archaeology: A Summary. *Science* 156 (3772): 175–191.

Grinnell, George B. 1923. *The Cheyenne Indians*. 2 vols. New Haven: Yale University Press.

———. 1961. *Pawnee Hero Stories and Folk Tales*. Lincoln: University of Nebraska Press.

———. 1962. *Blackfoot Lodge Tales*. Lincoln: University of Nebraska Press.

———. 1962. *By Cheyenne Campfires*. New Haven: Yale University Press.

Hall, Robert L. 1983. "The Evolution of the Calumet Pipe." In *Prairie Archaeology: Papers in Honor of David Baerreis*. Edited by Guy E. Gibbon. Publications in Anthropology, No. 3, Minneapolis: University of Minnesota.

Heizer, Robert F., and Alan Almquist. 1971. *The Other Californians*. Berkeley: University of California Press.

Heizer, Robert F., and M. A. Whipple. 1951. *The California Indians*. Berkeley: University of California Press.

Hickerson, Harold. 1970. *The Chippewa and Their Neighbors: A Study in Ethnohistory* (reissued 1988). Prospect Heights, IL: Waveland Press.

Hoffecker, John F., W. Roger Powers, and Ted Goebel. 1993. The Colonization of Beringia and the Peopling of the New World. *Science* 259: 46–53.

Hoffman, Walter J. 1891. *The Medewiwin or "Grand Medicine Society" of the Ojibwa*. ARBAE 7:143–300.

———. 1893. *The Menomini Indians*. ARBAE 15:11–328.

Honigman, John J. 1954. *The Kaska Indians*. YUPA 51.

Hudson, Charles. 1980. *The Southeastern Indians*. Knoxville: University of Tennessee Press.

Hudson, Charles, Marvin Smith, David Hally, Richard Polhemus, and Chester DePratter. 1985. Coosa: A Chiefdom in the Sixteenth-Century Southeastern United States. *American Antiquity* 50(4): 723–737.

Huyltkranz, Ake. 1987. *Native Religions of North America*. New York: Harper and Row.

Innis, H. A. 1976. *The Fur Trade in Canada*. Toronto: University of Toronto Press.

Inverarity, Robert B. 1950. *Art of the Northwest Coast Indians*. Berkeley: University of California Press.

Jenness, Diamond. 1928. *The People of the Twilight*. Chicago: University of Chicago Press.

______. 1955. *The Indians of Canada*. Bulletin 65. 3d ed. Ottawa: Canadian National Museum.

Jennings, Jesse D. 1989. *Prehistory of North America*. 3d ed. Mountain View, CA: Mayfield Publishing Company.

Jennings, Jesse D., ed. 1983. *Ancient North Americans*. New York: W. H. Freeman and Company.

Jones, David E. 1972. *Sanapia: Comanche Medicine Woman* (reissued 1984). Prospect Heights, IL: Waveland Press.

Joseph, Alice, R. B. Spicer, and Jane Chesky. 1949. *The Desert People: A Study of the Papago Indians*. Chicago: University of Chicago Press.

Josephy, Alvin M. 1965. *The Nez Perce Indians and the Opening of the Northwest*. New Haven: Yale University Press.

______. 1968. *The Indian Heritage of America*. New York: Alfred A. Knopf.

Kluckhohn, Clyde. 1944. *Navaho Witchcraft*. Boston: Beacon Press.

Kluckhohn, Clyde, and Dorothea Leighton. 1962. *The Navaho*. Rev. ed. New York: Doubleday.

Krause, Aurel. 1956. *The Tlingit Indians*. MAES 26.

Kroeber, Alfred L. 1925. *Handbook of the Indians of California*. BBAE 78.

______. 1939. *Cultural and Natural Areas of Native North America*. UCPAA 38.

Kroeber, Theodora. 1961. *Ishi in Two Worlds*. Berkeley: University of California Press.

LaFarge, Oliver. 1956. *A Pictorial History of the American Indians*. New York: Crown Publishers.

LaFlesche, Francis. 1963. *The Middle Five*. Madison: University of Wisconsin Press.

Landes, Ruth. 1968. *Ojibwa Religion*. Madison: University of Wisconsin Press.

______. 1970. *The Prairie Potawatomi*. Madison: University of Wisconsin Press.

Lange, Charles H. 1958. *Cochici, a New Mexico Pueblo*. Austin: University of Texas Press.

Lantis, Margaret. 1947. *Alaskan Eskimo Ceremonialism*. MAES 11.

______. 1960. *Eskimo Childhood and Interpersonal Relationships*. MAES 33.

Lapham, I. A. 1855. *The Antiquities of Wisconsin, as Surveyed and Described.* Smithsonian Contributions to Knowledge 7. Washington, D.C.: Smithsonian Institution.

Leacock, Eleanor. 1954. *The Montagnais Hunting Territory and the Fur Trade.* MAAA 78.

Leacock, Eleanor, and Nancy O. Lurie. 1971. *North American Indians in Historical Perspective* (reissued 1988). Prospect Heights, IL: Waveland Press.

Lehmer, Donald J. 1971. *Introduction to Middle Missouri Archaeology.* U.S. Department of the Interior, National Park Service, Anthropological Papers 1. Washington, D.C.: U.S. Government Printing Office.

Levine, Stuart, and Nancy O. Lurie, eds. 1970. *The American Indian Today.* Baltimore: Penguin Books.

Lewis, Theodore, and Madeline Kneberg. 1958. *Tribes that Slumber: Indian Tribes in the Tennessee Region.* Knoxville: University of Tennessee Press.

Lowie, Robert. 1910. *The Assiniboine.* APAMNH 4:1–270.

———. 1916. *Plains Indian Age Societies.* APAMNH 11:877–992.

———. 1935. *The Crow Indians.* New York: Holt, Rinehart and Winston.

———. 1954. *Indians of the Plains.* New York: McGraw-Hill.

Lurie, Nancy O. 1966. *Mountain Wolf Woman.* Ann Arbor: University of Michigan Press.

McFee, Malcolm. 1972. *Modern Blackfeet: Montanans on a Reservation* (reissued 1986). Prospect Heights, IL: Waveland Press.

Marriott, Alice. 1945. *The Ten Grandmothers.* Norman: University of Oklahoma Press.

———. 1948. *Maria, the Potter of San Ildefonso.* Norman: University of Oklahoma Press.

Martin, Paul S., George Quimby, and Donald Collier. 1947. *Indians before Columbus.* Chicago: University of Chicago Press.

Mason, Ronald. 1981. *Great Lakes Archaeology.* New York: Academic Press.

Maxwell, Moreau S. 1985. *Prehistory of the Eastern Arctic.* New York: Academic Press.

Meggers, Betty, Clifford Evans, and Emilio Estrada. 1965. *Early Formative Period of Coastal Ecuador.* Smithsonian Contributions to Anthropology I. Washington, D.C.: U.S. Government Printing Office.

Milanich, Jerald T., and Charles H. Fairbanks. 1980. *Florida Archaeology.* New York: Academic Press.

Mishkin, Bernard. 1940. *Rank and Warfare among Plains Indians.* MAES 3.

Mooney, James. 1965. *The Ghost Dance Religion.* Chicago: University of Chicago Press.

Moratto, Michael J. 1984. *California Archaeology.* New York: Academic Press.

Morgan, Lewis H. 1851. *League of the Ho-De-No-Sau-Nee or Iroquois.* (Several editions.)

———. 1965. *Houses and House-Life of the American Aborigines.* Chicago: University of Chicago Press.

Morse, Dan F., and Phyllis A. Morse. 1983. *Archaeology of the Central Mississippi Valley*. New York: Academic Press.

Mowat, Farley. 1954. *People of the Deer*. London: Pyramid.

Muller, Jon. 1986. *Archaeology of the Lower Ohio River Valley*. New York: Academic Press.

Murdock, George P. 1972. *Ethnographic Bibliography of North America*. New Haven: Human Relations Area Files.

Nabokov, Peter. 1967. *Two Leggings: The Making of a Crow Warrior*. New York: Crowell.

Neihardt, John G. 1951. *When the Tree Flowered*. Lincoln: University of Nebraska Press.

______. 1961. *Black Elk Speaks*. Lincoln: University of Nebraska Press.

Oberg, Kalvero. 1973. *The Social Economy of the Tlingit Indians*. MAES 55.

O'Brien, Sharon. 1989. *American Indian Tribal Governments*. Norman: University of Oklahoma Press.

O'Donnell, Janet. 1991. *The Dispossession of the American Indian, 1887–1934*. Bloomington: Indiana University Press.

Opler, Morris E. 1941. *An Apache Life-way*. Chicago: University of Chicago Press.

Ortiz, Alfonso. 1969. *The World of the Tewa Indians*. Chicago: University of Chicago Press.

Osgood, Cornelius. 1936. *Contributions to the Ethnography of the Kutchin*. YUPA 14.

______. 1937. *The Ethnography of the Tanaina*. YUPA 16.

Parsons, Elsie C. 1939. *Pueblo Indian Religion*. 2 vols. Chicago: University of Chicago Press.

Patterson, E. Palmer. 1972. *The Canadian Indian: A History Since 1500*. Toronto: Collier-MacMillan Canada.

Phillips, James L., and James A. Brown, eds. 1983. *Archaic Hunters and Gatherers in the American Midwest*. New York: Academic Press.

Price, John. 1979. *Indians of Canada*. Scarborough, Ontario: Prentice-Hall of Canada, Ltd.

Prucha, Francis P. 1962. *American Indian Policy in the Formative Years*. Cambridge: Harvard University Press.

______. 1971. *The Indian in American History*. New York: Holt, Rinehart and Winston.

______. 1977. *A Bibliographical Guide to the History of Indian-White Relations in the U.S.* Chicago: University of Chicago Press.

______. 1984. *The Great Father: The United States and the American Indians*. 2 vols. Lincoln: University of Nebraska Press.

Quimby, George. 1960. *Indian Life in the Upper Great Lakes*. Chicago: University of Chicago Press.

Radin, Paul. 1926. *Crashing Thunder, the Autobiography of a Winnebago Indian*. New York: Appleton-Century.

———. 1956. *The Trickster: A Study in American Indian Mythology*. New York: Philosophical Library.

———. 1971. *The Winnebago Tribe*. Madison: University of Wisconsin Press.

Ray, Verne F. 1963. *Primitive Pragmatists: The Modoc Indians of Northern California*. MAES 38.

Reichard, Gladys A. 1950. *Navaho Indian Religion*. New York: Pantheon Press.

Ritzenthaler, Robert E., and Pat Ritzenthaler. 1970. *The Woodland Indians of the Western Great Lakes*. Garden City, NY: Natural History Press.

Rohner, Ronald, and E. C. Bettauer. 1970. *The Kwakiutl: Indians of British Columbia* (reissued 1986). Prospect Heights, IL: Waveland Press.

Secoy, Frank R. 1953. *Changing Military Patterns of the Great Plains*. MAES 21.

Simmons, Leo W. 1963. *Sun Chief: The Autobiography of a Hopi Indian*. New Haven: Yale University Press.

Slobodin, Richard. 1966. *Metins of the MacKenzie District*. Ottawa: Saint Paul University.

Smith, Bruce D. 1978. *Mississippian Settlement Patterns*. New York: Academic Press.

———. 1992. *Rivers of Change: Essays on Early Agriculture in Eastern North America*. Washington, D.C.: Smithsonian Institution Press.

Smith, Bruce D., ed. 1990. *The Mississippian Emergence*. Washington, D.C.: Smithsonian Institution Press.

Snow, Dean R. 1980. *The Archaeology of New England*. New York: Academic Press.

———. 1989. *The Archaeology of North America*. New York: Chelsea House Publishers.

Speck, Frank G. 1907. *Ethnology of the Yuchi Indians*. UPMAP 1.

———. 1919. *Functions of Wampum among the Eastern Algonkian*. MAAA 6.

———. 1935. *Naskapi*. Norman: University of Oklahoma Press.

———. 1940. *Penobscot Man*. Philadelphia: University of Pennsylvania Press.

Spencer, Robert. 1959. *The North Alaskan Eskimo*. BBAE 171.

Spicer, Edward H. 1962. *Cycles of Conquest*. Tucson: University of Arizona Press.

Spier, Leslie. 1921. *The Sun Dance of the Plains Indians*. APAMNH 16:451–527.

———. 1928. *Havasupai Ethnography*. APAMNH 29:81–391.

———. 1930. *Klamath Ethnography*. UCPAA 30.

Spinden, Herbert J. 1908. *The Nez Perce Indians*. MAAA 2:165–274.

Spindler, George, and Louise Spindler. 1971. *Dreamers with Power: The Menominee* (reissued 1984). Prospect Heights, IL: Waveland Press.

Spindler, Louise. 1962. *Menominee Women and Culture Change*. MAAA 91.

Stern, Theodore. 1966. *The Klamath Tribe*. MAES 41.

Stevenson, Matilde C. 1904. *The Zuni Indians*. ARBAE 23.

Steward, Julian H. 1933. *Ethnography of the Owens Valley Paiute*. UCPAA 33:233–350.

______. 1938. *Basin-Plateau Aboriginal Socio-political Groups*. BBAE 120.

Stewart, Omer C. 1941. *Northern Paiute*. Anthropological Records of the University of California (Berkeley) 4:361–446.

Strong, William D. 1929. *Aboriginal Society in Southern California*. UCPAA 26.

Sturtevant, William C., general ed. 1978. et. seq. *Handbook of North American Indians*. Washington, D.C.: Smithsonian Institution Press. Volumes 4, 5, 6, 7, 8, 9, 10, 11, and 15 currently available.

Swanton, John R. 1911. *Indian Tribes of the Lower Mississippi Valley*. BBAE 43.

______. 1946. *The Indians of the Southeastern United States*. BBAE 137.

______. 1952. *The Indian Tribes of North America*. BBAE 145.

Tanner, Clara Lee. 1957. *Southwest Indian Painting*. Tucson: University of Arizona Press.

Tanner, Helen Hornbeck, ed. 1987. *Atlas of Great Lakes Indian History*. Norman: University of Oklahoma Press.

Teicher, Morton I. 1960. "Windigo Psychosis." In *Proceedings of the 1960 Annual Spring Meeting of the American Ethnological Society*, Verne F. Ray, ed. Seattle: University of Washington Press.

Thompson, Laura, and Alice Joseph. 1944. *The Hopi Way*. Chicago: University of Chicago Press.

Thompson, Stith. 1971. *Tales of the North American Indians*. Bloomington: Indiana University Press.

Thwaites, Reuben G., ed. 1896–1901. *The Jesuit Relations and Allied Documents*. Cleveland: Burrows Bros.

Trigger, Bruce G. 1990. *The Huron, Farmers of the North*. Ft. Worth, TX: Holt, Rinehart and Winston.

Underhill, Ruth. 1956. *The Navajos*. Norman: University of Oklahoma Press.

______. 1979. *Papago Woman* (reissued 1985). Prospect Heights, IL: Waveland Press.

Van Stone, James W. 1962. *Point Hope: An Eskimo Village in Transition*. MAES 36.

______. 1967. *Eskimos of the Nushagak River*. Seattle: University of Washington Press.

Viola, Herman J. 1990. *After Columbus: The Smithsonian Chronicle of the North American Indians*. Washington, D.C.: Smithsonian Books.

Voegelin, Carl, and F. M. Voegelin. 1966. *Map of North American Indians Languages*. American Ethnological Society. Seattle: University of Washington Press.

Wallace, Ernest, and E. A. Hoebel. 1952. *The Comanches, Lords of the South Plains*. Norman: University of Oklahoma Press.

Washburn, Wilcomb E. 1964. *The Indian and the White Man*. Garden City, NY: Doubleday.

———. 1971. *Red Man's Land—White Man's Law*. New York: Charles Scribner's Sons.

White, Robert H. 1991. *Tribal Assets: The Rebirth of Native America*. New York: Henry Holt & Co.

Williams, Stephen. 1991. *Fantastic Archaeology: The Wild Side of North American Prehistory*. Philadelphia: University of Pennsylvania Press.

Wilson, Edmund. 1960. *Apologies to the Iroquois*. Includes Joseph Mitchell, "The Mohawks in High Steel." New York: Random House.

Wilson, Gilbert L. 1924. *The Horse and the Dog in Hidatsa Culture*. APAMNH 15:125–311.

Wissler, Clark. 1916. *Costumes of the Plains Indians*. APAMNH 17:39–91.

———. 1938. *The American Indian*. New York: Oxford University Press.

Wood, W. Raymond. 1967. *An Interpretation of Mandan Culture History*. Smithsonian Institution, Bureau of American Ethnology, Bulletin 198. Washington, D.C.: U.S. Government Printing Office.

FILMS AND VIDEOS

These films and videos are commonly available and may be useful for courses about Native American cultural heritage. For information about availability in film and video format, it is suggested that potential users contact the suppliers directly.

The following fifteen films and videos are in the American Indian Film Series, produced by the University of California, Center for Media and Independent Learning, 2000 Center Street, Fourth Floor, Berkeley, California, 94704. All of these are in color and are available in 16mm film or one-half inch VHS videocassette formats. Other video formats may also be available.

Acorns: Staple Food of California Indians. 28 min. 1962.

Basketry of the Pomo: Introductory. 30 min. 1962.

Basketry of the Pomo: Forms and Ornamentation. 21 min. 1962.

Basketry of the Pomo: Techniques. 33 min. 1962.

Beautiful Trees—Chishkale (about California Indians and acorns). 20 min. 1965.

Buckeyes: Food of California Indians. 13 min. 1961.

Calumet, Pipe of Peace (Great Plains). 23 min. 1964.

Dream Dances of the Kashia Pomo. 30 min. 1964.

Game of Staves (California games). 10 min. 1962.

Kashia Men's Dances: Southwestern Pomo Indians. 40 min. 1963.

Obsidian Point Making (Tolowa). 13 min. 1964.

Pine Nuts (Great Basin). 13 min. 1961.

Sinew-backed Bow and Its Arrows (Yurok Indians of California). 24 min. 1961.

Totem Pole (Kwakiutl Indians of the Northwest Coast). 27 min. 1963.

Wooden Box: Made by Steaming and Bending (Kwakiutl Indians of the Northwest Coast). 33 min. 1962.

Other films available from the University of California Extension Media Center, in formats as previously noted:

1492 Revisited (alternative perspective on the impact of European contact on Native American peoples). 28 min. Color. 1992.

4-Butte-1: A Lesson in Archaeology (excavation of a Maidu Village in California). 33 min. Color. 1968.

Another Wind is Moving (history and impact of American Indian boarding schools). 59 min. Color. 1986.

The California Missions (the meeting of two cultures). 22 min. Color. 1990.

The Exiles (three Native Americans living in Los Angeles). 72 min. B&W. 1961.

Fonseca: In Search of Coyote (Native American artist's work depicting coyote). 30 min. Color. 1983.

Full Circle (Native American cultural and economic renaissance in Washington State). 50 min. Color. 1990.

Haa Shagoon (Tlingit ceremony in Alaska). 29 min. Color. 1983.

Ishi, the Last Yahi (recent documentary providing a thorough examination of Ishi and the Yahi lifeway). 57 min. Color. 1993.

The Longest Trail (more than fifty Native American dances and a recounting of the original settlement of the New World by peoples from Asia). 58 min. Color. 1986.

Medicine Fiddle (fiddling and step-dancing among Native and Mètis families on both sides of the U.S.-Canadian border). 81 min. Color. 1992.

Pomo Shaman (Pomo shamanistic curing ceremony, shortened version of *Sucking Doctor*, below). 20 min. B&W. 1964.

Primitive Process Pottery (how ceramic pottery was made by prehistoric peoples, especially those of the American Southwest). 60 min. Color. 1993.

Return to Sovereignty (impact of the Indian Self-Determination and Education Assistance Act of 1975 on the Kansas Kickapoo). 46 min. Color. 1987.

Separate Visions (profiles of four American Indian artists). 40 min. Color. 1989.

The Spirit of the Mask (the spiritual and psychological power of masks among the Northwest Coast peoples). 50 min. Color. 1992.

Sucking Doctor (Pomo shamanistic curing ceremony). 45 min. B&W. 1964.

The following nine films on the Netsilik Eskimos were made by Dr. Asen Balikci in collaboration with the Educational Development Center and the National Film Board of Canada. These are comprehensive films, complete with natural soundtrack, of the seasonal camps of the Netsilik in traditional times. For further information, contact the National Film Board of Canada, 1251 Avenue of the Americas, New York, NY 10020.

Caribou Hunting at the Crossing Place I. 32 min. Color. 1967.

Caribou Hunting at the Crossing Place II. 29 min. Color. 1967.

At the Spring Sea-Ice Camp I. 27 min. Color. 1968.

At the Spring Sea-Ice Camp II. 27 min. Color. 1968.

At the Spring Sea-Ice Camp III. 27 min. Color. 1968.

At the Winter Sea-Ice Camp I and II. 60 min. Color. 1969.

At the Winter Sea-Ice Camp III. 33 min. Color. 1969.

At the Winter Sea-Ice Camp IV. 35 min. Color. 1967.

The following six videos are in the America's Indians Series, available through Films for the Humanities and Sciences, PO Box 2053, Princeton, NJ 08543. All of these are in color and each lasts 13 minutes.

The Indians Were There First (prehistoric arrival of humans to the New World; Iroquois and other tribal groups' location and culture).

When the White Man Came (Indian life among major tribes of the United States at the time of European contact).

The Bison Hunters (George Catlin's description of 19th century customs among Plains Indians).

The Trail of Tears (the forced removal of Indians from their homelands during the 19th century).

The Warpath (conflicts between Indian groups and white pioneers largely due to abrogation of treaties).

The Death of the Bison (focus on the events at Wounded Knee in 1973 and modern Native American issues that remain unresolved).

The first eight of the following sixteen videos are in the Legends of the Indians Series (designated by *), the second eight are in the More Legends of the Indians Series (designated by **). Both eight-part series are available through Films for the Humanities and Sciences, PO Box 2053, Princeton, NJ 08543. All of these videos are in color and each lasts 26 minutes.

The Return of the Child (Algonquin legend of a young man's unwillingness to let go of the dead).*

The Legend of Corn (Ojibway legend telling how the Great Manitou sent corn to the Indians to relieve their hunger).*

The Winter Wife (Lake Huron Chippewa legend about divesting one's self to learn the true meaning of life).*

Moowis, Where Are You, Moowis? (Algonquin legend concerning love, pride, and jealousy).*

Glooscap (how the intended harmony between humans and animals was upset by the intervention of evil).*

The Path of Souls (first part of a three-part Ojibway story about Gujek's attempt to find his beloved wife Wabana, who has died).*

The World Between (second part of Gujek's story).*

The Path of Life (third and final part of Gujek's story).*

Windigo (the evil spirit Windigo and the people of two neighboring villages).**

The Pleiades (the origin of Okt-kwa-tah, the constellation known as the Pleiades, from the dance of seven children who were turned into stars).**

The Magic Box (a magic box contains wisdom regarding true love).**

Pitchie the Robin (where the robin came from, and the story of a young man's search for peace through the beauty of music).**

The Spirit of the Dead Chief (the mutual obligations between a chief and his people, and the story of how a chief told his people about his experiences along the Path of Souls).**

The Path Without End (the trickery of the spirit world and a selfish young man's attempt to possess beauty).**

The Invisible Man (the story of an invisible man who explained to the Indians where the rainbow came from).**

Megmoowesoo (why we must not despise poor people but must help them, no matter what).**

Films by other producers:

America's Indian Heritage: Rediscovering Columbus [Ohio] (Study of the prehistoric earthworks of North America). 56 min. Color. Films for the Humanities and Sciences, PO Box 2053, Princeton, NJ 08543.

The Anasazi and Chaco Canyon. 43 min. Color. Films for the Humanities and Sciences, PO Box 2053, Princeton, NJ 08543.

The Ancients of North America (archaeological study of a 7000-year-old prehistoric culture of southeastern Utah). 28 min. Color. Films for the Humanities and Sciences, PO Box 2053, Princeton, NJ 08543.

Before Columbus: Teaching Indians to Be White (Seminole, Miccosukee, and Cree cultural responses to schools teaching their children to integrate into outside society). 28 min. Color. Films for the Humanities and Sciences, PO Box 2053, Princeton, NJ 08543.

Before Columbus: The Indian Experience in the 20th Century (cultural challenges facing Native American societies in the present century). 28 min. Color. Films for the Humanities and Sciences, PO Box 2053, Princeton, NJ 08543.

Cahokia: A Prehistoric Legacy (description of this very important prehistoric site and what archaeological research has revealed about Middle Mississippian culture). 17 min. Color. 1989. Cahokia Mounds Museum Society, PO Box 382, Collinsville, IL 62234.

Caribou Hunters (Cree and Chippewa). 18 min. Color. National Film Board of Canada, 1251 Avenue of the Americas, New York, NY 10020.

A Choice for K'aila: May Parents Refuse a Transplant for Their Child? (examines a situation in which Western medical practices conflict with traditional Native American religious beliefs). 28 min. 1993. Filmakers Library, 124 East 40th Street, New York, NY 10016.

Circle of the Sun (Blood Indians of Alberta). 30 min. Color. 1960. Contemporary Films/McGraw Hill, 1221 Avenue of the Americas, New York, NY 10020.

Columbus Didn't Discover Us: Native People's Perspective on the Columbus Quincentennial (interviews with members of Indian nations of North,

Central, and South America). 24 min. Color. Turning Tide Productions, PO Box 864, Wendell, MA 01379.

Coppermine (culture contact and change among the Native American peoples in Canada's central Arctic region). 56 min. National Film Board of Canada, 1251 Avenue of the Americas, New York, NY 10020.

Corn and the Origins of Settled Life in Mesoamerica. Parts I and II. 40 min. Color. Educational Services, Inc., 1730 Eye Street, N.W., Washington, DC 20006.

Cry of the Yurok (the problems that have beset this northern California tribe since the beginning of contact with the white world). 58 min. Color. Films for the Humanities and Sciences, PO Box 2053, Princeton, NJ 08543.

The Death March of De Soto (the archaeological study of De Soto's trail across the Southeast and the native cultures he encountered 450 years ago). 28 min. Color. Films for the Humanities and Sciences, PO Box 2053, Princeton, NJ 08543.

Dineh Nation: The Navajo Story (perspectives on the Navajo culture and the current difficulties involving the exploitation of mineral deposits and resultant pollution on their reservation lands). 26 min. 1992. Filmakers Library, 124 East 40th Street, New York, NY 10016.

Fishing at the Stone Weir (Netsilik Eskimo). 40 min. Color. 1964. Educational Services, Inc., 1730 Eye Street, N.W., Washington, DC 20006.

Frontline: The Spirit of Crazy Horse (story of the Lakota People from the era of the Indian Wars to the present). 60 min. Color. 1991. PBS Home Video. Pacific Arts Video Publishing, 50 N. La Cienega Blvd., Beverly Hills, CA 90211.

Geronimo and the Apache Resistance (the American Experience series program that explores 19th century transformation of the Apache lifeway in the Southwest). 60 min. Color. 1988. PBS Video, 1320 Braddock Place, Alexandria, VA 22314–1698.

Ghost Dance (an examination and commemoration of events at Wounded Knee Creek, South Dakota, 1890, 100 years later). 9 min. Color. 1990. New Day Films, 121 W. 27th St., Suite 902, New York, NY 10001.

Honorable Nations: The Seneca's Land Rights (study of the relationship between the townspeople of Salamanca, the only city in the United States situated entirely on land owned by Native Americans, and the Seneca Indians who own the land). 54 min. 1993. Filmakers Library, 124 East 40th Street, New York, NY 10016.

Hopi: Songs of the Fourth World (examination of Hopi spirituality, art, philosophy, and life, and the preservation of the Hopi way). 60 min. Color. 1983. New Day Films, 121 W. 27th Street, Suite 902, New York, NY 10001.

Hunters and Bombers: The Innu Fight Back (indigenous inhabitants of Labrador-Quebec resist the use of their region by European air forces for supersonic low-level bomber training). 52 min. Color. Films for the Humanities and Sciences, PO Box 2053, Princeton, NJ 08543.

Hunters of the Seal: A Time of Change (impact of culture change among the Netsilik seal hunters of the Canadian Arctic). 30 min. Color. (NOVA) 1976. Time-Life Video, 100 Eisenhower Drive, Paramus, NJ 07652.

Indians, Outlaws, and Angie Debo (the American Experience series program outlining the research conducted by Debo concerning a major swindle that victimized the five civilized tribes of Oklahoma). 60 min. Color. 1988. PBS Video, 1320 Braddock Place, Alexandria, VA 22314–1698.

In the White Man's Image (the American Experience series program exploring the longterm consequences of the Carlisle School for Indians' efforts to "civilize" Native Americans between the 1870s and 1930s). 60 min. Color. 1988. PBS Video, 1320 Braddock Place, Alexandria, VA 22314–1698.

Ishi in Two Worlds (documentary of the last Yahi Indian of California). 19 min. Color. 1967. McGraw-Hill. CRM Films, 2233 Faraday Ave., Carlsbad, CA 92008.

Kwa'Nu'Te": Micmac and Maliseet Artists (the spiritual basis of the work of eight Native American artists). 41 min. National Film Board of Canada, 1251 Avenue of the Americas, New York, NY 10020.

The Lake Man (mixed blood Indian in western Canada). 27 min. B&W. National Film Board of Canada, 1251 Avenue of the Americas, New York, NY 10020.

The Longhouse People (Iroquois who still practice the Longhouse Religion). 25 min. Color. 1950. Encyclopedia Britannica Educational Corp., 425 N. Michigan Ave., Chicago, IL 60611.

The Loon's Necklace. Restored Edition. (Northwest Coast legend filmed with masks; excellent). 11 min. Color. Encyclopedia Britannica Educational Corp., 425 N. Michigan Ave., Chicago, IL 60611.

A Matter of Respect (recent changes in the Tlingit lifeway explored through interviews with contemporary members of one community). 30 min. Color. New Day Films, 121 W. 27th St., Suite 902, New York, NY 10001.

Midway: A Vision of the Past (contemporary archaeological research at a prehistoric Oneota village site in western Wisconsin). 29 min. Color. 1989. Studio A Teleproductions, University of Wisconsin-La Crosse, La Crosse, WI 54601.

More than Bows and Arrows (contributions of Native Americans to the development of the United States and Canada). 60 min. Color. 1992. Camera One Productions, PO Box 75556, Seattle, WA 98125.

Nanook of the North (documentary of Itivimiut Eskimo life in 1922, by Robert Flaherty). Restored version 64 min. 1976. B&W. Films Inc., Public Media, Inc., 5547 Ravenswood Avenue, Chicago, IL 60640.

Nanook Revisited (a revisit to the scene of Robert Flaherty's documentary). 60 min. Color. Films for the Humanities and Sciences, PO Box 2053, Princeton, NJ 08543.

Native American Folklore (a collection of five Native American stories or legends). Includes *Christmas at Moose Factory* (Cree, 13 min.), *Salmon People* (West Coast, 25 min.), *The Man, the Snake and the Fox* (Ojibwa,

12 min.), *Medoonak the Stormmaker* (Micmac, 13 min.), and *Summer Legend* (Micmac, 8 min.). 71 min. total. National Film Board of Canada, 1251 Avenue of the Americas, New York, NY 10020.

Navajo Moon (an examination of the lives of three children on the Navajo reservation). 28 min. Color. 1988. Films for the Humanities and Sciences, PO Box 2053, Princeton, NJ 08543.

Navajo Night Dances. 12 min. Color. 1957. Coronet Instructional Media, Division of Esquire, 65 E. S. Water St., Chicago, IL 60601.

Now That the Buffalo's Gone (how Europeans seeking freedom in America neglected the same freedoms of the Native Americans). 20 min. Color. Films for the Humanities and Sciences, PO Box 2053, Princeton, NJ 08543.

Odyssey: The Chaco Legacy (prehistoric Anasazi culture of Chaco Canyon, New Mexico). 59 min. Color. 1980. PBS Home Video. Pacific Arts Video Publishing, 50 N. La Cienega Blvd., Beverly Hills, CA 90211.

Odyssey: Myths and Moundbuilders (the story of research into the nature and origin of aboriginal mounds and earthworks in eastern North America). 58 min. Color. 1981. PBS Home Video. Pacific Arts Video Publishing, 50 N. La Cienega Blvd., Beverly Hills, CA 90211.

Oneota Longhouse People (the reconstruction of prehistoric Oneota Upper Mississippian life through the archaeological excavation of a summer village in northeastern Iowa occupied several hundred years ago). 14 min. Color. 1973. University of Iowa AV Center, Media Library C-5, East Hall, Iowa City, IA 52242.

People of the Klamath: Of Land and Life (legal efforts of the Karuk of northern California to protect their sacred lands from environmental desecration). 28 min. Color. New Day Films, 121 W. 27th St., Suite 902, New York, NY 10001.

People of the Klamath: Preserving a Way of Life (the loss of culture through the process of assimilation during the 20th century and attempts to preserve traditional lifeway). 28 min. Color. New Day Films, 121 W. 27th St., Suite 902, New York, NY 10001.

People of the Potlatch. 21 min. Color. National Film Board of Canada, 1251 Avenue of the Americas, New York, NY 10020.

The Reindeer Queen: The Story of Alaska's Sinrock Mary (story of an Eskimo woman who became owner of the largest herd of introduced Siberian reindeer in the North). 28 min. 1993. Filmakers Library, 124 East 40th Street, New York, NY 10016.

The Right to Be Mohawk (a contemporary look at the Mohawk effort to protect and build their culture and nation). 17 min. Color. New Day Films, 121 W. 27th St., Suite 902, New York, NY 10001.

River People: Behind the Case of David Sohappy (story of a Native American spiritual leader sent to prison for selling salmon from the Columbia River out of season, and its relationship to the historic conflict over the use of resources in the Northwest). 50 min. 1991. Filmakers Library, 124 East 40th Street, New York, NY 10016.

Sacajawea (Sacajawea's recounting of events during the Lewis and Clark Expedition across America). 24 min. Color. 1984. Films for the Humanities and Sciences, PO Box 2053, Princeton, NJ 08543.

The Search for the First Americans (NOVA program exploring the earliest human inhabitants of the New World). 60 min. Color. 1992. Films for the Humanities and Sciences, PO Box 2053, Princeton, NJ 08543.

Secrets of the Little Bighorn (modern archaeological study prompts rethinking of the traditional views of this famous battle). 28 min. Color. Films for the Humanities and Sciences, PO Box 2053, Princeton, NJ 08543.

Spirits of the Canyon: Ancient Art of the Pecos Indians (study of paintings and pictographs among the southwest Texas canyons). 30 min. Color. Films for the Humanities and Sciences, PO Box 2053, Princeton, NJ 08543.

The Spirit Within (a unique rehabilitation program helping Native American prison inmates). 51 min. National Film Board of Canada, 1251 Avenue of the Americas, New York, NY 10020.

Summer of the Loucheux (traditional Loucheux methods of taking large fish and preparing them for winter use). 27 min. Color. New Day Films, 121 W. 27th St., Suite 902, New York, NY 10001.

Transitions (the impact of the disappearance of the Blackfeet tribal language between 1890 and 1990). 1991. Montana Public Television, Bozeman, MT 59717.

Tule Technology: Northern Paiute Uses of Marsh Resources in Western Nevada. 1981. Pennsylvania State University, University Park, PA 16802.

Vision Quest (traditional quest of Plains Indians re-enacted). 30 min. Color. 1961. Montana State University, Bozeman, MT 59715.

Washoe (cultural transition of Washoe Indians of Nevada from traditional customs to 20th century life). 56 min. B&W. McGraw-Hill Films, 1220 Avenue of the Americas, New York, NY 10020.

Waterborne: Gift of the Indian Canoe (the revival of the art of canoe building and racing by modern Suquamish Indians of Washington State). 13 min. Color. New Day Films, 121 W. 27th St., Suite 902, New York, NY 10001.

PHOTO AND ILLUSTRATION CREDITS

Part I opener: Photo courtesy of Milwaukee Public Museum

Chapter One: p. 5, photo courtesy of Robert F. Boszhardt, Mississippi Valley Archaeology Center at the University of Wisconsin-LaCrosse; p. 14, 25, 28, 32, 37, 38, McGraw-Hill, redrawn from *Prehistory of North America*, Jesse Jennings; p. 19, Thames & Hudson, Ltd., London: redrawn from *The First Americans*, G.H.S. Bushnell; p. 35, 40, Ohio Historical Society

Chapter Two: p. 55, 59, McGraw-Hill, redrawn from *Prehistory of North America*, Jesse Jennings; p. 57, photo by Jesse L. Nusbaum, courtesy Museum of New Mexico, Neg. No. 43170; p. 60, Peabody Museum, Harvard University, photograph by F. P. Orchard; p. 68, 70, University of Chicago Press: redrawn from *Indians Before Columbus*, Martin, Quimby, and Collier, 1947; p. 69, Time-Life, redrawn from *The First Americans*; p. 81, 82, Cahokia Mounds State Historic Site; p. 83, Indiana Historical Society: redrawn after *Drawing in Angel Site, Vandenberg County Indiana*, an Introduction by Glenn Black, Prehistory Research Series II, 5, Indianapolis, 1944

Part II opener: The Bettmann Archive

Chapter Three: p. 108, 114, redrawn from *The North Alaskan Eskimo, A Study in Ecology and Society*, Robert Spencer, Bureau of Ethnology Bulletin, 1959; p. 111, The Bettmann Archive; p. 117, Smithsonian Institution, Neg. No. 55,019

Chapter Four: p. 145, University of Chicago Press, redrawn from *Indians Before Columbus*, Martin, Quimby, and Collier, 1947; p. 162, Neg. No. 32955, Courtesy Department of Library Services, American Museum of Natural History; p. 164, Smithsonian Institution, Neg. No. 74-3623

Chapter Five: p. 187, 197, Phoebe A. Hearst Museum of Anthropology, The University of California at Berkeley; p. 189, University of California Press, redrawn from *The California Indians*, Second Edition, R. E. Heizer and M. A. Whipple, 1971; p. 191, Henry E. Huntington Library; p. 201, Neg. No. 32706 B, Courtesy Department of Library Services, American Museum of Natural History; p. 208, Courtesy of the Southwest Museum, Los Angeles, Photo N. 20051

Chapter Six: p. 240, The Philbrook Museum of Art, Tulsa, Oklahoma; p. 252, Neg. No. 2A3642, Courtesy Department of Library Services, American Museum of Natural History

Chapter Seven: p. 269, 271, Philadelphia Museum of Art: Purchased with funds from the American Museum of Photography; p. 270, The University Museum, University of Pennsylvania (Neg. No. 58-78495); p. 288, 1961.146 The Buffalo Hunt No. 39, Charles M. Russell, oil on canvas, 1919, Amon Carter Museum, Fort Worth

Chapter Eight: p. 321, Kane, Paul, Canadian 1810-1871, *Indian Encampment on Lake Huron*, c. 1845-50, oil on canvas, 48.3 x 73.7 cm, Art Gallery of Ontario, Toronto; p. 325, The Bettmann Archive; p. 330, Smithsonian Institution, Neg. No. 817-A

Part III opener: Smithsonian Institution, Neg. No. 85-9753

Chapter Nine: p. 370, Courtesy Museum of New Mexico, Neg. No. 36175; p. 379, redrawn from American Museum of Natural History; p. 382, Arizona State Museum, University of Arizona, F. Hannah, Photographer

Chapter Ten: p. 394, P1979.228.497, Grandmother and Baby in Cradle Chaco Area, Laura Gilpin, safety negative, 1954, Copyright Amon Carter Museum, Laura Gilpin Collection; p. 404, Smithsonian Institution, Neg. No. 56,258

Part IV opener: Smithsonian Institution, Neg. No. 690-A

Chapter Eleven: p. 444, Photo courtesy of Milwaukee Public Museum; p. 445, South Dakota Historical Society; p. 448, Courtesy of Arizona Historical Society, Tucson, photo no. 19841

Chapter Twelve: p. 469, 480, 487, AP/Wide World Photos

INDEX

Abnaki Confederation, 311
Aboriginal groups, of Subarctic region, 127
Acoma, language of, 233
Adaptations, defined, 94
Adena culture, 33, 35-37, 38, 302
Adobe, 236
Adoption, 391-392
Age-graded associations, 402
Agriculture. *See also* Cultivation; Farming
  of Adena, 36
  Anasazi, 65
  cultivation and cultures, 49-91
  of Eastern Archaic forest people, 30-31
  of Hohokam, 62
  of Hopewell, 41-42
  Mandan, 293-294
  Mississippian, 78-79
  Southwestern beginnings of, 55-57
Agua Caliente Reservation, 450
AIM. *See* American Indian Movement
Alabama, 303
  Moundville in, 79
Alaska, 9. *See also* Subarctic region
  Archaic people in, 30
  early sites in, 8
  Eskimo groups in, 107
  glaciation and, 8
Alaska Eskimo, 107, 108-115. *See also* Eskimos; Inuit
  carvings of, 112
  home life of, 113-115
  Northwest Coast peoples and, 156
  spring whaling, 109-110
  summer activities, 110-112
  winter life, 112-115
Alaska Native Brotherhood, 485
Alcohol and alcoholism, 453, 466
Aleut language and people, 7, 106
  population by state, 461
Algonkian languages and people, 45, 76, 127, 129, 265, 278, 299, 302, 307, 318. *See also* Subarctic people
  Central Atlantic, 328-331
  European contact with, 436, 437
  French and, 429-430
  kinship organization, 320
  leadership of, 312-313
  legend of, 298
  Midewiwin, 380
  New England, 307-313
  Ojibwa and, 134
  Prairie region, 321-322
  political organization of Northeast, 308-311
  religion and, 374, 376
  village life of Northeast, 308
Allotment, 434-435, 436
Allotment Act (1887), 434-435, 474
Alphabet, Cherokee, 478
American Indian Movement (AIM), 489
American Indians. *See* Indians; Native Americans
American Revolution, 426
  Indian policy after, 433

Amerind, 2
Anasazi, 65–73, 227
  artifacts of, 71
  pueblos of, 66–73
Ancestors. *See* Religion
Animals, migration of, 9
Antelope Society, 241
Apache, 227, 246–248, 286
  ceremonies of, 372
  death and, 398
  economic success of, 484
  European impact on, 448
  inheritance and, 413
  language, 228
  life-style of, 246–247
  religion of, 247–248
  social organization of, 247
  Spanish impact on, 447
Apalachee, 334
Arapaho, 265, 276
  associations of, 402
  sacred objects of, 384
Archaeological sites, 11
Archaic period, 23–33. *See also* Cultivation; Farming societies; Southwestern region
  Arctic people, 29–30
  artifacts from, 28
  Coastal Archaic people, 27–29
  Desert Archaic people, 24–27
  forest people of Eastern, 30–33
  in Great Plains, 86–87
  Subarctic people, 29–30
Arctic region
  adapting to, 106–107
  as culture area, 102–108
  culture areas and tribes, *map*, 105
  environment of, 103–104
  Eskimo in, 104–108
  fishing and, 351
  language in, 104–106
  warfare in, 415
  white contact with, 454–455
Arctic Small Tool tradition, 29–30
Argillite, artwork in, 486
Arikara, 89, 265, 266, 291, 431
Arizona
  Anasazi in, 65–66
  Hohokam in, 61
  pueblos in, 65
  voting rights in, 436
Arkansas River, 86
Arrowheads, 349–350
Arrow Renewal Ceremony, 284
Artifacts
  Archaic period, 28
  bones and, 18
  Hohokam, 64
  preservation of, 490–492
Arts and crafts, 363–370. *See also* Artifacts; Clothing; Dramatic arts
  basketry, 368
  body decoration, 362–363
  bone and horn in, 364
  contemporary, 485–486
  of Hopewell people, 39–41
  leather work, 366–367
  metal work, 367–368
  of Northwest Coast region, 159–160, 165–166
  painting, dyes, and pigments, 368–369
  pottery, 364–365
  stone working, 365–366
  textiles, 369–370
  toys, 370
  woodworking, 364
Asia, movement of people from, 7–8, 9
Assimilation, 474
Assiniboine creation myth, 260–261
Associations, 401–403
  of Plains region, 273–274
Athabaskan (Na Dene) language and people, 7, 8, 127, 228
  legend of, 125–126
  Spanish and, 447–448
  Tlingit language and, 166
  warfare of, 416

Athabaskan movement, 72
Athabaskan society, 128, 129, 130. *See also* Subarctic people
  Apache, 246–248
  Chipewyan, 133–134
  migration south of, 245–246
  Navajo, 248–255
  Southern, 245–255
Athletics. *See* Games and recreation
Atlantic seaboard region, culture after European contact, 437–438
Atlantic states, 307
Atlatl, 20, 21, 348
Atsina, associations of, 402
Aztec-Tanoan languages and people, 97, 99, 228, 233,,

Babiche, 129
Ball courts, of Hohokam, 62–64
Band
  defined, 128
  as social organization, 15–16
Band List, 457
Banks, as political organization, 407
Bark canoe, 359. *See also* Canoes
Barren Grounds, 107, 115
Basketry, 368
  in Archaic period, 25
  in California region, 188
  contemporary, 486
  of Great Basin people, 221
  Paiute, 224
  Pomo, 200–201
Bast, 369
Beans, 50–51, 351
  domestication of, 54
Bear
  Menominee and, 322, 323
  and sacrificial ceremonies, 383
Bella Coola, 157
  religion and, 376
Benedict, Ruth, 244
Beothuk, 45, 127, 437
Berdache, 277
Bering, Vitus, 426
Beringia, 9
Bering land bridge, 9, 10, 24
Big Cypress Seminole Reservation, 484
Big Game Hunters
  decline in Archaic period, 24
  Folsom people, 18–19
  in Great Plains, 86–87
  Paleo Indians as, 16–23
Birchbark canoe, 31–32
Birth, rites of passage and, 393–395
Bison antiquus, 18–19
Black Drink, 326
Blackfoot, 265, 277, 278–283
  associations of, 402
  equestrian, 279–280
  medicine man of, 379
  organization of, 280–281
  pedestrian, 278–279
  religion of, 281
  seasonal life of, 280
  tipis of, 271
  visions and, 377
  warfare of, 281–282
Blood, 278
Blowguns, 350
Boats, 359. *See also* Canoes
  Eskimo, 116
Body decoration, 362–363
  hair, 362
  jewelry, 363
  paint and tattoos, 362–363
Bone and horn, in arts and crafts, 364
Bones, and artifacts, 18
Botanical evidence, for transoceanic contacts, 42–43
Bow and arrow, 30, 73, 268–269
  types of, 348–349
Bow drill, 366
Boys. *See* Puberty rites
Bridewealth, 389
British North America Act (1867), 455
Buffalo, 263–264, 288, 293–294

end of, 442–443
and sacrificial ceremonies, 383
Bull boat, 359
Bull Society, 281
Bureau of Indian Affairs (BIA), 433–434, 458, 466–470
California land assets and, 450
occupation of building, 489–490
organizational chart, 467
after World War II, 474
Burial mounds, 33
of Adena people, 35–37
of Hopewell people, 39–41
Burial practices, 397–398
of Great Plains people, 88–89
preservation of remains, 490–491
Busk Dance. See Green Corn (Busk) Dance
Buzzard Cult, 77
Buzzard man, 397–398

Cabot, John, 424, 425
Cabrillo, Juan Rodrigues, 449
Caddoan languages and people, 265, 303
Cahokia, Illinois, 79–83, 301, 322
decline of, 83–85
pyramid mound in, 77
Calhoun, John C., 466
California (state), Indians in, 460
California region, 157, 181–212
ceremonies of, 382
clothing in, 361
culture after European contact, 449–450
culture areas and tribes of, *map*, 184
death and, 398
environment of, 183–186
folklore of, 373
food resources of, 186–188
gold in, 442
Maidu creation myth, 182
Northern California, 183–185
political organization in, 189–190, 409
puberty rites of, 397
religion in, 190
shamans and, 379
Southern California, 204–211
Spanish in, 427
technology of, 188–189
warfare in, 416
Calumets (pipes), 320
trade and, 414
Calusa, 299, 327, 335, 337
Campbell, Ben Whitehorse, 465
Canada. *See also* Subarctic region
Archaic people in, 30
casino gaming in, 488
economic development in, 493–494
education in, 495
enfranchisement in, 456–457
Eskimo in, 107–108, 485
government policy of, 455–458
hunting and fishing rights in, 494–495
land claims in, 492–493
potlatching ban by, 453–454
reservations in, 434
status Indian population in, 458
Cannibalism, 132–133
by Iroquois, 315
Canoes, 31–32, 159, 359
California region, 188, 189
Nootka, 172
Carib Indians, 432
Caribou Eskimo, 107, 115
food of, 128
Carlisle Indian School, 479
Carnivores, 17
Carson, Kit, 447
Cartier, Jacques, 425, 455
Casino gaming
in Canada, 494
in U.S., 486–488
Catawba, 326
Catlin, George, 174, 365, 431
Cayuga, 313
Cayuse, 450

horses and, 150
Central Atlantic Algonkians, 328–331
rites of passage, 393
Central California, environment of, 185
Ceremonies. *See also* Religion
Adena, 36
Apache, 247–248
Cheyenne, 284–285
fire-making and, 354
Hopi, 239–241
of Iroquois League, 317
of Katcina Cult, 239–240, 241
of Kuksu Cult, 203–204
Luiseño, 207–208
Mandan, 292
of Mississippian people, 76–77
Navajo, 250–252
paraphernalia of, 384–385
of Plateau tribes, 147
of Pueblo (people), 235
regional rituals, 381–383
religious, 380–385
sacrifice, 383–384
Sun Dance, 276–277
Toloache Cult, 207–209
Chaco Canyon, Anasazi in, 67, 70
Cherokee, 303, 326, 337, 438
chief of, 330
and Eastern tribes, 302
Sequoyah and, 478
Chert, 79
Cheyenne, 265, 273, 276, 283–286
behavior of, 285–286
ceremonies of, 284
childhood and, 393
divorce and, 390
marriage and, 388
religion of, 285
sacred objects of, 384
seasonal life of, 283
social and political organization of, 284
Chicago American Indian Center, 477
Chickahominy, 328
Chickasaw, 337
Chickee, 471
Chief
Central Atlantic Algonkian, 329–331
defined, 408-409
Nez Perce, 149
Chief Joseph, 451–452
Children. *See also* Birth
childhood and, 392–393
Eskimo, 121
Chilkat
art of, 166
weavers, 369–370
Chillicothe, Ohio, mounds at, 36
Chinook, 157, 173–175, 453
head flattening of, 174
religion of, 175
Chipewyan, as Athabaskan group, 133–134
Chippewa, 134, 319, 322
casino of, 487
legend of, 318
name of, 99
Chiricahua, 246
Chitimacha, 334
Choctaw, 303, 337, 438
language of, 76
Christianity, 482. *See also* Europeans; Religion
European contact and, 430–431
Handsome Lake and, 440–441, 482
Chukchi language, 104
Chumash, 188, 204–205
Chunkey, 80, 403
Churches, 472
Cibola, 425
Circumpolar Conference, 485
Cities. *See also* Relocation policy
adjustment to life in, 477
Mississippian, 79–80
Citizenship, 435–436
in Canada, 456–457
Civilization Fund, 478

Civil War, 434
Clans
  in California region, 189
  and other groupings, 398–403
  rights and duties of, 400
  Western Pueblo, 235–236
Class system, of Natchez, 333–334
Cliff dwellings. *See* Pueblos
Cliff Palace, Mesa Verde, 68–69
Climate
  in Archaic period, 24, 26
  in California region, 188–189. *See also* Environment
  Desert Archaic people and, 24
  Great Basin, 217
  in late Pleistocene period, 16–17, 22
  and Mississippian cultures, 84
  of Northeast region, 307
  of Northwest Coast region, 155
  of Plains region, 263
  of Pueblo (people), 234
  of Southwest, 56
  of Subarctic region, 126–127
Clothing, 360–363
  of Adena people, 36–37
  body decoration and, 362
  in California region, 188
  Central Atlantic Algonkian, 329
  of Eastern region, 304
  footwear, 361–362
  kinds of, 360–361
  Paiute, 222–224
  of Plains region, 269–271
  Pomo, 200
  Pueblo, 238
  of River Yumans, 229–230
  styles of, 361
  in Subarctic region, 130
Clovis, New Mexico, 19
Coastal Archaic people, 27–29
Coast Salish group, 157
Cochise, 246, 448
Cochiti, 242–244
  clowns association, 243–244
  language of, 233
  social and political organization of, 242–244
  witchcraft of, 244
Colleges and universities, 479–481
  English, 429
Colombia, Valdivia complex pottery and, 45
Colonial America, Indian policies of, 432–433
Colorado
  Anasazi in, 65–66
  pueblos in, 65
Colorado Plateau, pueblo abandonments and, 70, 71
Columbus, Christopher, 2, 424
Comanche, 246, 265, 266, 286–288
  horses and, 150, 286–288
  marriage and, 389
  removal of, 434
Commerce, trade and, 413–415
Communal rights. *See* Economic systems
Communication, in Plains region, 271–272
Community colleges, 480
Confederacies
  Abnaki, 311
  Algonkian, 308
  Leni Lenape, 311–312
  Mahicans, 311, 312
  Massachuset, 311
  Narraganset, 311–312
Conflict, intercultural, 419–458. *See also* Warfare
Controls. *See* Social control
Cook, James, 426
Cooking, 354
Cooper, James Fenimore, 308
Coosa, 303
Copper
  in arts and crafts, 367
  tools of, 31, 32
Copper Eskimo, 107
Coppers (plaques), 166

Cordilleran Glacier, 9
Corn (maize), 41, 50-51, 351. *See also* Maize
  development of, 55
  domesticated, 54
  in Eastern region, 301
  in Southwest, 55-56
Coronado, 89, 445
Coronation Gulf region, 107
Costanoans, 204, 205
Cotton, 43
Council of Forty-four, 284
Councils, as political organization, 409-410
Coup stick, 275
Coyote Dance, of Pomo, 204
Crafts. *See* Arts and crafts
Creation myths. *See* Myths and legends
Cree, 279, 280
  pseudo-kinship and, 401
Creek, 334, 335, 337, 438
  language of, 76
  moiety organization and, 401
  name of, 99
  priests of, 380
Creek Confederacy, 303
Cremation, 398
Crops. *See* Agriculture; Cultivation
Crow, 265, 273, 289-291
  raids by, 289-291
Cucurbits, 31
Cultigens, 45, 51, 53
  corn as, 301
  Mississippians and, 78-79
  spread of, 431-432
Cultivation, 30-31, 351-352. *See also* Agriculture; Farming
  and American cultures, 49-91
  Hopewell, 41-42
  Hopi, 238-239
  Mandan, 291-292
  in Mexico, 50-54
  in Southwest, 54-73
  women and, 405
Cults, Mississippian, 77. *See also* Religion; individual cults
Cultural borrowing, 16
Cultural conflict, 419-458
Cultural diffusion, 42-45
  defined, 94
  Mexico-Hohokam, 64
Cultural evidence, for transoceanic contacts, 43-45
Cultural evolution, defined, 94
Cultural isolation, defined, 94
Culture areas
  adaptation to Plains region, 261
  Arctic, 102-108
  California, 184
  defined, 94
  Eastern, 299, 300
  European impact on, 436-455
  Great Basin and Southwest, 218
  language, 97-99
  language map, 98
  lifestyle reconstructions, 96
  map, 93
  of North America, 93-100
  Northeast, 307-318
  of Northwest Coast, 142
  Plains region, 262
  of Plateau, 141, 142
  population, 97
  as scheme, 94-97
  Southeast, 325-337
  Western Great Lakes, 318-324
Cultures
  Anasazi, 57, 65-73
  in Archaic period, 23-24
  cultivation and, 49-91
  defined, 94
  Eastern Archaic forest people, 30-33
  Great Plains people, 86-89
  Hohokam, 57, 61-65
  Late Woodland developments, 73-76
  Mississippian tradition and, 76-86
  Mogollon, 57-61

prehistoric, 6–48
Cumberland Gap, 414
Custer, George, 443

Dakota, 265
Dalles, 141, 143, 150
Chinook and, 173–175
Dance(s), 371. *See also* Ceremonies; Religion
of Kuksu Cult, 203–204
Navajo, 251
of Toloache Cult, 207–208
Yurok, 195–196
Deadfalls, 348
Death, 397–398. *See also* Burial mounds
disposal of bodies, 397–398
mortuary practices and, 74–76
mourning, 398
rites, of Southern Californian Indians, 209–211
Deganawidah, 316
legend of, 313–314
Deities, 374–375. *See also* Religion; Supernatural
Hopi, 241–242
De la Vente (French trader), 84–85
Delaware (people). *See* Leni Lenape
Dene, 457, 493
Dentalia
as medium of exchange, 414
Nootka, 172–173
Yurok, 193–194
Department of Indian Affairs and Northern Development (DIAND) (Canada), 458
Desert Archaic tradition, 24–27, 87
Paiute and, 225
Southwestern cultures and, 227
De Soto, Hernando, 76, 303, 425
DIAND. *See* Canada; Department of Indian Affairs and Northern Development
Diegueño, 205, 206
Diet
of Anasazi, 69–70
in California region, 186–188
of Desert Archaic people, 24–25
Eskimo, 115–116
late Paleo Indian period, 22–23
Mexican, 50–51
of prehistoric people, 13–15
Tlingit, 167
Diggers, 219
Dine, 2
meaning of, 253
Disease, 456
European-borne, 84–85, 431
Division of labor, Eskimo, 118–119
Divorce, 389–390
among Chipewyan, 134
Eskimo, 120
of Nez Perce, 150
Dogs
Alaska Eskimo and, 110–111
domesticated, 26
as sacrificial offerings, 383
Dog sled, 118
Dog Soldiers, 274
Domestication, of animals, 26, 53. *See also* Cultivation
Dramatic arts, 371–374
Dreams, Paiute and, 224–225
Dugout canoe, 359. *See also* Canoes

Earth Diver, 373
Earth lodges, 266–268, 356
Earth mounds, 33. *See also* Burial mounds; Religion
of Late Woodland period, 74–76
Eastern Agricultural Complex, 31
Eastern Archaic people, 30–33
Eastern cultures. *See also* Adena culture; Hopewell culture
influence on Great Plains people, 88
late Woodland developments in, 73–76
Mississippian tradition in, 76–86
Eastern region, 297–343

ancestors and descendants in, 302
culture area and tribes of, *map*, 300
divisions of, 299
early life in, 299-306
European contact with, 301-303
European struggles in, 426
folklore of, 373-374
lifestyles of, 305-307
New England Algonkian legend, 298
prehistory of, 299-301
resources and technology of, 303-305
scalping and, 417
warfare in, 415
Economics, of Plains region, 272-273
Economic success, 484-485
future of, 485-488
Economic systems, 412-415
inheritance, 413
property rights and land tenure, 412-413
trade and commerce, 413-415
Education
in Canada, 495
contemporary, 479-481
and employment, 484
English, of Indians, 429
Indian schools, 479
Sequoyah and, 478
in U.S., 477-481
Effigy mounds, 35. *See also* Burial mounds; Moundbuilders
of Late Woodland period, 74-76
Employment, 483-484
Enemy Way, 251
Enfranchisement, in Canada, 456-457
English, 301
Algonkian warfare with, 313
exploration by, 425
goals of, 427-429
English language, Algonkian expressions in, 308, 313
Environment
Arctic, 103-104
of California region, 183-186
and culture, 96
of Northwest Coast region, 155-156
of Plateau, 141
of Pueblo (people), 234-235
and River Yumans, 229-230
of Southwestern region, 226-227
Subarctic, 126-127
Epicanthic eye folds, 7
Ericson, Leif, 424
Eskimos, 7, 29, 45, 104-108. *See also* Inuit
adaptation of, 106-107
Alaska Eskimo, 107, 108-115
boats of, 359
as Canadian native group, 457
clothing of, 360-361
creation myth of, 102-103
death and, 397
diet of, 115-116
economic success of, 485
folklore of, 373
general lifestyle and culture, 115-124
language of, 104-106
marriage and, 390
political organization of, 406-407
population by state, 461
regional variations among, 107-108
religion and, 121-122, 374, 376
sacred objects of, 385
shamans and, 378, 379
social control among, 411
social organization of, 118-121
technology of, 116-118
toys of, 370
white contact with, 454-455
Ethnographic analogy, 13
Etowah, Georgia, 79, 303
Europeans. *See also* English; French; Spanish

consequences of contact with Indians, 430–432
contact with Eastern tribes, 301–303
contact with North America, 424
early exploration by, 424–430
goals of, 427–430
Indian policies of, 432–436
Mississippian tradition and, 76
spread of disease and, 431
Exchange, media of, 414–415. *See also* Trade
Exogamy, 398, 400
in moieties, 401
Exploration, early European, 424–430
Extended family, 391

False Face Society, 317
Family life, 391–393. *See also* Clans; Divorce; Marriage; Matrilineal society; individual groups by name
adoption and, 391–392
childhood, 392–393
Eskimo, 118–119, 120
language, 97
Nootka, 170
Tlingit, 166–167
Farming. *See also* Agriculture; Cultivation
Hopi, 238–239
in Northeast region, 307
in Plains region, 265
in Southwest, 56–57
Farming societies
Anasazi, 65–73
Hohokam, 61–65
Mogollon, 57–61
Southwestern, 227
Feathered headdress, 270
Females. *See* Women
Fernandeño, 205
Fetishes, 384–385
Nez Perce and, 149
Fictive kinship, 401
Fire Dance, 251
Fire-making, cooking and, 354–355
Fire plough, 355
Fishing, 32, 351
in Plateau region, 144–145
rights to, 412, 494, 495
Five Civilized Tribes, 337
removal and, 434
Flathead Indians, 174
Flint, 18
Flood irrigation, 61–62
Florida, 76
annexation of, 337
cultural displacement in, 337
French in, 425
Seminole in, 334, 335–337
Spanish in, 425
Flute Society, 241
Folklore, 371–374
characters in, 372–373
themes of, 373–374
Folsom, New Mexico, 18
Foods. *See also* Diet; Hunters and hunting
of Adena people, 36
Blackfoot, 279
of Central Atlantic Algonkians, 331
cooking, 354
cultivation and, 351–352
of Desert Archaic people, 24–25
of Eastern region, 304
fire-making and, 354–355
fishing and, 351
gathering, 346–347
of Great Basin people, 217–221
hunting for, 347–350
of Klamath, 152–154
of Natchez, 334
of Nez Perce, 148–149
obtaining, 346–352
Paiute, 222–224
of Paleo Indians, 22
of Pimans, 231–232

of Plateau, 143
of Pomo, 189–199
preparing, 352–355
preservation and storage, 353–354
Pueblo, 233, 234
of Subarctic region, 128
of Western Lakes region, 320
Footwear, 361–362
Foraging, of Desert Archaic people, 24–25
Fort Ancient culture, 86, 302
Fossils, of primitive humans, 6
Fox, 319, 322
name of, 99
Fraser River, fishing rights on, 495
French, 301
exploration by, 425
goals of, 429–430
Indian relationships with, 429–430
French and Indian War (1755–1763), 426
Fur trade, 436–437, 442
Russian, 453
trappers, 451

Gabrielino, 205, 207
language, 207
Gambling, 403, 486–488
in Canada, 494
Game animals, 347–348
sacrifice of, 384
Games and recreation, 403, 404. *See also* Ball courts
General List, 457
Genetics, Native American origins and, 7–8
Georgia, 303
Etowah in, 79
Geronimo, 246, 448
Geronticide, 397
Eskimo, 121
Ghost Dance, 443–444, 448, 452, 483
Ghosts and spirits
Navajo, 252–253
Pomo, 204. *See also* Myths and legends; Religion
Gift-giving, 415
Gilbert, Humphrey, 425
Girls. *See* Puberty rites; Women
Glaciers, 8–9
expansion and contraction of, 9
Glottochronology, 99
Gold rush, 442
Government, Indian policies of, 432–436. *See also* Political organization
Grand Medicine Society, 320–321
Great Basin region, 216–225
bands of, 407
birth and, 395
culture after European contact, 450–452
culture areas of, *map*, 218
death and, 398
environment of, 217–219
food of, 220–221
housing in, 219–220
marriage and, 390
Paiute, 222–225
people of, 219–225
relations with whites, 451–452
Shoshoni, 216, 225
social organization in, 221–222
technology in, 221
Ute, 225
warfare in, 415
weavers of, 369
Great Lakes region
culture after European contact, 439–441
Eastern and Lower, 307
exploration of, 425
tools near, 31
tribes, of prairies, 319
Western region, 318–324
Great Plains region
people, 17–23, 86–89
prehistoric animals in, 17
relations with whites, 451

village tradition in, 87–89
Great Spirit, 374
Great Sun (Natchez ruler), 331–333, 380, 409, 410
treaties and, 433
Green Corn (Busk) Dance, 327, 337, 383, 401
Greenland, Viking voyages to, 45
Greenland Eskimo, 108
Grinding, 352–353
stones, 25
Guayule plant, 62
Guns, 268–269

Habitations, 355–358. *See also* Archaic people; Housing; Paleo Indians
Adena, 36, 37
Apache, 247
Apache hogan, 248
in Cahokia, 82
in California region, 188–189
earth lodges, 266–268, 356
Eskimo, 113, 114, 116–117
Great Basin people, 220
Havasupai, 229
hogans, 249, 357
Hohokam, 62
Iroquois, 314, 315, 358
Mandan, 291
Mississippian cities, 79–80
Mogollon, 58–59
Northeast bark tipi, 309
Northwest Coast region, 158–159
pithouses, 58–59, 66
in Plains region, 266–268
plank houses, 357–358
of Plateau, 143
Pomo, 199–200
Pueblo adobe, 236, 237
pueblos, 66–73
sweathouses, 358
tipis, 247, 271, 291, 309, 355–356
Tlingit, 167
village life, 53
wattle and daub house, 356–357
wickiups, 220, 355
wigwams, 310, 355
Yurok, 191
Haida, 157, 165
Hair pipes, 363
Hair styles, of Eastern region, 305
Handsome Lake, 440–441, 482
Hand trembler, 251
Hano, 447
Happy Hunting Ground, 374, 376
Hariot, Thomas, 328
Harvesting
Adena people and, 36
of Eastern Archaic forest people, 30–31
tools for, 352
Haskell Institute (Kansas), 479
Havasupai, 228–229
Hawkins, John, 432
Head flattening, 174
Head gates, 61
Headman
in California region, 190
in Plateau region, 145–146
Health and healing. *See* Medicine; Religion; Shaman
reservation services, 481–482
shaman and, 378
Herodotus, scalping and, 417
Hidatsa, 89, 265, 266, 273, 291
associations of, 402
Hogans, 248, 249, 357, 470
Hohokam, 57, 61–65, 227
decline of, 65
irrigation of, 61–62
Mexican contacts with, 62–64
subsistence and settlements of, 62
Hokan languages and people, 99, 185, 192, 219, 228
Home life
Alaska Eskimo, 113–115
of Klamath, 151–152
Homestead Act (1862), 434, 442
Hoop and pole, 403

Hoopa Valley Reservation, 450
Hootch, origins of term, 174
Hopewell culture, 33, 38-42, 302
  decline of, 41-42
Hopi, 238-242
  ceremonies of, 239-241, 382
  death and, 398
  deities of, 241-242
  Katcina Cult of, 239-240, 241, 402
  land cultivation by, 238-239
  languages of, 228, 233
  Navajo and, 448
  political organization of, 409
  pseudo-kinship and, 401
  witchcraft of, 242
Hopi land settlement. *See* Navajo reservation
Horses
  Apache and, 246
  Blackfoot and, 279-280, 282-283
  Comanche and, 286-288
  Crow and, 289
  culture of, 265-266
  economic changes and, 272-273
  equipment for, 268
  and Nez Perce, 150
  in Plains region, 264-265
Housing, 355-358. *See also* Habitations
  pueblos, 357
  on reservations, 470-471
  in Subarctic region, 130
Human remains, preservation of, 490-492
Human sacrifice, 383
Hunters and hunting, 347-351. *See also* Big Game Hunters and hunting; Paleo Indians
  Alaska Eskimo, 111, 112
  buffalo, 288
  caribou, 115
  Mandan, 292, 293-294
  methods of, 350
  migration and, 16
  Paiute, 222-224
  Paleo Indian, 20-22
  by prehistoric people, 13, 15
  rabbit hunt, 27
  rights to, in Canada, 494-495
  seal, 111, 112
  weapons for, 348-350
Hupa, 157, 191
  medium of exchange of, 414-415
  shamans of, 379
Huron, 313, 318, 319, 430
  Cartier and, 425
  fur trade and, 436-437
Huskface Society, 317

Ice Age, Mississippian cultures and, 84
Igloo, 114, 116-117
Illinois (people), 319
Illinois (state)
  Cahokia in, 77, 79-83
  tribes in, 322
Impounds, 348
Incest taboo, 388
Indian Act (1876), 457
  1985 amendment to, 458
Indian Economic Development Fund (Canada), 493-494
Indian Register, 458
Indian removal, 433-434
Indian Removal Act (1830), 434
Indian Reorganization Act (1934), 436, 466, 474
  economic future and, 485-486
Indians, 2-3. *See also* Eskimos; Native Americans; groups by name
  as Canadian native group, 457
  changes after World War II, 473-477
  contemporary, 459-496
  economic success of, 484-485
  in general population, 460
  origins of name, 2
  population by state, 461
Indian schools, 479

Indian Self-Determination and Education Assistance Act (1975), 468
Indian Service, 466. *See also* Bureau of Indian Affairs (BIA)
Indian Territory (Oklahoma), 326, 434, 438, 460
  Seminole move to, 337
Infanticide, 392
  Eskimo, 121
Inheritance, 413
Initiation rites, of Central Atlantic Algonkians, 331. *See also* Ceremonies; Toloache Cult
Intermarriage, 437, 438
  citizenship and, 456–457
  French and, 429–430
  Scots and, 429
Inuit, 493. *See also* Eskimos
  Canadian use of name, 457
  population of (1990), 458
Inuit-Nunavut settlement, 493
Inuit Tapirisat, 485
Iroquoian languages and people, 299, 302, 313
  adoption and, 392
  clan rights and duties, 400
  False Face Society of, 402
  Keepers of the Faith, 380
  longhouses of, 358
  marriage and, 389
  sacrifice and, 383
  shamans and, 378
  slavery and, 405
Iroquois League, 313–318
  ceremonies and societies of, 317
  religion of, 317–318
  social organization of, 316
  village life of, 314
  warfare of, 314–315
Irrigation, Hohokam, 61–62

Jackson, Andrew, 337
  Indian removal and, 434
Jaguar Cave, Idaho, 26
James Bay and Northern Quebec Agreement (1978), 493
James River, Virginia, 328
Jamestown, Virginia, 425
Japan, Valdivia complex pottery and, 44
Jenner, Edward, 431
Jicarilla, 246
Johnson-O'Malley Act (1934), 468
Joliet, Louis, 425
Jomon, Japan, 44
Joseph, Chief. *See* Chief Joseph
Juaneño, 205–206
Jumping Dance, of Yurok, 196, 197

Kamchadal language, 104
Kansa, 265, 273
Kansas, 434
Karok, 157, 191
Kashia, 199
Kaskaskia, 322
Katcina Cult, 239–240, 241
  as association, 402
Katcinas, 235, 364
Kayak, 107, 108, 116, 359
Kepel fish dam, ceremony at, 196–197
Keresan languages and people, 233, 236, 242
Keresan origin myth, 225–226
Kerlsefni, Thorfinn, 424
Kinnikinnik, 320
Kinship. *See also* Associations
  groupings by, 400–401
  Navajo, 250
  in Plains region, 273
  Pomo, 202
  property rights and, 413
  pseudo, 401
Kiowa, 265, 274
  removal of, 434
Kiowa Apache, 246
Kiva, 381–382, 447. *See also* Pueblo (people), social organization of
  defined, 235

Klamath, 150-154
  bands of, 407
  home life of, 151-152
  termination and, 474
  work and success of, 154
Kuksu Cult, 202-204, 402
Kunti, 327
Kwakiutl, 157, 175-177
  art of, 165
  associations of, 402
  village of, 162

Labrador, 424
Labrets, 107
Lacrosse, 403
Land bridge, 9, 10
Land claims
  in Canada, 457, 492-493
Land management, 470
Land tenure, 412-413
Land transportation, 360
Languages, 97-99. *See also* Communication
  Algonkian, 127
  Athabaskan, 127
  California culture area, 186
  chart of, 179-180, 213-214, 296, 339
  Chinook, 174
  Eskimo, 104-106
  map, 98
  of Mississippian people, 76
  North American, 98
  phyla of, 99
  Pueblo, 233
  in Southwestern region, 227-228
  table of, 138
  Tlingit, 166
  and tribal names, 99
  written, 478
  Yurok, Karok, and Hupa, 191-192
Last of the Mohicans, The, 308
Late Woodland period, 73-76
  mortuary practices of, 74-76
Laurentide Glacier, 9
Laws. *See* laws by name
Leadership, Eskimo, 119
League of the Iroquois, 313. *See also* Iroquois League
  adoption of tribe by, 392
  French and, 430
Leather work, 366-367
Legends. *See* Myths and legends
Le Moyne, Jacques, 335
Leni Lenape (Delaware) confederation, 311-312
Lewis and Clark, 442
  Chinook and, 174
  Nez Perce and, 148, 150
  Sacajawea and, 451
Life-style. *See also* specific groups
  in Archaic period, 24-26
  of Eastern region, 305-306
  of Luiseño, 206
  Navajo, 248-250
Linguistic groups, tribes as, 160-161 groups
Linguistics. *See* Languages
Lipan, 246
Liquor. *See* Alcohol and alcoholism
Little Bighorn, battle of (1876), 443
Little Egypt, Georgia, 303
Little Ice Age, 84
Llama, 53
Lodges. *See* Earth lodges
Longhouse, 314, 315
Longhouse People, 472
Long Walk, 447
Lost tribes of Israel, 3
Louisiana Purchase (1803), 434
Lower Creek, 335
Lower Loup River, Nebraska, 89
Luiseño, 206-211
  life-style of, 206
  religion of, 207-208
  social and political organization of, 206-207
  Toloache Cult of, 207-209

MacIntosh, Chilly and William, 429

Macro-Algonkian languages and people, 99, 192
Macro-Siouan languages and people, 99
Mahican confederation, 311, 312
Maidu, 186
  creation myth of, 182
Maize, 41, 50–51, 73. *See also* Corn
Manabozho, 374
Manabush, 323–324
Mandan, 89, 265, 266, 273, 291–294
  associations of, 402
  communities of, 291
  cultivation and hunting of, 291–292
  food preservation and storage by, 353–354
  religion of, 292
  smallpox and, 431
  social and political organization of, 292
Manifest destiny, 433
Manitu, 317, 375
Mano, 25, 238, 353
Marquette, Jacques, 425
Marriage, 388–391
  affection, divorce, and, 389–390
  arranging, 388–390
  bridewealth and, 389
  Chipewyan, 134
  Eskimo, 120
  interracial, 437, 438
  Nez Perce, 149–150
  polygamy, 390–391
  residence and, 389
  Tlingit, 168–169
Martinez, Maria, 486
Mascouten, 319
Masks, religious uses of, 385
Massachuset confederation, 311
Massachusetts (colony), 425
Mathematics, of Pomo, 202
Mather, Cotton, 428
Matrilineal society, 128, 398. *See also* Social organization
  Cochiti, 242
  in Northwest Coast region, 161
  of Pueblo, 235–236
  Tlingit and, 168
  tribes with, 400
McGillivray, Alexander, 429
McJunkin, George, 18
Meadowcroft Rockshelter, 11
Media of exchange, 414–415
Medicine. *See also* Health and healing; Religion; Shaman
  Paiute dreams and curing, 224–225
  priests and, 380
  shaman and, 124, 378
Medicine Arrows, 284
Medicine bundles, 276, 280
Medicine Creek Treaty (1854), 489
Medicine Dance, 320–321
Medicine Lodge ceremony, 285
Medicine man, Navajo, 251, 253. *See also* Shamans
Medicine societies
  Cochiti, 243
  Menominee, 323
Menominee, 319, 322, 322–324, 439
  religion of, 323–324
  social and political organization of, 322–323
  termination and, 475
  warfare of, 323
Mesas, 65–66
Mesa Verde, abandonment of, 70
Mesa Verde National Park, Colorado, 65, 68
Mescalero, 246
Mesoamerica. *See also* Mexico
  cultivation in, 50–54
  impact on Mississippian traditions, 77–79
Mesquaki, 99
Metal work, 367
Metate, 25, 236, 353
Métis, 457, 493
Mexican Indians, 2–3. *See also* Native Americans
Mexico
  cultivation and culture in, 50–54

Hohokam contacts with, 62-64
impact on Mississippian traditions, 77-79
Microblades, 29
Middle Mississippian cultures, 77, 85. *See also* Mississippian tradition
Middle Woodland cultures, 73. *See also* Woodland tradition
Midewiwin Society, 131, 323, 380, 402-403
Midwest, 85-86, 318. *See also* Great Lakes entries; Western Great Lakes region
Midwest. *See also* Great Plains people; Mississippian traditions
burial mounds in, 74
culture after European contact, 439-441
Migrations, 8-11, 12
of animals, 9
into cities, 460-462
to New World, 6
waves of, 7-8
in Western Great Lakes region, 319-321
Mikasuki (Lower Creek), 335, 438
language, 337
Milling stones, 353
Mission Indians, 205-206, 449-450
Mission Relief Act (1881), 450
Missions and missionaries, 449
Mississippian tradition, 76-86, 303
Cahokia, 79-83
cities, 79-80
decline of cities, 83-85
Eastern region and, 301, 301
Great Plains people, 87-89
Mexican influence on, 77-79
mound building and ceremonial objects, 76-77
Upper Mississippian cultures, 85-86
Mississippi basin, 425
Missouri River, 86, 89
people of, 266-267
Miwok, 186
Moccasins, 361
Mogollon, 57-61, 227
Mohawk, 312, 313, 314
economic success of, 484-485
Mohegan. *See* Mahican confederation
Moiety, 401
of Cochiti, 243
defined, 167-168
of Menominee, 322
of southern Mission Indians, 206-207
Mojave region, shamans and, 379
Money, 414
Monks Mound, 77, 81-82
Monogamy, 390
Monotheism, 374
Montagnais, French and, 429
Monte Verde, 11
Mortality. *See* Death
Mortars, 353
Mother-in-law taboo. *See* Apache; Navajo
Moundbuilders, Adena people as, 35-37
Mounds, 33, 35-37, 85
in Cahokia, 77, 81-83
in Eastern region, 301
Hohokam platform, 64
of Late Woodland period, 74-76
of Mississippian societies, 76-77
Moundville, Alabama, 79, 303
Mourning, 398
Mukluks, 494
Music, 371, 372
Pomo, 201
Muskogean languages and people, 76, 299
childhood and, 392
of Southeast, 326
Trickster Tale of, 324-325
Muskogee (Upper Creek), 335
language, 337
Myths and legends, 371-374
Assiniboine creation myth, 260-261

Chippewa, 318
creation, 373
Eskimo creation, 102–103
Keresan origin myth, 225–226
Maidu creation myth, 182
Muskoean Trickster Tale, 324–325
Navajo creation myth, 253–255
New England Algonkian legend, 298
Nootka Wolf Dance and, 173
Northern Athabaskan Legend, 125–126
Pueblo, 233
Salishan Trickster Tale, 140
Shoshonean, 216
Tlingit-Haida creation, 154–155

Na-Dene languages and people, 7, 8, 99, 192
Naja, 486
Naming, as rite of passage, 395–396
Narragansett confederation, 311
Narragansett Indians, 460
Naskapi, 129, 130
Natchez, 84–85, 303, 326, 331–334, 438
class system of, 333–334
customs of, 333–334
Great Sun ruler of, 331–333, 380, 409, 410
mourning and, 398
naming and, 395
political organization of, 409
slavery and, 405
White Woman of, 333
Nation, defined, 408
National Indian Gaming Commission, 487
National Indian Youth Council, 488–489
National Tribal Chairmen's Association, 490
Native American, use of name, 2. *See also* Indians
Native American Church, 472, 483
Natural resources. *See* Food resources; Resources
Navajo, 227, 248–255
ceremonies of, 250–252, 372
children and, 394
death and, 398
Dine as name for, 2
inheritance and, 413
language of, 228
life-style of, 248–250
religion and, 250–255
reservation. *See* Navajo reservation
silver work of, 486
sings of, 250–251
social and political organization of, 250
Spanish impact on, 447
textiles of, 370, 486
Navajo Community College, 480–481
Navajo-Hopi land settlement. *See* Navajo reservation
Navajo reservation, 448, 462
colleges on, 480
facilities on, 465–466
Navajo-Hopi land settlement and, 469–470
Nebraska, 434
Lower Loup River, 89
Neutral (people), 313
New England, 307. *See also* Northeast
Algonkians of, 298, 307–313
Newfoundland, 45, 424, 425
New Mexico
Anasazi in, 66
Mogollon in, 58
voting rights in, 435
New World, peopling of, 8–11, 12
Nez Perce, 147–150, 265, 450
Chief Joseph of, 451–452
chiefs of, 149
guardian spirits of, 149
marriage of, 149–150
seasonal life of, 148–149
Smohalla cult and, 452

Nomads
  Apaches as, 246–247
  in Plains region, 265–266
Non-status Indian, 457
Nootka, 157, 170–173
  bilateral organization of, 170
  dentalia of, 172–173
  social organization of, 170–171
  whaling of, 171–172
  Wolf Dance of, 173
Norsemen, 2
Norse voyages, 45
North America
  culture areas of. *See* Culture areas
  European exploration of, 424–430
  Great Plains Indians of, 17–23
  introduction to culture areas of, 93–100
  languages of, 98
  migration into, 11
Northeast region, 299, 307–313
  Abnaki confederation, 311
  clothing in, 361
  culture after European contact, 436
  hunting methods in, 350
  Iroquois League, 313-318
  Leni Lenape (Delaware), 311
  Mahican confederation, 311, 312
  Massachuset confederation, 311
  Narragansett confederation, 311
  resources in, 312
Northern California region, 183–185
Northwest Coast region, 154–178. *See also* Coastal Archaic people; Klamath; Plateau region
  art(s) of, 159–160, 165–166
  basketry of, 368
  ceremonies of, 382–383
  Chinook, 173–175
  clothing, in, 361
  culture areas and tribes of, *map*, 142
  death and, 398
  environment of, 155–156
  European exploration of, 426
  fishing and, 351
  fishing rights in, 412
  folklore of, 373
  habitations in, 158–159, 357–358
  Indian economic success in, 485
  languages of, 179
  marriage and, 388, 389
  masks of, 385
  naming and, 395
  Nootka of, 170–173
  painting in, 369
  potlatch in, 162–164
  priests of, 380
  puberty rites and, 396–397
  relations with whites, 453–454
  rites of passage in, 393, 396–397
  scalping and, 417
  secret societies in, 402
  slavery in, 405, 406
  social control in, 411
  technology in, 158–160
  textiles of, 369–370
  Tlingit of, 166–170
  tribes of, 166–177
  warfare in, 415
  woodworking of, 364
Northwest Territories, Canada, 457, 493
Nova Scotia, 424
Nuclear family, 391
  Eskimo as, 118
  Klamath, 152

Obsidian, 366
Ohio (state), tribal population near, 302
Ohio Valley region, 86
Ojibwa, 134–137, 439
  Midewiwin (Grand Medicine Society), 131, 320–321
  religion of, 136–137
Okipa, 292
Oklahoma, 303, 438. *See also* Indian Territory
  Indians in, 460

as Indian Territory, 326, 434
Spiro in, 79
Old Copper Culture, 31
Old Whaling People, 109
Omaha, 265, 273
clan rights and duties, 400
religion and, 376
Oneida, 313
Oneota culture, 85–86
Onondaga, 313, 314
Oraibi, 65
Oregon Trail, 414
Orenda, 317, 375
Osage, 265, 460
Ossuaries, 398
Oto, 273
Ottawa, 136, 319, 439
name of, 99
Outfit, Navajo families, 250

Pacific Northwest region. *See* Northwest Coast region
Paint and tattoos, 362–363
Painting, dyes, and pigments, 368–369
Paiute, 26, 222–225
bands of, 407
dreams and curing of, 224–225
Wovoka, 443
Paleo-Arctic tradition, 29
Paleo Indians, 16–23
Clovis people, 19
Folsom people, 18–19
hunting by, 20–22, 86
in Northwest Coast region, 156
Paleolithic people, 9
Paleontologists, 18
Paleo-Siberian languages, 99, 104
Palisades, 314
Pamlico, 328
Pamunkey, 328
Papago, 65, 227
as Piman tribe, 231–233
Parfleche, 268, 270, 367
Partnerships, Eskimo, 118–119
Passamaquoddy, 311
Patayan people, 228
Patrilineal society, 398, 399, 400. *See also* Social organization
tribes with, 400
Pawnee, 89, 265, 291
religion of, 375
Peace pipe, 320
trade and, 414
Pectorals, 269
Pedra Furada, 11
Pelts, as medium of exchange, 414
Pemmican, 128
Penn, William, 428
Penobscot, 311
Penutian languages and people, 99, 228, 233
Chinook as, 174
Peoria (tribe), 322
Personal property, 412
inheritance and, 413
Pestle, 353
Peyote Cult, 483
Phratries, 400–401
Phyla, language, 97–99
Physical anthropologists, 6–7
Physical appearance, 3, 6–7
Piegan, 278
Pima, 65, 227, 231–233
name of, 99
languages and people, 228
social organization of, 232–233
subsistence of, 231–232
Pine Ridge Reservation, 489
Pine Tree Chiefs, 316
Pipes, 320
Pipestone, 365
Pisgah culture, 303
Pithouses, 58–59, 66
Alaskan, 113, 114
Klamath, 151
Piñon nuts, 26
Plains region, 259–296. *See also* Forest people; Great Plains region
adaptation to, 261

Assiniboine creation myth, 260–261
associations of, 402
battles in, 416
Blackfoot, 278–283
ceremonies of, 381
Cheyenne, 283–286
clothing of, 269–271, 361
Comanche, 286–288
communication in, 271–272
Crow, 289–291
culture after European impact, 441–445
culture area and tribes of, *map*, 262, 277–294
economic change in, 272–273
equipment of, 268–268
folklore of, 373
horse in, 264–265
housing in, 267–268
Indian removal and, 434
jewelry in, 363
Mandan, 291–294
marriage in, 389, 390–391
misfits in, 277
Plateau peoples and, 146, 150
prehistory of, 263–264
property rights in, 412
scalping and, 417
shamans and, 378
social organization of, 273–275
Spanish impact on, 264–265
technology of, 266–271
trade of, 273
values and beliefs of, 275–277
warfare in, 415–416
Plank houses, of Northwest, 357–358
Plants, 15. *See also* Agriculture; Cultivation
botanical evidence of transoceanic contacts, 42–43
exchange of, 53–54. *See also* Cultigens
Plateau region, 140–154
communities of, 144–146
as cultural transition zone, 141
culture after European contact, 450–452
culture areas and tribes of, 142
environment of, 141
fishing and, 351
folklore of, 373
Klamath of, 150–154
languages of, 179
life on, 143–154
Nez Perce of, 147–150
prehistory of, 141–143
religion in, 146–147
resources of, 144
rivers of, 140, 141
Smohalla cult in, 452
Platform mounds, 64, 77
Pleistocene Epoch, 8
Pocahontas, 328, 437
Political movements, 488–490
American Indian Movement (AIM), 489
National Indian Youth Council, 488–489
occupation of BIA building, 489–490
and preservation of human remains, 490–492
property repatriation and, 492
Political organization, 406–410. *See also* Social and political systems
Algonkian, 308–311
bands as, 407
Blackfoot, 280–281
in California region, 189–190
Central Atlantic Algonkian, 329–331
Cheyenne, 284
chiefdoms as, 408–409
Chinook, 175
Cochiti, 243–244
councils as, 409–410
in Great Basin, 221–222
of Hopewell people, 41

Iroquois, 316
Luiseño, 206–207
Mandan, 292
Menominee, 322–323
Natchez, 333–334
Navajo, 250
of Nez Perce, 149
of Northeast Algonkian, 312–313
in Northwest Coast region, 160–161
in Plains region, 273
in Plateau region, 145–146
of Pomo, 199–200
of Pueblo (people), 244–245
tribes as, 407–408
Yurok, 192–193
Political systems, 387–422
Polyandry, 390
Polygamy, 390–391
Polygyny, 274, 390
Pomo, 198–204
background of, 199
basketry of, 368
food resources of, 198–199
ghosts and spirits of, 204
Kuksu Cult of, 202–204
organization of, 199–200
sexual equality of, 202
technology of, 200–202
Ponce de Leon, Juan, 424
Pontiac, 426
Popé uprising, 446–447
Population, 97
American Indian, Eskimo, Aleut, by state, 461
and decline of Cahokia, 84
of Subarctic region, 127
Potawatomi, 136, 319, 322, 439
Potlatch, 162–164
baby naming and, 395
Canadian ban on, 453–454
origins of term, 174
Potomac, 328
Pottery, 364–365. *See also* Adena culture; Hopewell culture
of Adena, 36
contemporary, 486
of Eastern region, 304
in Mexico, 53
of Mogollon people, 59–60
Valdivia complex, 44
Powamu Society, 240–241
Powhatan (Chief), 328, 329–331
Powhatan (tribe), 328, 329–331
treaties and, 433
Prairies, 85
Prairie tribes
Algonkians, 321–322
Potawatomi (Mascouten), 319
Precipitation, in Southwest, 56
Pre-Columbian transoceanic contacts, 42–45
Prehistoric people and cultures, 2–3, 6–48
Archaic Period, 23–33
earliest evidence in Americas, 11
Eastern region, 299–301
lives of, 13–15
Northwest Coast region, 156–157
Paleo Indians, 16–23
physical appearance of, 6–7
Plateau region, 141–143
social organization in bands, 15–16
transoceanic contacts of, 42–45
Woodland tradition, 33–42
Preservation, food, 353–354
Priests, 380
Proclamation of 1763, 455–456
Property. *See also* Wealth and property
repatriation of, 490–492
rights and land tenure, 412–413
Pseudo-kinship, 401
Puants, 333
Puberty rites, 396–397. *See also* Ceremonies; Religion
Public Law 95-561, 468
Pueblo (people), 227, 233–245
ceremonies of, 381–382

clothing of, 361-362
Cochiti, 242-244
contemporary housing of, 471
dramatic arts of, 371
environment of, 234-235
hair styles of, 362
Hopi as, 238-242
marriage and, 389
masks of, 385
medium of exchange of, 415
organization of, 244-245
political organization of, 409
priests of, 380
religion of, 235
sacred objects of, 384
shamans and, 379
silver work of, 368
social organization of, 235-236
Spanish and, 425, 445-446
technology of, 236-238
trade of, 273
warfare of, 416
weaving of, 369, 370
women of, 405
Pueblo Bonito, 67, 69
Pueblos (habitations), 357
abandonment of, 70-73
Anasazi, 66-73
artifacts from, 71
Pyramid mounds, of Mississippian people, 76-77. *See also* Mounds

Quapaw, removal of, 434
Quebec, Canada, 492-493
Quileute, 157
Quivira, 89

Rabbit hunt, 27
Raids
Blackfoot, 282-283
Crow, 289-291
Rain dance, 294, 380
Rainfall. *See* Precipitation
Raleigh, Walter, 425
Rancherias, 450, 462
Rancheria Termination Act (1958), 450
Rank, in Northwest Coast society, 161-162
Rappahannock, 328
Recreation, on reservations, 472
Regalia, Yurok, 195-196
Religion, 374-385. *See also* Myths and legends
Apache, 247-248
behavior and, 376-377
Blackfoot, 279, 281
in California region, 190
Central Atlantic Algonkian temples, 328-329
ceremonies, 380-385. *See also* Ceremonies
Cheyenne, 285
Chinook, 175
contemporary, 482
of Eastern region, 306
Eskimo, 121-122
European contact and, 429-431
in Great Basin region, 221-222
Handsome Lake and, 440-441
Hopi beliefs, 239-242
Iroquois, 317-318
Luiseño, 207-208
Mandan, 292
Menominee, 323-324
of Natchez, 334
Native American Church, 483
Navajo, 250-255
Nez Perce, 149
Ojibwa, 136-137
Paiute dreams and curing, 224-225
paraphernalia of, 384-385
of Plains region, 275-277
of Plateau tribes, 146-147
political organization and, 409
Pomo, 202
priests, 380
Pueblo (people), 235

of River Yumans, 230–231
shamans, 115, 124–125, 377–380
souls and, 376
Southeastern, 327
specialists in, 377–380
spirit helpers, 146–147
in Subarctic region, 130–131
Tlingit, 169–170
Western Great Lakes region, 320–321
Yurok, 195–197
Relocation policy, 473, 475–477
placement centers for, 475–476
success of, 476–477
Repatriation, of property, 490–492
Reservations, 434
culture of, 473
facilities on, 465–466
health services on, 481–482
housing on, 470–471
Indian rights on, 462–465
Indians and Eskimos on, 460
Indian-white relations and, 472
jurisdictions of, 462
land area in, 470
life on, 471–472
list of, 463–464
for Northwest and Western Subarctic Indians, 453–454
in Oklahoma, 460
relocation policy, 473, 475–477
system, 433
termination policy, 473, 474–475
tribal governments on, 436
in United States, 462–473
work and recreation on, 472
Resettlement, forcible, 438
Residence, marriage and, 389
Resources. *See also* Food resources; Foods
California region, 186–188
on Canadian reserves, 494
of Eastern region, 303–305
of Northeast region, 307, 312
of Northwest Coast region, 155–156, 157–158, 160
of Plateau region, 144
Revitalization movements, 440
Rhode Island, Indians in, 460
Rice. *See* Wild rice
Rights, on reservations, 462–465. *See also* Voting rights
Rio Grande (river), 50
Rio Grande peoples, 234, 236
languages of, 233
Rio Grande pueblos, 446–447
Rites of passage, 393–398
birth, 393–395
death, 397–398
naming, 395–396
potlatches and, 163
puberty, 396–397
River Yumans, 229–231
environment and, 229–230
religion of, 230–231
social organization of, 230
Roach (hair), 362
Roanoke Island, 425
Rocky Mountains, 9
Rolfe, John, 437
Ross, John, 429

Sacajawea, 174, 451
Sachems, 312, 316
Sacred objects, in religious ceremonies, 384–385
Sacrifice, 383–384
human, 383
Sagamores, 312
Salishan Trickster Tale, 140
Salmon
catching, 145
in Northwest Coast region, 157
San Diego, mission of, 449
Sand painting, Navajo, 252
San Idefonso Pueblo, 486
Santa Fe, 445–446
Santa Fe Trail, 414
Sarci, 264
Sauk, 319, 322
Savages, English views of, 428

Scalping, 417
Crow and, 289
in Eastern region, 306
Scalp lock, 305
Schools, Indian, 479. *See also* Education
Scottish settlers, 428–429
Scrapers, 20–21
Sculpture, of Hopewell people, 41
Scythians, scalping by, 417
Seal hunt, 112–113
Seasonal life-style changes, 26
Secret societies, 402
Security, pueblos and, 67
Sedna creation myth, 102–103, 115, 374
Self-determination, BIA and, 468–469
Self-mutilation, 383
Seminole, 334–337, 438
adoption and, 392
babies of, 395
casino gaming of, 487
contemporary housing of, 471
establishment of, 335–337
move to Indian Territory, 337
Seminole War (1835–1843), 337
Seneca, 313, 314
Handsome Lake, 440
Sequoia National Park, 478
Sequoyah, 478
Serpent Mound, 35
Settlements. *See* Habitations
of Great Plains people, 87–89
Hohokam, 62, 64
Seven Cities of Gold, 425, 445
Sex. *See* Marriage
Sex discrimination, in Canada, 457, 458
Sexual equality, of Pomo, 202
Shakers, 482
Northwest Indians and, 454
Shamans, 377–380
in California region, 190
Central Atlantic Algonkian, 329
in Eastern region, 306
Eskimo, 115, 124–125
in Great Basin region, 221–222
Klamath, 152
Menominee, 323
Ojibwa, 136
Pomo, 202
in Subarctic society, 131
Western Great Lakes region, 321
Shasta, religion and, 376
Shells, of Eastern region, 304
Shoshonean languages and people, 26, 185, 219, 225, 265, 286, 451
legend, 216
"Shovel-shaped" incisors, 7
Siberia, 9
Siblings, 388
Sickness. *See* Health; Medicine; Shamans
Siksika, 278
Silver work, 368
contemporary, 486
Sings, Navajo, 250–251
Siouan languages and people, 76, 265, 291, 299, 302
Siouan Winnebago, 318
Sioux, 276
Southeastern, 326
Six Nations, 392
Six-Point-Cloud People, 241
Skraellings, 424
Slash-and-burn agriculture, 307
Slavery, 405–406
and Northwest Coast social rank, 161–162
Slocum, John, 454
Smallpox, 431
Smith, John, 328, 331
Smohalla cult, 452
Smoking, 36
Snake Society, 241
Snowshoes, 128–129, 360
Social and political systems, 387–422

clans and other large groupings, 398–403
economic systems, 412–415
family, 391–393
games and recreation, 403, 404
marriage, 388–391
rites of passage, 393–398
slavery, 405–406
warfare and, 415–418
women's status in, 404–405. *See also* Women
Social control, 410–411
of adults, 411
supernatural and, 410–411
Socialization, folklore and, 372
Social organization. *See also* Social and political systems
Apache, 247
bands, 15–16
Blackfoot, 280–281
Cheyenne, 284
Cochiti, 242–243
Eskimo, 118–121
in Great Basin region, 221–222
Iroquois, 316
Klamath, 152
Luiseño, 206–207
Mandan, 292
Menominee, 322–323
Natchez, 333–334
Navajo, 250
Nootka, 170–171
Northwest Coast region, 160–162
Piman, 232–233
of Plains region, 273–275
Pomo, 199–200
potlatch and, 162–164
of Pueblo (people), 235–236
of River Yumans, 230
Tlingit, 167–168
Western Great Lakes region, 320–321
Yurok, 192–193
Society, prehistoric, 15–16. *See also* Prehistoric people and cultures
Song duels, Eskimo, 121
Souls, 376
South America, migrations to, 8 , 11
Southeast region, 299, 325–337
ancestors and descendants in, 303
basketry of, 368
Central Atlantic Algonkians, 328–331
clothing in, 361
communities of, 326–327
culture after European contact, 438
death and, 397
early culture of, 326–327
folklore of, 374
hunting methods in, 350
moiety organization in, 401
Natchez, 331–334
paint and tattoos in, 361
political organization of, 409
priests of, 380
religious ceremonies in, 380–381
Seminole, 334–337
textiles of, 369
women in, 405
Southern Athabaskans, 245–255
Apache, 246–248
Navajo, 248–255
Southern California region, 204–211
environment of, 185
Mission Indians in, 205–206
Southern Death Cult, 77
Southwest region, 225–255. *See also* Desert Archaic people; West
agriculture in, 55–57
Anasazi, 65–73
Apache, 246–248
Athabaskan movement and, 72
Cochiti, 242–245
cultivation and culture in, 54–73
culture after European contact, 445–448
culture areas of, *map*, 218
early peoples of, 227–233
Hohokam, 61–65
Hopi, 238–242

Keresan Origin myth in, 225–226
masks of, 385
Mogollon, 57–61
Navajo, 248–255
Pimans, 231–233
prehistoric, 50
Pueblo (people) of, 233–245
River Yumans, 229–231
sacrifice in, 383
Southern Athabaskans, 245–255
Upland Yumans, 228–229
Southwestern Polytechnic Institute (Albuquerque), 480
Soyal Ceremony, 239–240
Spanish, 301, 303
Comanche and, 286
contact with North America, 424
exploration by, 425
goals of, 427
impact on Plains region, 264–265
impact on Southeast region, 438
Spears, 20, 21, 348
arrowheads and, 349–350
Spirit helpers, 146–147
Spiro site, Oklahoma, 79, 303
Sports. *See* Ball courts; Games and recreation
Squanto, 308
Squash, 50–51
domesticated, 54, 351
Squaw Dance (Navajo), 251
Status Indian, 457, 458
population of (1990), 458
Stereotypes, 342
Stockbridge, 312
Stone tools, 23
microblades, 29
Stone working, 365–366
Strachey, William, 328
Subarctic Archaic people, 29–30
Subarctic region, 125–137
aboriginal population of, 127
Chipewyan, 133–134
clothing in, 130
culture areas and tribes, *map*, 105
environment of, 126–127
fishing and, 351
fishing rights in, 412
folklore of, 374
food of, 128
housing in, 130
life in, 127–128
Ojibwa, 134–137
religion in, 130–131
technology of, 128–130
warfare in, 415
Windigo in, 131–132
Sun Dance, 276–277, 280, 281, 285, 286, 381, 384
Sun Watcher, Hopi, 239
Supernatural, 374. *See also* Religion
control of, 410–411
Eskimo belief in, 122–124
Iroquois, 317–318
and Nez Perce, 149
power of, 374–376
in Subarctic religion, 130–131
and Yurok, 195
Sweathouses, 358
Sycuan gaming center, 487

Taboos, 375
incest, 388
of Plateau tribes, 147
Taos, trade at, 273
Tattoos, 362–363
Taxation, and reservations, 465
Technology. *See also* Tools
art, religion, and, 341–385
in California region, 188–189
clothing and, 360–363
of Eastern region, 303–305
Eskimo, 116–118
food and, 346–355
of Great Basin people, 221
housing, 355–358. *See also* Habitations
Northwest Coast region, 158–160
Paiute, 222–224
of Plains region, 266–271

Pomo, 200–202
of Pueblo (people), 236–238
of Subarctic region, 128–130
transportation, 358–360. *See also* Transportation
of Western Great Lakes region, 320
Tecumseh, 426
Tehuacán Valley, 51
Ten lost tribes of Israel, 3
Teosinte, 50
Termination policy, 473, 474–475
Textiles, 369–370
contemporary, 486
Theocracy, Chiciti and Hopi as, 244
Thorpe, Jim, 479
Three Fires alliance, 136
Tierra del Fuego, people in, 11
Timucua, 334, 335, 438
Tipis, 130, 355–356
Apache, 247
Blackfoot, 271
Mandan, 291
Northeast bark, 309
in Plains region, 268
Tirawa, 375
Tlingit, 157, 166–170, 485
aggression by, 169
art of, 165
religion of, 169–170
seasonal life of, 166–167
slavery and, 406
social organization of, 167–168
Tlingit-Haida creation myth, 154–155
Tobacco (people), 313
Tobacco, 36
in religious ceremonies, 383, 384
spread of, 432
Toboggan, 128, 129
Toloache Cult, 207–209
Tomahawks, 306
Tools
in Archaic period, 23
Arctic Small Tool tradition, 29–30
copper, 31, 32
for cultivation, 352
for drilling, 14
of Eastern Archaic forest people, 31
Eskimo, 117–118
making, 14
microblades, 29
of Mississippian people, 88
of Mogollon people, 59
prehistoric, 13
stone, 366
Torture, by Iroquois, 315
Totem pole, 159–160, 364
Toys, 370
Trade
of Alaska Eskimo, 111–112
of Chinook, 173–175
and commerce, 413–415
gift-giving and, 415
of Hopewell people, 38–39
media of exchange for, 414–415
of Northwest Coast Indians, 453
of Plains region, 273
routes, 414
Trail of Broken Treaties, 489–490
Traits, of Native American and North Asian populations, 7
Transoceanic contacts, 42–45
botanical evidence of, 42–43
cultural evidence of, 43–45
Transportation, 358–360. *See also* Trade
in California region, 188
canoes, 31–32, 159, 172
Eskimo, 116
land, 360
travois, 269
water, 359
Trapping, 350, 451
Travois, 269
Treaties, 432–433
cessation of new, 436
Indian removal and, 434
Tribal governments, 436
Tribelets

California, 409
Klamath, 152
Tribes. *See also* Culture areas; regions by name; tribes by name
defined, 160
of Great Basin, 218, 219–221
as linguistic groups, 160–161
names of, 99
of Northwest Coast region, 166–177
in Plains region, 273
as political units, 407–408
Trickster tales, 373
Salishan, 140
Tsimshian, 157, 165
religion and, 376
Tumpline, 360
Tundra, 103
Tungus, language and people, 377
Tunica, 334
Tuscarora
adoption of, 392
and Eastern tribes, 302

Umiaks, 107, 108, 116, 359
Unilineal society, 398
of Pomo, 202
United States
California as part of, 450
changes after World War II, 473–477
development of Indian policies, 473–474
Universities. *See* Colleges and universities
Upland Yumans, 228–229
Upper Creek, 335
Upper Mississipian cultures, 85–86
Oneota culture, 85–86
Upper Paleolithic sites, 8
Urbanization, 476–477
Utah, Anasazi in, 66
Ute, 26, 225
Uto-Aztecan languages and people, 219
Valdivia complex, Ecuador, 44
Vancouver, George, 426
Vancouver Island
Kwakiutl warriors on, 175–177
Nootka of, 170–173
Vegetation, late Pleistocene, 22. *See also* Agriculture; Climate; Cultivation; Diet; Foods; Plants
Viking voyages, 45
Villages, life in, 53. *See also* Habitations; Pueblos
Vinland, 45, 424
Vision quest, 146, 376–377
Cheyenne, 285
of Plains region, 275–276
Voegelin, Carl, 99
Voting rights, 435–436
in Canada, 456–458

Wahunsonacock, 328
Wakonda, 317, 375
Walapai, 228
Wampanoag, 308
Wampum, 314, 414
Warbonnet, 270
Warfare, 415–418
battles, 416–417
Blackfoot, 281–282
chiefdoms and, 409
Crow, 289
of Eastern region, 305–306
Iroquois, 314–315
Kwakiutl and, 175–177
in Late Woodland period, 74
Menominee, 323
of Northeast Algonkian, 312–313
of Pimans, 232
of Plains region, 268–269
preparation for, 416
and Pueblo (people), 236
of River Yumans, 230
scalping, 417

Southeastern, 327
of Tlingit, 169
Warp and weft, 369
Warriors' societies, 274
Washo, 219
Water transportation, 359
Wattle and daub house, 356–357
Way (Navajo sing), 251
Wealth
of Plains region, 272–273
Yurok, 193–194
Weapons
Eskimo, 117–118
of Plains region, 268–269
prehistoric, 13
Weaving, 369–370
Navajo, 249–250
Weir, 32
Western Apache, 246
Western Great Lakes region
Chippewa legend, 318
food and technology of, 320
Great Lakes tribes of, 319–320
Menominee, 322–324
metal work in, 367
prairie people, 321–322
priests of, 380
property rights in, 412
Woodland tribes of, 319
Whaling, 109–110, 115
Nootka, 171–172
White, John, 328
White Deerskin Dance, of Yurok, 196, 197
White Dog Ceremony, 383
Whites, relations with, 424–458
White Woman, in Natchez custom, 333
Wichita, 89, 265
removal of, 434
Wickiups, 355
Wigwams, 355
Northeast or Western Great Lakes, 310
Wild rice, 30, 319, 324, 325
Williams, Roger, 428
Windigo, 131–132
and cannibalism, 132–133
Winnebago, 318, 319, 439
Wintun, 186
Wisconsin (state), termination policy and, 475
Witchcraft, 375, 410
Cochiti, 244
Hopi and, 242
Navajo, 252–253
Women. *See also* Marriage; Matrilineal society
Anasazi, 69–70
Apache puberty rites, 247–248, 250
in Archaic period, 25
birth and, 393–395
Blackfoot, 281
Cheyenne, 286
Chipewyan, 134
cooking and, 354
as cultivators, 352
discrimination against, 457, 458
of Eastern Archaic forest people, 30
Eskimo, 118–119
gathering food and, 346
in Iroquois league, 316
leather work of, 366–367
Navajo, 249–250
in Plains region, 274–275
in Plateau region, 146, 147
Pomo, 202
pottery and, 364–365
puberty rites of, 396
Southeastern, 327
status of, 404–405
in Subarctic society, 129, 131
Toloache adolescence ceremony, 209
in warfare, 417
Wood carvings, of Northwest Coast region, 160
Woodland tradition, 33–42. *See also* Eastern area
Adena culture, 33
beginning of, 301

Hopewell culture, 33
late developments in eastern area, 73–76
late Woodland period, 73–76
Plains region and, 263
tribes of Western Great Lakes, 319–320
Woodworking, 364
World Renewal, Yurok, Karok, and Hupa ceremonies of, 195
World War II, changes after, 473–477
Wounded Knee, South Dakota (1973), 489
massacre at, 444–445
Wovoka, 443, 444
Written language, Sequoyah and Cherokee, 478

Yamasee, 334, 438
Yavapai, 228
Yei, Navajo Holy People, 255
Yeibeichai dance, 251
Yokuts, 186, 190
Yuchi, 326, 334
language of, 76
Yuman languages and people, 206, 227, 228
River, 229–231
Upland, 228–229
Yurok, 157, 190–197
fishing areas of, 412
religion of, 195–197
social and political organization of, 192–193
subsistence of, 192
wealth and property of, 193–194

Zuni
language of, 227, 233
sacred objects of, 385
silver work of, 486
Zuni Pueblo, 425